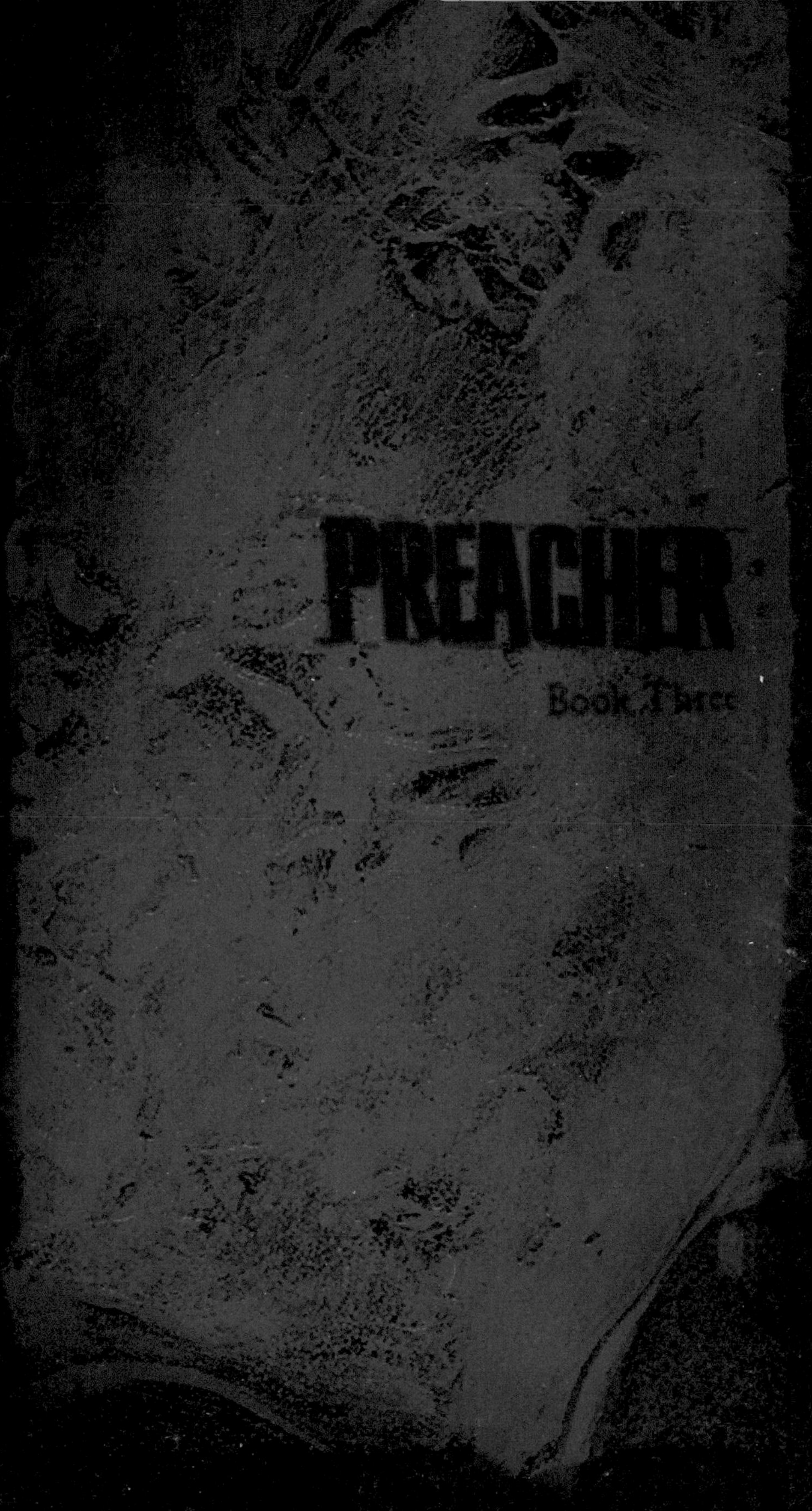

# PREACHER

Book Three

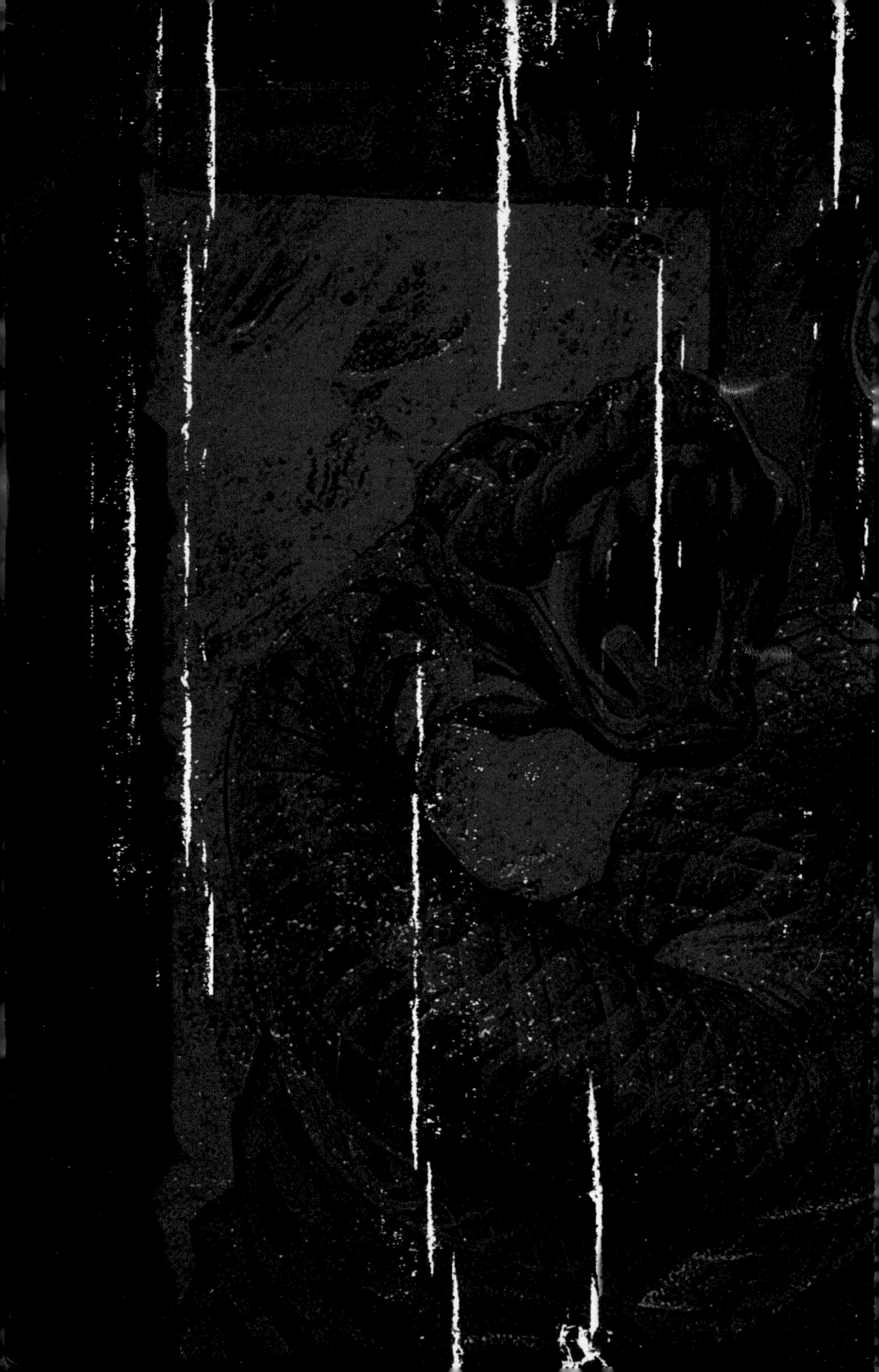

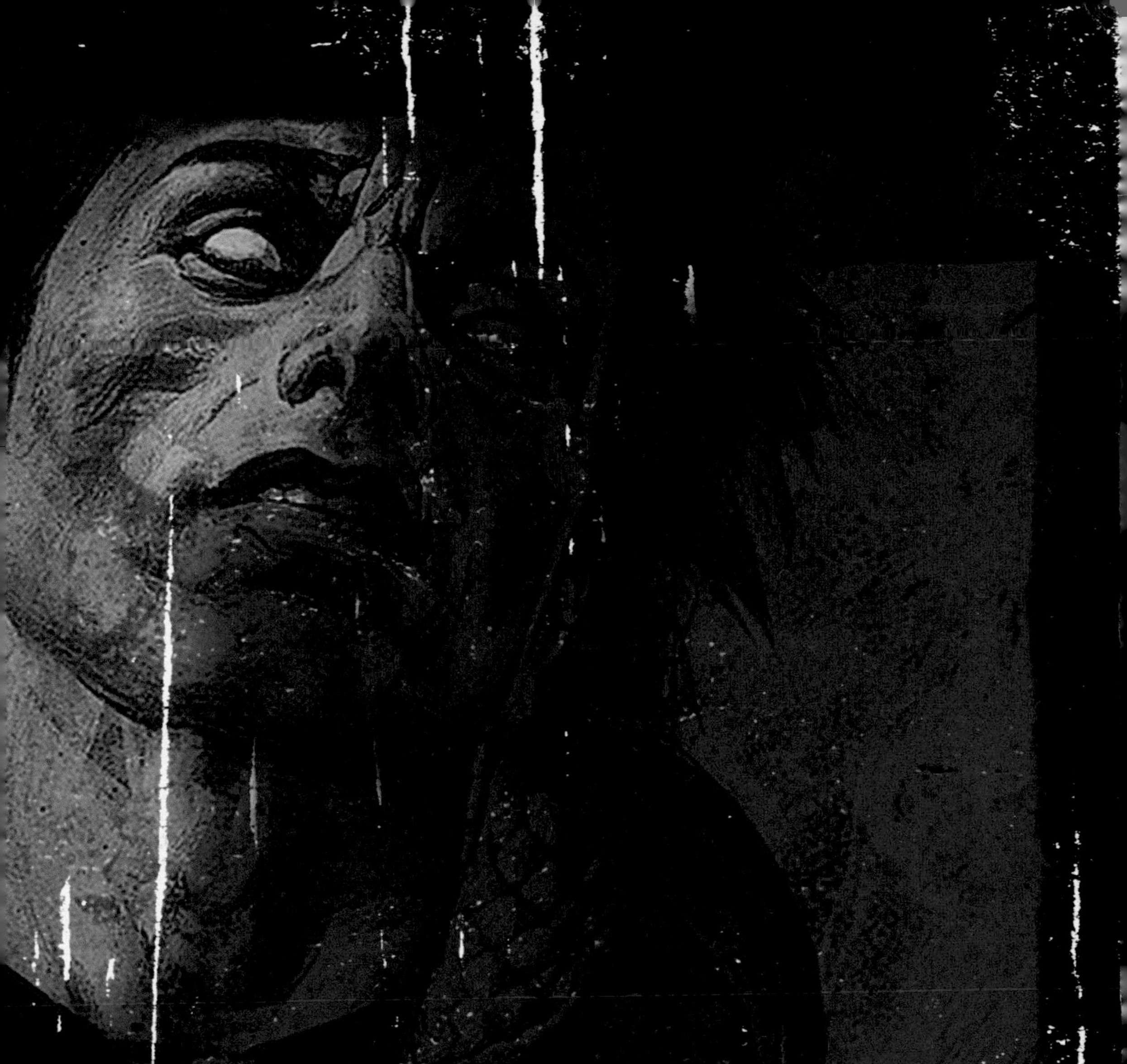

# PREACHER

## Book Three

Garth Ennis Writer

Steve Dillon Steve Pugh Carlos Ezquerra Artists

Pamela Rambo Matt Hollingsworth James Sinclair Colorists

Clem Robins Letterer Cover Art and Original Series Covers by Glenn Fabry

Preacher created by Garth Ennis and Steve Dillon

Axel Alonso  Julie Rottenberg Editors – Original Series  Jeb Woodard Group Editor – Collected Editions
Scott Nybakken Editor – Collected Edition  Robbin Brosterman Design Director – Books  Louis Prandi Publication Design

Shelly Bond VP & Executive Editor – Vertigo

Diane Nelson President Dan DiDio and Jim Lee Co-Publishers  Geoff Johns Chief Creative Officer
Amit Desai Senior VP – Marketing & Global Franchise Management  Nairi Gardiner Senior VP – Finance  Sam Ades VP – Digital Marketing
Bobbie Chase VP – Talent Development  Mark Chiarello Senior VP – Art, Design & Collected Editions  John Cunningham VP – Content Strategy
Anne DePies VP – Strategy Planning & Reporting  Don Falletti VP – Manufacturing Operations
Lawrence Ganem VP – Editorial Administration & Talent Relations  Alison Gill Senior VP – Manufacturing & Operations
Hank Kanalz Senior VP – Editorial Strategy & Administration  Jay Kogan VP – Legal Affairs
Derek Maddalena Senior VP – Sales & Business Development  Jack Mahan VP – Business Affairs  Dan Miron VP – Sales Planning & Trade Development
Nick Napolitano VP – Manufacturing Administration  Carol Roeder VP – Marketing  Eddie Scannell VP – Mass Account & Digital Sales
Courtney Simmons Senior VP – Publicity & Communications  Jim (Ski) Sokolowski VP – Comic Book Specialty & Newsstand Sales
Sandy Yi Senior VP – Global Franchise Management

## PREACHER BOOK THREE

Library of Congress Cataloging-in-Publication Data

Ennis, Garth, author.
  Preacher, book three / Garth Ennis ; illustrated by Steve Dillon.
    pages cm
  ISBN 978-1-4012-4501-6 (pbk.)
  1.   Custer, Jesse (Fictitious character)—Comic books, strips, etc. 2.  Clergy—Comic books, strips, etc.
Vigilantes—Comic books, strips, etc. 4.  Vampires—Comic books, strips, etc. 5.  Graphic novels. I. Dillon, Steve,
illustrator. II. Title.
  PN6727.E56P7333 2014
  741.5'973—dc23

                              2013036107

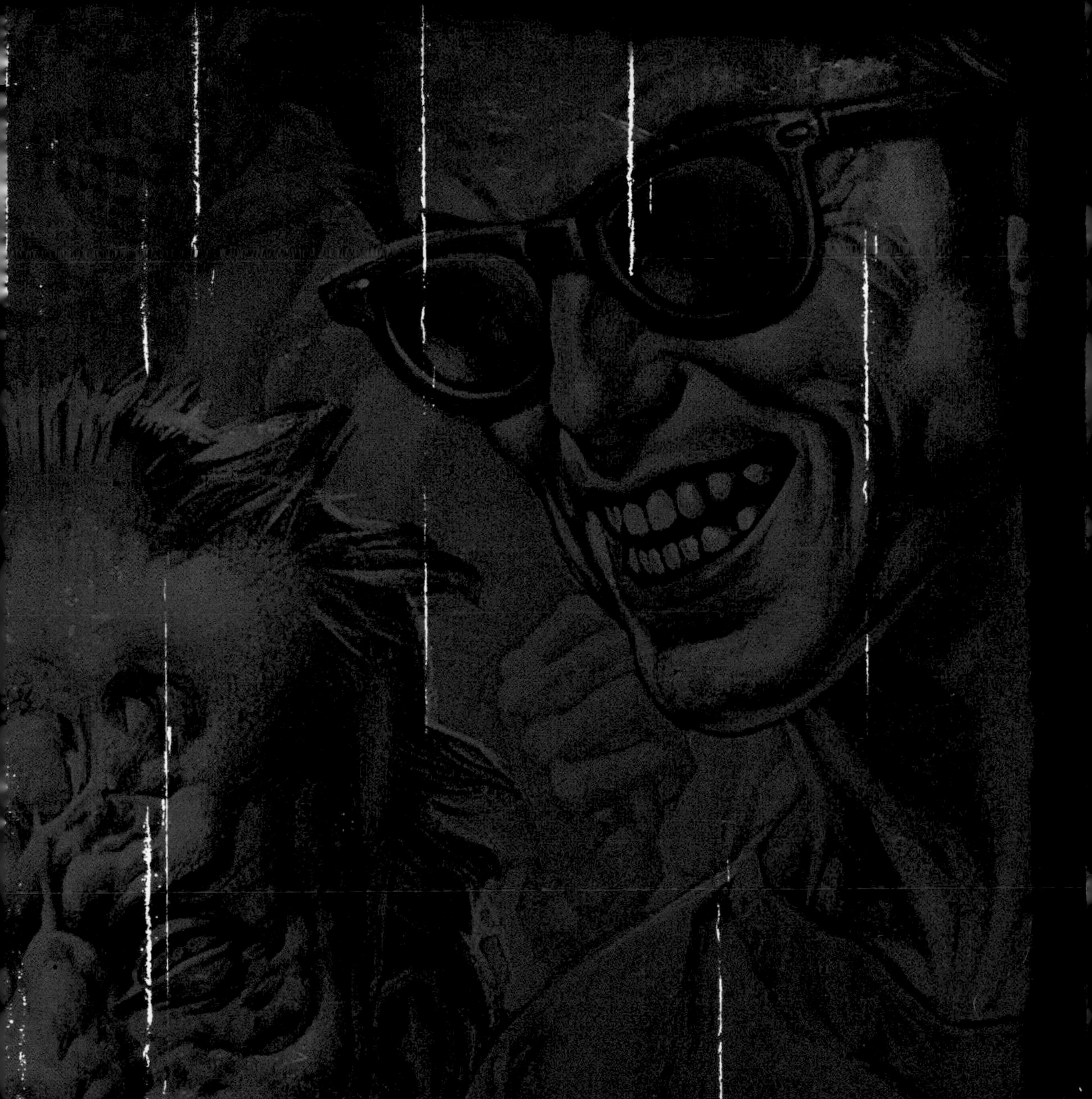

# Table of Contents

# My Bar Gone By, I Miss It So

The Blarney Stone has gone to God. The other day I steeled myself and walked down 32nd street, already knowing what I'd see, heart sinking all the same. Sure enough, it seemed like half the block was gone, with just a construction site to fill the gap and not a sign the place had ever been there.

What was the Blarney Stone? Just a bar, an Irish sports bar in the heart of New York City. I first went there in 'ninety-two, when Steve and I arrived for a convention at the nearby Pennsylvania Hotel. He'd been there before, he told me, and it was a nice little place and it was handy. In we went. I was almost drunk on sensation already, mind awhirl at what I'd decided instantly was the greatest city in the world, and here I was walking into my first New York bar. Would it be like *Goodfellas*, or *State of Grace*, or some as yet undreamed-of drinker's paradise wreathed in smoke and hidden dangers?

The barman looked up, saw us, smiled without surprise. No drama here.

"How're yeh, Steve?"

"You *remember* me?"

The barman's name was Martin, and I'd get to know him and Jimmy and all the others well in the years to come. He remembered Mr. Dillon. Our hero had spent two weeks there, six years earlier, and even though this was more a comment on him than Martin's memory, I still recall thinking — *Hmmm... this looks like the place for me.*

Here's what it was like: the bar itself began just inside the door, grew out in a long curve of worn-out wood that turned inwards and straightened out again, then ended halfway down the room. To your left as you entered was the luncheon counter, packed with what Amanda Conner christened "mystery meat" (a fair description; it was cheap and tasty and came in mighty platefuls, but every time you ate it you were dicing with the shits), and as you walked along the bar you came in sight of the booths and tables at the rear.

There was a little room at the very back, where you could play darts if you wanted, or just carry on talking shite if you preferred. There was the latest in a long line of cats, two of which I remember in my time there: Blarney the tortoiseshell, who eventually succumbed to the gigantic growth that blossomed on his cheek, and his powder-grey replacement Blarney, who presumably made it to the end. There was all sorts of crap stuck up on the walls, with little gems in amongst the Hurley sticks and shamrocks — that classic shot of Ollie gaping at the flame on Stan's thumb comes to mind, as do half a dozen ancient ads for Michelob and Schlitz. There was beer and whiskey and people and bullshit, and I loved every second of it. They do not make them like that anymore.

Now, fear not, this is not about to become another drawn-out whine about gentrification, or how there are no soapdodgers left in the East Village. This is a lament for a bar, one single place, and the only lesson to be drawn from its passing is that nothing lasts forever. It sat in the shadows of giants built of brick and iron, huge towers arranged in orderly rows but reaching madly for the heavens. *That* New

York, that steel-hard stretch where people go but rarely live, where the incomers off the boats — micks, wops, krauts and polacks — must have stopped and stared, gazing up and up and up at things beyond their old world understanding. The Blarney Stone was of that time and of that place, and so it resolutely remained.

It was not cool. It was not hip. It did not have a happening jukebox. There was a digital one towards the end, which I remember nothing from, and before that a plastic wreck loaded up with Irish favorites that no one ever played — *You English Bastards It's All Your Fault*, or *When I'm Shooting Soldiers*, stuff like that. The one song I do associate with the place is *She's Always a Woman*, and only then because I was once (quietly) amused to note the biggest and most dangerous man I'd ever seen weeping into his liquor while it played. No beautiful people ever went there, nor any hipsters, unless a bunch of college kids had wandered in by accident. If there was a game on at the Garden the place exploded with Rangers shirts or Knicks caps; if the Dead were playing it would be a sea of tie-dye. Otherwise it was just ordinary fuckers.

I drank in the Blarney Stone for fifteen years, for the simple reason that every time I walked through the door I felt like I was home. I sent John Constantine to have a beer there, and Dougie and Ivor from *Dicks*, and Jesse, Tulip, Cassidy and Amy in the story you're about to read. Most of the friends I've made or kept in my adult life went there at one time or another, and at least half of them loathed it, which I got a secret, perverse enjoyment out of. My good pal Keith Harrington was there with me on the very last night the place was in business, and some time afterwards he stared at me suspiciously and ventured —

"It's gone?"

"It is."

"Definitely?"

"No doubt about it. Smashed to the ground."

"Good. I'll never have to go to that horrible, dark, fucking little shithole ever again. Thank Christ."

Keith had come three thousand miles for the last night of the Blarney Stone. I suppose you can take that any way you like.

— Garth Ennis

New York City, August 2010

# PREACHER

Book Three

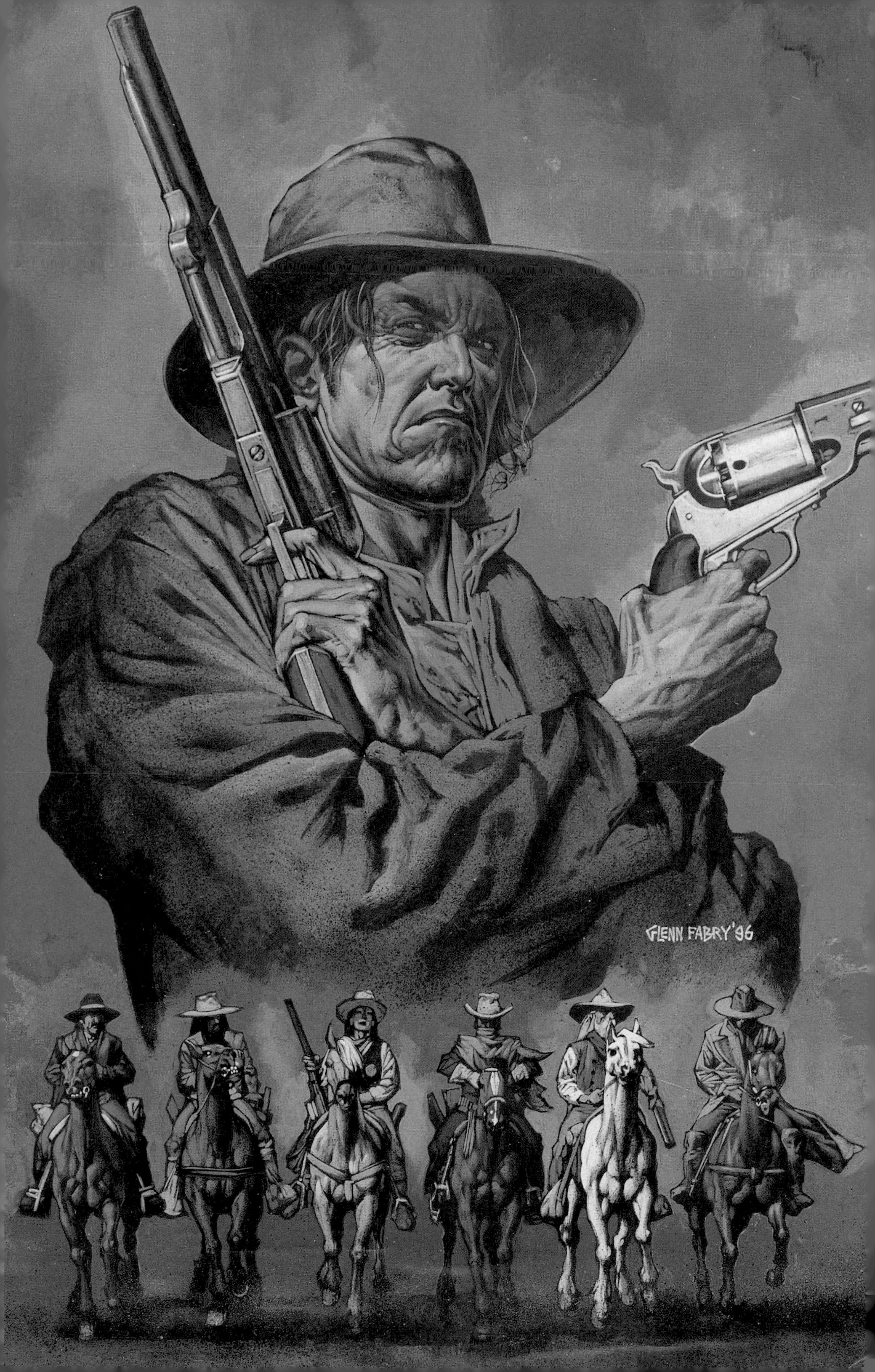
GLENN FABRY '96

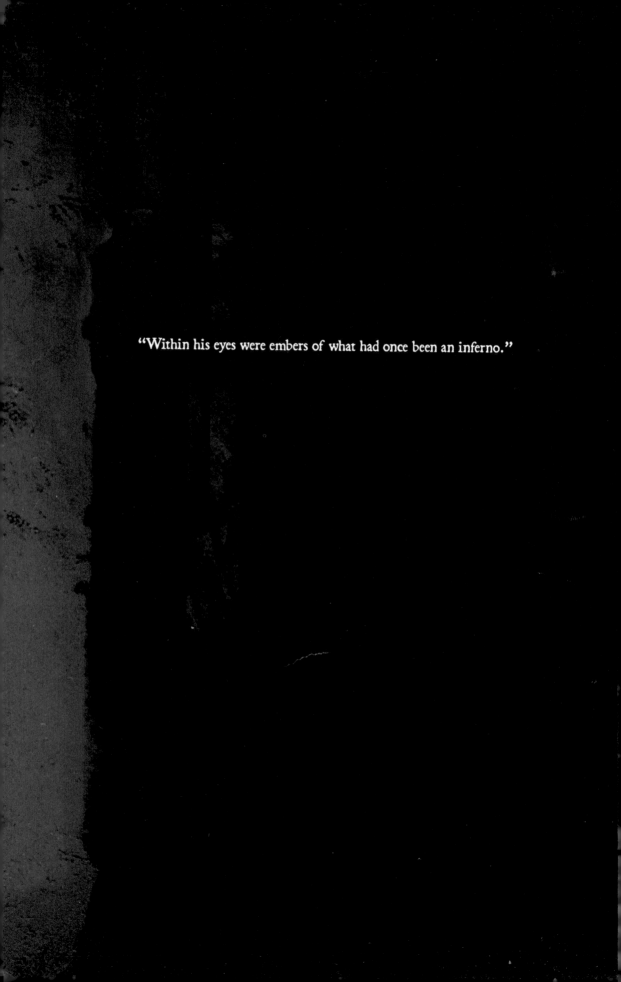

"Within his eyes were embers of what had once been an inferno."

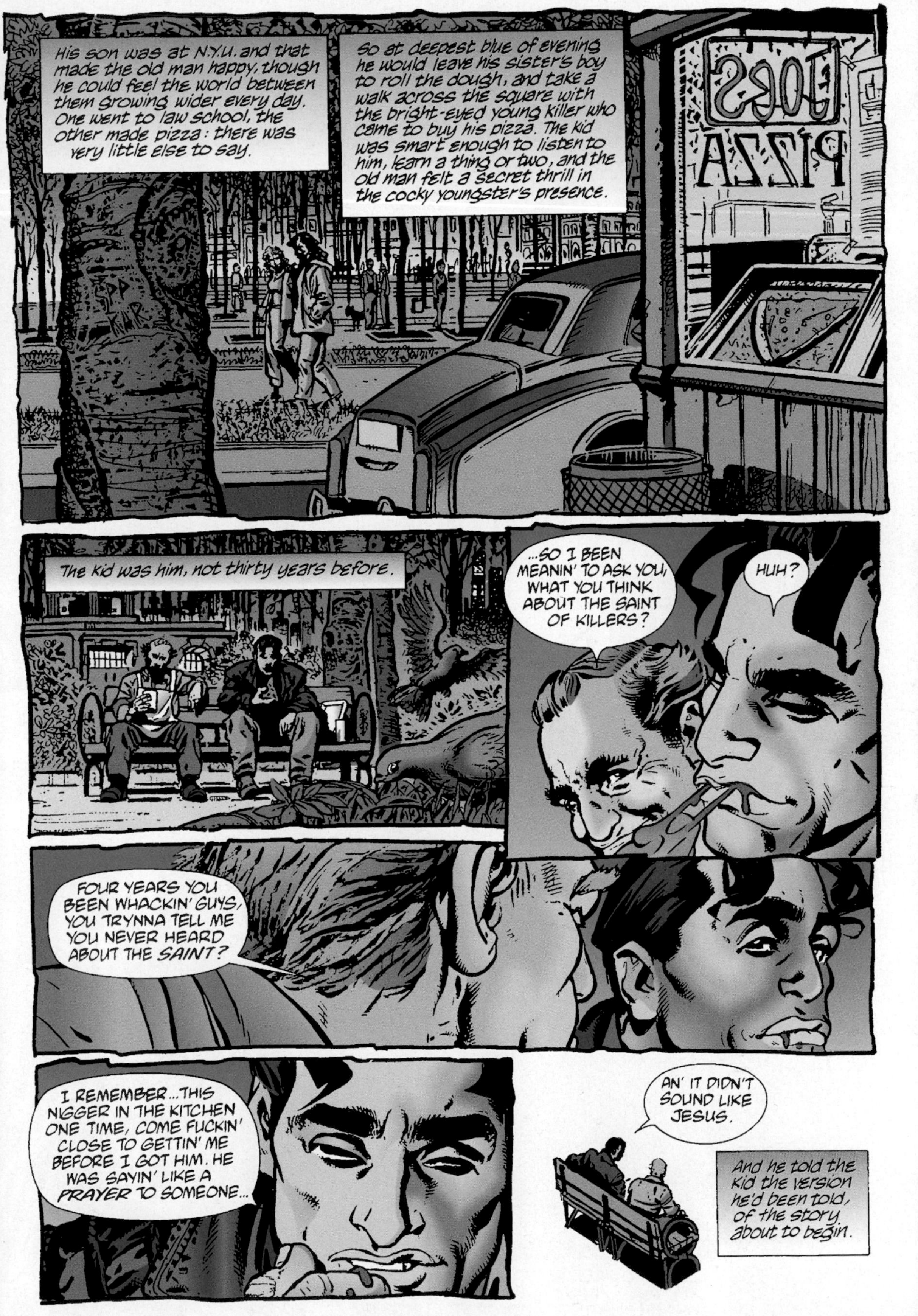

His son was at N.Y.U. and that made the old man happy, though he could feel the world between them growing wider every day. One went to law school, the other made pizza: there was very little else to say.
So at deepest blue of evening he would leave his sister's boy to roll the dough, and take a walk across the square with the bright-eyed young killer who came to buy his pizza. The kid was smart enough to listen to him, learn a thing or two, and the old man felt a secret thrill in the cocky youngster's presence.
JOE'S
PIZZA
The kid was him, not thirty years before.
...SO I BEEN MEANIN' TO ASK YOU, WHAT YOU THINK ABOUT THE SAINT OF KILLERS?
HUH?
FOUR YEARS YOU BEEN WHACKIN' GUYS, YOU TRYNNA TELL ME YOU NEVER HEARD ABOUT THE SAINT?
I REMEMBER... THIS NIGGER IN THE KITCHEN ONE TIME, COME FUCKIN' CLOSE TO GETTIN' ME BEFORE I GOT HIM. HE WAS SAYIN' LIKE A PRAYER TO SOMEONE...
AN' IT DIDN'T SOUND LIKE JESUS.
And he told the kid the version he'd been told, of the story about to begin.

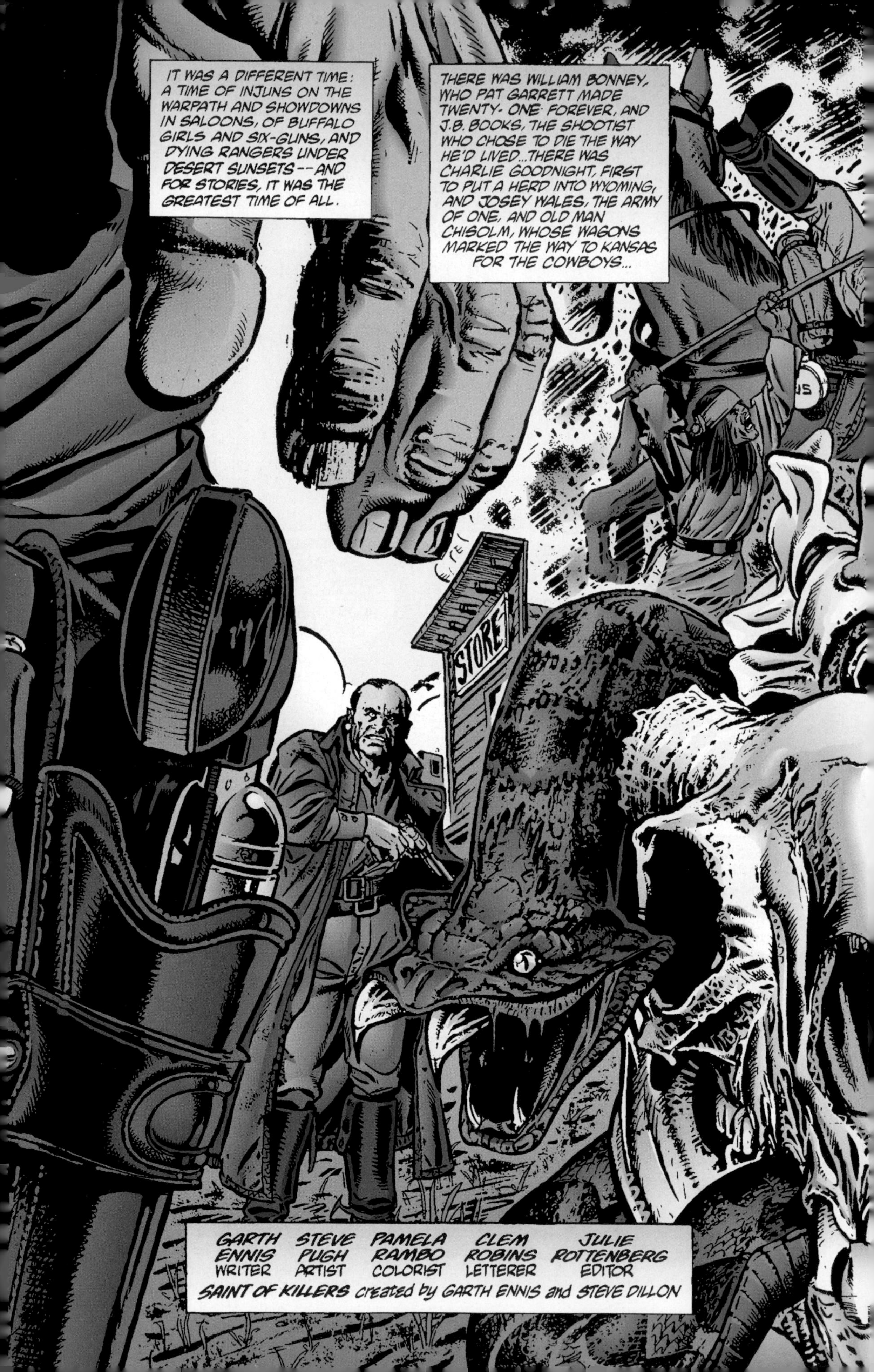
IT WAS A DIFFERENT TIME: A TIME OF INJUNS ON THE WARPATH AND SHOWDOWNS IN SALOONS, OF BUFFALO GIRLS AND SIX-GUNS, AND DYING RANGERS UNDER DESERT SUNSETS -- AND FOR STORIES, IT WAS THE GREATEST TIME OF ALL.
THERE WAS WILLIAM BONNEY, WHO PAT GARRETT MADE TWENTY-ONE FOREVER, AND J.B. BOOKS, THE SHOOTIST WHO CHOSE TO DIE THE WAY HE'D LIVED...THERE WAS CHARLIE GOODNIGHT, FIRST TO PUT A HERD INTO WYOMING, AND JOSEY WALES, THE ARMY OF ONE, AND OLD MAN CHISOLM, WHOSE WAGONS MARKED THE WAY TO KANSAS FOR THE COWBOYS...
STORE
GARTH ENNIS WRITER
STEVE PUGH ARTIST
PAMELA RAMBO COLORIST
CLEM ROBINS LETTERER
JULIE ROTTENBERG EDITOR
SAINT OF KILLERS created by GARTH ENNIS and STEVE DILLON

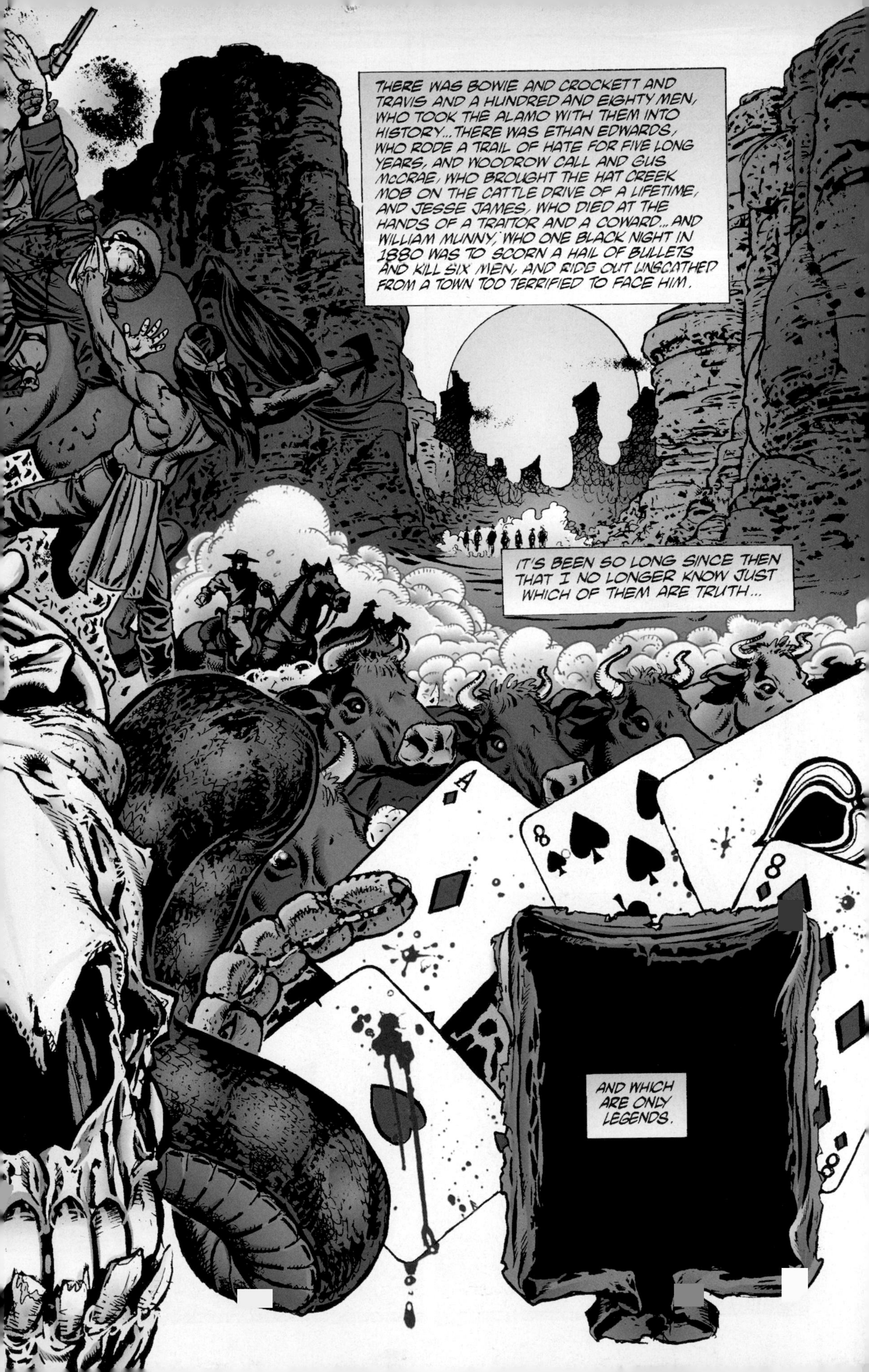
THERE WAS BOWIE AND CROCKETT AND TRAVIS AND A HUNDRED AND EIGHTY MEN, WHO TOOK THE ALAMO WITH THEM INTO HISTORY... THERE WAS ETHAN EDWARDS, WHO RODE A TRAIL OF HATE FOR FIVE LONG YEARS, AND WOODROW CALL AND GUS McCRAE, WHO BROUGHT THE HAT CREEK MOB ON THE CATTLE DRIVE OF A LIFETIME, AND JESSE JAMES, WHO DIED AT THE HANDS OF A TRAITOR AND A COWARD... AND WILLIAM MUNNY, WHO ONE BLACK NIGHT IN 1880 WAS TO SCORN A HAIL OF BULLETS AND KILL SIX MEN, AND RIDE OUT UNSCATHED FROM A TOWN TOO TERRIFIED TO FACE HIM.
IT'S BEEN SO LONG SINCE THEN THAT I NO LONGER KNOW JUST WHICH OF THEM ARE TRUTH...
AND WHICH ARE ONLY LEGENDS.

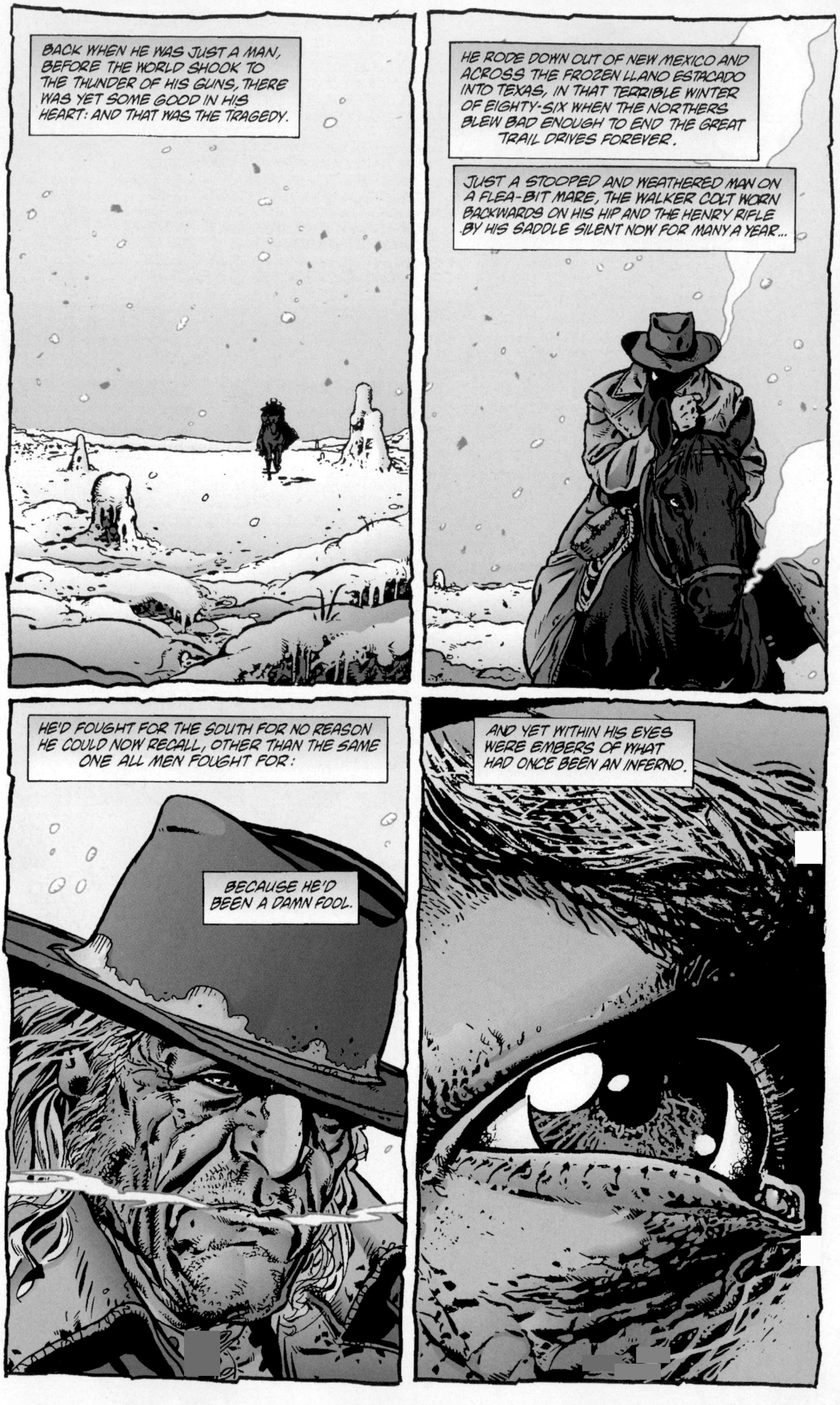
BACK WHEN HE WAS JUST A MAN, BEFORE THE WORLD SHOOK TO THE THUNDER OF HIS GUNS, THERE WAS YET SOME GOOD IN HIS HEART: AND THAT WAS THE TRAGEDY.
HE RODE DOWN OUT OF NEW MEXICO AND ACROSS THE FROZEN LLANO ESTACADO INTO TEXAS, IN THAT TERRIBLE WINTER OF EIGHTY-SIX WHEN THE NORTHERS BLEW BAD ENOUGH TO END THE GREAT TRAIL DRIVES FOREVER.
JUST A STOOPED AND WEATHERED MAN ON A FLEA-BIT MARE, THE WALKER COLT WORN BACKWARDS ON HIS HIP AND THE HENRY RIFLE BY HIS SADDLE SILENT NOW FOR MANY A YEAR...
HE'D FOUGHT FOR THE SOUTH FOR NO REASON HE COULD NOW RECALL, OTHER THAN THE SAME ONE ALL MEN FOUGHT FOR:
BECAUSE HE'D BEEN A DAMN FOOL.
AND YET WITHIN HIS EYES WERE EMBERS OF WHAT HAD ONCE BEEN AN INFERNO.

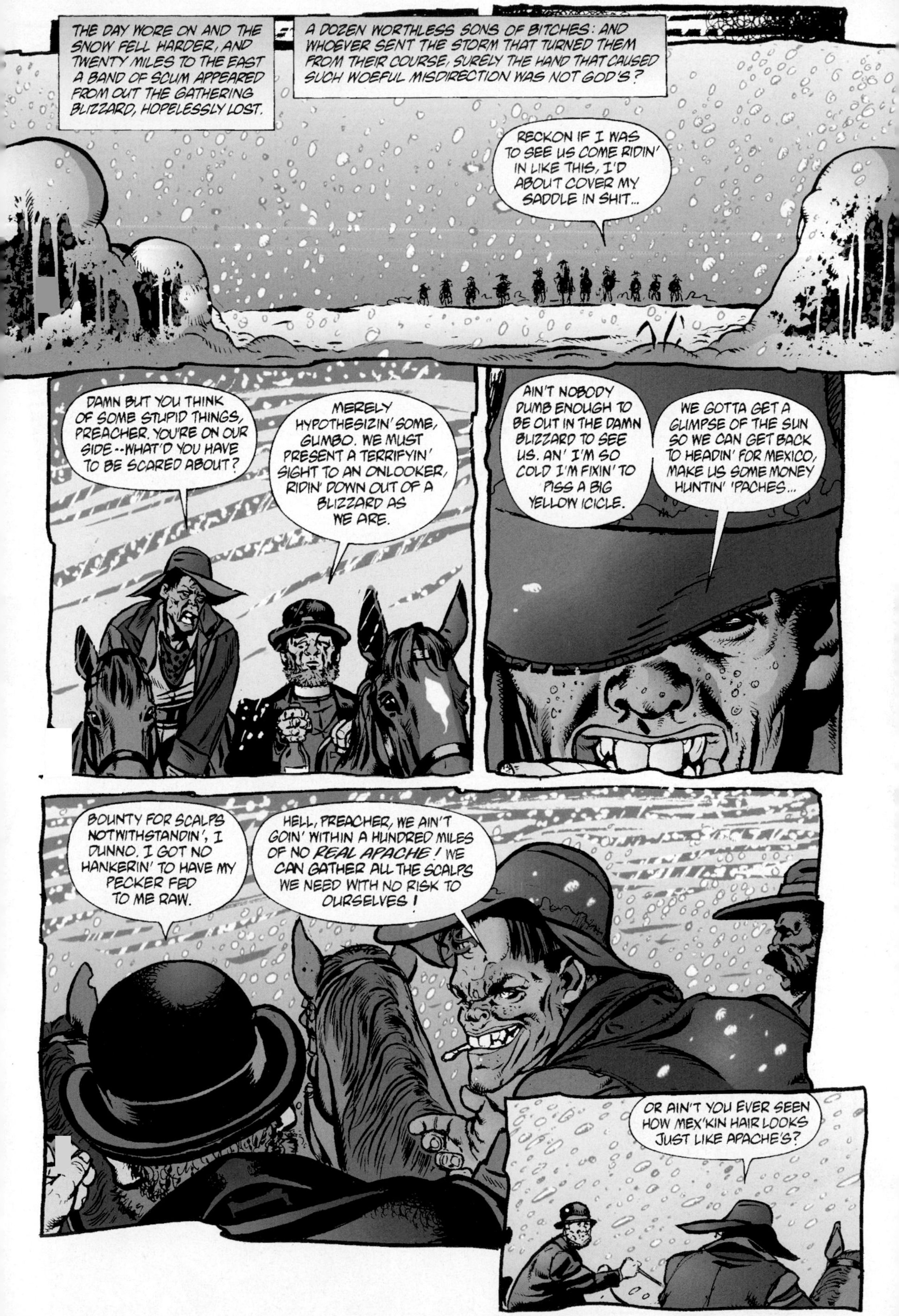
THE DAY WORE ON AND THE SNOW FELL HARDER, AND TWENTY MILES TO THE EAST A BAND OF SCUM APPEARED FROM OUT THE GATHERING BLIZZARD, HOPELESSLY LOST.
A DOZEN WORTHLESS SONS OF BITCHES: AND WHOEVER SENT THE STORM THAT TURNED THEM FROM THEIR COURSE, SURELY THE HAND THAT CAUSED SUCH WOEFUL MISDIRECTION WAS NOT GOD'S?
RECKON IF I WAS TO SEE US COME RIDIN' IN LIKE THIS, I'D ABOUT COVER MY SADDLE IN SHIT...
DAMN BUT YOU THINK OF SOME STUPID THINGS, PREACHER. YOU'RE ON OUR SIDE--WHAT'D YOU HAVE TO BE SCARED ABOUT?
MERELY HYPOTHESIZIN' SOME, GUMBO. WE MUST PRESENT A TERRIFYIN' SIGHT TO AN ONLOOKER, RIDIN' DOWN OUT OF A BLIZZARD AS WE ARE.
AIN'T NOBODY DUMB ENOUGH TO BE OUT IN THE DAMN BLIZZARD TO SEE US. AN' I'M SO COLD I'M FIXIN' TO PISS A BIG YELLOW ICICLE.
WE GOTTA GET A GLIMPSE OF THE SUN SO WE CAN GET BACK TO HEADIN' FOR MEXICO, MAKE US SOME MONEY HUNTIN' 'PACHES...
BOUNTY FOR SCALPS NOTWITHSTANDIN', I DUNNO. I GOT NO HANKERIN' TO HAVE MY PECKER FED TO ME RAW.
HELL, PREACHER, WE AIN'T GOIN' WITHIN A HUNDRED MILES OF NO REAL APACHE! WE CAN GATHER ALL THE SCALPS WE NEED WITH NO RISK TO OURSELVES!
OR AIN'T YOU EVER SEEN HOW MEX'KIN HAIR LOOKS JUST LIKE APACHE'S?

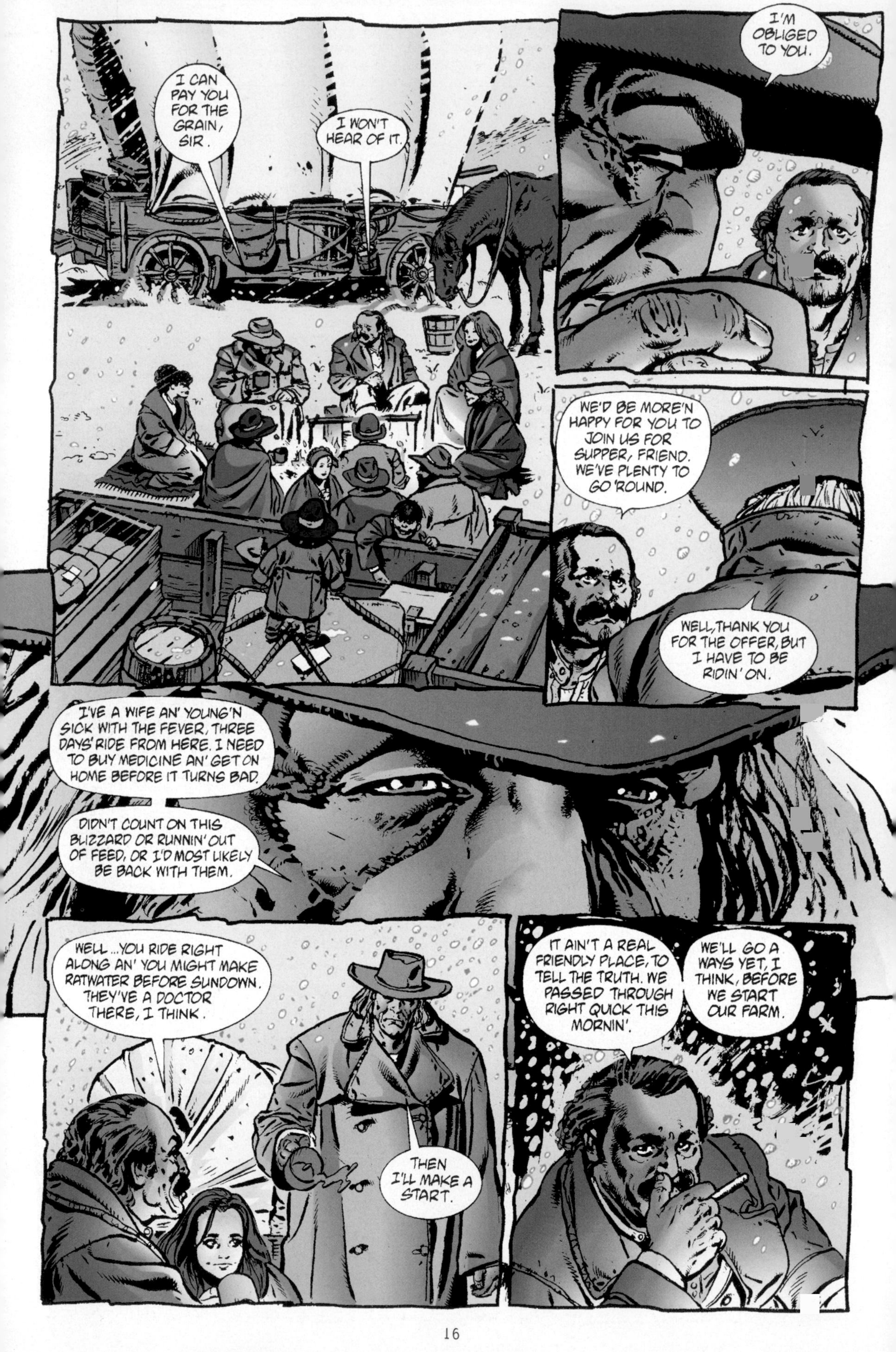
I CAN PAY YOU FOR THE GRAIN, SIR.
I WON'T HEAR OF IT.
I'M OBLIGED TO YOU.
WE'D BE MORE'N HAPPY FOR YOU TO JOIN US FOR SUPPER, FRIEND. WE'VE PLENTY TO GO 'ROUND.
WELL, THANK YOU FOR THE OFFER, BUT I HAVE TO BE RIDIN' ON.
I'VE A WIFE AN' YOUNG'N SICK WITH THE FEVER, THREE DAYS' RIDE FROM HERE. I NEED TO BUY MEDICINE AN' GET ON HOME BEFORE IT TURNS BAD.
DIDN'T COUNT ON THIS BLIZZARD OR RUNNIN' OUT OF FEED, OR I'D MOST LIKELY BE BACK WITH THEM.
WELL... YOU RIDE RIGHT ALONG AN' YOU MIGHT MAKE RATWATER BEFORE SUNDOWN. THEY'VE A DOCTOR THERE, I THINK.
THEN I'LL MAKE A START.
IT AIN'T A REAL FRIENDLY PLACE, TO TELL THE TRUTH. WE PASSED THROUGH RIGHT QUICK THIS MORNIN'.
WE'LL GO A WAYS YET, I THINK, BEFORE WE START OUR FARM.

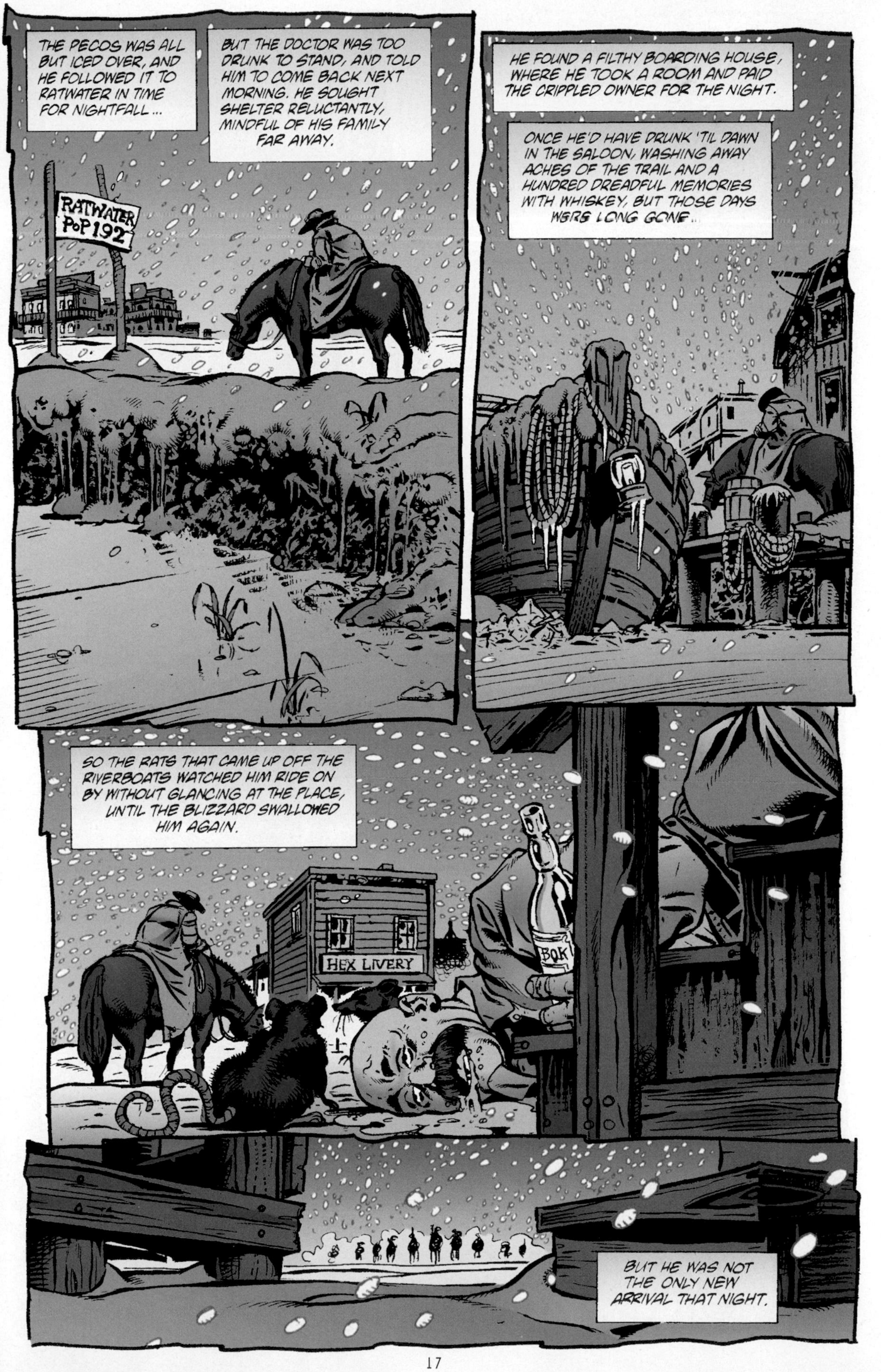
THE PECOS WAS ALL BUT ICED OVER, AND HE FOLLOWED IT TO RATWATER IN TIME FOR NIGHTFALL ...
BUT THE DOCTOR WAS TOO DRUNK TO STAND, AND TOLD HIM TO COME BACK NEXT MORNING. HE SOUGHT SHELTER RELUCTANTLY, MINDFUL OF HIS FAMILY FAR AWAY.
RATWATER
PoP 192
HE FOUND A FILTHY BOARDING HOUSE, WHERE HE TOOK A ROOM AND PAID THE CRIPPLED OWNER FOR THE NIGHT.
ONCE HE'D HAVE DRUNK 'TIL DAWN IN THE SALOON, WASHING AWAY ACHES OF THE TRAIL AND A HUNDRED DREADFUL MEMORIES WITH WHISKEY, BUT THOSE DAYS WERE LONG GONE...
SO THE RATS THAT CAME UP OFF THE RIVERBOATS WATCHED HIM RIDE ON BY WITHOUT GLANCING AT THE PLACE, UNTIL THE BLIZZARD SWALLOWED HIM AGAIN.
HEX LIVERY
BUT HE WAS NOT THE ONLY NEW ARRIVAL THAT NIGHT.

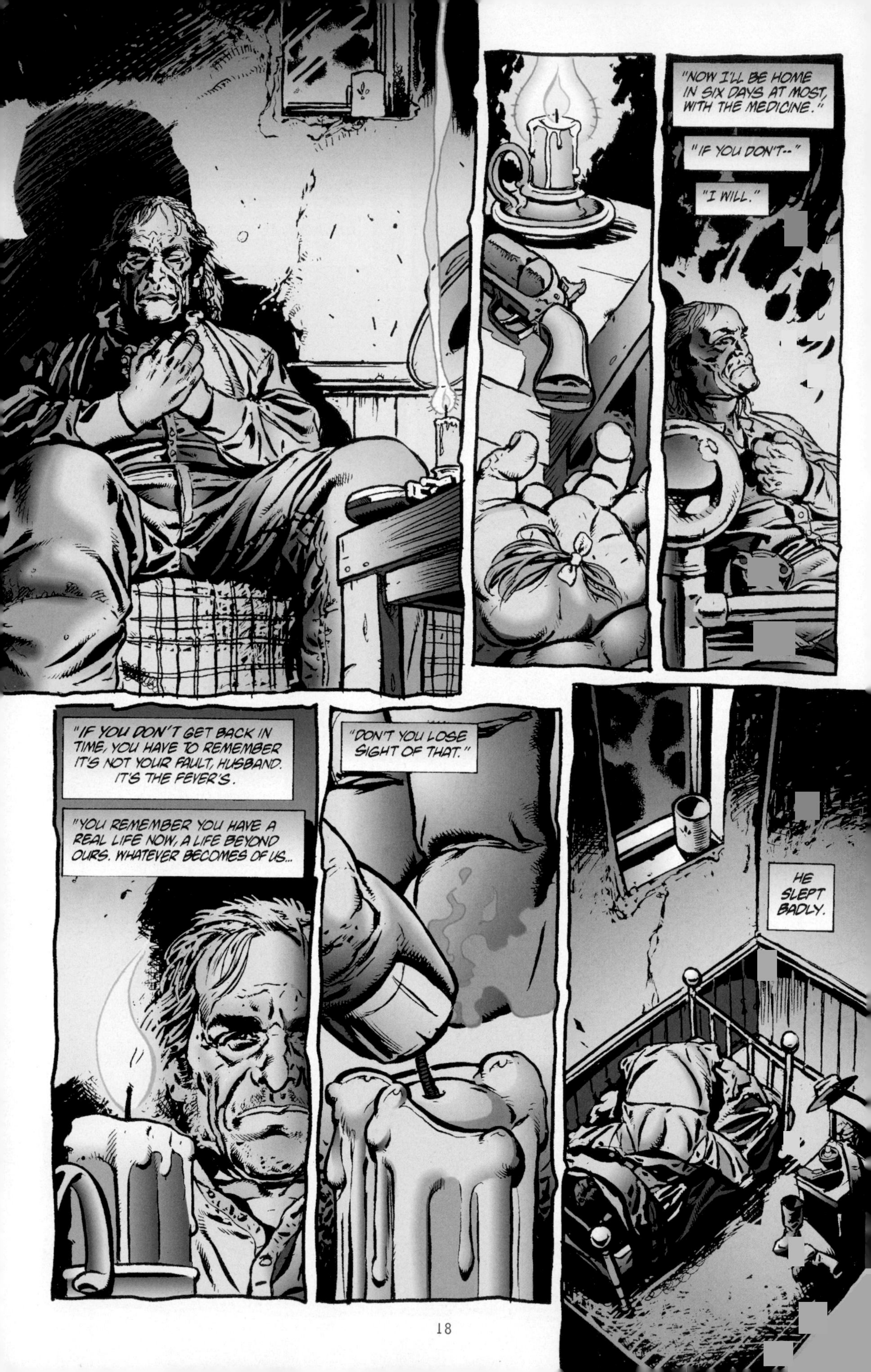
"NOW I'LL BE HOME IN SIX DAYS AT MOST, WITH THE MEDICINE."
"IF YOU DON'T--"
"I WILL."
"IF YOU DON'T GET BACK IN TIME, YOU HAVE TO REMEMBER IT'S NOT YOUR FAULT, HUSBAND. IT'S THE FEVER'S.
"YOU REMEMBER YOU HAVE A REAL LIFE NOW, A LIFE BEYOND OURS. WHATEVER BECOMES OF US...
"DON'T YOU LOSE SIGHT OF THAT."
HE SLEPT BADLY.

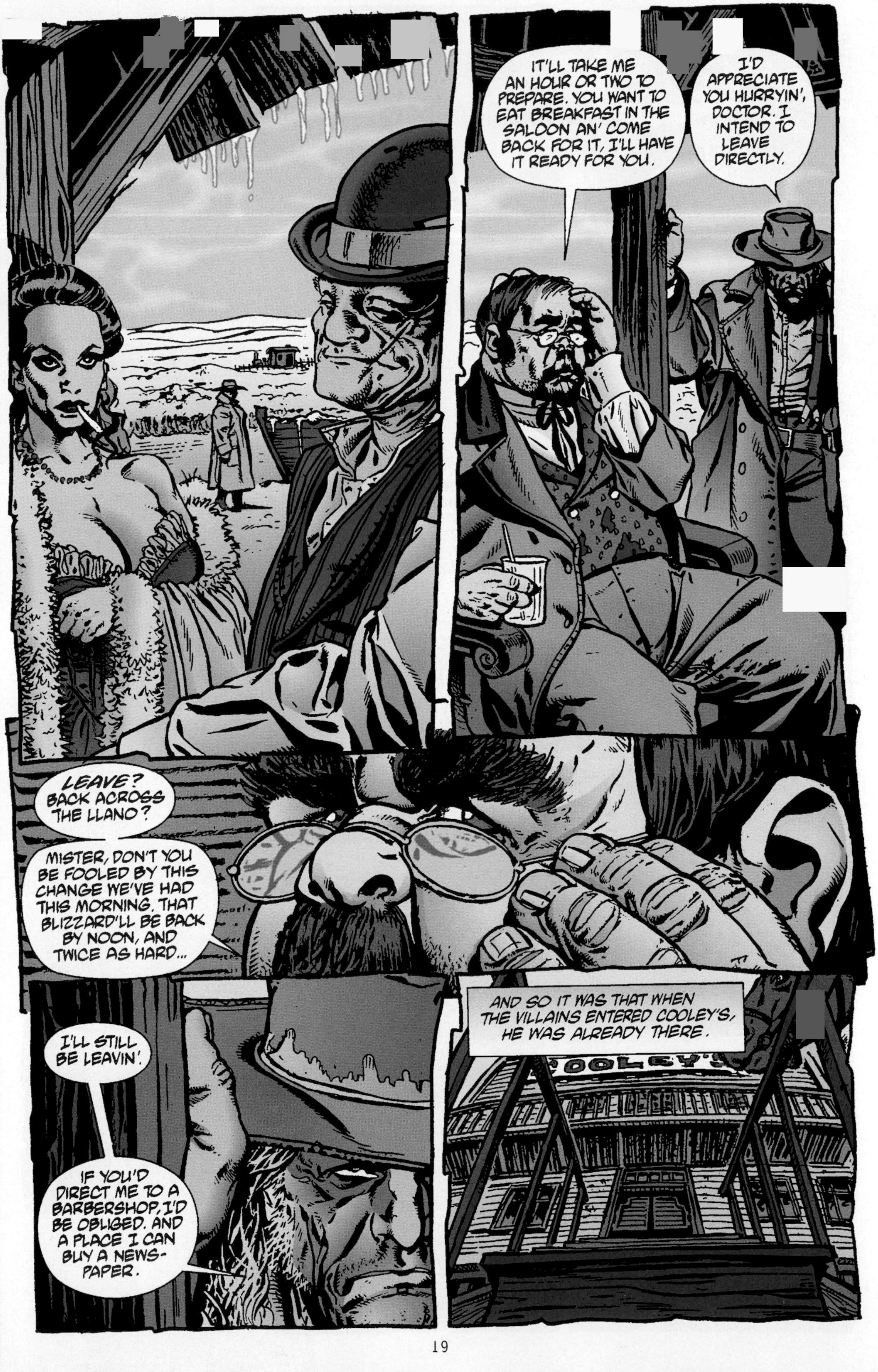

IT'LL TAKE ME AN HOUR OR TWO TO PREPARE. YOU WANT TO EAT BREAKFAST IN THE SALOON AN' COME BACK FOR IT, I'LL HAVE IT READY FOR YOU.
I'D APPRECIATE YOU HURRYIN', DOCTOR. I INTEND TO LEAVE DIRECTLY.
LEAVE? BACK ACROSS THE LLANO?
MISTER, DON'T YOU BE FOOLED BY THIS CHANGE WE'VE HAD THIS MORNING. THAT BLIZZARD'LL BE BACK BY NOON, AND TWICE AS HARD...
I'LL STILL BE LEAVIN'.
IF YOU'D DIRECT ME TO A BARBERSHOP, I'D BE OBLIGED. AND A PLACE I CAN BUY A NEWS-PAPER.
AND SO IT WAS THAT WHEN THE VILLAINS ENTERED COOLEY'S, HE WAS ALREADY THERE.

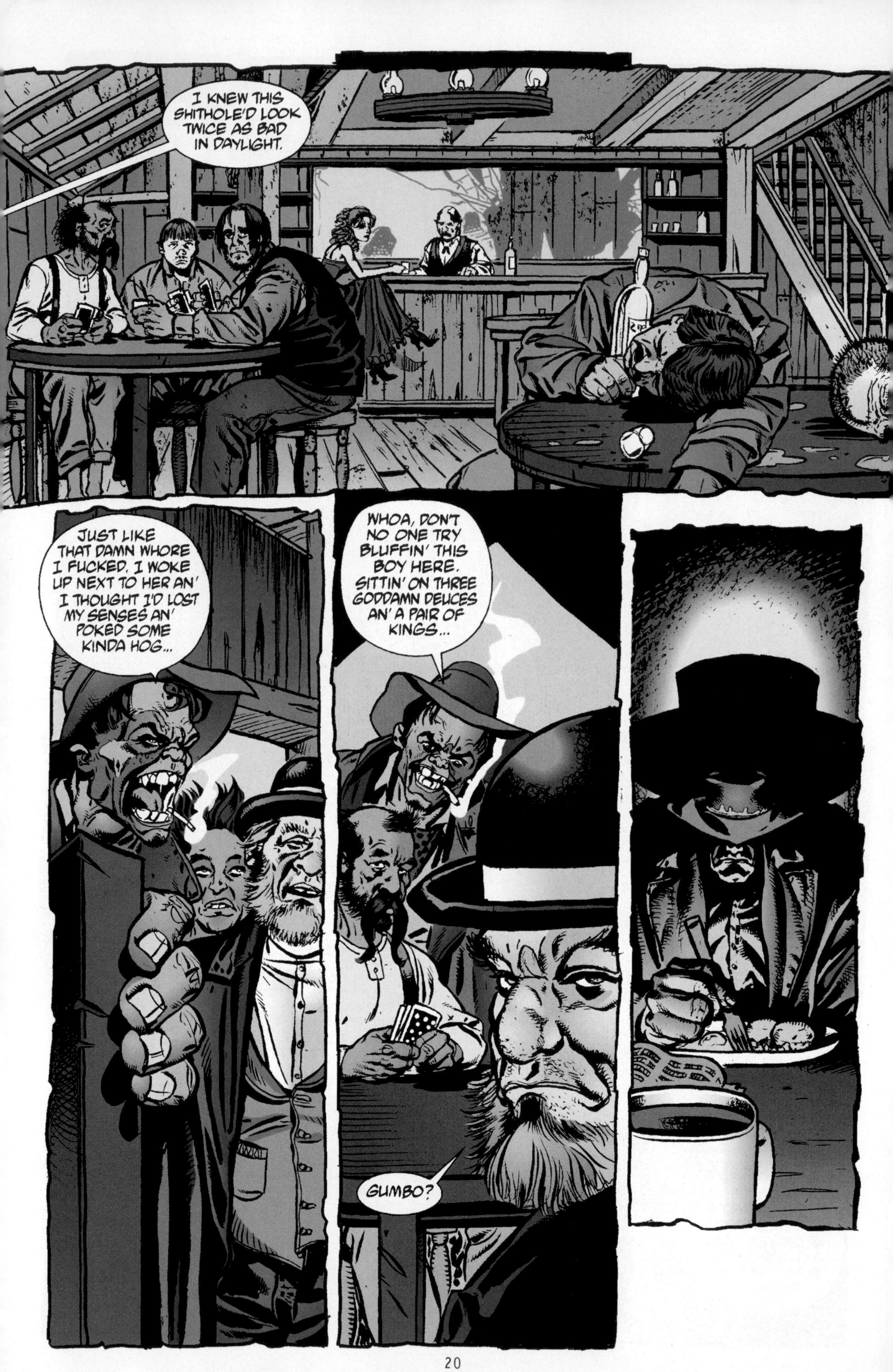
I KNEW THIS SHITHOLE'D LOOK TWICE AS BAD IN DAYLIGHT.
JUST LIKE THAT DAMN WHORE I FUCKED. I WOKE UP NEXT TO HER AN' I THOUGHT I'D LOST MY SENSES AN' POKED SOME KINDA HOG...
WHOA, DON'T NO ONE TRY BLUFFIN' THIS BOY HERE. SITTIN' ON THREE GODDAMN DEUCES AN' A PAIR OF KINGS...
GUMBO?

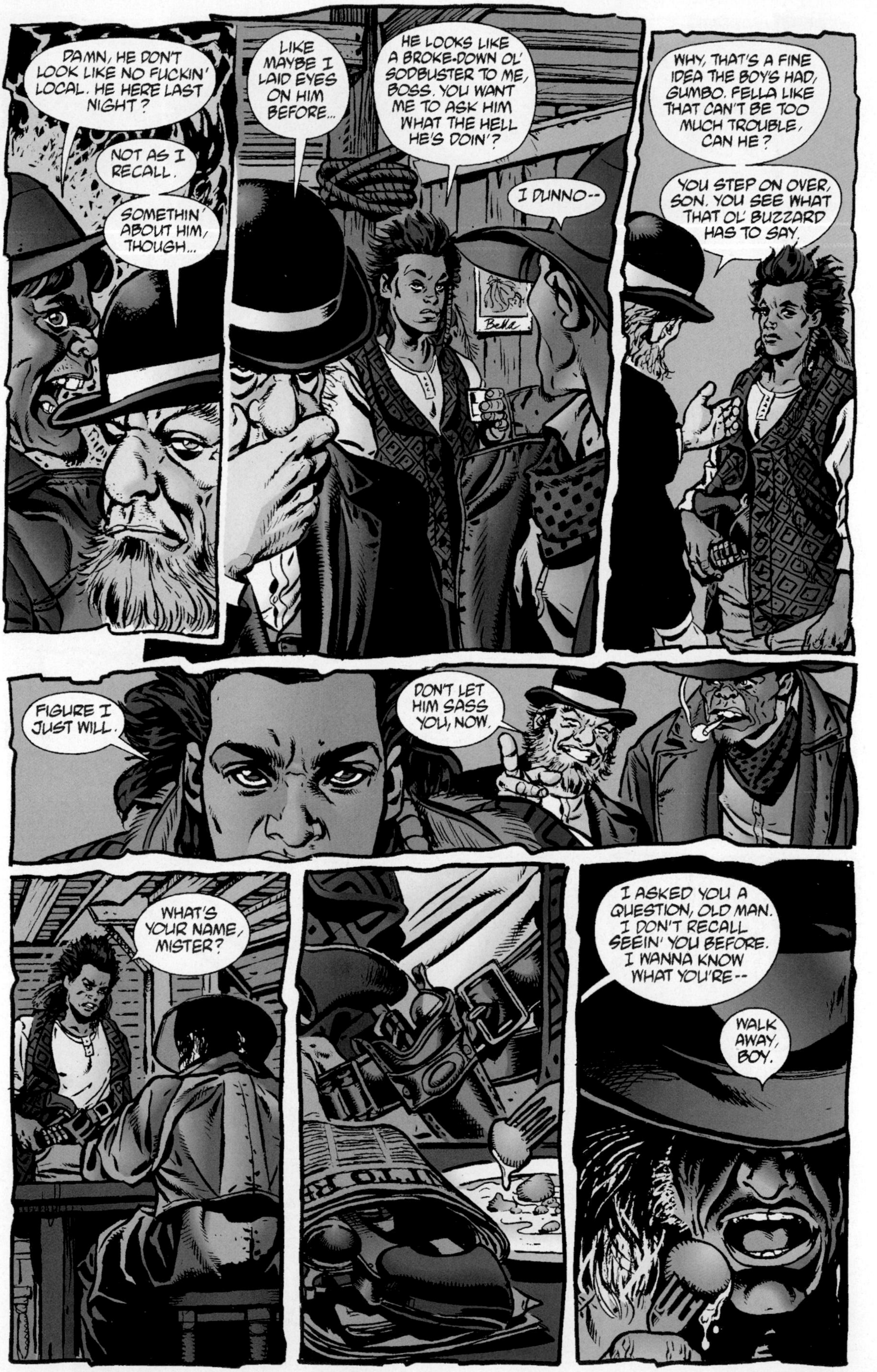
DAMN, HE DON'T LOOK LIKE NO FUCKIN' LOCAL. HE HERE LAST NIGHT?
NOT AS I RECALL.
SOMETHIN' ABOUT HIM, THOUGH...
LIKE MAYBE I LAID EYES ON HIM BEFORE...
HE LOOKS LIKE A BROKE-DOWN OL' SODBUSTER TO ME, BOSS. YOU WANT ME TO ASK HIM WHAT THE HELL HE'S DOIN'?
I DUNNO--
WHY, THAT'S A FINE IDEA THE BOY'S HAD, GUMBO. FELLA LIKE THAT CAN'T BE TOO MUCH TROUBLE, CAN HE?
YOU STEP ON OVER, SON. YOU SEE WHAT THAT OL' BUZZARD HAS TO SAY.
FIGURE I JUST WILL.
DON'T LET HIM SASS YOU, NOW.
WHAT'S YOUR NAME, MISTER?
I ASKED YOU A QUESTION, OLD MAN. I DON'T RECALL SEEIN' YOU BEFORE. I WANNA KNOW WHAT YOU'RE--
WALK AWAY, BOY.

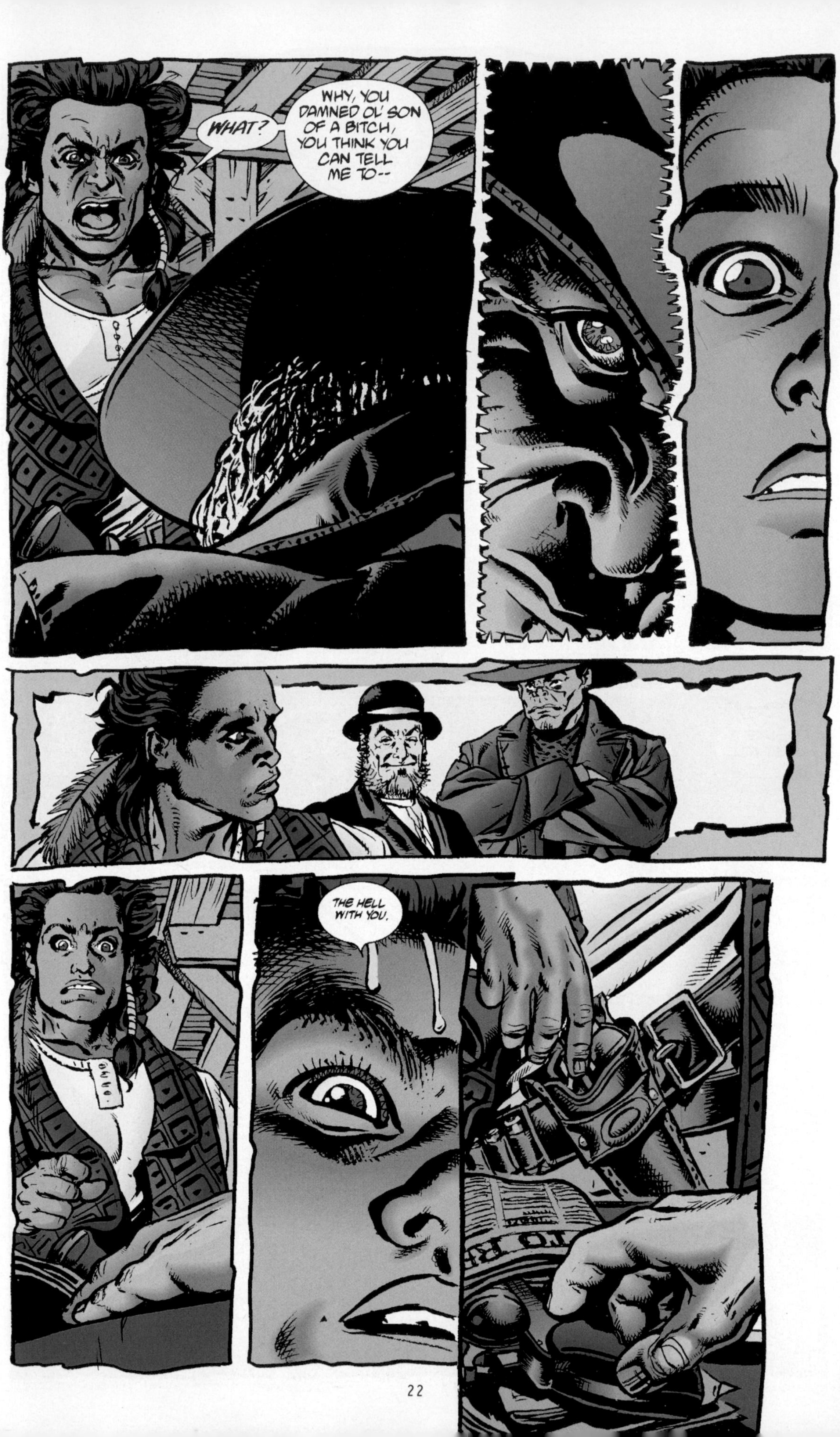
WHAT?
WHY, YOU DAMNED OL' SON OF A BITCH, YOU THINK YOU CAN TELL ME TO--
THE HELL WITH YOU.

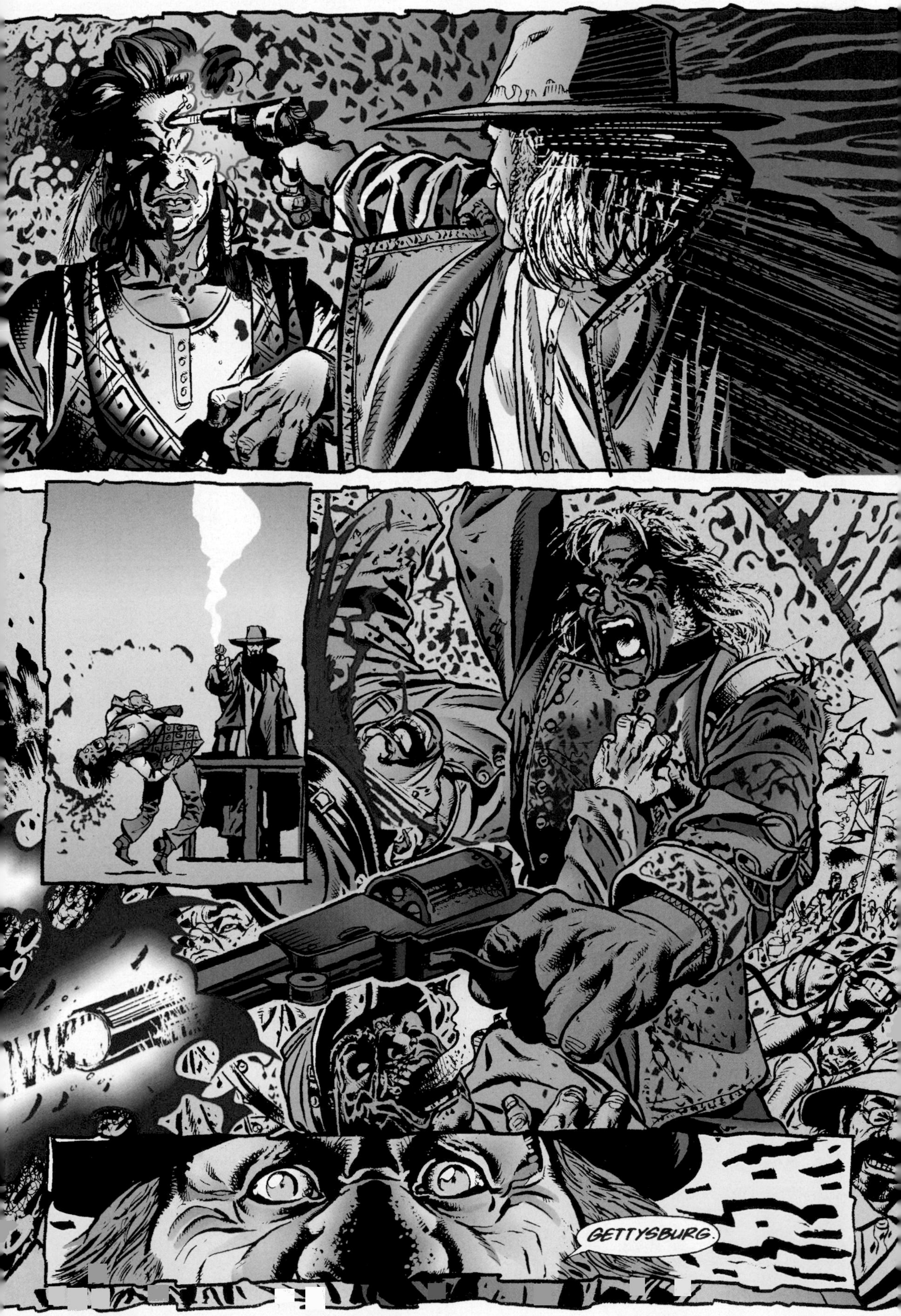
GETTYSBURG.

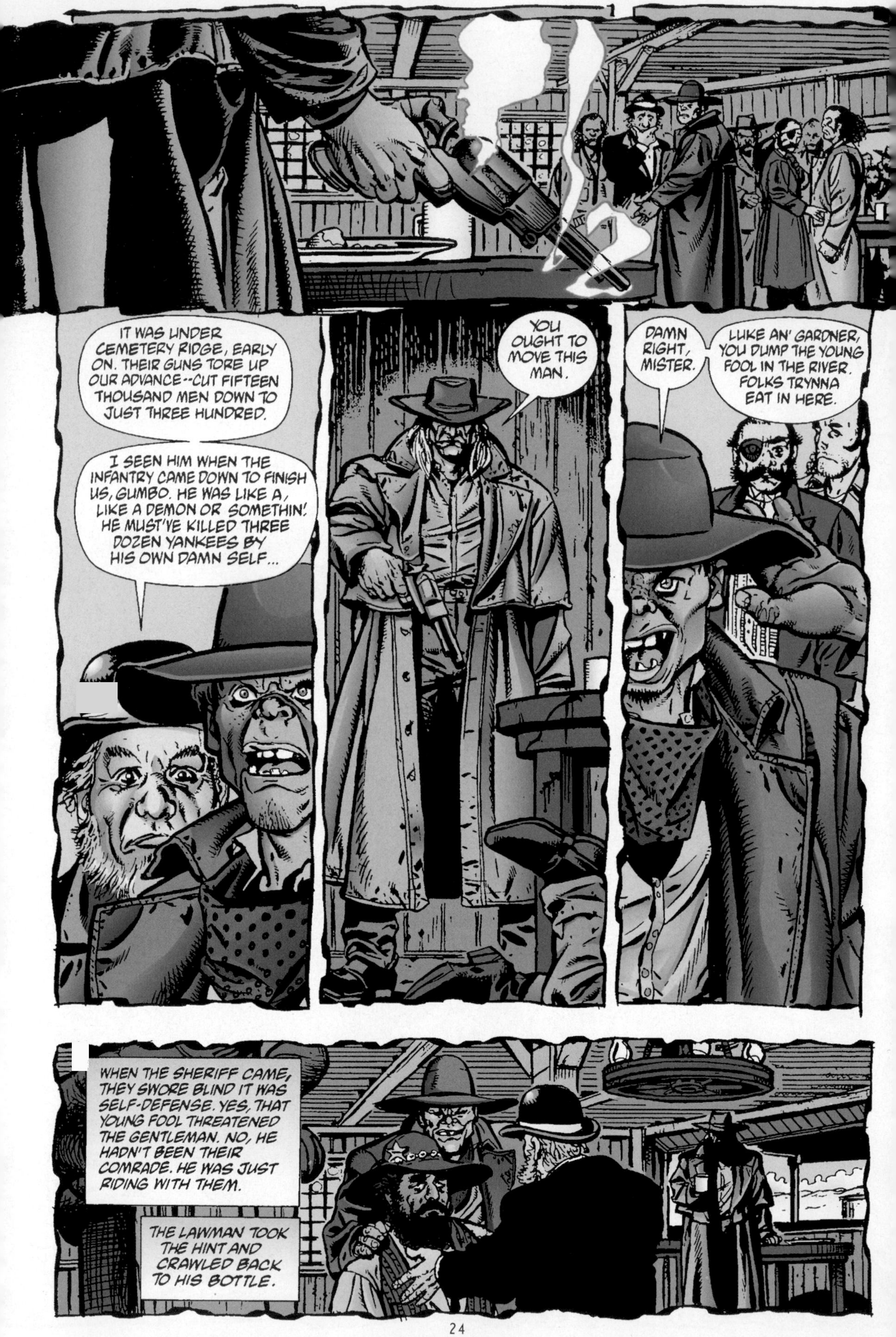
IT WAS UNDER CEMETERY RIDGE, EARLY ON. THEIR GUNS TORE UP OUR ADVANCE--CUT FIFTEEN THOUSAND MEN DOWN TO JUST THREE HUNDRED.
I SEEN HIM WHEN THE INFANTRY CAME DOWN TO FINISH US, GUMBO. HE WAS LIKE A, LIKE A DEMON OR SOMETHIN'. HE MUST'VE KILLED THREE DOZEN YANKEES BY HIS OWN DAMN SELF...
YOU OUGHT TO MOVE THIS MAN.
DAMN RIGHT, MISTER.
LUKE AN' GARDNER, YOU DUMP THE YOUNG FOOL IN THE RIVER. FOLKS TRYNNA EAT IN HERE.
WHEN THE SHERIFF CAME, THEY SWORE BLIND IT WAS SELF-DEFENSE. YES, THAT YOUNG FOOL THREATENED THE GENTLEMAN. NO, HE HADN'T BEEN THEIR COMRADE. HE WAS JUST RIDING WITH THEM.
THE LAWMAN TOOK THE HINT AND CRAWLED BACK TO HIS BOTTLE.

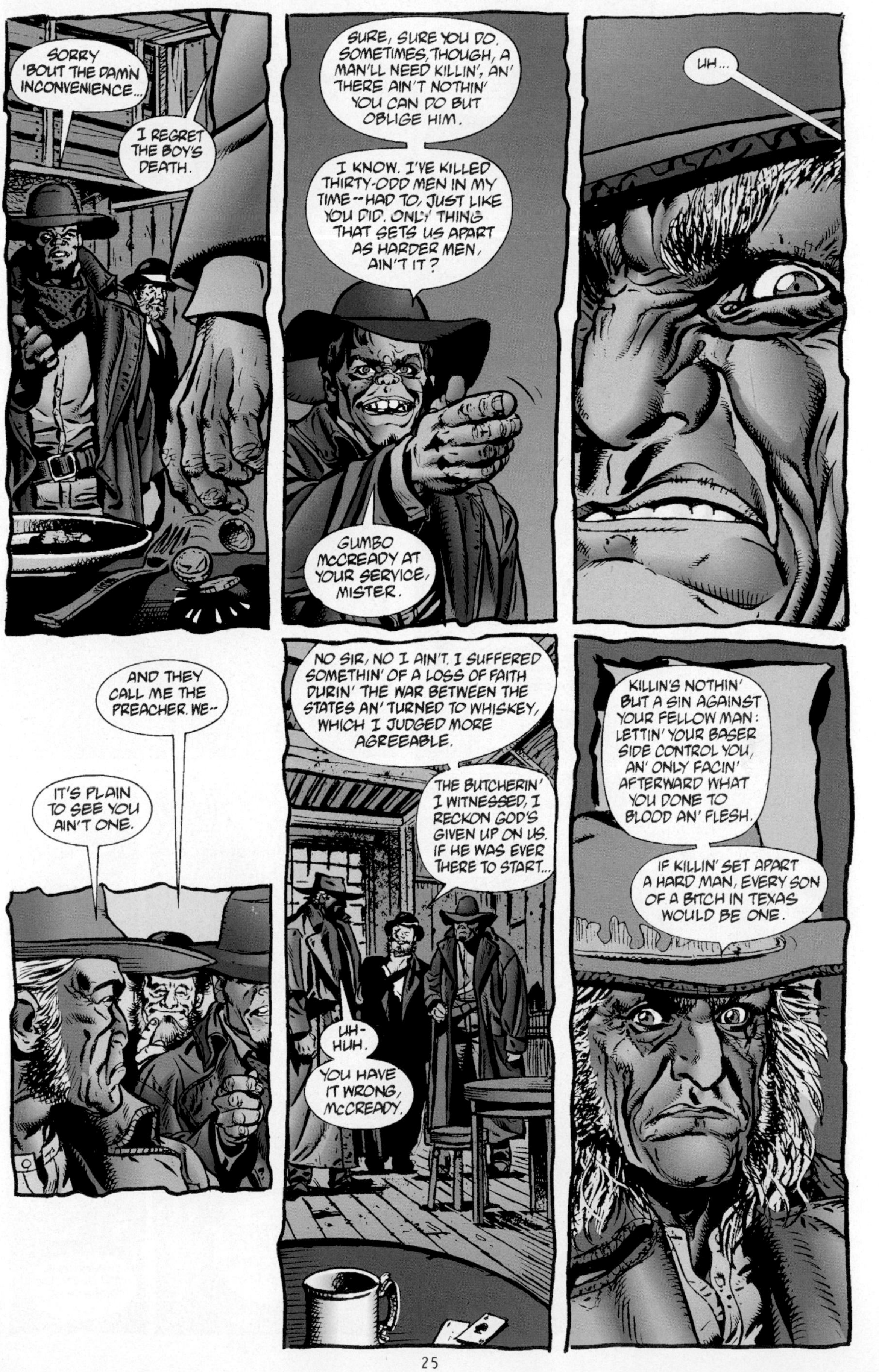
SORRY 'BOUT THE DAMN INCONVENIENCE...
I REGRET THE BOY'S DEATH.
SURE, SURE YOU DO. SOMETIMES, THOUGH, A MAN'LL NEED KILLIN', AN' THERE AIN'T NOTHIN' YOU CAN DO BUT OBLIGE HIM.
I KNOW. I'VE KILLED THIRTY-ODD MEN IN MY TIME--HAD TO, JUST LIKE YOU DID. ONLY THING THAT SETS US APART AS HARDER MEN, AIN'T IT?
GUMBO McCREADY AT YOUR SERVICE, MISTER.
UH...
AND THEY CALL ME THE PREACHER. WE--
IT'S PLAIN TO SEE YOU AIN'T ONE.
NO SIR, NO I AIN'T. I SUFFERED SOMETHIN' OF A LOSS OF FAITH DURIN' THE WAR BETWEEN THE STATES AN' TURNED TO WHISKEY, WHICH I JUDGED MORE AGREEABLE.
THE BUTCHERIN' I WITNESSED, I RECKON GOD'S GIVEN UP ON US. IF HE WAS EVER THERE TO START...
UH-HUH.
YOU HAVE IT WRONG, McCREADY.
KILLIN'S NOTHIN' BUT A SIN AGAINST YOUR FELLOW MAN: LETTIN' YOUR BASER SIDE CONTROL YOU, AN' ONLY FACIN' AFTERWARD WHAT YOU DONE TO BLOOD AN' FLESH.
IF KILLIN' SET APART A HARD MAN, EVERY SON OF A BITCH IN TEXAS WOULD BE ONE.

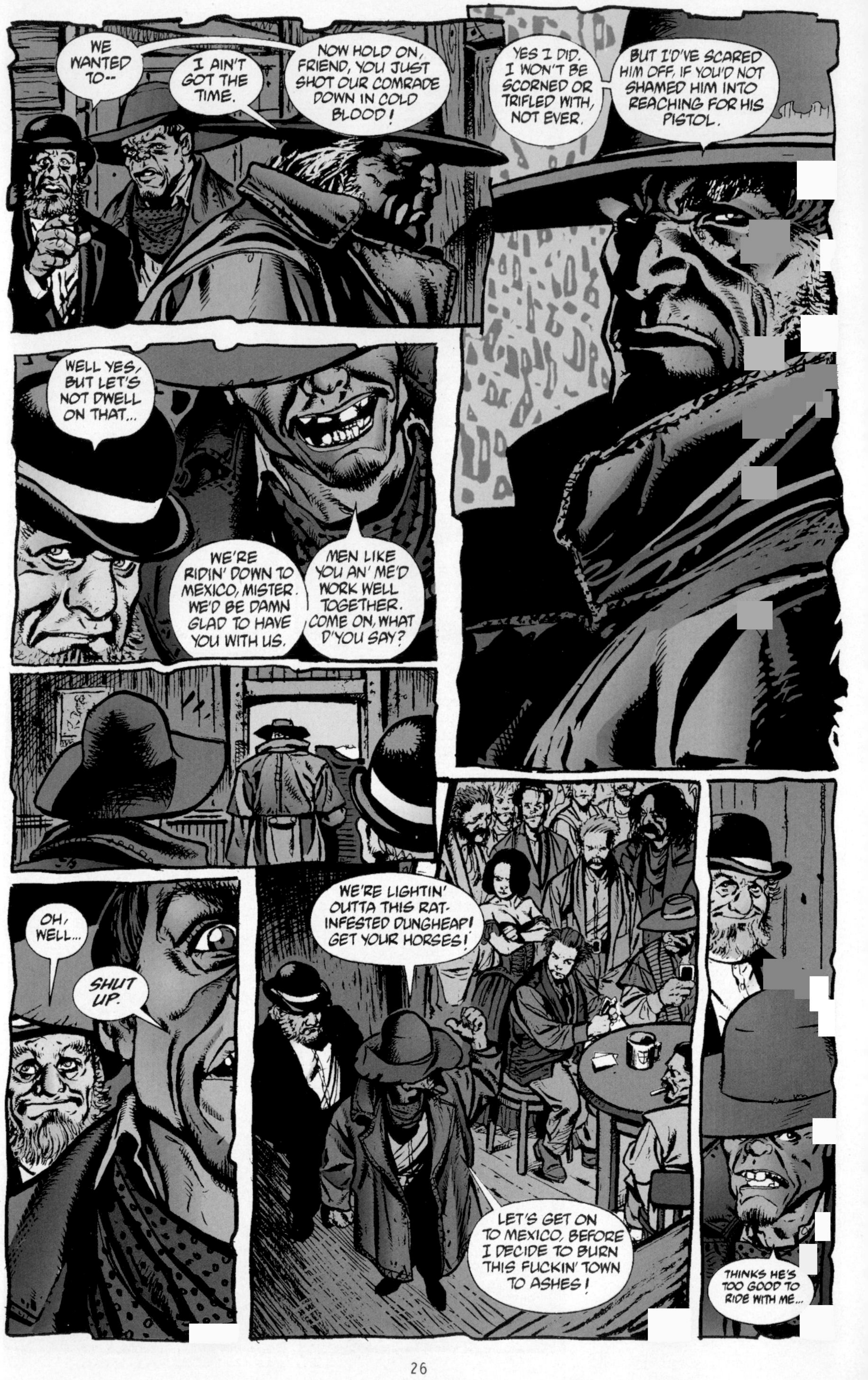
WE WANTED TO--
I AIN'T GOT THE TIME.
NOW HOLD ON, FRIEND, YOU JUST SHOT OUR COMRADE DOWN IN COLD BLOOD!
YES I DID. I WON'T BE SCORNED OR TRIFLED WITH, NOT EVER.
BUT I'D'VE SCARED HIM OFF, IF YOU'D NOT SHAMED HIM INTO REACHING FOR HIS PISTOL.
WELL YES, BUT LET'S NOT DWELL ON THAT...
WE'RE RIDIN' DOWN TO MEXICO, MISTER. WE'D BE DAMN GLAD TO HAVE YOU WITH US.
MEN LIKE YOU AN' ME'D WORK WELL TOGETHER. COME ON, WHAT D'YOU SAY?
OH, WELL...
SHUT UP.
WE'RE LIGHTIN' OUTTA THIS RAT-INFESTED DUNGHEAP! GET YOUR HORSES!
LET'S GET ON TO MEXICO, BEFORE I DECIDE TO BURN THIS FUCKIN' TOWN TO ASHES!
THINKS HE'S TOO GOOD TO RIDE WITH ME...

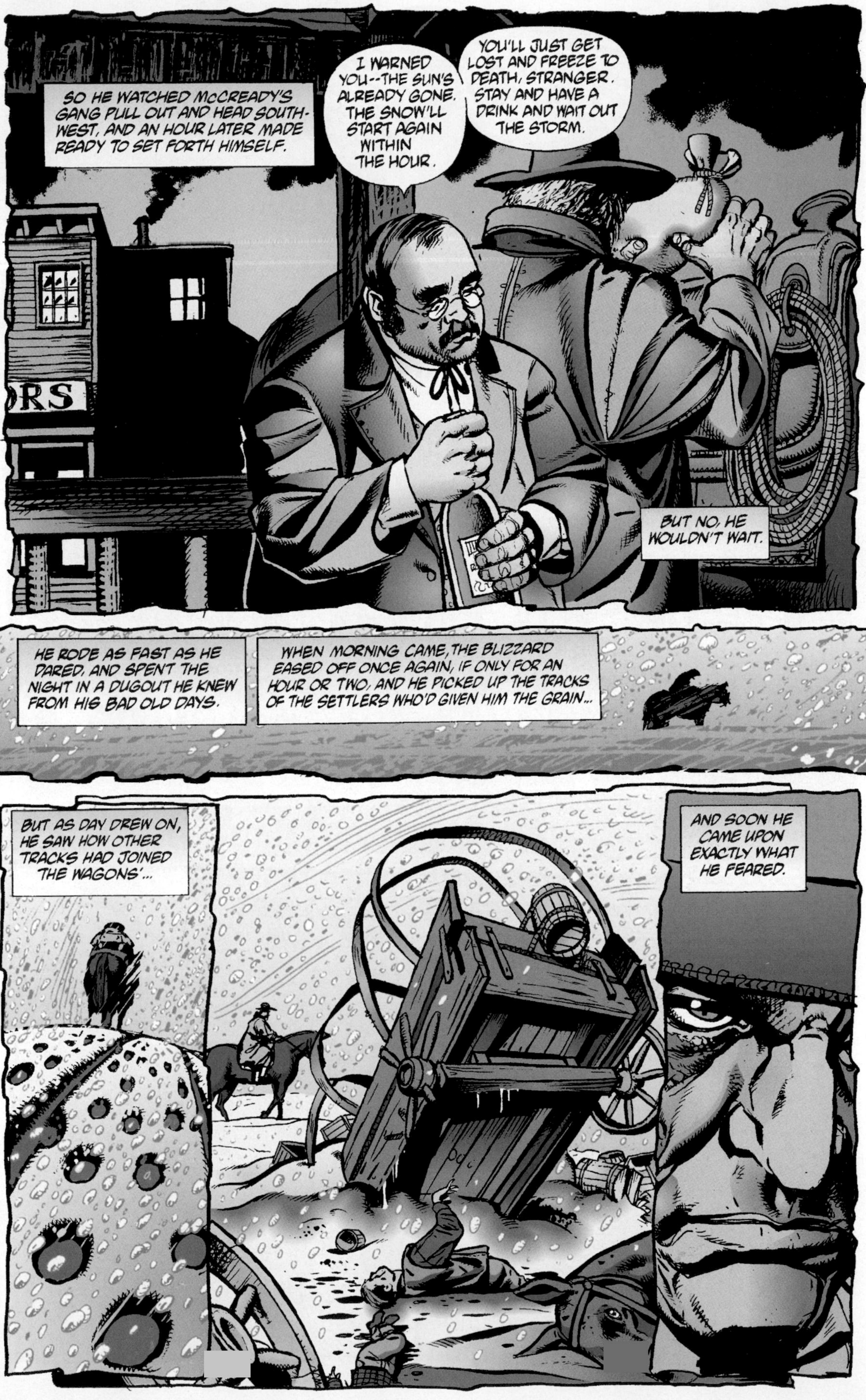
SO HE WATCHED McCREADY'S GANG PULL OUT AND HEAD SOUTH-WEST, AND AN HOUR LATER MADE READY TO SET FORTH HIMSELF.
I WARNED YOU--THE SUN'S ALREADY GONE. THE SNOW'LL START AGAIN WITHIN THE HOUR.
YOU'LL JUST GET LOST AND FREEZE TO DEATH, STRANGER. STAY AND HAVE A DRINK AND WAIT OUT THE STORM.
BUT NO, HE WOULDN'T WAIT.
HE RODE AS FAST AS HE DARED, AND SPENT THE NIGHT IN A DUGOUT HE KNEW FROM HIS BAD OLD DAYS.
WHEN MORNING CAME, THE BLIZZARD EASED OFF ONCE AGAIN, IF ONLY FOR AN HOUR OR TWO, AND HE PICKED UP THE TRACKS OF THE SETTLERS WHO'D GIVEN HIM THE GRAIN...
BUT AS DAY DREW ON, HE SAW HOW OTHER TRACKS HAD JOINED THE WAGONS'...
AND SOON HE CAME UPON EXACTLY WHAT HE FEARED.

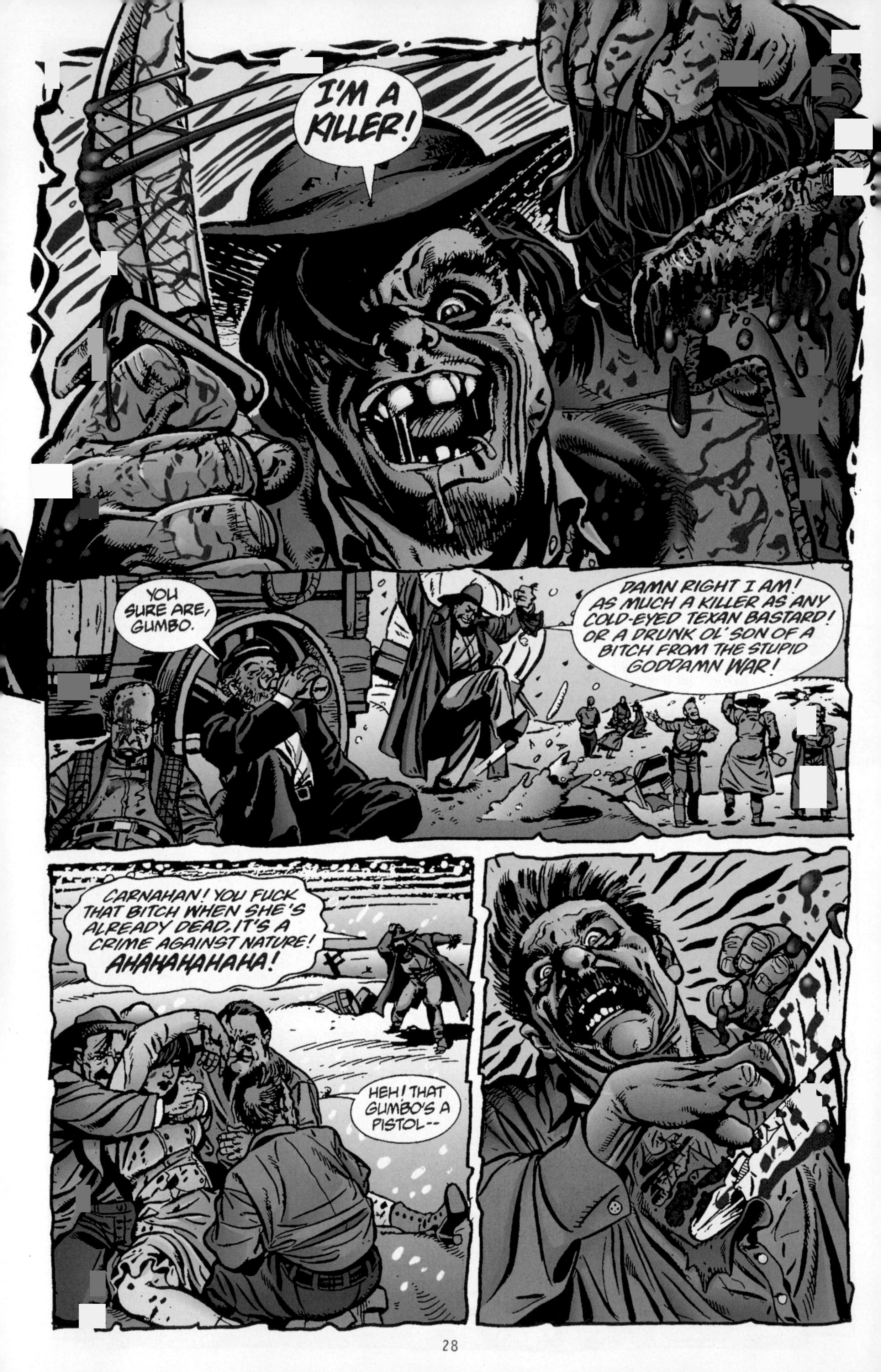
I'M A KILLER!
YOU SURE ARE, GUMBO.
DAMN RIGHT I AM! AS MUCH A KILLER AS ANY COLD-EYED TEXAN BASTARD! OR A DRUNK OL' SON OF A BITCH FROM THE STUPID GODDAMN WAR!
CARNAHAN! YOU FUCK THAT BITCH WHEN SHE'S ALREADY DEAD. IT'S A CRIME AGAINST NATURE! AHAHAHAHAHA!
HEH! THAT GUMBO'S A PISTOL--

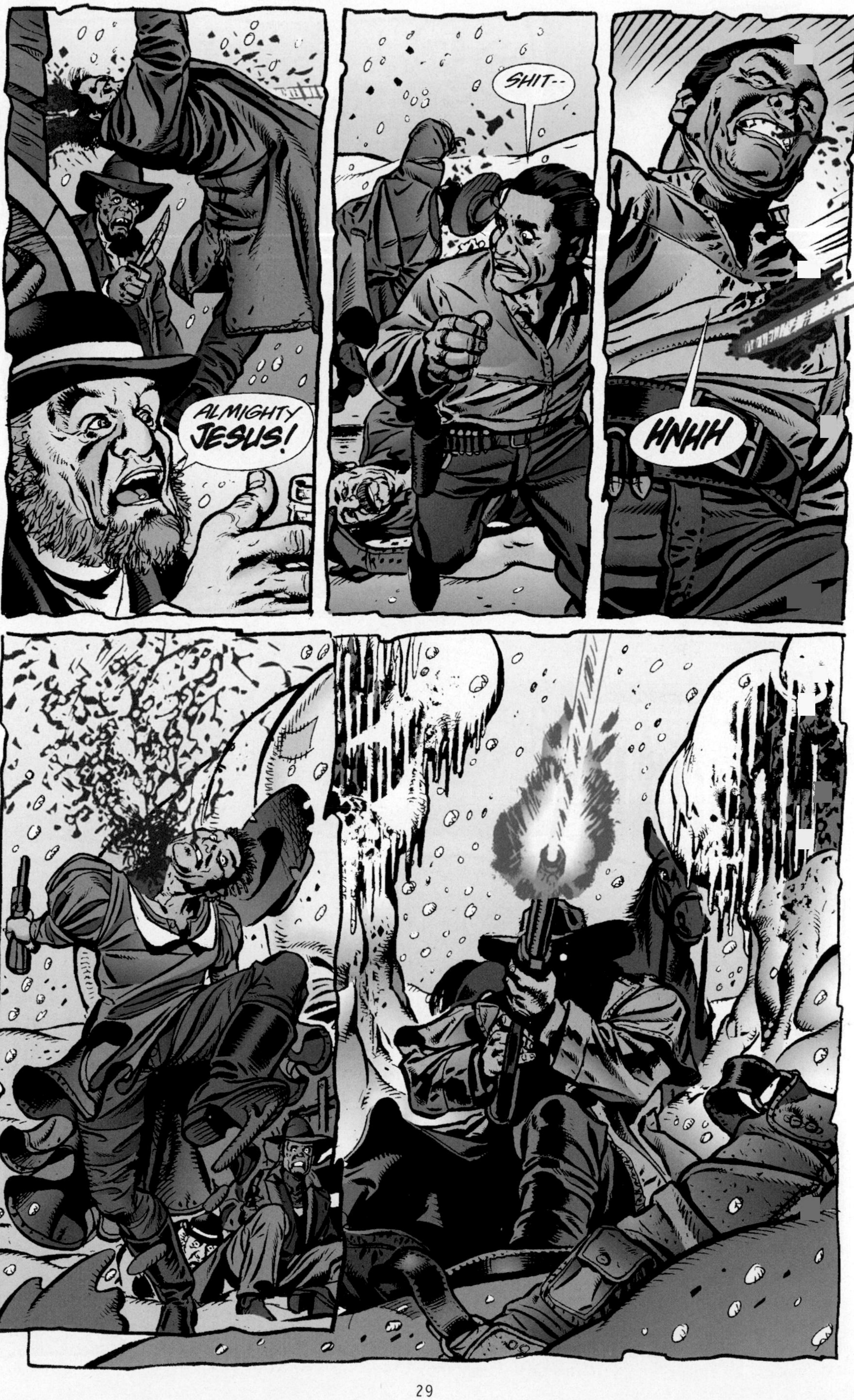
ALMIGHTY JESUS!
SHIT--
UNNH

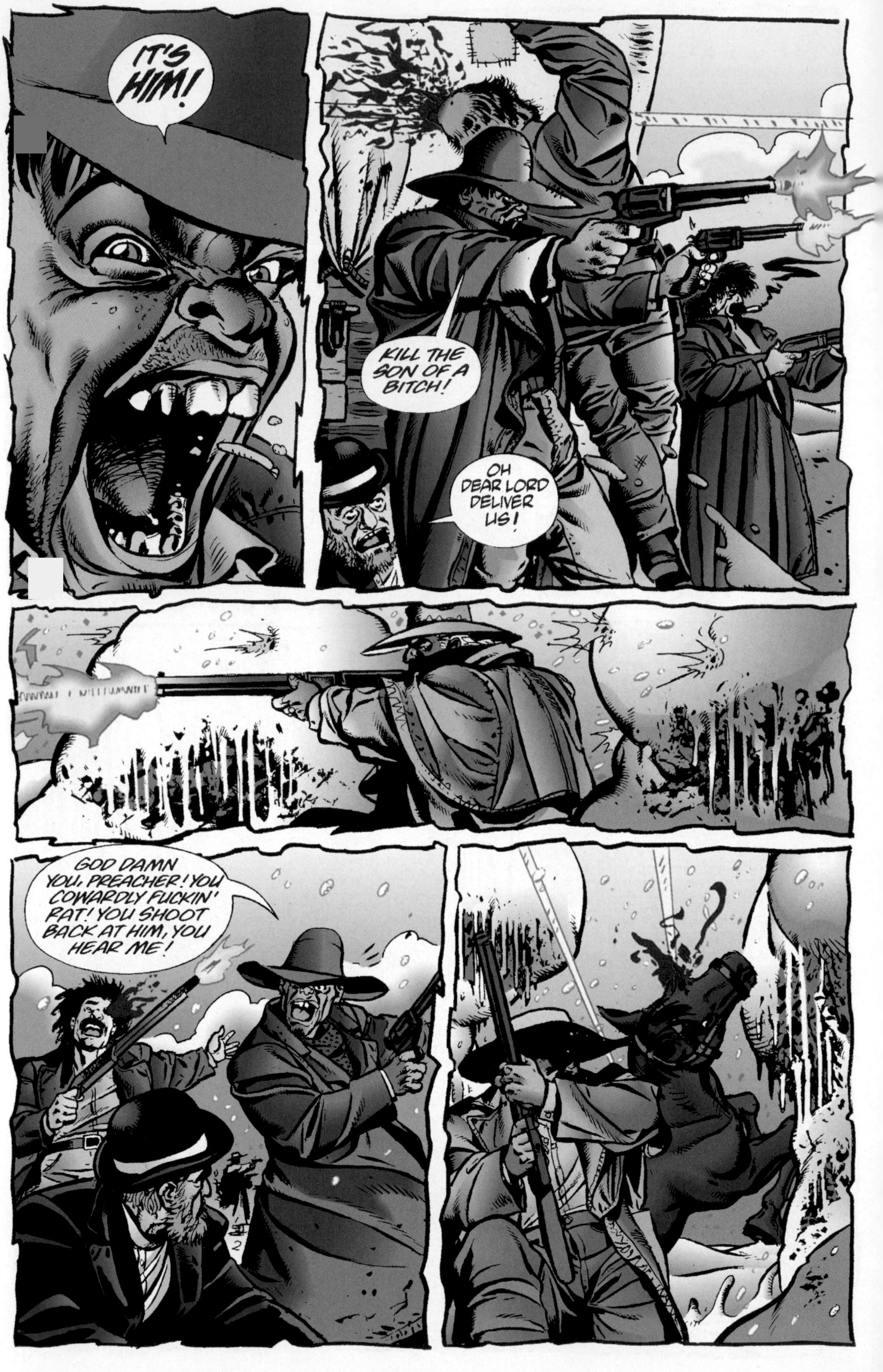
IT'S HIM!
KILL THE SON OF A BITCH!
OH DEAR LORD DELIVER US!
GOD DAMN YOU, PREACHER! YOU COWARDLY FUCKIN' RAT! YOU SHOOT BACK AT HIM, YOU HEAR ME!

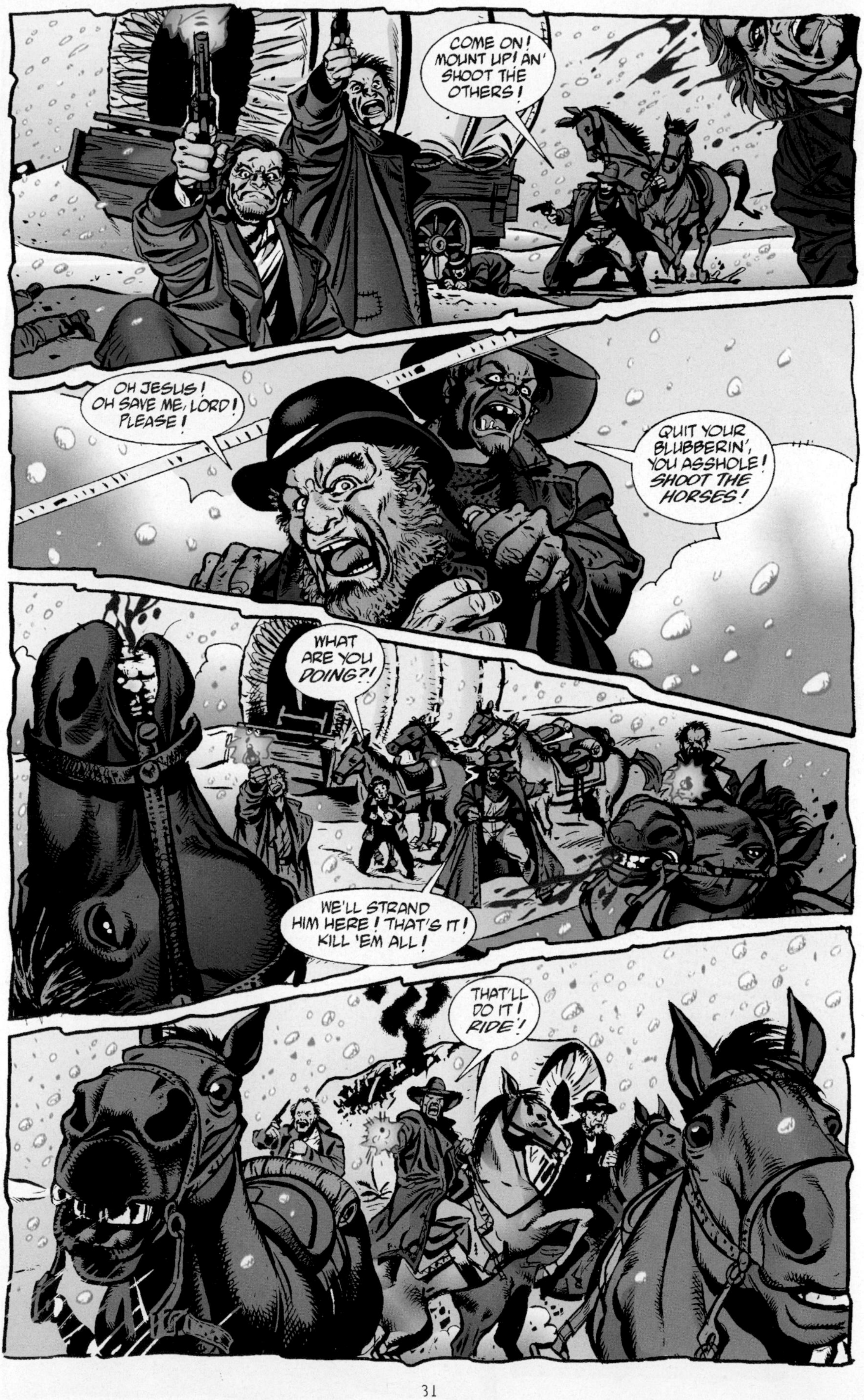
COME ON! MOUNT UP! AN' SHOOT THE OTHERS!
OH JESUS! OH SAVE ME, LORD! PLEASE!
QUIT YOUR BLUBBERIN', YOU ASSHOLE! SHOOT THE HORSES!
WHAT ARE YOU DOING?!
WE'LL STRAND HIM HERE! THAT'S IT! KILL 'EM ALL!
THAT'LL DO IT! RIDE!

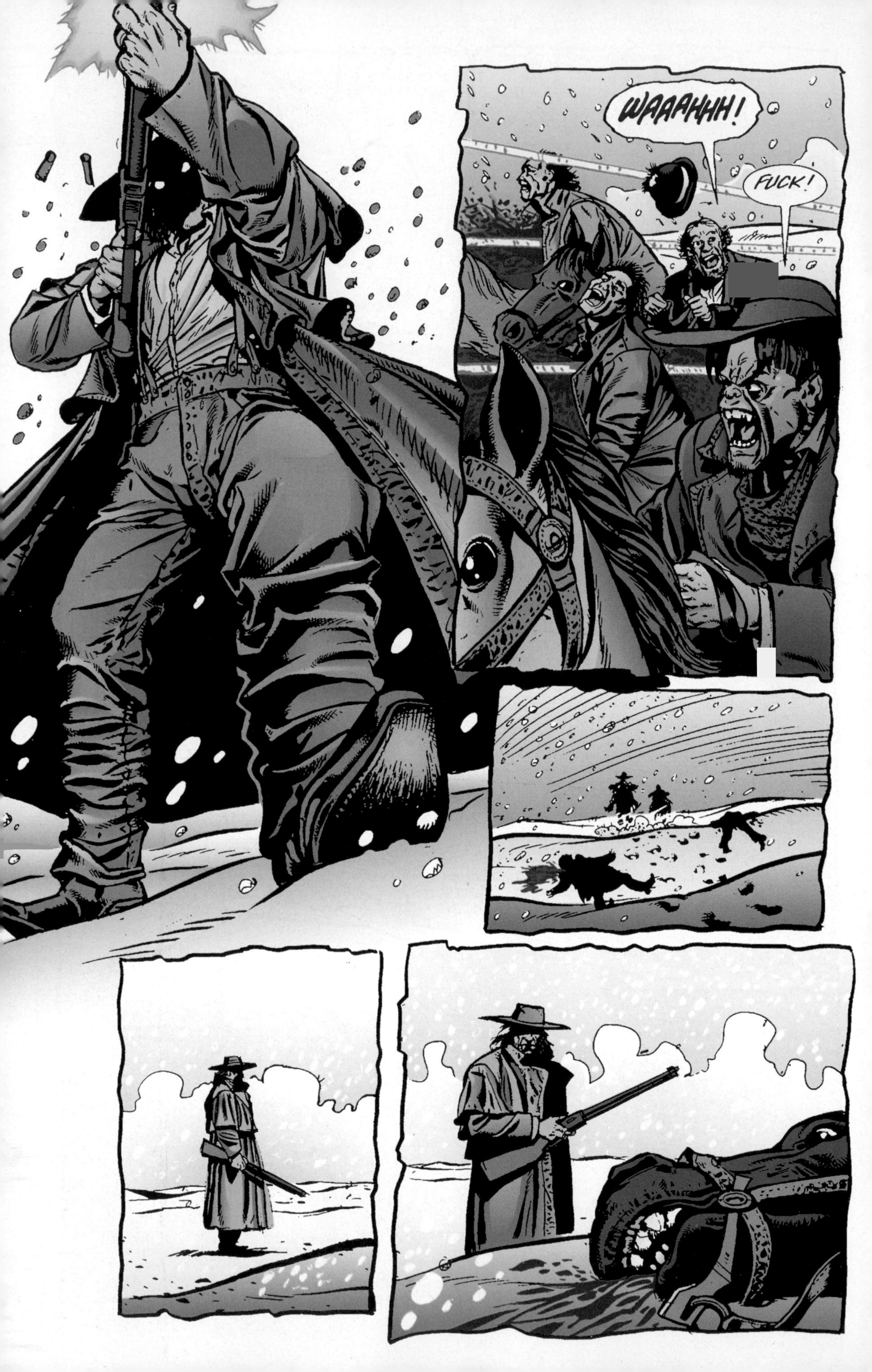
WAAAHHH!
FUCK!

HIS HOPES OF A FRESH MOUNT DIED STRAIGHT AWAY: NOTHING WAS STILL LIVING.

NOTHING THAT SHOULD HAVE BEEN.

HHH--

HHLL MHH

HHLL MHH

TOO LATE TO SAVE THE PEOPLE WHO HAD HELPED HIM.

NO TIME AT ALL TO BURY THEM.

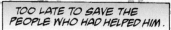

HE CUT MEAT FROM THE HORSES, AND STARTED WALKING WEST.

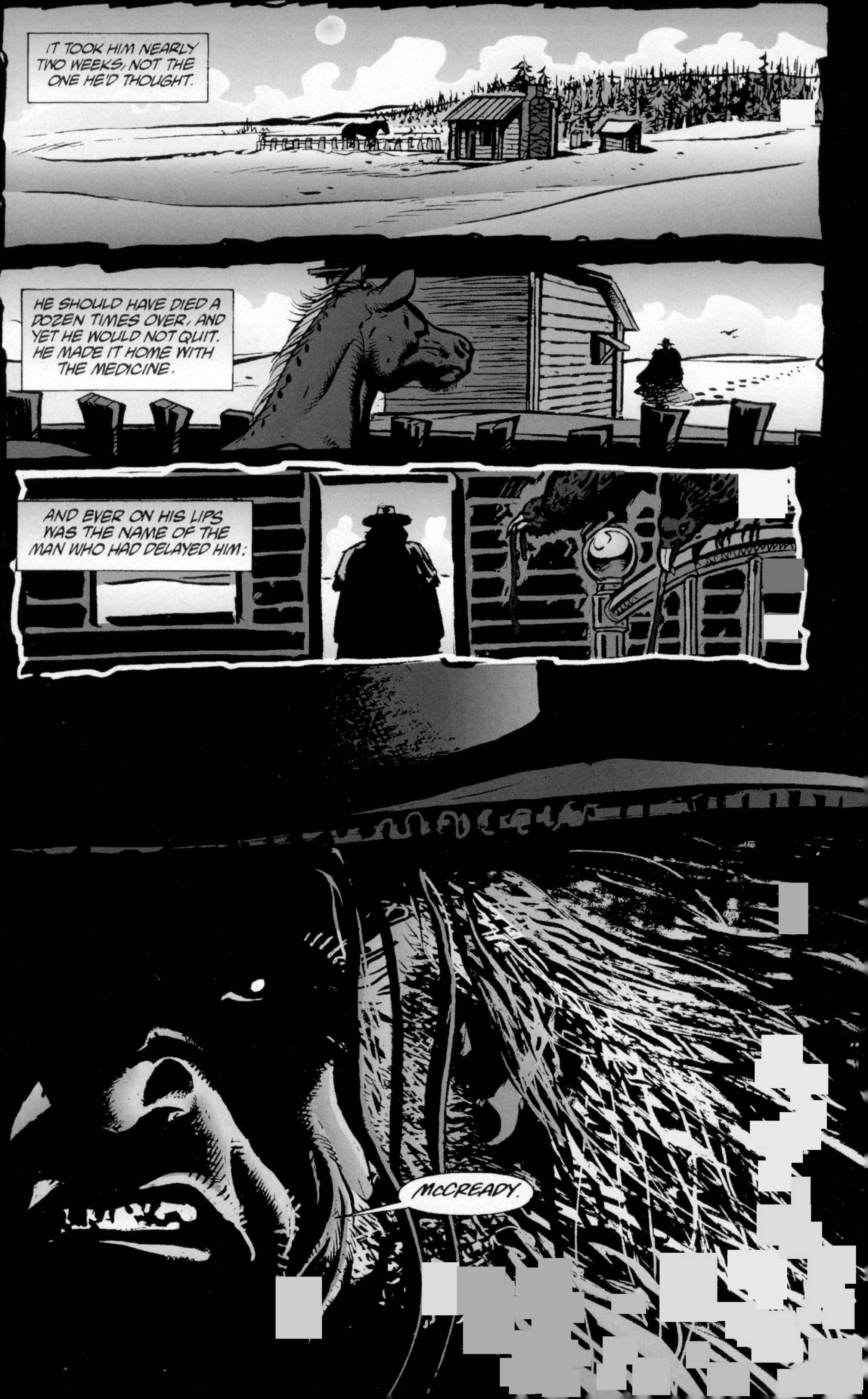
IT TOOK HIM NEARLY TWO WEEKS, NOT THE ONE HE'D THOUGHT.
HE SHOULD HAVE DIED A DOZEN TIMES OVER, AND YET HE WOULD NOT QUIT. HE MADE IT HOME WITH THE MEDICINE.
AND EVER ON HIS LIPS WAS THE NAME OF THE MAN WHO HAD DELAYED HIM:
McCREADY.

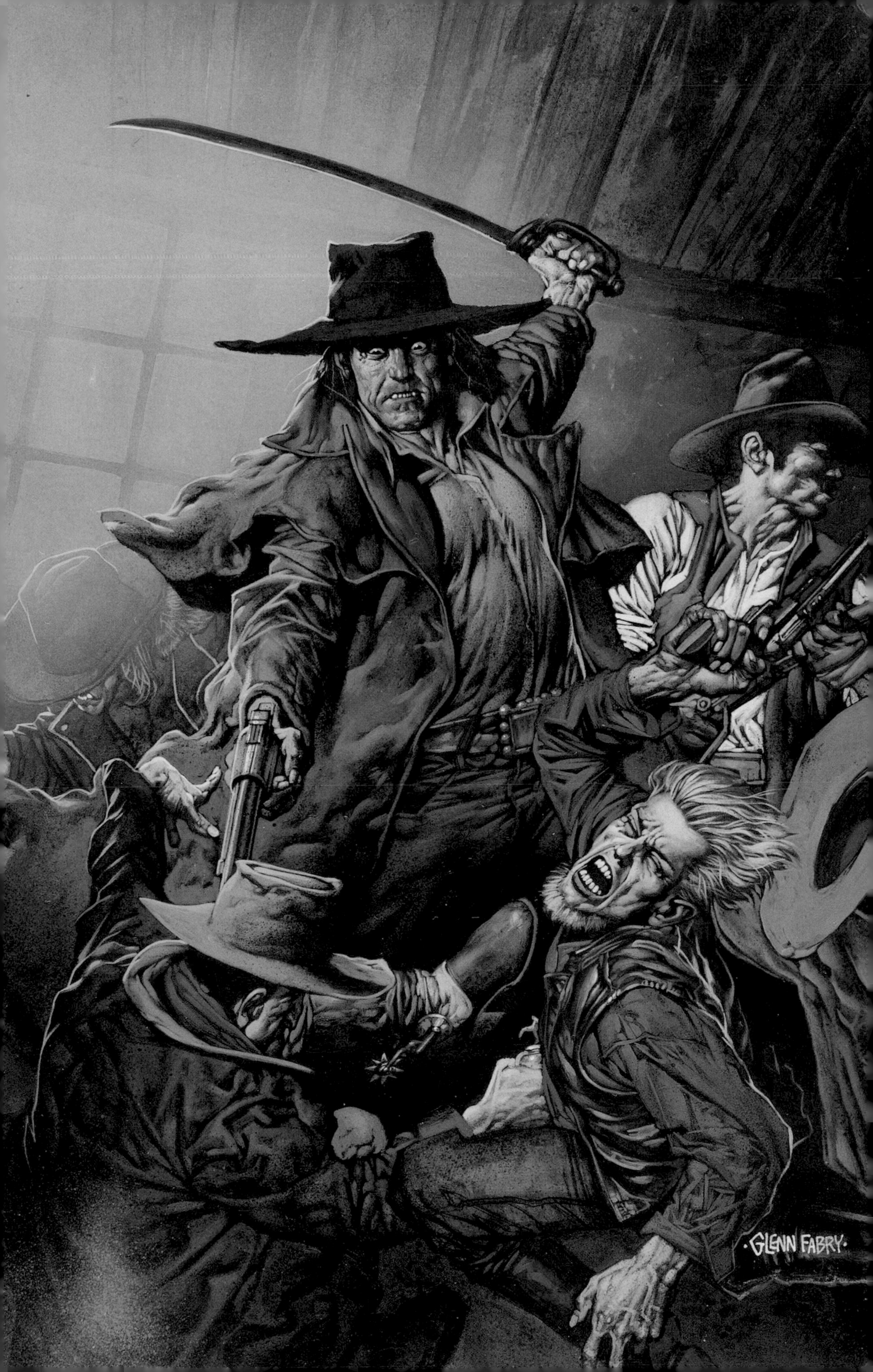
·GLENN FABRY·

"Those ten years he'd fooled himself
were crawling like a demon in his gut."

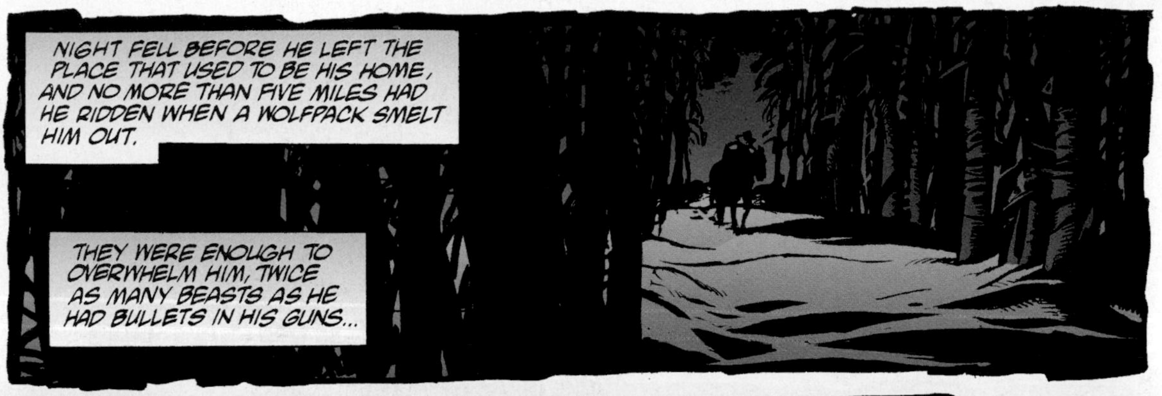
NIGHT FELL BEFORE HE LEFT THE PLACE THAT USED TO BE HIS HOME, AND NO MORE THAN FIVE MILES HAD HE RIDDEN WHEN A WOLFPACK SMELT HIM OUT.
THEY WERE ENOUGH TO OVERWHELM HIM, TWICE AS MANY BEASTS AS HE HAD BULLETS IN HIS GUNS...

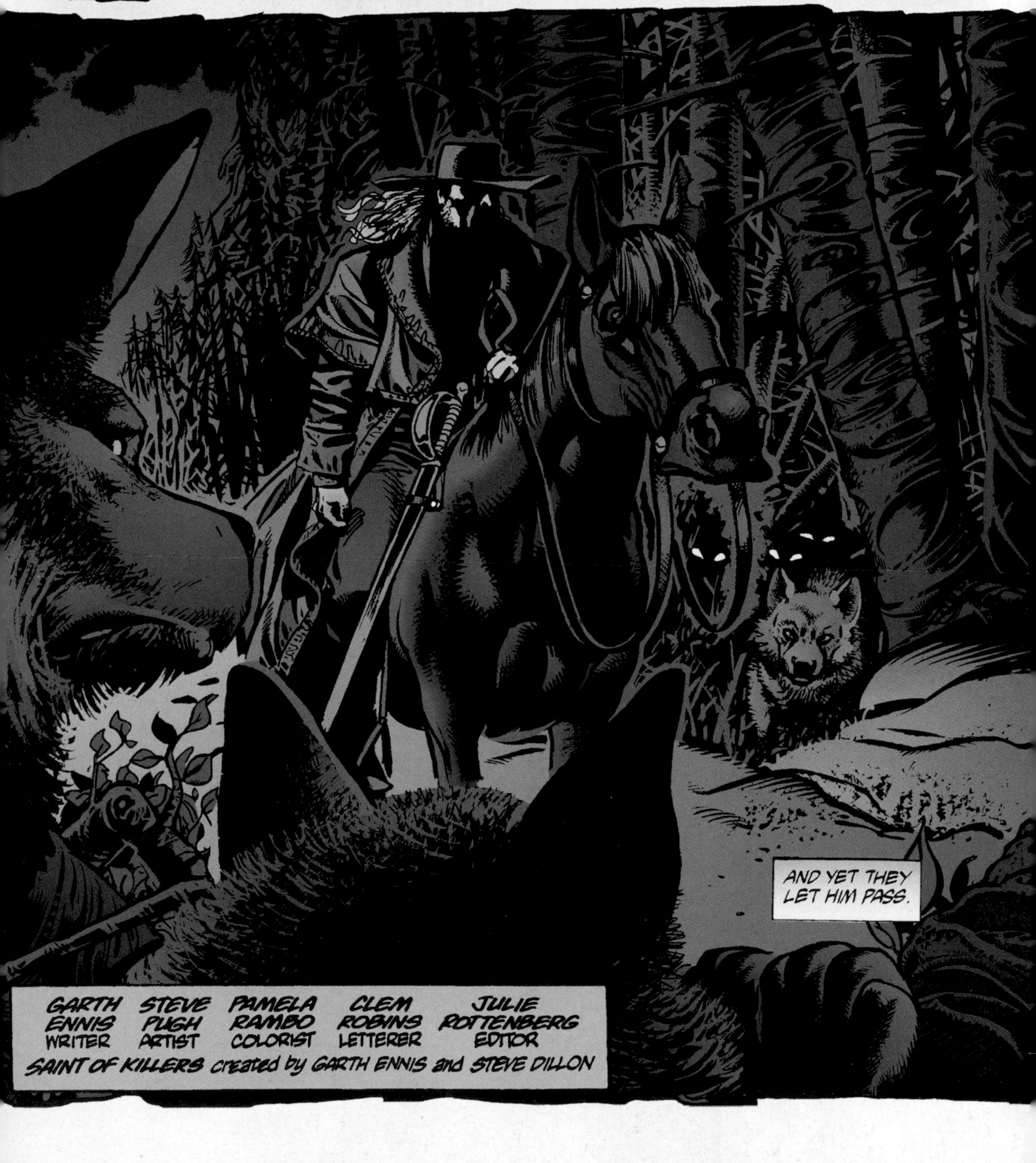
AND YET THEY LET HIM PASS.
GARTH ENNIS WRITER
STEVE PUGH ARTIST
PAMELA RAMBO COLORIST
CLEM ROBINS LETTERER
JULIE ROTTENBERG EDITOR
SAINT OF KILLERS created by GARTH ENNIS and STEVE DILLON

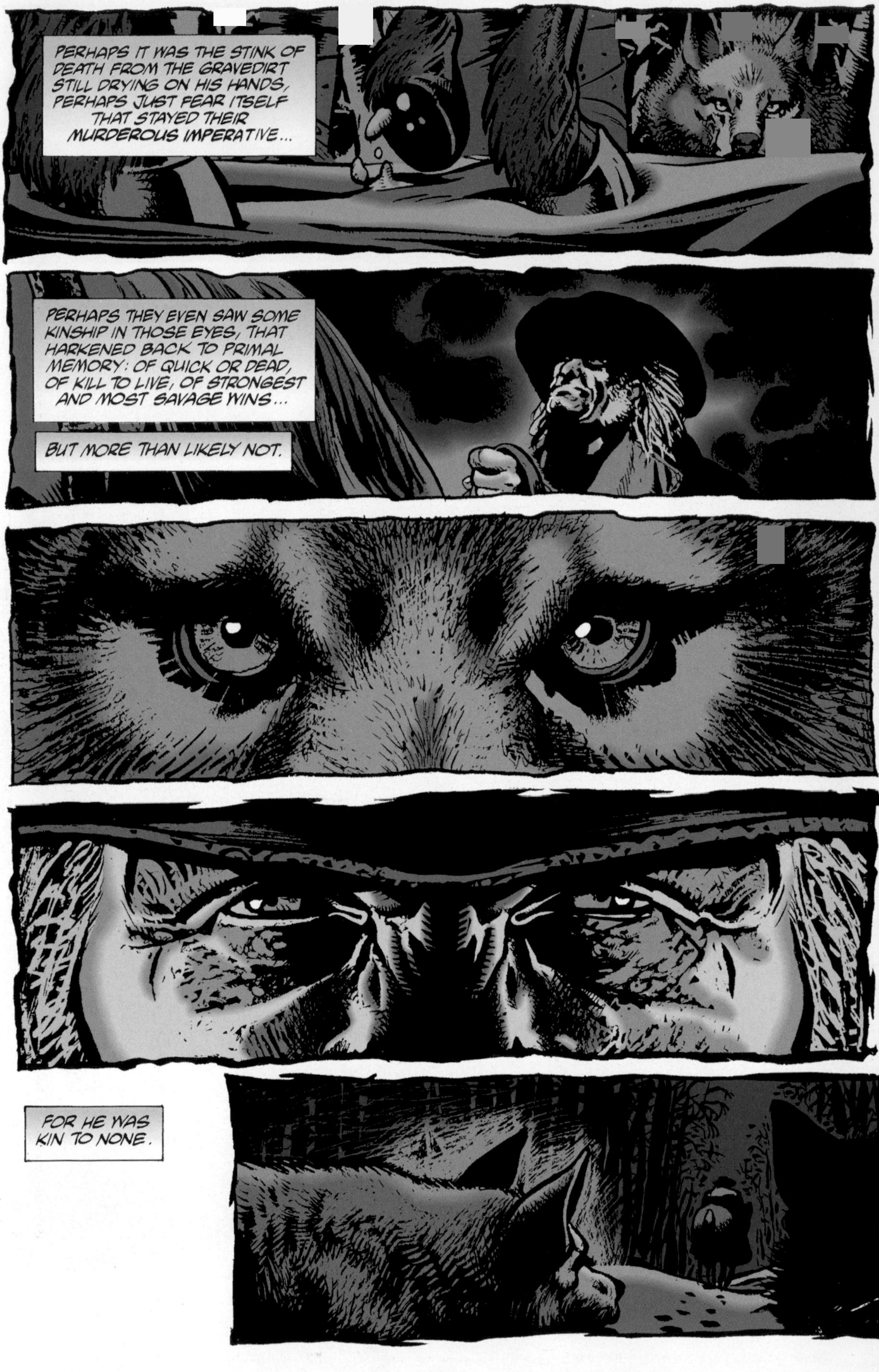
PERHAPS IT WAS THE STINK OF DEATH FROM THE GRAVEDIRT STILL DRYING ON HIS HANDS, PERHAPS JUST FEAR ITSELF THAT STAYED THEIR MURDEROUS IMPERATIVE...
PERHAPS THEY EVEN SAW SOME KINSHIP IN THOSE EYES, THAT HARKENED BACK TO PRIMAL MEMORY: OF QUICK OR DEAD, OF KILL TO LIVE, OF STRONGEST AND MOST SAVAGE WINS...
BUT MORE THAN LIKELY NOT.
FOR HE WAS KIN TO NONE.

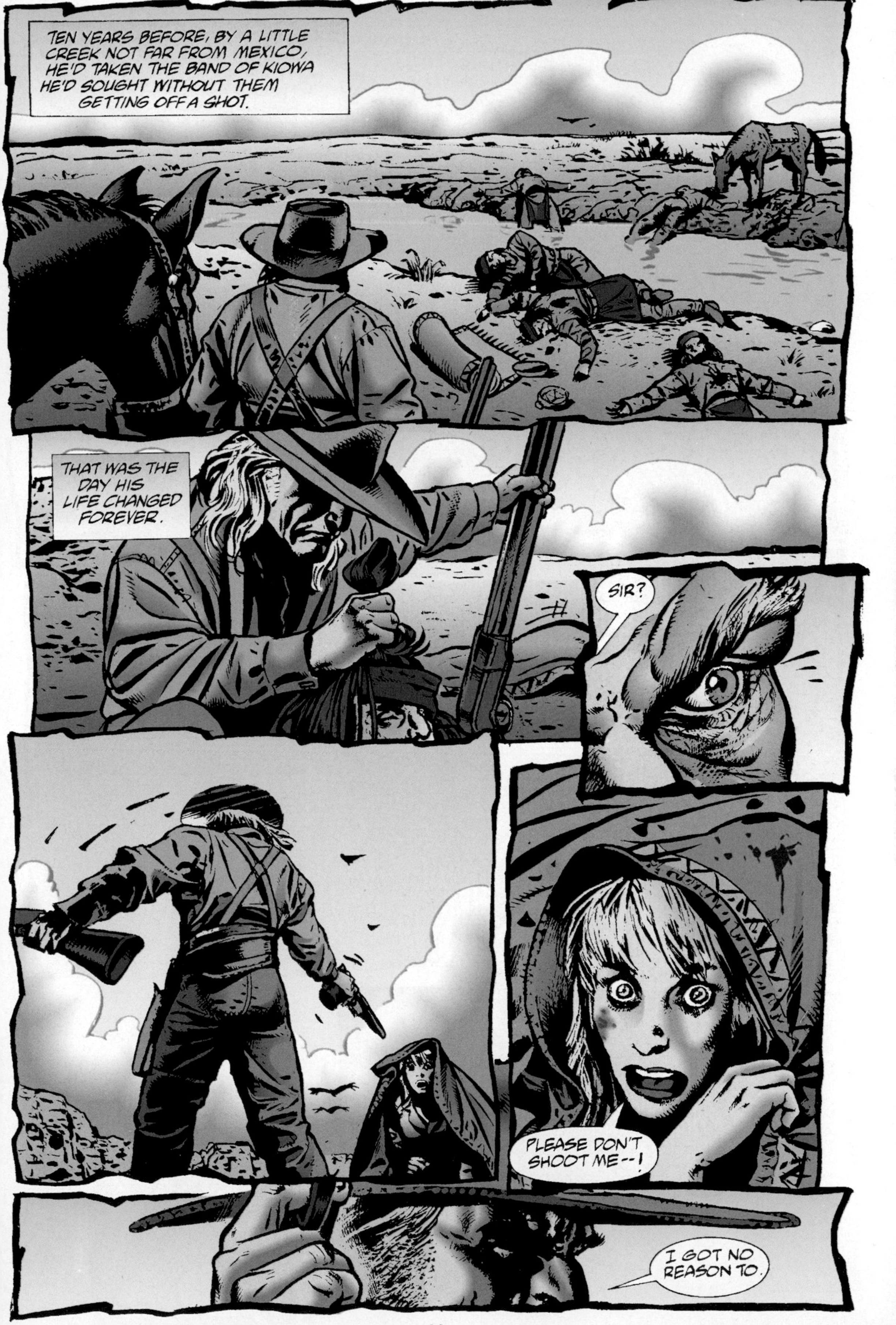
TEN YEARS BEFORE, BY A LITTLE CREEK NOT FAR FROM MEXICO, HE'D TAKEN THE BAND OF KIOWA HE'D SOUGHT WITHOUT THEM GETTING OFF A SHOT.
THAT WAS THE DAY HIS LIFE CHANGED FOREVER.
SIR?
PLEASE DON'T SHOOT ME--!
I GOT NO REASON TO.

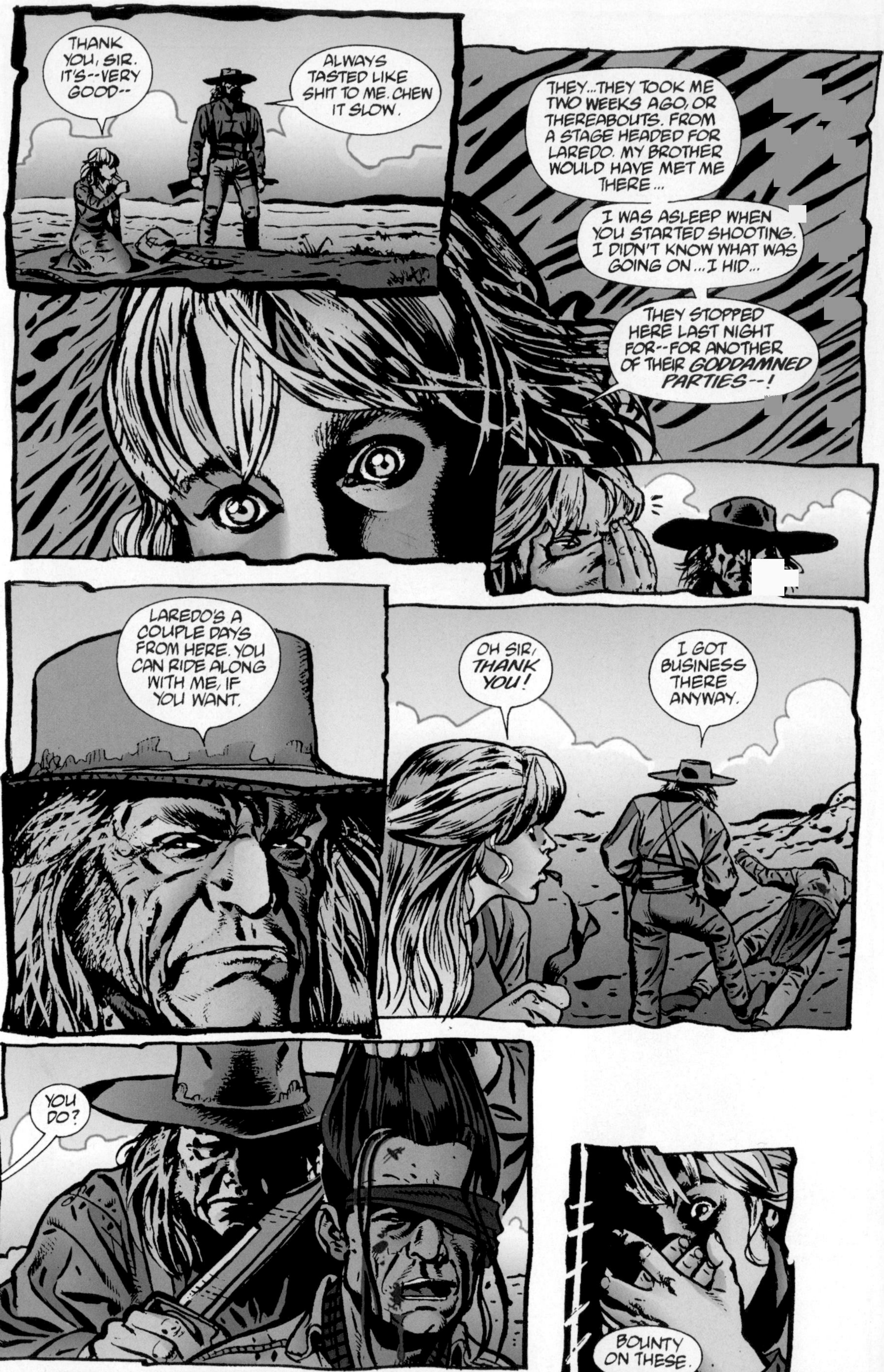
THANK YOU, SIR. IT'S--VERY GOOD--
ALWAYS TASTED LIKE SHIT TO ME. CHEW IT SLOW.
THEY...THEY TOOK ME TWO WEEKS AGO, OR THEREABOUTS. FROM A STAGE HEADED FOR LAREDO. MY BROTHER WOULD HAVE MET ME THERE...
I WAS ASLEEP WHEN YOU STARTED SHOOTING. I DIDN'T KNOW WHAT WAS GOING ON... I HID...
THEY STOPPED HERE LAST NIGHT FOR--FOR ANOTHER OF THEIR GODDAMNED PARTIES--!
LAREDO'S A COUPLE DAYS FROM HERE. YOU CAN RIDE ALONG WITH ME, IF YOU WANT.
OH SIR, THANK YOU!
I GOT BUSINESS THERE ANYWAY.
YOU DO?
BOUNTY ON THESE.

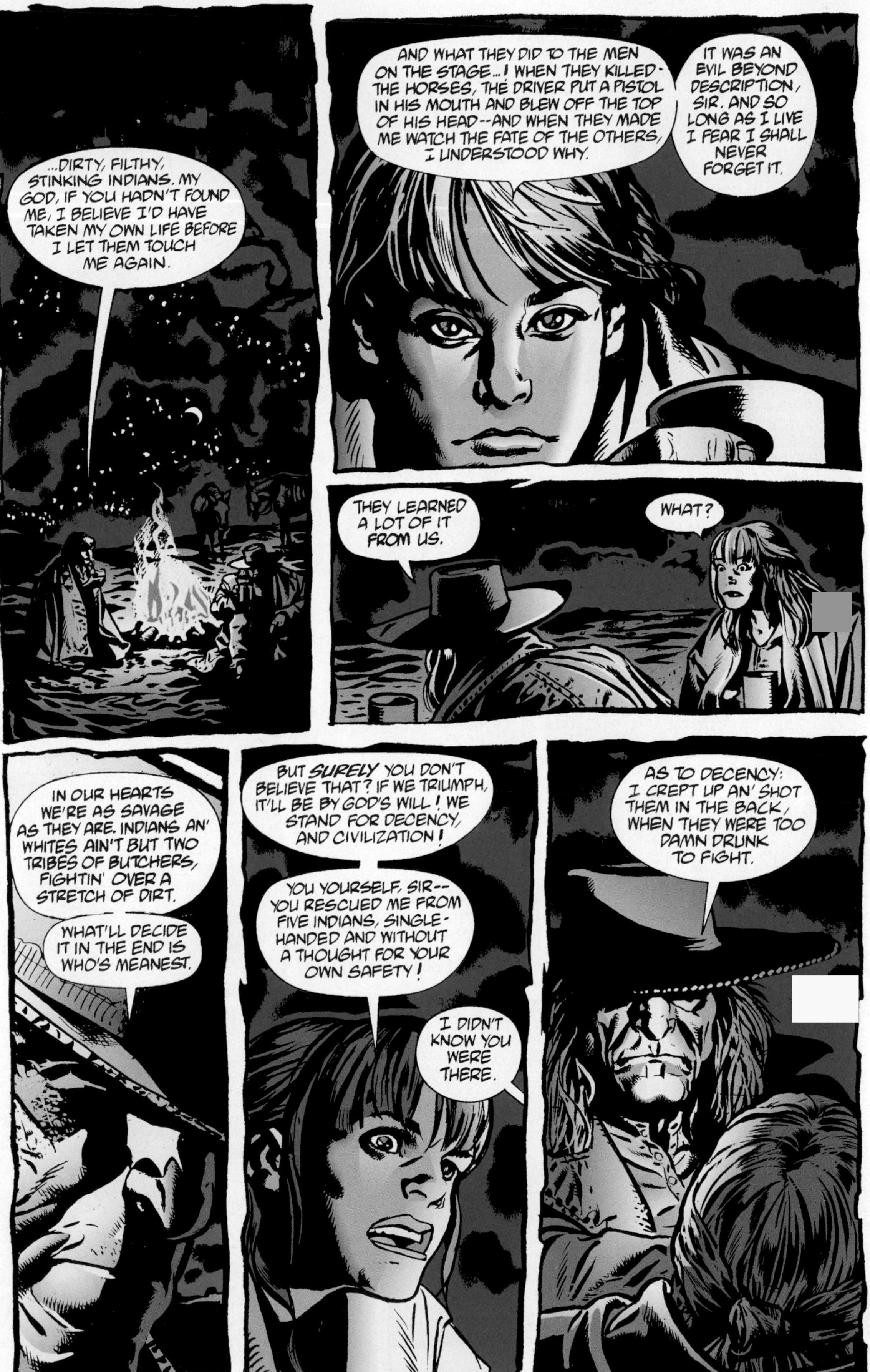
...DIRTY, FILTHY, STINKING INDIANS. MY GOD, IF YOU HADN'T FOUND ME, I BELIEVE I'D HAVE TAKEN MY OWN LIFE BEFORE I LET THEM TOUCH ME AGAIN.
AND WHAT THEY DID TO THE MEN ON THE STAGE...! WHEN THEY KILLED THE HORSES, THE DRIVER PUT A PISTOL IN HIS MOUTH AND BLEW OFF THE TOP OF HIS HEAD--AND WHEN THEY MADE ME WATCH THE FATE OF THE OTHERS, I UNDERSTOOD WHY.
IT WAS AN EVIL BEYOND DESCRIPTION, SIR. AND SO LONG AS I LIVE I FEAR I SHALL NEVER FORGET IT.
THEY LEARNED A LOT OF IT FROM US.
WHAT?
IN OUR HEARTS WE'RE AS SAVAGE AS THEY ARE. INDIANS AN' WHITES AIN'T BUT TWO TRIBES OF BUTCHERS, FIGHTIN' OVER A STRETCH OF DIRT.
WHAT'LL DECIDE IT IN THE END IS WHO'S MEANEST.
BUT SURELY YOU DON'T BELIEVE THAT? IF WE TRIUMPH, IT'LL BE BY GOD'S WILL! WE STAND FOR DECENCY, AND CIVILIZATION!
YOU YOURSELF, SIR-- YOU RESCUED ME FROM FIVE INDIANS, SINGLE-HANDED AND WITHOUT A THOUGHT FOR YOUR OWN SAFETY!
I DIDN'T KNOW YOU WERE THERE.
AS TO DECENCY: I CREPT UP AN' SHOT THEM IN THE BACK, WHEN THEY WERE TOO DAMN DRUNK TO FIGHT.

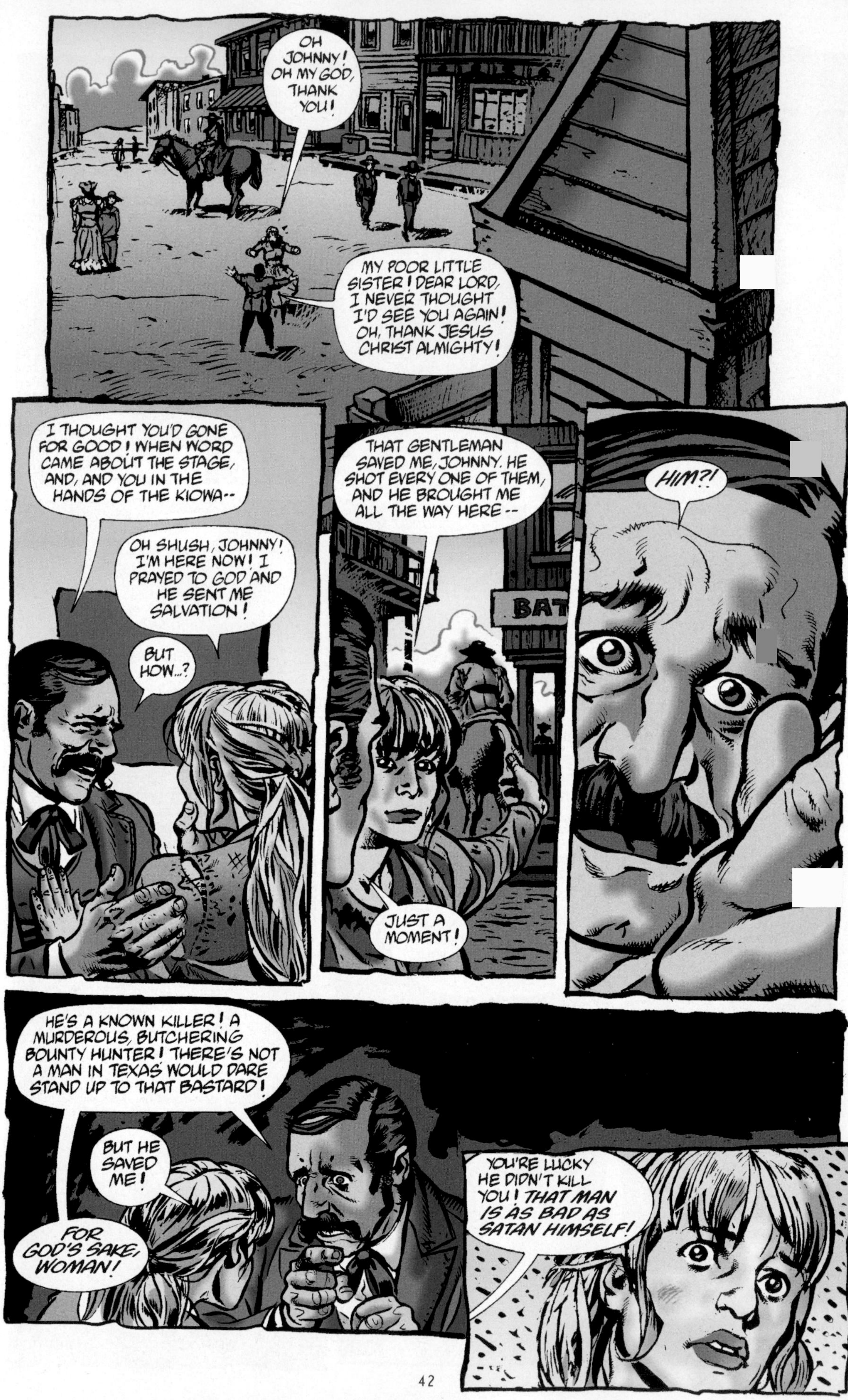
OH JOHNNY! OH MY GOD, THANK YOU!
MY POOR LITTLE SISTER! DEAR LORD, I NEVER THOUGHT I'D SEE YOU AGAIN! OH, THANK JESUS CHRIST ALMIGHTY!
I THOUGHT YOU'D GONE FOR GOOD! WHEN WORD CAME ABOUT THE STAGE, AND, AND YOU IN THE HANDS OF THE KIOWA--
OH SHUSH, JOHNNY! I'M HERE NOW! I PRAYED TO GOD AND HE SENT ME SALVATION!
BUT HOW...?
THAT GENTLEMAN SAVED ME, JOHNNY. HE SHOT EVERY ONE OF THEM, AND HE BROUGHT ME ALL THE WAY HERE--
BAT
JUST A MOMENT!
HIM?!
HE'S A KNOWN KILLER! A MURDEROUS, BUTCHERING BOUNTY HUNTER! THERE'S NOT A MAN IN TEXAS WOULD DARE STAND UP TO THAT BASTARD!
BUT HE SAVED ME!
FOR GOD'S SAKE, WOMAN!
YOU'RE LUCKY HE DIDN'T KILL YOU! THAT MAN IS AS BAD AS SATAN HIMSELF!

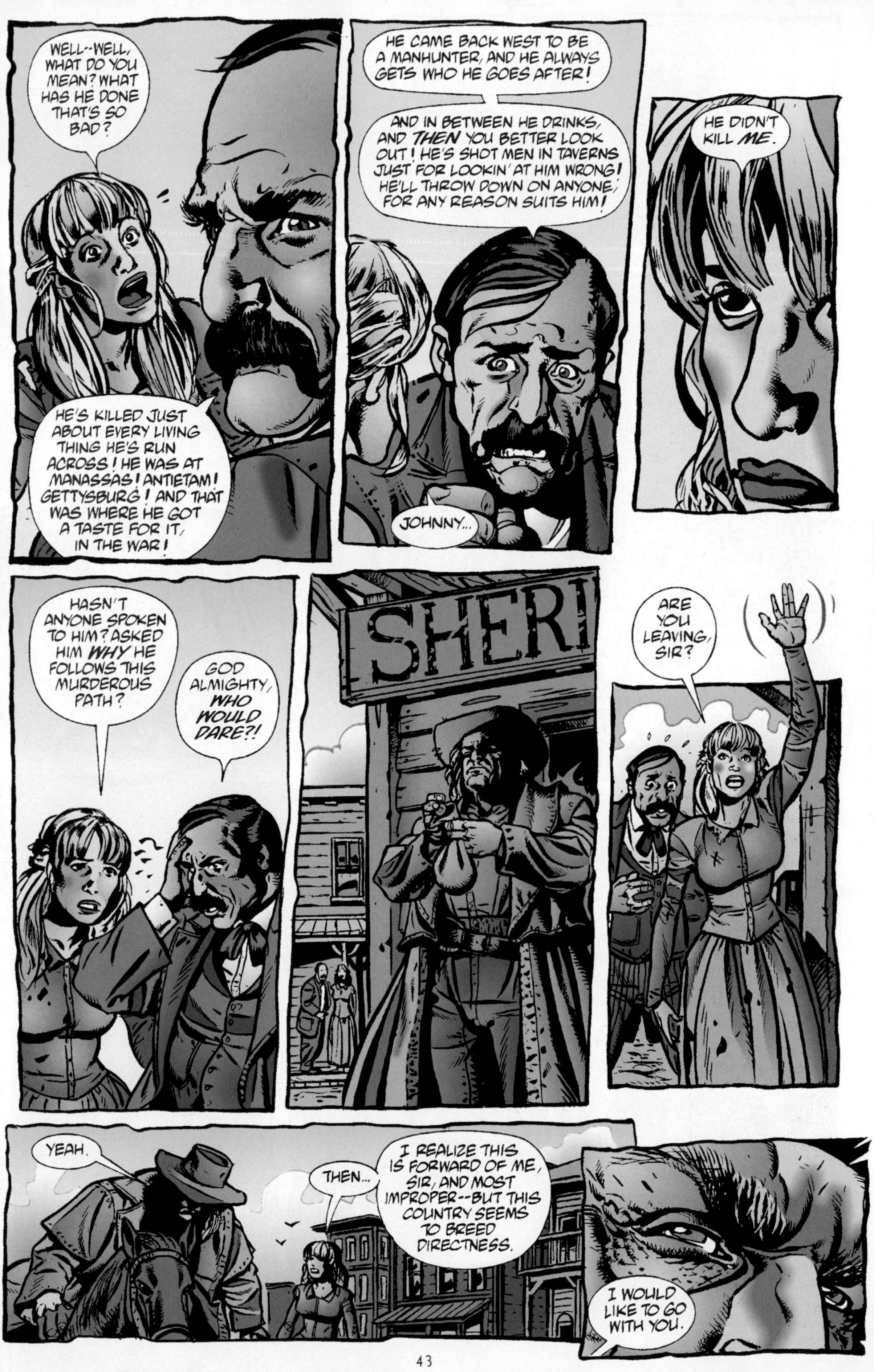

WELL--WELL, WHAT DO YOU MEAN? WHAT HAS HE DONE THAT'S SO BAD?
HE'S KILLED JUST ABOUT EVERY LIVING THING HE'S RUN ACROSS! HE WAS AT MANASSAS! ANTIETAM! GETTYSBURG! AND THAT WAS WHERE HE GOT A TASTE FOR IT, IN THE WAR!
HE CAME BACK WEST TO BE A MANHUNTER, AND HE ALWAYS GETS WHO HE GOES AFTER!
AND IN BETWEEN HE DRINKS, AND THEN YOU BETTER LOOK OUT! HE'S SHOT MEN IN TAVERNS JUST FOR LOOKIN' AT HIM WRONG! HE'LL THROW DOWN ON ANYONE, FOR ANY REASON SUITS HIM!
JOHNNY...
HE DIDN'T KILL ME.
HASN'T ANYONE SPOKEN TO HIM? ASKED HIM WHY HE FOLLOWS THIS MURDEROUS PATH?
GOD ALMIGHTY, WHO WOULD DARE?!
SHERI
ARE YOU LEAVING, SIR?
YEAH.
THEN...
I REALIZE THIS IS FORWARD OF ME, SIR, AND MOST IMPROPER--BUT THIS COUNTRY SEEMS TO BREED DIRECTNESS.
I WOULD LIKE TO GO WITH YOU.

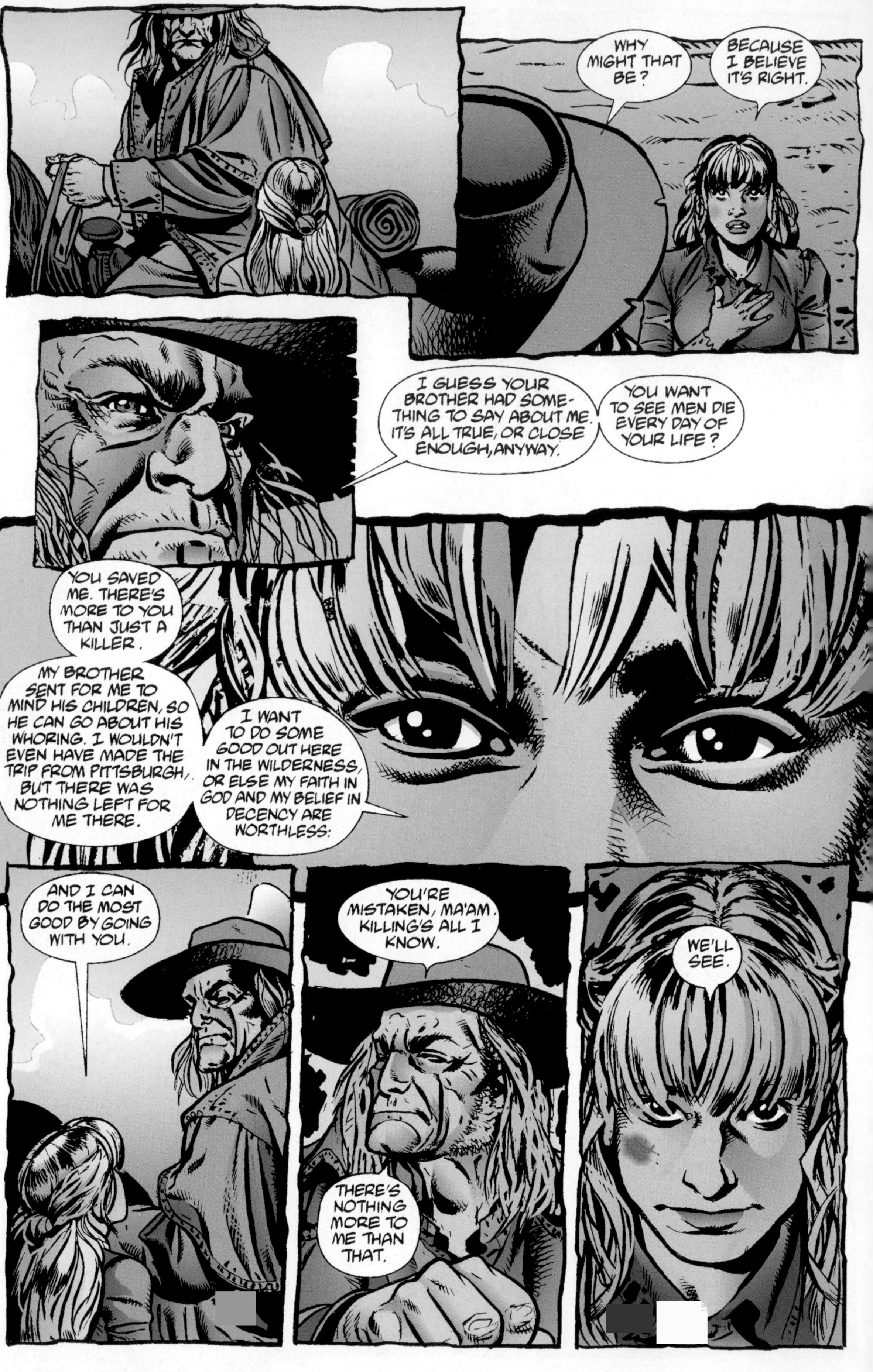
WHY MIGHT THAT BE?
BECAUSE I BELIEVE IT'S RIGHT.
I GUESS YOUR BROTHER HAD SOME-THING TO SAY ABOUT ME. IT'S ALL TRUE, OR CLOSE ENOUGH, ANYWAY.
YOU WANT TO SEE MEN DIE EVERY DAY OF YOUR LIFE?
YOU SAVED ME. THERE'S MORE TO YOU THAN JUST A KILLER.
MY BROTHER SENT FOR ME TO MIND HIS CHILDREN, SO HE CAN GO ABOUT HIS WHORING. I WOULDN'T EVEN HAVE MADE THE TRIP FROM PITTSBURGH, BUT THERE WAS NOTHING LEFT FOR ME THERE.
I WANT TO DO SOME GOOD OUT HERE IN THE WILDERNESS, OR ELSE MY FAITH IN GOD AND MY BELIEF IN DECENCY ARE WORTHLESS.
AND I CAN DO THE MOST GOOD BY GOING WITH YOU.
YOU'RE MISTAKEN, MA'AM. KILLING'S ALL I KNOW.
THERE'S NOTHING MORE TO ME THAN THAT.
WE'LL SEE.

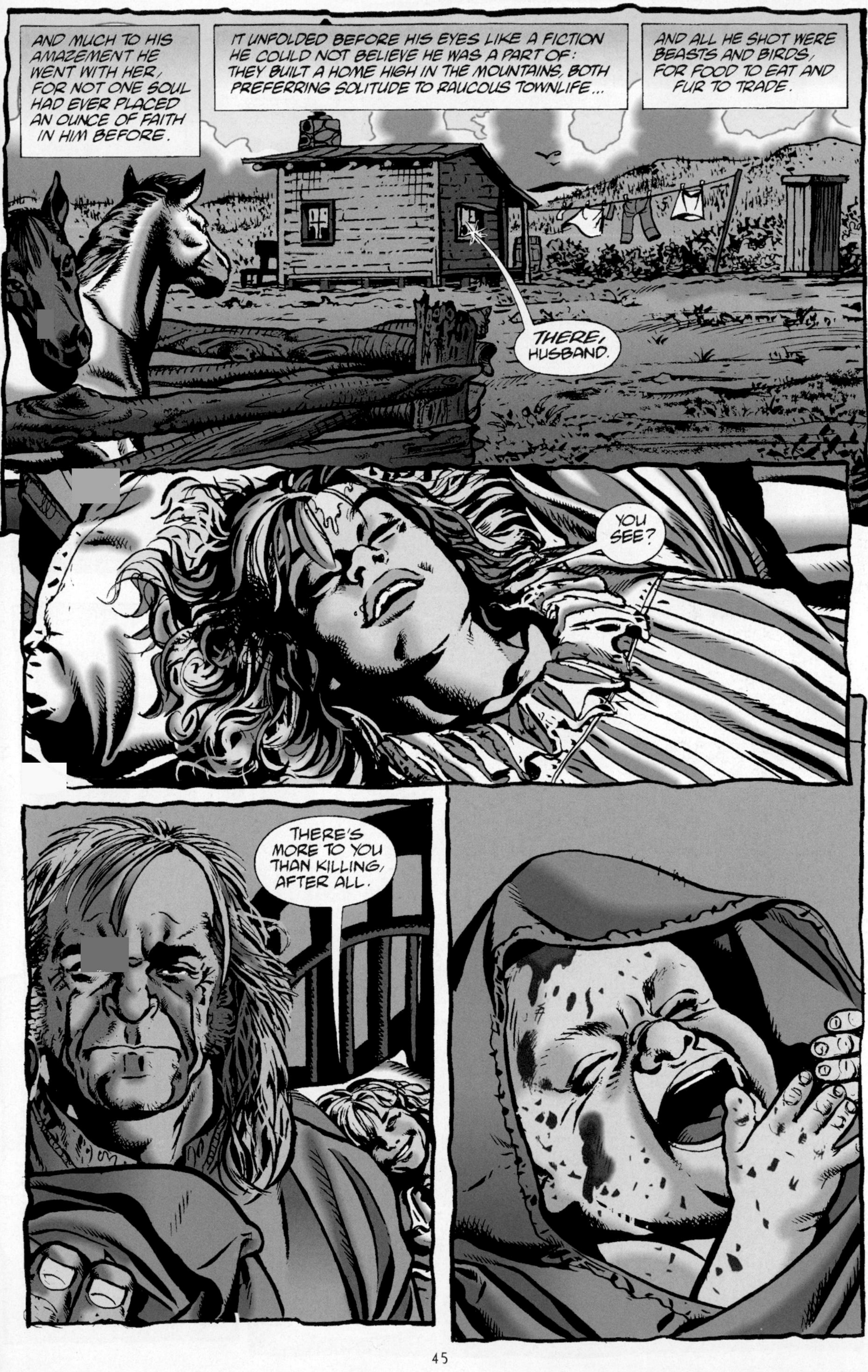
AND MUCH TO HIS AMAZEMENT HE WENT WITH HER, FOR NOT ONE SOUL HAD EVER PLACED AN OUNCE OF FAITH IN HIM BEFORE.
IT UNFOLDED BEFORE HIS EYES LIKE A FICTION HE COULD NOT BELIEVE HE WAS A PART OF: THEY BUILT A HOME HIGH IN THE MOUNTAINS, BOTH PREFERRING SOLITUDE TO RAUCOUS TOWNLIFE...
AND ALL HE SHOT WERE BEASTS AND BIRDS, FOR FOOD TO EAT AND FUR TO TRADE.
THERE, HUSBAND.
YOU SEE?
THERE'S MORE TO YOU THAN KILLING, AFTER ALL.

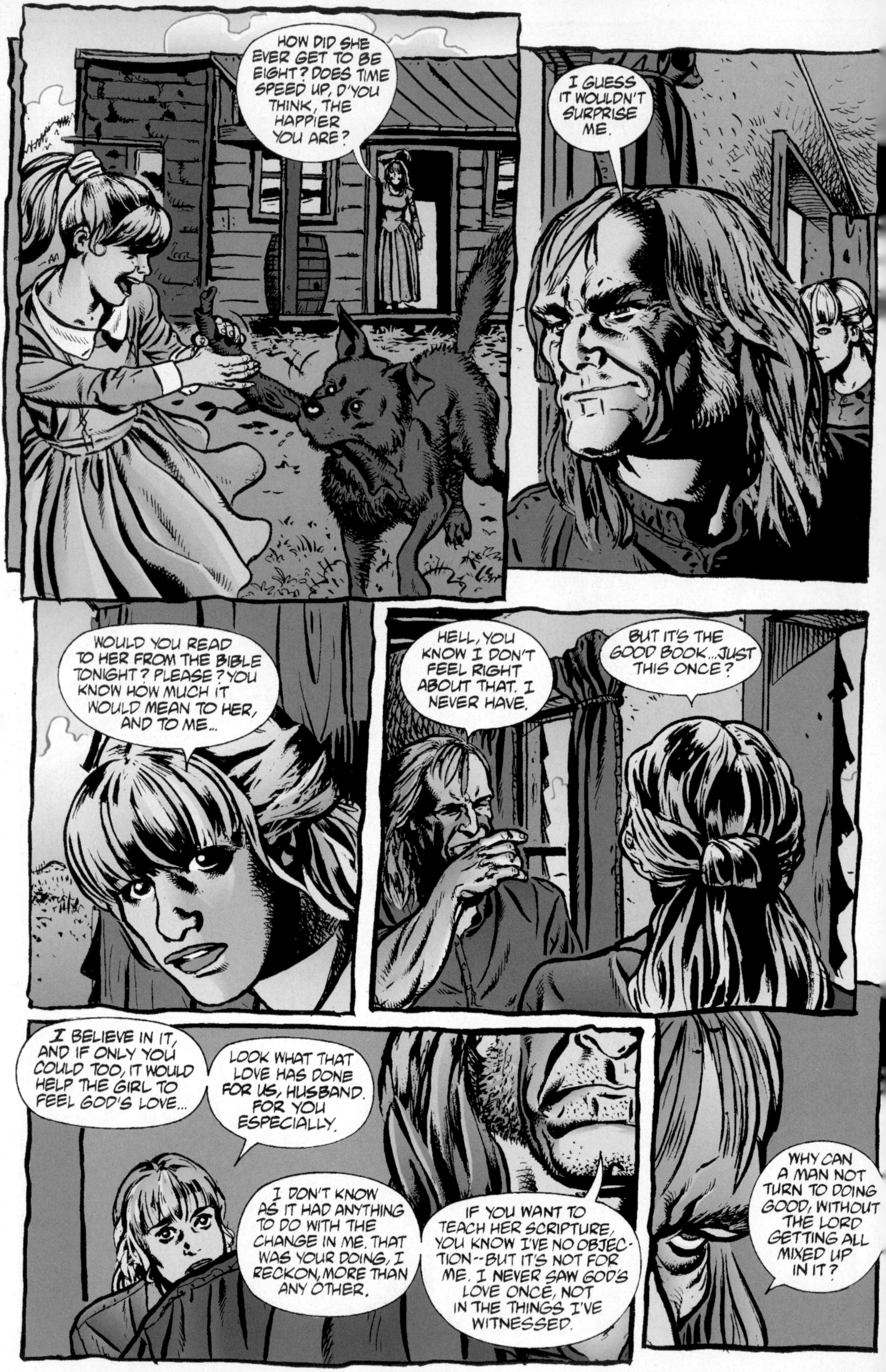
HOW DID SHE EVER GET TO BE EIGHT? DOES TIME SPEED UP, D'YOU THINK, THE HAPPIER YOU ARE?
I GUESS IT WOULDN'T SURPRISE ME.
WOULD YOU READ TO HER FROM THE BIBLE TONIGHT? PLEASE? YOU KNOW HOW MUCH IT WOULD MEAN TO HER, AND TO ME...
HELL, YOU KNOW I DON'T FEEL RIGHT ABOUT THAT. I NEVER HAVE.
BUT IT'S THE GOOD BOOK...JUST THIS ONCE?
I BELIEVE IN IT, AND IF ONLY YOU COULD TOO, IT WOULD HELP THE GIRL TO FEEL GOD'S LOVE...
LOOK WHAT THAT LOVE HAS DONE FOR US, HUSBAND. FOR YOU ESPECIALLY.
I DON'T KNOW AS IT HAD ANYTHING TO DO WITH THE CHANGE IN ME. THAT WAS YOUR DOING, I RECKON, MORE THAN ANY OTHER.
IF YOU WANT TO TEACH HER SCRIPTURE, YOU KNOW I'VE NO OBJECTION--BUT IT'S NOT FOR ME. I NEVER SAW GOD'S LOVE ONCE, NOT IN THE THINGS I'VE WITNESSED.
WHY CAN A MAN NOT TURN TO DOING GOOD, WITHOUT THE LORD GETTING ALL MIXED UP IN IT?

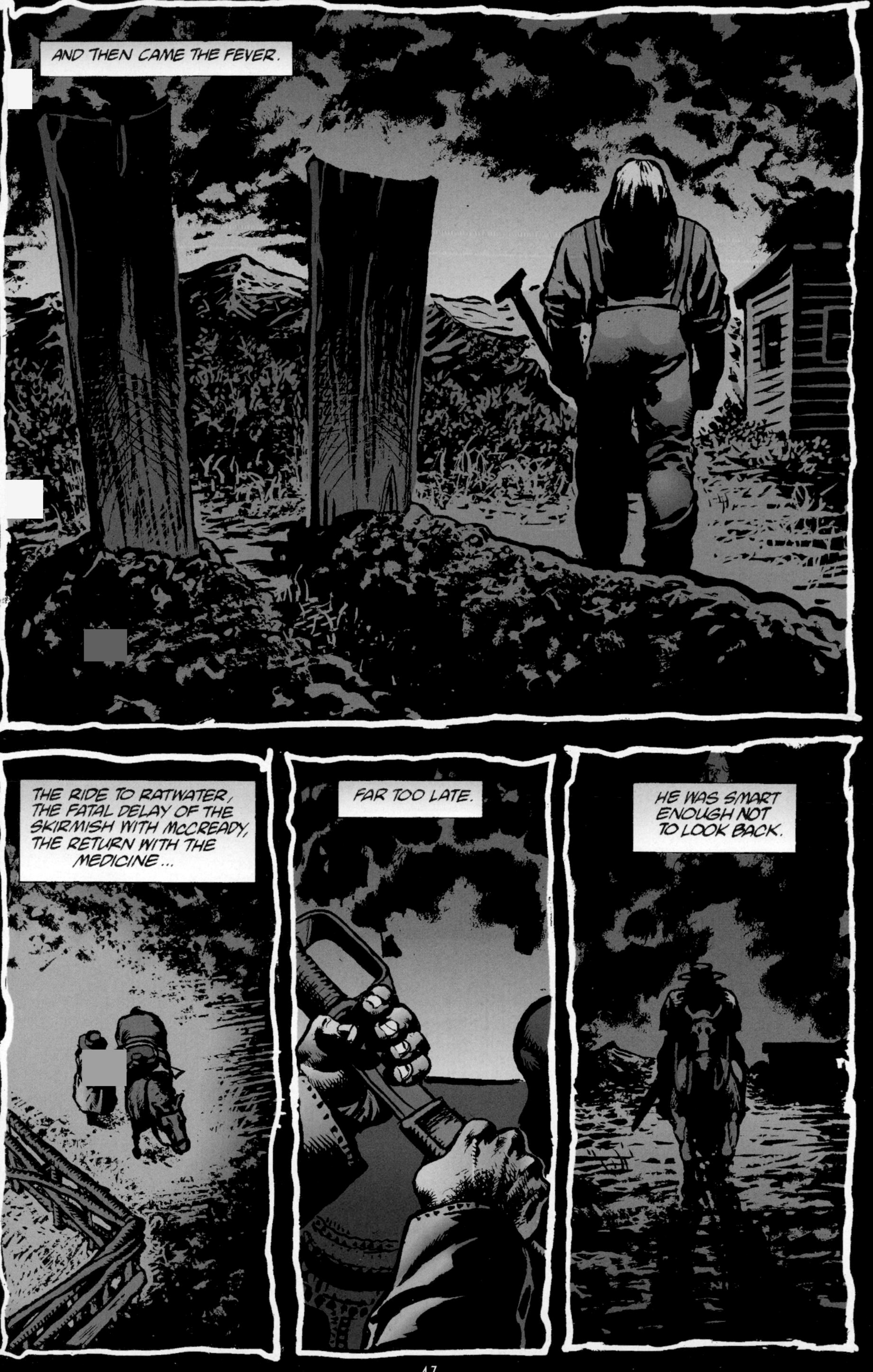
AND THEN CAME THE FEVER.
THE RIDE TO RATWATER, THE FATAL DELAY OF THE SKIRMISH WITH McCREADY, THE RETURN WITH THE MEDICINE...
FAR TOO LATE.
HE WAS SMART ENOUGH NOT TO LOOK BACK.

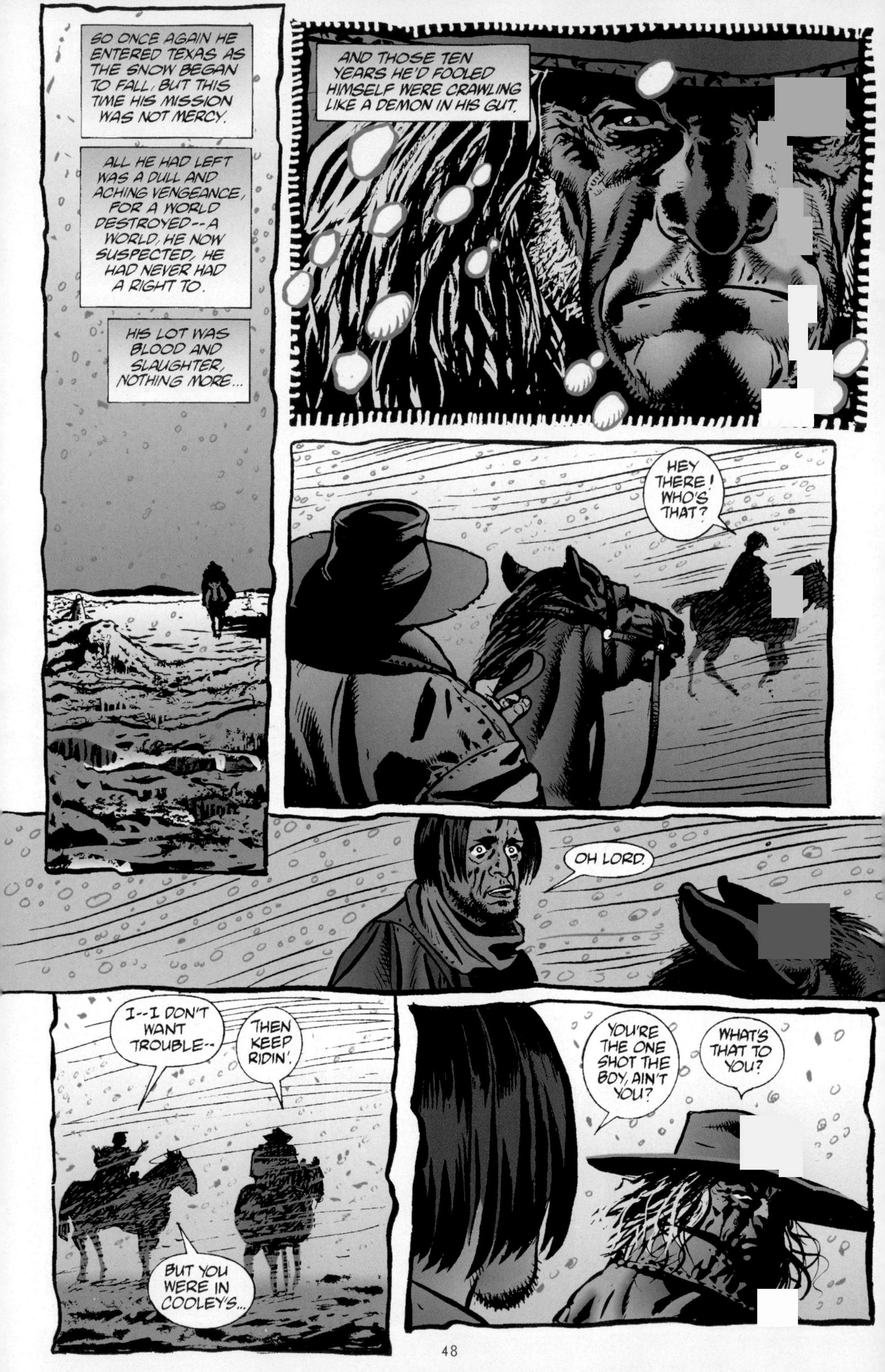
SO ONCE AGAIN HE ENTERED TEXAS AS THE SNOW BEGAN TO FALL, BUT THIS TIME HIS MISSION WAS NOT MERCY.
ALL HE HAD LEFT WAS A DULL AND ACHING VENGEANCE, FOR A WORLD DESTROYED--A WORLD, HE NOW SUSPECTED, HE HAD NEVER HAD A RIGHT TO.
HIS LOT WAS BLOOD AND SLAUGHTER, NOTHING MORE...
AND THOSE TEN YEARS HE'D FOOLED HIMSELF WERE CRAWLING LIKE A DEMON IN HIS GUT.
HEY THERE! WHO'S THAT?
OH LORD.
I--I DON'T WANT TROUBLE--
THEN KEEP RIDIN'.
BUT YOU WERE IN COOLEY'S...
YOU'RE THE ONE SHOT THE BOY, AIN'T YOU?
WHAT'S THAT TO YOU?

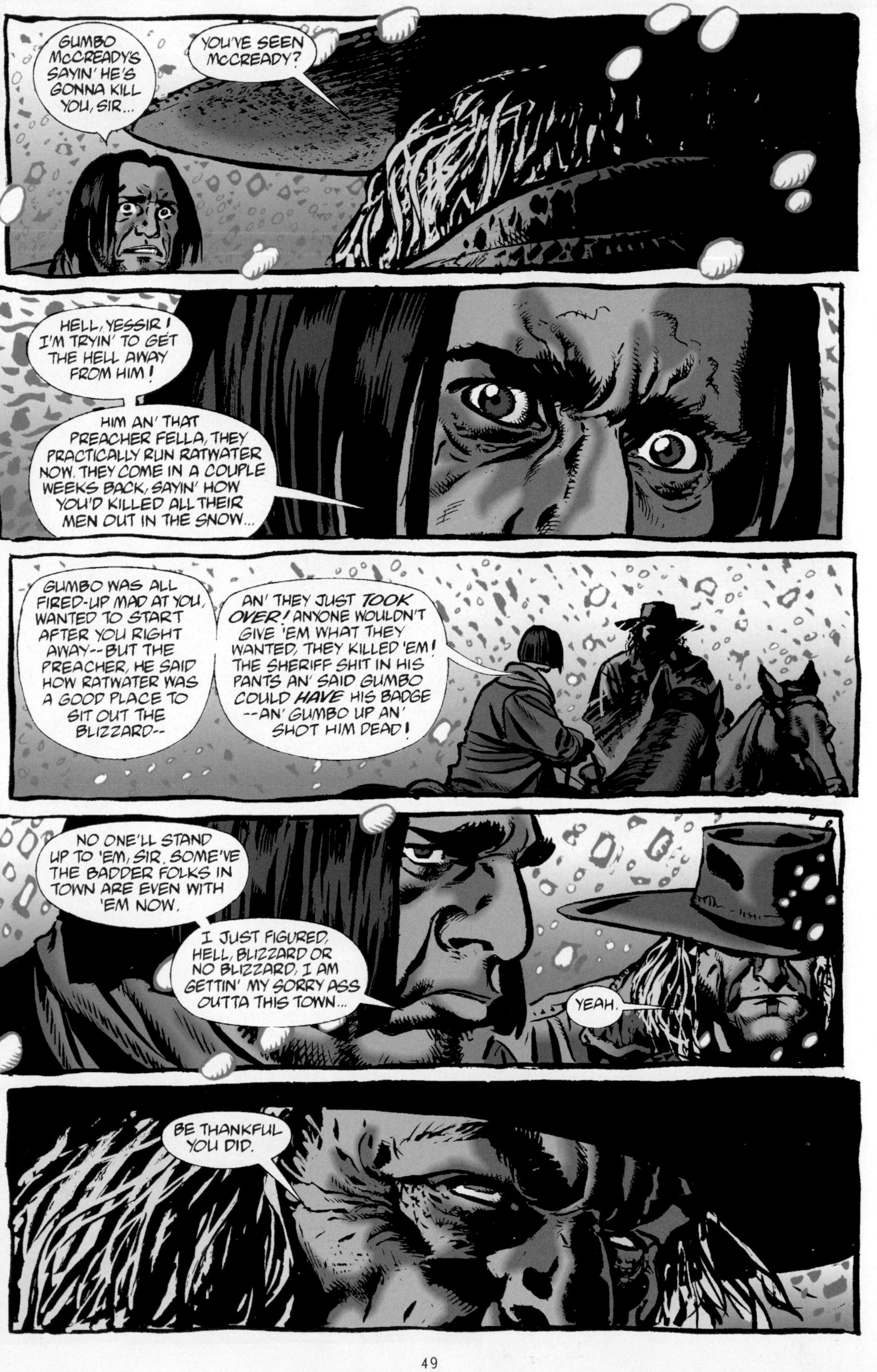
GUMBO McCREADY'S SAYIN' HE'S GONNA KILL YOU, SIR...
YOU'VE SEEN McCREADY?
HELL, YESSIR! I'M TRYIN' TO GET THE HELL AWAY FROM HIM!
HIM AN' THAT PREACHER FELLA, THEY PRACTICALLY RUN RATWATER NOW. THEY COME IN A COUPLE WEEKS BACK, SAYIN' HOW YOU'D KILLED ALL THEIR MEN OUT IN THE SNOW...
GUMBO WAS ALL FIRED-UP MAD AT YOU, WANTED TO START AFTER YOU RIGHT AWAY--BUT THE PREACHER, HE SAID HOW RATWATER WAS A GOOD PLACE TO SIT OUT THE BLIZZARD--
AN' THEY JUST TOOK OVER! ANYONE WOULDN'T GIVE 'EM WHAT THEY WANTED, THEY KILLED 'EM! THE SHERIFF SHIT IN HIS PANTS AN' SAID GUMBO COULD HAVE HIS BADGE --AN' GUMBO UP AN' SHOT HIM DEAD!
NO ONE'LL STAND UP TO 'EM, SIR. SOME'VE THE BADDER FOLKS IN TOWN ARE EVEN WITH 'EM NOW.
I JUST FIGURED, HELL, BLIZZARD OR NO BLIZZARD, I AM GETTIN' MY SORRY ASS OUTTA THIS TOWN...
YEAH.
BE THANKFUL YOU DID.

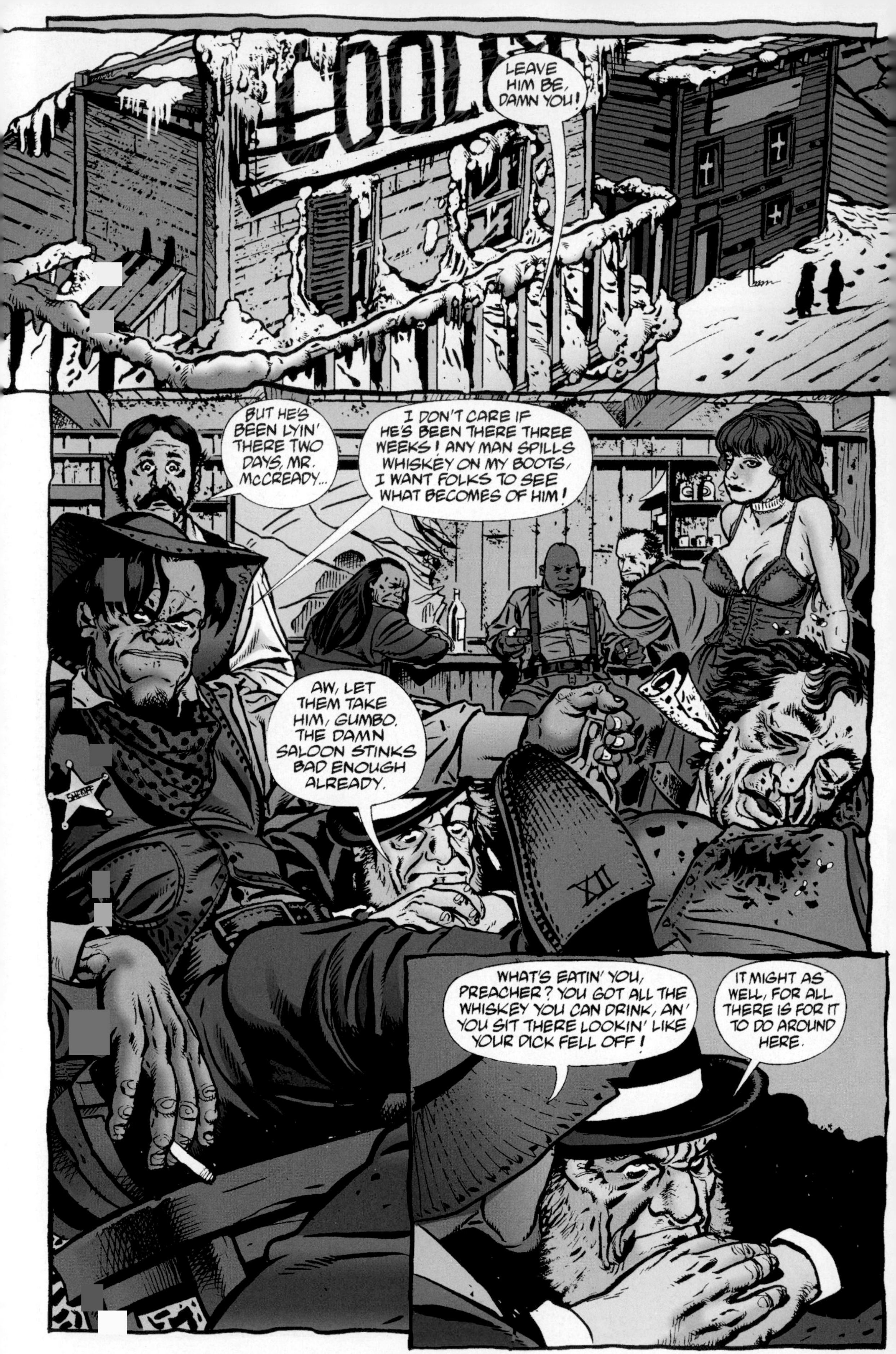
LEAVE HIM BE, DAMN YOU!
BUT HE'S BEEN LYIN' THERE TWO DAYS, MR. McCREADY...
I DON'T CARE IF HE'S BEEN THERE THREE WEEKS! ANY MAN SPILLS WHISKEY ON MY BOOTS, I WANT FOLKS TO SEE WHAT BECOMES OF HIM!
AW, LET THEM TAKE HIM, GUMBO. THE DAMN SALOON STINKS BAD ENOUGH ALREADY.
WHAT'S EATIN' YOU, PREACHER? YOU GOT ALL THE WHISKEY YOU CAN DRINK, AN' YOU SIT THERE LOOKIN' LIKE YOUR DICK FELL OFF!
IT MIGHT AS WELL, FOR ALL THERE IS FOR IT TO DO AROUND HERE.

ALL I WANT FROM LIFE IS DRINK AN' FORNICATION, BUT THE HAND I BEEN DEALT IS SO WRETCHED IT SEEMS LIKE EVEN THAT'S TOO MUCH TO ASK.

IF THERE IS A GOD, HE MUST'VE WIPED HIS ASS ON TEXAS --AN' RATWATER'S JUST THE SHITSTAIN LEFT BEHIND...

YOU SAID IT WOULD BE A GOOD PLACE TO WAIT OUT THE BLIZZARD, YOU DRUNK FOOL!

YOU LISTENED TO ME.

WELL, ONCE IT CLEARS WE'RE RIDIN' TO TAKE OUR REVENGE ON THAT MURDERIN' SON OF A BITCH...

I THOUGHT YOU GAVE UP ON HIM.

WHAT FOR? WE GOT ANOTHER GANG NOW, AIN'T WE?

THIS BUNCH?

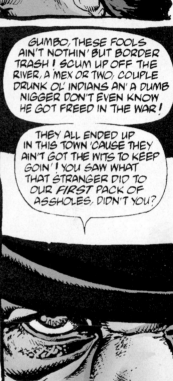

GUMBO, THESE FOOLS AIN'T NOTHIN' BUT BORDER TRASH! SCUM UP OFF THE RIVER, A 'MEX OR TWO, COUPLE DRUNK OL' INDIANS AN' A DUMB NIGGER DON'T EVEN KNOW HE GOT FREED IN THE WAR!

THEY ALL ENDED UP IN THIS TOWN 'CAUSE THEY AIN'T GOT THE WITS TO KEEP GOIN'! YOU SAW WHAT THAT STRANGER DID TO OUR FIRST PACK OF ASSHOLES, DIDN'T YOU?

SO WHAT D'YOU THINK HE'LL--

AND A PISTOLSHOT TURNED THE PREACHER'S BLOOD TO ICE.

51

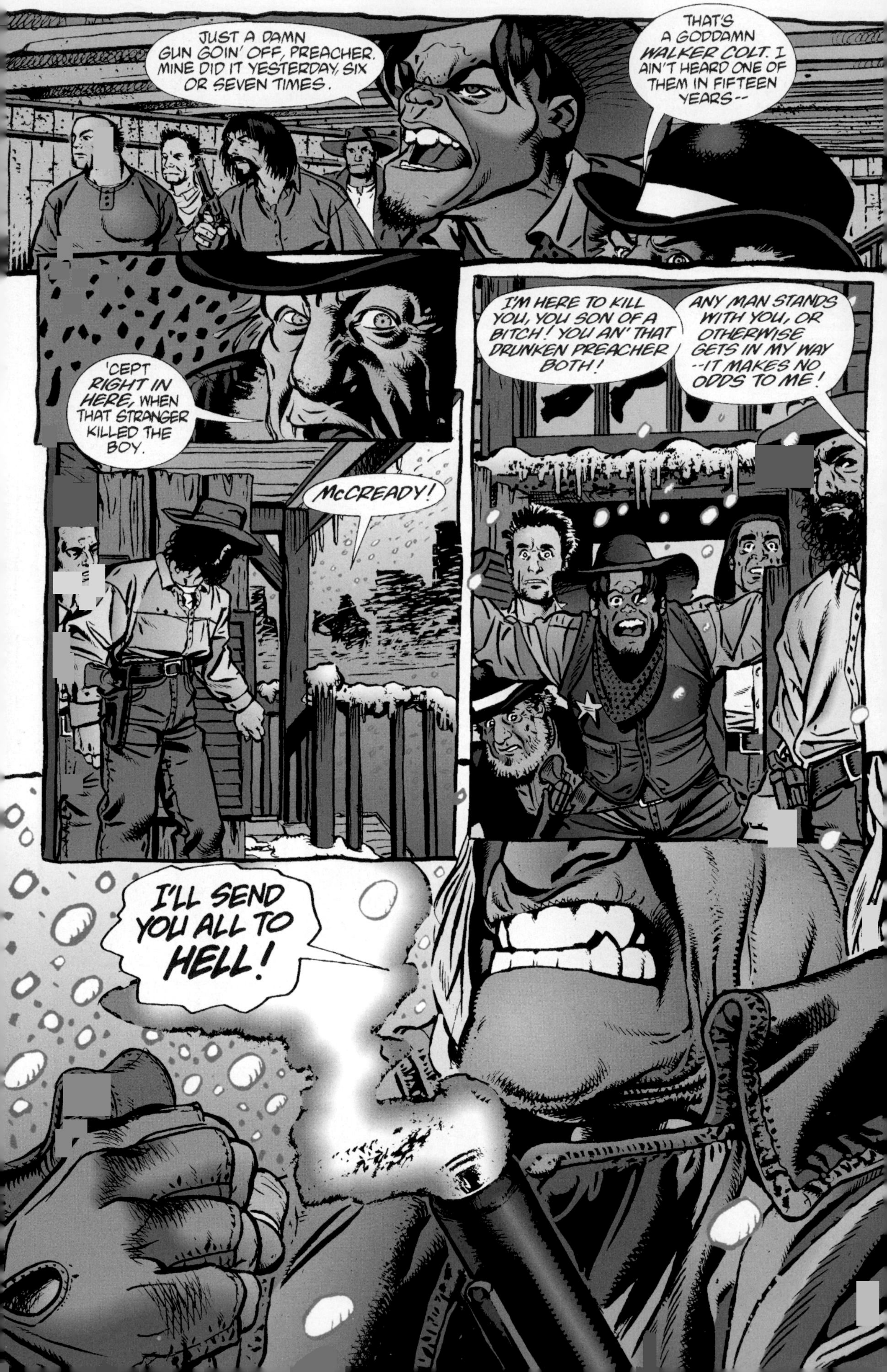
JUST A DAMN GUN GOIN' OFF, PREACHER. MINE DID IT YESTERDAY, SIX OR SEVEN TIMES.
THAT'S A GODDAMN WALKER COLT. I AIN'T HEARD ONE OF THEM IN FIFTEEN YEARS--
'CEPT RIGHT IN HERE, WHEN THAT STRANGER KILLED THE BOY.
McCREADY!
I'M HERE TO KILL YOU, YOU SON OF A BITCH! YOU AN' THAT DRUNKEN PREACHER BOTH!
ANY MAN STANDS WITH YOU, OR OTHERWISE GETS IN MY WAY --IT MAKES NO ODDS TO ME!
I'LL SEND YOU ALL TO HELL!

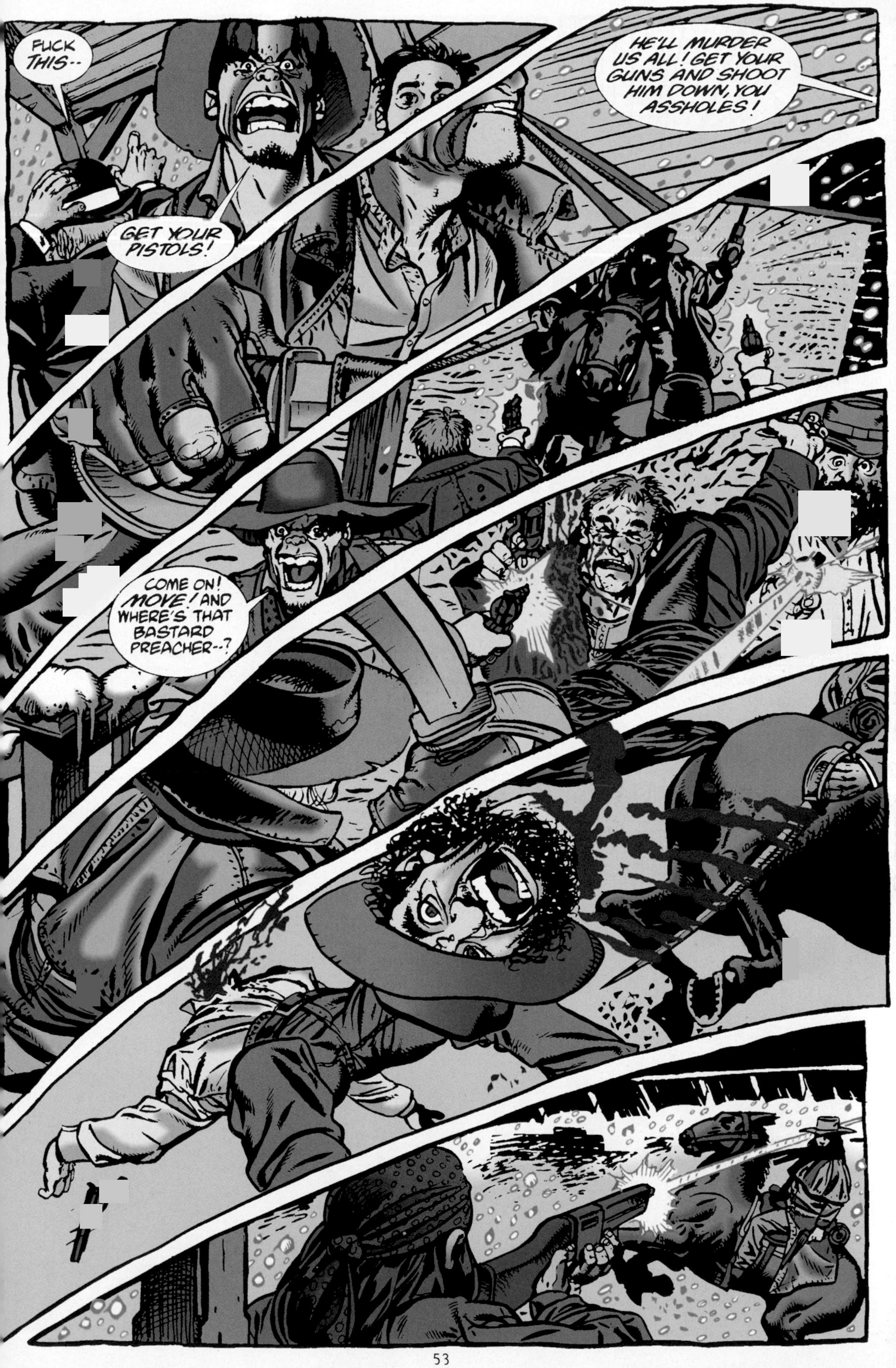
FUCK THIS--
GET YOUR PISTOLS!
HE'LL MURDER US ALL! GET YOUR GUNS AND SHOOT HIM DOWN, YOU ASSHOLES!
COME ON! MOVE! AND WHERE'S THAT BASTARD PREACHER--?

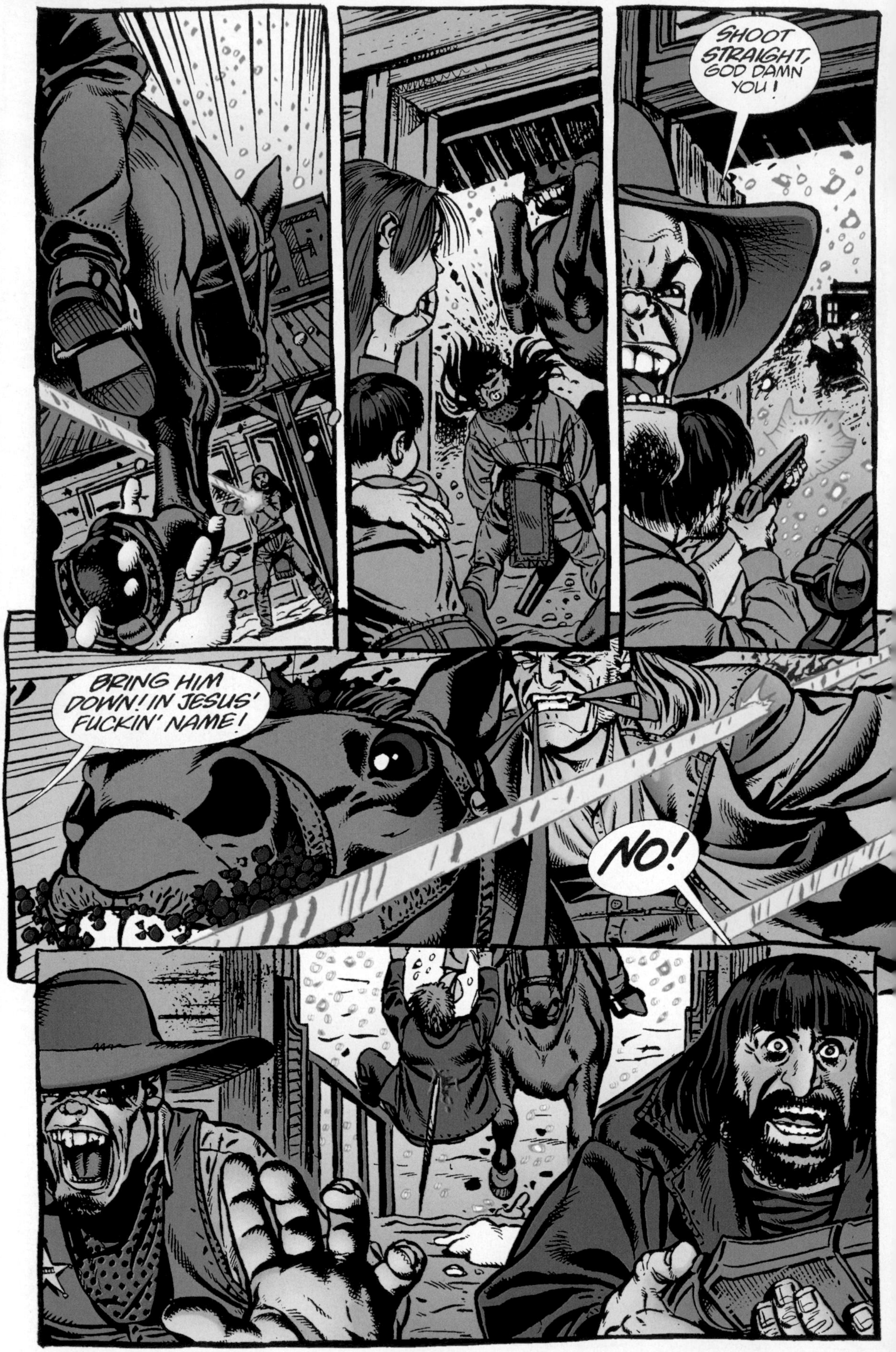
SHOOT STRAIGHT, GOD DAMN YOU!
BRING HIM DOWN! IN JESUS' FUCKIN' NAME!
NO!

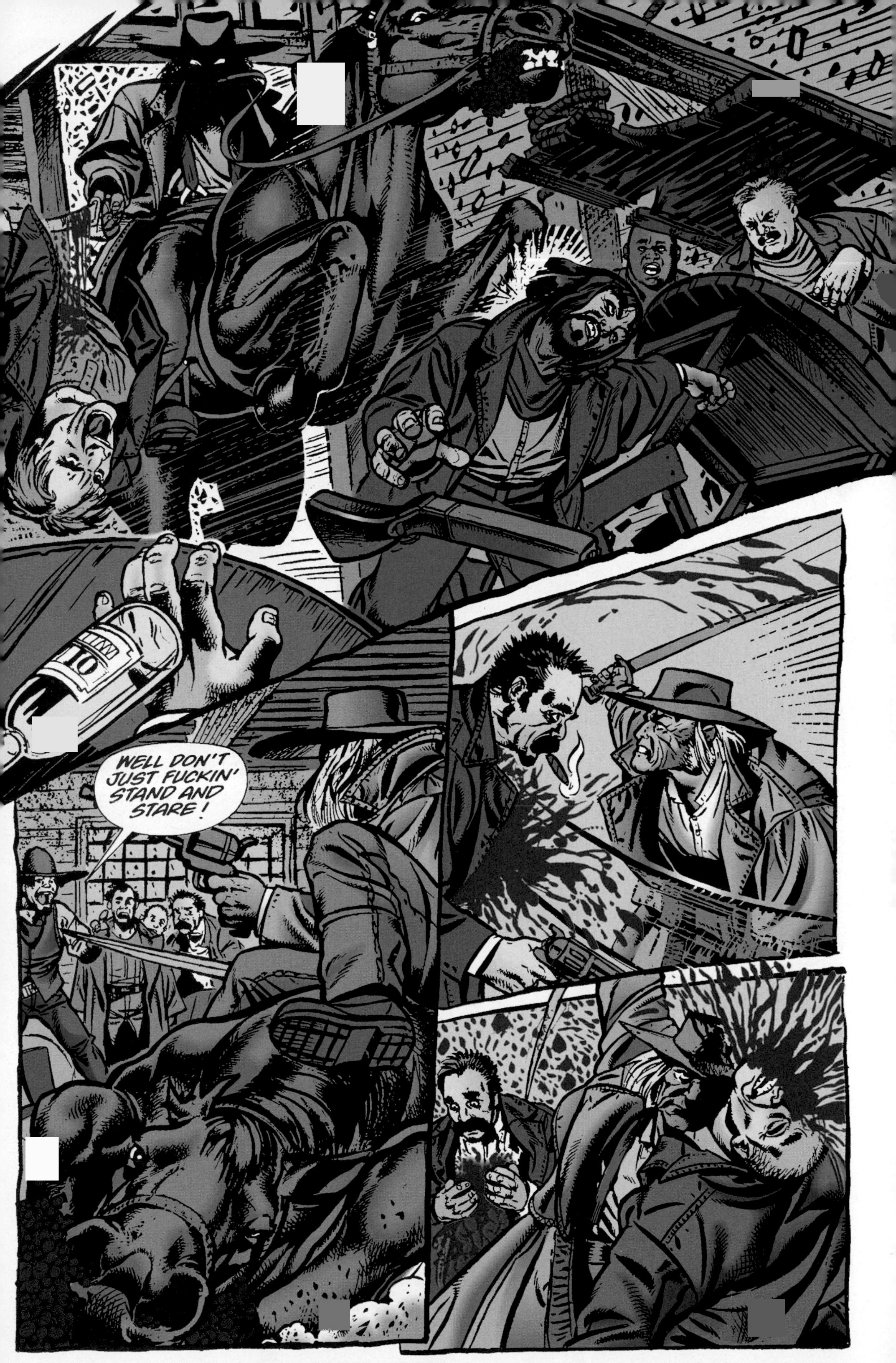
WELL DON'T JUST FUCKIN' STAND AND STARE!

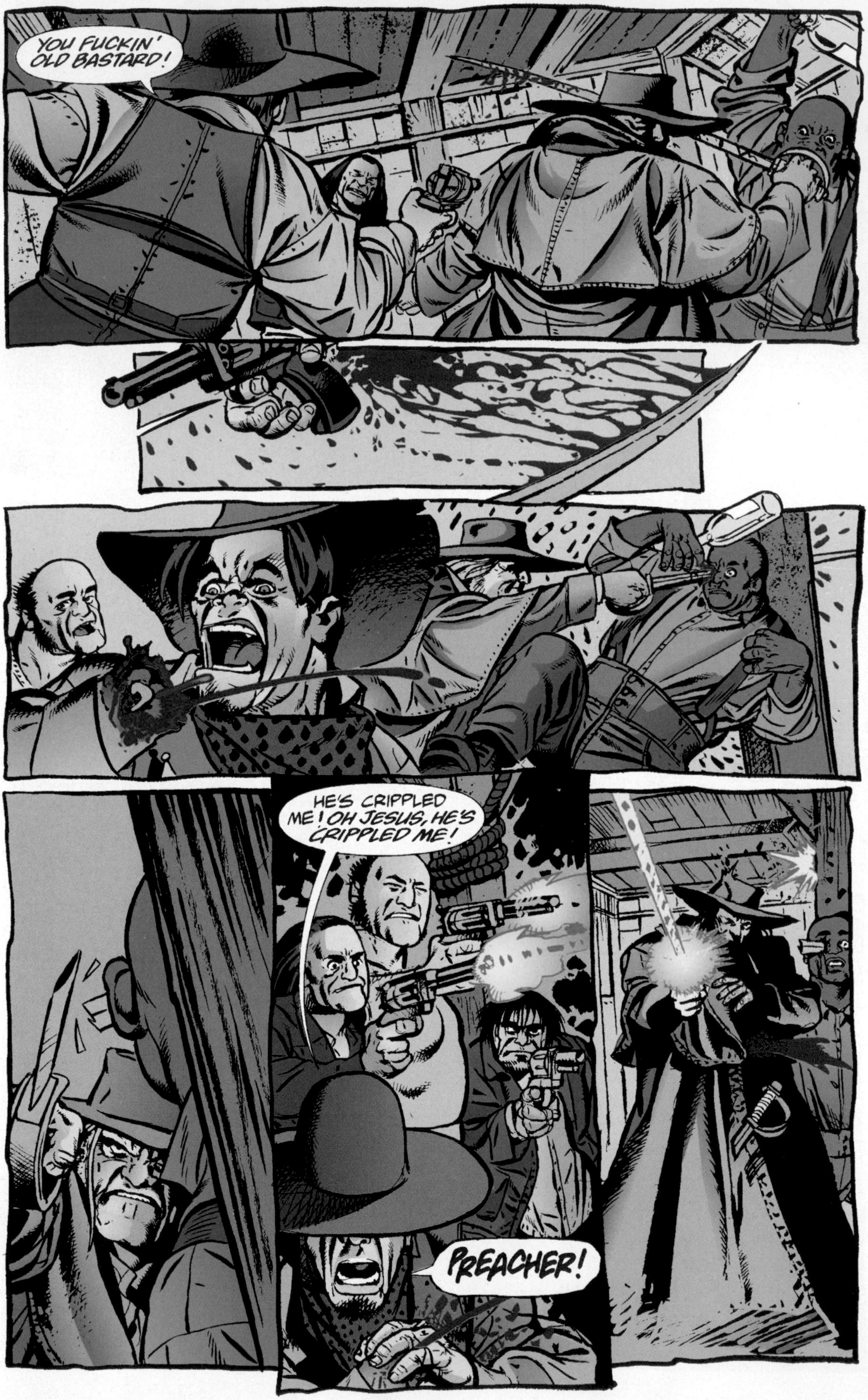
YOU FUCKIN' OLD BASTARD!
HE'S CRIPPLED ME! OH JESUS, HE'S CRIPPLED ME!
PREACHER!

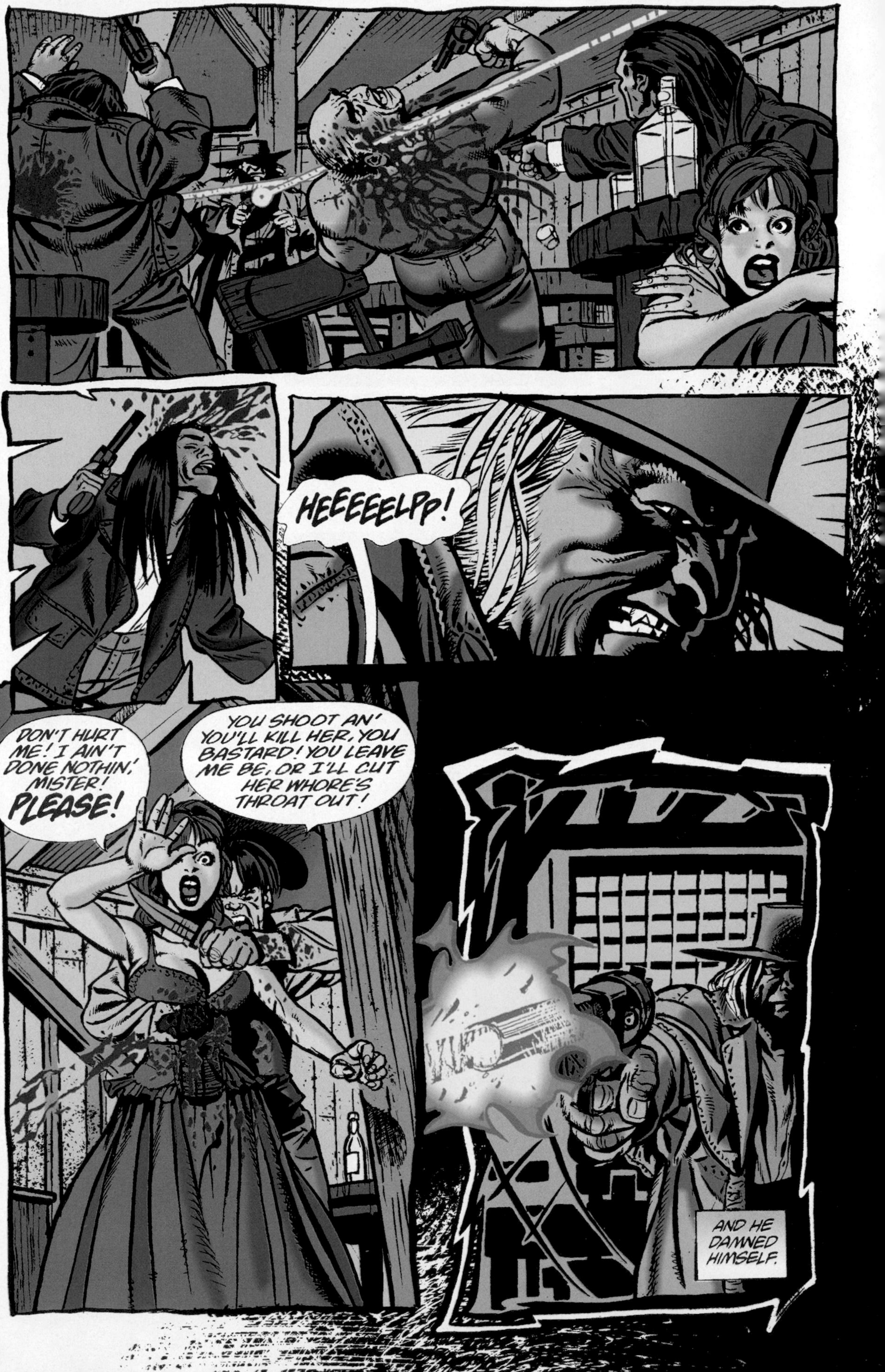
HEEEEEELPP!
DON'T HURT ME! I AIN'T DONE NOTHIN', MISTER! PLEASE!
YOU SHOOT AN' YOU'LL KILL HER, YOU BASTARD! YOU LEAVE ME BE, OR I'LL CUT HER WHORE'S THROAT OUT!
AND HE DAMNED HIMSELF.

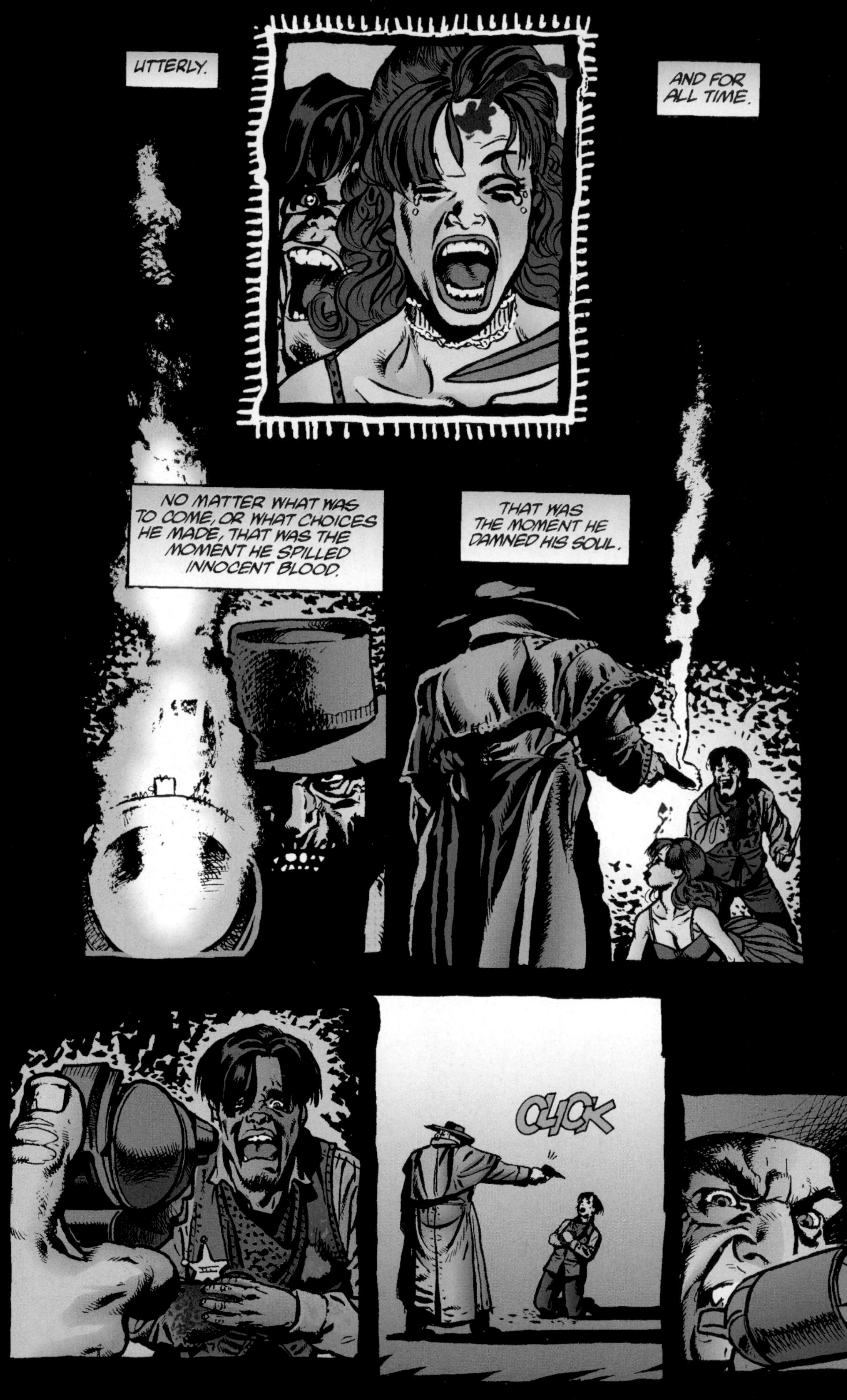
UTTERLY.
AND FOR ALL TIME.
NO MATTER WHAT WAS TO COME, OR WHAT CHOICES HE MADE, THAT WAS THE MOMENT HE SPILLED INNOCENT BLOOD.
THAT WAS THE MOMENT HE DAMNED HIS SOUL.
CLICK

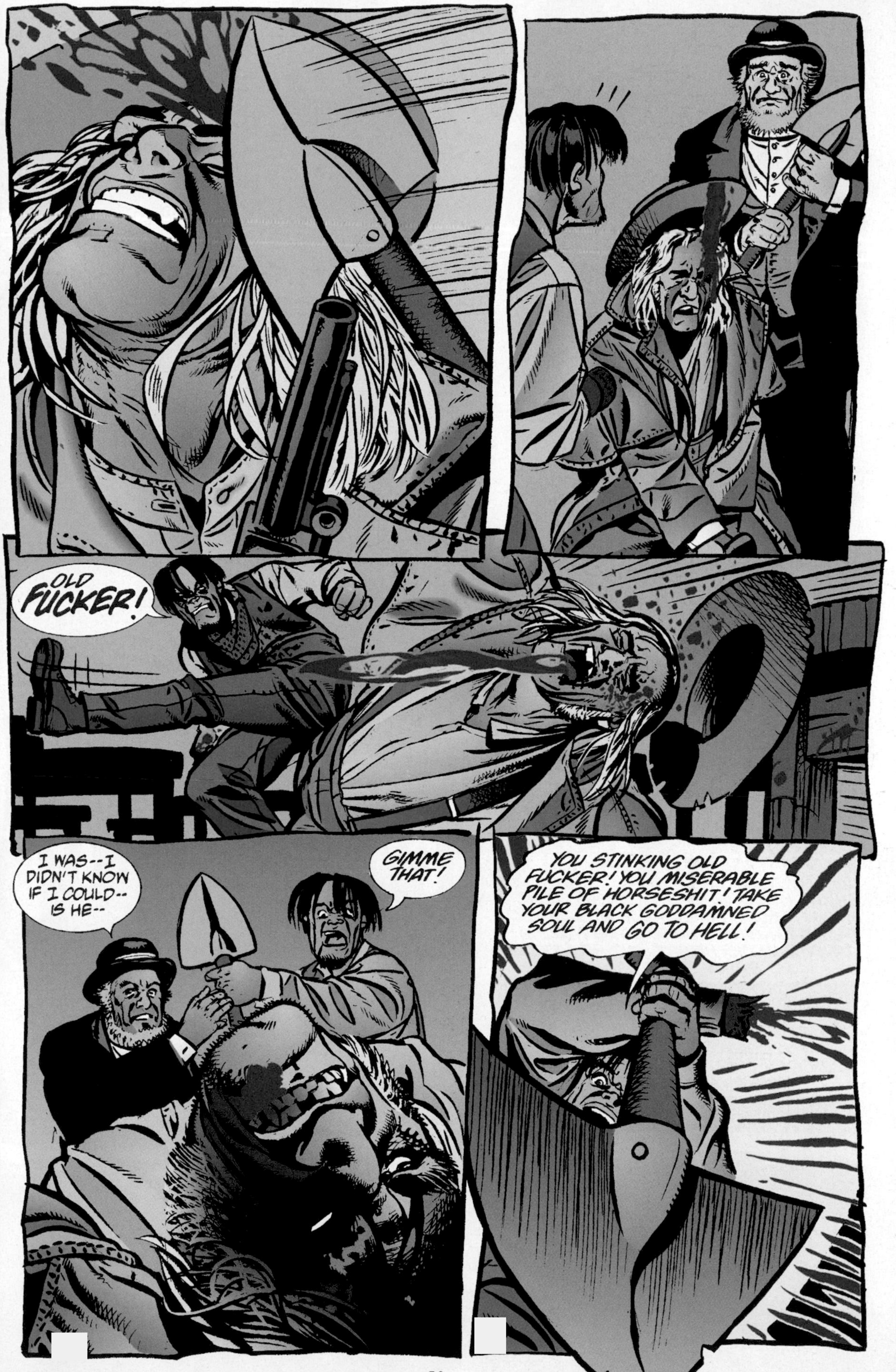
OLD FUCKER!
I WAS--I DIDN'T KNOW IF I COULD--IS HE--
GIMME THAT!
YOU STINKING OLD FUCKER! YOU MISERABLE PILE OF HORSESHIT! TAKE YOUR BLACK GODDAMNED SOUL AND GO TO HELL!

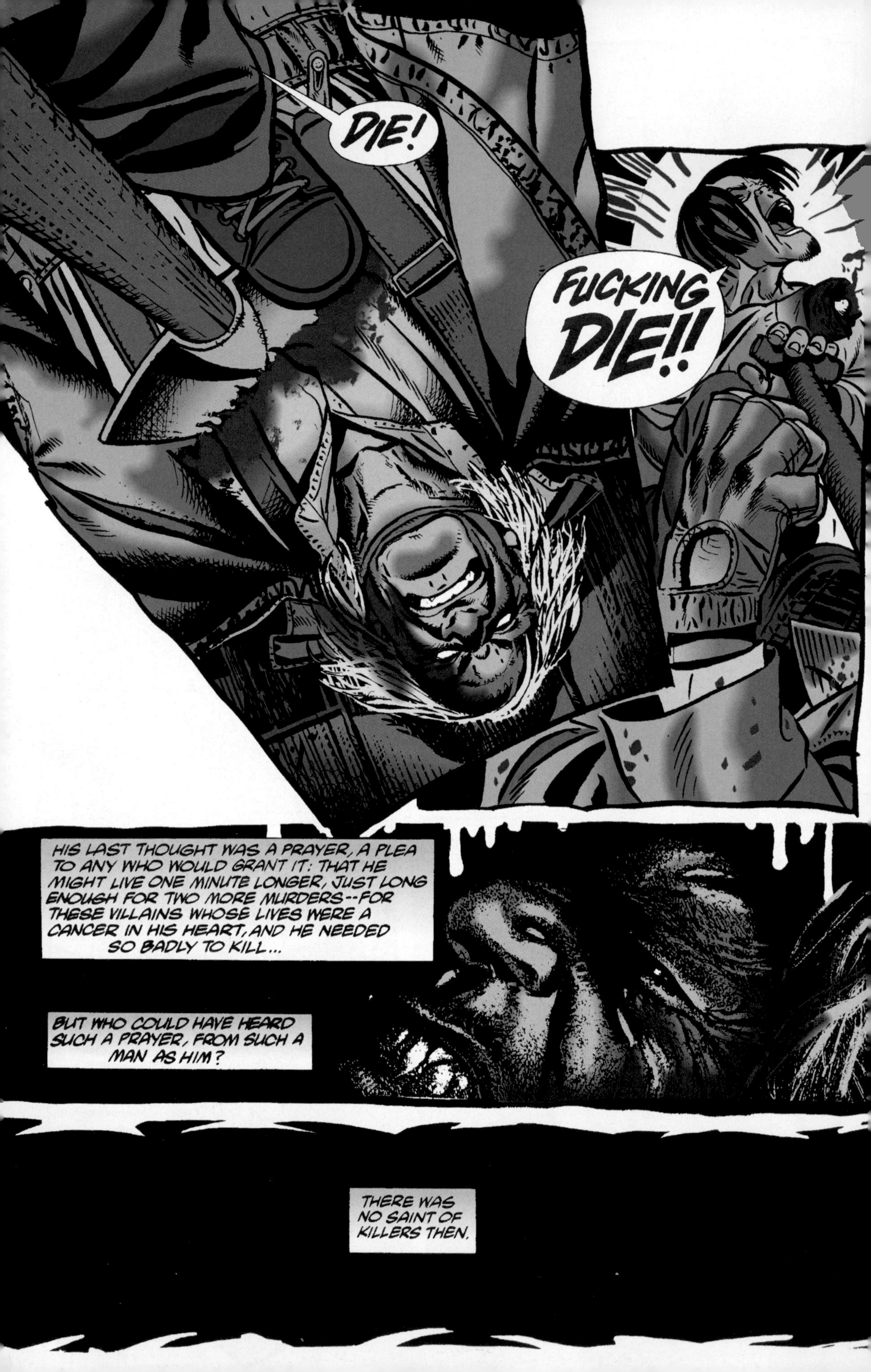
DIE!
FUCKING DIE!!
HIS LAST THOUGHT WAS A PRAYER, A PLEA TO ANY WHO WOULD GRANT IT: THAT HE MIGHT LIVE ONE MINUTE LONGER, JUST LONG ENOUGH FOR TWO MORE MURDERS--FOR THESE VILLAINS WHOSE LIVES WERE A CANCER IN HIS HEART, AND HE NEEDED SO BADLY TO KILL...
BUT WHO COULD HAVE HEARD SUCH A PRAYER, FROM SUCH A MAN AS HIM?
THERE WAS NO SAINT OF KILLERS THEN.

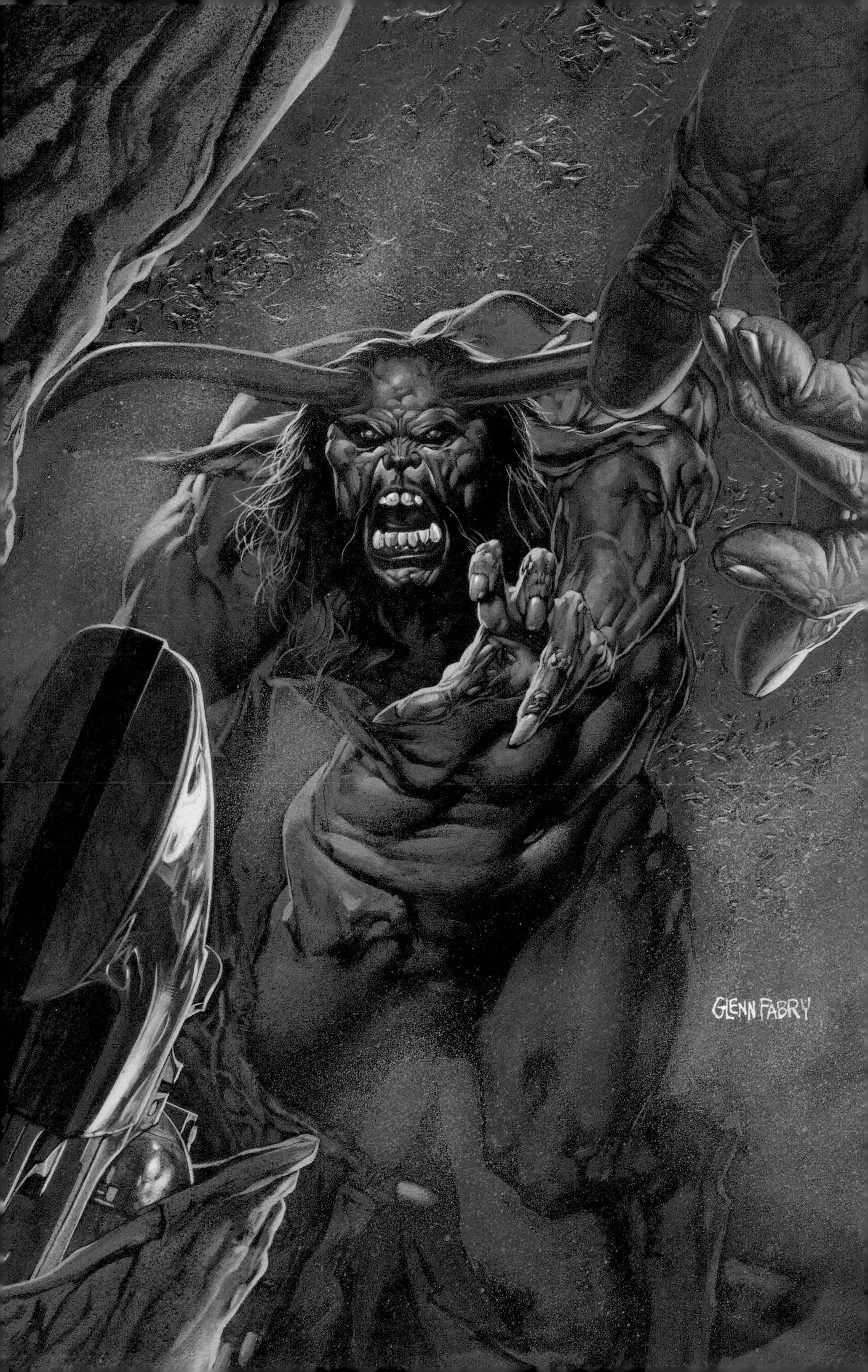
GLENN FABRY

"What they should have done was wept.
For the world. And for the future."

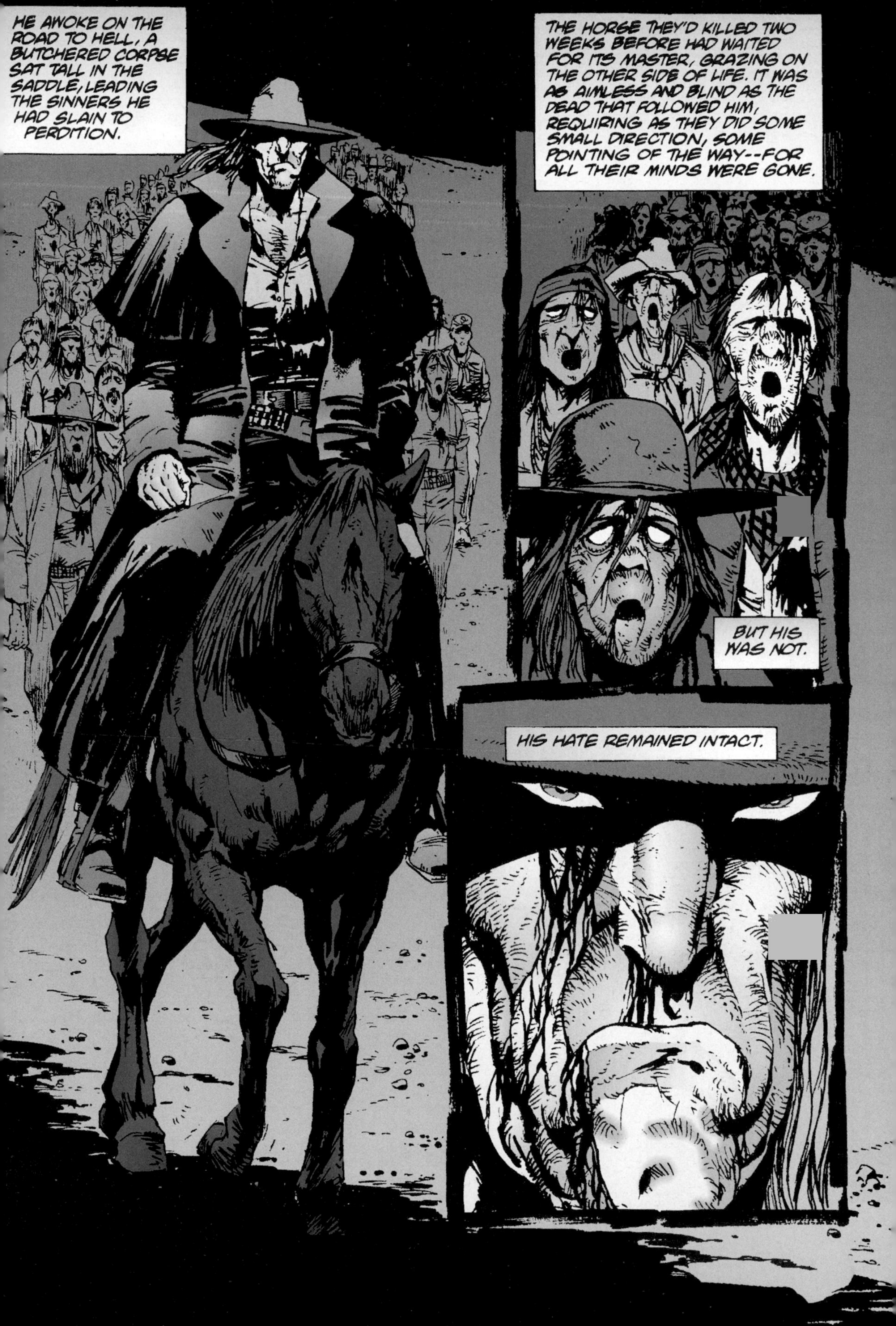
HE AWOKE ON THE ROAD TO HELL, A BUTCHERED CORPSE SAT TALL IN THE SADDLE, LEADING THE SINNERS HE HAD SLAIN TO PERDITION.
THE HORSE THEY'D KILLED TWO WEEKS BEFORE HAD WAITED FOR ITS MASTER, GRAZING ON THE OTHER SIDE OF LIFE. IT WAS AS AIMLESS AND BLIND AS THE DEAD THAT FOLLOWED HIM, REQUIRING AS THEY DID SOME SMALL DIRECTION, SOME POINTING OF THE WAY--FOR ALL THEIR MINDS WERE GONE.
BUT HIS WAS NOT.
HIS HATE REMAINED INTACT.

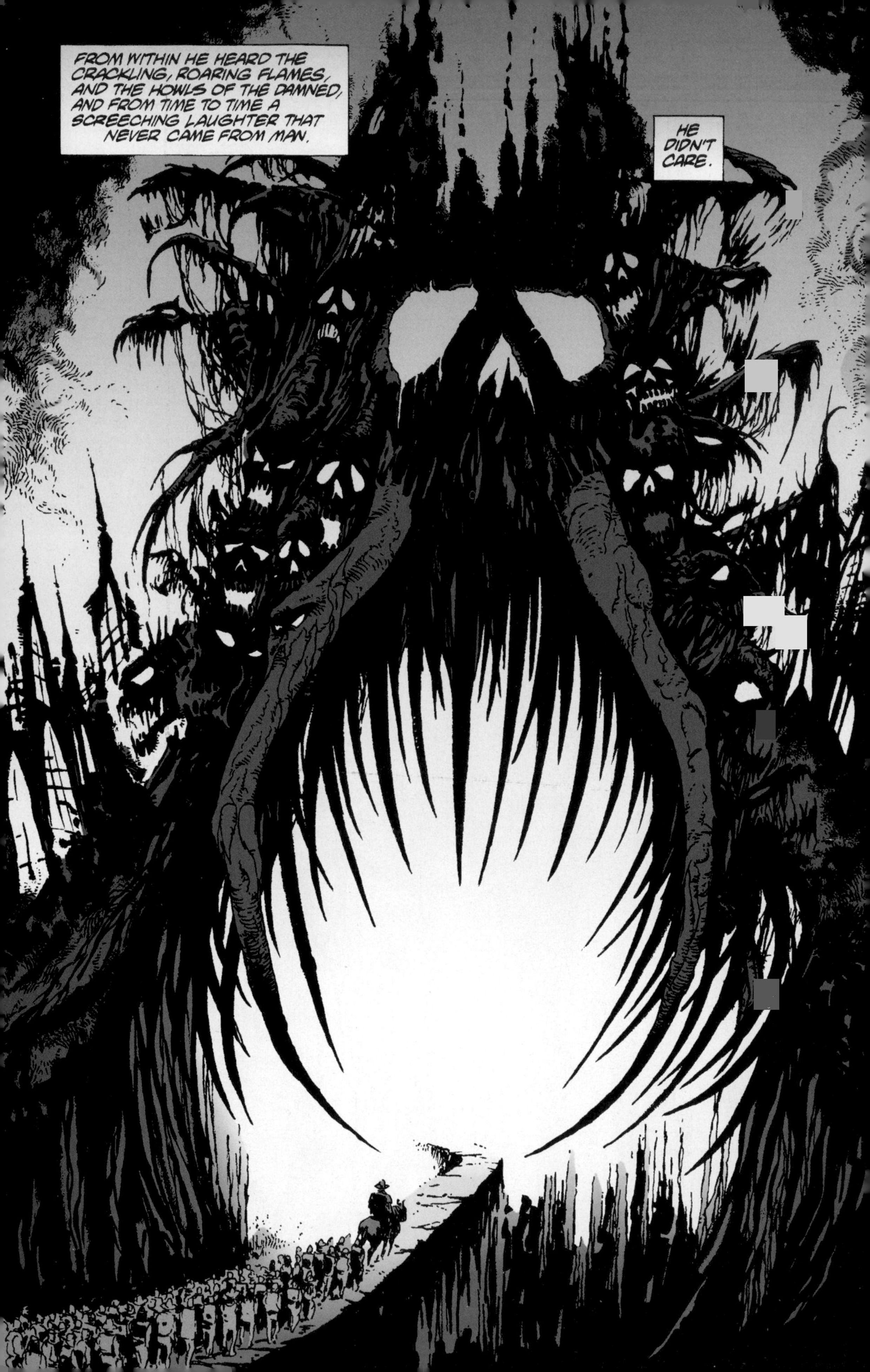
FROM WITHIN HE HEARD THE CRACKLING, ROARING FLAMES, AND THE HOWLS OF THE DAMNED, AND FROM TIME TO TIME A SCREECHING LAUGHTER THAT NEVER CAME FROM MAN.
HE DIDN'T CARE.

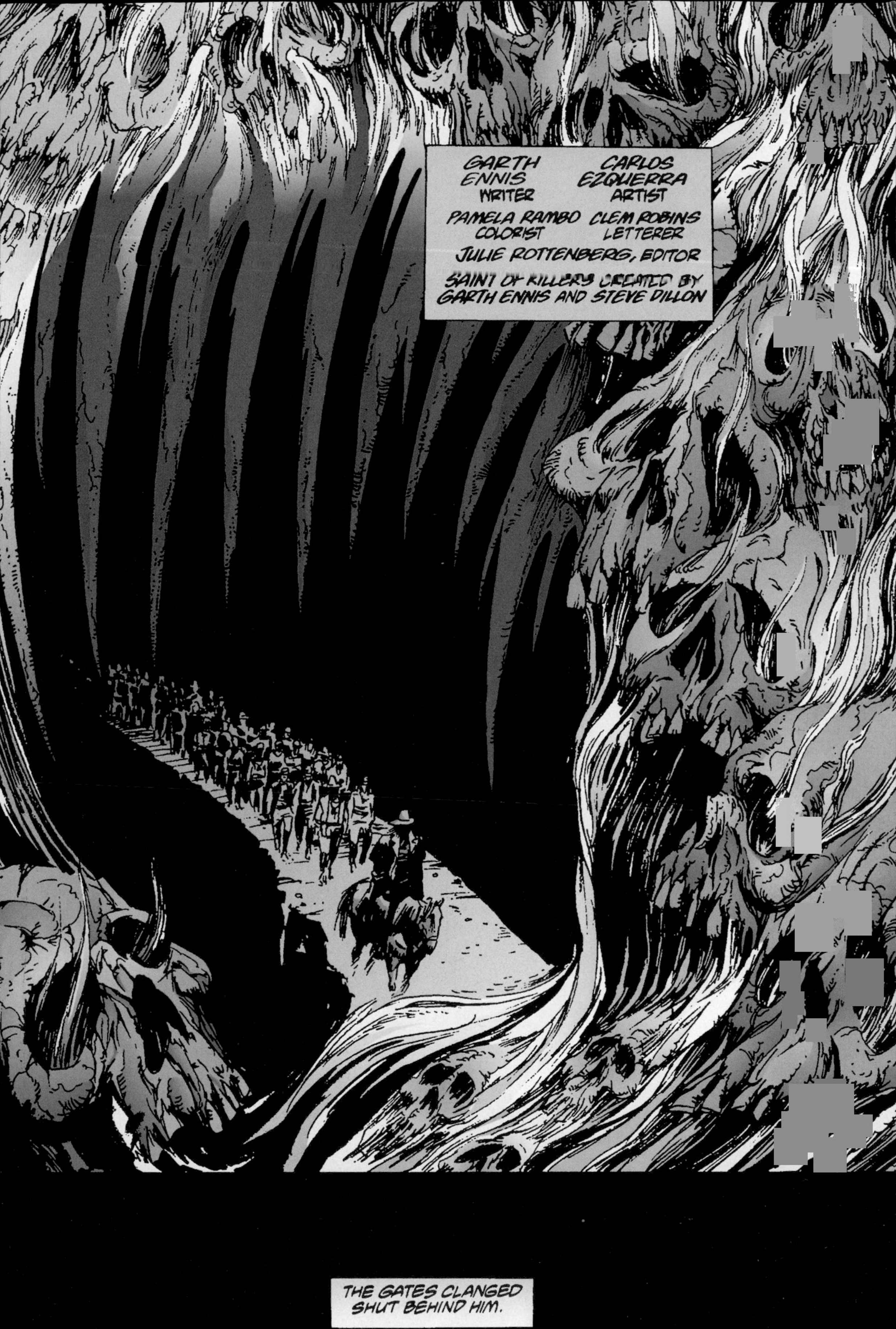
GARTH ENNIS WRITER
CARLOS EZQUERRA ARTIST
PAMELA RAMBO COLORIST
CLEM ROBINS LETTERER
JULIE ROTTENBERG, EDITOR
SAINT OF KILLERS CREATED BY GARTH ENNIS AND STEVE DILLON
THE GATES CLANGED SHUT BEHIND HIM.

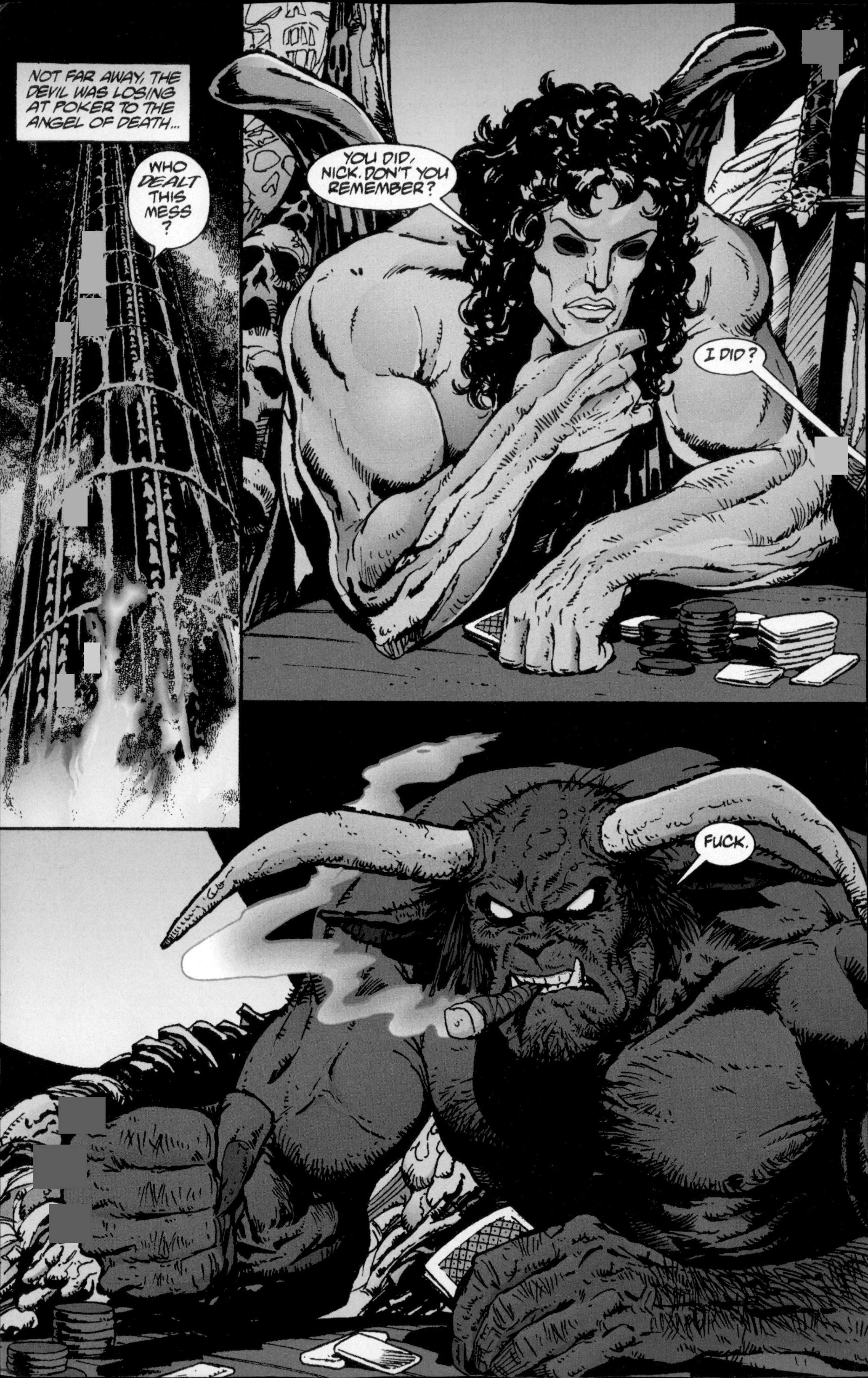
NOT FAR AWAY, THE DEVIL WAS LOSING AT POKER TO THE ANGEL OF DEATH...
WHO DEALT THIS MESS?
YOU DID, NICK. DON'T YOU REMEMBER?
I DID?
FUCK.

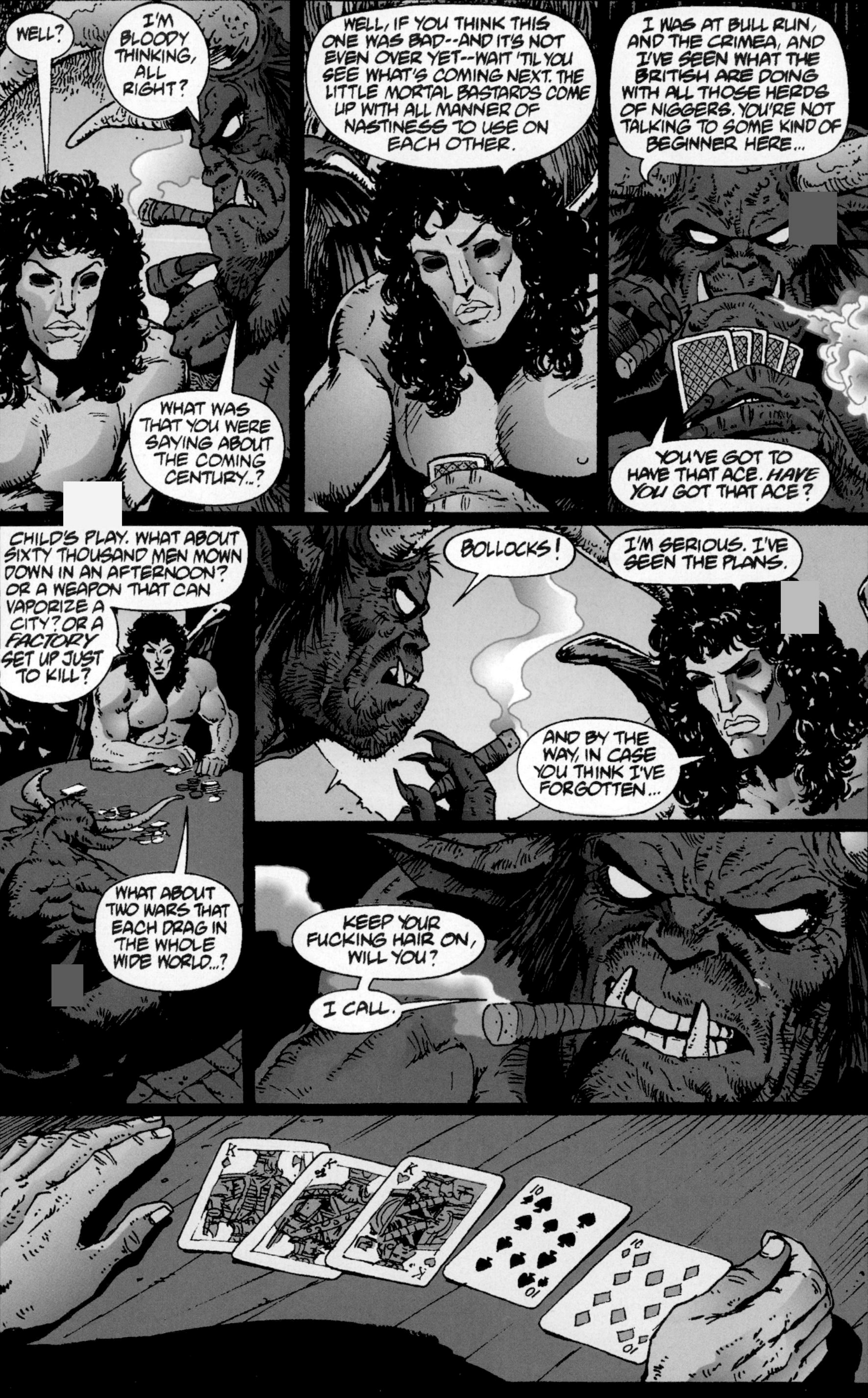
WELL?
I'M BLOODY THINKING, ALL RIGHT?
WHAT WAS THAT YOU WERE SAYING ABOUT THE COMING CENTURY..?
WELL, IF YOU THINK THIS ONE WAS BAD--AND IT'S NOT EVEN OVER YET--WAIT 'TIL YOU SEE WHAT'S COMING NEXT. THE LITTLE MORTAL BASTARDS COME UP WITH ALL MANNER OF NASTINESS TO USE ON EACH OTHER.
I WAS AT BULL RUN, AND THE CRIMEA, AND I'VE SEEN WHAT THE BRITISH ARE DOING WITH ALL THOSE HERDS OF NIGGERS. YOU'RE NOT TALKING TO SOME KIND OF BEGINNER HERE...
YOU'VE GOT TO HAVE THAT ACE. *HAVE YOU* GOT THAT ACE?
CHILD'S PLAY. WHAT ABOUT SIXTY THOUSAND MEN MOWN DOWN IN AN AFTERNOON? OR A WEAPON THAT CAN VAPORIZE A CITY? OR A *FACTORY* SET UP JUST TO KILL?
WHAT ABOUT TWO WARS THAT EACH DRAG IN THE WHOLE WIDE WORLD..?
BOLLOCKS!
I'M SERIOUS. I'VE SEEN THE PLANS.
AND BY THE WAY, IN CASE YOU THINK I'VE FORGOTTEN...
KEEP YOUR FUCKING HAIR ON, WILL YOU?
I CALL.

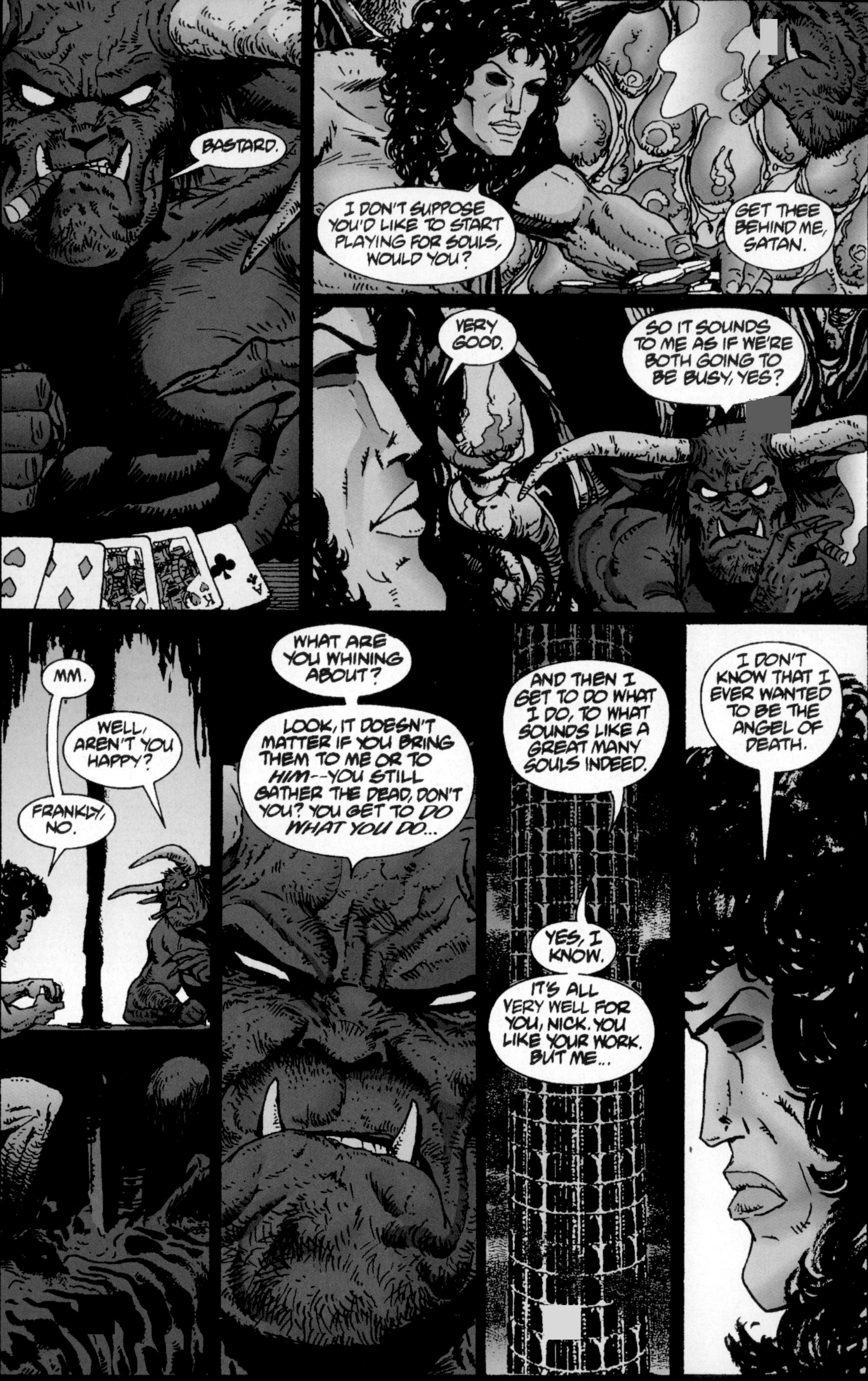
BASTARD.
I DON'T SUPPOSE YOU'D LIKE TO START PLAYING FOR SOULS, WOULD YOU?
GET THEE BEHIND ME, SATAN.
VERY GOOD.
SO IT SOUNDS TO ME AS IF WE'RE BOTH GOING TO BE BUSY, YES?
MM.
WELL, AREN'T YOU HAPPY?
FRANKLY, NO.
WHAT ARE YOU WHINING ABOUT?
LOOK, IT DOESN'T MATTER IF YOU BRING THEM TO ME OR TO *HIM*--YOU STILL GATHER THE DEAD, DON'T YOU? YOU GET TO *DO WHAT YOU DO*...
AND THEN I GET TO DO WHAT I DO, TO WHAT SOUNDS LIKE A GREAT MANY SOULS INDEED.
YES, I KNOW.
IT'S ALL VERY WELL FOR YOU, NICK. YOU LIKE YOUR WORK. BUT ME...
I DON'T KNOW THAT I EVER WANTED TO BE THE ANGEL OF DEATH.

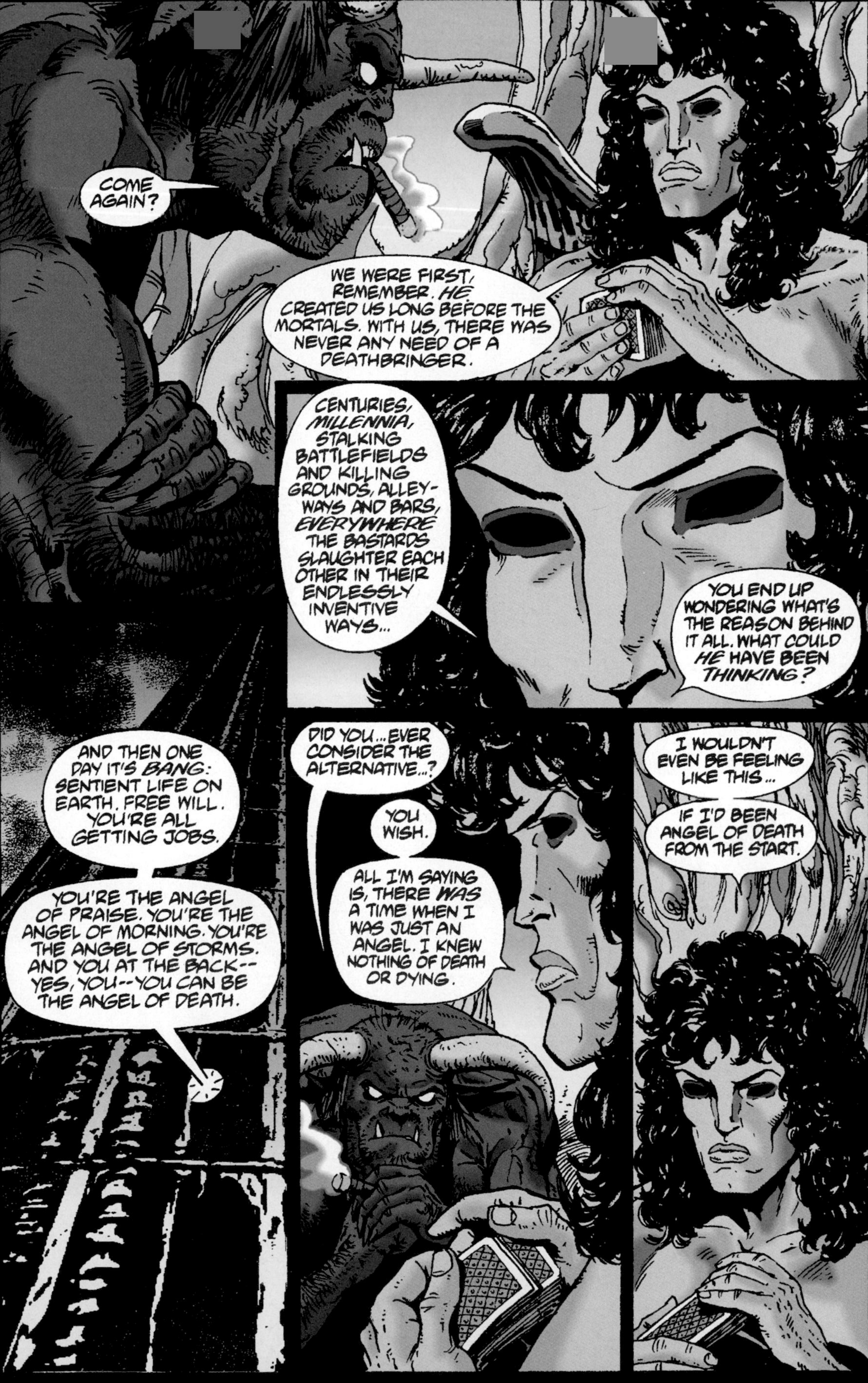
COME AGAIN?
WE WERE FIRST, REMEMBER. *HE* CREATED US LONG BEFORE THE MORTALS. WITH US, THERE WAS NEVER ANY NEED OF A DEATHBRINGER.
CENTURIES, *MILLENNIA*, STALKING BATTLEFIELDS AND KILLING GROUNDS, ALLEY-WAYS AND BARS, *EVERYWHERE* THE BASTARDS SLAUGHTER EACH OTHER IN THEIR ENDLESSLY INVENTIVE WAYS...
YOU END UP WONDERING WHAT'S THE REASON BEHIND IT ALL. WHAT COULD *HE* HAVE BEEN *THINKING*?
AND THEN ONE DAY IT'S *BANG*: SENTIENT LIFE ON EARTH. FREE WILL. YOU'RE ALL GETTING JOBS.
YOU'RE THE ANGEL OF PRAISE. YOU'RE THE ANGEL OF MORNING. YOU'RE THE ANGEL OF STORMS. AND YOU AT THE BACK-- YES, YOU--YOU CAN BE THE ANGEL OF DEATH.
DID YOU...EVER CONSIDER THE ALTERNATIVE...?
YOU WISH.
ALL I'M SAYING IS, THERE *WAS* A TIME WHEN I WAS JUST AN ANGEL. I KNEW NOTHING OF DEATH OR DYING.
I WOULDN'T EVEN BE FEELING LIKE THIS...
IF I'D BEEN ANGEL OF DEATH FROM THE START.

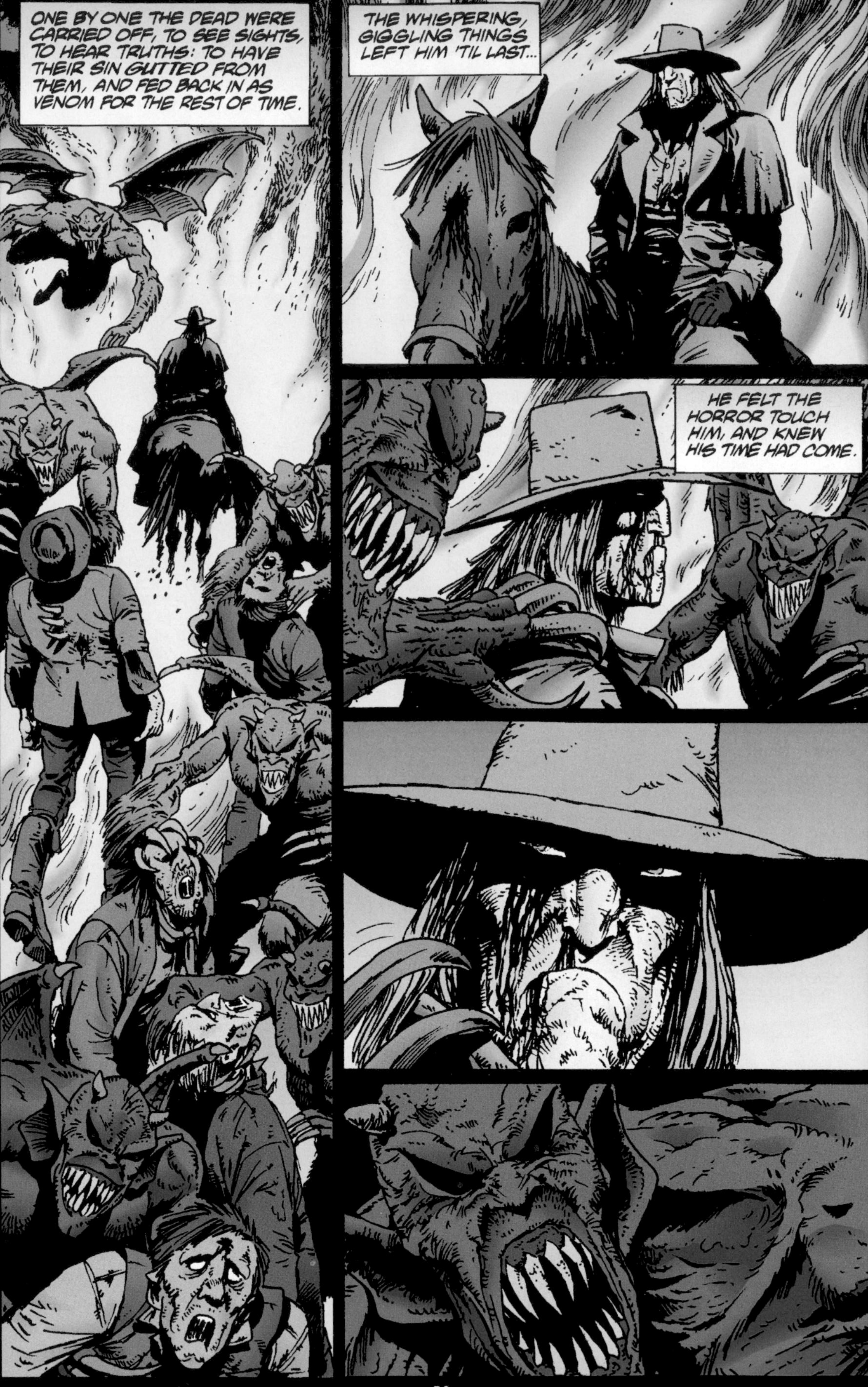
ONE BY ONE THE DEAD WERE CARRIED OFF, TO SEE SIGHTS, TO HEAR TRUTHS: TO HAVE THEIR SIN GUTTED FROM THEM, AND FED BACK IN AS VENOM FOR THE REST OF TIME.
THE WHISPERING, GIGGLING THINGS LEFT HIM 'TIL LAST...
HE FELT THE HORROR TOUCH HIM, AND KNEW HIS TIME HAD COME.

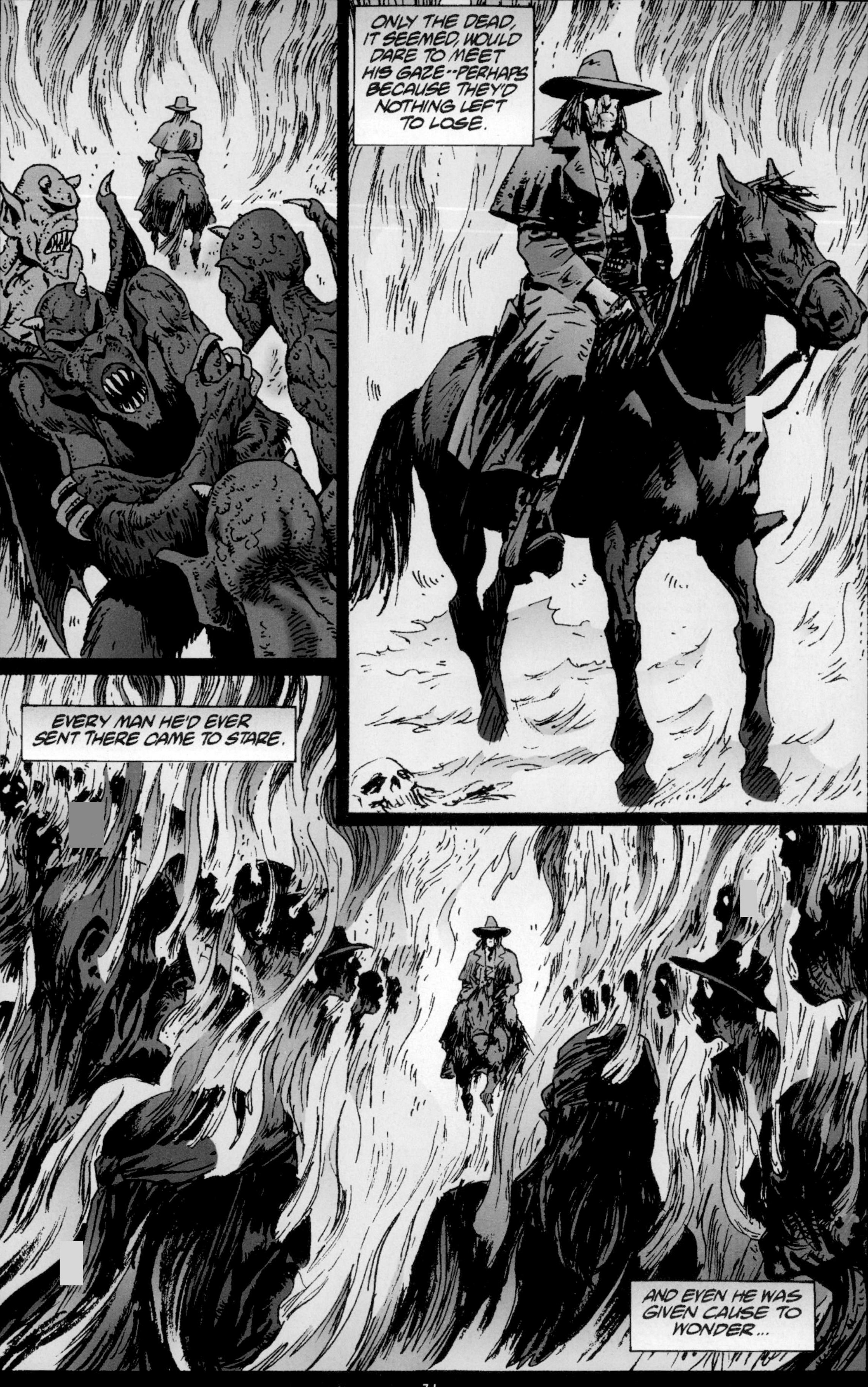
ONLY THE DEAD, IT SEEMED, WOULD DARE TO MEET HIS GAZE--PERHAPS BECAUSE THEY'D NOTHING LEFT TO LOSE.
EVERY MAN HE'D EVER SENT THERE CAME TO STARE.
AND EVEN HE WAS GIVEN CAUSE TO WONDER...

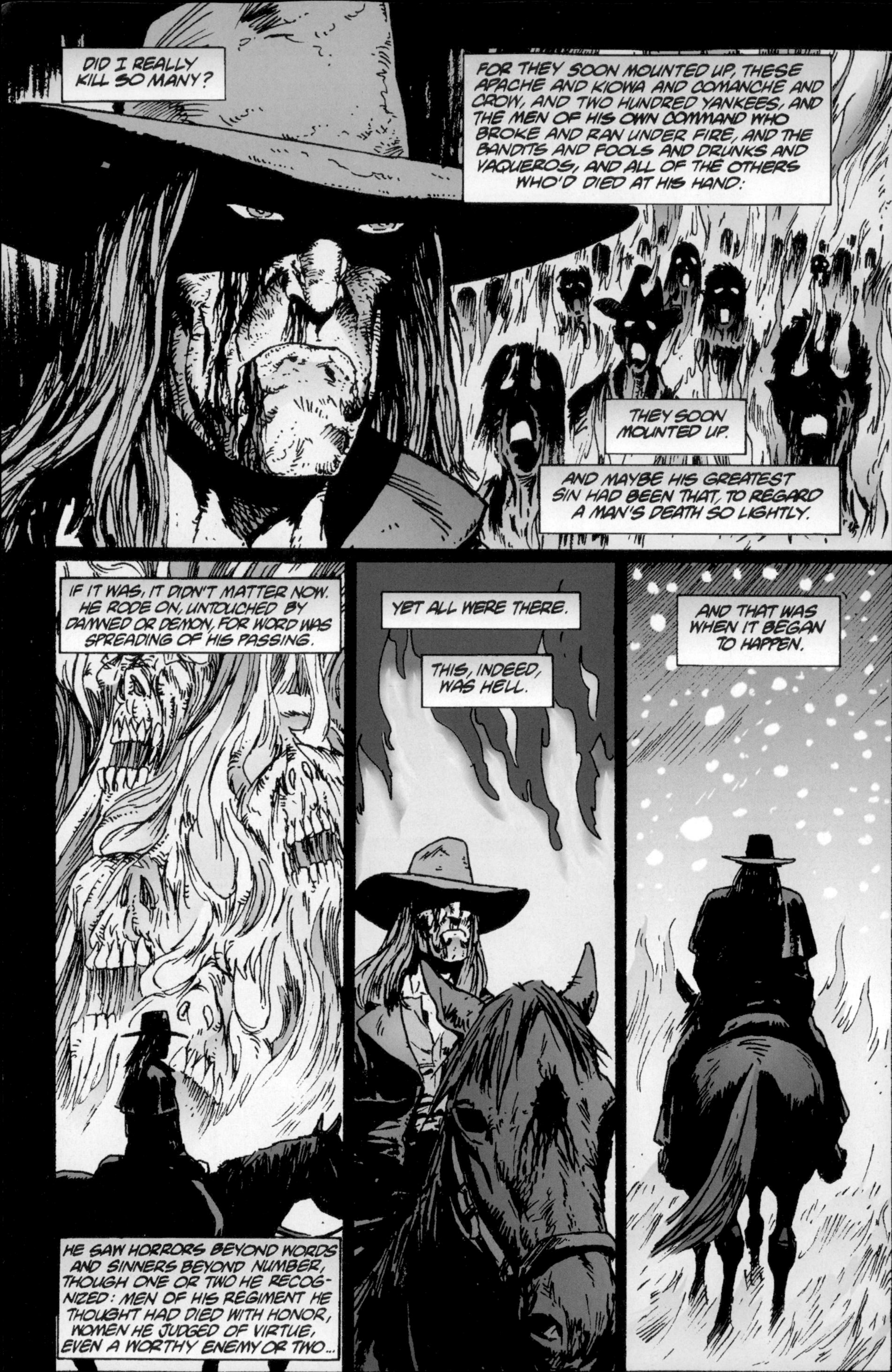
DID I REALLY KILL SO MANY?
FOR THEY SOON MOUNTED UP, THESE APACHE AND KIOWA AND COMANCHE AND CROW, AND TWO HUNDRED YANKEES, AND THE MEN OF HIS OWN COMMAND WHO BROKE AND RAN UNDER FIRE, AND THE BANDITS AND FOOLS AND DRUNKS AND VAQUEROS, AND ALL OF THE OTHERS WHO'D DIED AT HIS HAND:
THEY SOON MOUNTED UP.
AND MAYBE HIS GREATEST SIN HAD BEEN THAT, TO REGARD A MAN'S DEATH SO LIGHTLY.
IF IT WAS, IT DIDN'T MATTER NOW. HE RODE ON, UNTOUCHED BY DAMNED OR DEMON, FOR WORD WAS SPREADING OF HIS PASSING.
HE SAW HORRORS BEYOND WORDS AND SINNERS BEYOND NUMBER, THOUGH ONE OR TWO HE RECOGNIZED: MEN OF HIS REGIMENT HE THOUGHT HAD DIED WITH HONOR, WOMEN HE JUDGED OF VIRTUE, EVEN A WORTHY ENEMY OR TWO...
YET ALL WERE THERE.
THIS, INDEED, WAS HELL.
AND THAT WAS WHEN IT BEGAN TO HAPPEN.

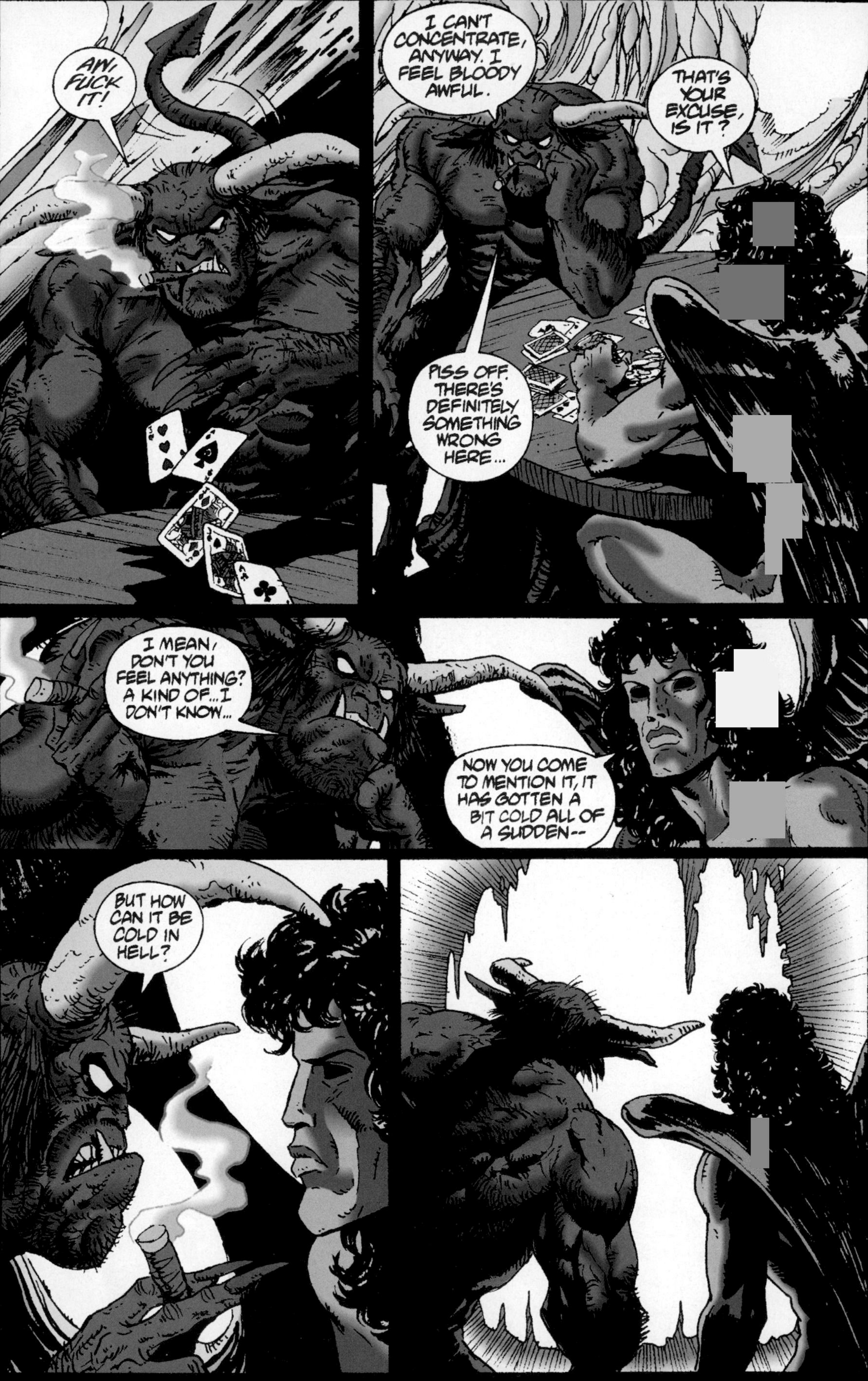
AW, FUCK IT!
I CAN'T CONCENTRATE, ANYWAY. I FEEL BLOODY AWFUL.
THAT'S YOUR EXCUSE, IS IT?
PISS OFF. THERE'S DEFINITELY SOMETHING WRONG HERE...
I MEAN, DON'T YOU FEEL ANYTHING? A KIND OF...I DON'T KNOW...
NOW YOU COME TO MENTION IT, IT HAS GOTTEN A BIT COLD ALL OF A SUDDEN--
BUT HOW CAN IT BE COLD IN HELL?

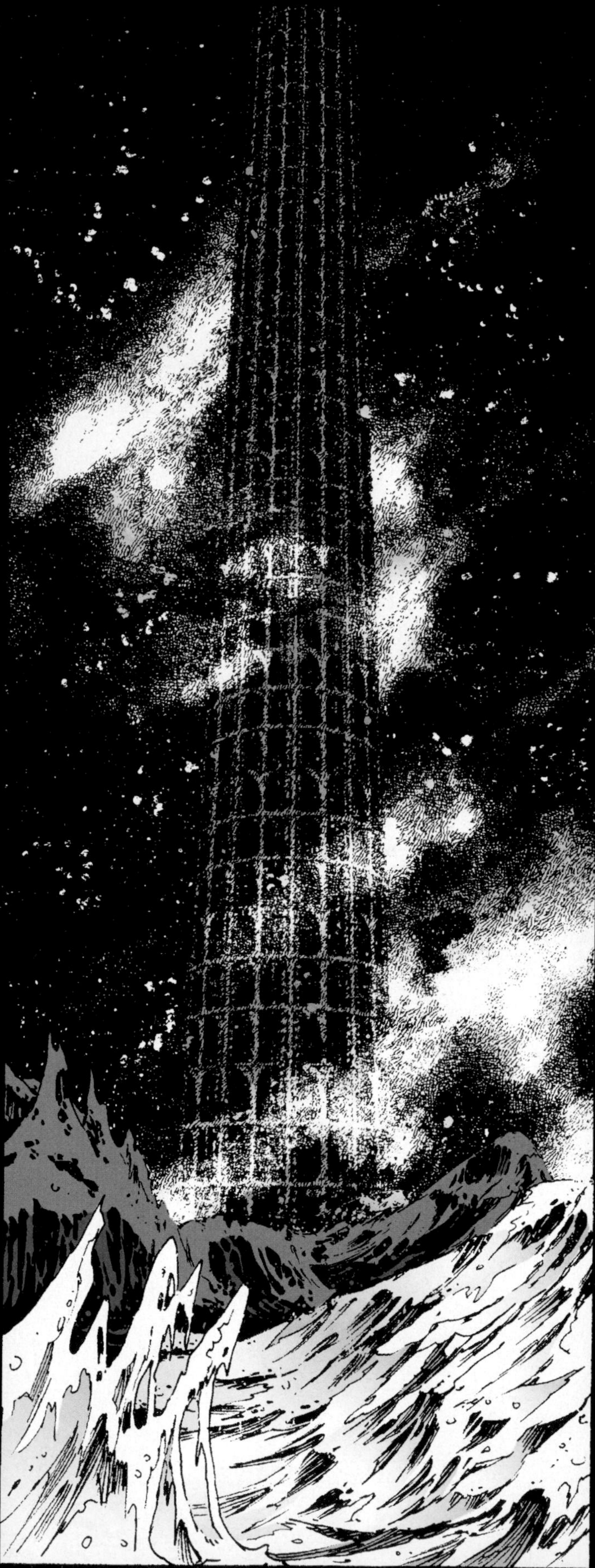

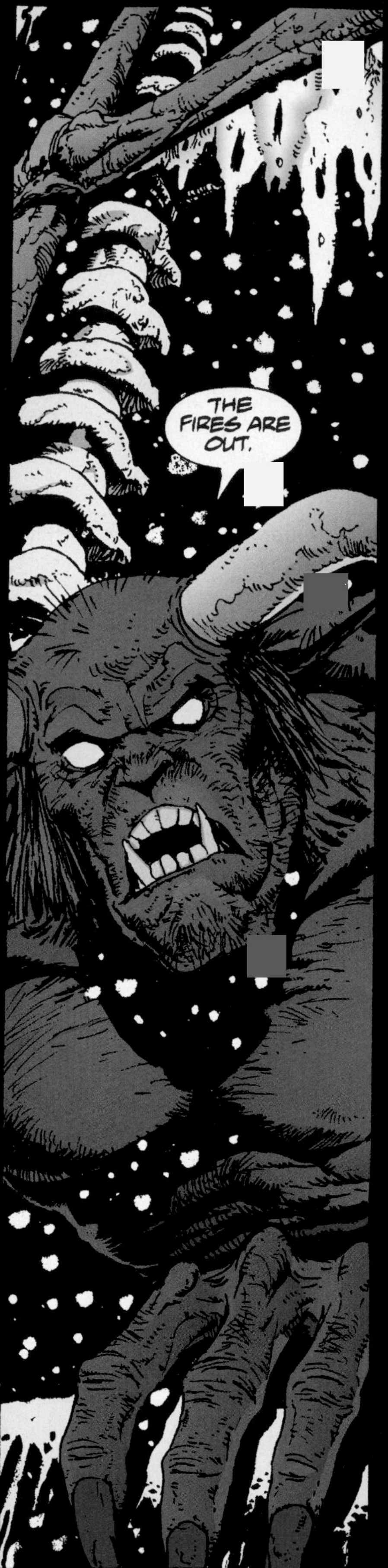
THE FIRES ARE OUT.

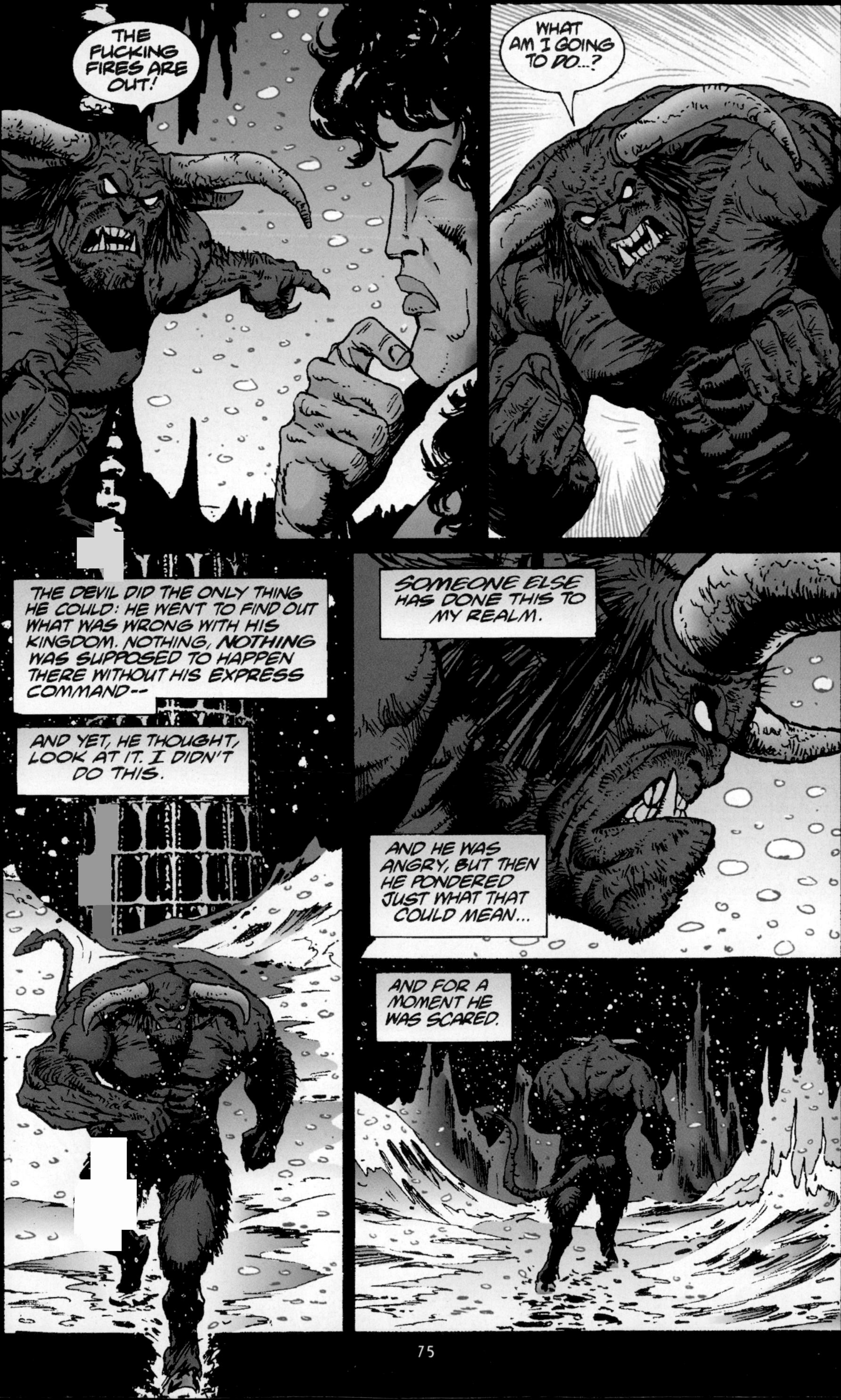

THE FUCKING FIRES ARE OUT!
WHAT AM I GOING TO DO...?
THE DEVIL DID THE ONLY THING HE COULD: HE WENT TO FIND OUT WHAT WAS WRONG WITH HIS KINGDOM. NOTHING, NOTHING WAS SUPPOSED TO HAPPEN THERE WITHOUT HIS EXPRESS COMMAND--
AND YET, HE THOUGHT, LOOK AT IT. I DIDN'T DO THIS.
SOMEONE ELSE HAS DONE THIS TO MY REALM.
AND HE WAS ANGRY, BUT THEN HE PONDERED JUST WHAT THAT COULD MEAN...
AND FOR A MOMENT HE WAS SCARED.

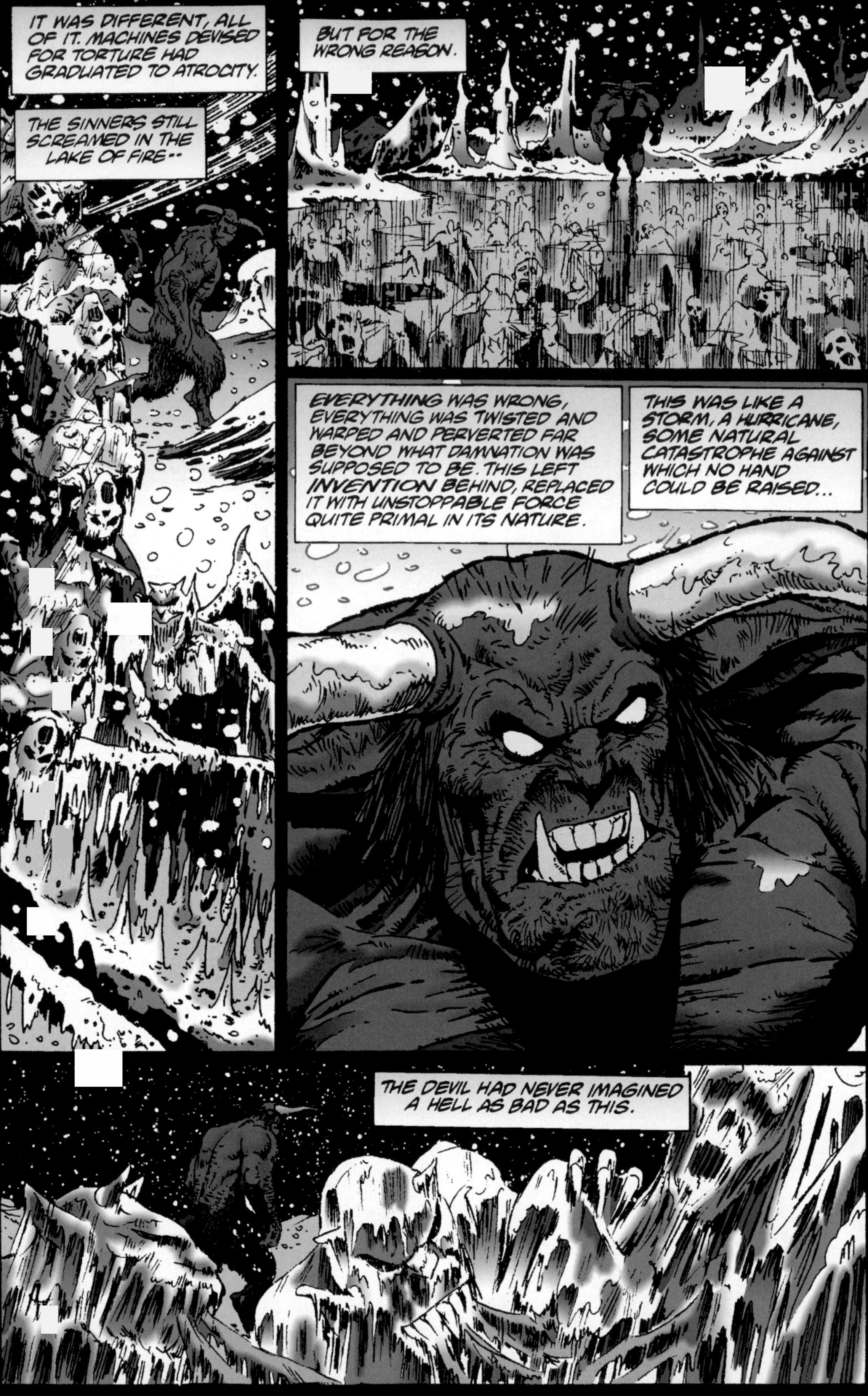
IT WAS DIFFERENT, ALL OF IT. MACHINES DEVISED FOR TORTURE HAD GRADUATED TO ATROCITY.
THE SINNERS STILL SCREAMED IN THE LAKE OF FIRE--
BUT FOR THE WRONG REASON.
EVERYTHING WAS WRONG, EVERYTHING WAS TWISTED AND WARPED AND PERVERTED FAR BEYOND WHAT DAMNATION WAS SUPPOSED TO BE. THIS LEFT INVENTION BEHIND, REPLACED IT WITH UNSTOPPABLE FORCE QUITE PRIMAL IN ITS NATURE.
THIS WAS LIKE A STORM, A HURRICANE, SOME NATURAL CATASTROPHE AGAINST WHICH NO HAND COULD BE RAISED...
THE DEVIL HAD NEVER IMAGINED A HELL AS BAD AS THIS.

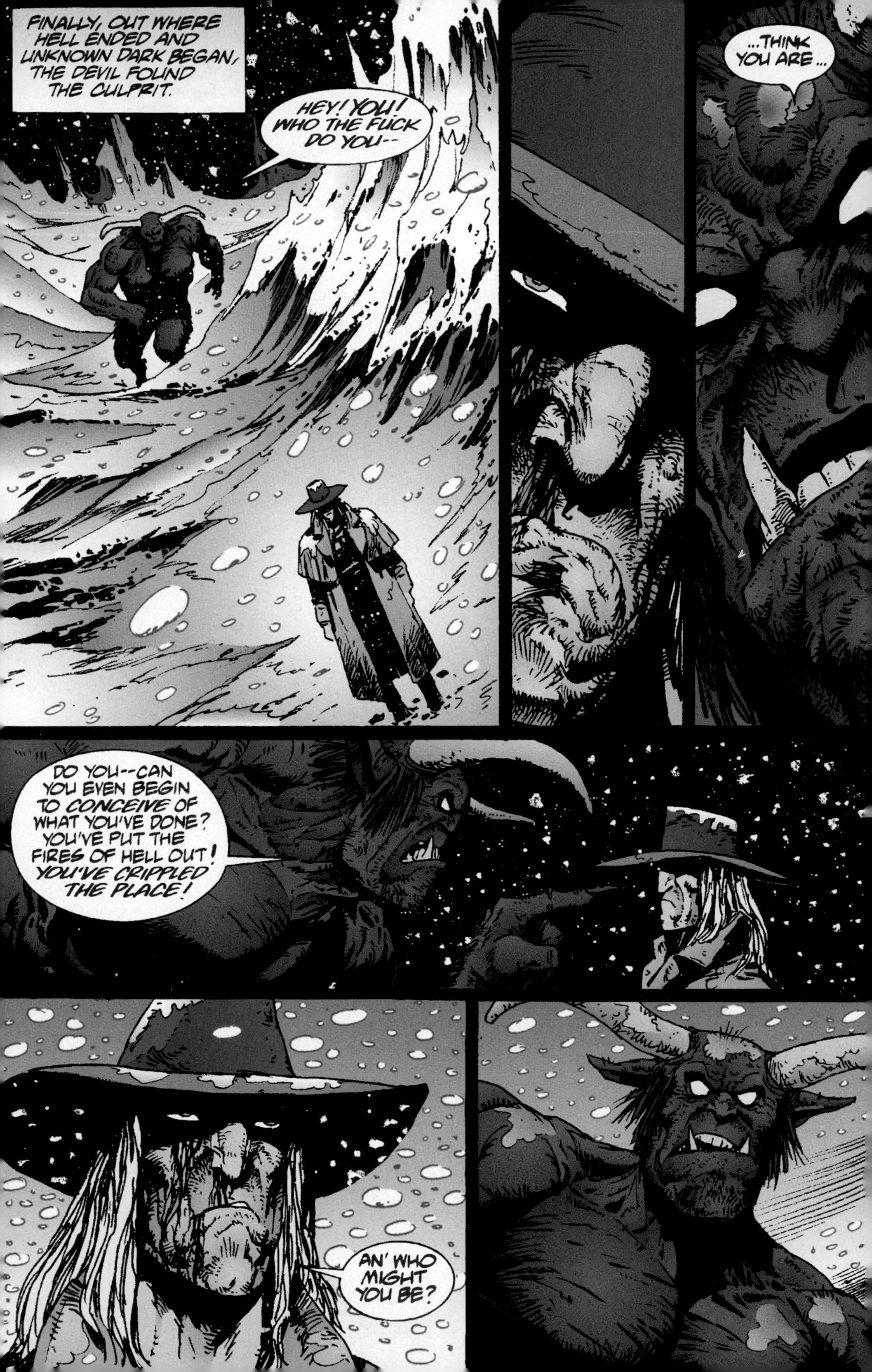

FINALLY, OUT WHERE HELL ENDED AND UNKNOWN DARK BEGAN, THE DEVIL FOUND THE CULPRIT.
HEY! YOU! WHO THE FUCK DO YOU--
...THINK YOU ARE...
DO YOU--CAN YOU EVEN BEGIN TO CONCEIVE OF WHAT YOU'VE DONE? YOU'VE PUT THE FIRES OF HELL OUT! YOU'VE CRIPPLED THE PLACE!
AN' WHO MIGHT YOU BE?

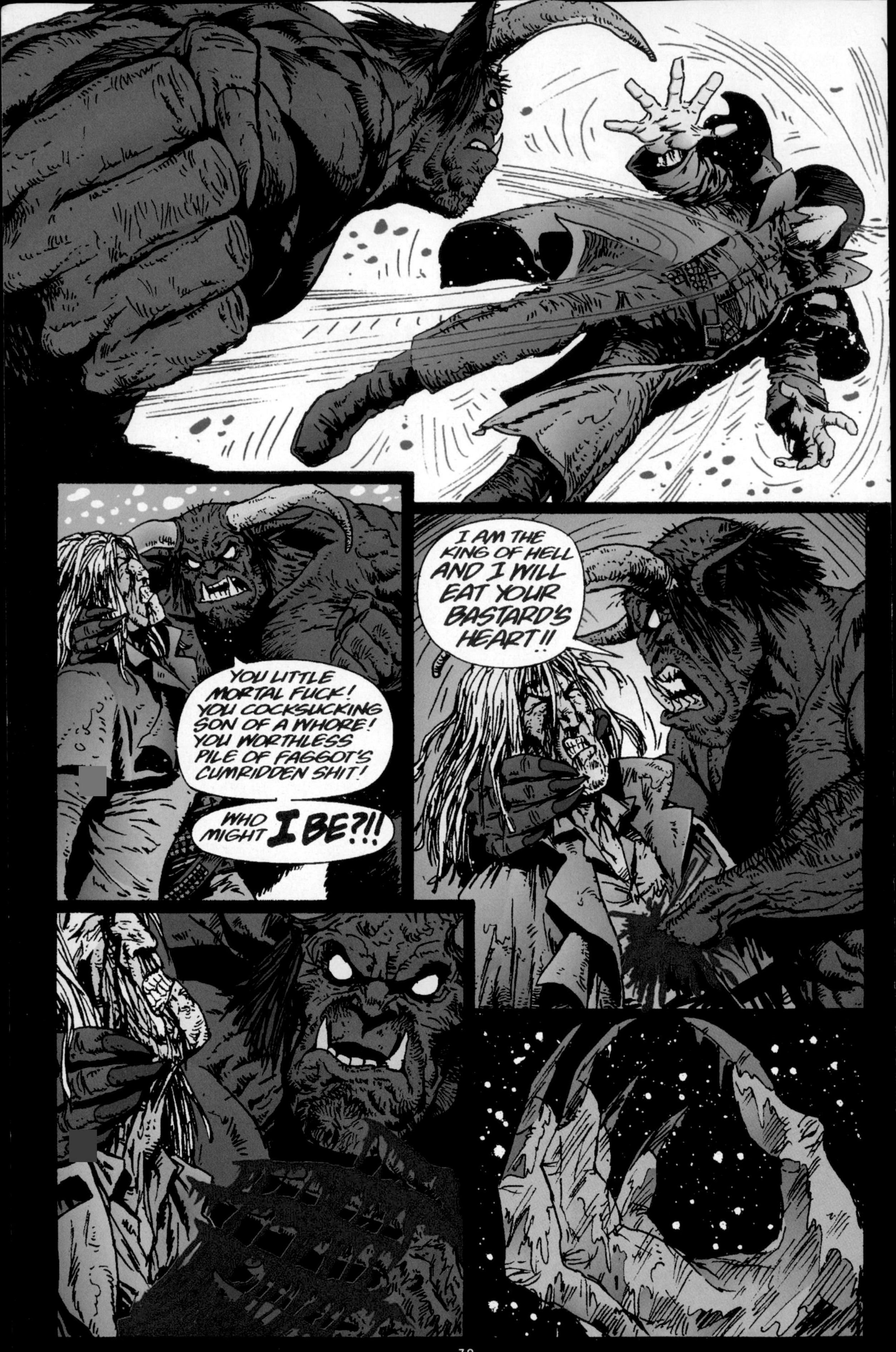
YOU LITTLE MORTAL FUCK! YOU COCKSUCKING SON OF A WHORE! YOU WORTHLESS PILE OF FAGGOT'S CUMRIDDEN SHIT!
WHO MIGHT I BE?!!
I AM THE KING OF HELL AND I WILL EAT YOUR BASTARD'S HEART!!

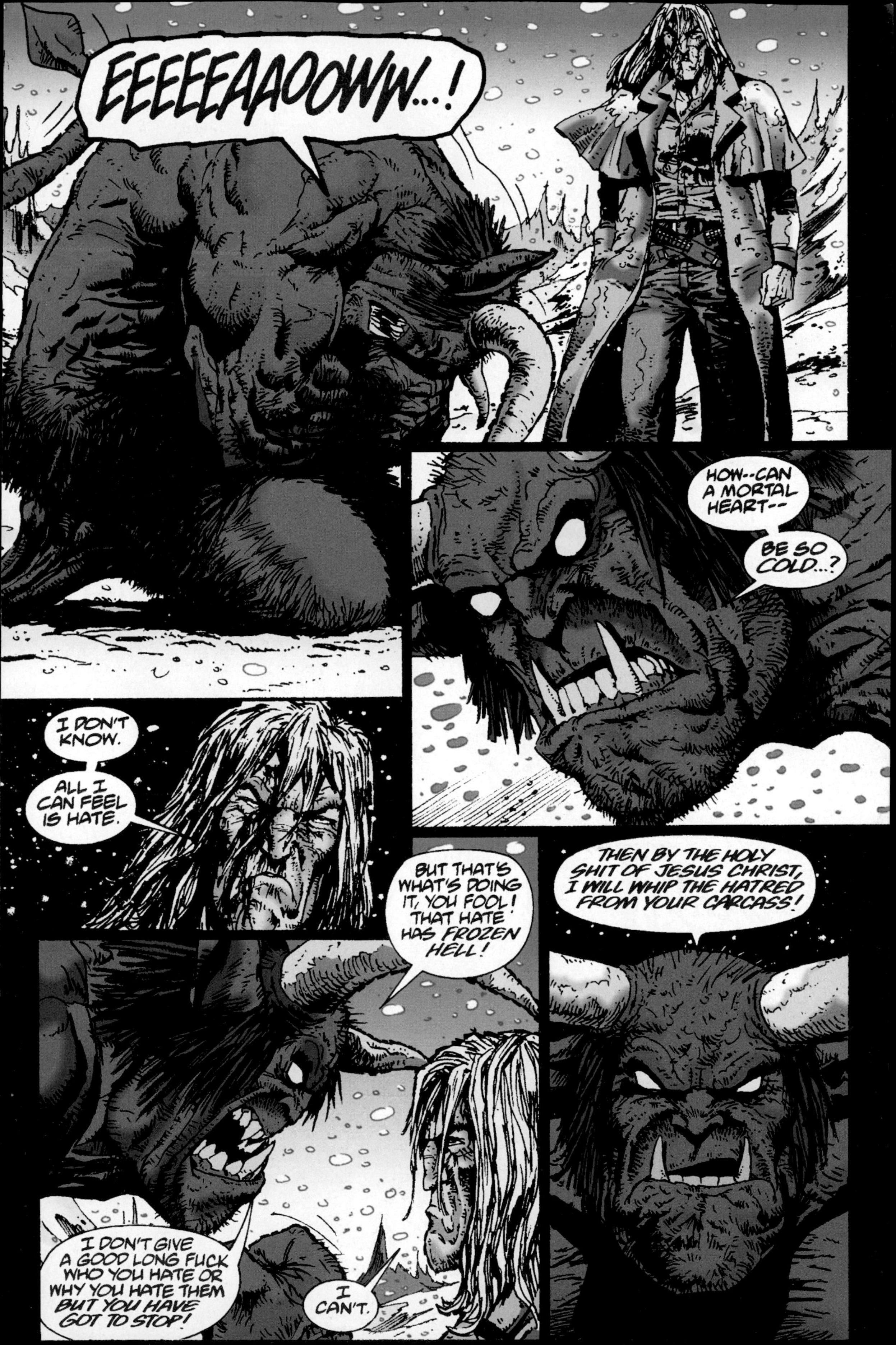
EEEEEAAOOWW...!
HOW--CAN A MORTAL HEART--
BE SO COLD...?
I DON'T KNOW.
ALL I CAN FEEL IS HATE.
BUT THAT'S WHAT'S DOING IT, YOU FOOL! THAT HATE HAS *FROZEN HELL*!
THEN BY THE HOLY SHIT OF JESUS CHRIST, I WILL WHIP THE HATRED FROM YOUR CARCASS!
I DON'T GIVE A GOOD LONG FUCK WHO YOU HATE OR WHY YOU HATE THEM *BUT YOU HAVE GOT TO STOP!*
I CAN'T.

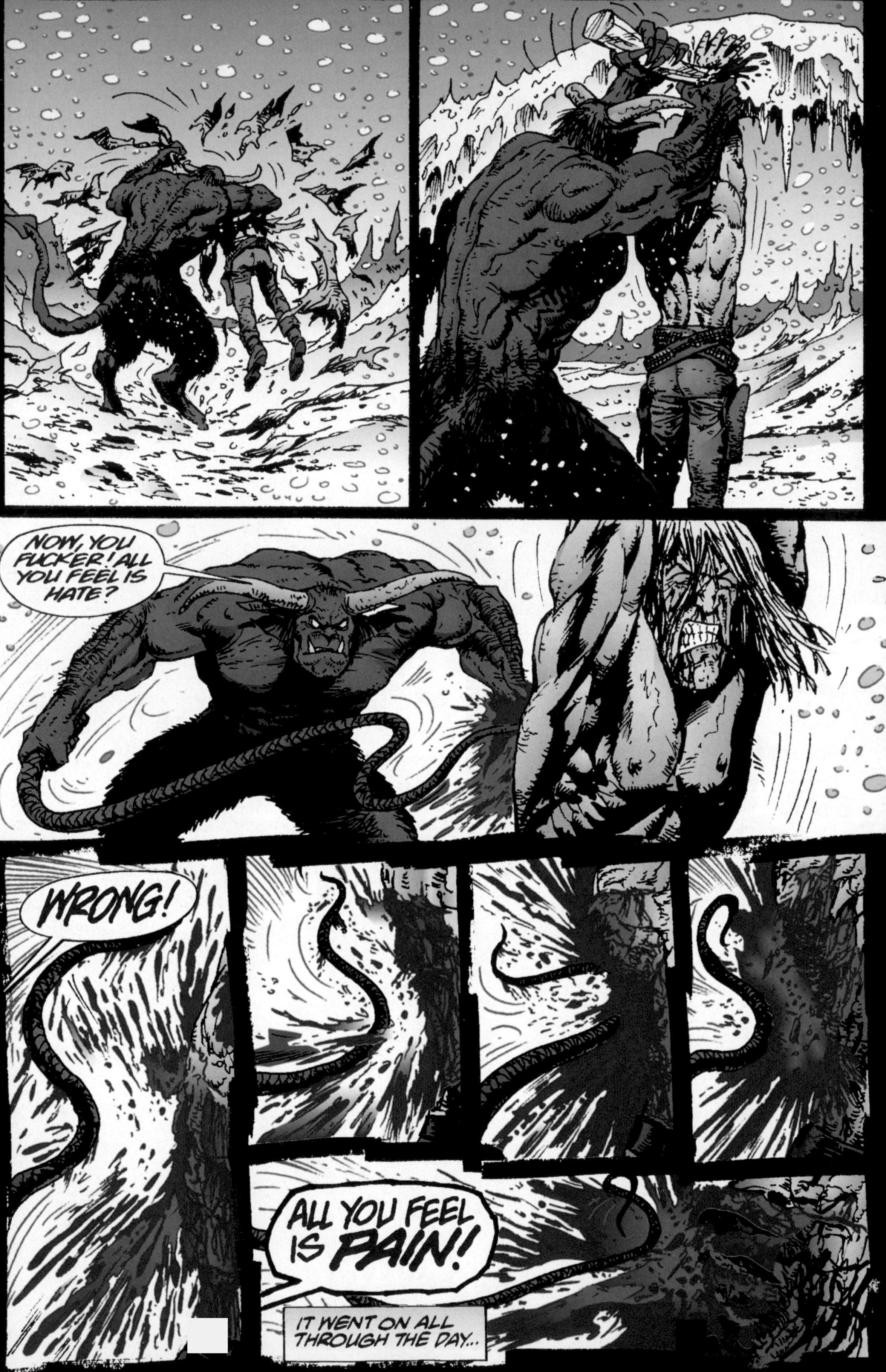
NOW, YOU FUCKER! ALL YOU FEEL IS HATE?
WRONG!
ALL YOU FEEL IS PAIN!
IT WENT ON ALL THROUGH THE DAY...

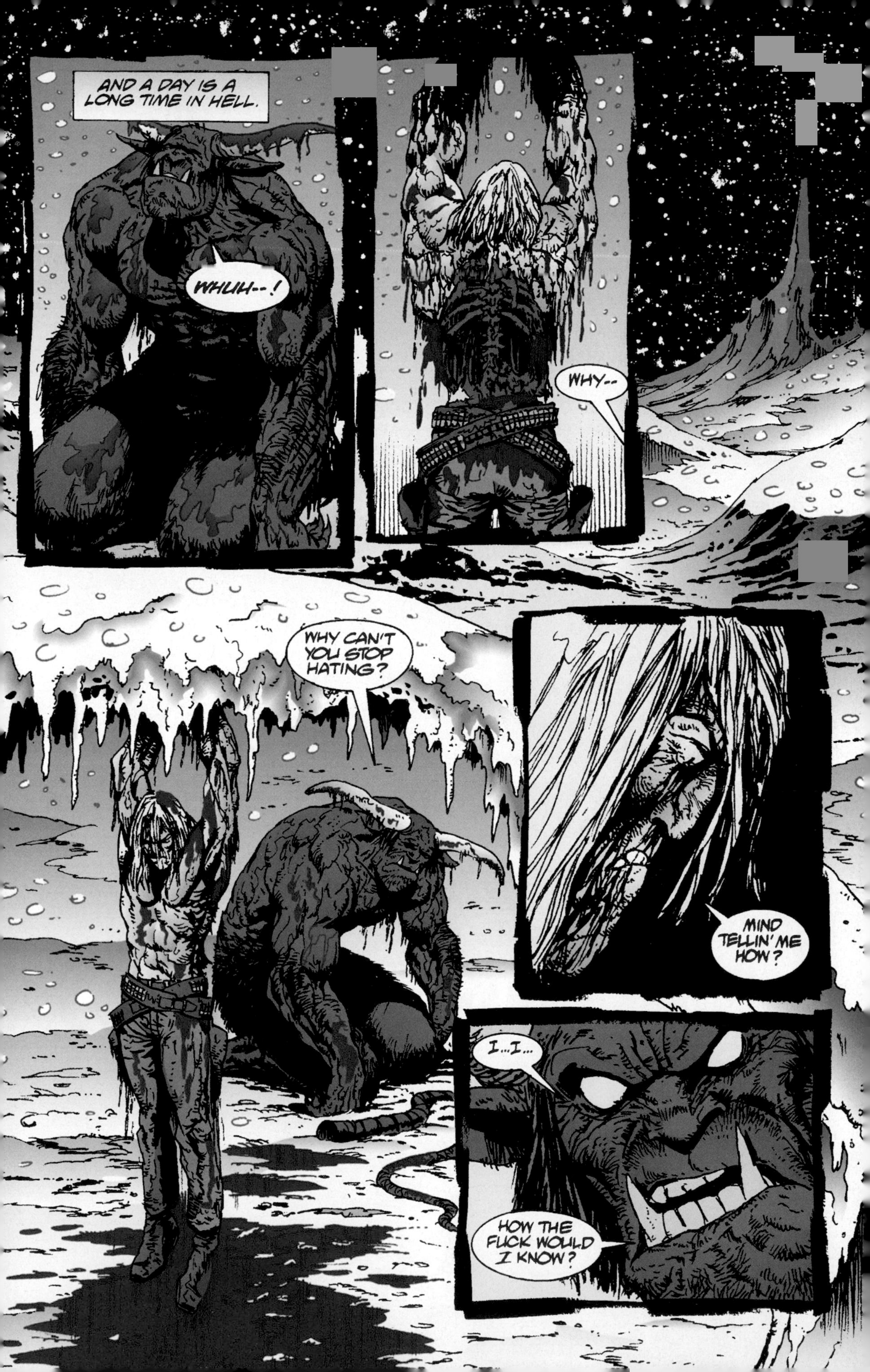
AND A DAY IS A LONG TIME IN HELL.
WHUH--!
WHY--
WHY CAN'T YOU STOP HATING?
MIND TELLIN' ME HOW?
I...I...
HOW THE FUCK WOULD I KNOW?

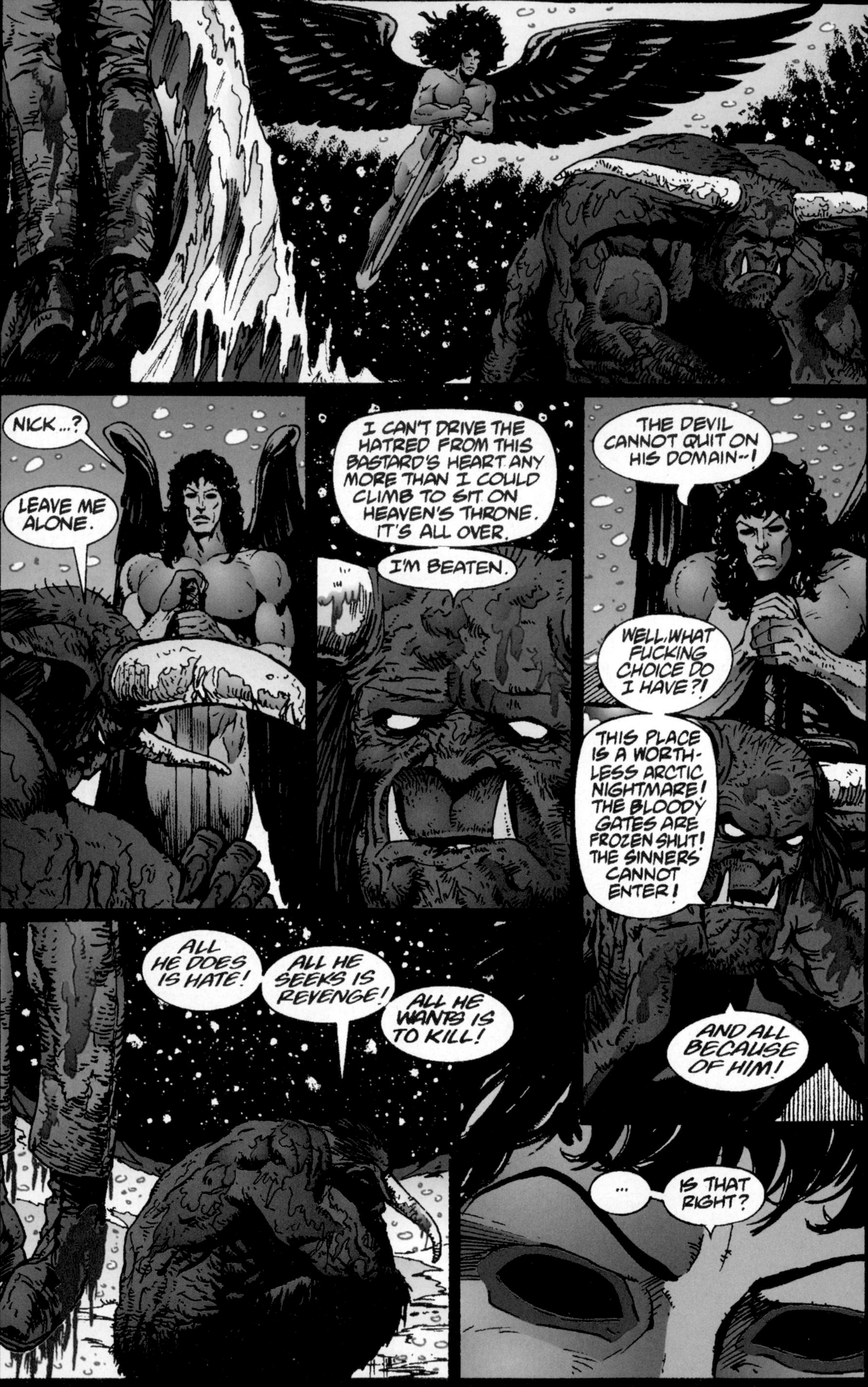

NICK...?
LEAVE ME ALONE.
I CAN'T DRIVE THE HATRED FROM THIS BASTARD'S HEART ANY MORE THAN I COULD CLIMB TO SIT ON HEAVEN'S THRONE. IT'S ALL OVER.
I'M BEATEN.
THE DEVIL CANNOT QUIT ON HIS DOMAIN--!
WELL, WHAT FUCKING CHOICE DO I HAVE?!
THIS PLACE IS A WORTHLESS ARCTIC NIGHTMARE! THE BLOODY GATES ARE FROZEN SHUT! THE SINNERS CANNOT ENTER!
ALL HE DOES IS HATE!
ALL HE SEEKS IS REVENGE!
ALL HE WANTS IS TO KILL!
AND ALL BECAUSE OF HIM!
...
IS THAT RIGHT?

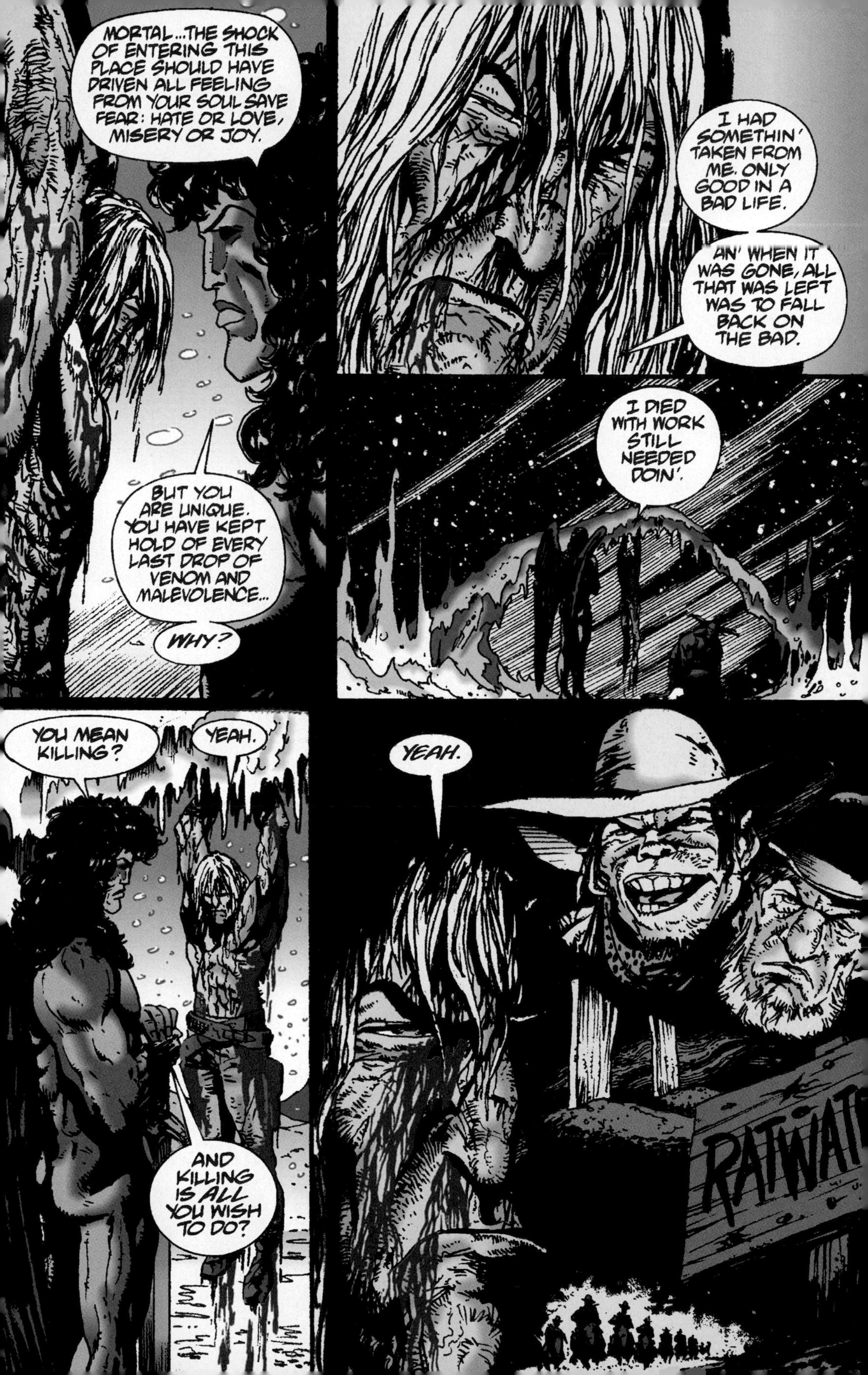
MORTAL...THE SHOCK OF ENTERING THIS PLACE SHOULD HAVE DRIVEN ALL FEELING FROM YOUR SOUL SAVE FEAR: HATE OR LOVE, MISERY OR JOY.
BUT YOU ARE UNIQUE. YOU HAVE KEPT HOLD OF EVERY LAST DROP OF VENOM AND MALEVOLENCE...
WHY?
I HAD SOMETHIN' TAKEN FROM ME. ONLY GOOD IN A BAD LIFE.
AN' WHEN IT WAS GONE, ALL THAT WAS LEFT WAS TO FALL BACK ON THE BAD.
I DIED WITH WORK STILL NEEDED DOIN'.
YOU MEAN KILLING?
YEAH.
AND KILLING IS ALL YOU WISH TO DO?
YEAH.
RATWAT

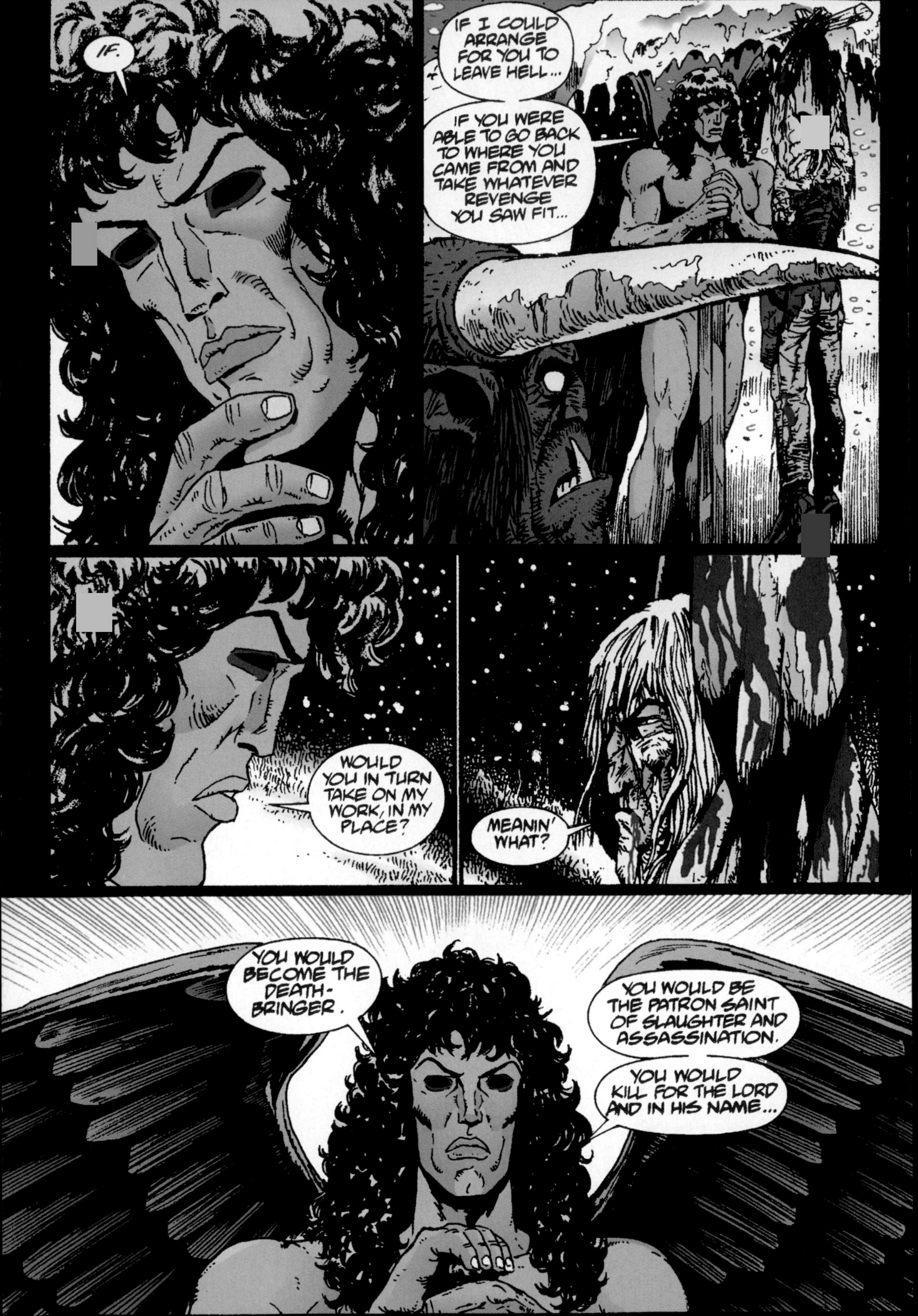
IF.
IF I COULD ARRANGE FOR YOU TO LEAVE HELL...
IF YOU WERE ABLE TO GO BACK TO WHERE YOU CAME FROM AND TAKE WHATEVER REVENGE YOU SAW FIT...
WOULD YOU IN TURN TAKE ON MY WORK, IN MY PLACE?
MEANIN' WHAT?
YOU WOULD BECOME THE DEATH-BRINGER.
YOU WOULD BE THE PATRON SAINT OF SLAUGHTER AND ASSASSINATION.
YOU WOULD KILL FOR THE LORD AND IN HIS NAME...

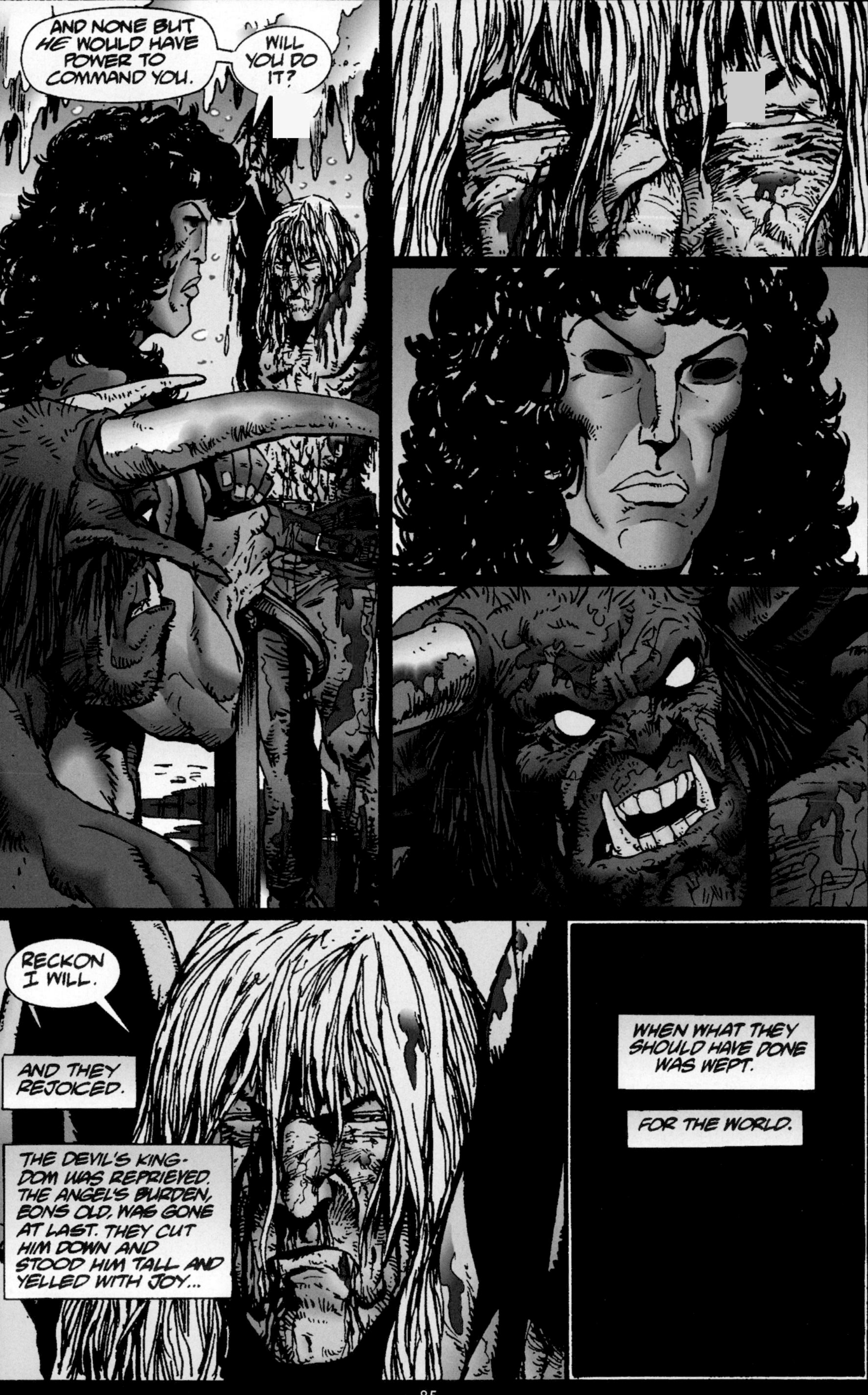

AND NONE BUT HE WOULD HAVE POWER TO COMMAND YOU.
WILL YOU DO IT?
RECKON I WILL.
AND THEY REJOICED.
THE DEVIL'S KING-DOM WAS REPRIEVED. THE ANGEL'S BURDEN, EONS OLD, WAS GONE AT LAST. THEY CUT HIM DOWN AND STOOD HIM TALL AND YELLED WITH JOY...
WHEN WHAT THEY SHOULD HAVE DONE WAS WEPT.
FOR THE WORLD.

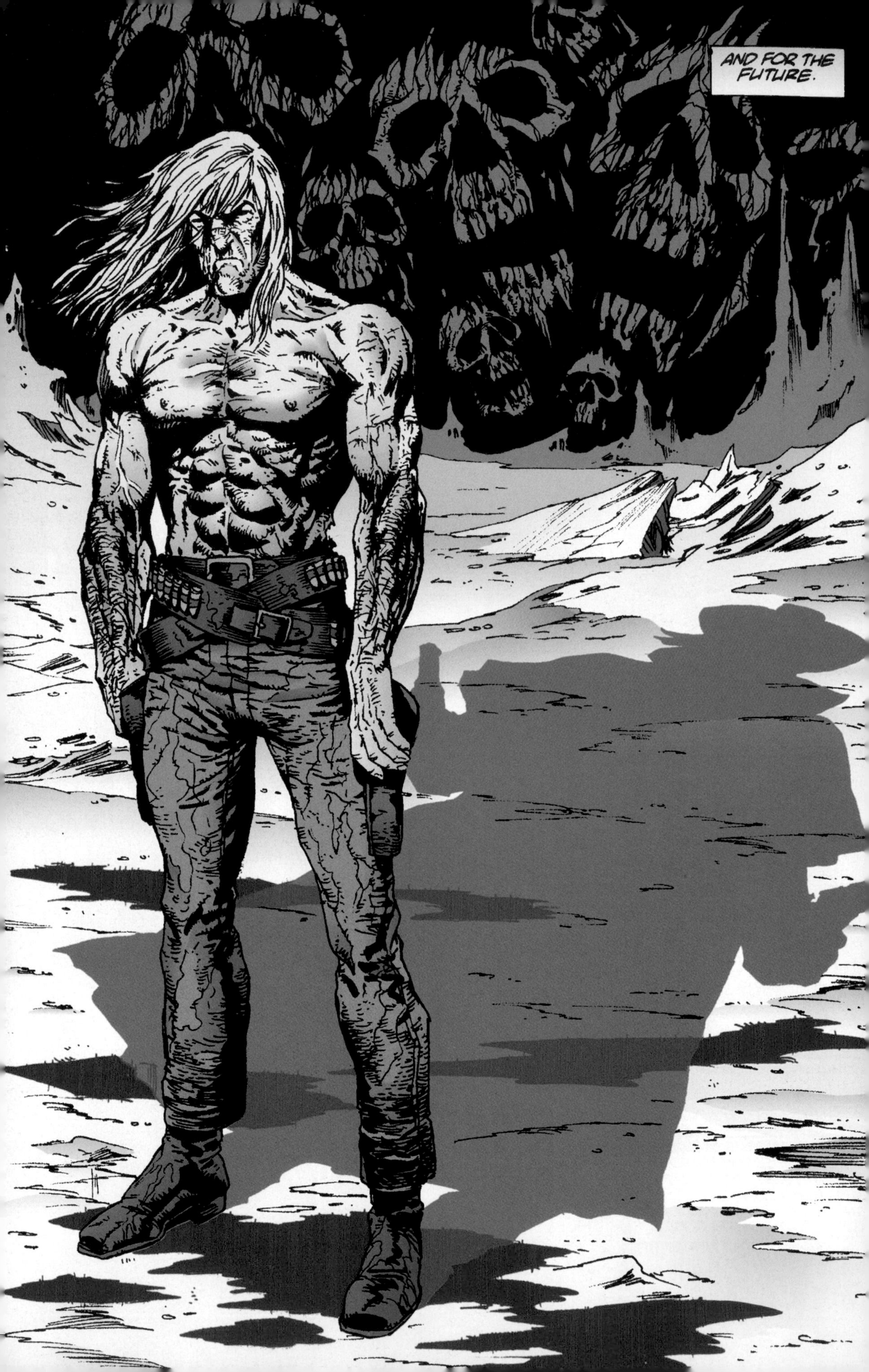
AND FOR THE FUTURE.

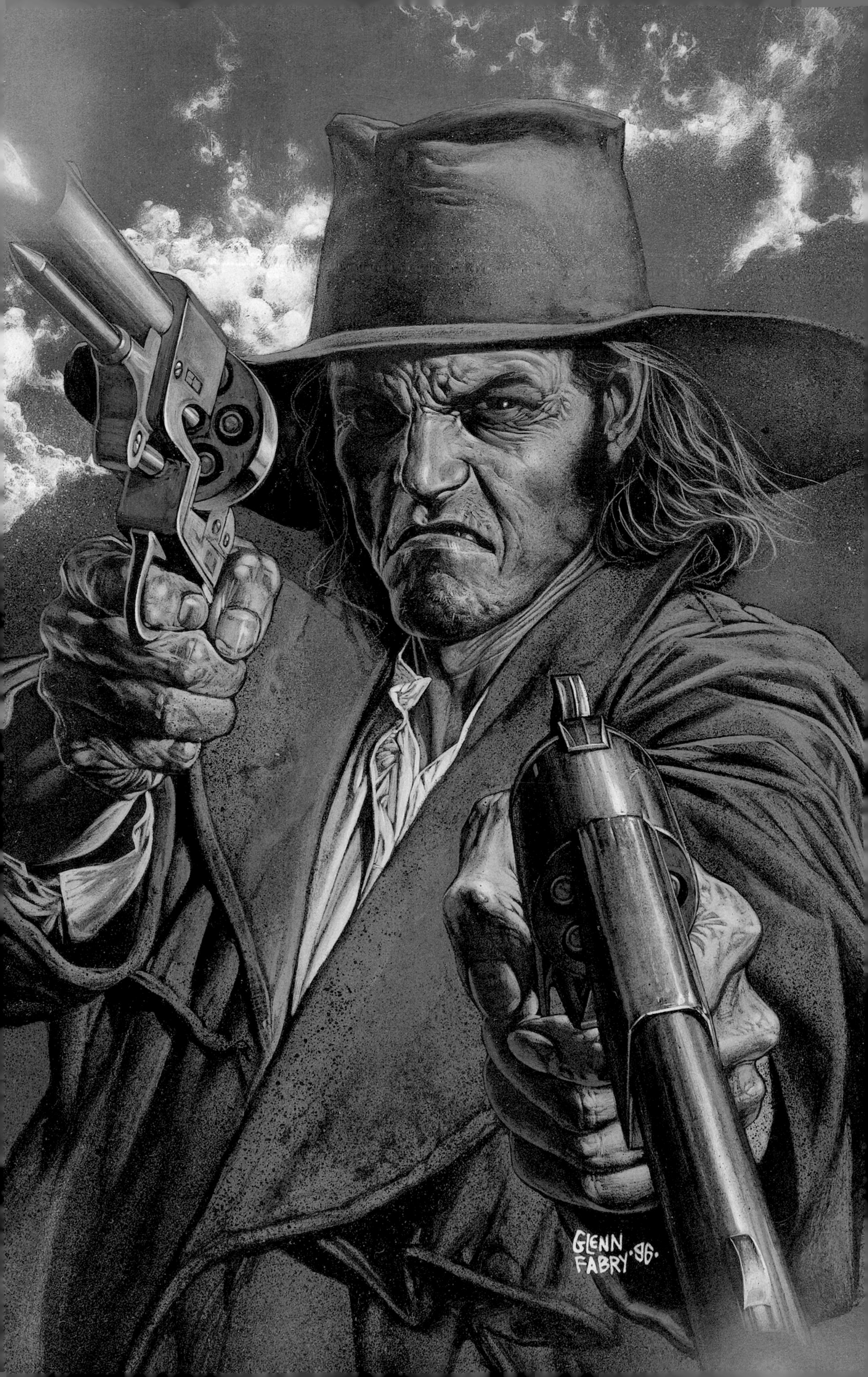
GLENN
FABRY ·96·

"It was a time when killers needed saints,
for so much of God's good work was being done."

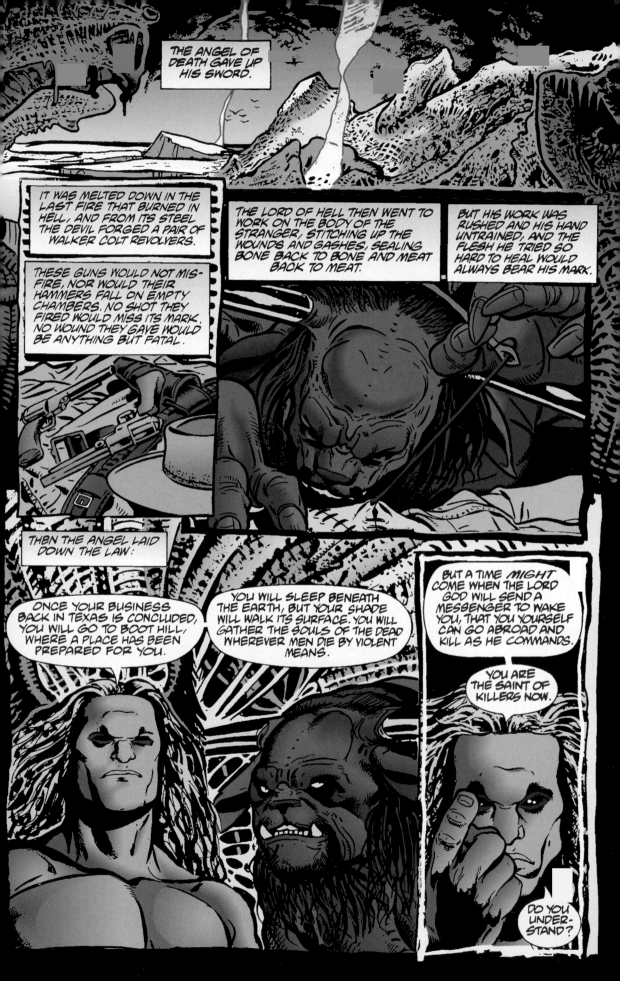

THE ANGEL OF DEATH GAVE UP HIS SWORD.

IT WAS MELTED DOWN IN THE LAST FIRE THAT BURNED IN HELL, AND FROM ITS STEEL THE DEVIL FORGED A PAIR OF WALKER COLT REVOLVERS.

THESE GUNS WOULD NOT MIS-FIRE, NOR WOULD THEIR HAMMERS FALL ON EMPTY CHAMBERS. NO SHOT THEY FIRED WOULD MISS ITS MARK. NO WOUND THEY GAVE WOULD BE ANYTHING BUT FATAL.

THE LORD OF HELL THEN WENT TO WORK ON THE BODY OF THE STRANGER, STITCHING UP THE WOUNDS AND GASHES, SEALING BONE BACK TO BONE AND MEAT BACK TO MEAT.

BUT HIS WORK WAS RUSHED AND HIS HAND UNTRAINED, AND THE FLESH HE TRIED SO HARD TO HEAL WOULD ALWAYS BEAR HIS MARK.

THEN THE ANGEL LAID DOWN THE LAW:

ONCE YOUR BUSINESS BACK IN TEXAS IS CONCLUDED, YOU WILL GO TO BOOT HILL, WHERE A PLACE HAS BEEN PREPARED FOR YOU.

YOU WILL SLEEP BENEATH THE EARTH, BUT YOUR SHADE WILL WALK ITS SURFACE. YOU WILL GATHER THE SOULS OF THE DEAD WHEREVER MEN DIE BY VIOLENT MEANS.

BUT A TIME *MIGHT* COME WHEN THE LORD GOD WILL SEND A MESSENGER TO WAKE YOU, THAT YOU YOURSELF CAN GO ABROAD AND KILL AS HE COMMANDS.

YOU ARE THE SAINT OF KILLERS NOW.

DO YOU UNDER-STAND?

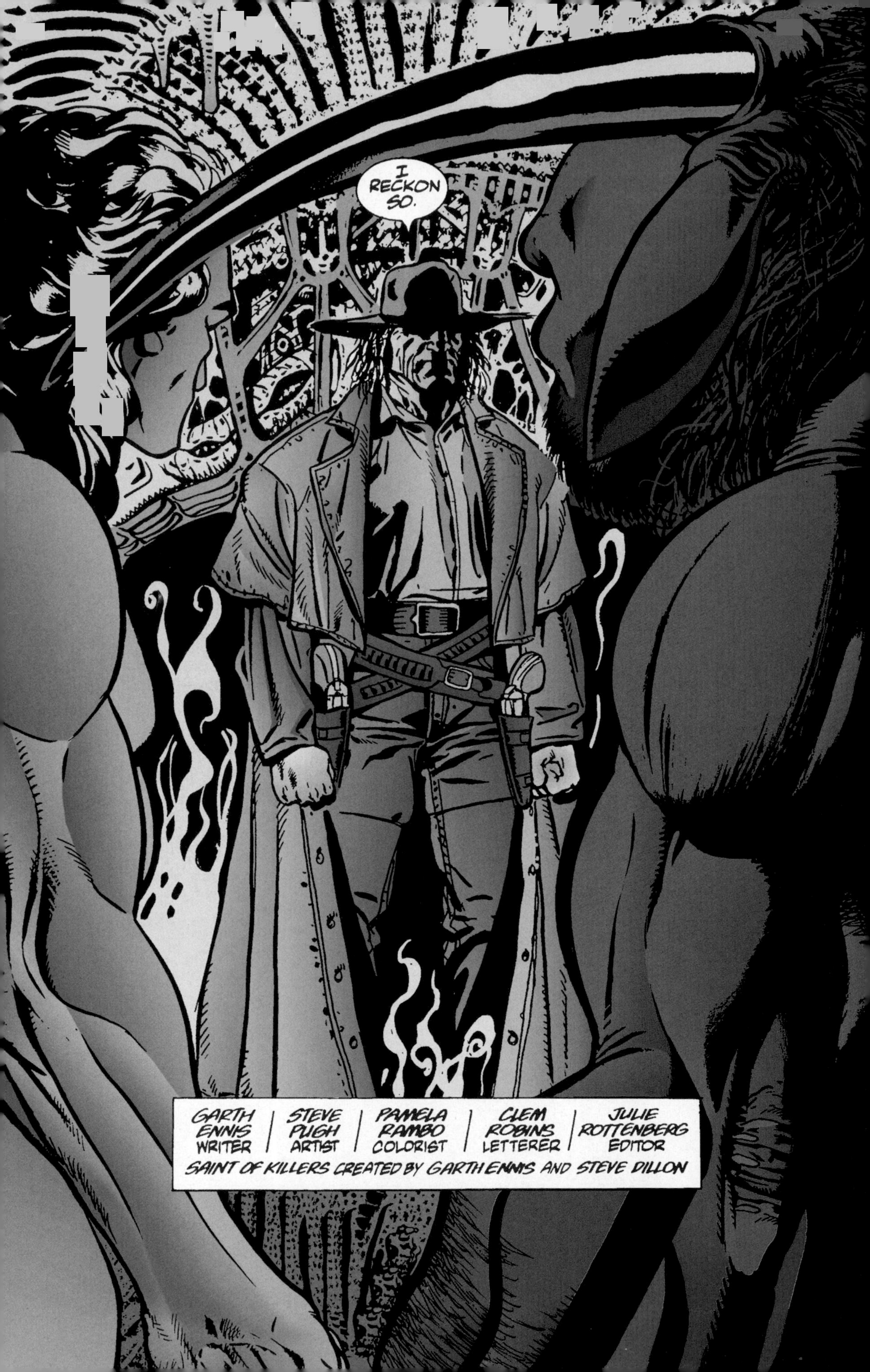
I RECKON SO.
GARTH ENNIS WRITER
STEVE PUGH ARTIST
PAMELA RAMBO COLORIST
CLEM ROBINS LETTERER
JULIE ROTTENBERG EDITOR
SAINT OF KILLERS CREATED BY GARTH ENNIS AND STEVE DILLON

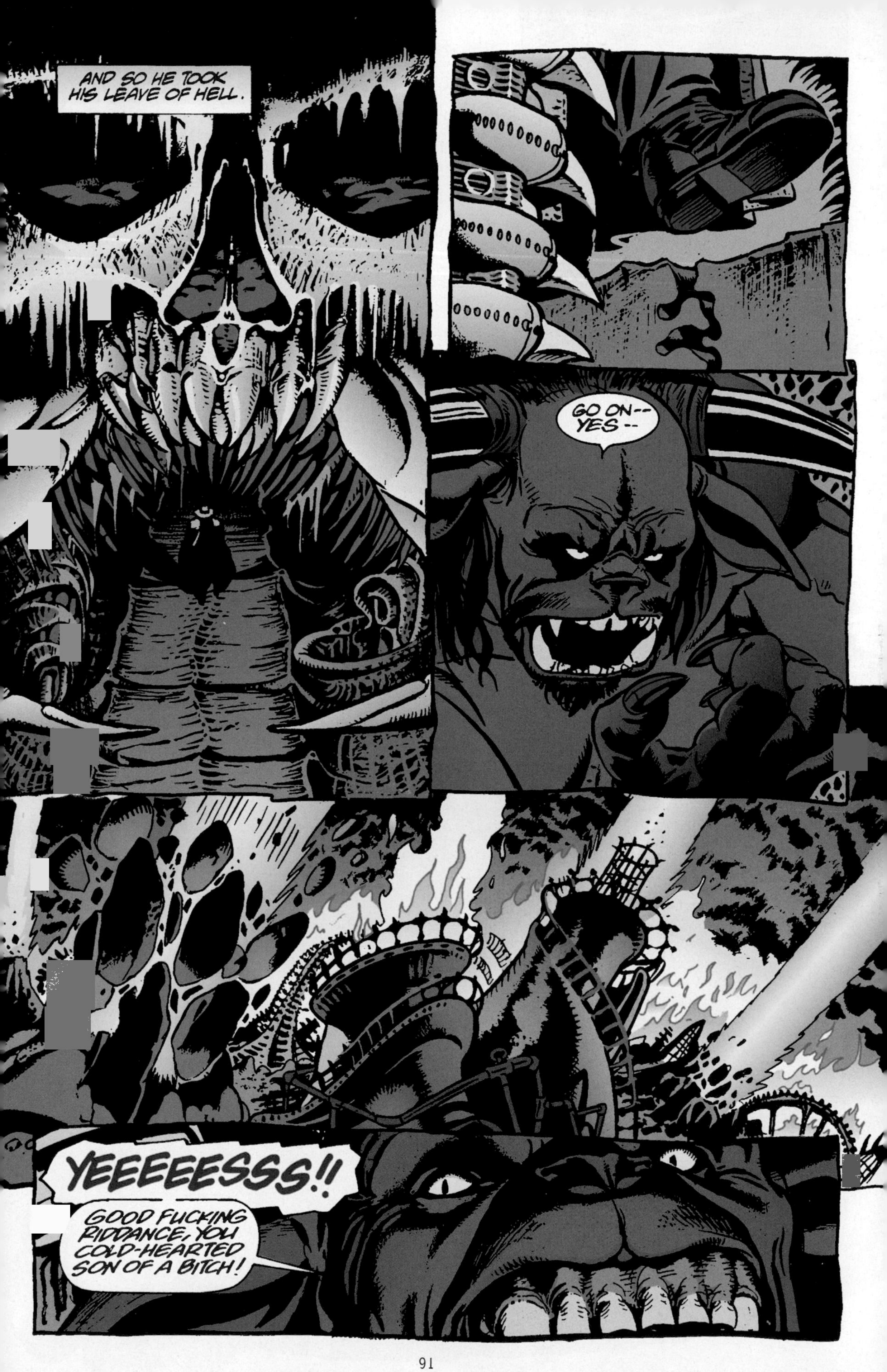
AND SO HE TOOK HIS LEAVE OF HELL.
GO ON-- YES--
YEEEEEESSS!!
GOOD FUCKING RIDDANCE, YOU COLD-HEARTED SON OF A BITCH!

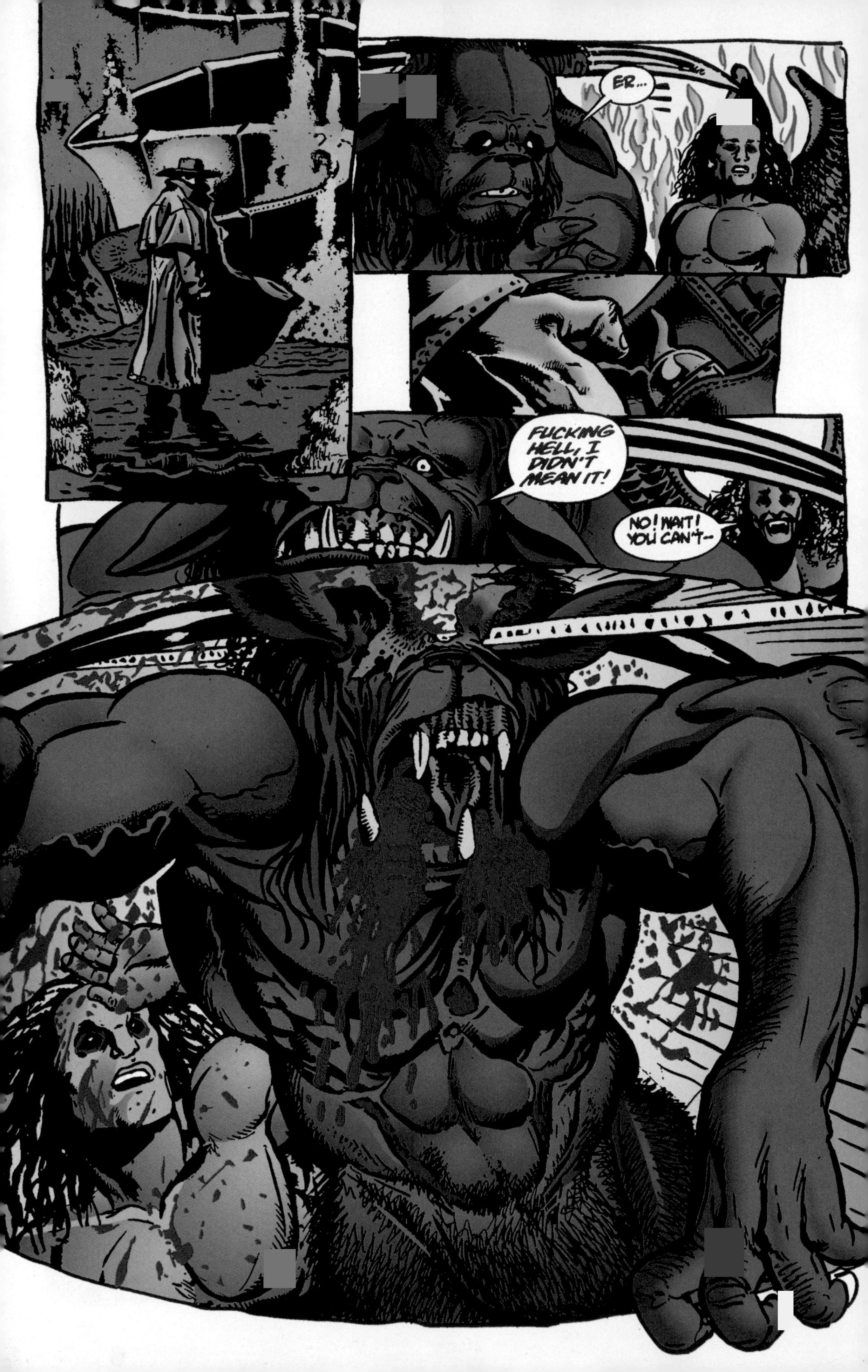
ER...
FUCKING HELL, I DIDN'T MEAN IT!
NO! WAIT! YOU CAN'T--

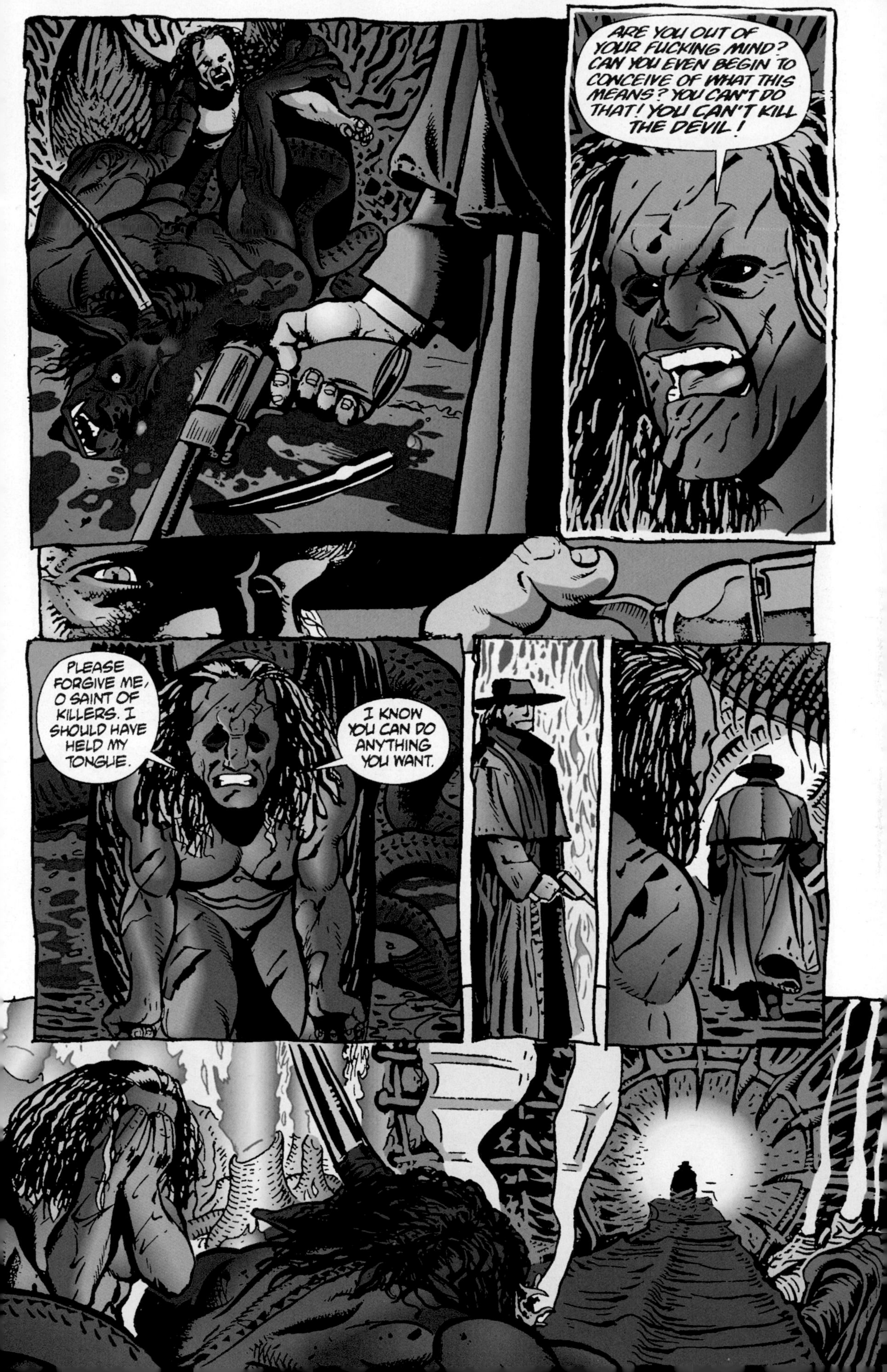
ARE YOU OUT OF YOUR FUCKING MIND? CAN YOU EVEN BEGIN TO CONCEIVE OF WHAT THIS MEANS? YOU CAN'T DO THAT! YOU CAN'T KILL THE DEVIL!
PLEASE FORGIVE ME, O SAINT OF KILLERS. I SHOULD HAVE HELD MY TONGUE.
I KNOW YOU CAN DO ANYTHING YOU WANT.

IT WAS CHRISTMAS IN RATWATER, AND GUMBO MCCREADY WAS A DYING MAN. THE STUMP OF HIS ARM HAD ROTTED. HIS BLOOD HAD TURNED TO POISON.

HE'D KILLED ABOUT A MAN A DAY SINCE HE'D ARRIVED IN TOWN, OUT OF SPITE OR MEANNESS FIRST, AND THEN BECAUSE THE EVIL IN HIS VEINS HAD SEIZED HIS WILL. YET NO ONE TRIED TO LEAVE, FOR FEAR THE BLIZZARD HOWLING ON THE LLANO WOULD DEVOUR THEM...

THE STORM HELD ONLY DEATH.

SONS OF WHORES!

SONS OF FUCKIN' WHORES...

WHERE IS EVERYONE?! S'POSED TO BE--FUCKIN' CHRISTMAS--!

AN' WE WON, GODDAMMIT! WE KILLED THAT OL' BASTARD OUTTA TEXAS...

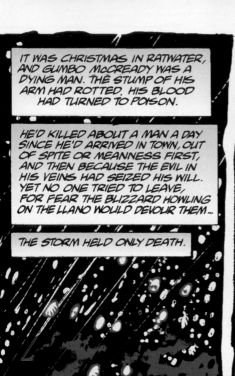

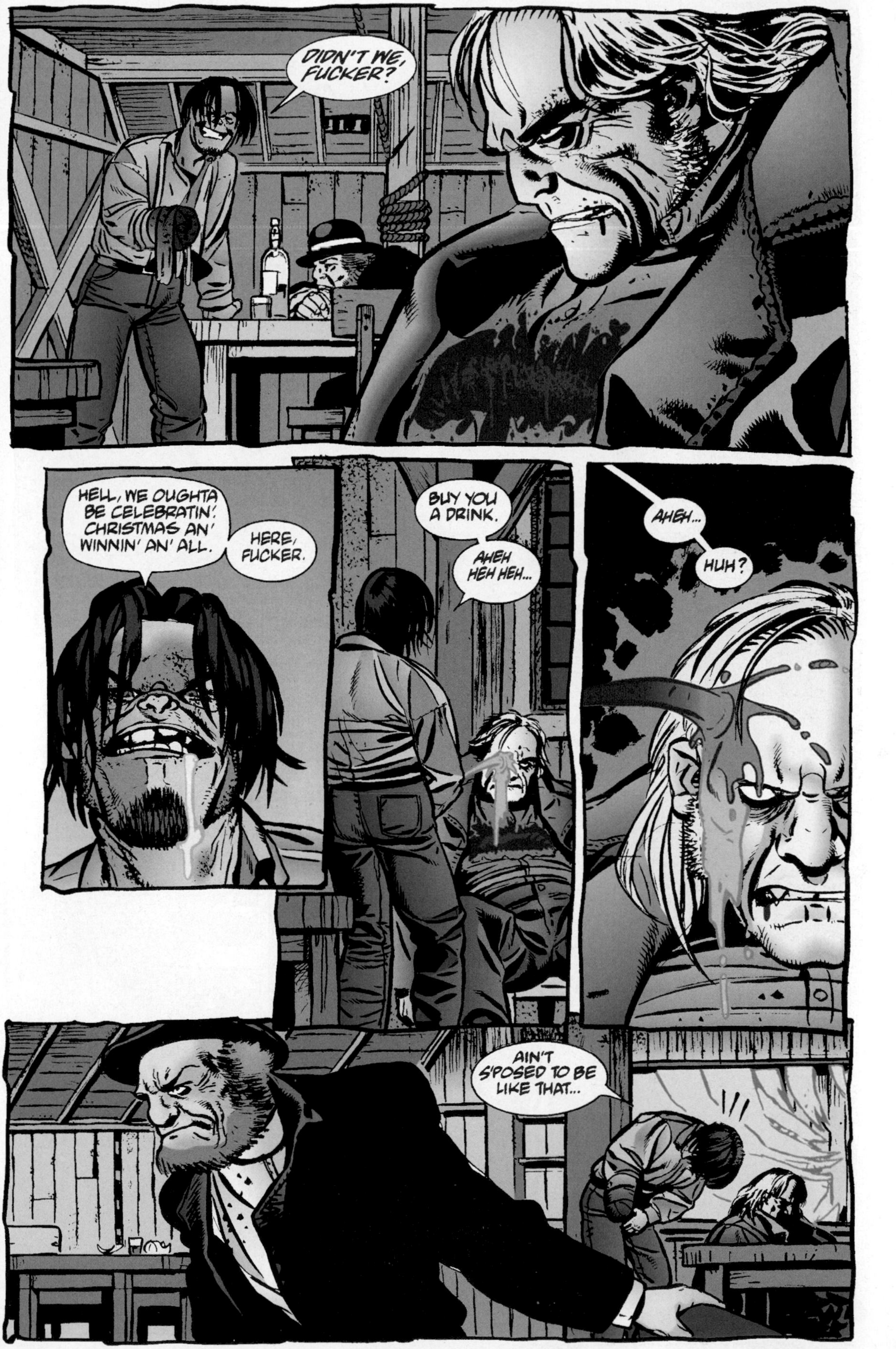
DIDN'T WE, FUCKER?
HELL, WE OUGHTA BE CELEBRATIN'. CHRISTMAS AN' WINNIN' AN' ALL.
HERE, FUCKER.
BUY YOU A DRINK.
AHEH HEH HEH...
AHEH...
HUH?
AIN'T S'POSED TO BE LIKE THAT...

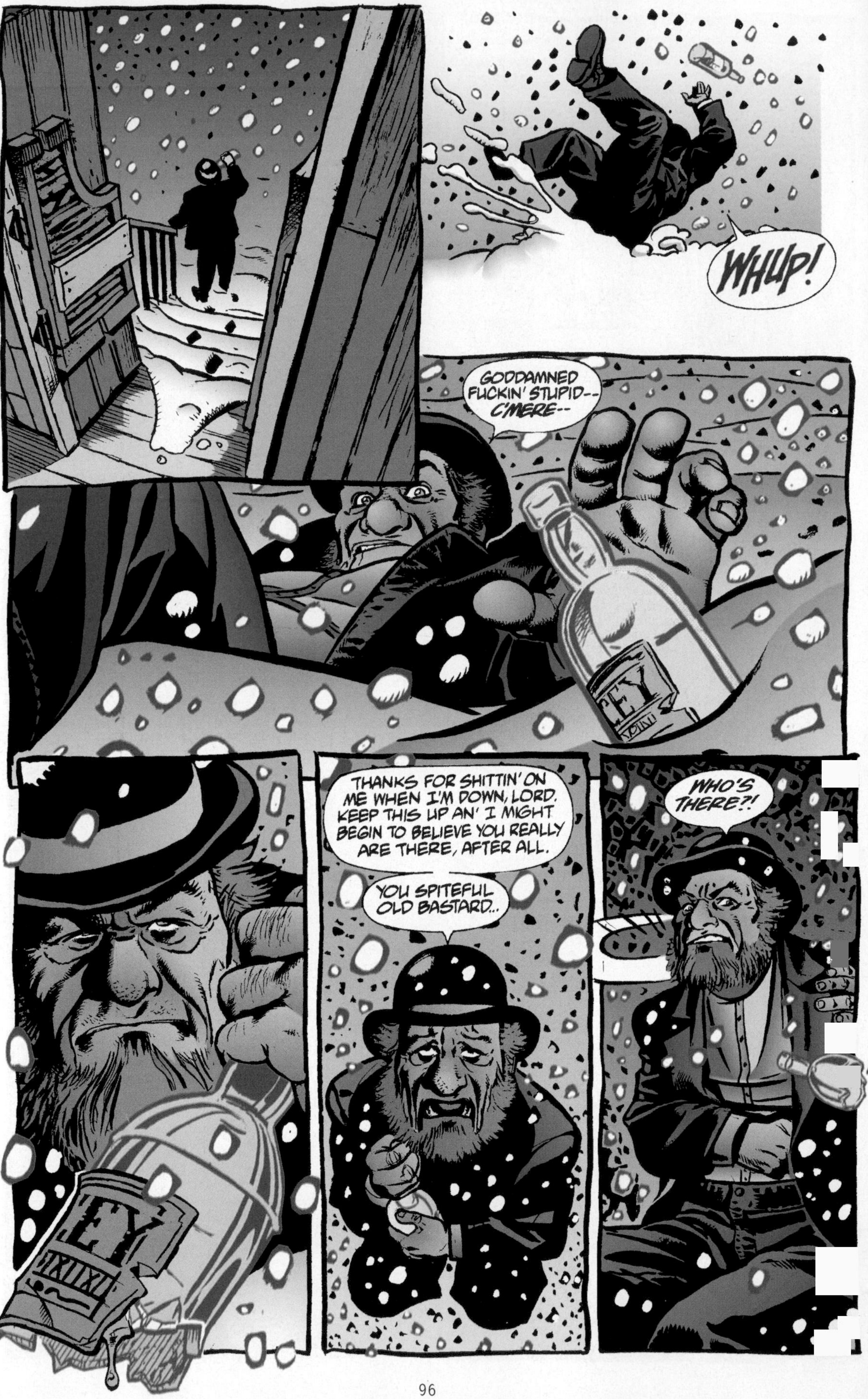
WHUP!
GODDAMNED FUCKIN' STUPID-- C'MERE--
THANKS FOR SHITTIN' ON ME WHEN I'M DOWN, LORD. KEEP THIS UP AN' I MIGHT BEGIN TO BELIEVE YOU REALLY ARE THERE, AFTER ALL.
YOU SPITEFUL OLD BASTARD...
WHO'S THERE?!

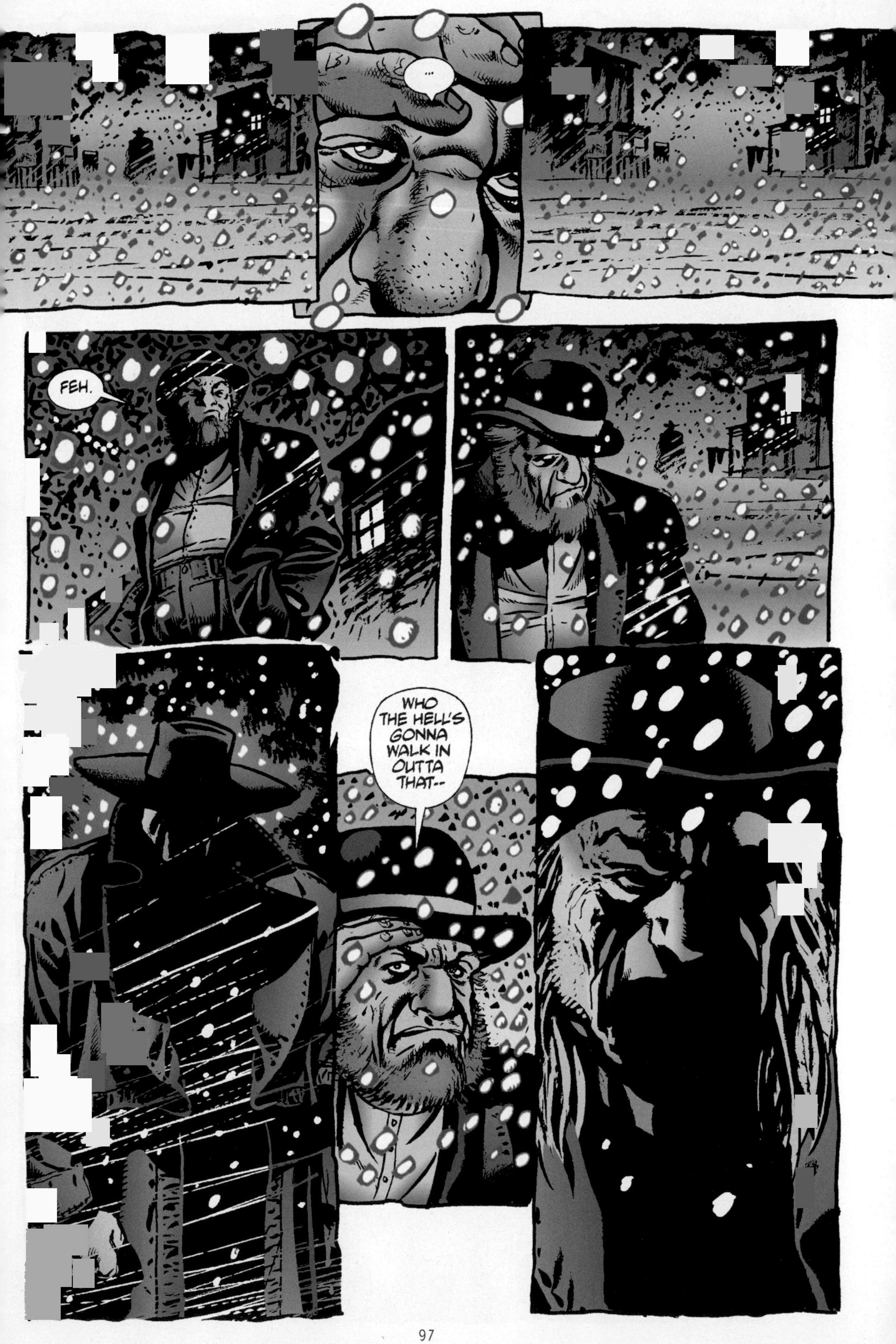
...
FEH.
WHO THE HELL'S GONNA WALK IN OUTTA THAT--

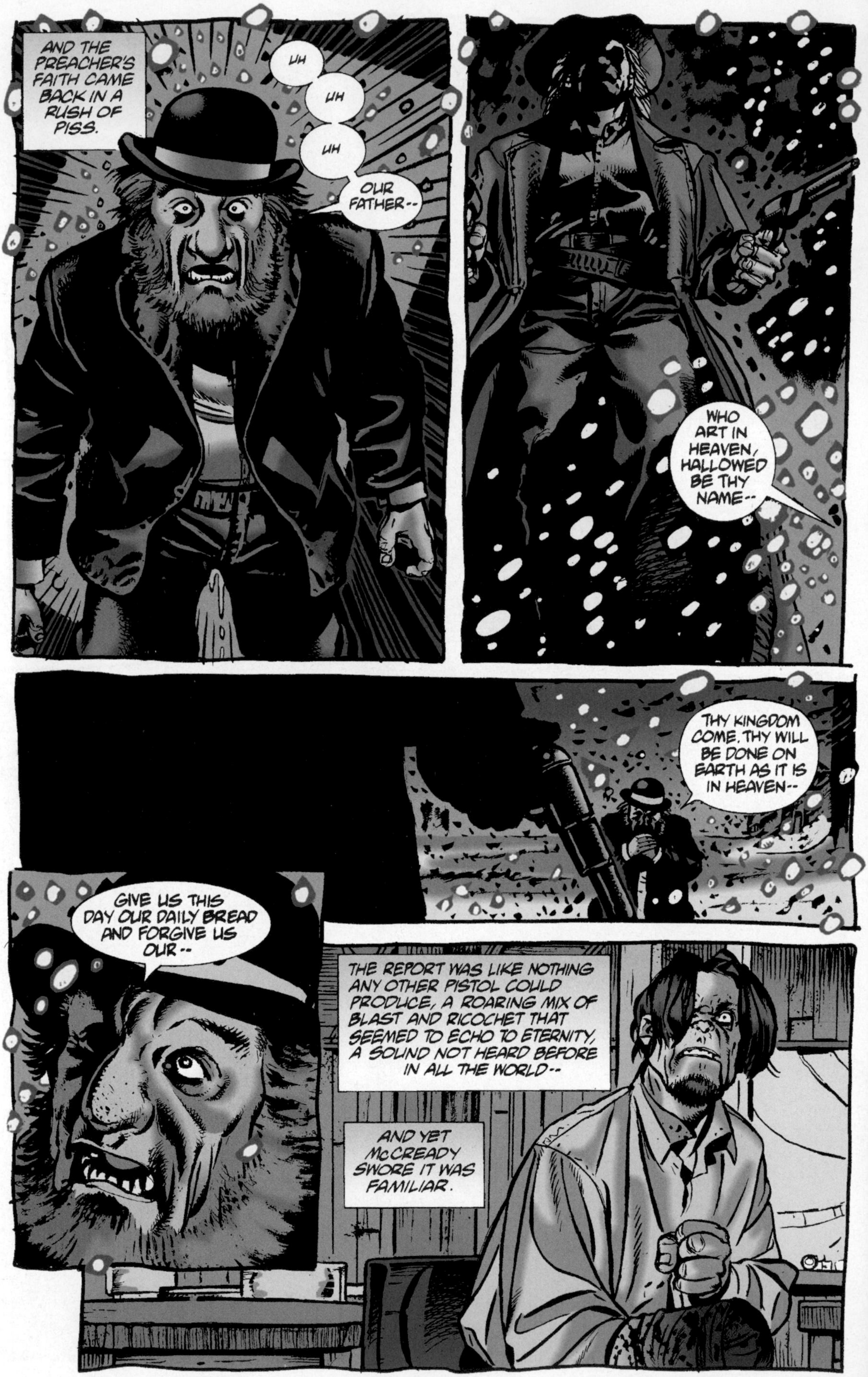
AND THE PREACHER'S FAITH CAME BACK IN A RUSH OF PISS.
UH
UH
UH
OUR FATHER--
WHO ART IN HEAVEN, HALLOWED BE THY NAME--
THY KINGDOM COME, THY WILL BE DONE ON EARTH AS IT IS IN HEAVEN--
GIVE US THIS DAY OUR DAILY BREAD AND FORGIVE US OUR--
THE REPORT WAS LIKE NOTHING ANY OTHER PISTOL COULD PRODUCE, A ROARING MIX OF BLAST AND RICOCHET THAT SEEMED TO ECHO TO ETERNITY, A SOUND NOT HEARD BEFORE IN ALL THE WORLD--
AND YET McCREADY SWORE IT WAS FAMILIAR.

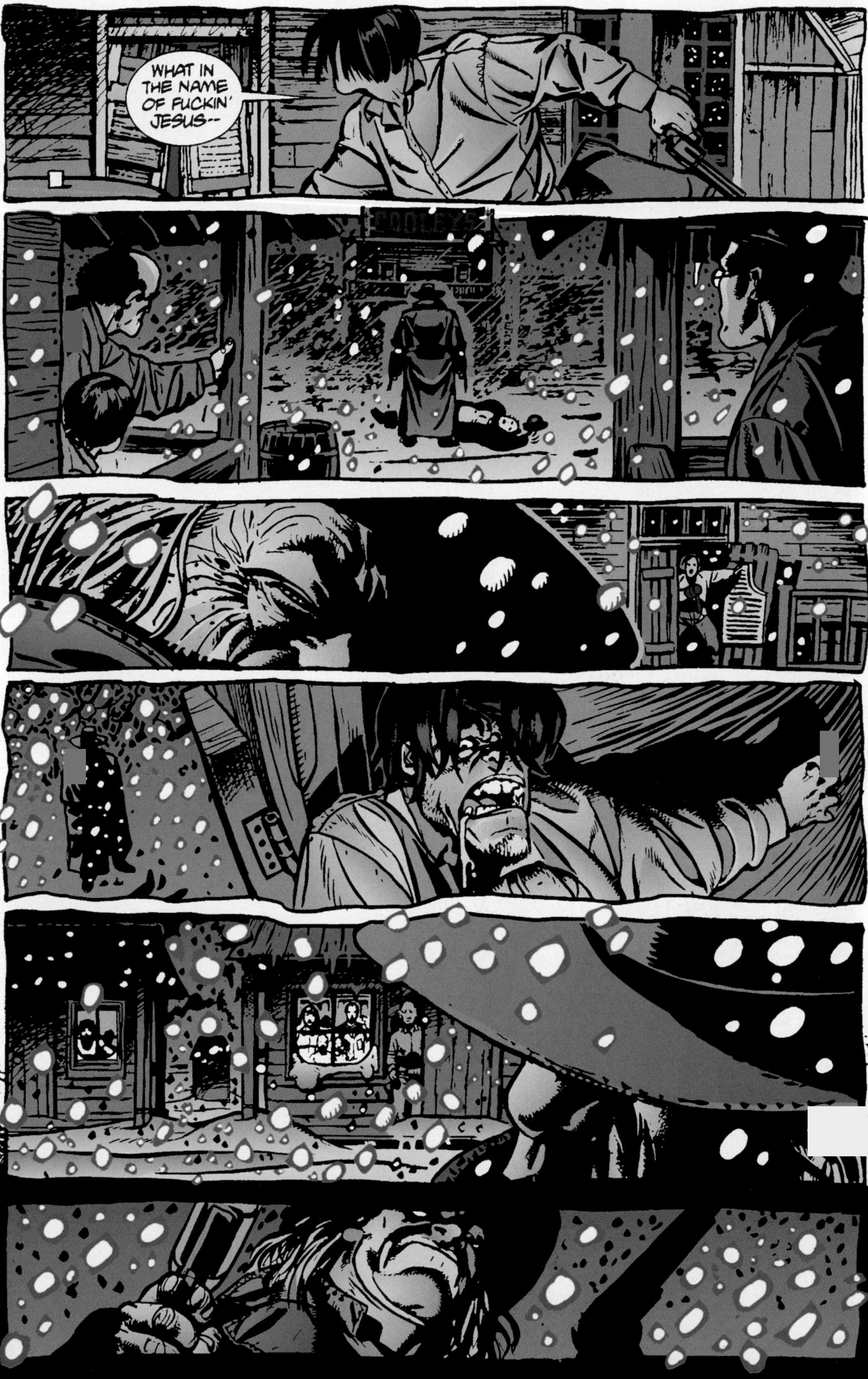
WHAT IN THE NAME OF FUCKIN' JESUS--
COOLEY'S

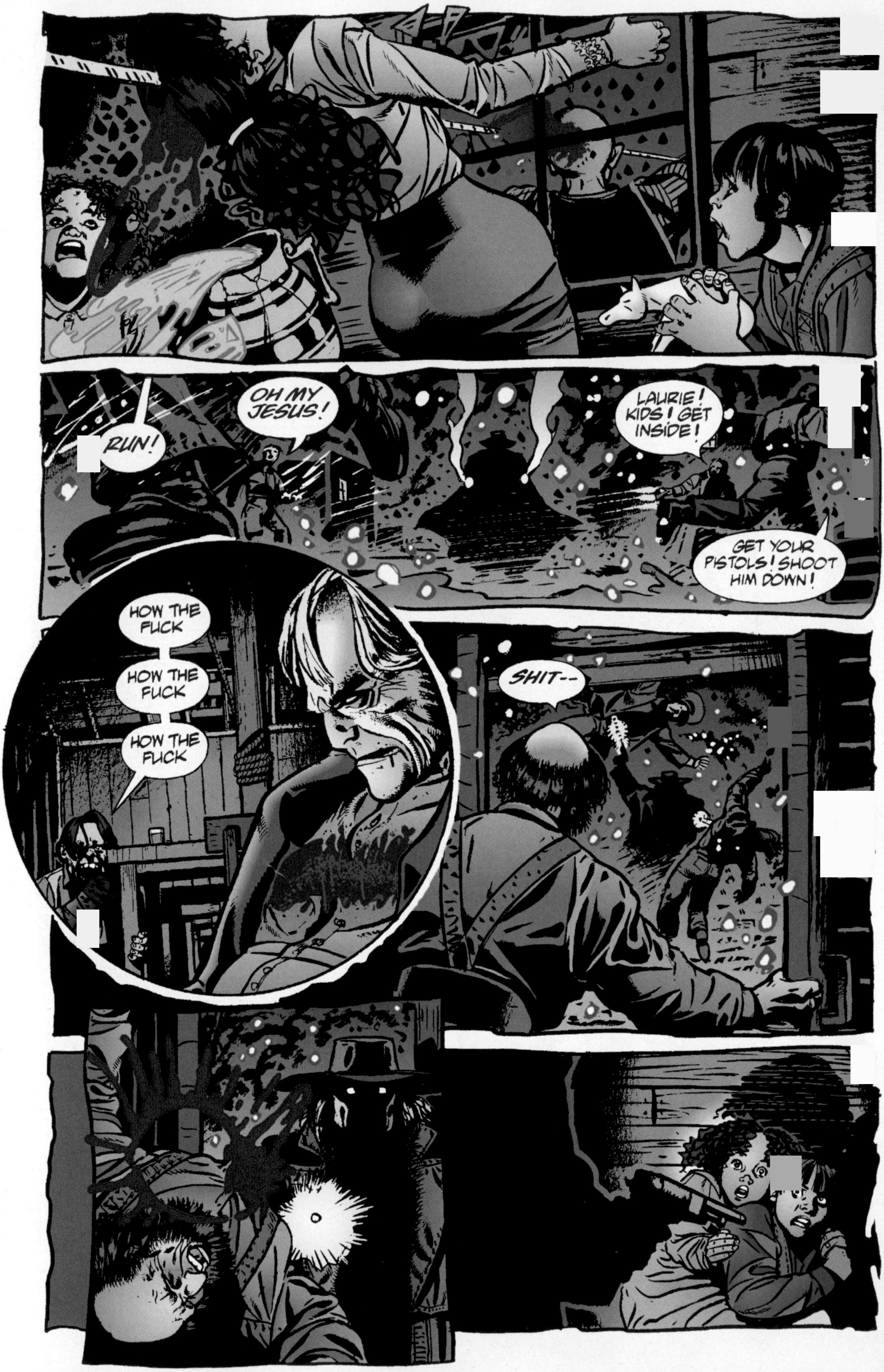
RUN!
OH MY JESUS!
LAURIE! KIDS! GET INSIDE!
GET YOUR PISTOLS! SHOOT HIM DOWN!
HOW THE FUCK
HOW THE FUCK
HOW THE FUCK
SHIT--

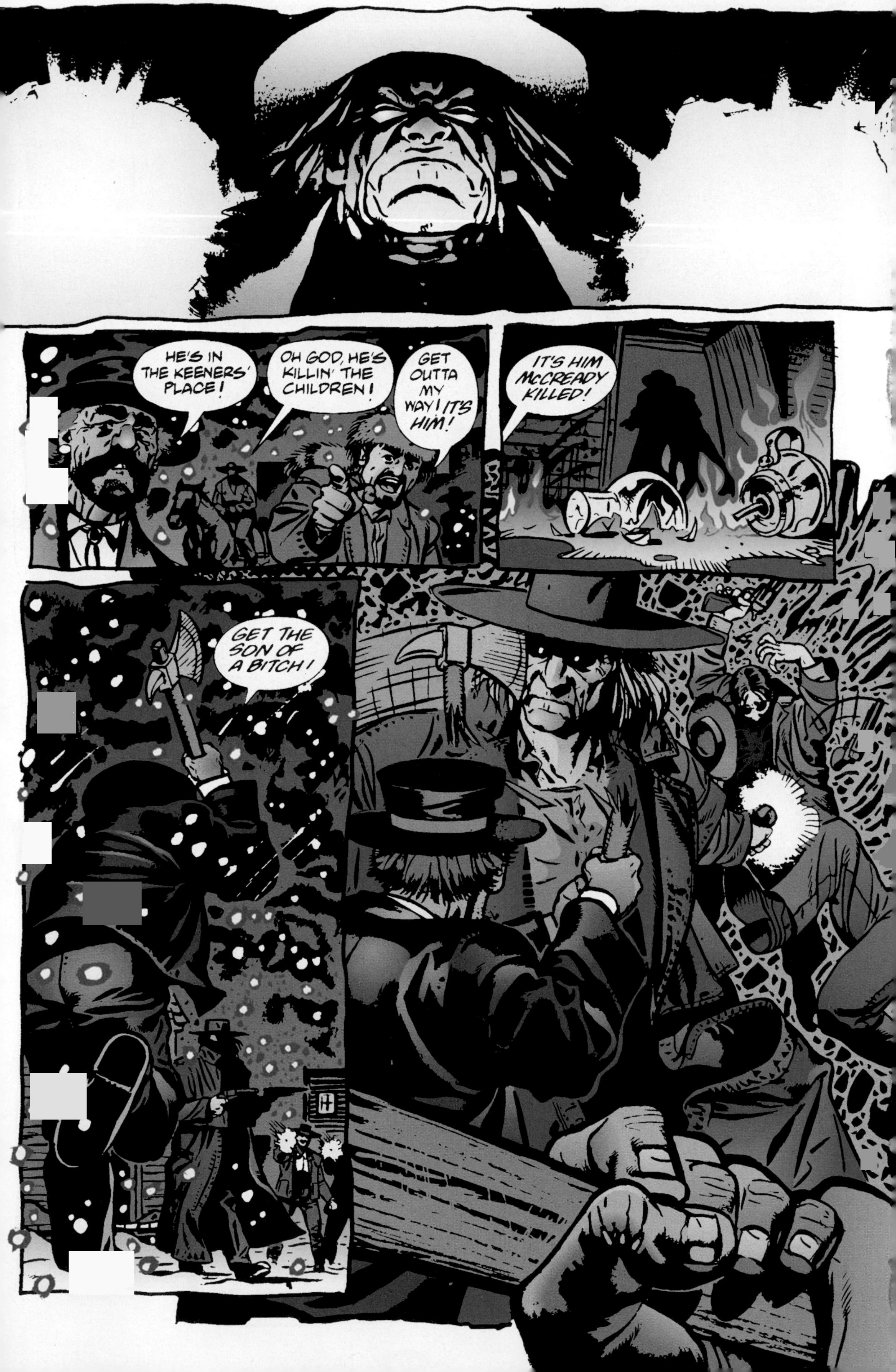
HE'S IN THE KEENERS' PLACE!
OH GOD, HE'S KILLIN' THE CHILDREN!
GET OUTTA MY WAY! IT'S HIM!
IT'S HIM McCREADY KILLED!
GET THE SON OF A BITCH!

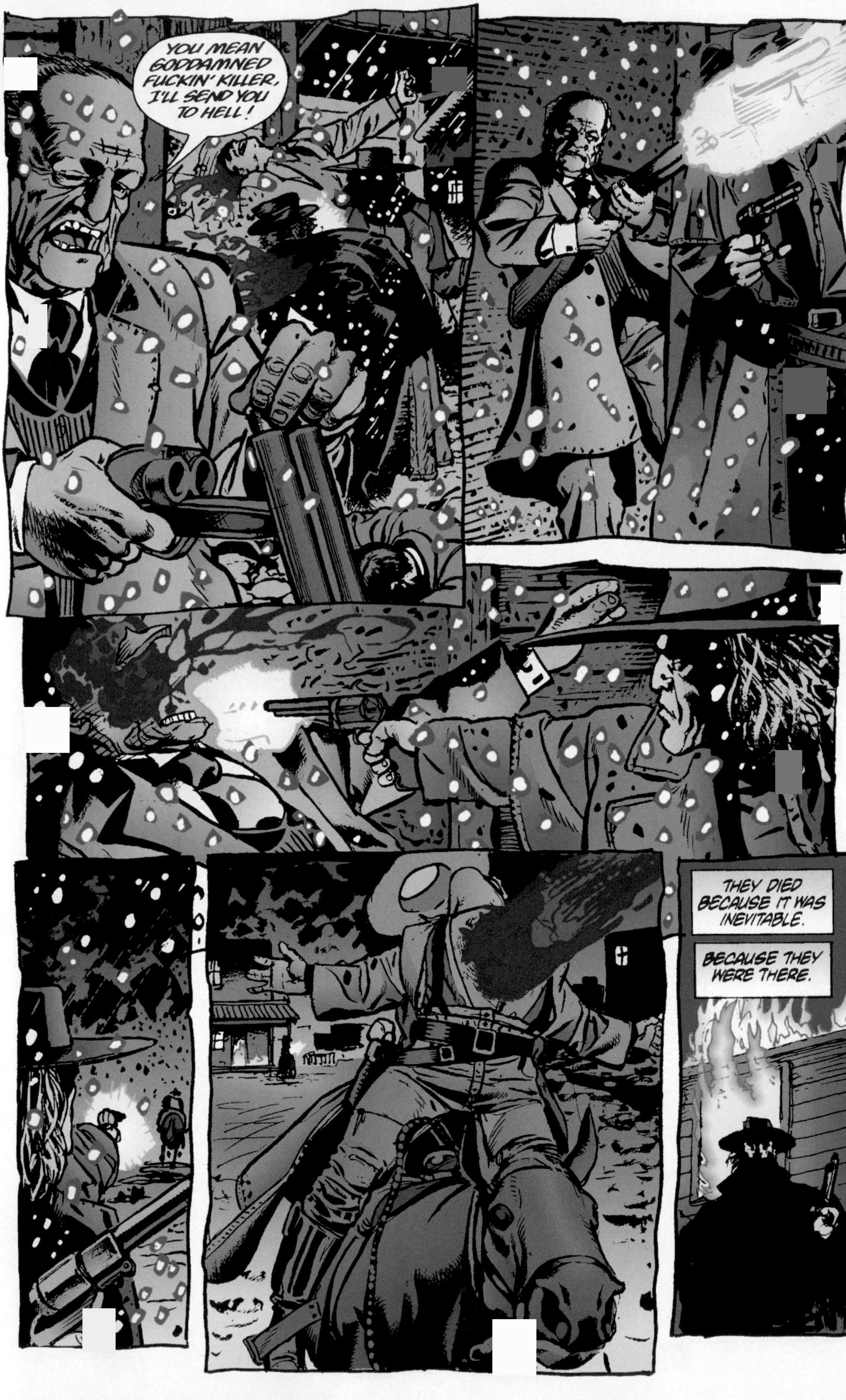
YOU MEAN GODDAMNED FUCKIN' KILLER, I'LL SEND YOU TO HELL!
THEY DIED BECAUSE IT WAS INEVITABLE.
BECAUSE THEY WERE THERE.

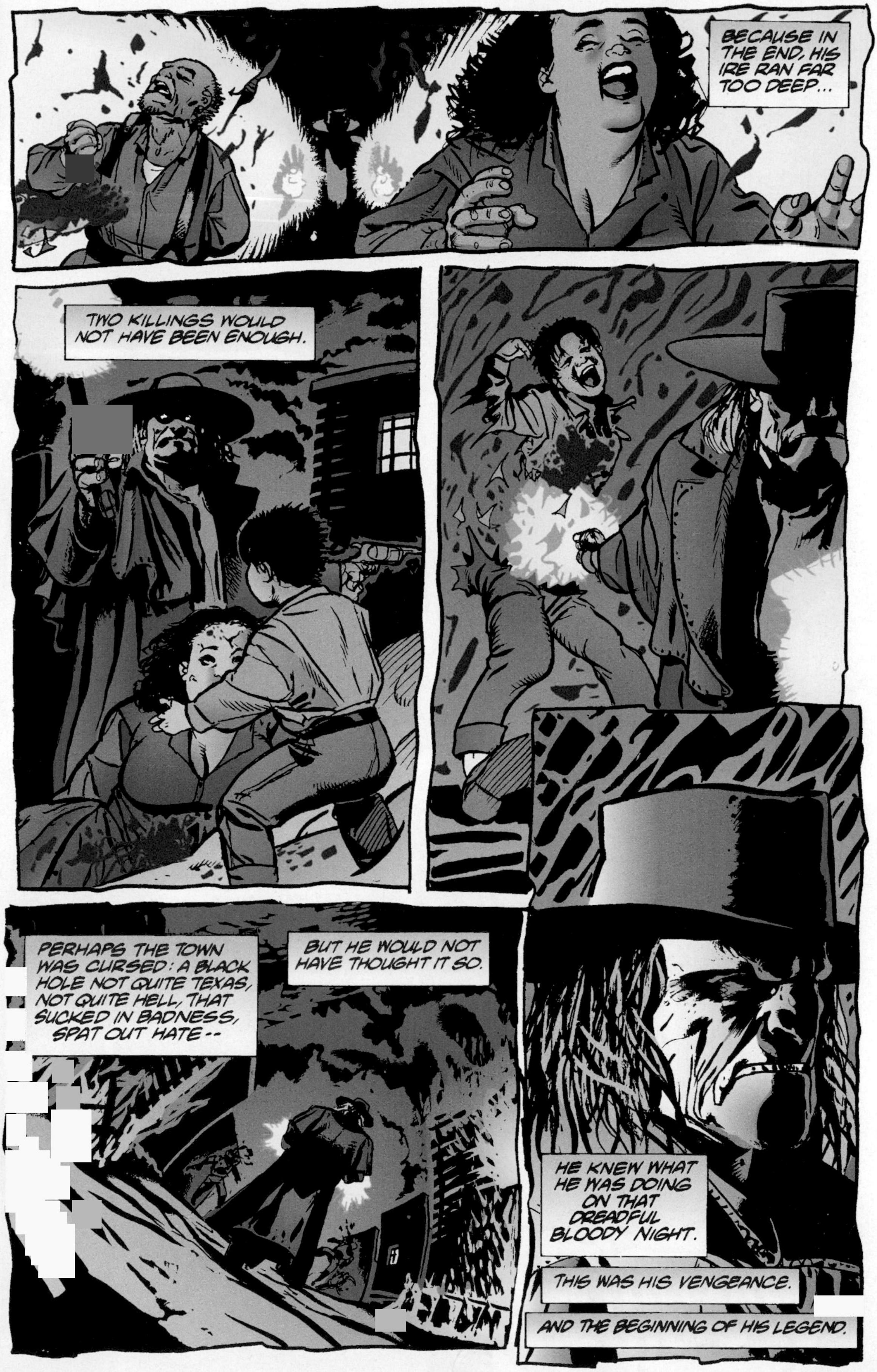
BECAUSE IN THE END, HIS IRE RAN FAR TOO DEEP...
TWO KILLINGS WOULD NOT HAVE BEEN ENOUGH.
PERHAPS THE TOWN WAS CURSED: A BLACK HOLE NOT QUITE TEXAS, NOT QUITE HELL, THAT SUCKED IN BADNESS, SPAT OUT HATE --
BUT HE WOULD NOT HAVE THOUGHT IT SO.
HE KNEW WHAT HE WAS DOING ON THAT DREADFUL BLOODY NIGHT.
THIS WAS HIS VENGEANCE.
AND THE BEGINNING OF HIS LEGEND.

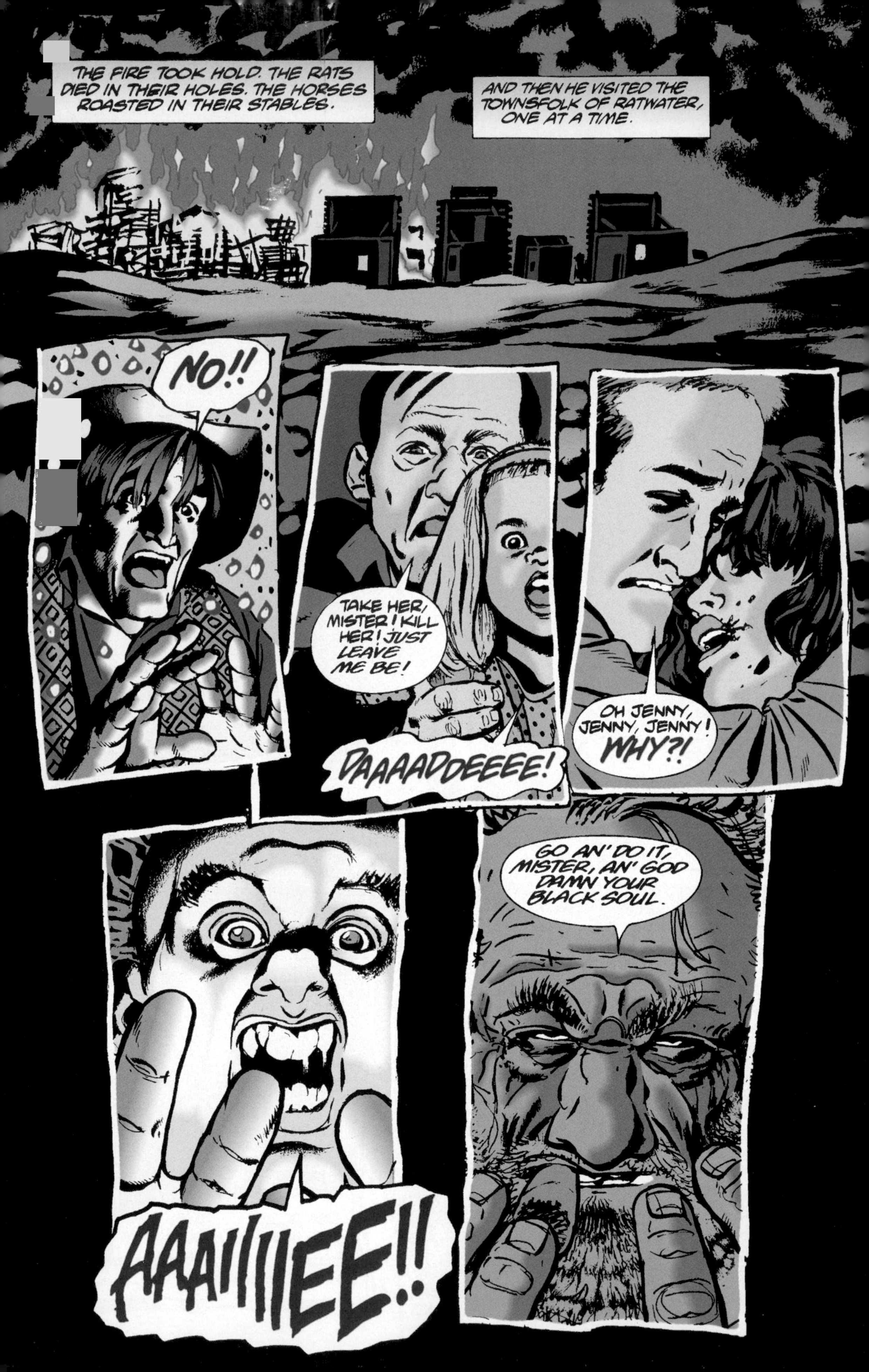
THE FIRE TOOK HOLD. THE RATS DIED IN THEIR HOLES. THE HORSES ROASTED IN THEIR STABLES.
AND THEN HE VISITED THE TOWNSFOLK OF RATWATER, ONE AT A TIME.
NO!!
TAKE HER, MISTER! KILL HER! JUST LEAVE ME BE!
DAAAADDEEEE!
OH JENNY, JENNY, JENNY! WHY?!
AAAIIIIEE!!
GO AN' DO IT, MISTER, AN' GOD DAMN YOUR BLACK SOUL.

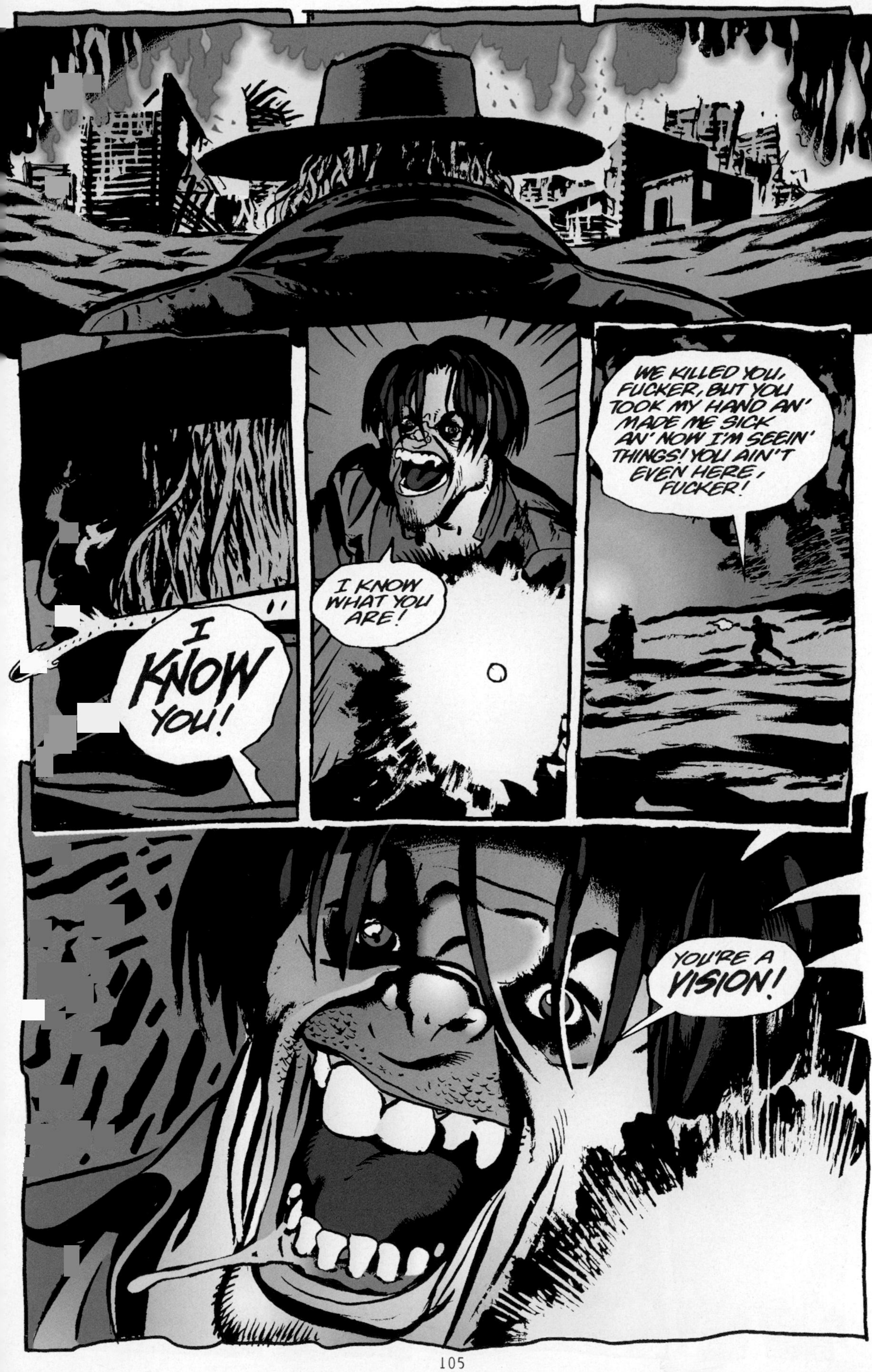
I KNOW YOU!
I KNOW WHAT YOU ARE!
WE KILLED YOU, FUCKER, BUT YOU TOOK MY HAND AN' MADE ME SICK AN' NOW I'M SEEIN' THINGS! YOU AIN'T EVEN HERE, FUCKER!
YOU'RE A VISION!

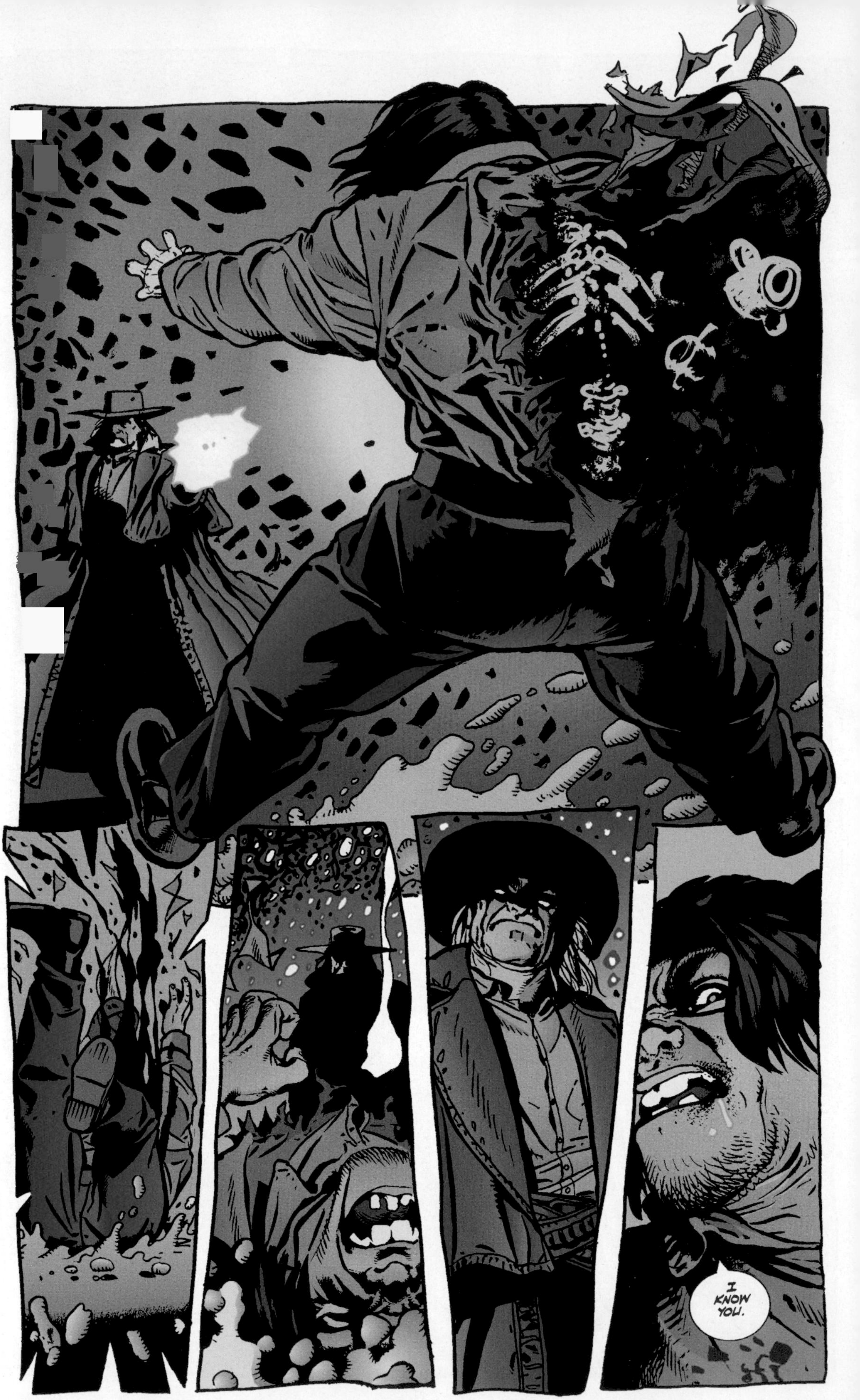
I KNOW YOU.

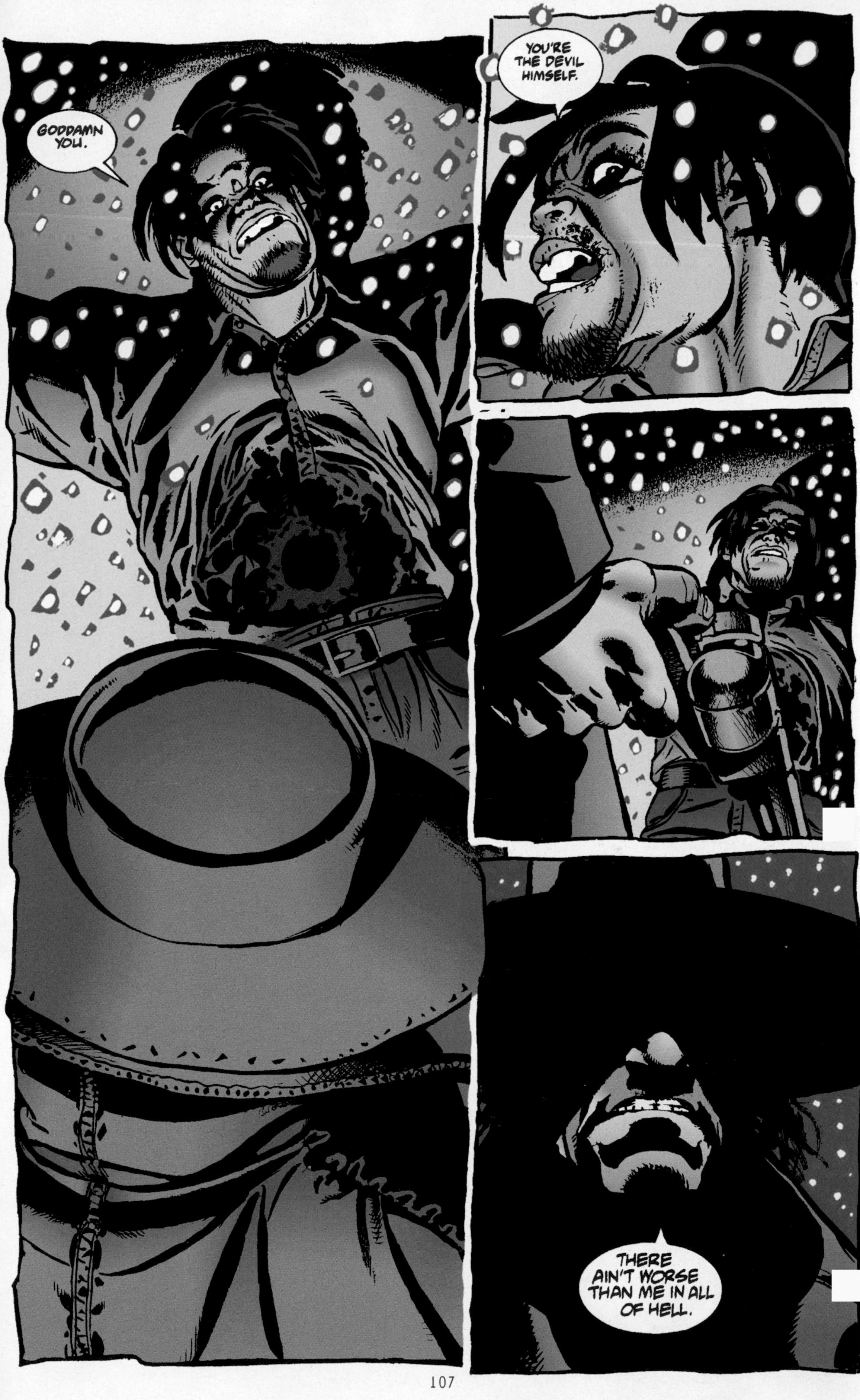
GODDAMN YOU.
YOU'RE THE DEVIL HIMSELF.
THERE AIN'T WORSE THAN ME IN ALL OF HELL.

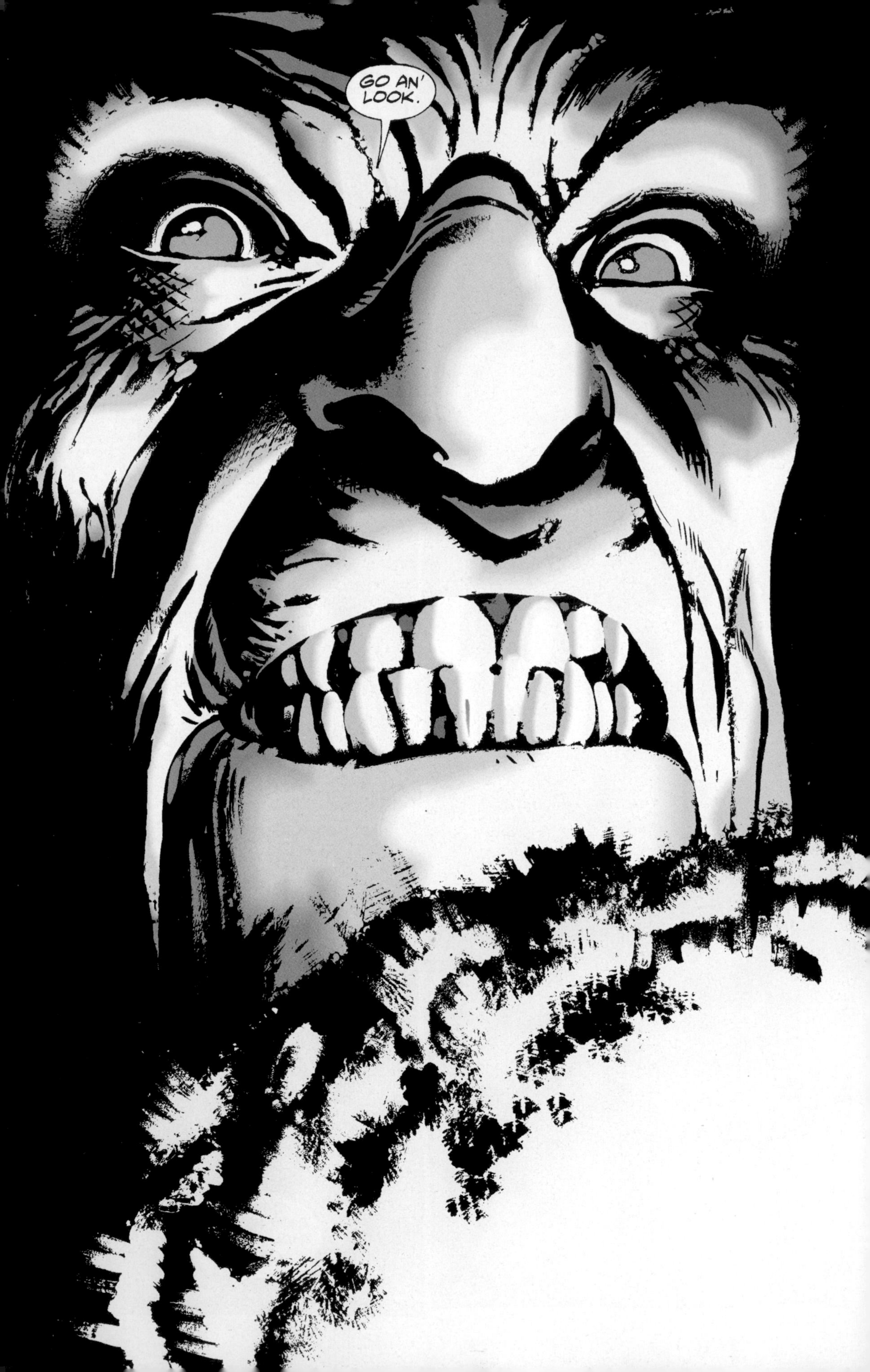
GO AN' LOOK.

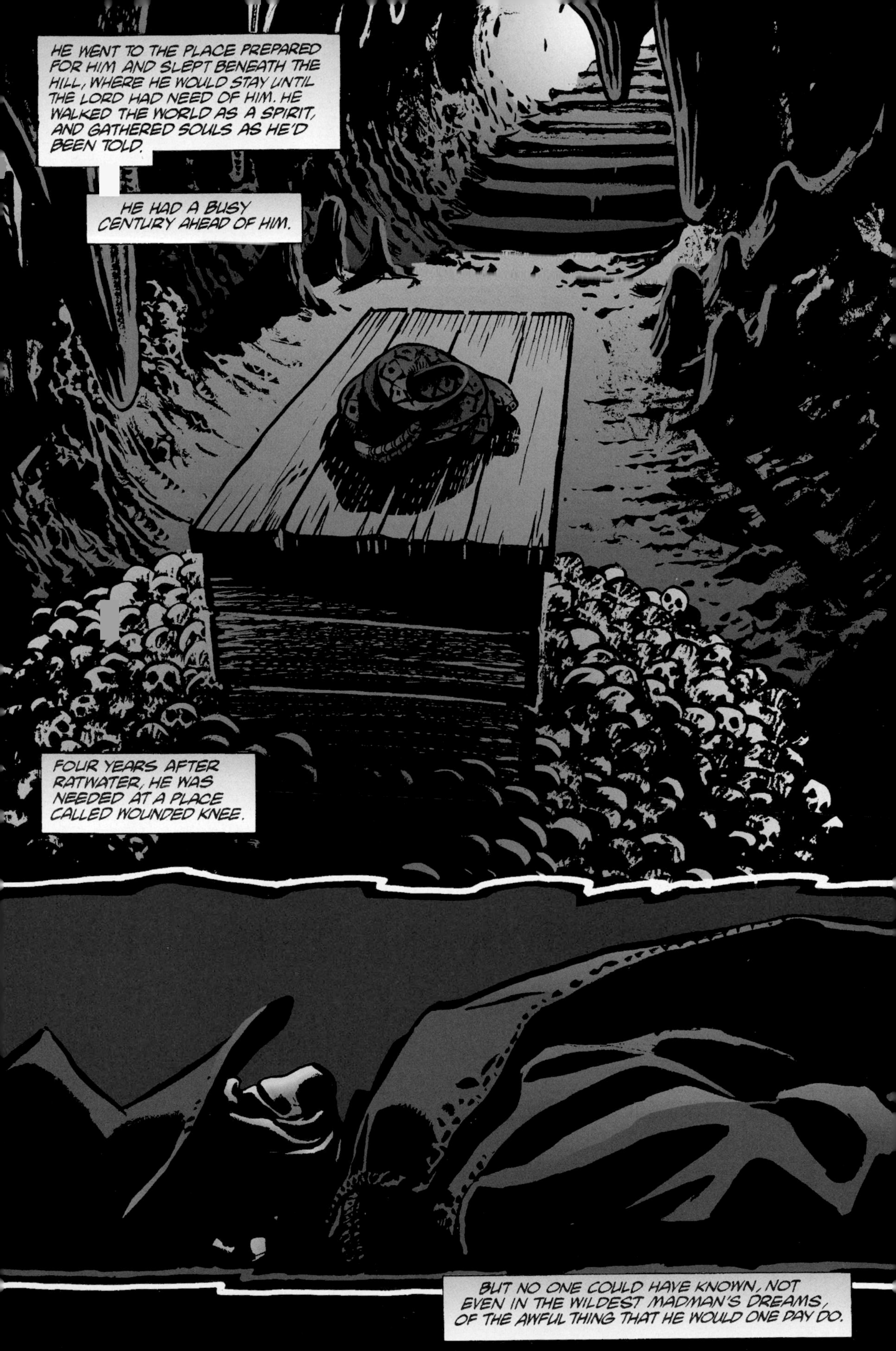
HE WENT TO THE PLACE PREPARED FOR HIM AND SLEPT BENEATH THE HILL, WHERE HE WOULD STAY UNTIL THE LORD HAD NEED OF HIM. HE WALKED THE WORLD AS A SPIRIT, AND GATHERED SOULS AS HE'D BEEN TOLD.
HE HAD A BUSY CENTURY AHEAD OF HIM.
FOUR YEARS AFTER RATWATER, HE WAS NEEDED AT A PLACE CALLED WOUNDED KNEE.
BUT NO ONE COULD HAVE KNOWN, NOT EVEN IN THE WILDEST MADMAN'S DREAMS, OF THE AWFUL THING THAT HE WOULD ONE DAY DO.

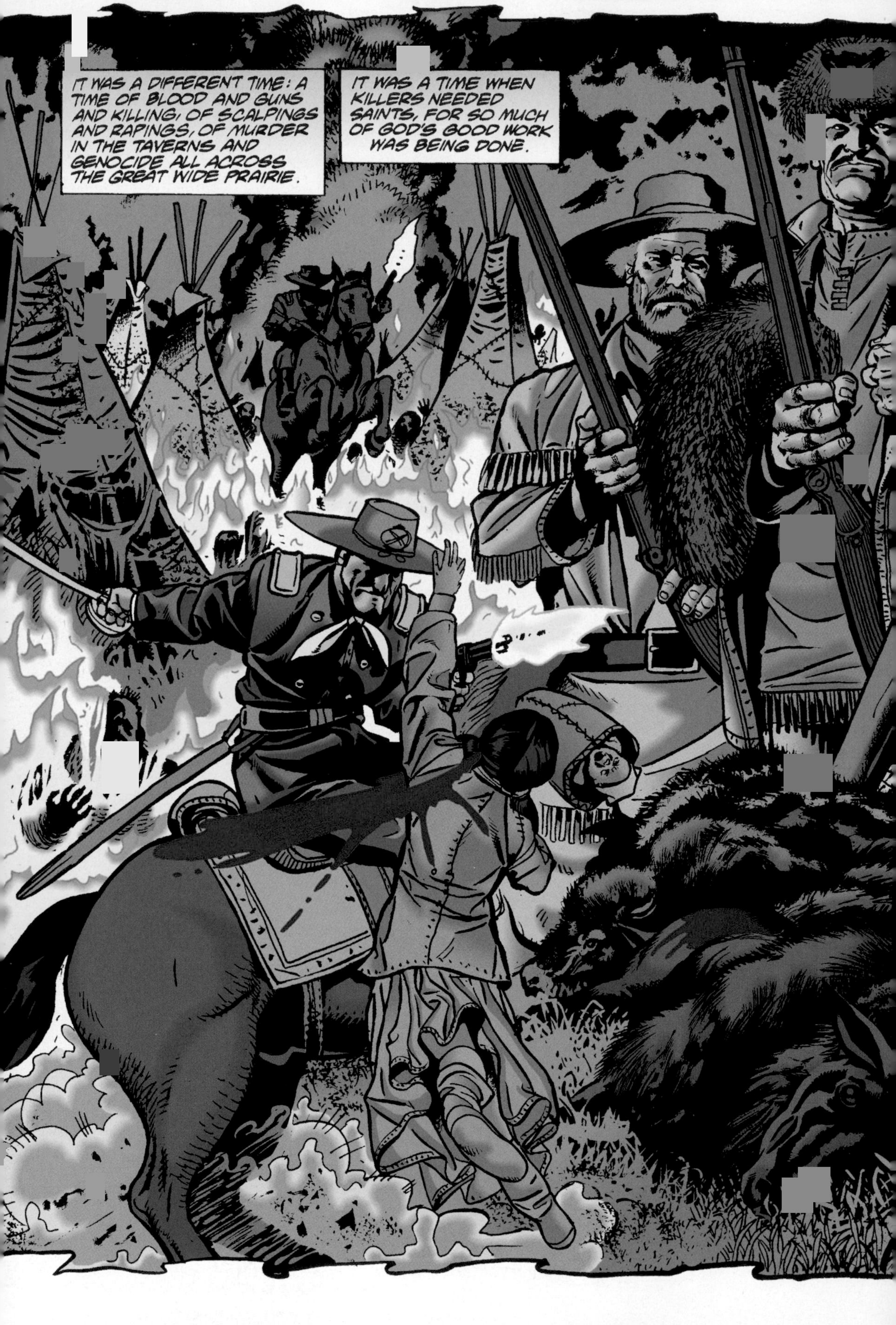
IT WAS A DIFFERENT TIME: A TIME OF BLOOD AND GUNS AND KILLING, OF SCALPINGS AND RAPINGS, OF MURDER IN THE TAVERNS AND GENOCIDE ALL ACROSS THE GREAT WIDE PRAIRIE.
IT WAS A TIME WHEN KILLERS NEEDED SAINTS, FOR SO MUCH OF GOD'S GOOD WORK WAS BEING DONE.

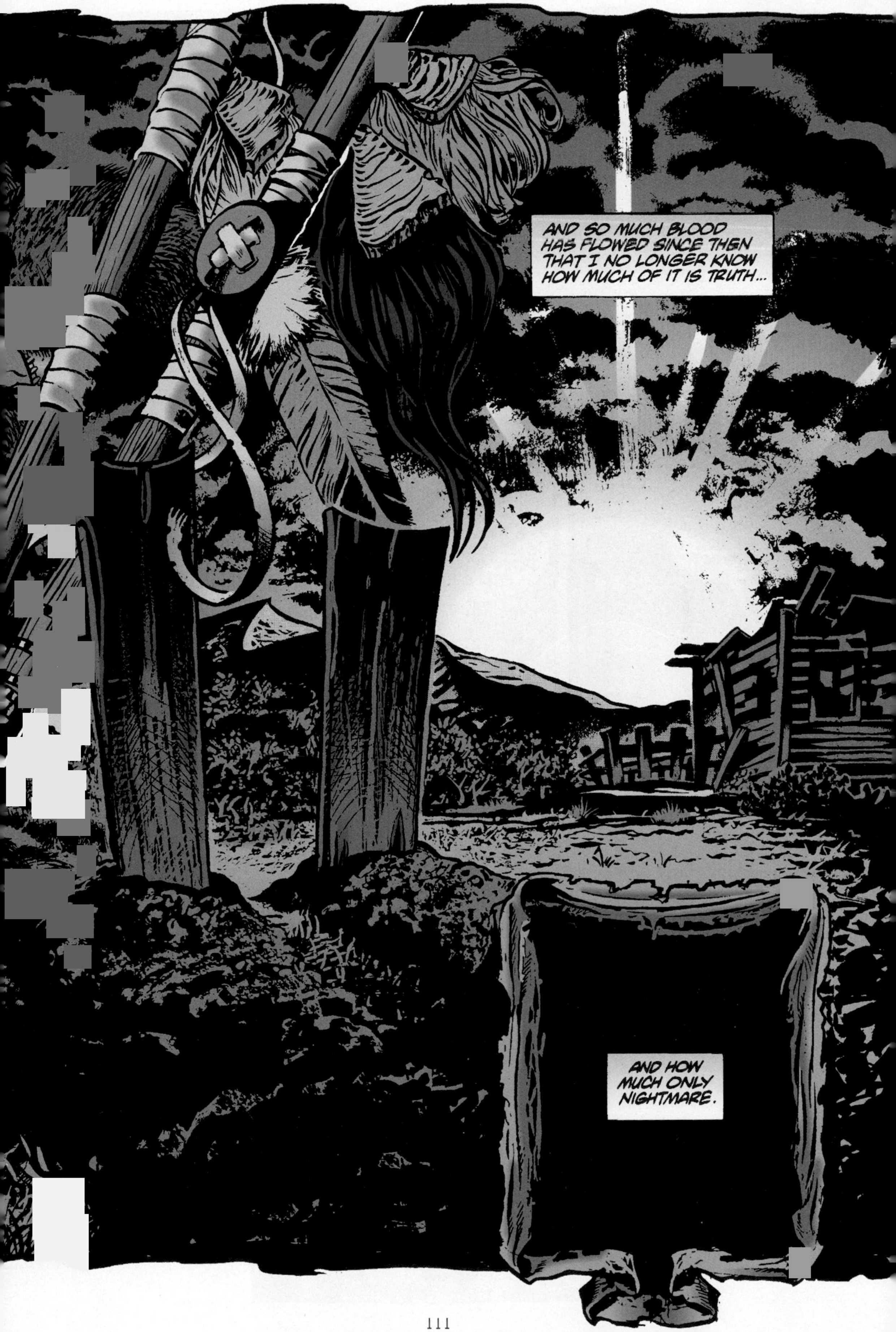
AND SO MUCH BLOOD HAS FLOWED SINCE THEN THAT I NO LONGER KNOW HOW MUCH OF IT IS TRUTH...
AND HOW MUCH ONLY NIGHTMARE.

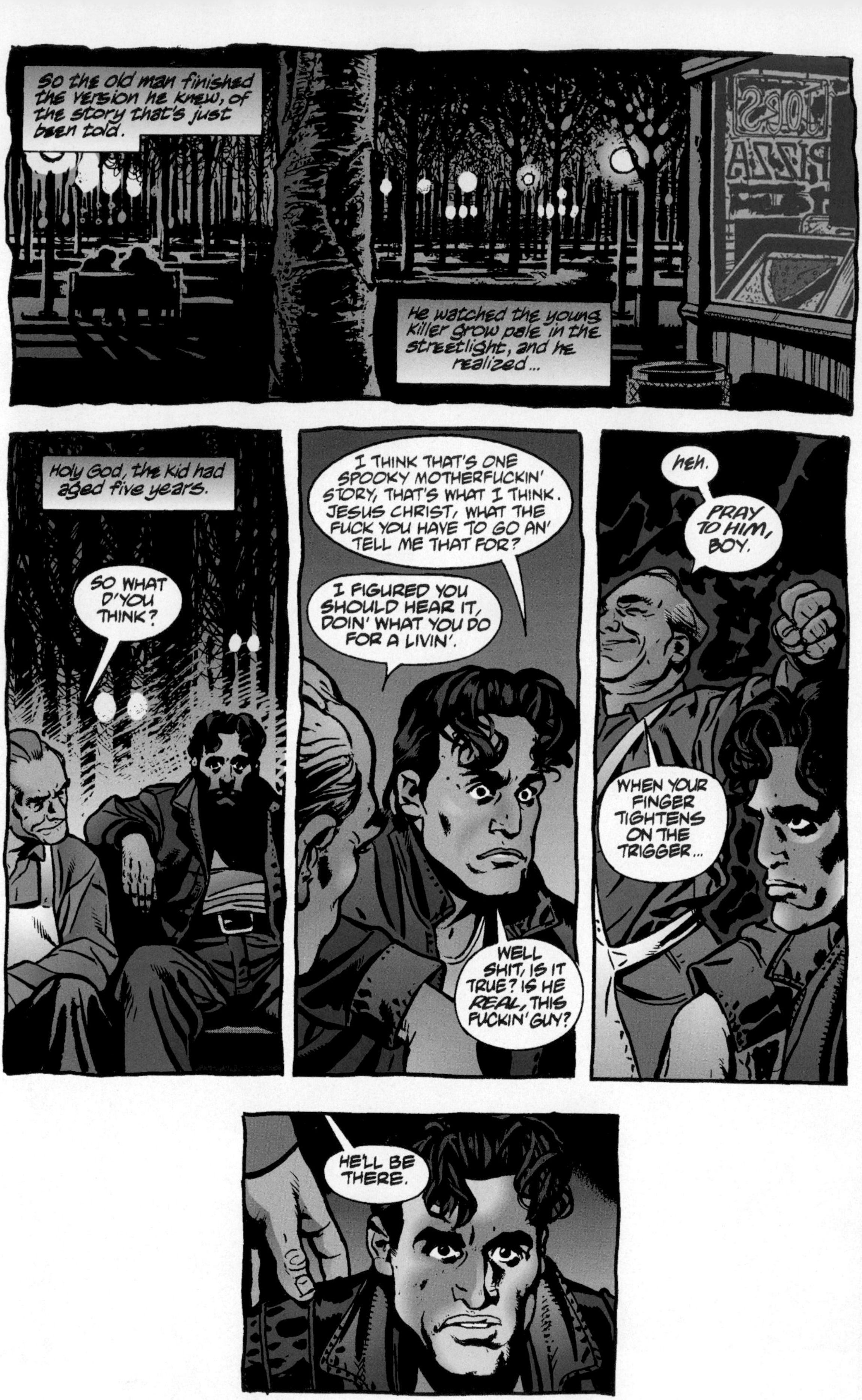
So the old man finished the version he knew, of the story that's just been told.
PIZZA
He watched the young killer grow pale in the streetlight, and he realized...
Holy God, the kid had aged five years.
SO WHAT D'YOU THINK?
I THINK THAT'S ONE SPOOKY MOTHERFUCKIN' STORY, THAT'S WHAT I THINK. JESUS CHRIST, WHAT THE FUCK YOU HAVE TO GO AN' TELL ME THAT FOR?
I FIGURED YOU SHOULD HEAR IT, DOIN' WHAT YOU DO FOR A LIVIN'.
WELL SHIT, IS IT TRUE? IS HE REAL, THIS FUCKIN' GUY?
heh.
PRAY TO HIM, BOY.
WHEN YOUR FINGER TIGHTENS ON THE TRIGGER...
HE'LL BE THERE.

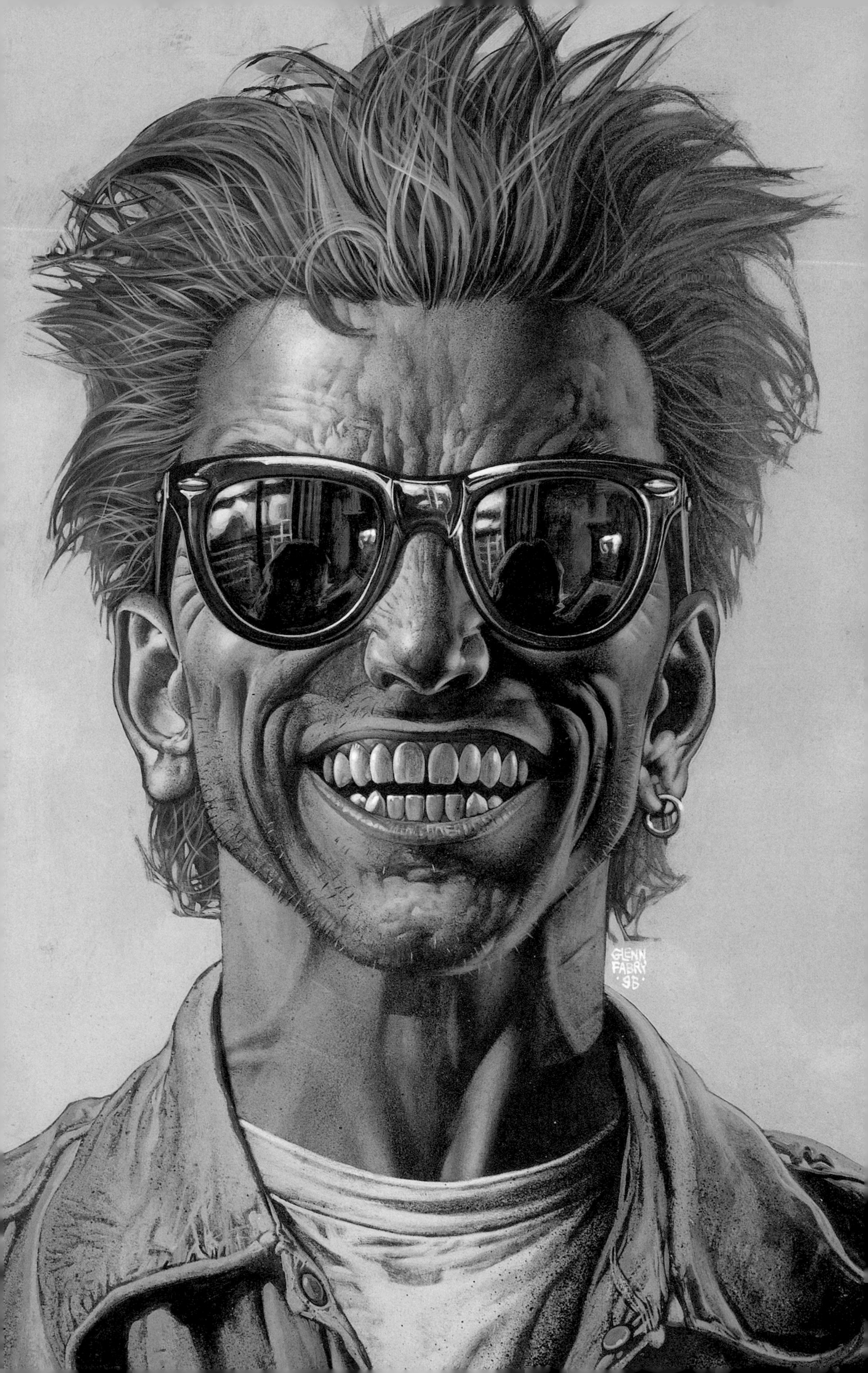
GLENN
FABRY
'96

"I finally find someone else who's gonna live forever an' — well.
It turns out he's a bit of a prick."

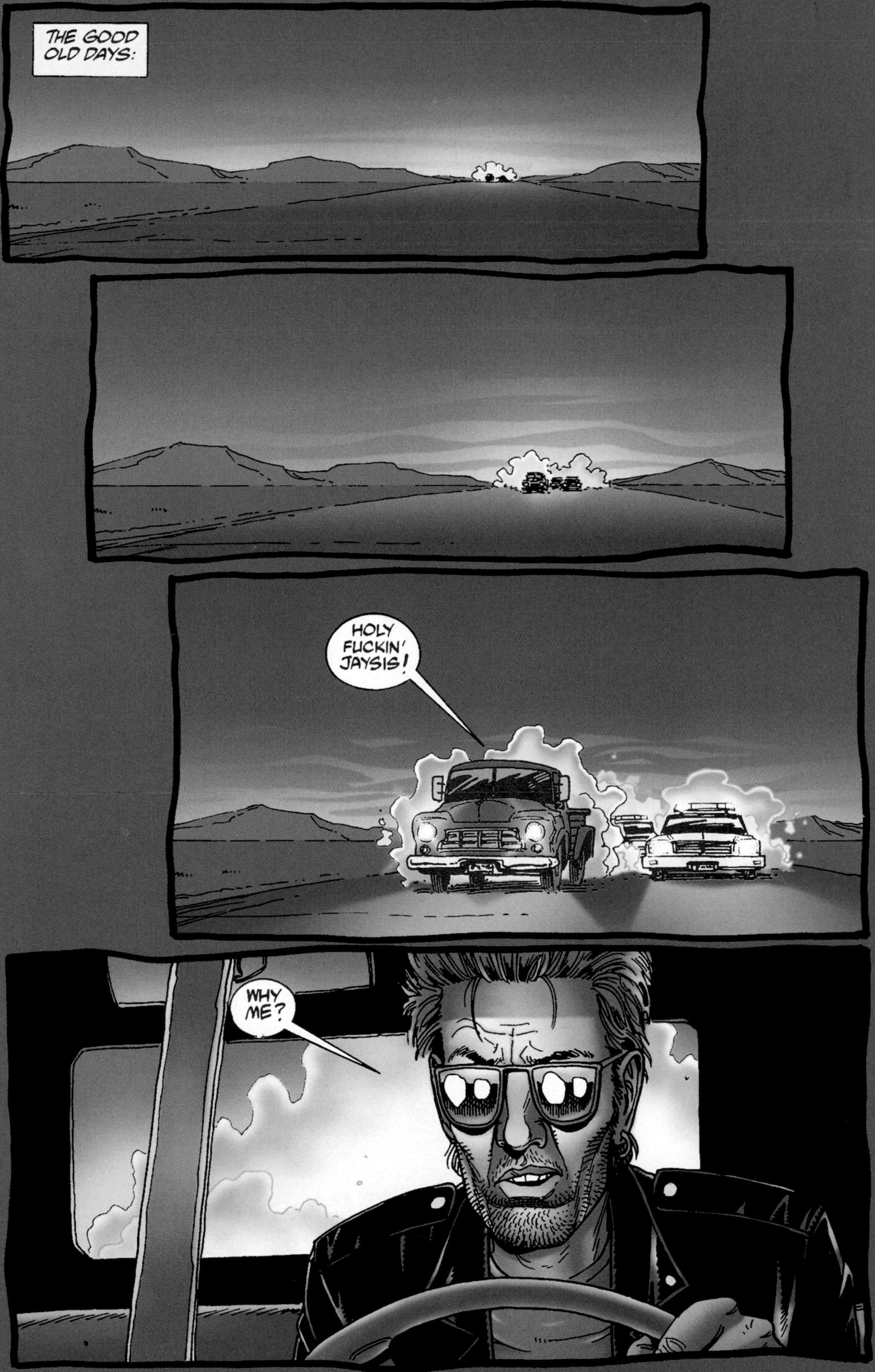
THE GOOD OLD DAYS:
HOLY FUCKIN' JAYSIS!
WHY ME?

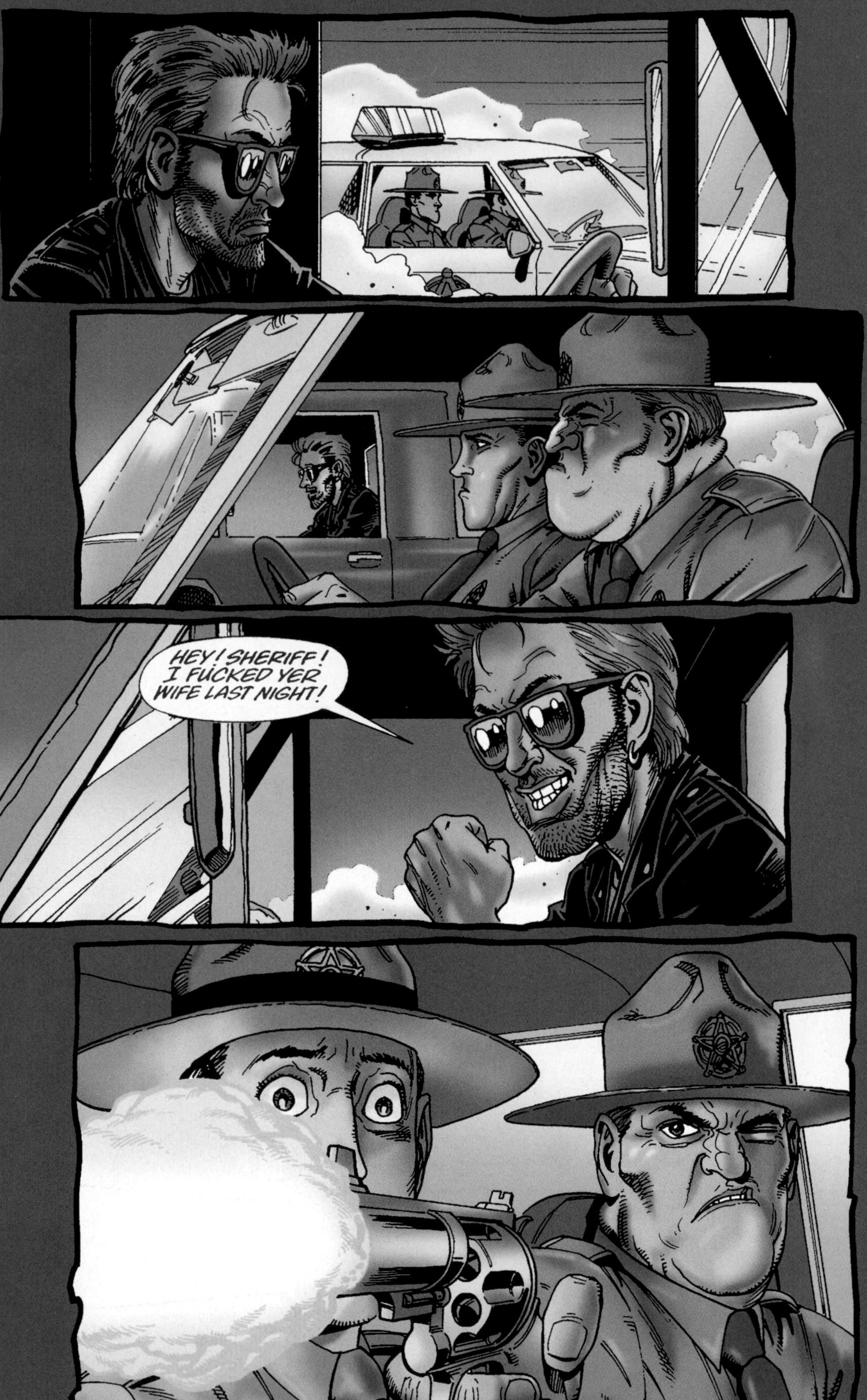
HEY! SHERIFF! I FUCKED YER WIFE LAST NIGHT!

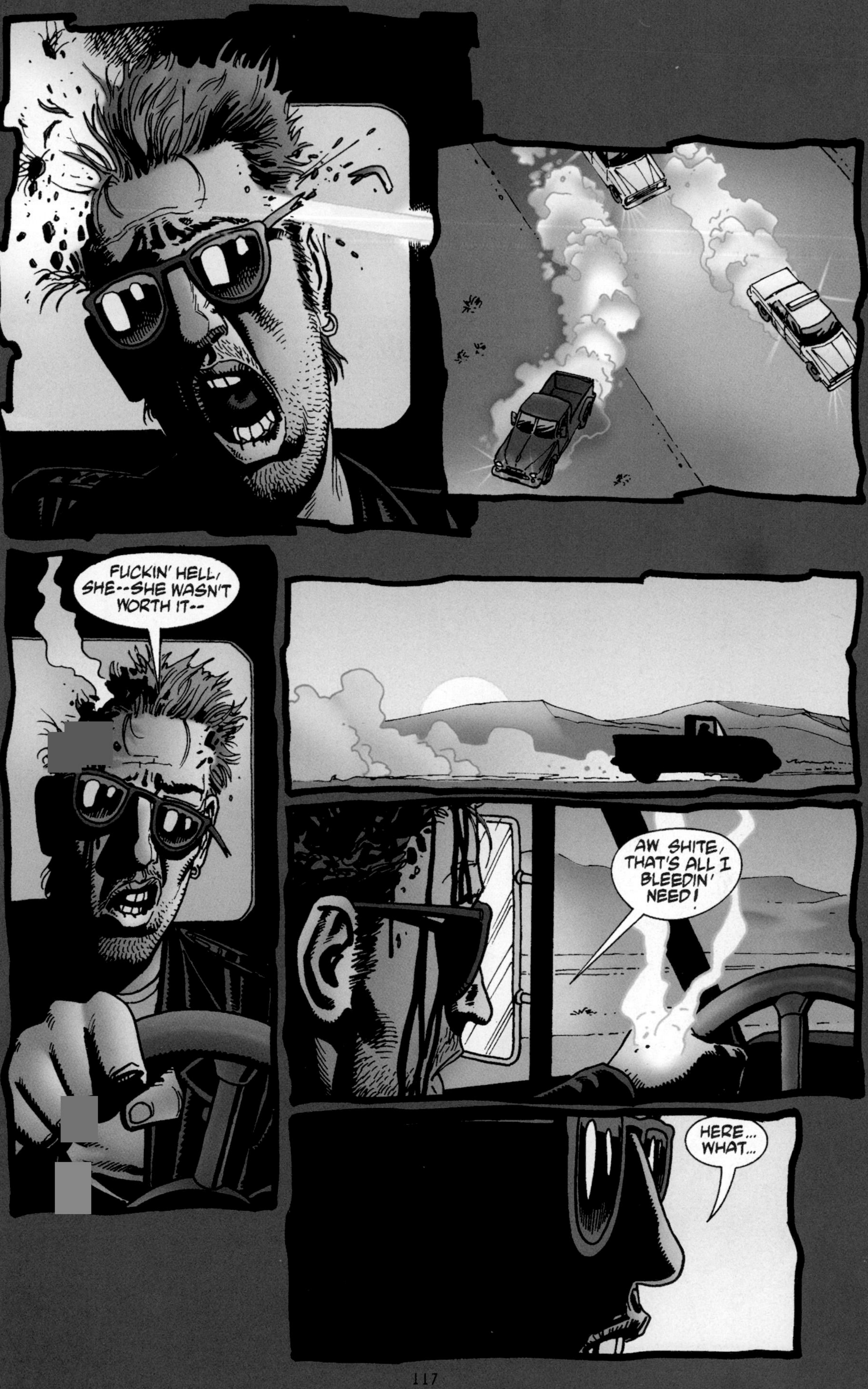
FUCKIN' HELL, SHE--SHE WASN'T WORTH IT--
AW SHITE, THAT'S ALL I BLEEDIN' NEED!
HERE... WHAT...

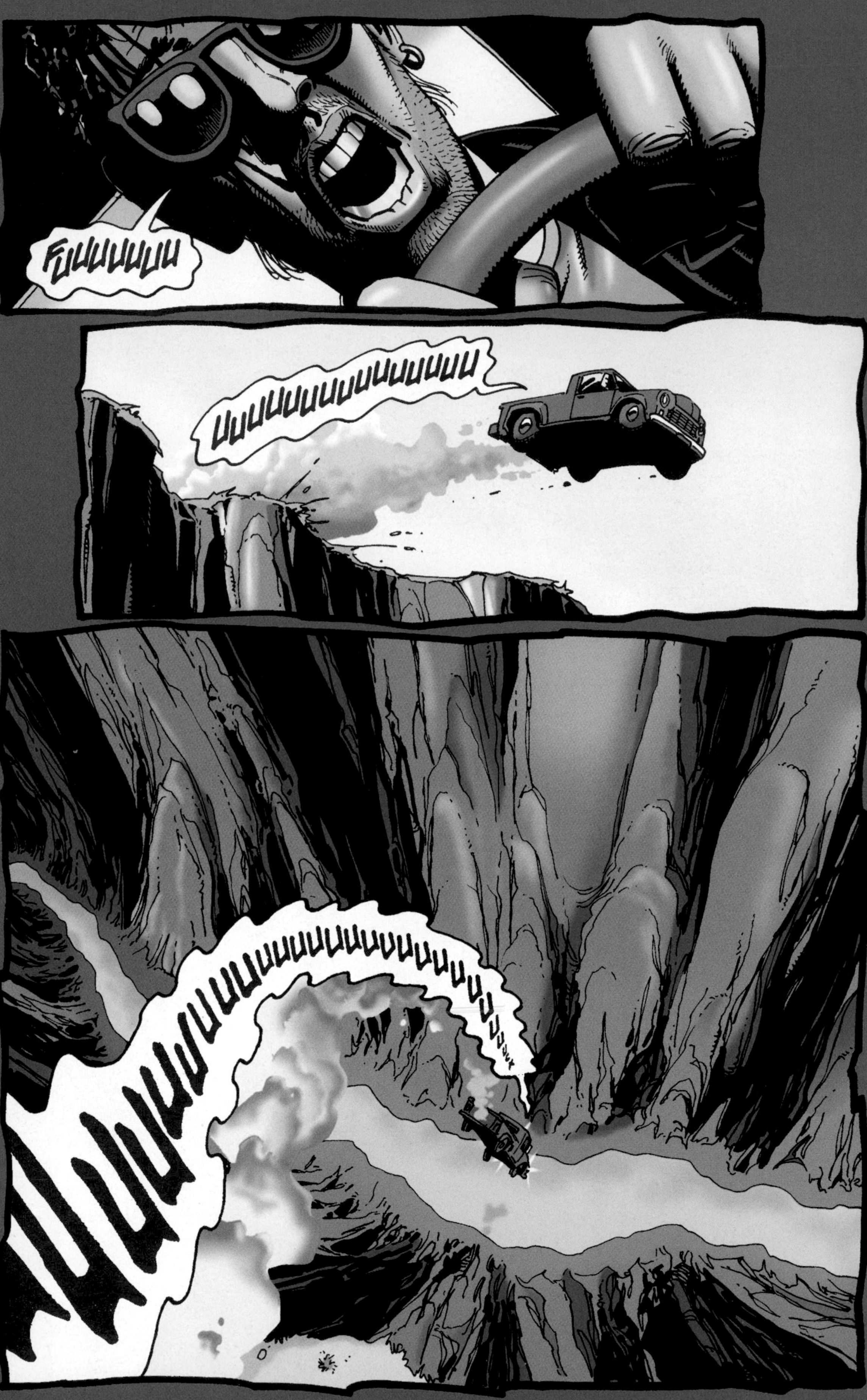
Fuuuuuuu
uuuuuuuuuuuuuuu
UUUUuuuuuuuuuuuuuuuuuuuuuuuuuuu

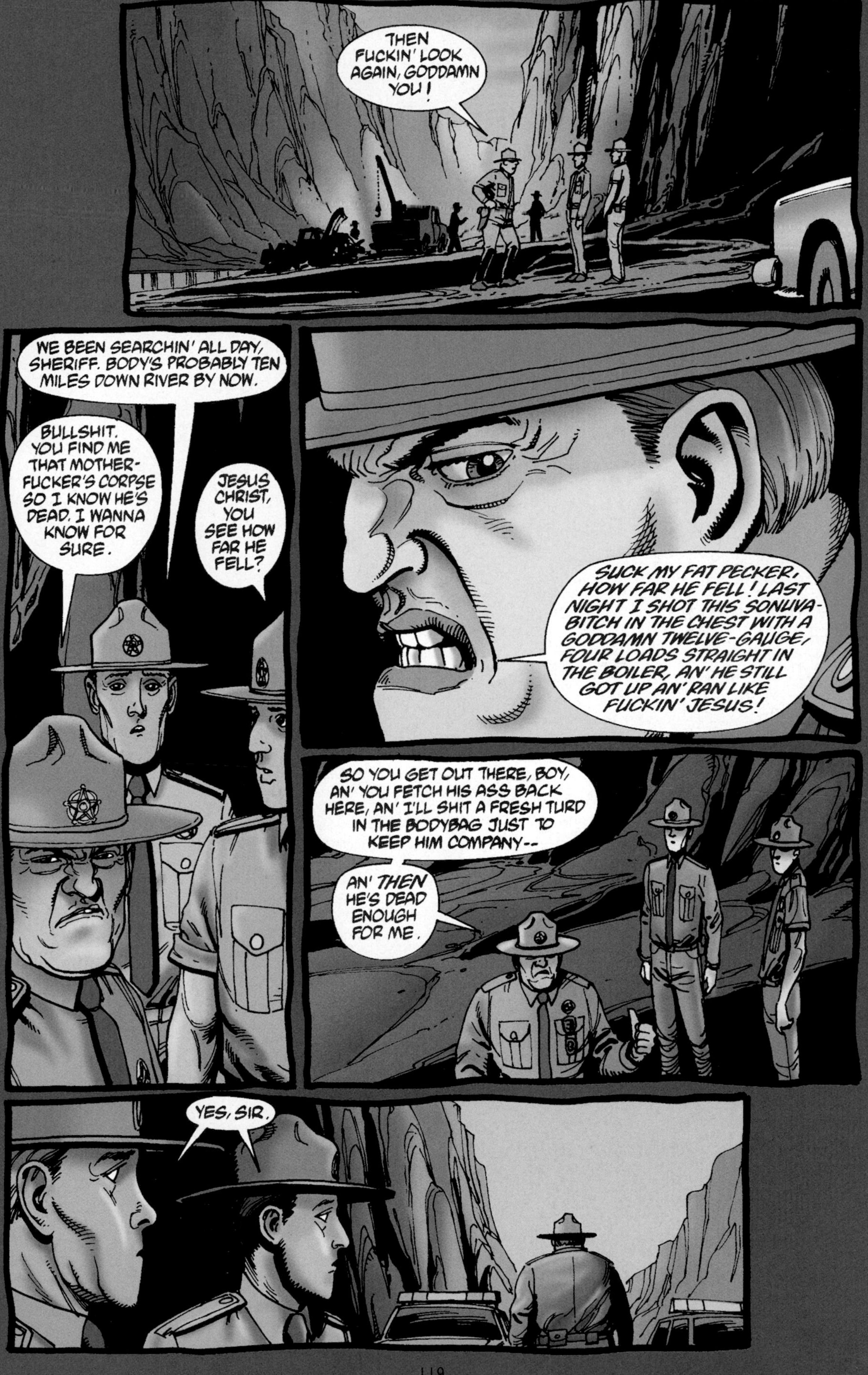
THEN FUCKIN' LOOK AGAIN, GODDAMN YOU!
WE BEEN SEARCHIN' ALL DAY, SHERIFF. BODY'S PROBABLY TEN MILES DOWN RIVER BY NOW.
BULLSHIT. YOU FIND ME THAT MOTHER-FUCKER'S CORPSE SO I KNOW HE'S DEAD. I WANNA KNOW FOR SURE.
JESUS CHRIST, YOU SEE HOW FAR HE FELL?
SUCK MY FAT PECKER, HOW FAR HE FELL! LAST NIGHT I SHOT THIS SONUVA-BITCH IN THE CHEST WITH A GODDAMN TWELVE-GAUGE, FOUR LOADS STRAIGHT IN THE BOILER, AN' HE STILL GOT UP AN' RAN LIKE FUCKIN' JESUS!
SO YOU GET OUT THERE, BOY, AN' YOU FETCH HIS ASS BACK HERE, AN' I'LL SHIT A FRESH TURD IN THE BODYBAG JUST TO KEEP HIM COMPANY--
AN' THEN HE'S DEAD ENOUGH FOR ME.
YES, SIR.

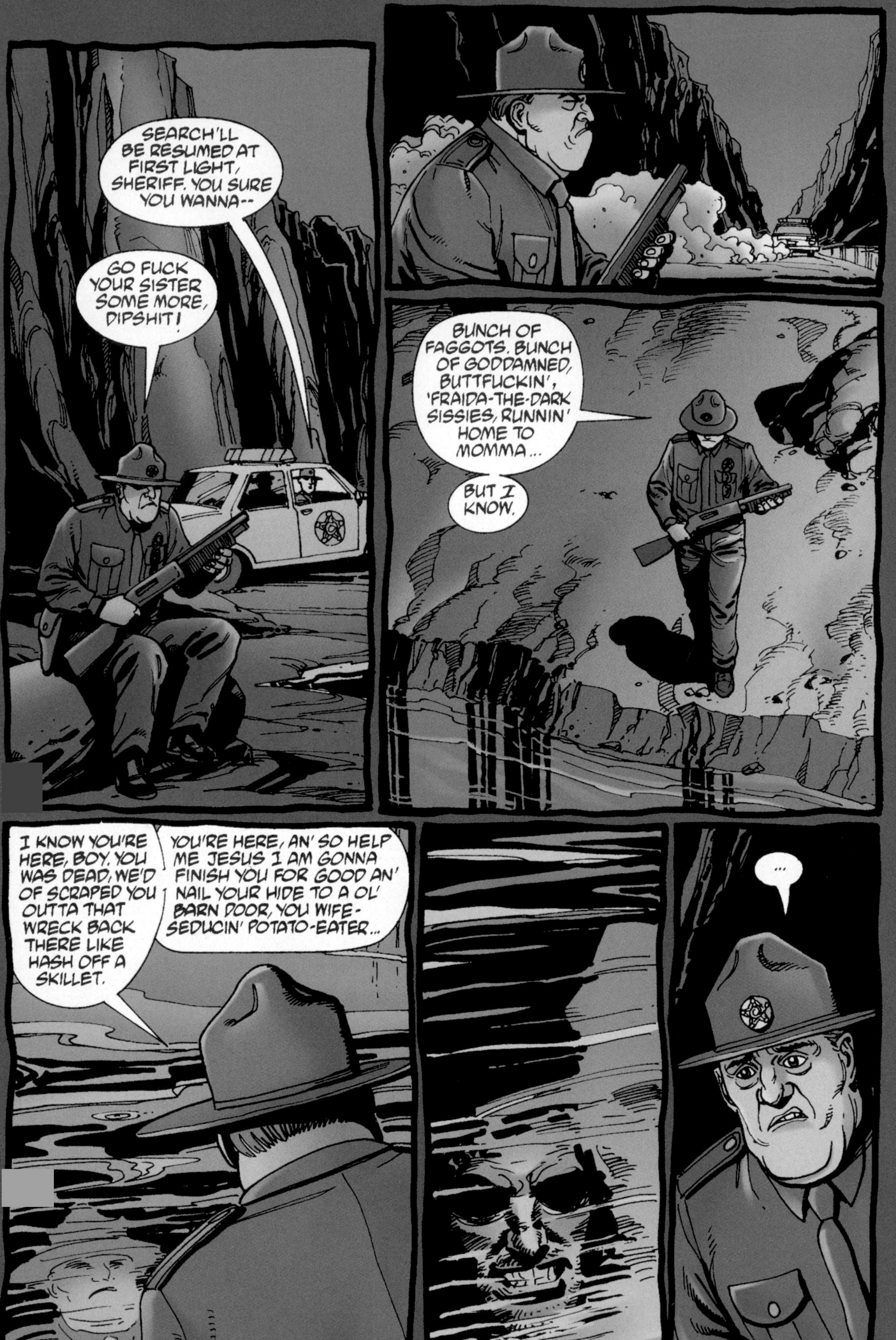
SEARCH'LL BE RESUMED AT FIRST LIGHT, SHERIFF. YOU SURE YOU WANNA--
GO FUCK YOUR SISTER SOME MORE, DIPSHIT!
BUNCH OF FAGGOTS. BUNCH OF GODDAMNED, BUTTFUCKIN', 'FRAIDA-THE-DARK SISSIES, RUNNIN' HOME TO MOMMA...
BUT I KNOW.
I KNOW YOU'RE HERE, BOY. YOU WAS DEAD, WE'D OF SCRAPED YOU OUTTA THAT WRECK BACK THERE LIKE HASH OFF A SKILLET.
YOU'RE HERE, AN' SO HELP ME JESUS I AM GONNA FINISH YOU FOR GOOD AN' NAIL YOUR HIDE TO A OL' BARN DOOR, YOU WIFE-SEDUCIN' POTATO-EATER...
...

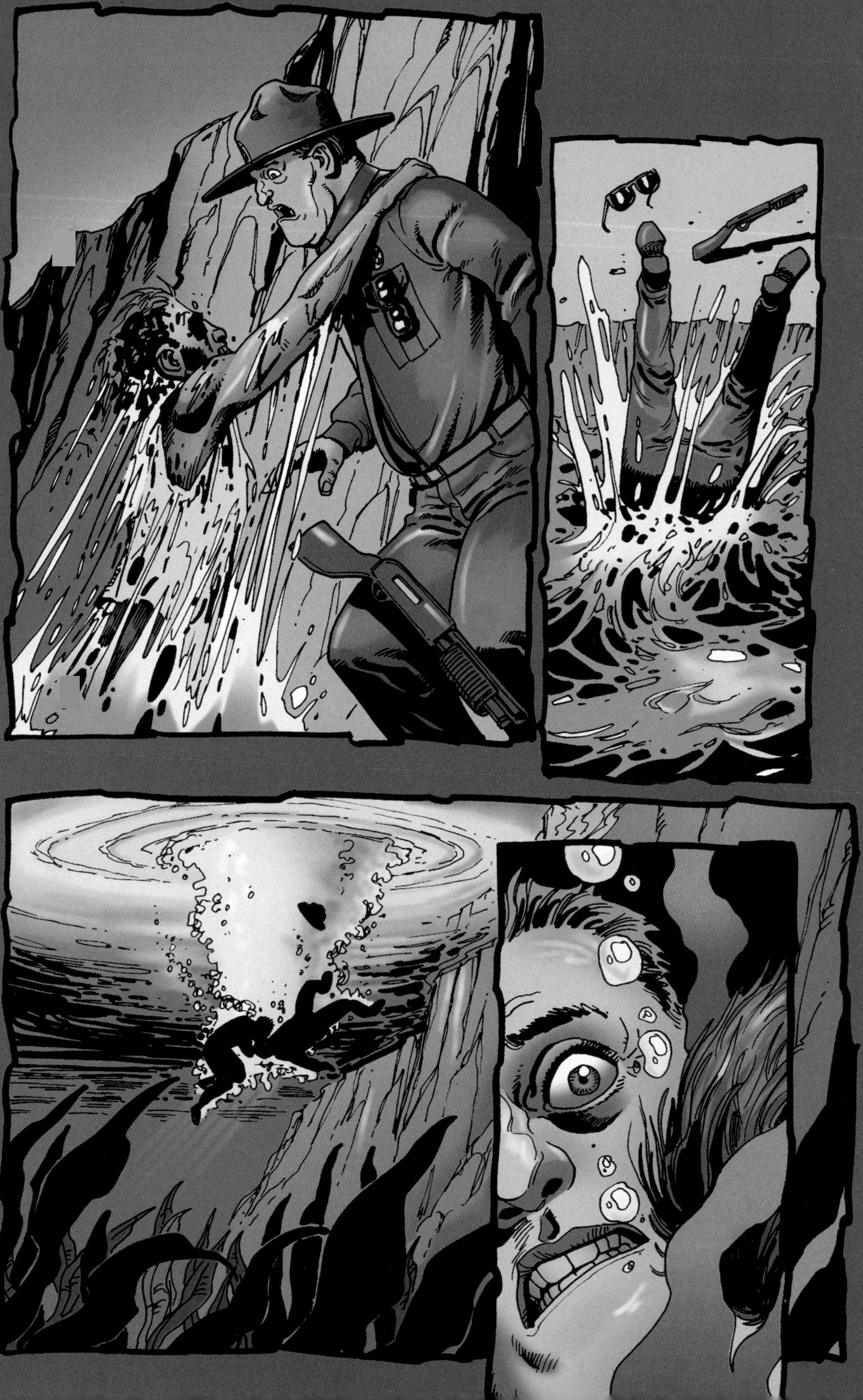

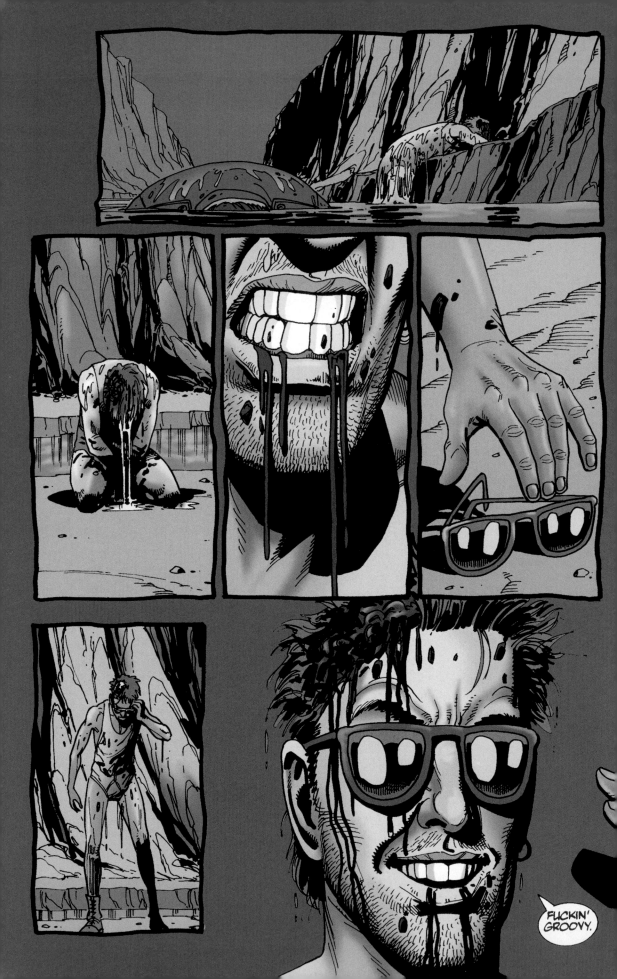

FUCKIN' GROOVY.

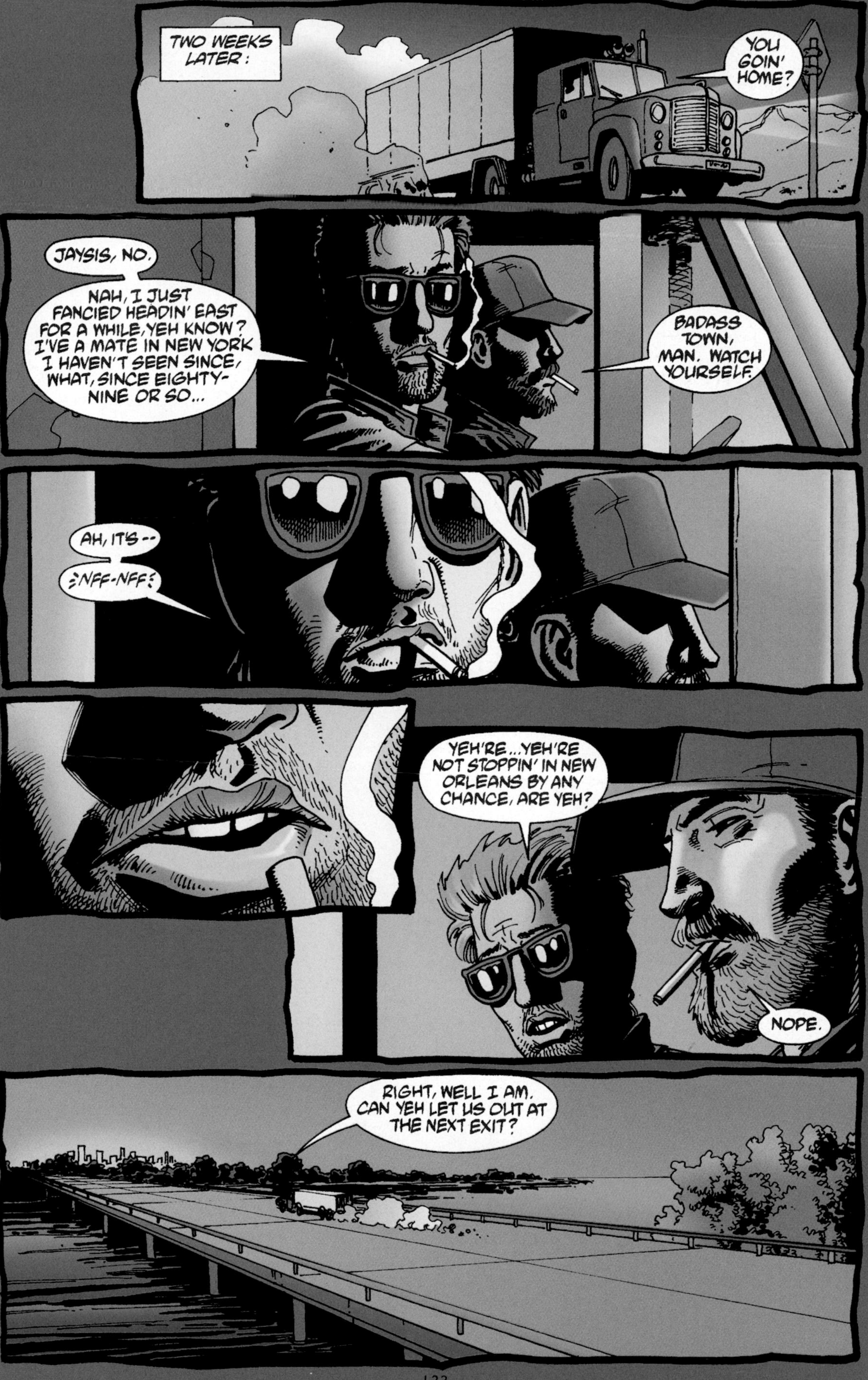
TWO WEEKS LATER:
YOU GOIN' HOME?
JAYSIS, NO.
NAH, I JUST FANCIED HEADIN' EAST FOR A WHILE, YEH KNOW? I'VE A MATE IN NEW YORK I HAVEN'T SEEN SINCE, WHAT, SINCE EIGHTY-NINE OR SO...
BADASS TOWN, MAN. WATCH YOURSELF.
AH, IT'S--
NFF-NFF
YEH'RE...YEH'RE NOT STOPPIN' IN NEW ORLEANS BY ANY CHANCE, ARE YEH?
NOPE.
RIGHT, WELL I AM. CAN YEH LET US OUT AT THE NEXT EXIT?

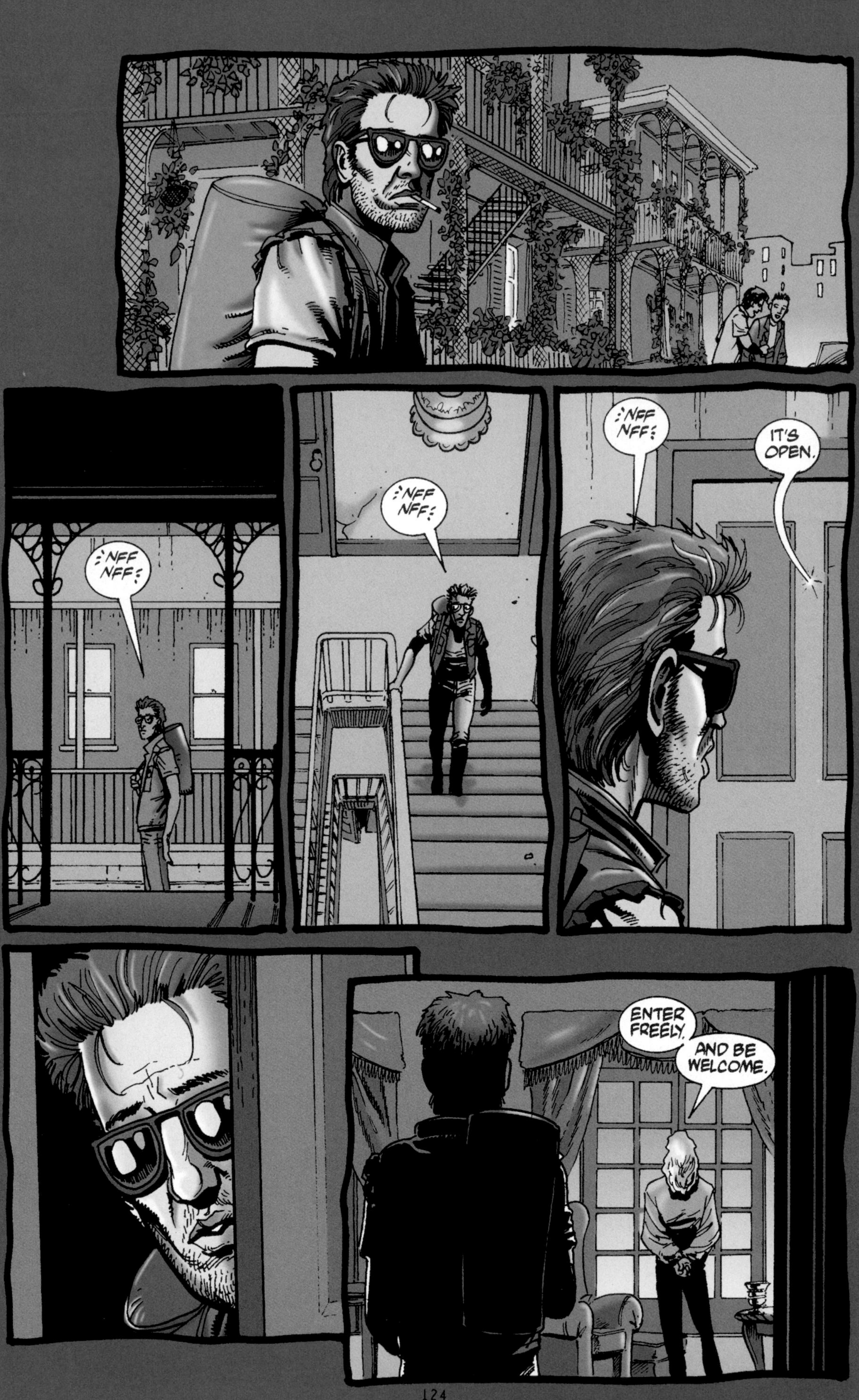
NFF NFF
NFF NFF
NFF NFF
IT'S OPEN.
ENTER FREELY.
AND BE WELCOME.

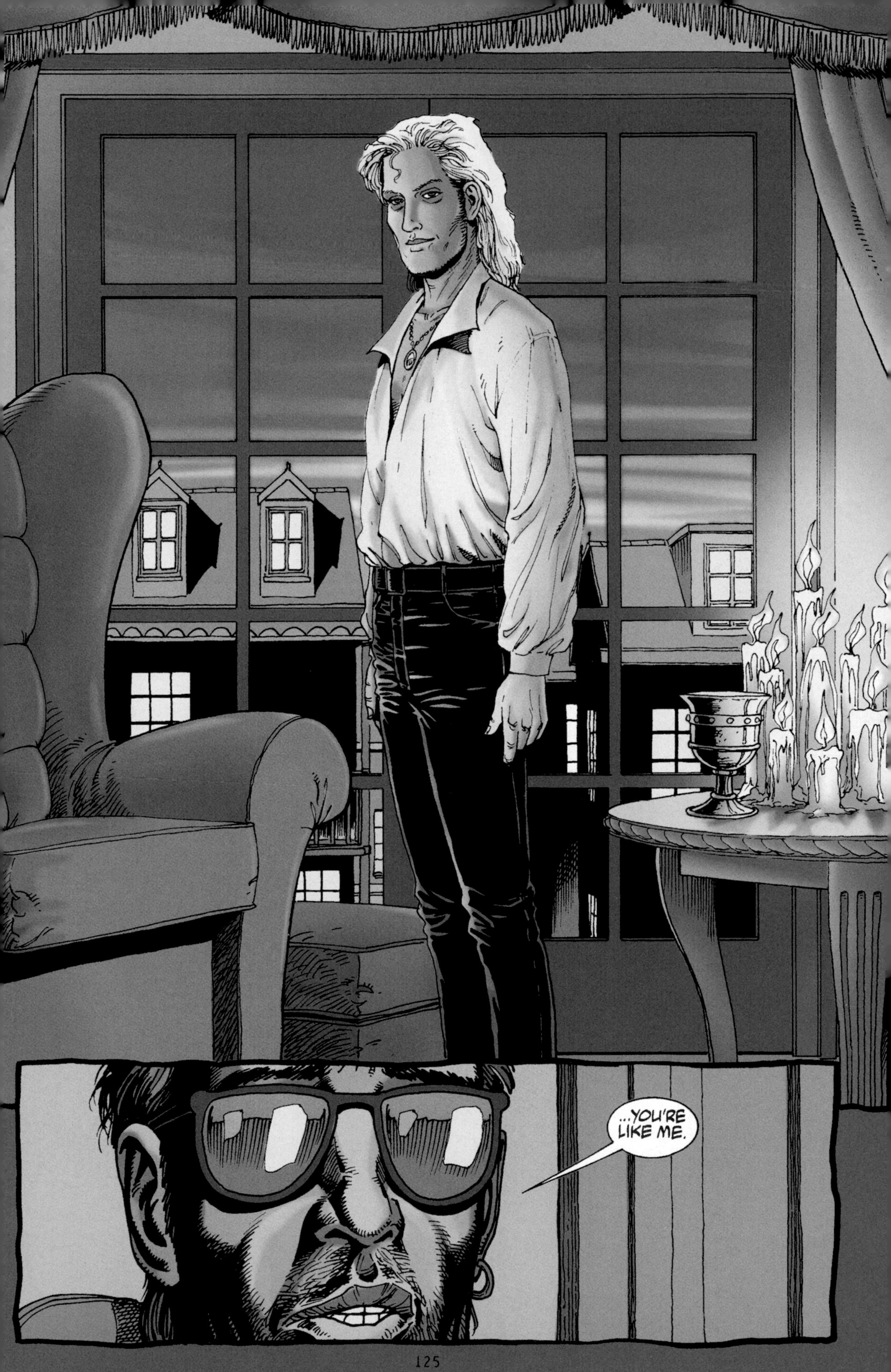
...YOU'RE LIKE ME.

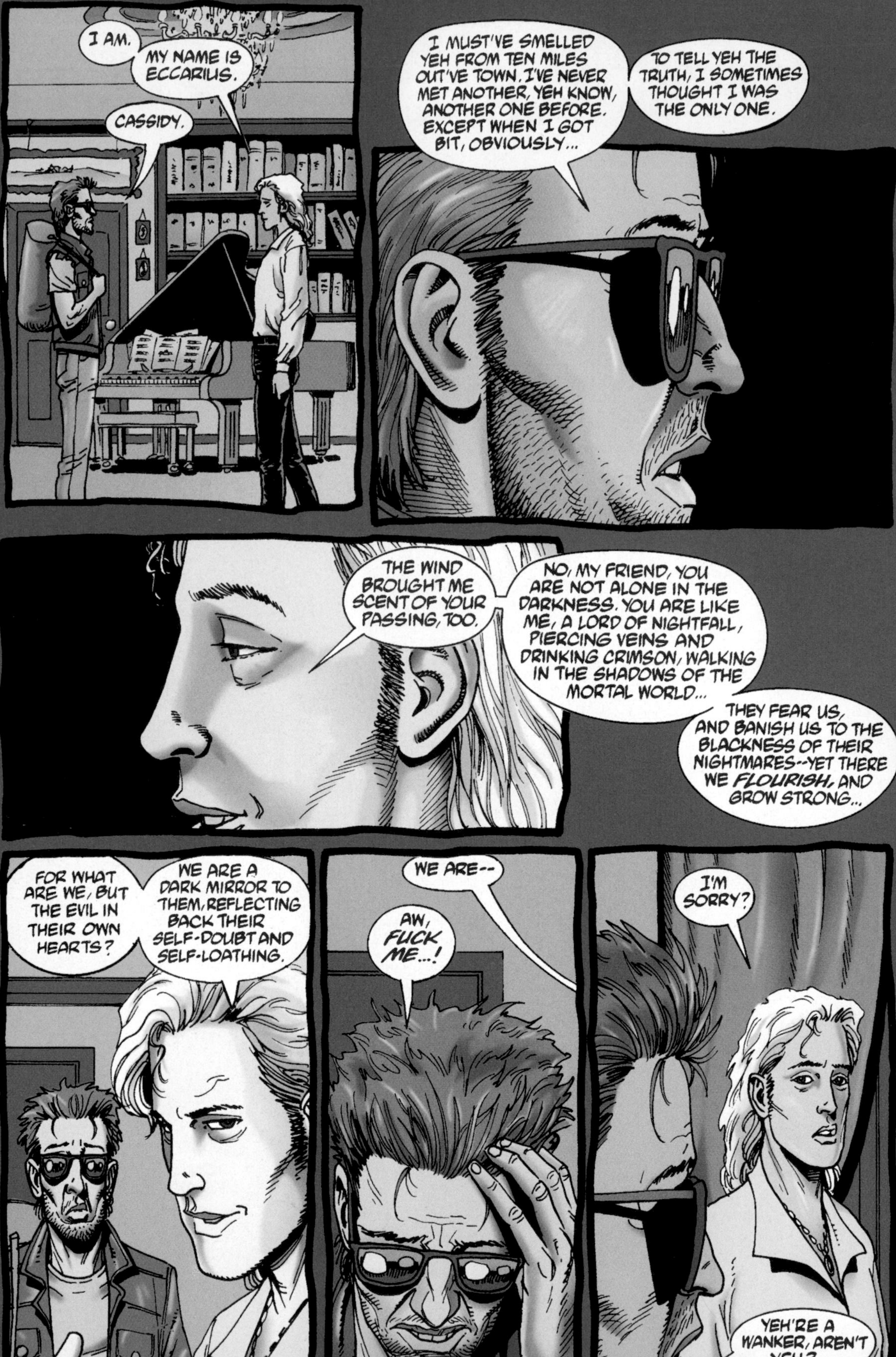
I AM.
MY NAME IS ECCARIUS.
CASSIDY.
I MUST'VE SMELLED YEH FROM TEN MILES OUT'VE TOWN. I'VE NEVER MET ANOTHER, YEH KNOW, ANOTHER ONE BEFORE. EXCEPT WHEN I GOT BIT, OBVIOUSLY...
TO TELL YEH THE TRUTH, I SOMETIMES THOUGHT I WAS THE ONLY ONE.
THE WIND BROUGHT ME SCENT OF YOUR PASSING, TOO.
NO, MY FRIEND, YOU ARE NOT ALONE IN THE DARKNESS. YOU ARE LIKE ME, A LORD OF NIGHTFALL, PIERCING VEINS AND DRINKING CRIMSON, WALKING IN THE SHADOWS OF THE MORTAL WORLD...
THEY FEAR US, AND BANISH US TO THE BLACKNESS OF THEIR NIGHTMARES--YET THERE WE *FLOURISH,* AND GROW STRONG...
FOR WHAT ARE WE, BUT THE EVIL IN THEIR OWN HEARTS?
WE ARE A DARK MIRROR TO THEM, REFLECTING BACK THEIR SELF-DOUBT AND SELF-LOATHING.
WE ARE--
AW, *FUCK ME...!*
I'M SORRY?
YEH'RE A WANKER, AREN'T YEH?

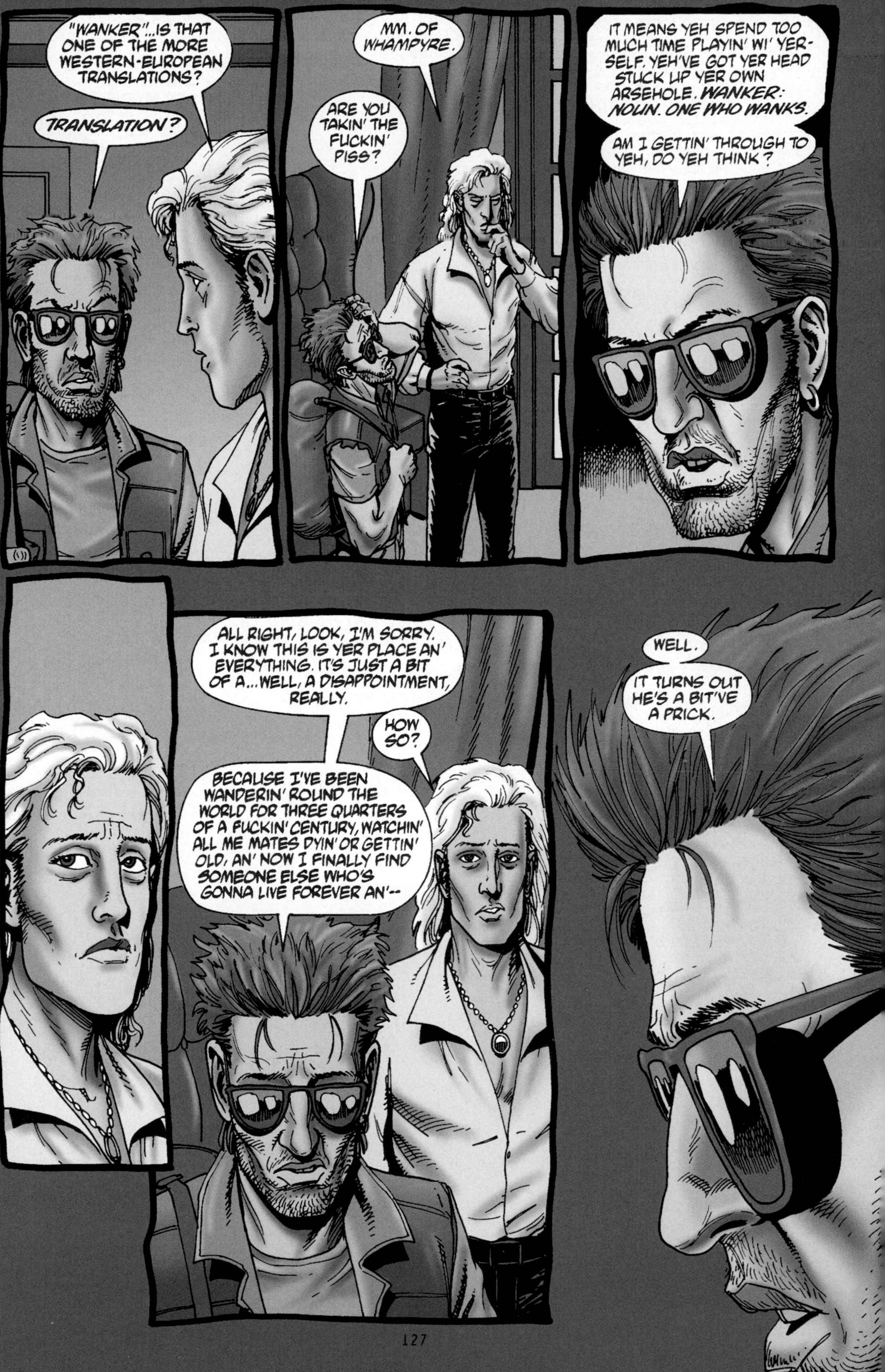
"WANKER"...IS THAT ONE OF THE MORE WESTERN-EUROPEAN TRANSLATIONS?
TRANSLATION?
MM. OF WHAMPYRE.
ARE YOU TAKIN' THE FUCKIN' PISS?
IT MEANS YEH SPEND TOO MUCH TIME PLAYIN' WI' YER-SELF. YEH'VE GOT YER HEAD STUCK UP YER OWN ARSEHOLE. WANKER: NOUN. ONE WHO WANKS.
AM I GETTIN' THROUGH TO YEH, DO YEH THINK?
ALL RIGHT, LOOK, I'M SORRY. I KNOW THIS IS YER PLACE AN' EVERYTHING. IT'S JUST A BIT OF A...WELL, A DISAPPOINTMENT, REALLY.
HOW SO?
BECAUSE I'VE BEEN WANDERIN' ROUND THE WORLD FOR THREE QUARTERS OF A FUCKIN' CENTURY, WATCHIN' ALL ME MATES DYIN' OR GETTIN' OLD, AN' NOW I FINALLY FIND SOMEONE ELSE WHO'S GONNA LIVE FOREVER AN'--
WELL.
IT TURNS OUT HE'S A BIT'VE A PRICK.

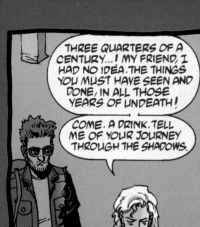

THREE QUARTERS OF A CENTURY...! MY FRIEND, I HAD NO IDEA. THE THINGS YOU MUST HAVE SEEN AND DONE, IN ALL THOSE YEARS OF UNDEATH!

COME. A DRINK. TELL ME OF YOUR JOURNEY THROUGH THE SHADOWS.

WHY, HOW LONG IS IT SINCE YEH WERE BIT YERSELF?

TEN YEARS.

TEN YEARS SINCE I PASSED OVER, EXPECTING AT LAST TO EXPLORE THE GREAT MYSTERY--ONLY TO FIND A MYRIAD OF GREATER MYSTERIES AWAITING ME IN THIS ETERNAL NIGHT...

*PWUUUSHH*

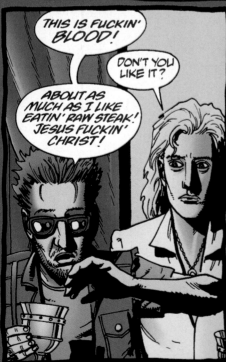

THIS IS FUCKIN' *BLOOD*!

DON'T YOU LIKE IT?

ABOUT AS MUCH AS I LIKE EATIN' RAW STEAK! JESUS FUCKIN' CHRIST!

WHAT I'M SAYIN' IS, THERE'S A TIME AN' A PLACE, YEH KNOW? HAVE YEH BEER?

I HAVE WINE...

DRY WHITE.

YOU SPOKE OF LOSING LOVED ONES AND COMPANIONS, CASSIDY. IT IS *EVER* OUR BURDEN, WE WHO STAND APART FROM MORTAL MAN.

AND YET, PERHAPS, YOU WILL FIND MORE SOLACE IN THIS CITY THAT YOU MIGHT AT FIRST HAVE THOUGHT.

OH AYE?

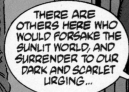

THERE ARE OTHERS HERE WHO WOULD FORSAKE THE SUNLIT WORLD, AND SURRENDER TO OUR DARK AND SCARLET URGING...

THERE'S MORE LIKE US, YEH MEAN?

NOT EXACTLY.

A SOCIETY THAT CONGREGATES IN A CELLAR DEEP BENEATH THE QUARTER, AND WHICH I SOMETIMES VISIT, THEY COVET THE LIFE THAT WE ALONE CAN LIVE, AND SEEK TO EMULATE IT...

AH. THEY AMUSE ME.

HOW COULD THEY KNOW THE TORMENT THAT WE FACE? OF NEVER QUITE BELONGING, ALWAYS LOOKING IN FROM OUT HERE IN THE COLD...THE EXQUISITE HELL OF A LIFE BOTH BLESSED AND CURSED...

AYE. TORMENT.

AT NEXT NIGHTFALL I WILL TAKE YOU TO THEM.

BUT COME, THE SUN IS RISING. OUR TIME IS ENDED. WE MUST REST.

I HAVE A PLACE PREPARED FOR YOU.

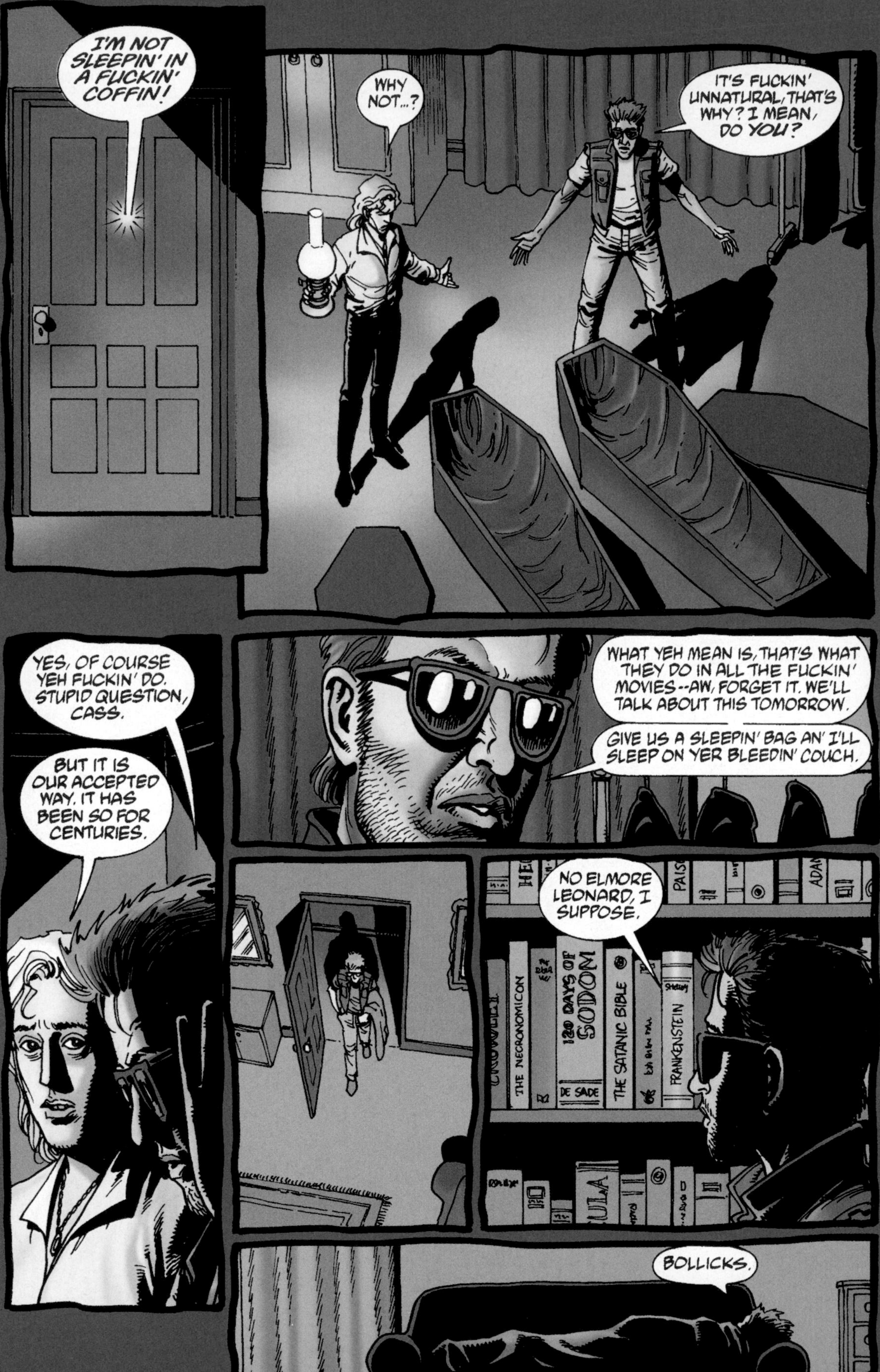
I'M NOT SLEEPIN' IN A FUCKIN' COFFIN!
WHY NOT...?
IT'S FUCKIN' UNNATURAL, THAT'S WHY? I MEAN, DO YOU?
YES, OF COURSE YEH FUCKIN' DO. STUPID QUESTION, CASS.
BUT IT IS OUR ACCEPTED WAY. IT HAS BEEN SO FOR CENTURIES.
WHAT YEH MEAN IS, THAT'S WHAT THEY DO IN ALL THE FUCKIN' MOVIES --AW, FORGET IT. WE'LL TALK ABOUT THIS TOMORROW.
GIVE US A SLEEPIN' BAG AN' I'LL SLEEP ON YER BLEEDIN' COUCH.
NO ELMORE LEONARD, I SUPPOSE.
THE NECRONOMICON
120 DAYS OF SODOM
DE SADE
THE SATANIC BIBLE
FRANKENSTEIN
BOLLICKS.

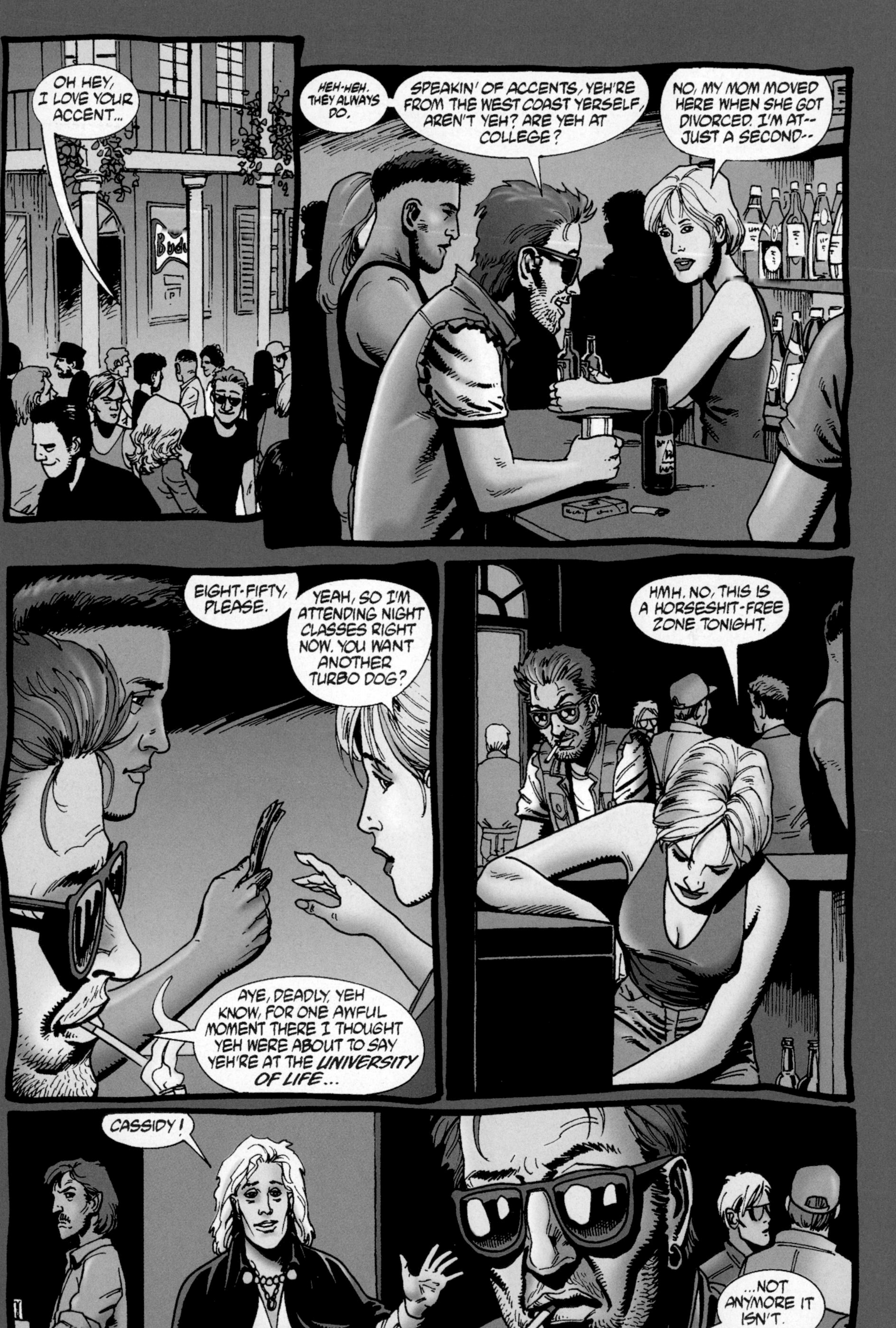
OH HEY, I LOVE YOUR ACCENT...
HEH-HEH. THEY ALWAYS DO.
SPEAKIN' OF ACCENTS, YEH'RE FROM THE WEST COAST YERSELF, AREN'T YEH? ARE YEH AT COLLEGE?
NO, MY MOM MOVED HERE WHEN SHE GOT DIVORCED. I'M AT-- JUST A SECOND--
EIGHT-FIFTY, PLEASE.
YEAH, SO I'M ATTENDING NIGHT CLASSES RIGHT NOW. YOU WANT ANOTHER TURBO DOG?
AYE, DEADLY. YEH KNOW, FOR ONE AWFUL MOMENT THERE I THOUGHT YEH WERE ABOUT TO SAY YEH'RE AT THE UNIVERSITY OF LIFE...
HMH. NO, THIS IS A HORSESHIT-FREE ZONE TONIGHT.
CASSIDY!
...NOT ANYMORE IT ISN'T.

I THOUGHT I'D LOST YOU IN THE CROWD, MY FRIEND.

AYE...LISTEN, YEH COULDN'T FUCK OFF AN' DO IT AGAIN, COULD YEH? CAUSE--

COME. WE MUST AWAY.

THIS IS NO PLACE FOR THE LIKES OF US. WE ARE EXPECTED AT A GATHERING BENEATH THE STREETS, AND THERE WE MUST HASTEN, AND GO DOWN.

er...

THERE OUR FAMILIARS AWAIT US, FAR AWAY FROM PRYING EYES. THERE WE MAY COMMIT THE DARK AND SECRET ACTS THAT OUR KIND LONG FOR, SAFE FROM HINDRANCE AND PERSECUTION.

COME, MY FRIEND! THE NIGHT AWAITS!

IT'S...IT'S NOT WHAT YEH THINK...

I LIKE HIS BATMAN OUTFIT.

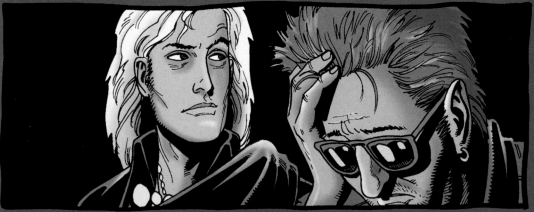

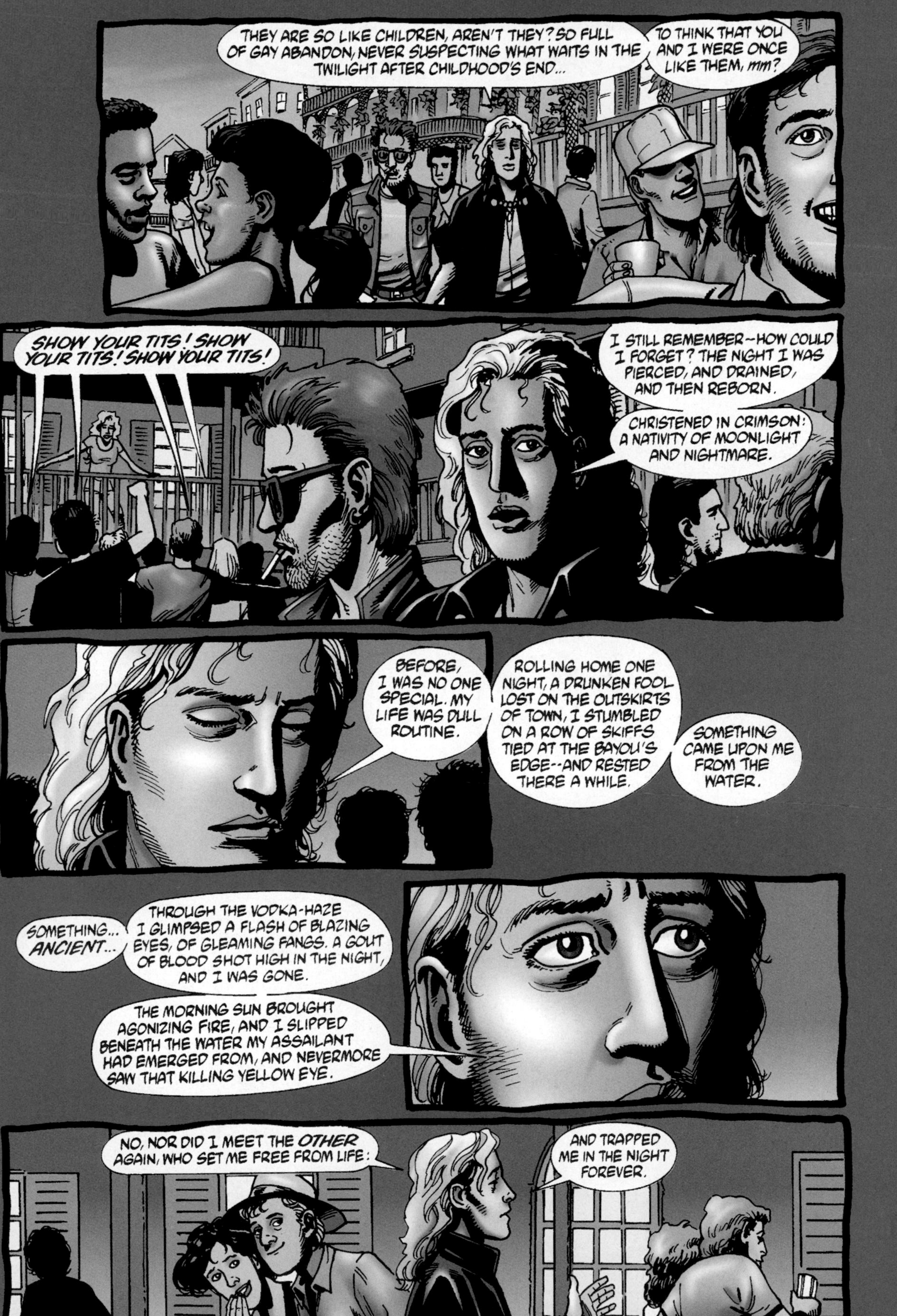
THEY ARE SO LIKE CHILDREN, AREN'T THEY? SO FULL OF GAY ABANDON, NEVER SUSPECTING WHAT WAITS IN THE TWILIGHT AFTER CHILDHOOD'S END...
TO THINK THAT YOU AND I WERE ONCE LIKE THEM, mm?
SHOW YOUR TITS! SHOW YOUR TITS! SHOW YOUR TITS!
I STILL REMEMBER--HOW COULD I FORGET? THE NIGHT I WAS PIERCED, AND DRAINED, AND THEN REBORN.
CHRISTENED IN CRIMSON: A NATIVITY OF MOONLIGHT AND NIGHTMARE.
BEFORE, I WAS NO ONE SPECIAL. MY LIFE WAS DULL ROUTINE.
ROLLING HOME ONE NIGHT, A DRUNKEN FOOL LOST ON THE OUTSKIRTS OF TOWN, I STUMBLED ON A ROW OF SKIFFS TIED AT THE BAYOU'S EDGE--AND RESTED THERE A WHILE.
SOMETHING CAME UPON ME FROM THE WATER.
SOMETHING... ANCIENT...
THROUGH THE VODKA-HAZE I GLIMPSED A FLASH OF BLAZING EYES, OF GLEAMING FANGS. A GOUT OF BLOOD SHOT HIGH IN THE NIGHT, AND I WAS GONE.
THE MORNING SUN BROUGHT AGONIZING FIRE, AND I SLIPPED BENEATH THE WATER MY ASSAILANT HAD EMERGED FROM, AND NEVERMORE SAW THAT KILLING YELLOW EYE.
NO, NOR DID I MEET THE OTHER AGAIN, WHO SET ME FREE FROM LIFE:
AND TRAPPED ME IN THE NIGHT FOREVER.

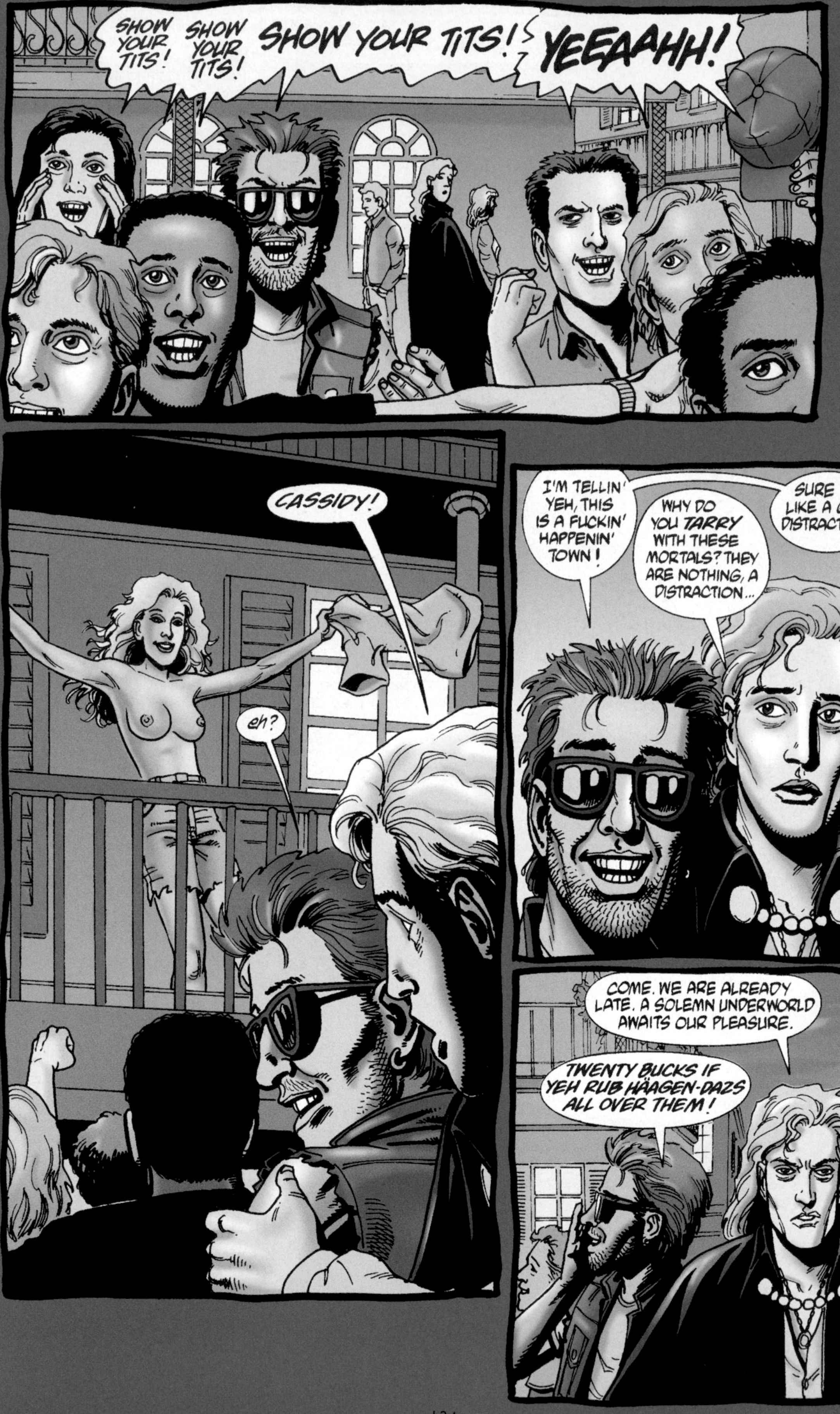
SHOW YOUR TITS!
SHOW YOUR TITS!
SHOW YOUR TITS!
YEEAAHH!
CASSIDY!
eh?
I'M TELLIN' YEH, THIS IS A FUCKIN' HAPPENIN' TOWN!
WHY DO YOU TARRY WITH THESE MORTALS? THEY ARE NOTHING, A DISTRACTION...
SURE I LIKE A GOOD DISTRACTION!
COME. WE ARE ALREADY LATE. A SOLEMN UNDERWORLD AWAITS OUR PLEASURE.
TWENTY BUCKS IF YEH RUB HÄAGEN-DAZS ALL OVER THEM!

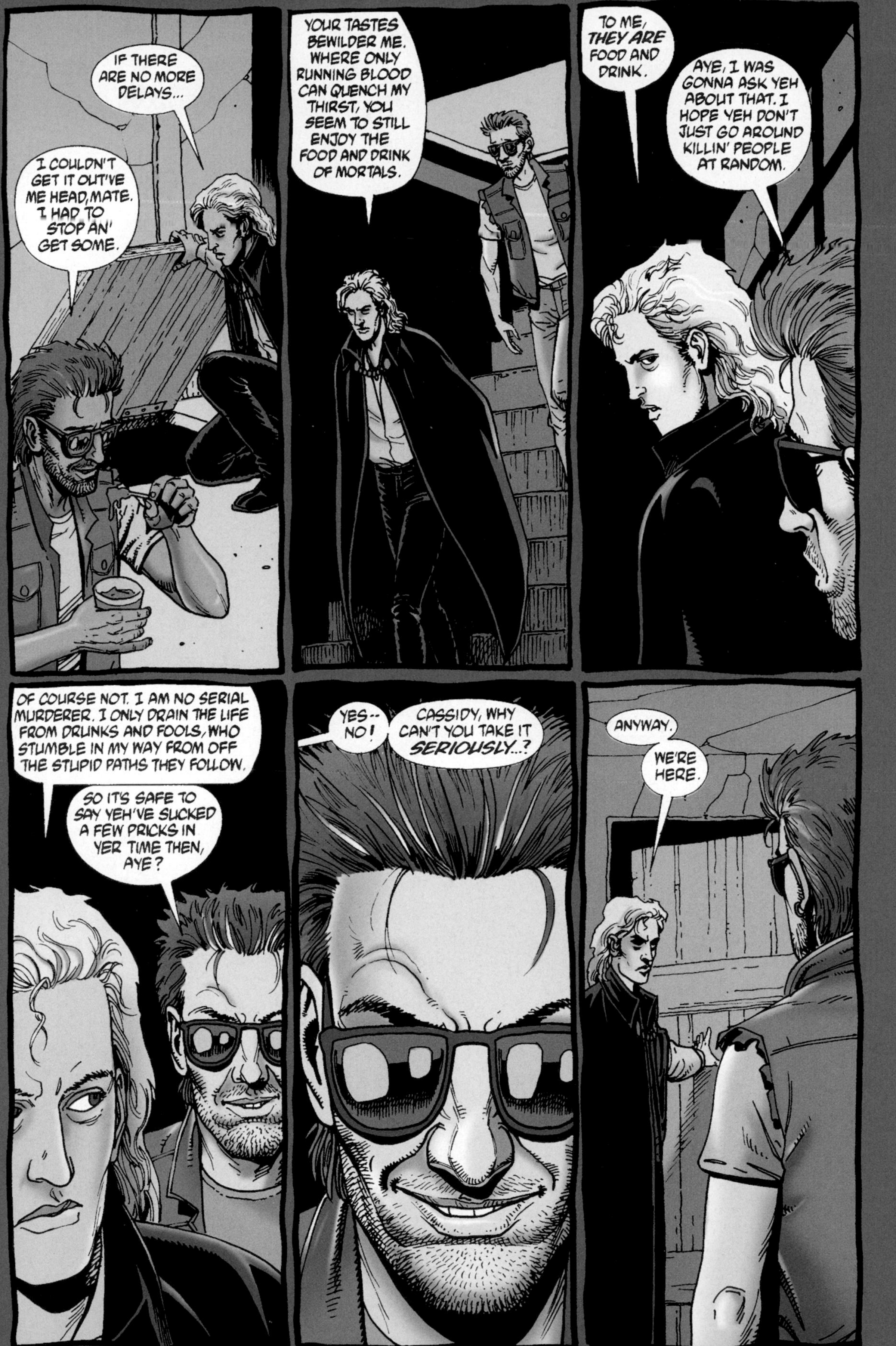
IF THERE ARE NO MORE DELAYS...
I COULDN'T GET IT OUT'VE ME HEAD, MATE. I HAD TO STOP AN' GET SOME.
YOUR TASTES BEWILDER ME. WHERE ONLY RUNNING BLOOD CAN QUENCH MY THIRST, YOU SEEM TO STILL ENJOY THE FOOD AND DRINK OF MORTALS.
TO ME, THEY ARE FOOD AND DRINK.
AYE, I WAS GONNA ASK YEH ABOUT THAT. I HOPE YEH DON'T JUST GO AROUND KILLIN' PEOPLE AT RANDOM.
OF COURSE NOT. I AM NO SERIAL MURDERER. I ONLY DRAIN THE LIFE FROM DRUNKS AND FOOLS, WHO STUMBLE IN MY WAY FROM OFF THE STUPID PATHS THEY FOLLOW.
SO IT'S SAFE TO SAY YEH'VE SUCKED A FEW PRICKS IN YER TIME THEN, AYE?
YES-- NO!
CASSIDY, WHY CAN'T YOU TAKE IT SERIOUSLY..?
ANYWAY.
WE'RE HERE.

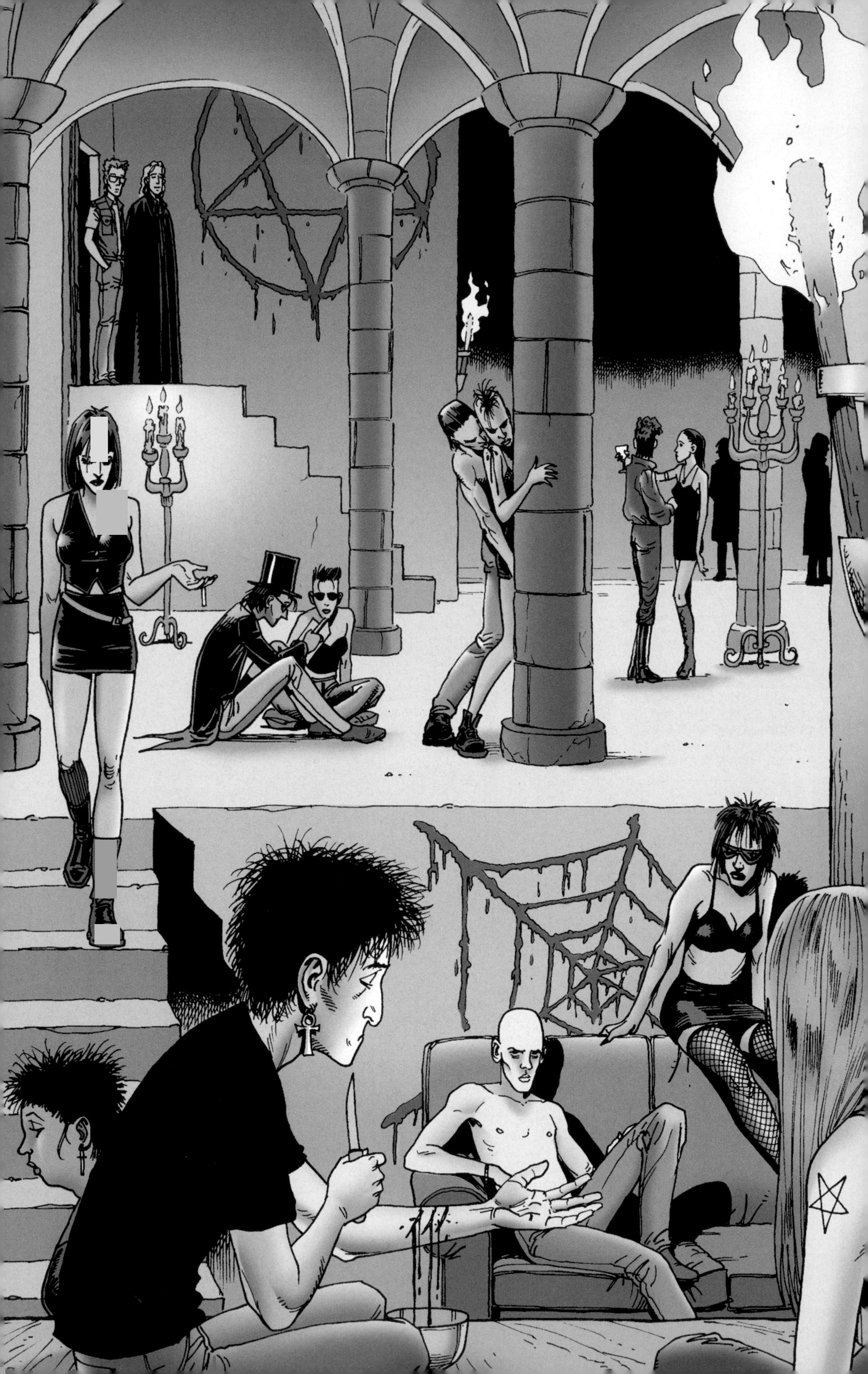

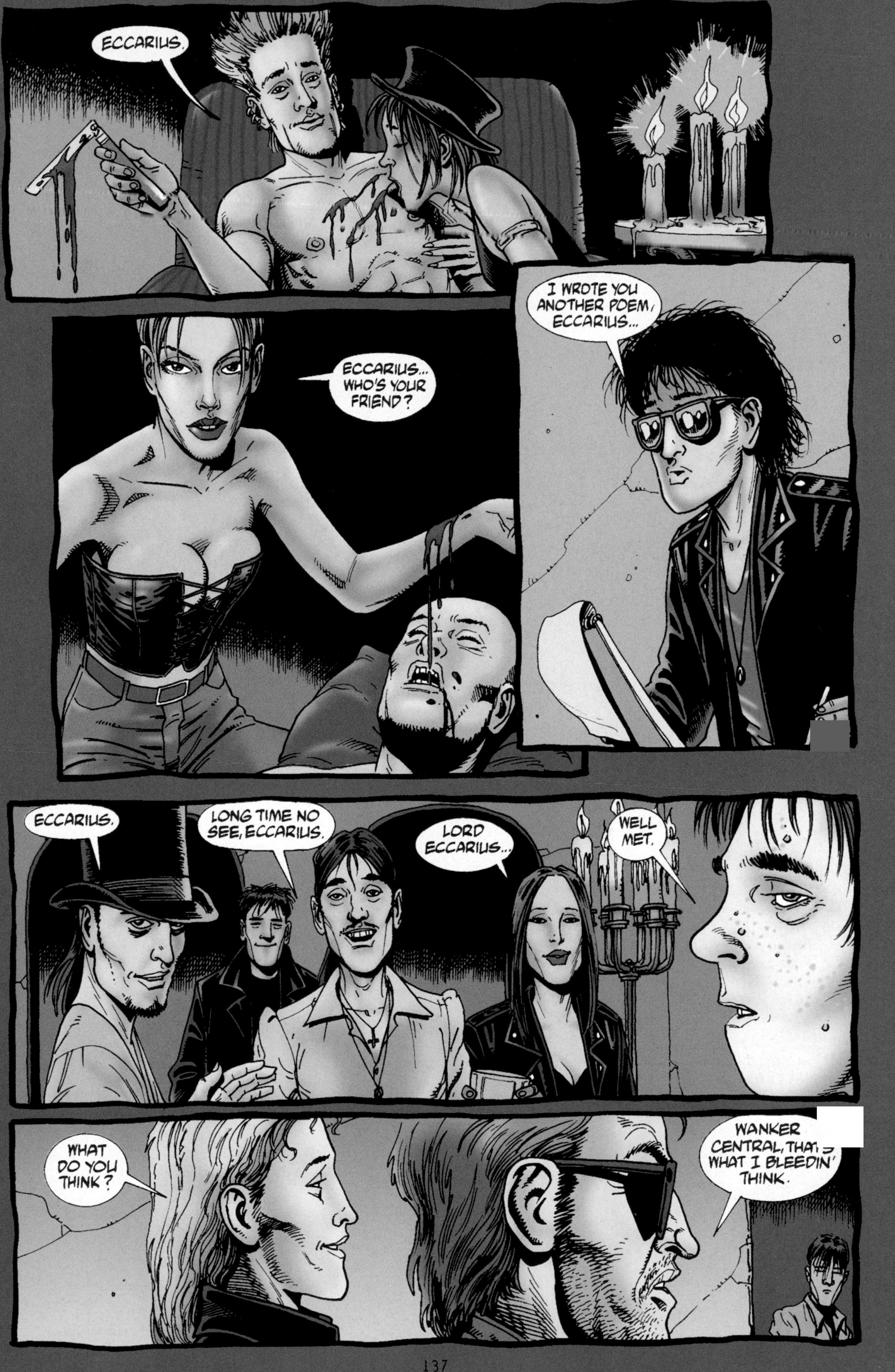
ECCARIUS.
ECCARIUS... WHO'S YOUR FRIEND?
I WROTE YOU ANOTHER POEM, ECCARIUS...
ECCARIUS.
LONG TIME NO SEE, ECCARIUS.
LORD ECCARIUS...
WELL MET.
WHAT DO YOU THINK?
WANKER CENTRAL, THAT
WHAT I BLEEDIN' THINK.

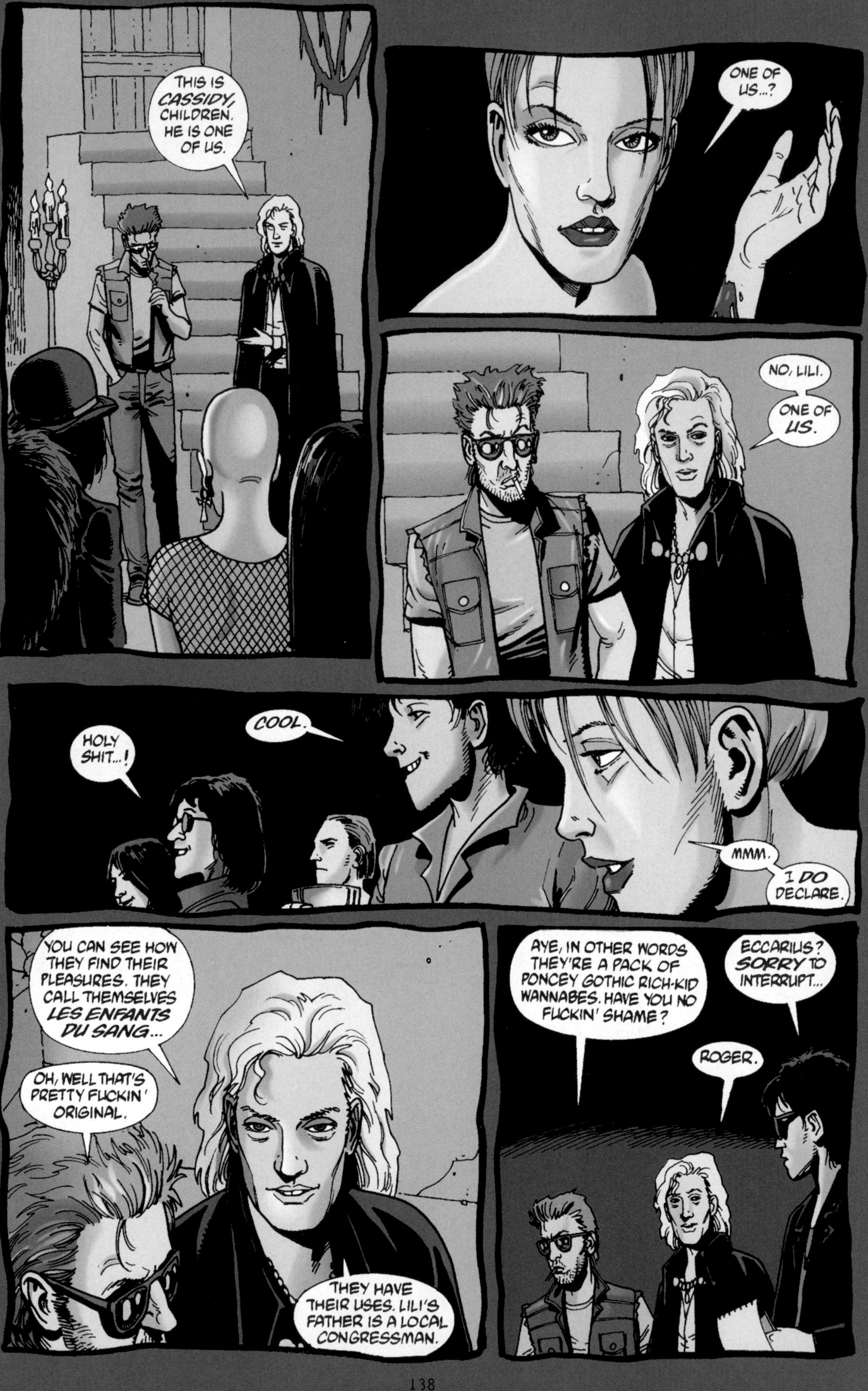

THIS IS CASSIDY, CHILDREN. HE IS ONE OF US.
ONE OF US...?
NO, LILI.
ONE OF US.
HOLY SHIT...!
COOL.
MMM. I DO DECLARE.
YOU CAN SEE HOW THEY FIND THEIR PLEASURES. THEY CALL THEMSELVES LES ENFANTS DU SANG...
OH, WELL THAT'S PRETTY FUCKIN' ORIGINAL.
THEY HAVE THEIR USES. LILI'S FATHER IS A LOCAL CONGRESSMAN.
AYE, IN OTHER WORDS THEY'RE A PACK OF PONCEY GOTHIC RICH-KID WANNABES. HAVE YOU NO FUCKIN' SHAME?
ECCARIUS? SORRY TO INTERRUPT...
ROGER.

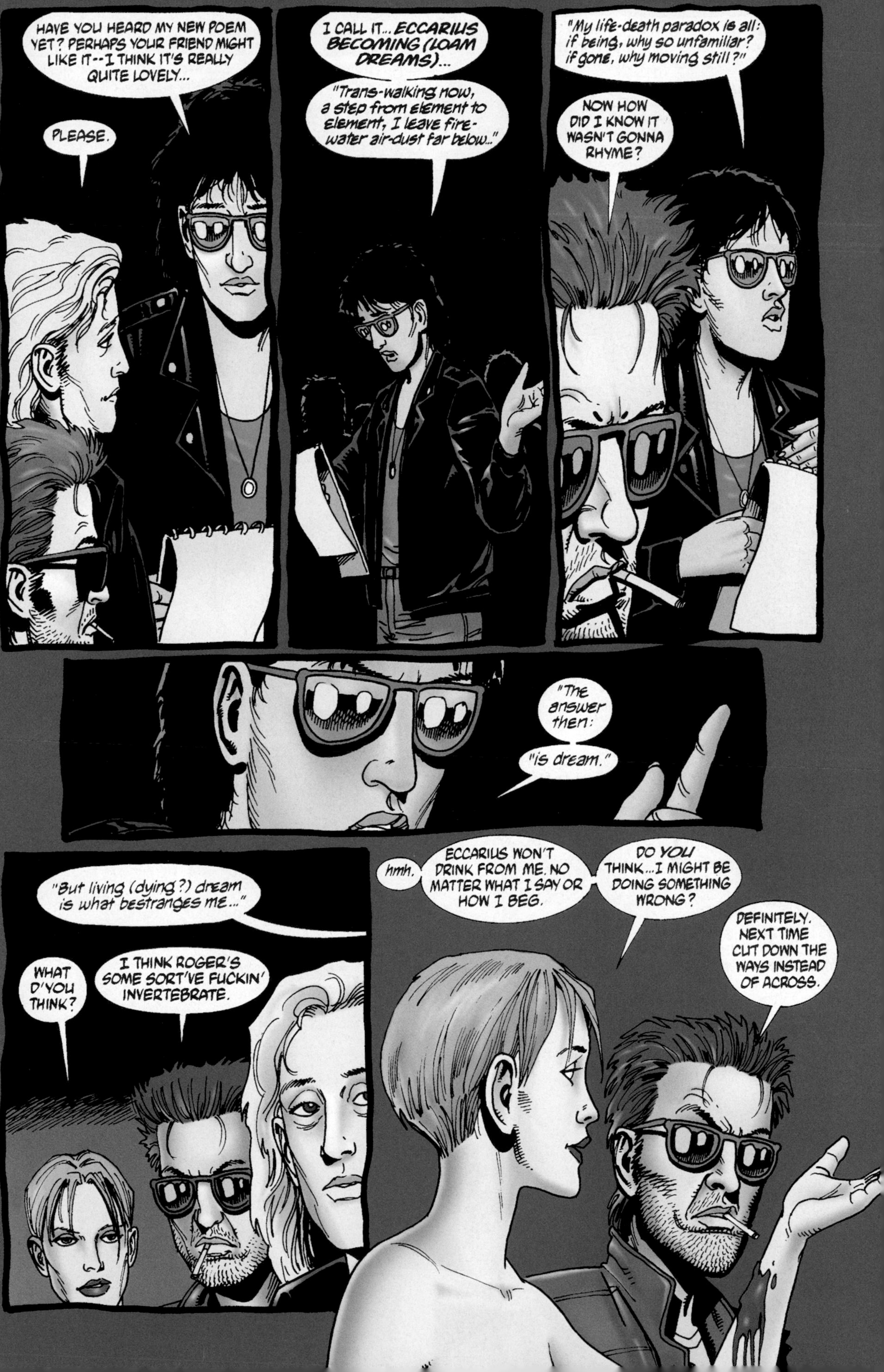
HAVE YOU HEARD MY NEW POEM YET? PERHAPS YOUR FRIEND MIGHT LIKE IT--I THINK IT'S REALLY QUITE LOVELY...
PLEASE.
I CALL IT... ECCARIUS BECOMING (LOAM DREAMS)...
"Trans-walking now, a step from element to element, I leave fire-water air-dust far below..."
"My life-death paradox is all: if being, why so unfamiliar? if gone, why moving still?"
NOW HOW DID I KNOW IT WASN'T GONNA RHYME?
"The answer then:
"is dream."
"But living (dying?) dream is what bestranges me..."
WHAT D'YOU THINK?
I THINK ROGER'S SOME SORT'VE FUCKIN' INVERTEBRATE.
hmh.
ECCARIUS WON'T DRINK FROM ME. NO MATTER WHAT I SAY OR HOW I BEG.
DO YOU THINK... I MIGHT BE DOING SOMETHING WRONG?
DEFINITELY. NEXT TIME CUT DOWN THE WAYS INSTEAD OF ACROSS.

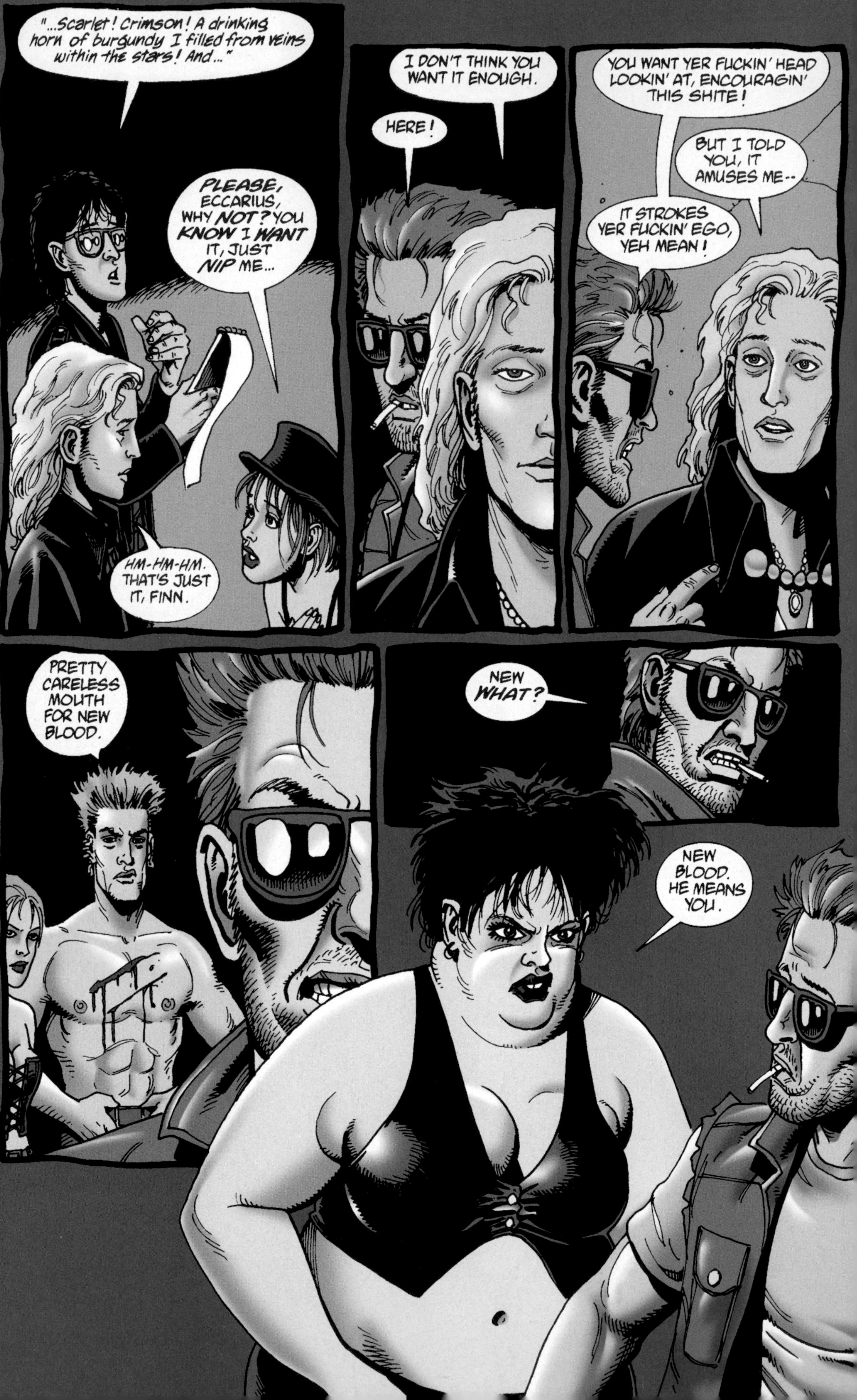
"...Scarlet! Crimson! A drinking horn of burgundy I filled from veins within the stars! And..."
PLEASE, ECCARIUS, WHY NOT? YOU KNOW I WANT IT, JUST NIP ME...
HM-HM-HM. THAT'S JUST IT, FINN.
I DON'T THINK YOU WANT IT ENOUGH.
HERE!
YOU WANT YER FUCKIN' HEAD LOOKIN' AT, ENCOURAGIN' THIS SHITE!
BUT I TOLD YOU, IT AMUSES ME--
IT STROKES YER FUCKIN' EGO, YEH MEAN!
PRETTY CARELESS MOUTH FOR NEW BLOOD.
NEW WHAT?
NEW BLOOD. HE MEANS YOU.

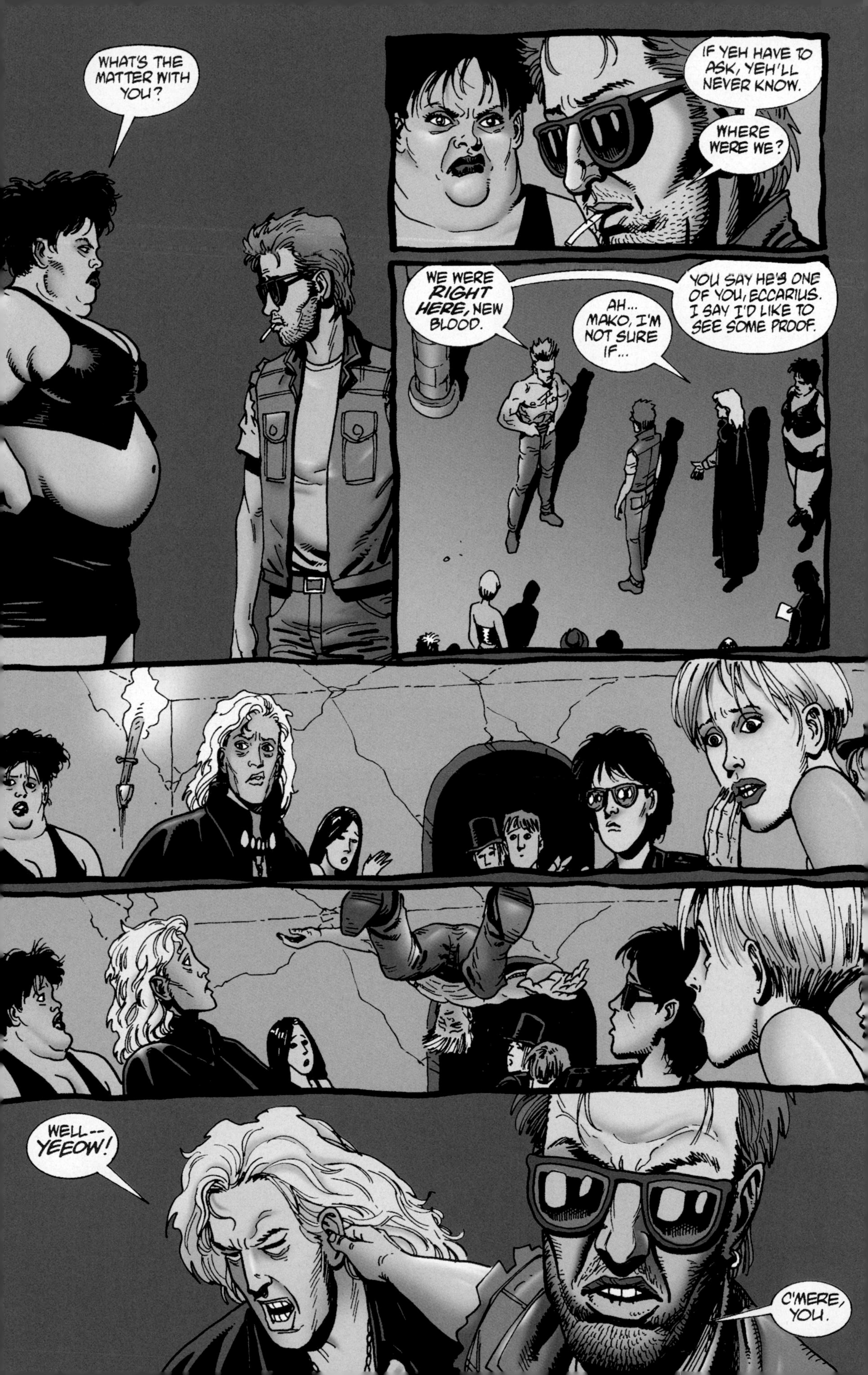
WHAT'S THE MATTER WITH YOU?
IF YEH HAVE TO ASK, YEH'LL NEVER KNOW.
WHERE WERE WE?
WE WERE *RIGHT HERE*, NEW BLOOD.
YOU SAY HE'S ONE OF YOU, ECCARIUS. I SAY I'D LIKE TO SEE SOME PROOF.
AH... MAKO, I'M NOT SURE IF...
WELL-- *YEEOW!*
C'MERE, YOU.

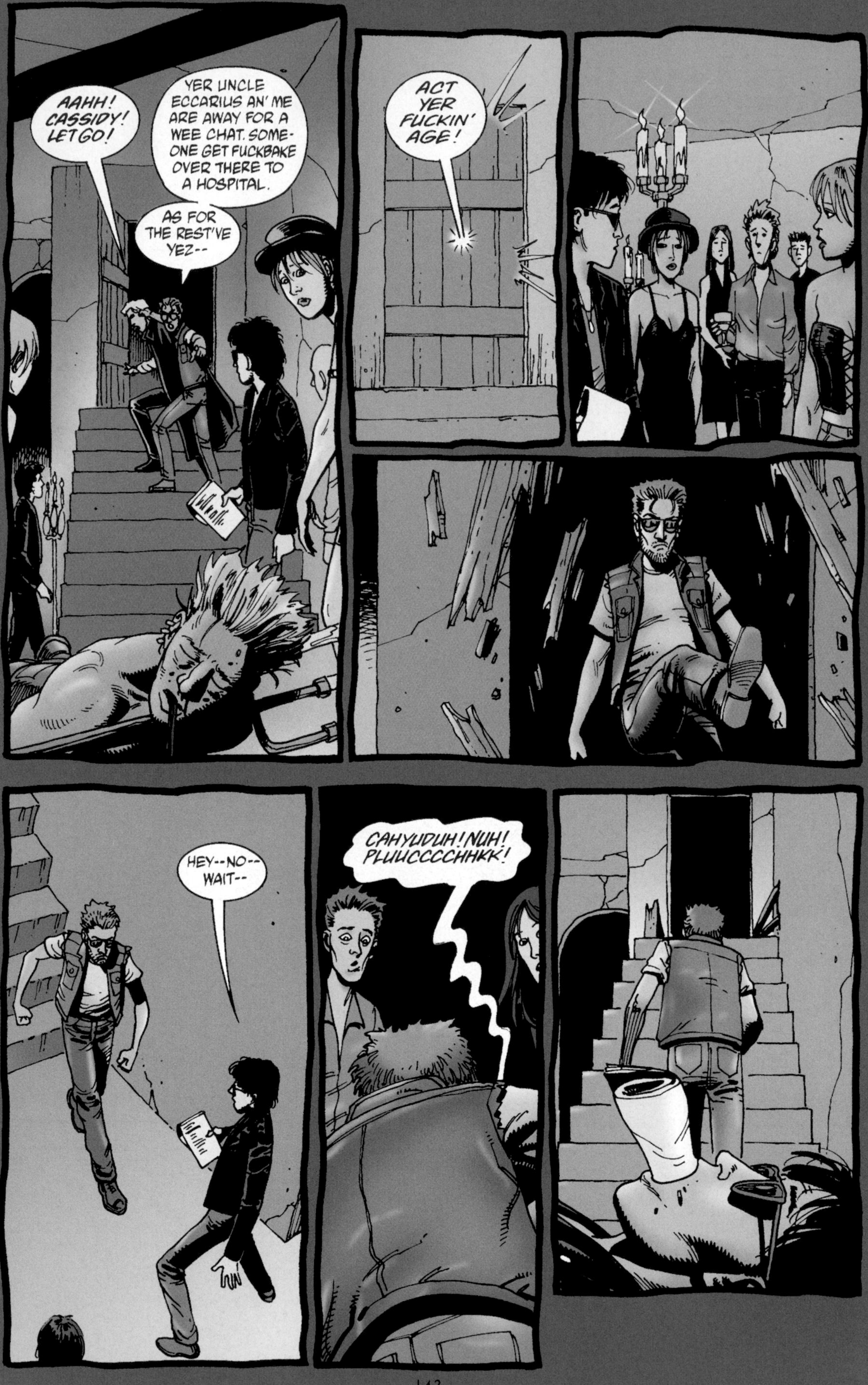
AAHH! CASSIDY! LETGO!
YER UNCLE ECCARIUS AN' ME ARE AWAY FOR A WEE CHAT. SOME-ONE GET FUCKBAKE OVER THERE TO A HOSPITAL.
AS FOR THE REST'VE YEZ--
ACT YER FUCKIN' AGE!
HEY--NO--WAIT--
CAHYUDUH! NUH! PLUUCCCCHHKK!

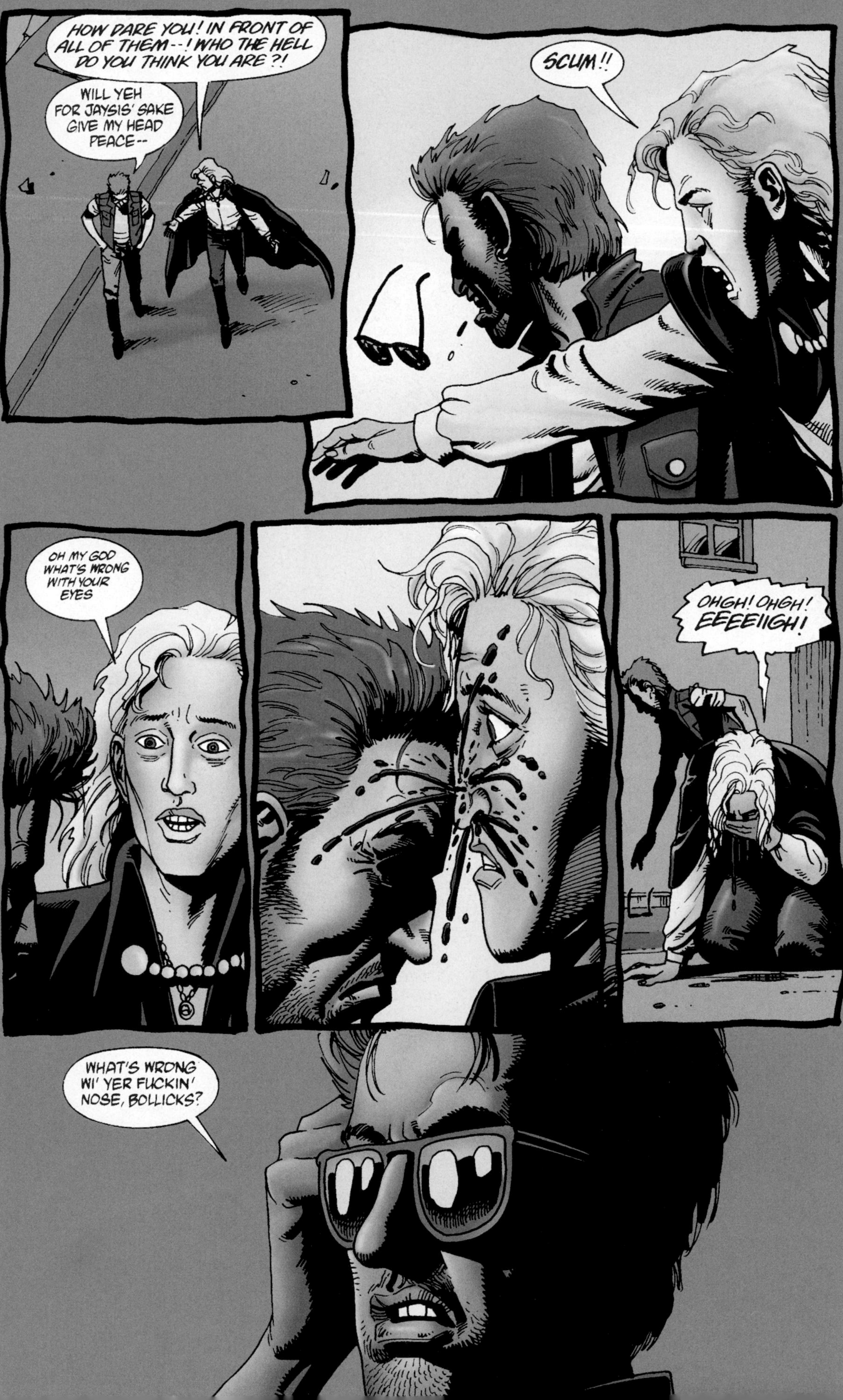
HOW DARE YOU! IN FRONT OF ALL OF THEM--! WHO THE HELL DO YOU THINK YOU ARE?!
WILL YEH FOR JAYSIS' SAKE GIVE MY HEAD PEACE--
SCUM!!
OH MY GOD WHAT'S WRONG WITH YOUR EYES
OHGH! OHGH! EEEEIIGH!
WHAT'S WRONG WI' YER FUCKIN' NOSE, BOLLICKS?

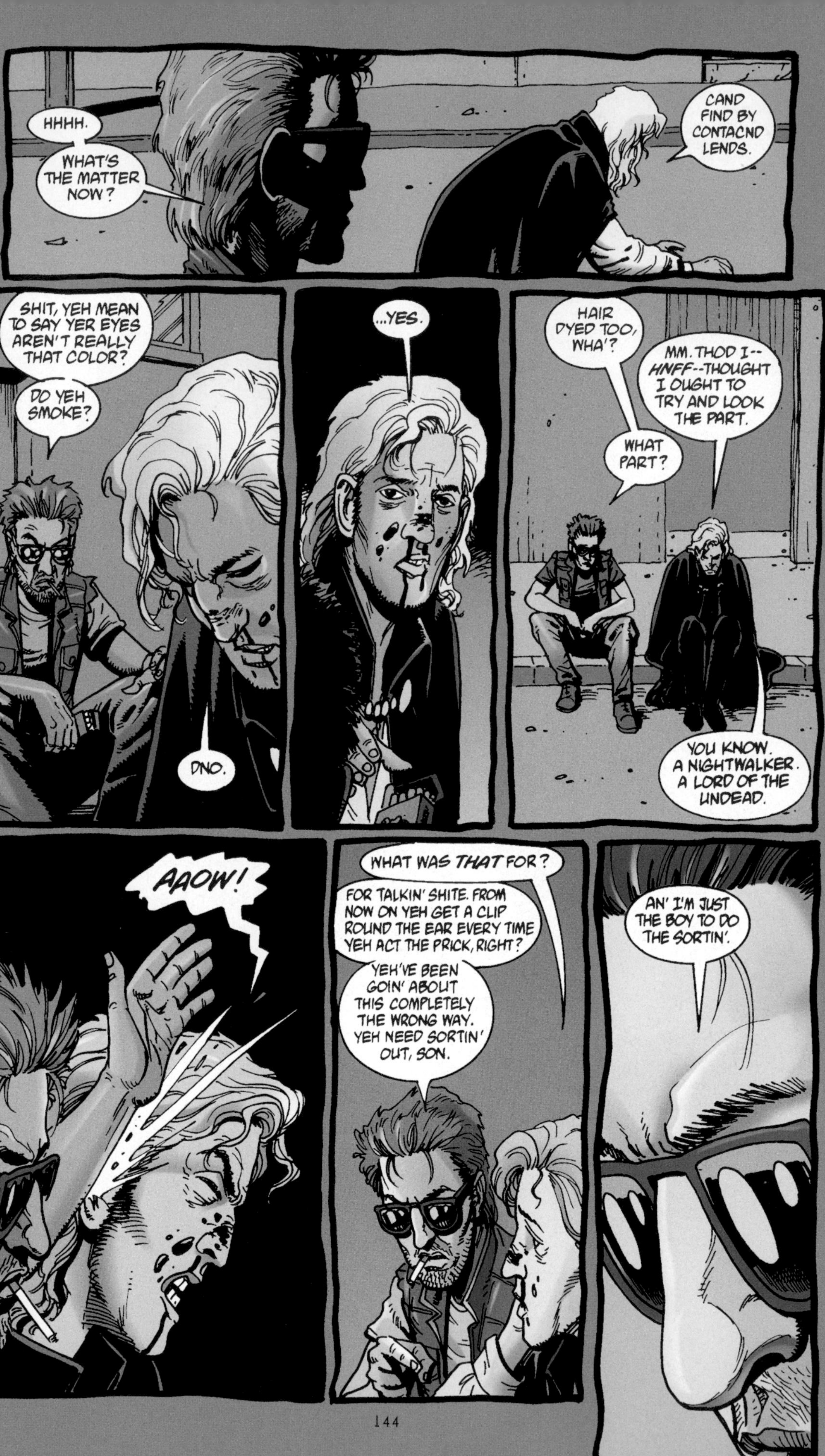

HHHH.
WHAT'S THE MATTER NOW?
CAND FIND BY CONTACND LENDS.
SHIT, YEH MEAN TO SAY YER EYES AREN'T REALLY THAT COLOR?
DO YEH SMOKE?
DNO.
...YES.
HAIR DYED TOO, WHA'?
MM. THOD I-- *HNFF*--THOUGHT I OUGHT TO TRY AND LOOK THE PART.
WHAT PART?
YOU KNOW. A NIGHTWALKER. A LORD OF THE UNDEAD.
AAOW!
WHAT WAS *THAT* FOR?
FOR TALKIN' SHITE. FROM NOW ON YEH GET A CLIP ROUND THE EAR EVERY TIME YEH ACT THE PRICK, RIGHT?
YEH'VE BEEN GOIN' ABOUT THIS COMPLETELY THE WRONG WAY. YEH NEED SORTIN' OUT, SON.
AN' I'M JUST THE BOY TO DO THE SORTIN'.

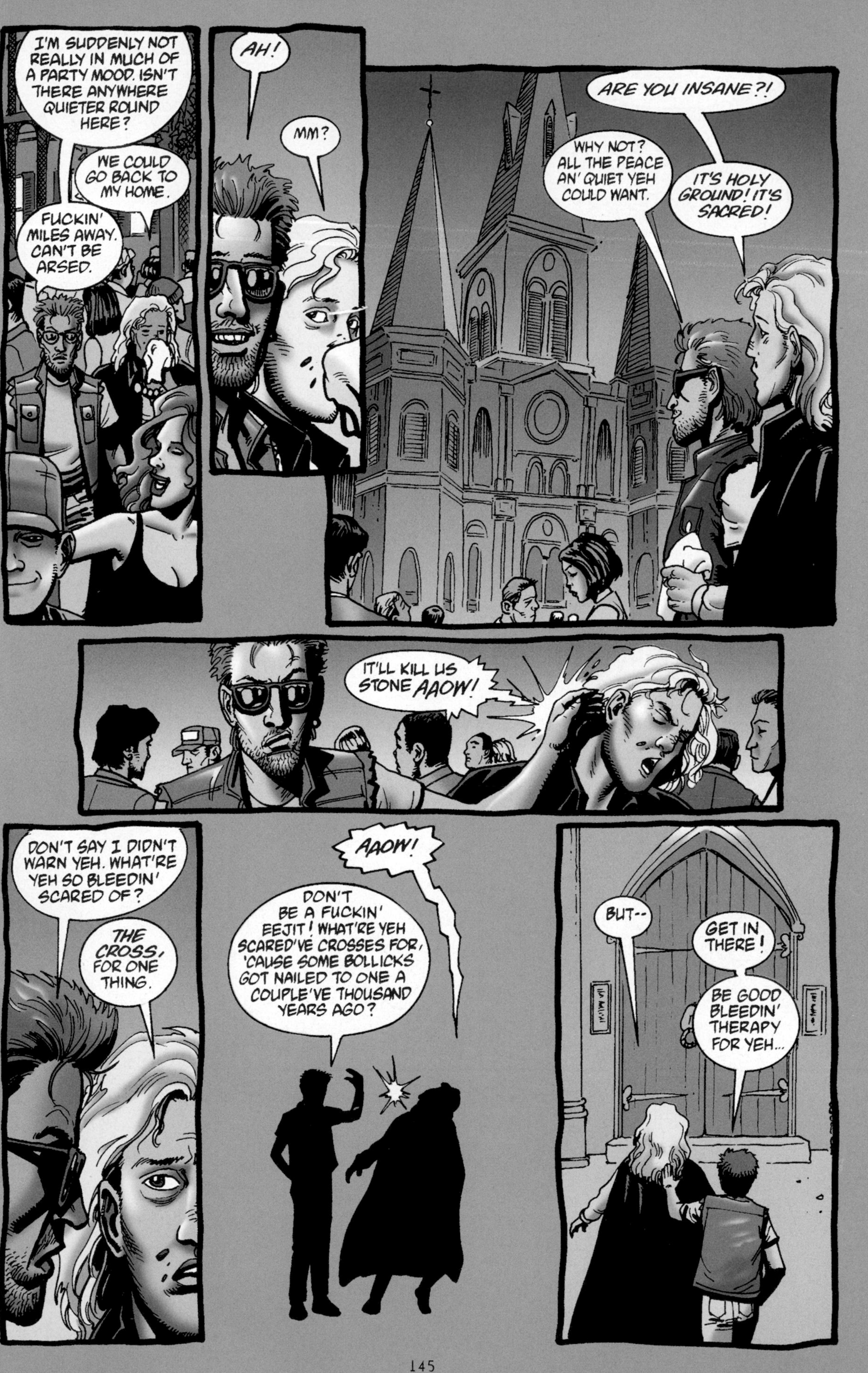
I'M SUDDENLY NOT REALLY IN MUCH OF A PARTY MOOD. ISN'T THERE ANYWHERE QUIETER ROUND HERE?
WE COULD GO BACK TO MY HOME.
FUCKIN' MILES AWAY. CAN'T BE ARSED.
AH!
MM?
ARE YOU INSANE?!
WHY NOT? ALL THE PEACE AN' QUIET YEH COULD WANT.
IT'S HOLY GROUND! IT'S SACRED!
IT'LL KILL US STONE AAOW!
DON'T SAY I DIDN'T WARN YEH. WHAT'RE YEH SO BLEEDIN' SCARED OF?
THE CROSS, FOR ONE THING.
AAOW!
DON'T BE A FUCKIN' EEJIT! WHAT'RE YEH SCARED'VE CROSSES FOR, 'CAUSE SOME BOLLICKS GOT NAILED TO ONE A COUPLE'VE THOUSAND YEARS AGO?
BUT--
GET IN THERE!
BE GOOD BLEEDIN' THERAPY FOR YEH...

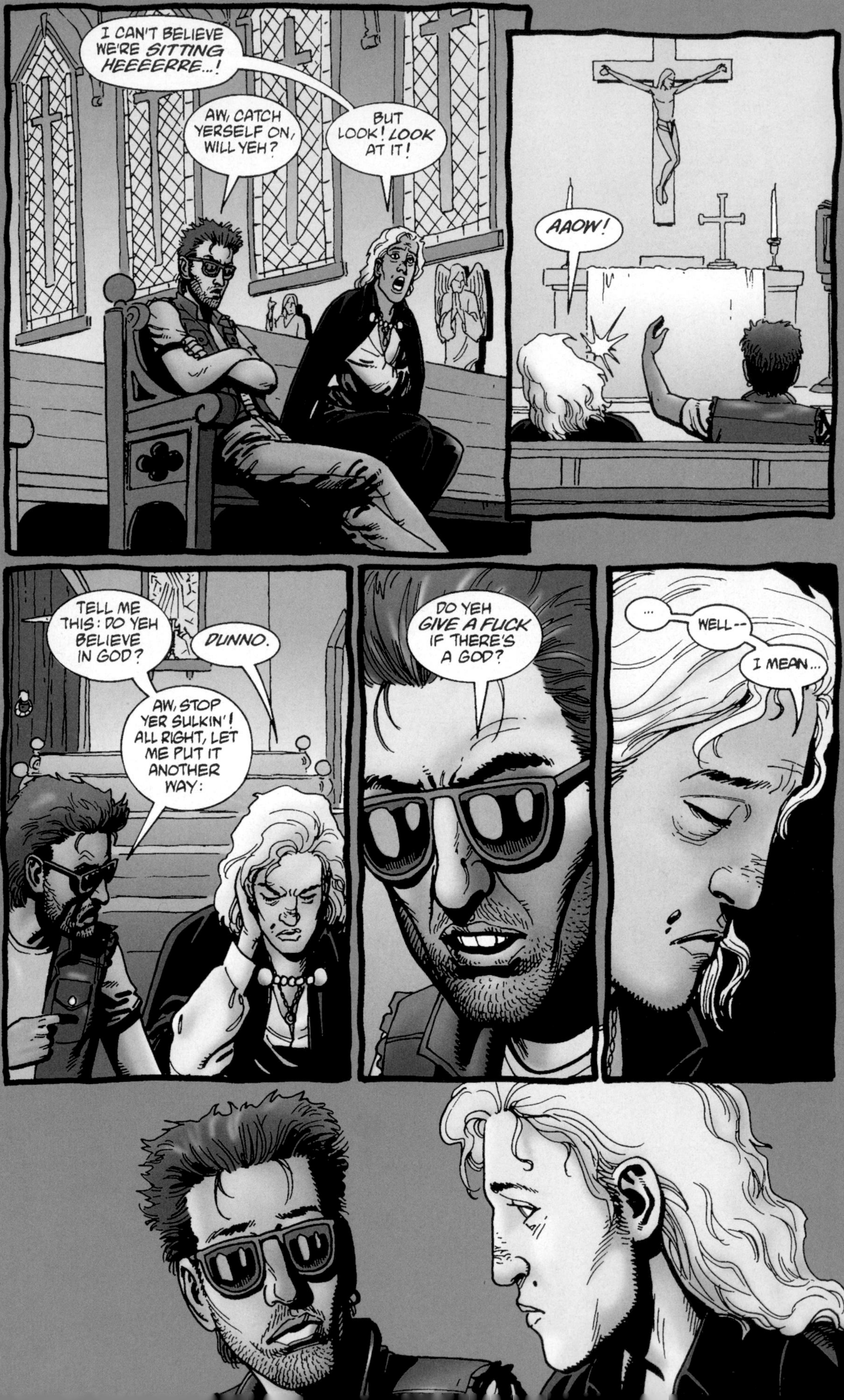
I CAN'T BELIEVE WE'RE *SITTING HEEEERRE*...!
AW, CATCH YERSELF ON, WILL YEH?
BUT LOOK! *LOOK* AT IT!
*AAOW!*
TELL ME THIS: DO YEH BELIEVE IN GOD?
*DUNNO.*
AW, STOP YER SULKIN'! ALL RIGHT, LET ME PUT IT ANOTHER WAY:
DO YEH *GIVE A FUCK* IF THERE'S A GOD?
...
WELL--
I MEAN...

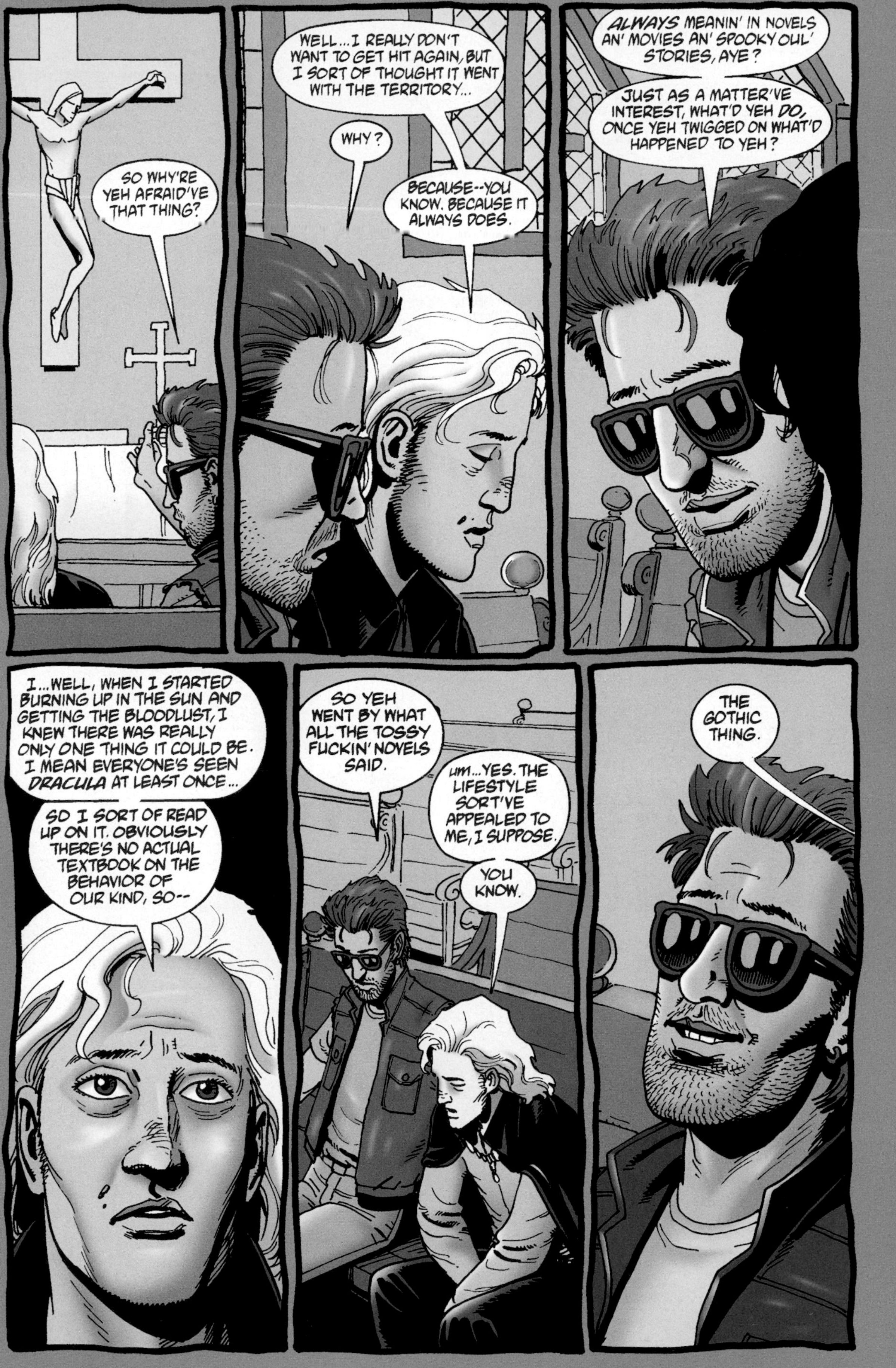
SO WHY'RE YEH AFRAID'VE THAT THING?
WELL...I REALLY DON'T WANT TO GET HIT AGAIN, BUT I SORT OF THOUGHT IT WENT WITH THE TERRITORY...
WHY?
BECAUSE--YOU KNOW. BECAUSE IT ALWAYS DOES.
ALWAYS MEANIN' IN NOVELS AN' MOVIES AN' SPOOKY OUL' STORIES, AYE?
JUST AS A MATTER'VE INTEREST, WHAT'D YEH DO, ONCE YEH TWIGGED ON WHAT'D HAPPENED TO YEH?
I...WELL, WHEN I STARTED BURNING UP IN THE SUN AND GETTING THE BLOODLUST, I KNEW THERE WAS REALLY ONLY ONE THING IT COULD BE. I MEAN EVERYONE'S SEEN DRACULA AT LEAST ONCE...
SO I SORT OF READ UP ON IT. OBVIOUSLY THERE'S NO ACTUAL TEXTBOOK ON THE BEHAVIOR OF OUR KIND, SO--
SO YEH WENT BY WHAT ALL THE TOSSY FUCKIN' NOVELS SAID.
UM...YES. THE LIFESTYLE SORT'VE APPEALED TO ME, I SUPPOSE.
YOU KNOW.
THE GOTHIC THING.

HAVE YEH EVER HAD A STAKE THROUGH THE HEART?

NO!

I HAVE. IT FUCKIN' HURTS. D'YEH EAT GARLIC?

NO...

I LOVE THE STUFF. THERE'S A PLACE IN SAN FRANCISCO, *THE STINKING ROSE,* THEY COOK EVERYTHING WITH IT. WHAT ABOUT HOLY WATER?

WHAT ABOUT IT?

EXACTLY.

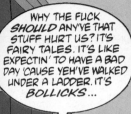

WHY THE FUCK *SHOULD* ANY'VE THAT STUFF HURT US? IT'S FAIRY TALES. IT'S LIKE EXPECTIN' TO HAVE A BAD DAY 'CAUSE YEH'VE WALKED UNDER A LADDER. IT'S *BOLLICKS...*

DID YEH EVER TRY JUMPIN' OFF A ROOF AN' TURNIN' INTO A BAT? OR RIDIN' MOON-BEAMS AS A CLOUD OF DUST?

I TRIED THE BAT THING ONCE.

BROKE BOTH MY FUCKING LEGS.

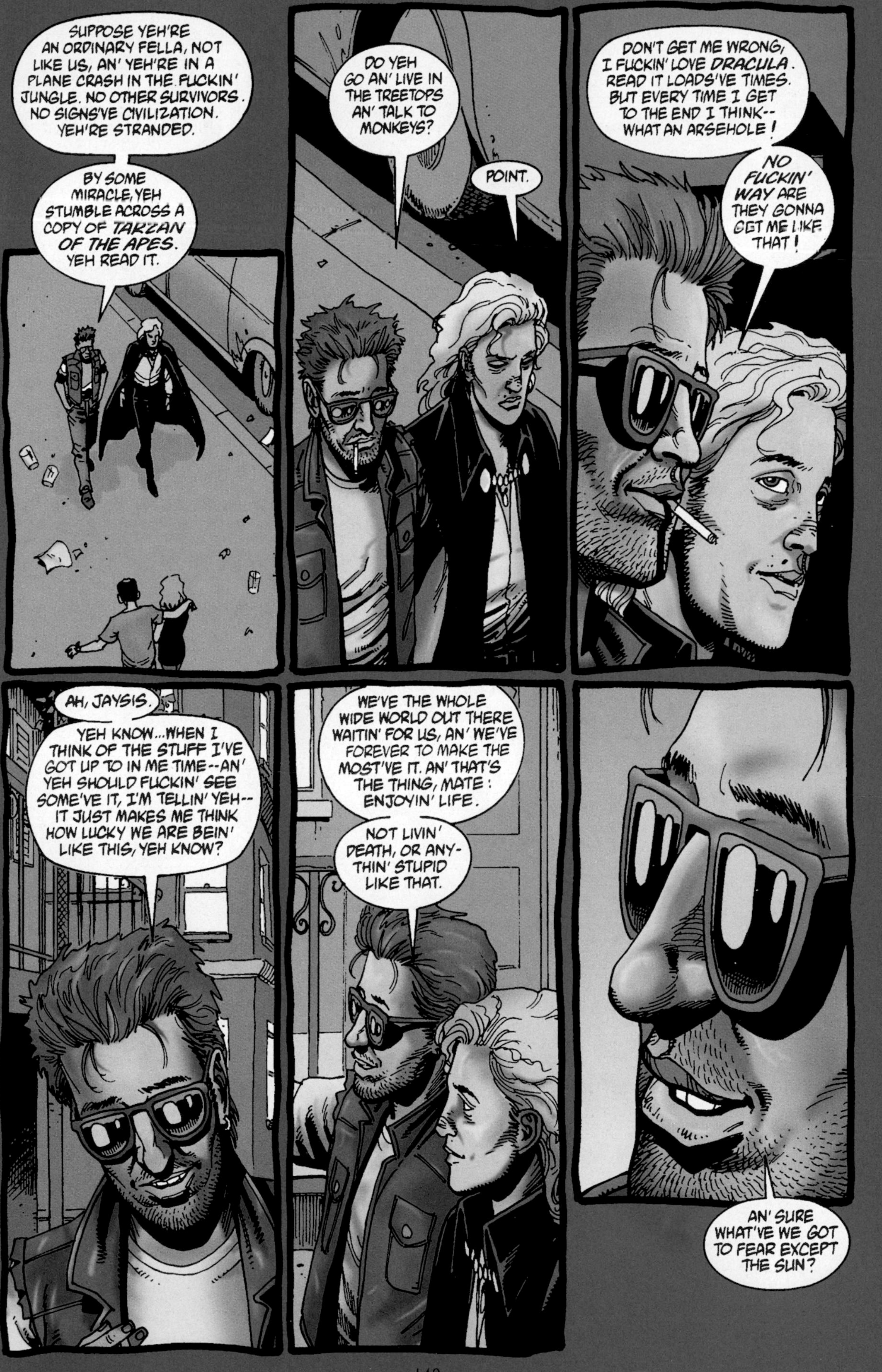
SUPPOSE YEH'RE AN ORDINARY FELLA, NOT LIKE US, AN' YEH'RE IN A PLANE CRASH IN THE FUCKIN' JUNGLE. NO OTHER SURVIVORS. NO SIGNS'VE CIVILIZATION. YEH'RE STRANDED.
BY SOME MIRACLE, YEH STUMBLE ACROSS A COPY OF TARZAN OF THE APES. YEH READ IT.
DO YEH GO AN' LIVE IN THE TREETOPS AN' TALK TO MONKEYS?
POINT.
DON'T GET ME WRONG, I FUCKIN' LOVE DRACULA. READ IT LOADS'VE TIMES. BUT EVERY TIME I GET TO THE END I THINK-- WHAT AN ARSEHOLE!
NO FUCKIN' WAY ARE THEY GONNA GET ME LIKE THAT!
AH, JAYSIS.
YEH KNOW...WHEN I THINK OF THE STUFF I'VE GOT UP TO IN ME TIME--AN' YEH SHOULD FUCKIN' SEE SOME'VE IT, I'M TELLIN' YEH-- IT JUST MAKES ME THINK HOW LUCKY WE ARE BEIN' LIKE THIS, YEH KNOW?
WE'VE THE WHOLE WIDE WORLD OUT THERE WAITIN' FOR US, AN' WE'VE FOREVER TO MAKE THE MOST'VE IT. AN' THAT'S THE THING, MATE: ENJOYIN' LIFE.
NOT LIVIN' DEATH, OR ANY-THIN' STUPID LIKE THAT.
AN' SURE WHAT'VE WE GOT TO FEAR EXCEPT THE SUN?

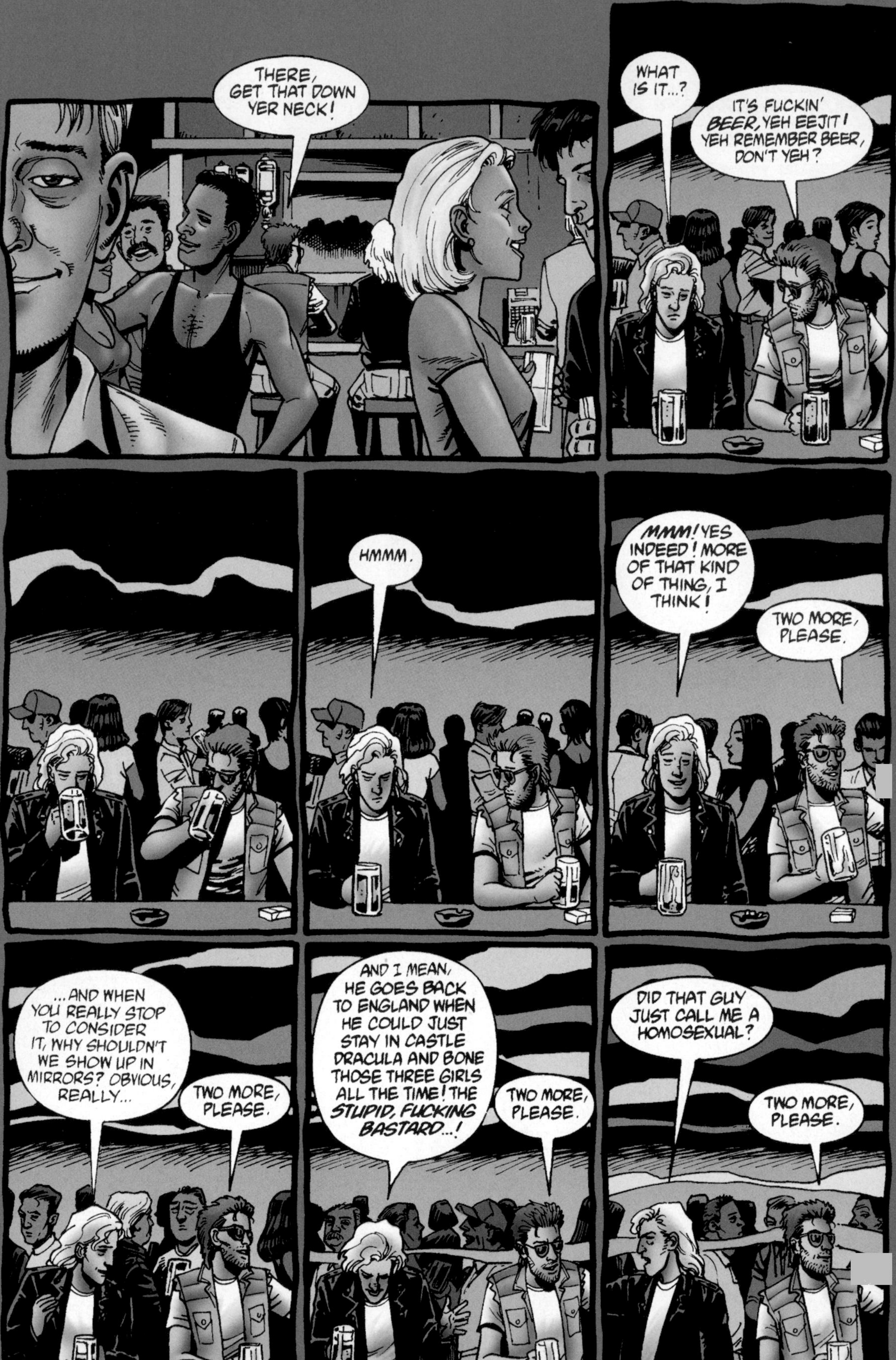
THERE, GET THAT DOWN YER NECK!
WHAT IS IT...?
IT'S FUCKIN' BEER, YEH EEJIT! YEH REMEMBER BEER, DON'T YEH?
HMMM.
MMM! YES INDEED! MORE OF THAT KIND OF THING, I THINK!
TWO MORE, PLEASE.
...AND WHEN YOU REALLY STOP TO CONSIDER IT, WHY SHOULDN'T WE SHOW UP IN MIRRORS? OBVIOUS, REALLY...
TWO MORE, PLEASE.
AND I MEAN, HE GOES BACK TO ENGLAND WHEN HE COULD JUST STAY IN CASTLE DRACULA AND BONE THOSE THREE GIRLS ALL THE TIME! THE STUPID, FUCKING BASTARD...!
TWO MORE, PLEASE.
DID THAT GUY JUST CALL ME A HOMOSEXUAL?
TWO MORE, PLEASE.

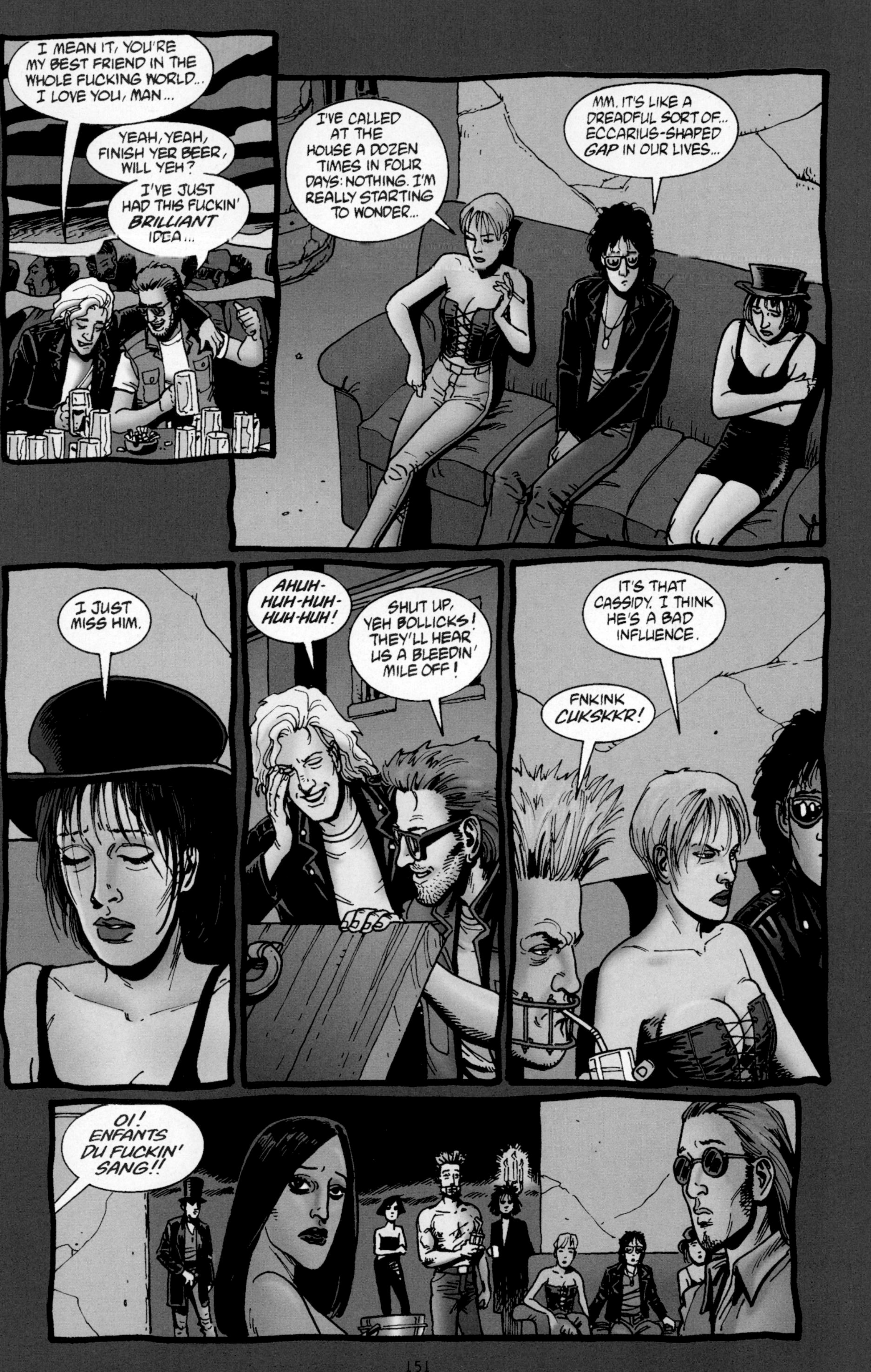
I MEAN IT, YOU'RE MY BEST FRIEND IN THE WHOLE FUCKING WORLD... I LOVE YOU, MAN...
YEAH, YEAH, FINISH YER BEER, WILL YEH?
I'VE JUST HAD THIS FUCKIN' BRILLIANT IDEA...
I'VE CALLED AT THE HOUSE A DOZEN TIMES IN FOUR DAYS: NOTHING. I'M REALLY STARTING TO WONDER...
MM. IT'S LIKE A DREADFUL SORT OF... ECCARIUS-SHAPED GAP IN OUR LIVES...
I JUST MISS HIM.
AHUH-HUH-HUH-HUH-HUH!
SHUT UP, YEH BOLLICKS! THEY'LL HEAR US A BLEEDIN' MILE OFF!
IT'S THAT CASSIDY. I THINK HE'S A BAD INFLUENCE.
FNKINK CUKSKKR!
OI! ENFANTS DU FUCKIN' SANG!!

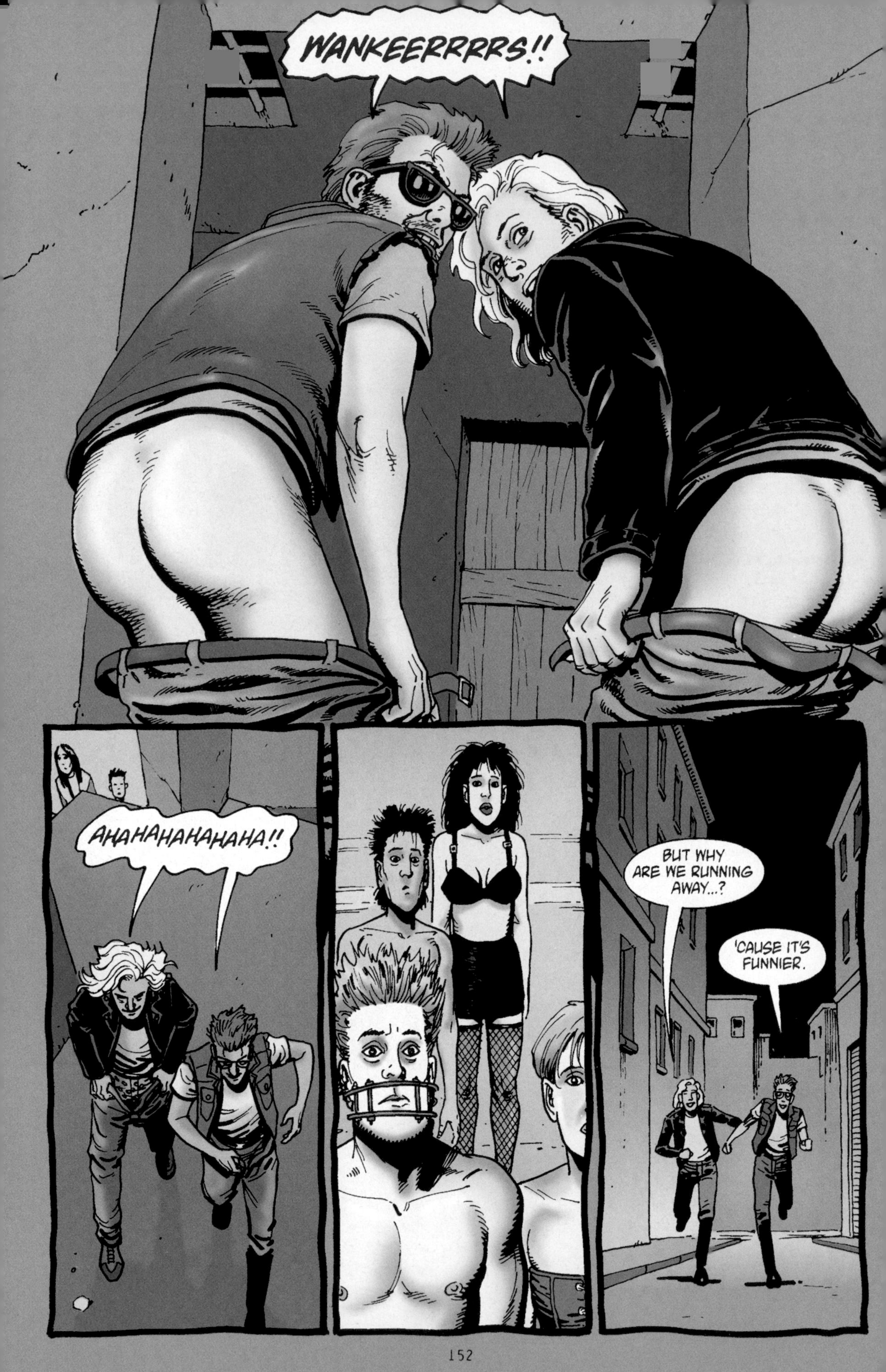
WANKEERRRRRS!!
AHAHAHAHAHAHAHA!!
BUT WHY ARE WE RUNNING AWAY...?
'CAUSE IT'S FUNNIER.

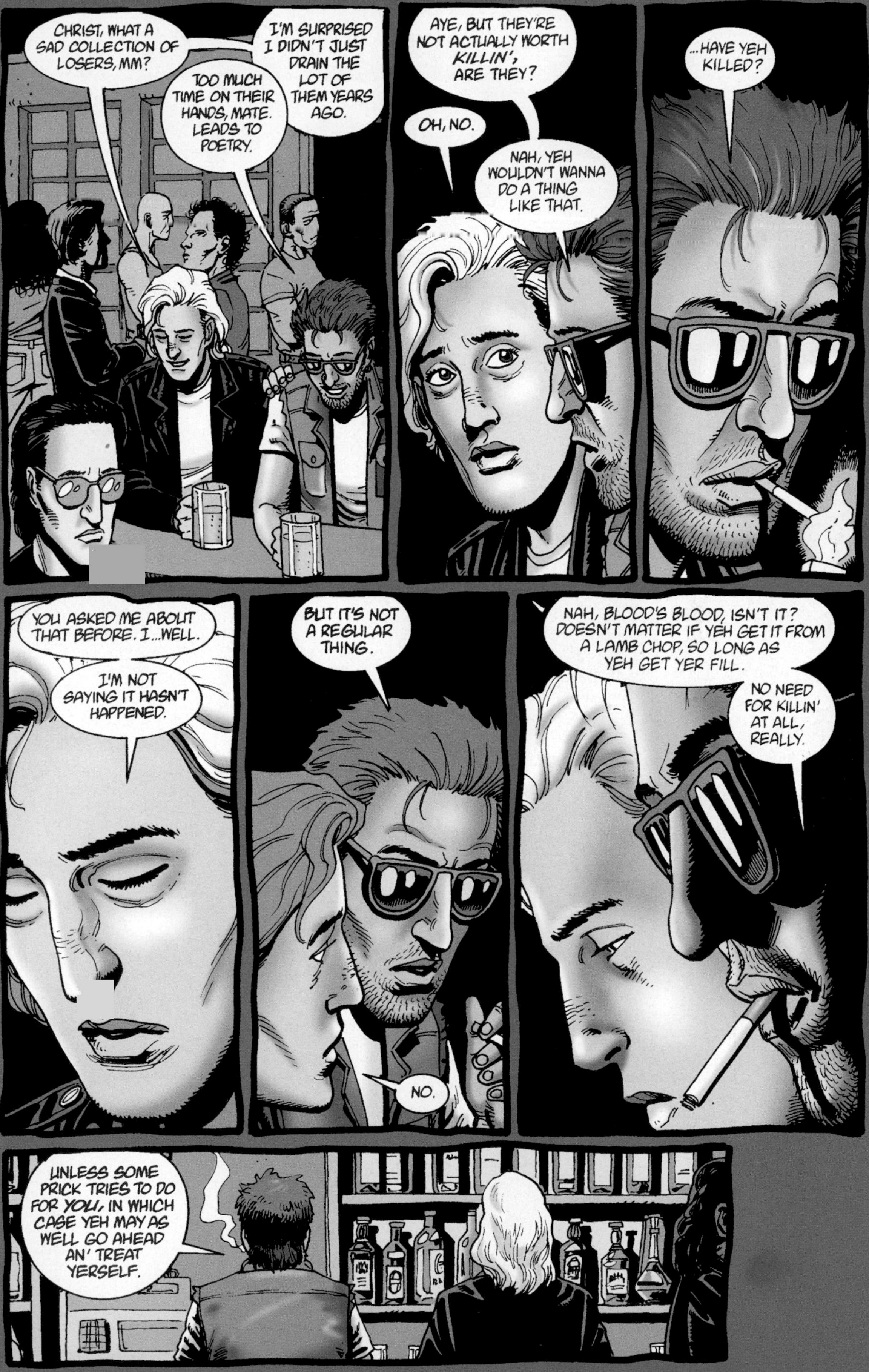
CHRIST, WHAT A SAD COLLECTION OF LOSERS, MM?
I'M SURPRISED I DIDN'T JUST DRAIN THE LOT OF THEM YEARS AGO.
TOO MUCH TIME ON THEIR HANDS, MATE. LEADS TO POETRY.
AYE, BUT THEY'RE NOT ACTUALLY WORTH *KILLIN'*, ARE THEY?
OH, NO.
NAH, YEH WOULDN'T WANNA DO A THING LIKE THAT.
...HAVE YEH KILLED?
YOU ASKED ME ABOUT THAT BEFORE. I...WELL.
I'M NOT SAYING IT HASN'T HAPPENED.
BUT IT'S NOT A REGULAR THING.
NO.
NAH, BLOOD'S BLOOD, ISN'T IT? DOESN'T MATTER IF YEH GET IT FROM A LAMB CHOP, SO LONG AS YEH GET YER FILL.
NO NEED FOR KILLIN' AT ALL, REALLY.
UNLESS SOME PRICK TRIES TO DO FOR *YOU*, IN WHICH CASE YEH MAY AS WELL GO AHEAD AN' TREAT YERSELF.

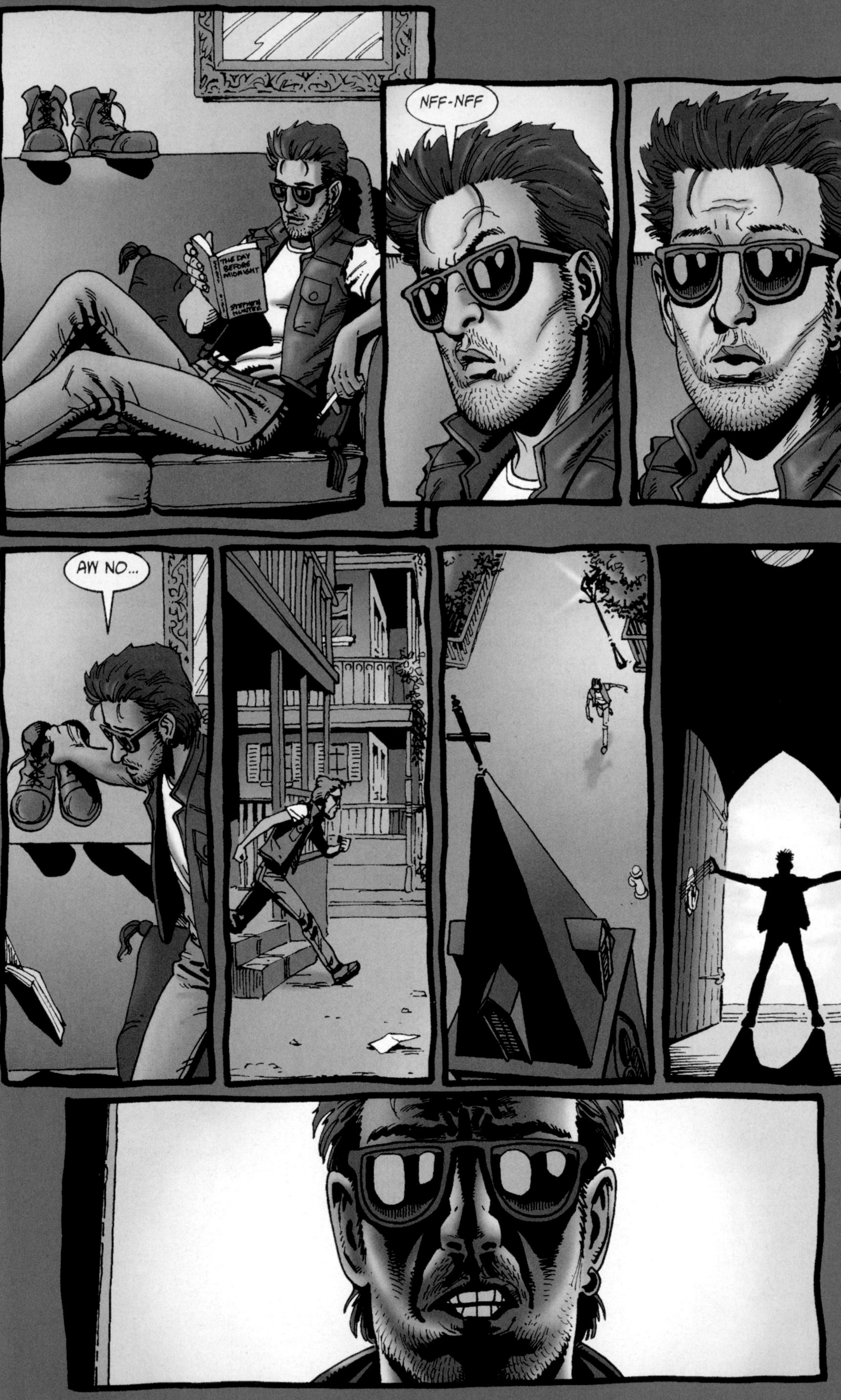
NFF-NFF
AW NO...

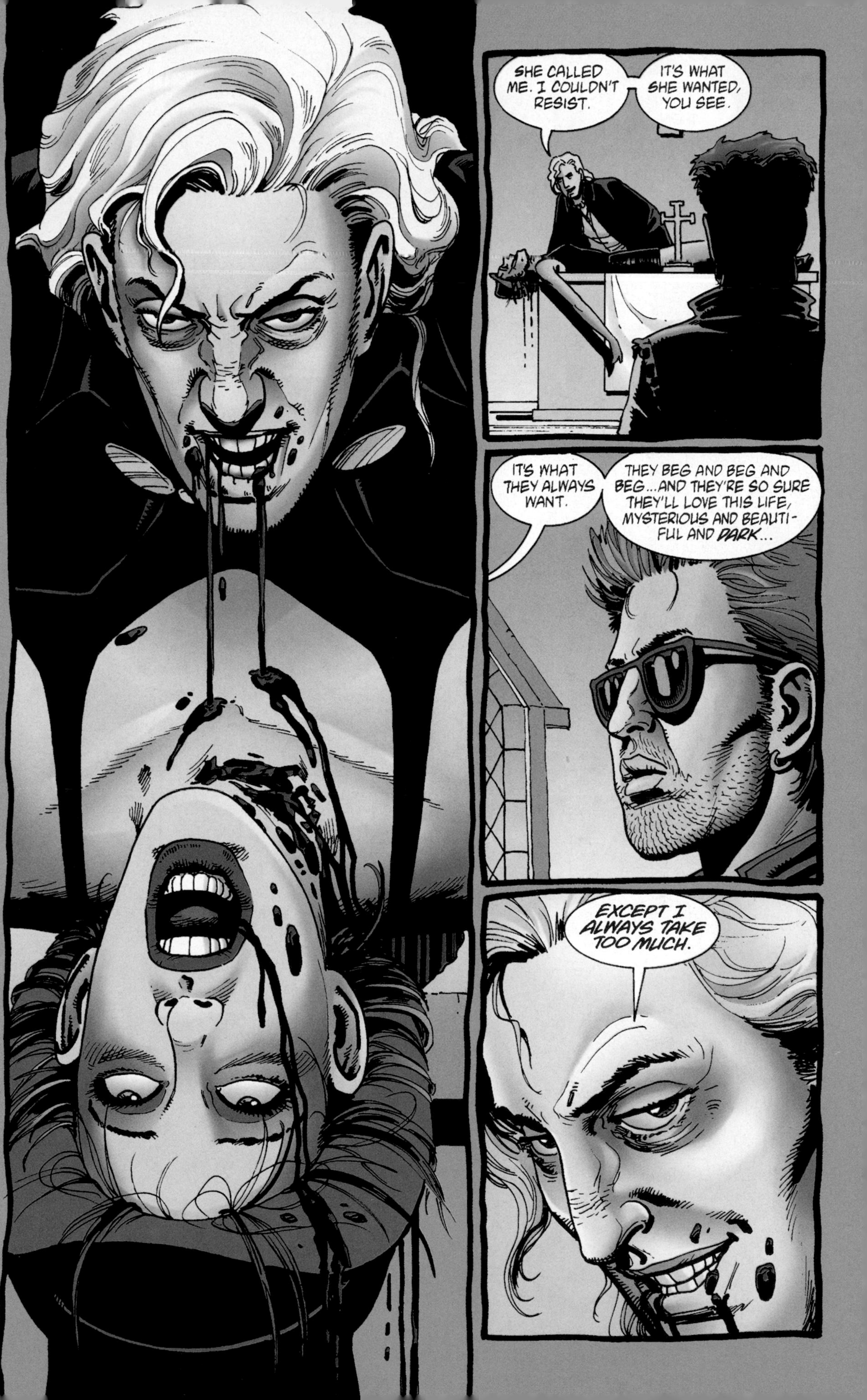
SHE CALLED ME. I COULDN'T RESIST.
IT'S WHAT SHE WANTED, YOU SEE.
IT'S WHAT THEY ALWAYS WANT.
THEY BEG AND BEG AND BEG...AND THEY'RE SO SURE THEY'LL LOVE THIS LIFE, MYSTERIOUS AND BEAUTIFUL AND DARK...
EXCEPT I ALWAYS TAKE TOO MUCH.

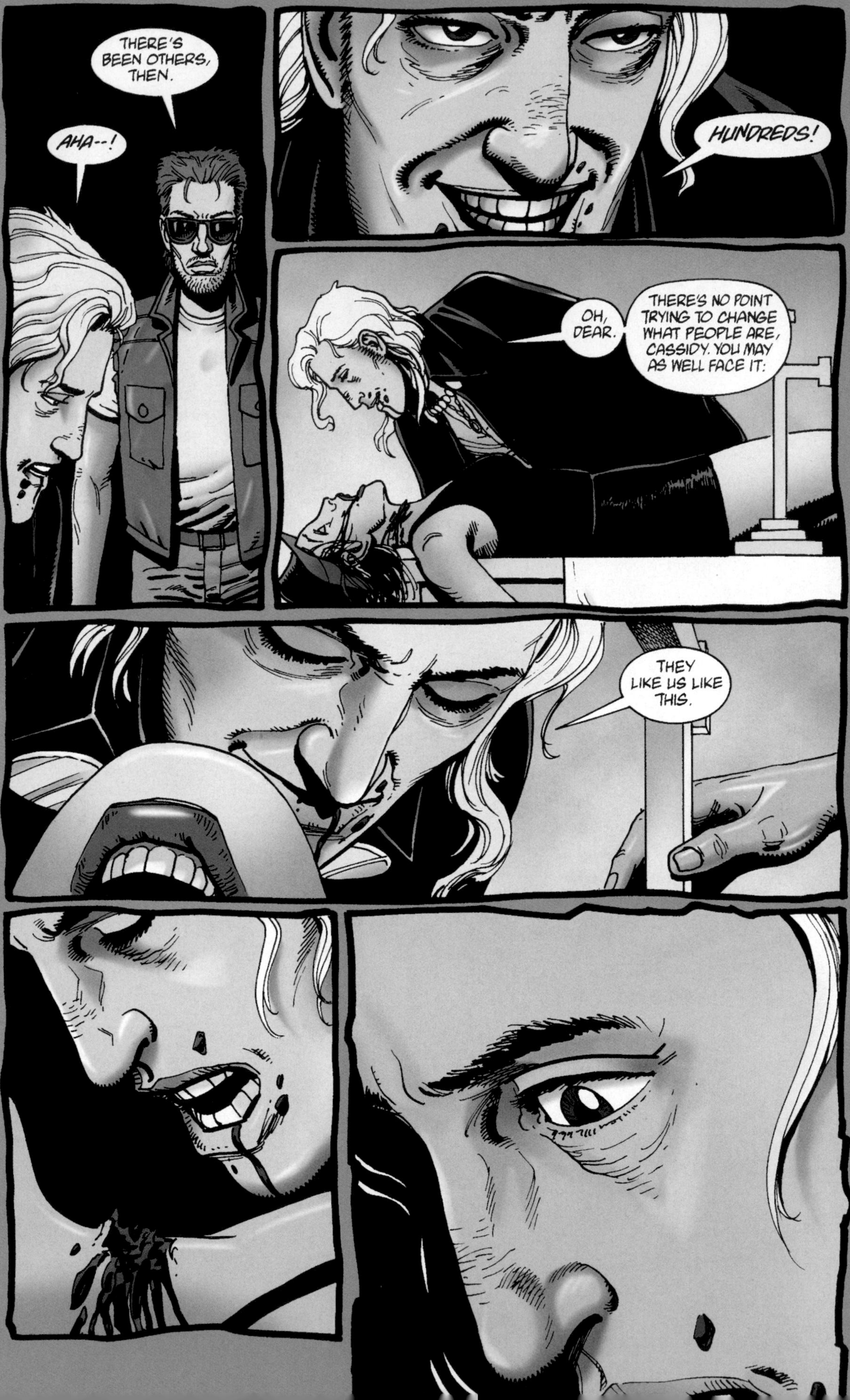
THERE'S BEEN OTHERS, THEN.
AHA--!
HUNDREDS!
OH, DEAR.
THERE'S NO POINT TRYING TO CHANGE WHAT PEOPLE ARE, CASSIDY. YOU MAY AS WELL FACE IT:
THEY LIKE US LIKE THIS.

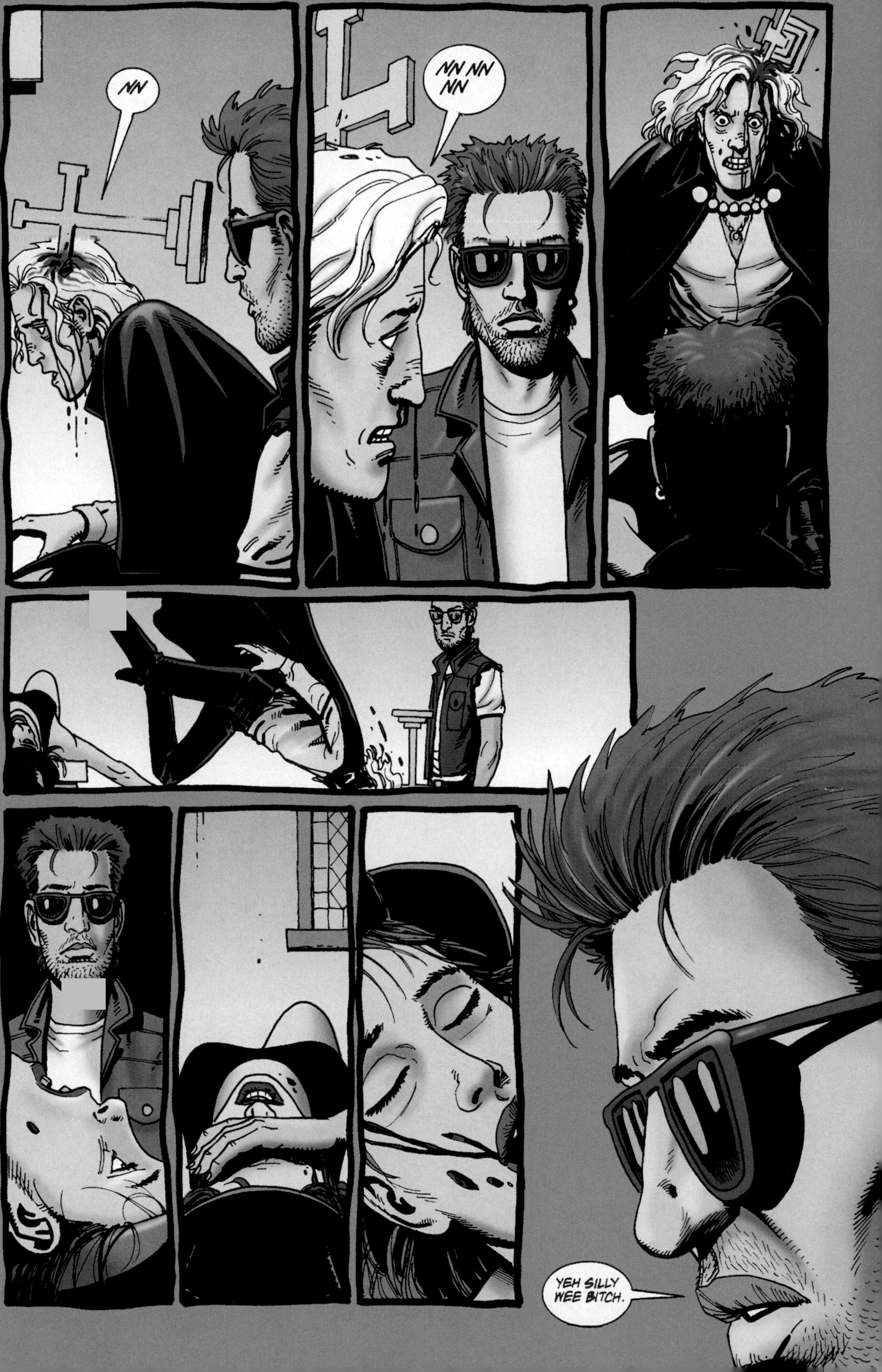
NN
NN NN NN
YEH SILLY WEE BITCH.

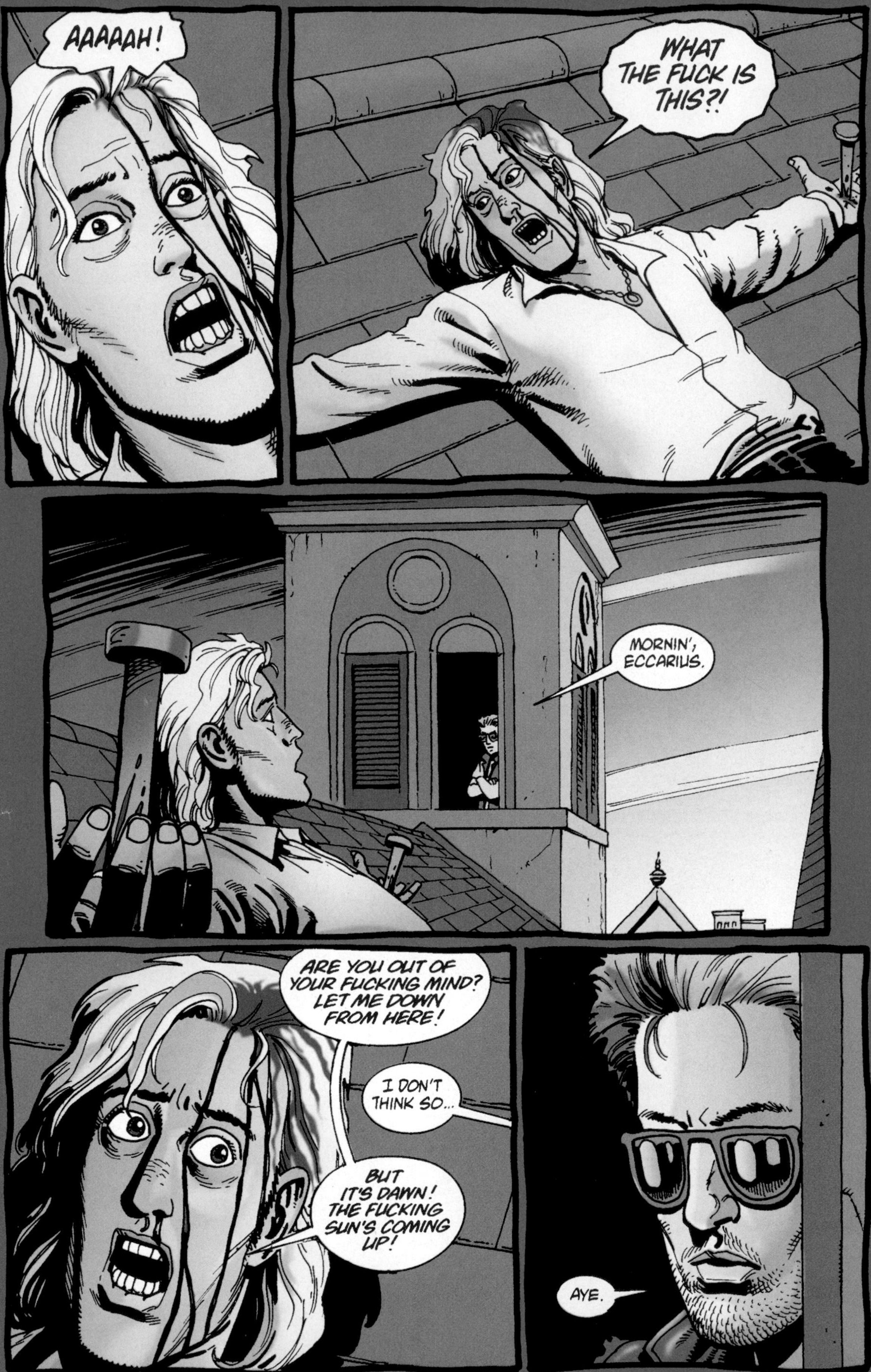
AAAAAH!
WHAT THE FUCK IS THIS?!
MORNIN', ECCARIUS.
ARE YOU OUT OF YOUR FUCKING MIND? LET ME DOWN FROM HERE!
I DON'T THINK SO...
BUT IT'S DAWN! THE FUCKING SUN'S COMING UP!
AYE.

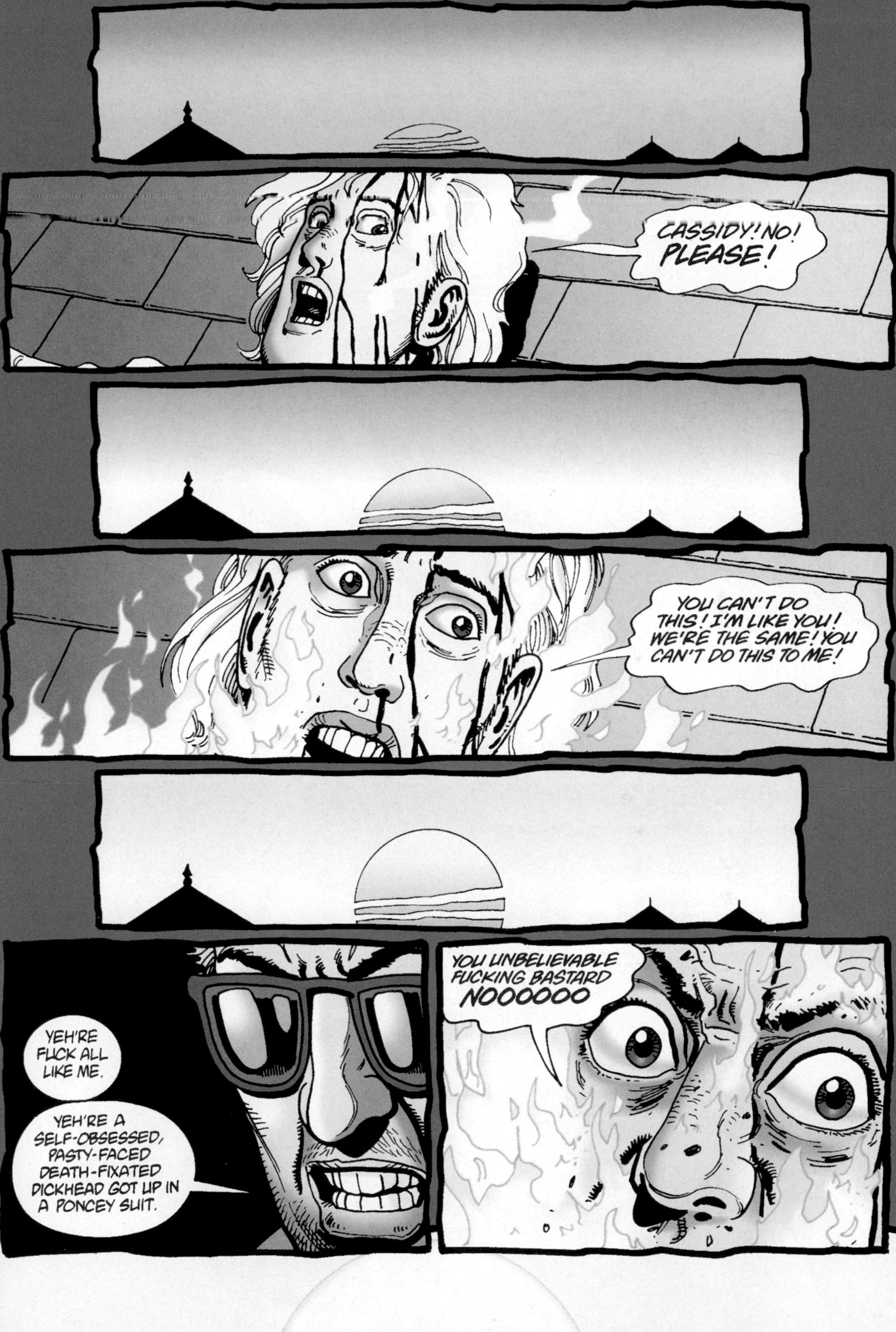
CASSIDY! NO! PLEASE!
YOU CAN'T DO THIS! I'M LIKE YOU! WE'RE THE SAME! YOU CAN'T DO THIS TO ME!
YEH'RE FUCK ALL LIKE ME.
YEH'RE A SELF-OBSESSED, PASTY-FACED DEATH-FIXATED DICKHEAD GOT UP IN A PONCEY SUIT.
YOU UNBELIEVABLE FUCKING BASTARD NOOOOOO

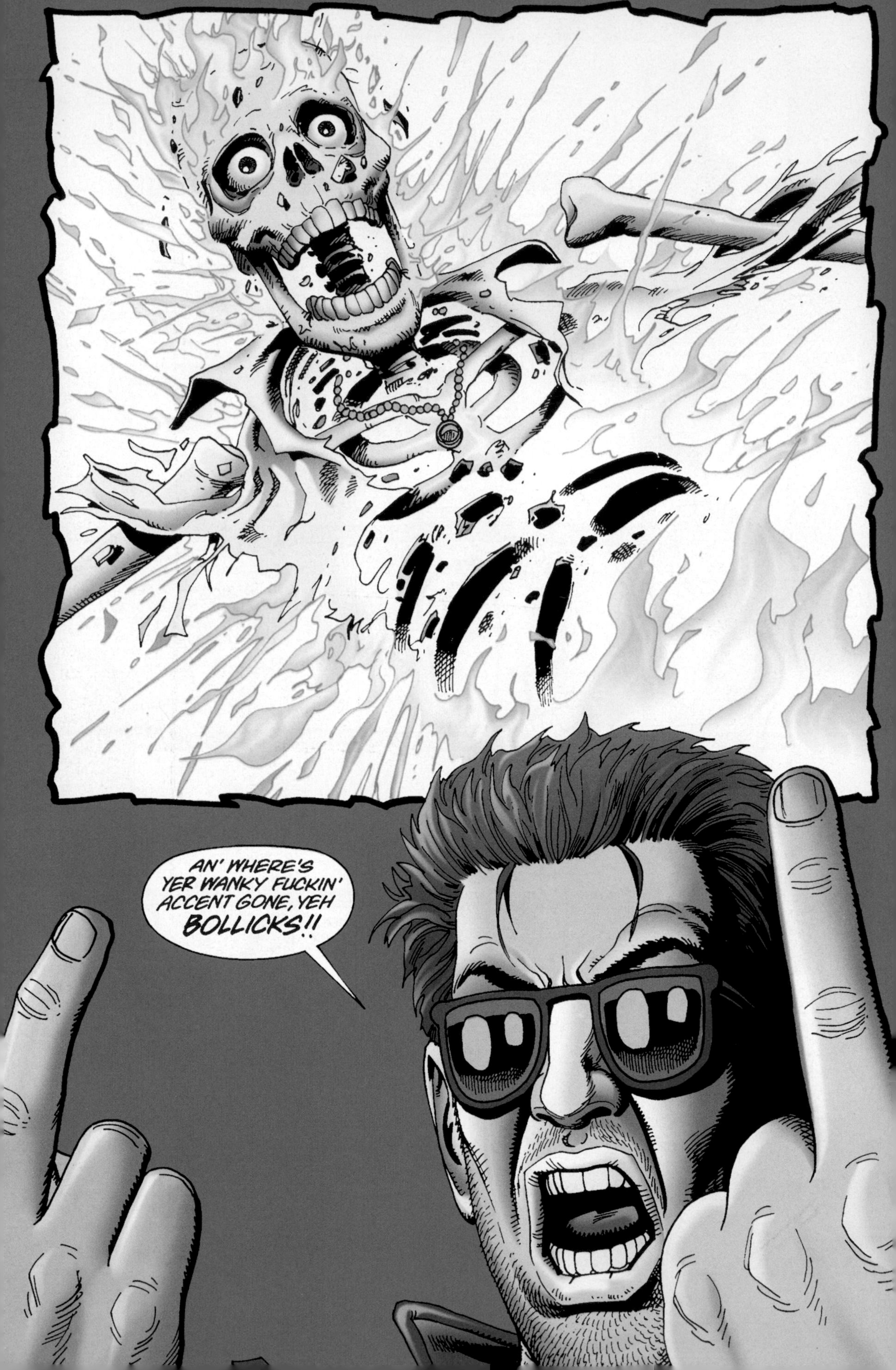
AN' WHERE'S YER WANKY FUCKIN' ACCENT GONE, YEH BOLLICKS!!

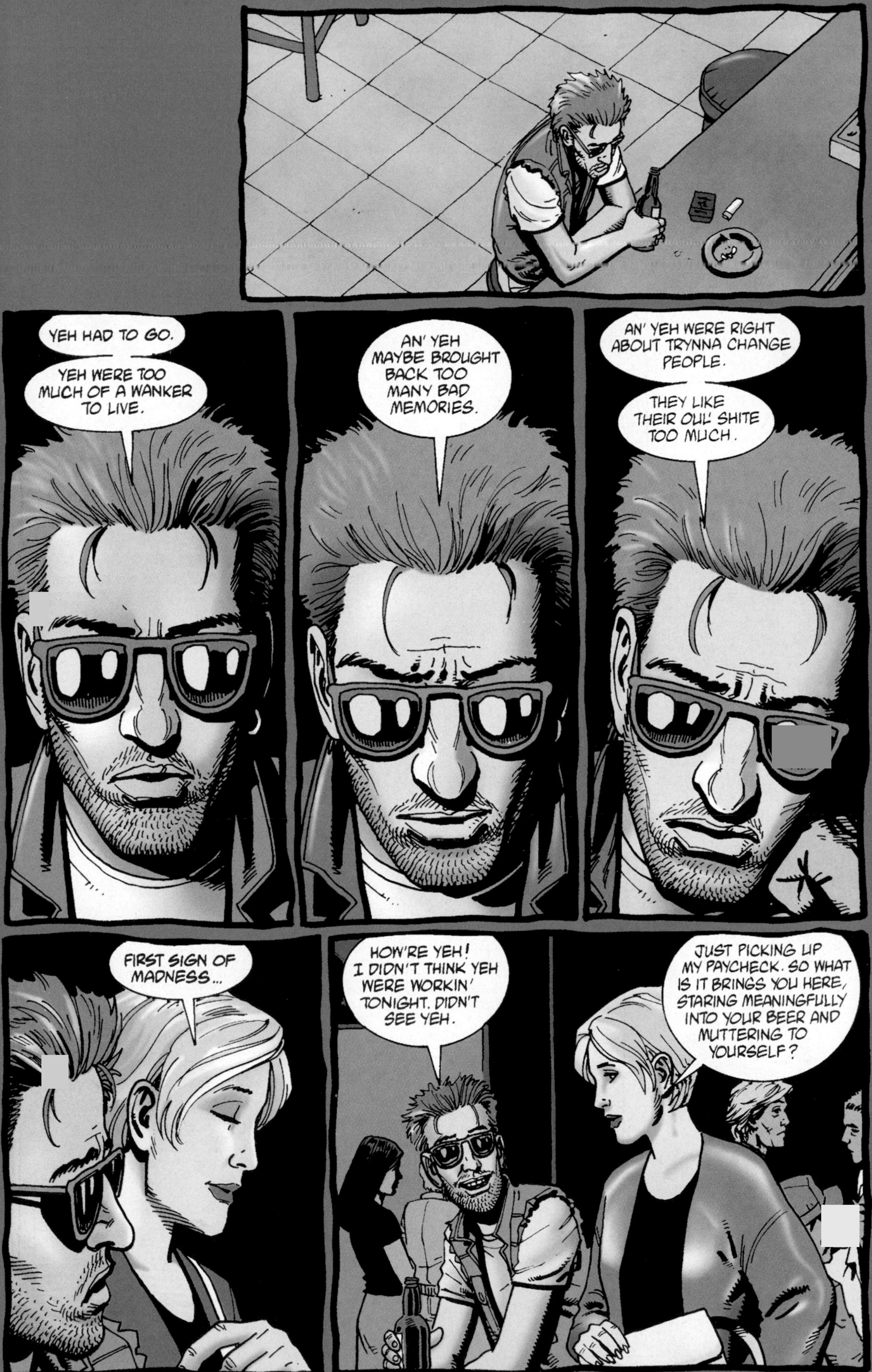
YEH HAD TO GO.
YEH WERE TOO MUCH OF A WANKER TO LIVE.
AN' YEH MAYBE BROUGHT BACK TOO MANY BAD MEMORIES.
AN' YEH WERE RIGHT ABOUT TRYNNA CHANGE PEOPLE.
THEY LIKE THEIR OUL' SHITE TOO MUCH.
FIRST SIGN OF MADNESS...
HOW'RE YEH! I DIDN'T THINK YEH WERE WORKIN' TONIGHT. DIDN'T SEE YEH.
JUST PICKING UP MY PAYCHECK. SO WHAT IS IT BRINGS YOU HERE, STARING MEANINGFULLY INTO YOUR BEER AND MUTTERING TO YOURSELF?

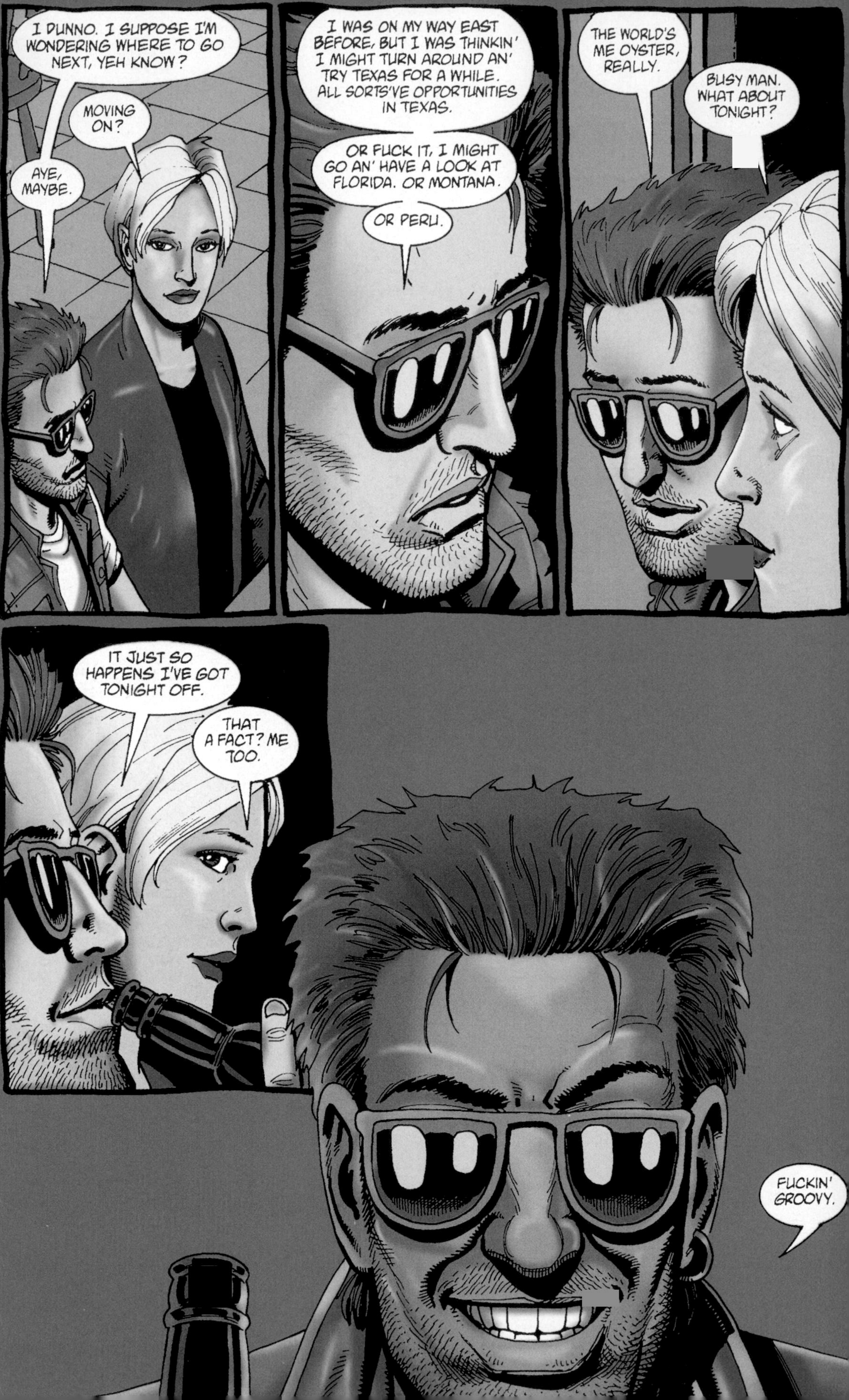
I DUNNO. I SUPPOSE I'M WONDERING WHERE TO GO NEXT, YEH KNOW?
MOVING ON?
AYE, MAYBE.
I WAS ON MY WAY EAST BEFORE, BUT I WAS THINKIN' I MIGHT TURN AROUND AN' TRY TEXAS FOR A WHILE. ALL SORTS'VE OPPORTUNITIES IN TEXAS.
OR FUCK IT, I MIGHT GO AN' HAVE A LOOK AT FLORIDA. OR MONTANA.
OR PERU.
THE WORLD'S ME OYSTER, REALLY.
BUSY MAN. WHAT ABOUT TONIGHT?
IT JUST SO HAPPENS I'VE GOT TONIGHT OFF.
THAT A FACT? ME TOO.
FUCKIN' GROOVY.

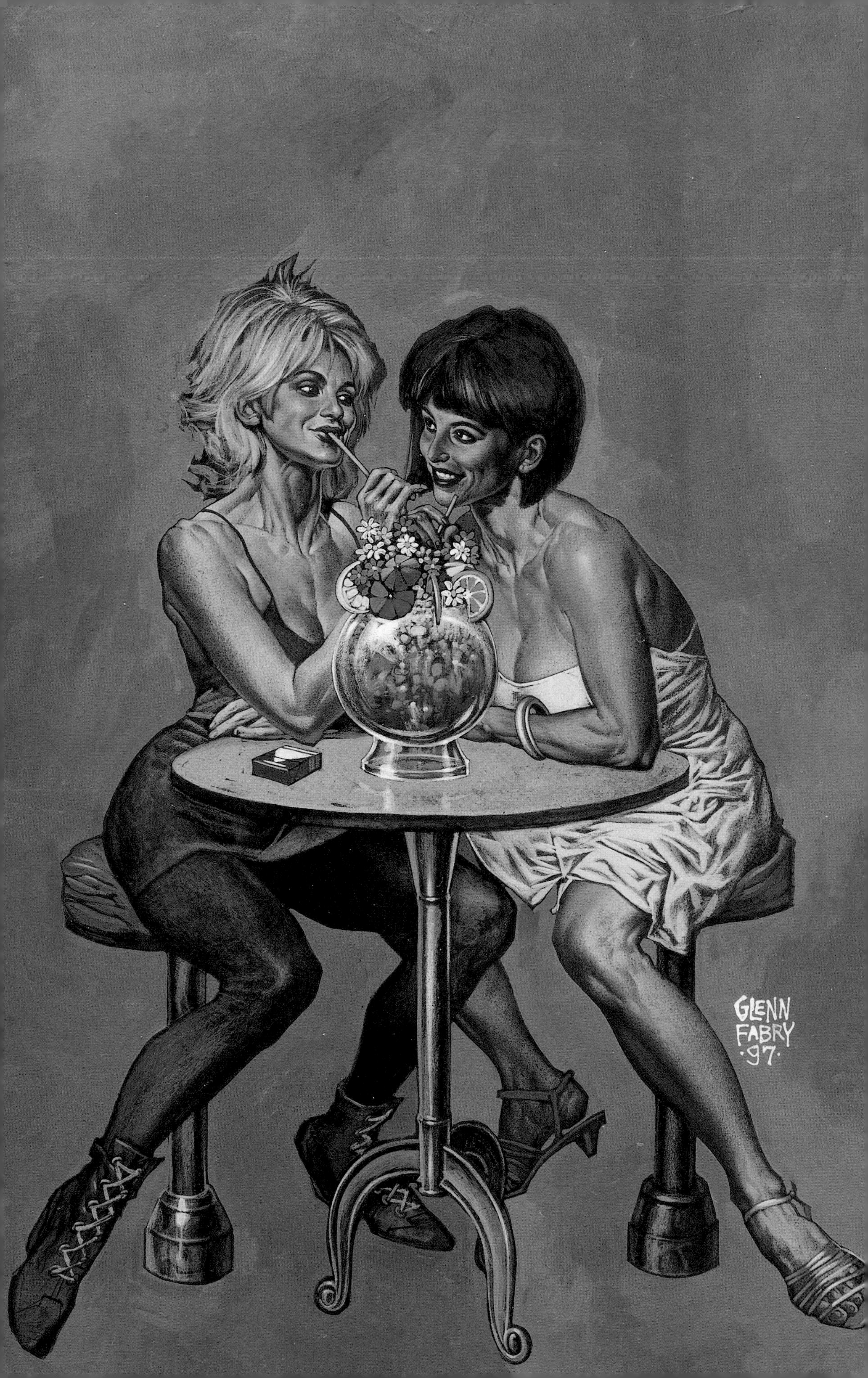
GLENN
FABRY
·97·

"Inbreeding, family feuds, bulimia, a retarded child —
always good for a laugh..."

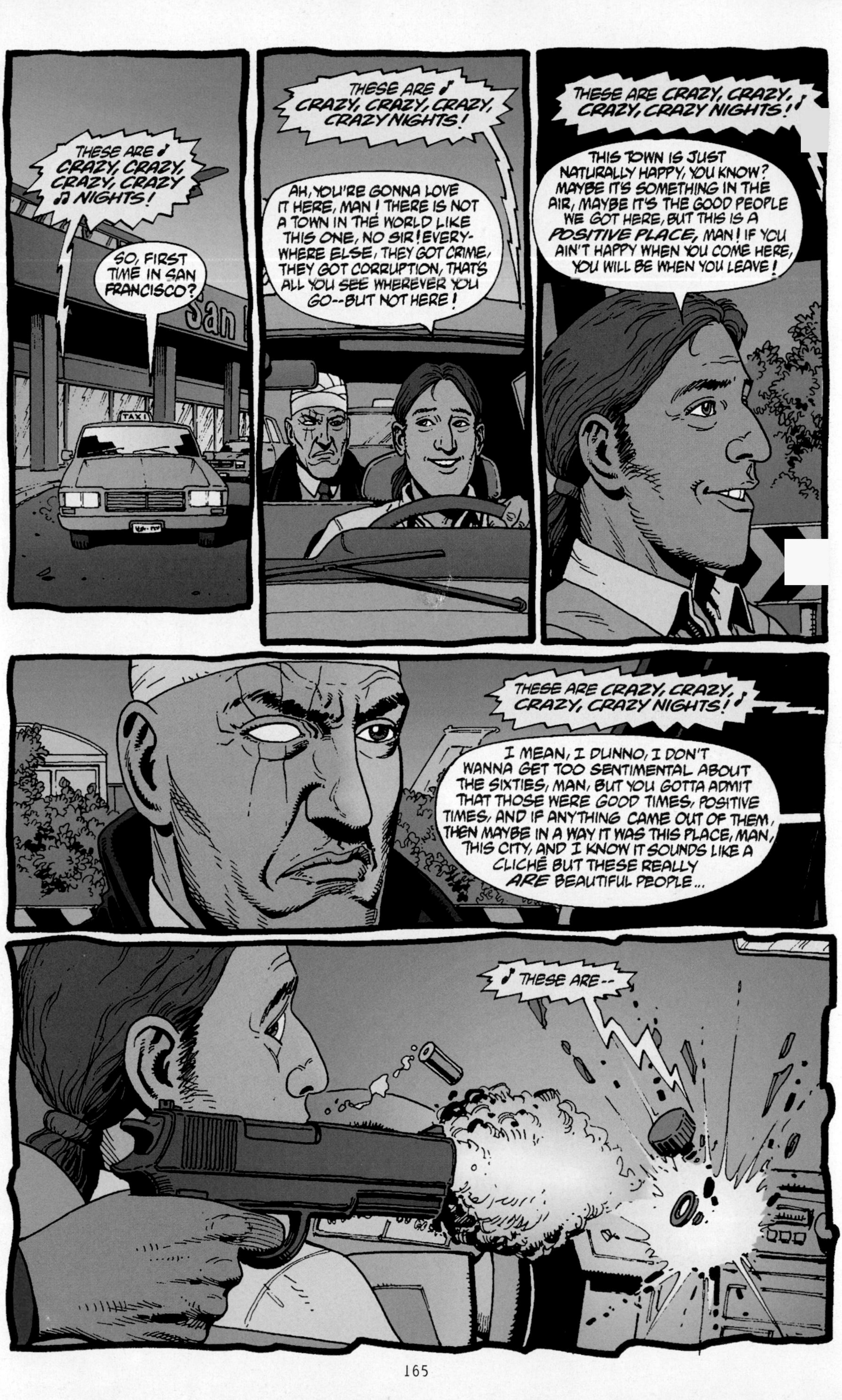
THESE ARE ♪ CRAZY, CRAZY, CRAZY, CRAZY ♫ NIGHTS!
SO, FIRST TIME IN SAN FRANCISCO?
San
TAXI
THESE ARE ♪ CRAZY, CRAZY, CRAZY, CRAZY NIGHTS!
AH, YOU'RE GONNA LOVE IT HERE, MAN! THERE IS NOT A TOWN IN THE WORLD LIKE THIS ONE, NO SIR! EVERYWHERE ELSE, THEY GOT CRIME, THEY GOT CORRUPTION, THAT'S ALL YOU SEE WHEREVER YOU GO--BUT NOT HERE!
THESE ARE CRAZY, CRAZY, CRAZY, CRAZY NIGHTS! ♪
THIS TOWN IS JUST NATURALLY HAPPY, YOU KNOW? MAYBE IT'S SOMETHING IN THE AIR, MAYBE IT'S THE GOOD PEOPLE WE GOT HERE, BUT THIS IS A POSITIVE PLACE, MAN! IF YOU AIN'T HAPPY WHEN YOU COME HERE, YOU WILL BE WHEN YOU LEAVE!
THESE ARE CRAZY, CRAZY, CRAZY, CRAZY NIGHTS! ♪
I MEAN, I DUNNO, I DON'T WANNA GET TOO SENTIMENTAL ABOUT THE SIXTIES, MAN, BUT YOU GOTTA ADMIT THAT THOSE WERE GOOD TIMES, POSITIVE TIMES, AND IF ANYTHING CAME OUT OF THEM, THEN MAYBE IN A WAY IT WAS THIS PLACE, MAN, THIS CITY, AND I KNOW IT SOUNDS LIKE A CLICHÉ BUT THESE REALLY ARE BEAUTIFUL PEOPLE...
♪ THESE ARE--

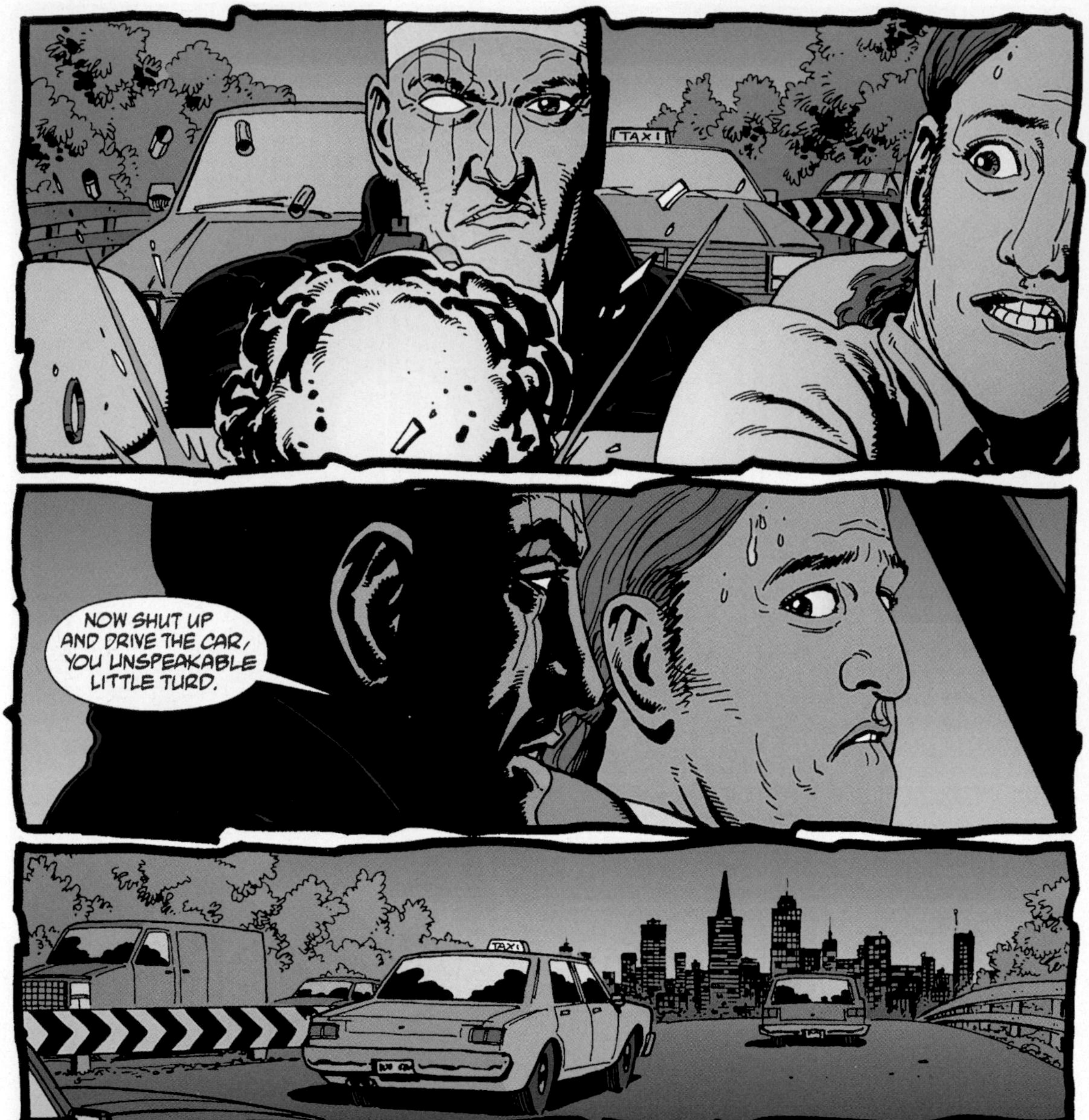
TAXI
NOW SHUT UP AND DRIVE THE CAR, YOU UNSPEAKABLE LITTLE TURD.

# GUNCHICKS

GARTH ENNIS - Writer STEVE DILLON - Artist
PAMELA RAMBO & MATT HOLLINGSWORTH – Color
CLEM ROBINS - Letterer AXEL ALONSO - Editor

PREACHER created by GARTH ENNIS and STEVE DILLON

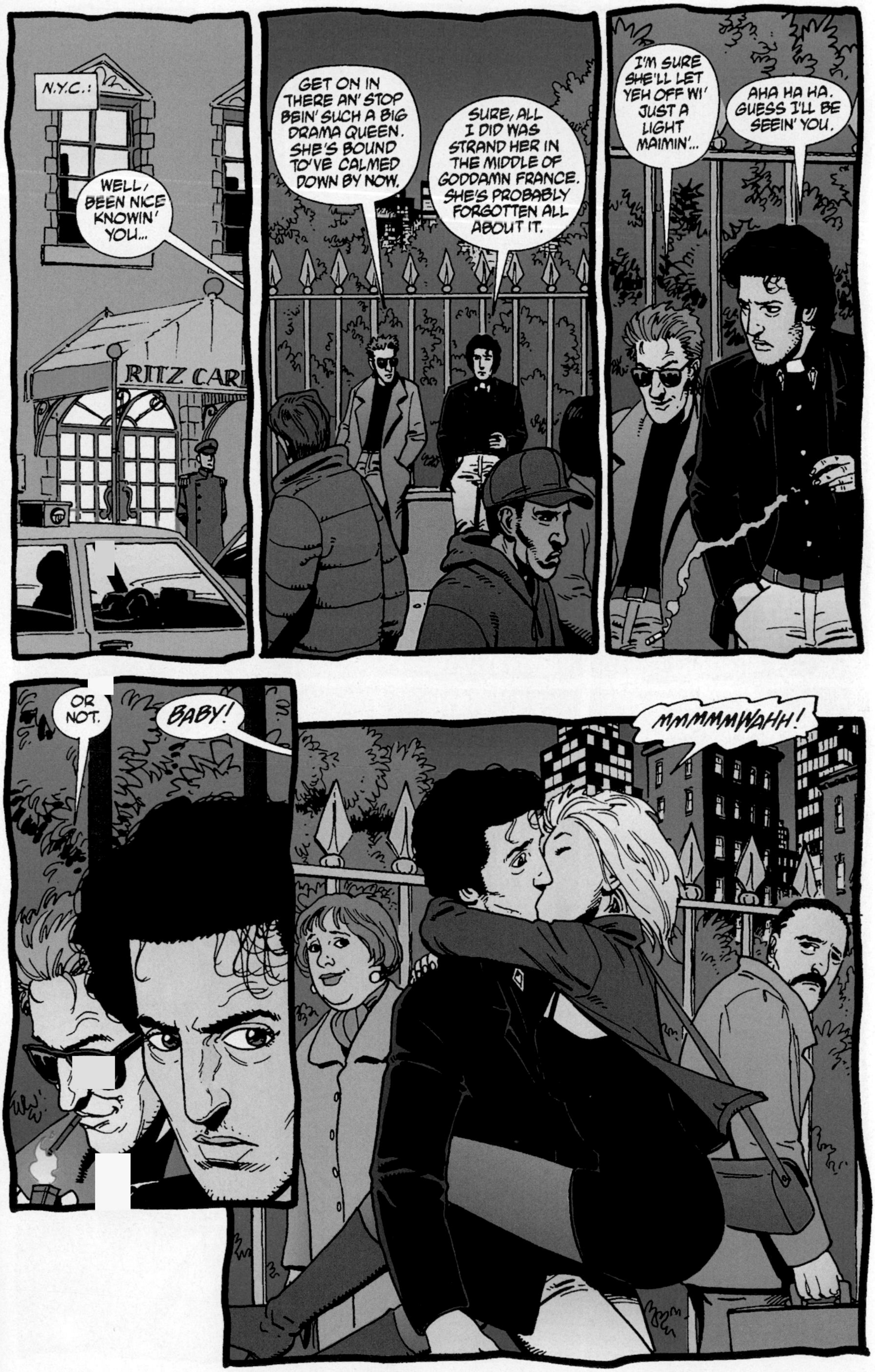
N.Y.C.:
WELL, BEEN NICE KNOWIN' YOU...
RITZ CAR
GET ON IN THERE AN' STOP BEIN' SUCH A BIG DRAMA QUEEN. SHE'S BOUND TO'VE CALMED DOWN BY NOW.
SURE, ALL I DID WAS STRAND HER IN THE MIDDLE OF GODDAMN FRANCE. SHE'S PROBABLY FORGOTTEN ALL ABOUT IT.
I'M SURE SHE'LL LET YEH OFF WI' JUST A LIGHT MAIMIN'...
AHA HA HA. GUESS I'LL BE SEEIN' YOU.
OR NOT.
BABY!
MMMMMWAHH!

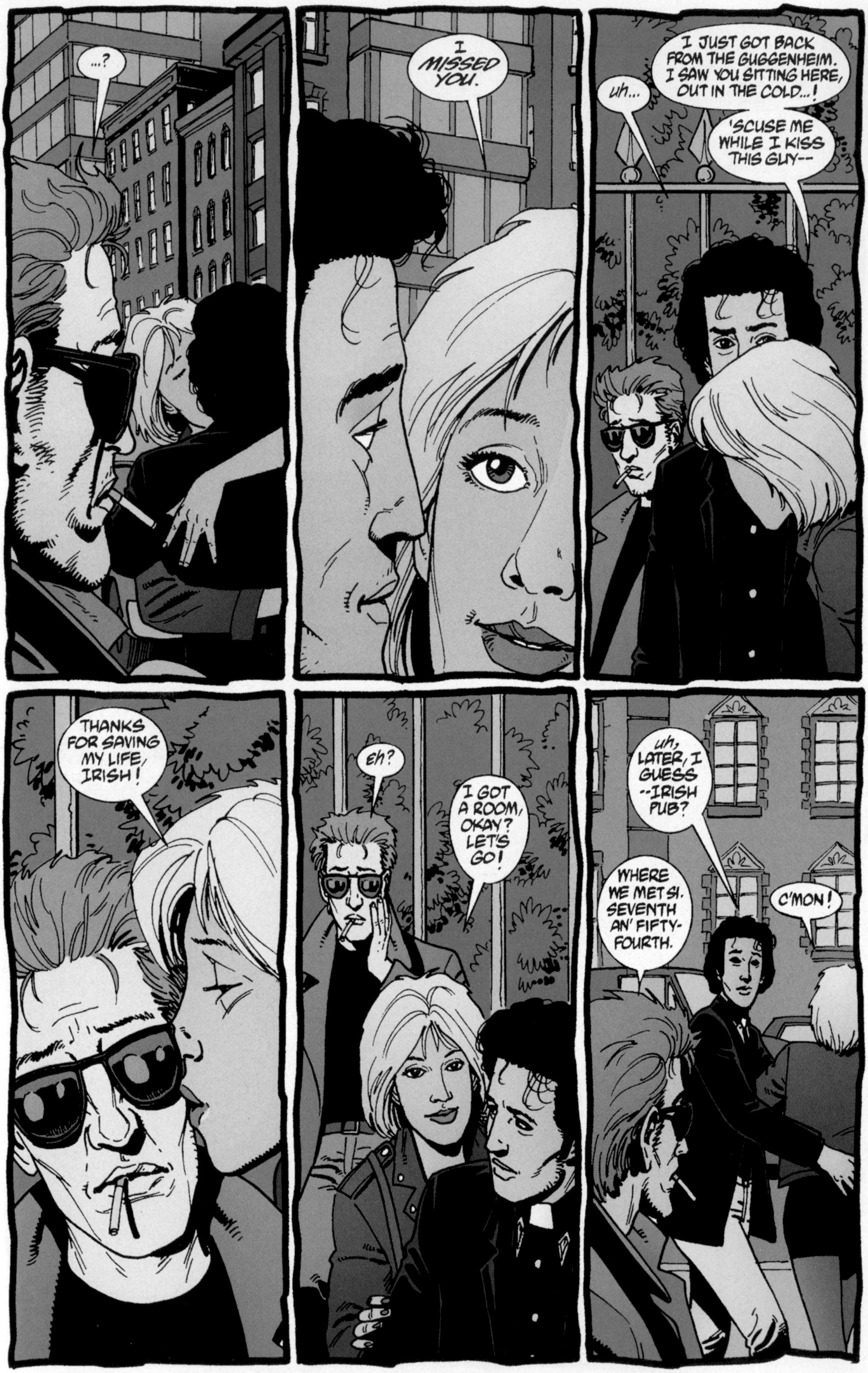
...?
I MISSED YOU.
uh...
I JUST GOT BACK FROM THE GUGGENHEIM. I SAW YOU SITTING HERE, OUT IN THE COLD...!
'SCUSE ME WHILE I KISS THIS GUY--
THANKS FOR SAVING MY LIFE, IRISH!
Eh?
I GOT A ROOM, OKAY? LET'S GO!
uh, LATER, I GUESS --IRISH PUB?
WHERE WE MET SI. SEVENTH AN' FIFTY-FOURTH.
C'MON!

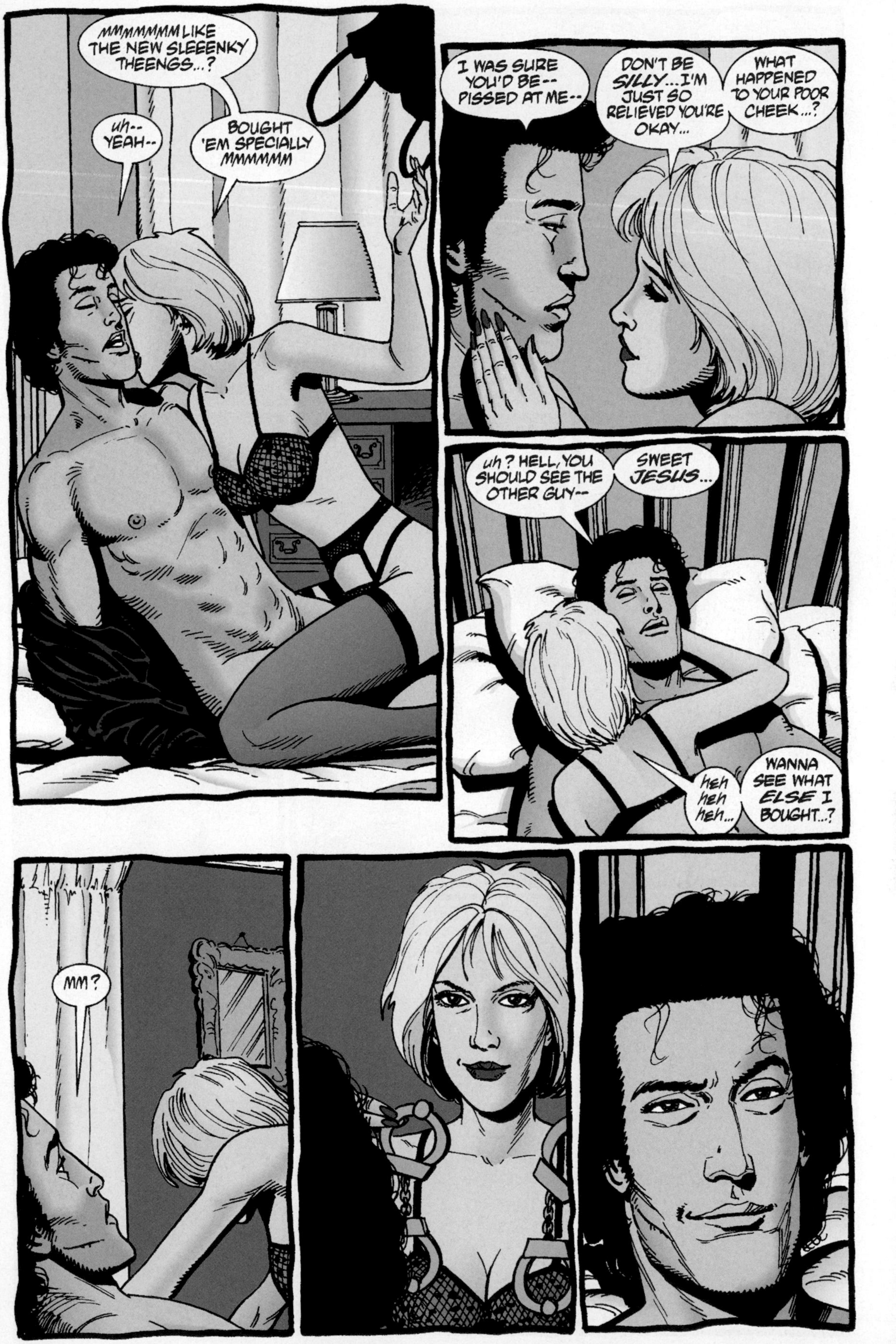
MMMMMMM LIKE THE NEW SLEEENKY THEENGS...?
uh-- YEAH--
BOUGHT 'EM SPECIALLY MMMMMM
I WAS SURE YOU'D BE-- PISSED AT ME--
DON'T BE SILLY...I'M JUST SO RELIEVED YOU'RE OKAY...
WHAT HAPPENED TO YOUR POOR CHEEK...?
uh? HELL, YOU SHOULD SEE THE OTHER GUY--
SWEET JESUS...
heh heh heh...
WANNA SEE WHAT ELSE I BOUGHT...?
MM?

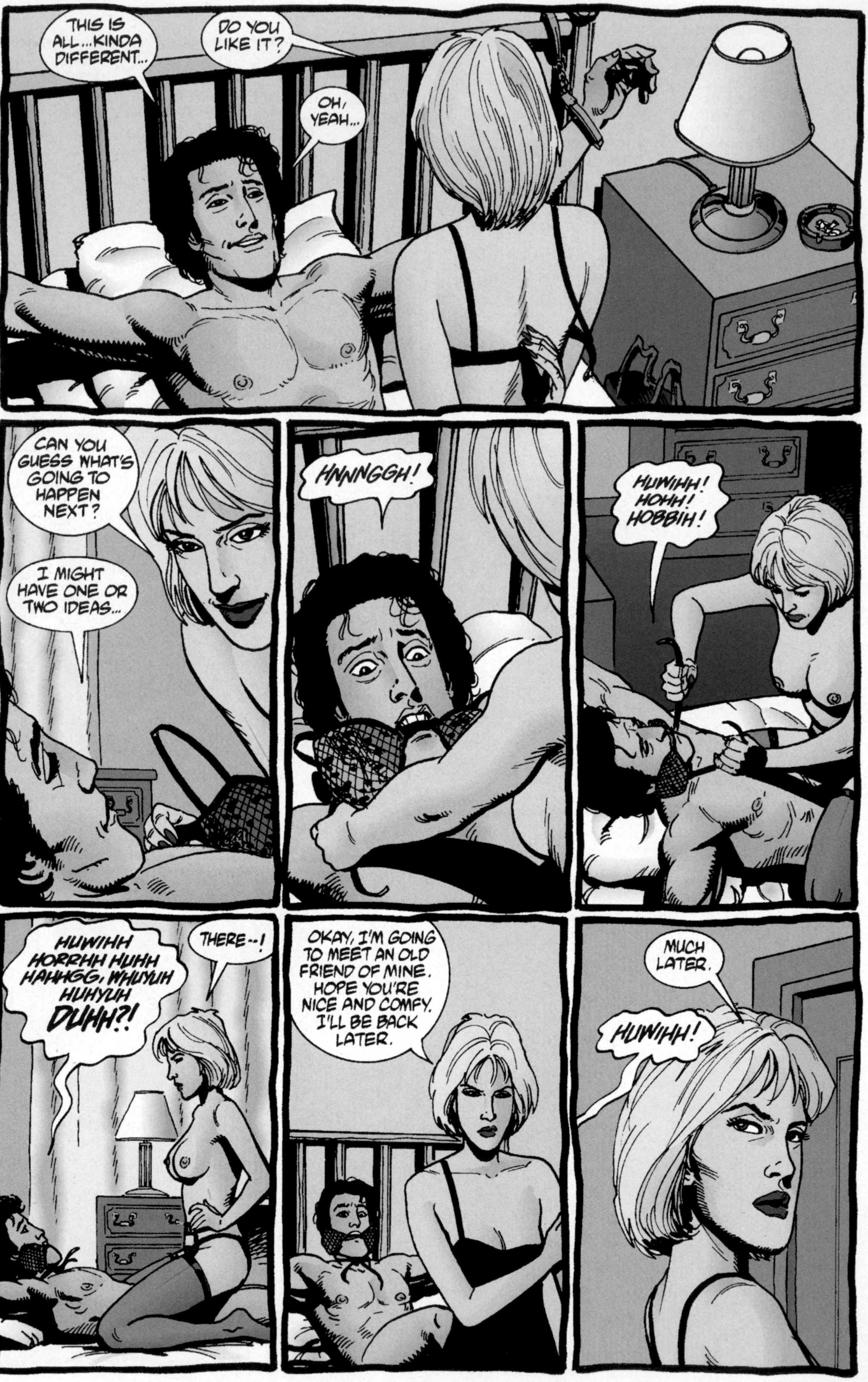
THIS IS ALL...KINDA DIFFERENT...
DO YOU LIKE IT?
OH, YEAH...
CAN YOU GUESS WHAT'S GOING TO HAPPEN NEXT?
I MIGHT HAVE ONE OR TWO IDEAS...
HNNNGGH!
HUWIHH! HOHH! HOBBIH!
HUWIHH HORRHH HUHH HAHHGG, WHUYUH HUHYUH DUHH?!
THERE--!
OKAY, I'M GOING TO MEET AN OLD FRIEND OF MINE. HOPE YOU'RE NICE AND COMFY. I'LL BE BACK LATER.
MUCH LATER.
HUWIHH!

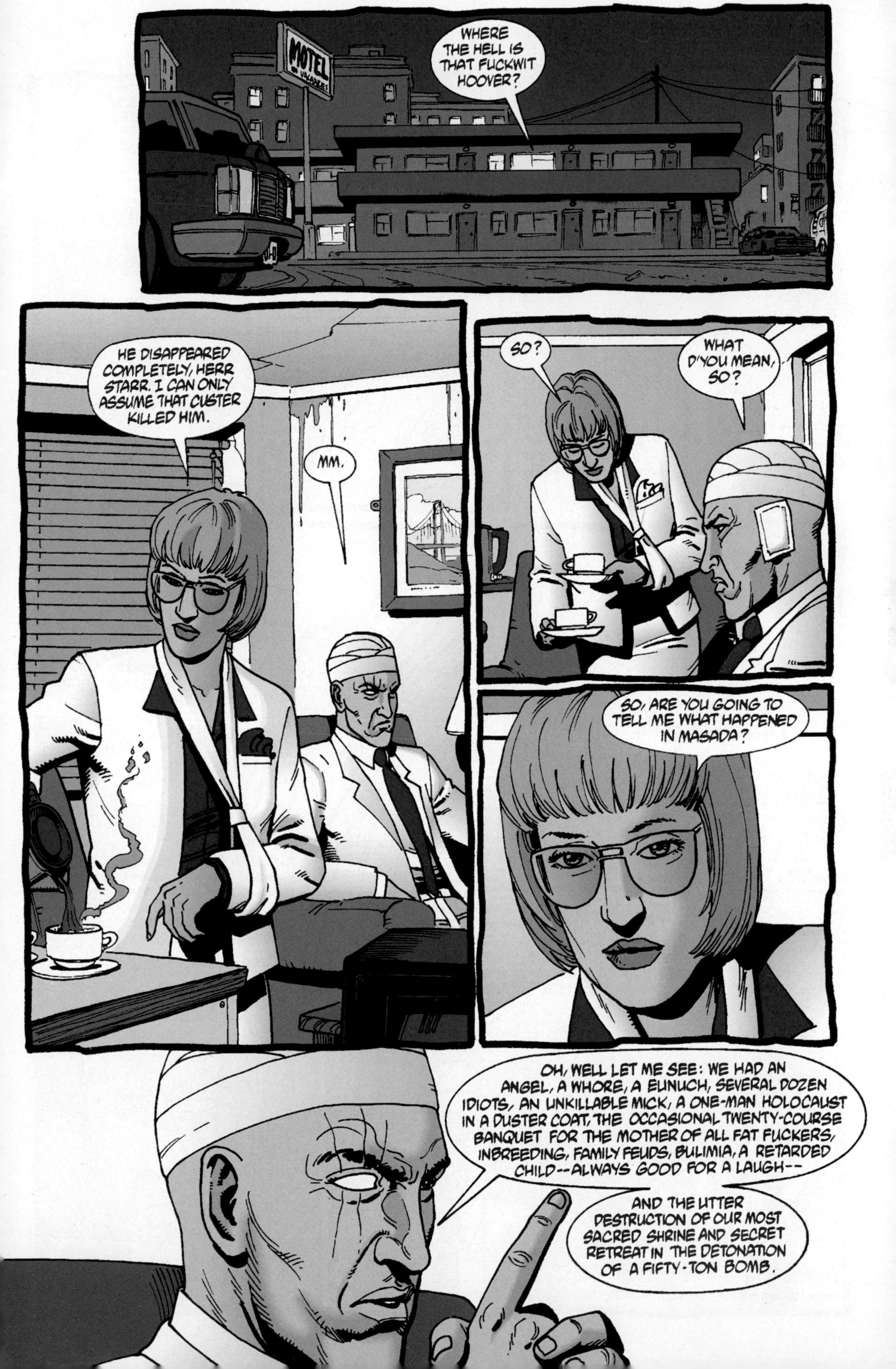

MOTEL
WHERE THE HELL IS THAT FUCKWIT HOOVER?
HE DISAPPEARED COMPLETELY, HERR STARR. I CAN ONLY ASSUME THAT CUSTER KILLED HIM.
MM.
SO?
WHAT D'YOU MEAN, SO?
SO, ARE YOU GOING TO TELL ME WHAT HAPPENED IN MASADA?
OH, WELL LET ME SEE: WE HAD AN ANGEL, A WHORE, A EUNUCH, SEVERAL DOZEN IDIOTS, AN UNKILLABLE MICK, A ONE-MAN HOLOCAUST IN A DUSTER COAT, THE OCCASIONAL TWENTY-COURSE BANQUET FOR THE MOTHER OF ALL FAT FUCKERS, INBREEDING, FAMILY FEUDS, BULIMIA, A RETARDED CHILD--ALWAYS GOOD FOR A LAUGH--
AND THE UTTER DESTRUCTION OF OUR MOST SACRED SHRINE AND SECRET RETREAT IN THE DETONATION OF A FIFTY-TON BOMB.

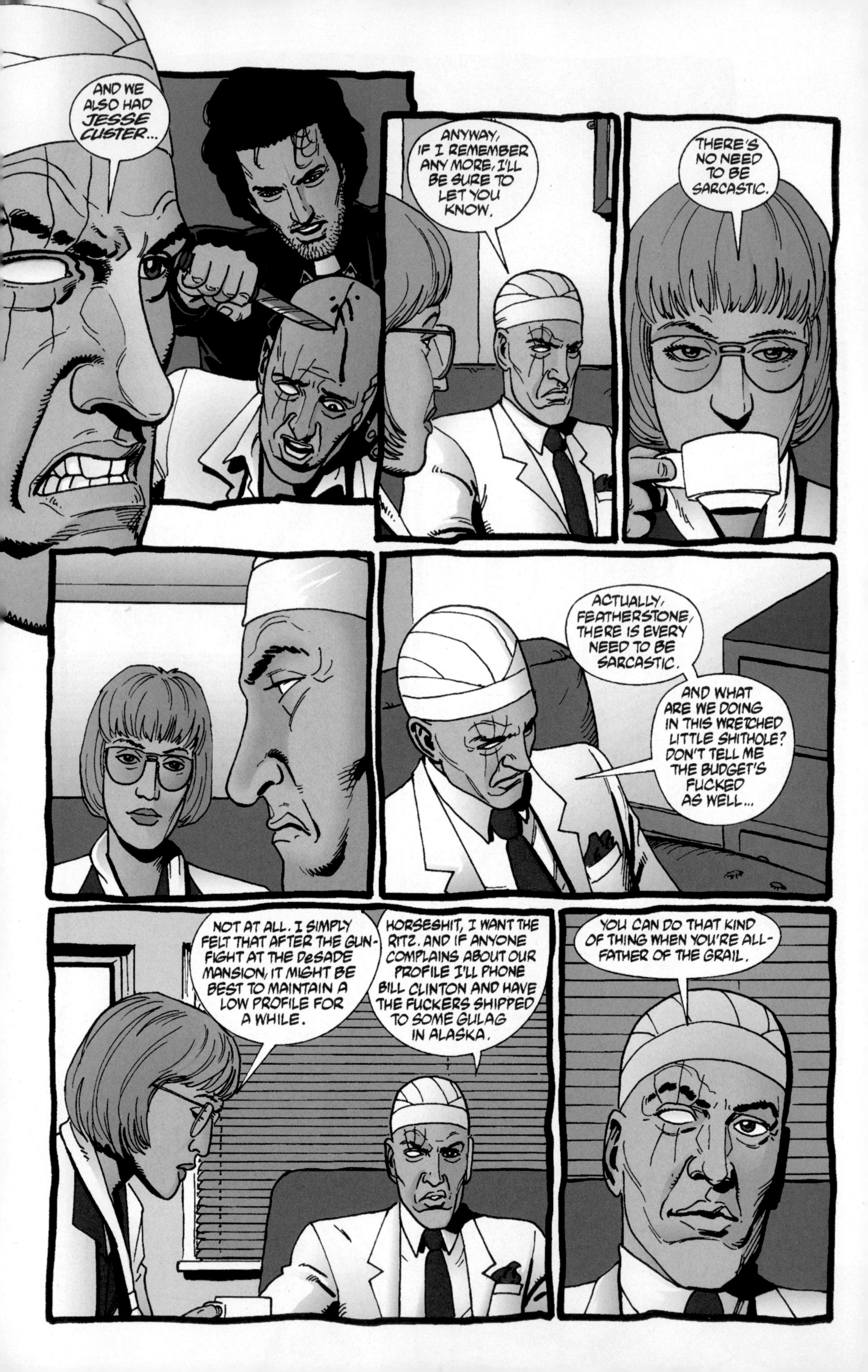
AND WE ALSO HAD JESSE CUSTER...
ANYWAY, IF I REMEMBER ANY MORE, I'LL BE SURE TO LET YOU KNOW.
THERE'S NO NEED TO BE SARCASTIC.
ACTUALLY, FEATHERSTONE, THERE IS EVERY NEED TO BE SARCASTIC.
AND WHAT ARE WE DOING IN THIS WRETCHED LITTLE SHITHOLE? DON'T TELL ME THE BUDGET'S FUCKED AS WELL...
NOT AT ALL. I SIMPLY FELT THAT AFTER THE GUN-FIGHT AT THE DeSADE MANSION, IT MIGHT BE BEST TO MAINTAIN A LOW PROFILE FOR A WHILE.
HORSESHIT, I WANT THE RITZ. AND IF ANYONE COMPLAINS ABOUT OUR PROFILE I'LL PHONE BILL CLINTON AND HAVE THE FUCKERS SHIPPED TO SOME GULAG IN ALASKA.
YOU CAN DO THAT KIND OF THING WHEN YOU'RE ALL-FATHER OF THE GRAIL.

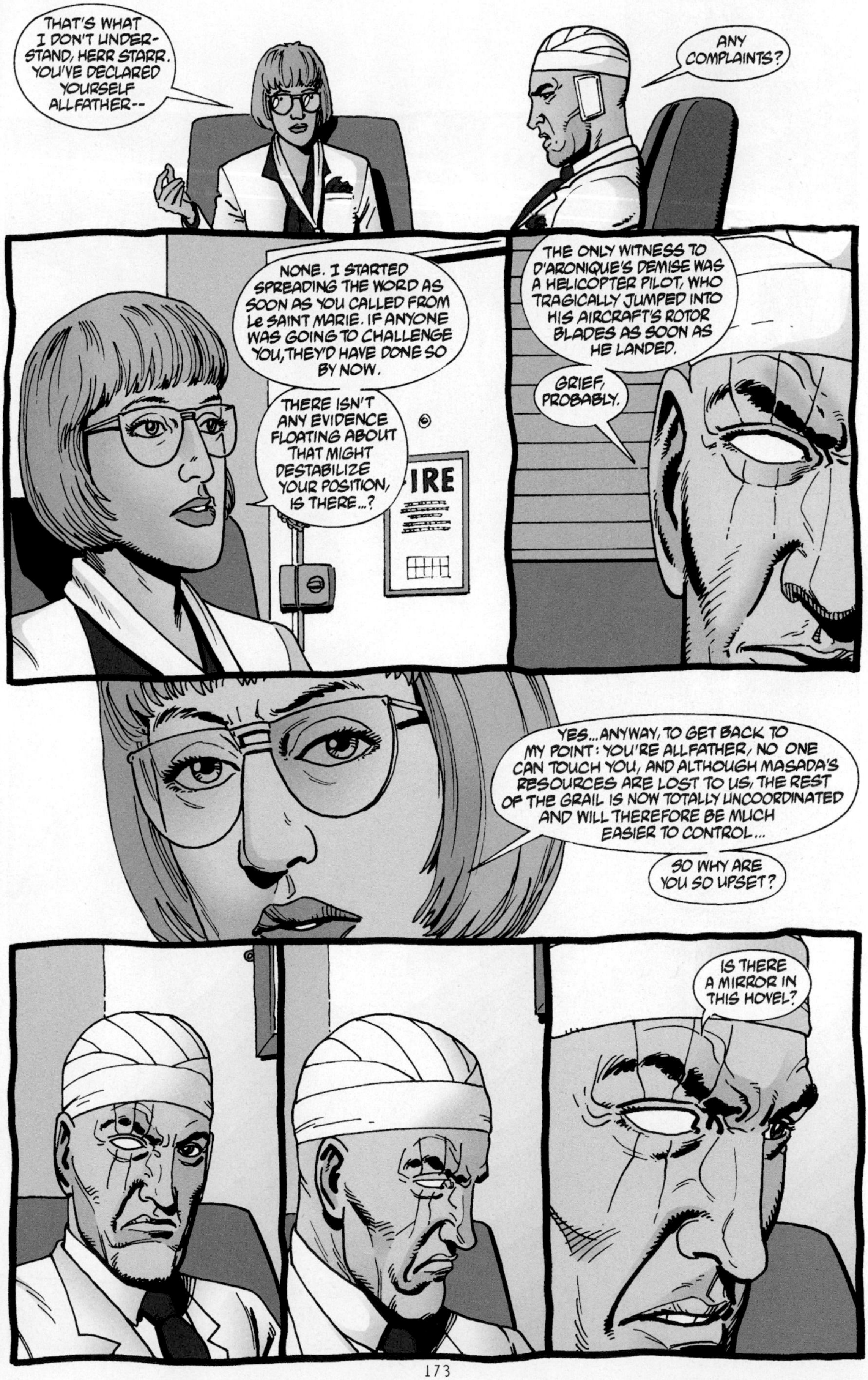
THAT'S WHAT I DON'T UNDER-STAND, HERR STARR. YOU'VE DECLARED YOURSELF ALLFATHER--
ANY COMPLAINTS?
NONE. I STARTED SPREADING THE WORD AS SOON AS YOU CALLED FROM Le SAINT MARIE. IF ANYONE WAS GOING TO CHALLENGE YOU, THEY'D HAVE DONE SO BY NOW.
THERE ISN'T ANY EVIDENCE FLOATING ABOUT THAT MIGHT DESTABILIZE YOUR POSITION, IS THERE...?
THE ONLY WITNESS TO D'ARONIQUE'S DEMISE WAS A HELICOPTER PILOT, WHO TRAGICALLY JUMPED INTO HIS AIRCRAFT'S ROTOR BLADES AS SOON AS HE LANDED.
GRIEF, PROBABLY.
YES... ANYWAY, TO GET BACK TO MY POINT: YOU'RE ALLFATHER, NO ONE CAN TOUCH YOU, AND ALTHOUGH MASADA'S RESOURCES ARE LOST TO US, THE REST OF THE GRAIL IS NOW TOTALLY UNCOORDINATED AND WILL THEREFORE BE MUCH EASIER TO CONTROL...
SO WHY ARE YOU SO UPSET?
IS THERE A MIRROR IN THIS HOVEL?

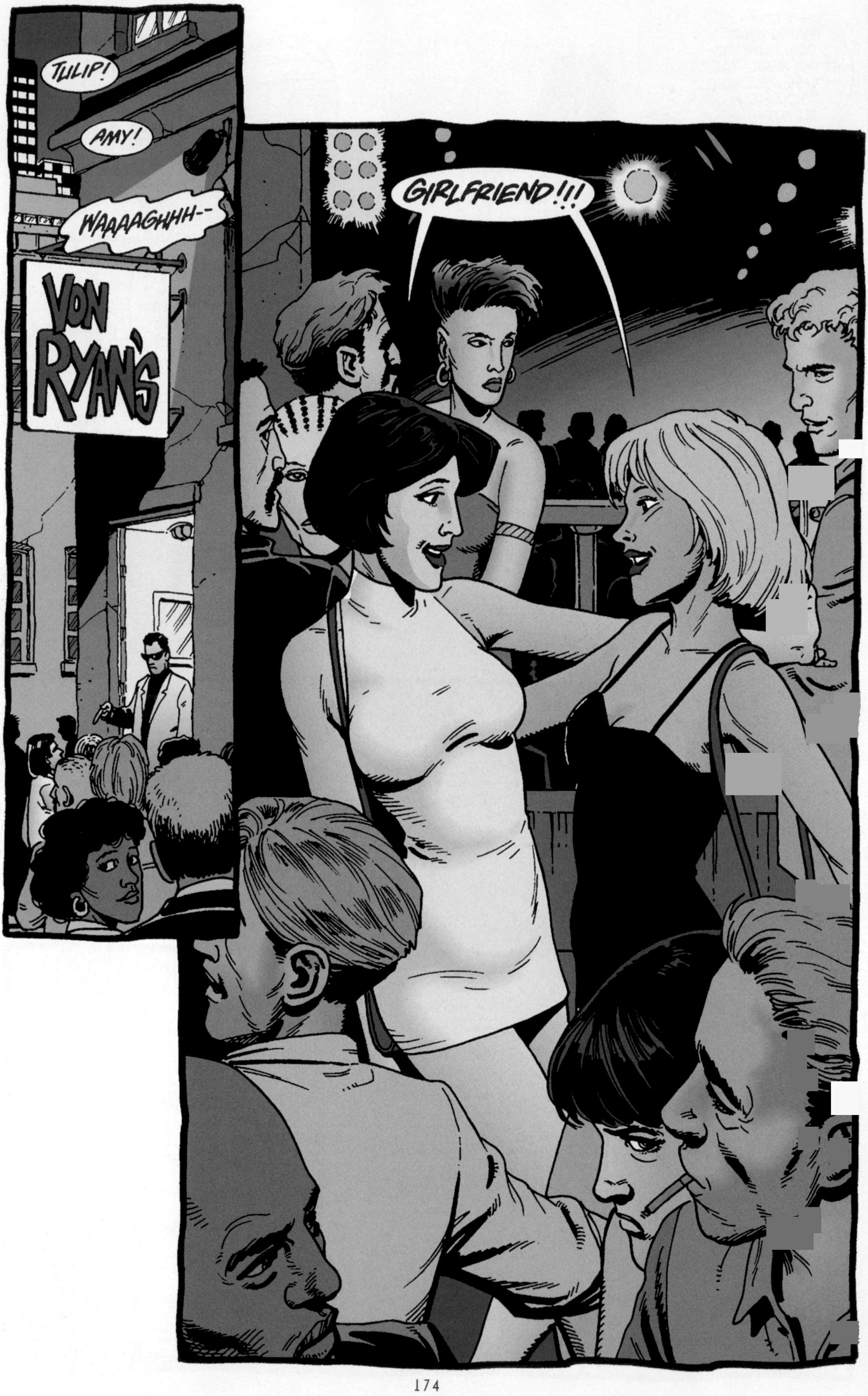
TULIP!
AMY!
WAAAAGHHH--
VON RYAN'S
GIRLFRIEND!!!

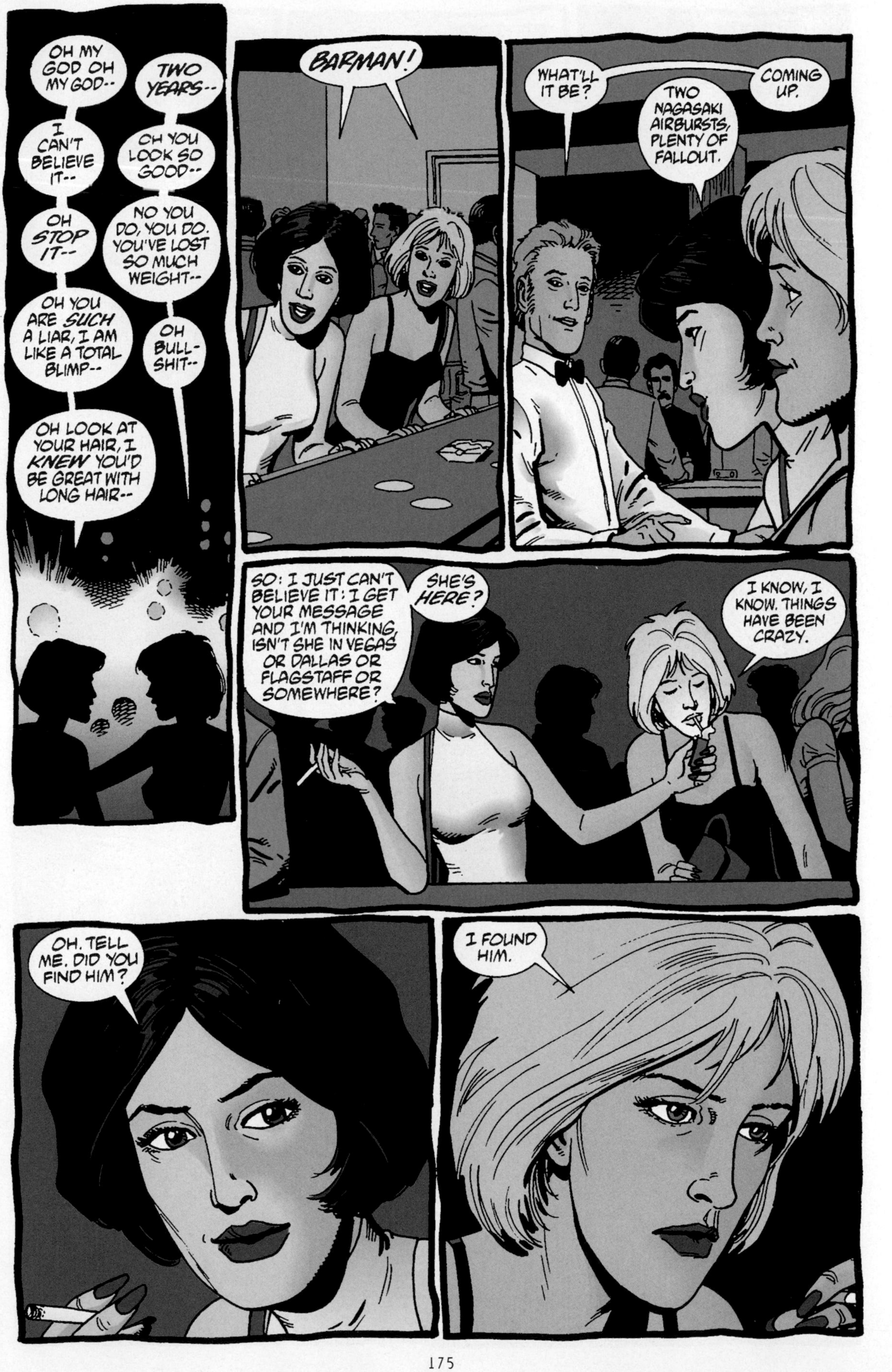
OH MY GOD OH MY GOD--
TWO YEARS--
I CAN'T BELIEVE IT--
OH YOU LOOK SO GOOD--
OH STOP IT--
NO YOU DO, YOU DO. YOU'VE LOST SO MUCH WEIGHT--
OH YOU ARE SUCH A LIAR, I AM LIKE A TOTAL BLIMP--
OH BULL-SHIT--
OH LOOK AT YOUR HAIR, I KNEW YOU'D BE GREAT WITH LONG HAIR--
BARMAN!
WHAT'LL IT BE?
TWO NAGASAKI AIRBURSTS, PLENTY OF FALLOUT.
COMING UP.
SO: I JUST CAN'T BELIEVE IT: I GET YOUR MESSAGE AND I'M THINKING, ISN'T SHE IN VEGAS OR DALLAS OR FLAGSTAFF OR SOMEWHERE?
SHE'S HERE?
I KNOW, I KNOW. THINGS HAVE BEEN CRAZY.
OH. TELL ME. DID YOU FIND HIM?
I FOUND HIM.

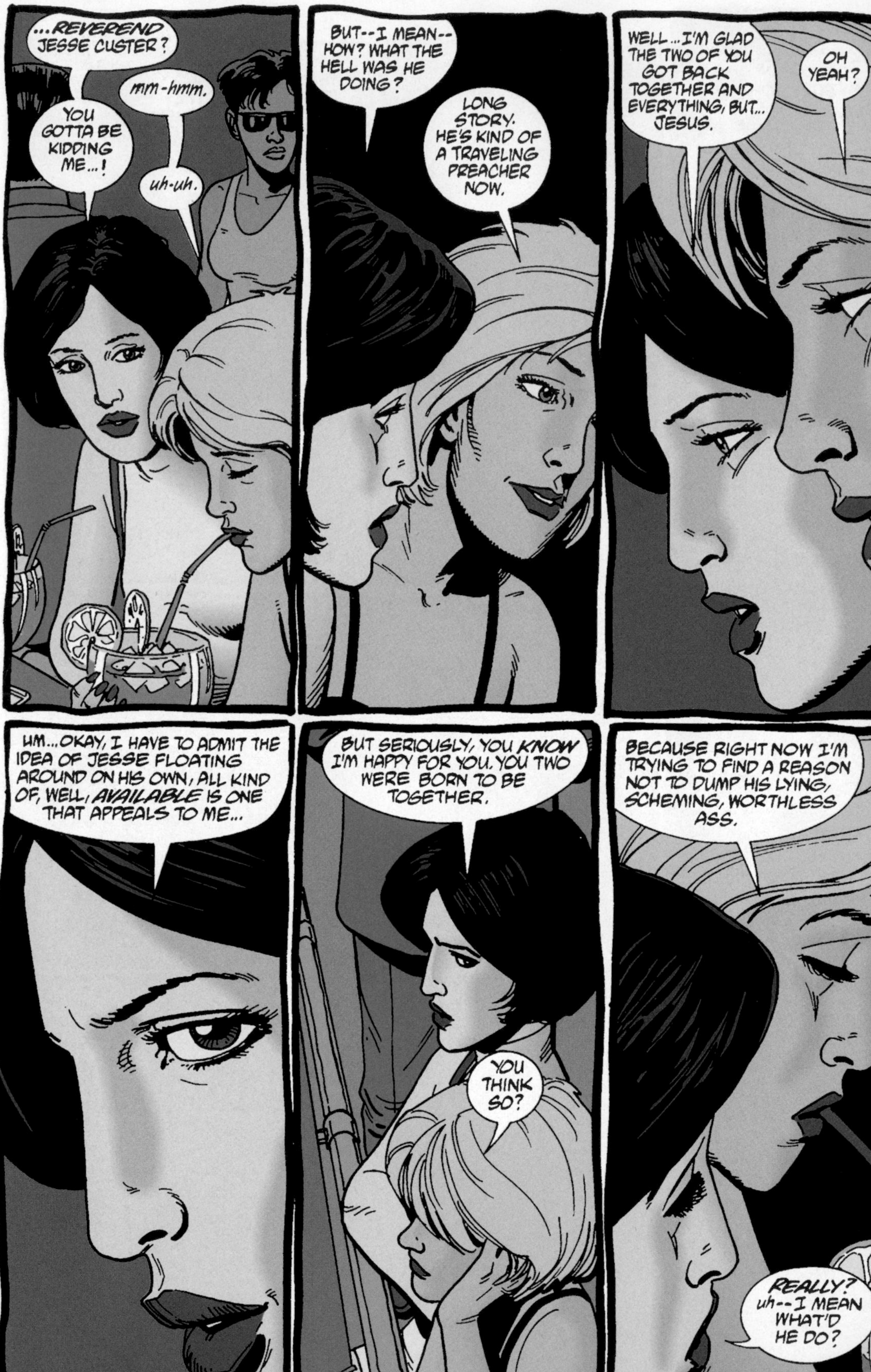

...REVEREND JESSE CUSTER?
mm-hmm.
YOU GOTTA BE KIDDING ME...!
uh-uh.
BUT--I MEAN--HOW? WHAT THE HELL WAS HE DOING?
LONG STORY. HE'S KIND OF A TRAVELING PREACHER NOW.
WELL...I'M GLAD THE TWO OF YOU GOT BACK TOGETHER AND EVERYTHING, BUT... JESUS.
OH YEAH?
UM...OKAY, I HAVE TO ADMIT THE IDEA OF JESSE FLOATING AROUND ON HIS OWN, ALL KIND OF, WELL, AVAILABLE IS ONE THAT APPEALS TO ME...
BUT SERIOUSLY, YOU KNOW I'M HAPPY FOR YOU. YOU TWO WERE BORN TO BE TOGETHER.
YOU THINK SO?
BECAUSE RIGHT NOW I'M TRYING TO FIND A REASON NOT TO DUMP HIS LYING, SCHEMING, WORTHLESS ASS.
REALLY? uh--I MEAN WHAT'D HE DO?

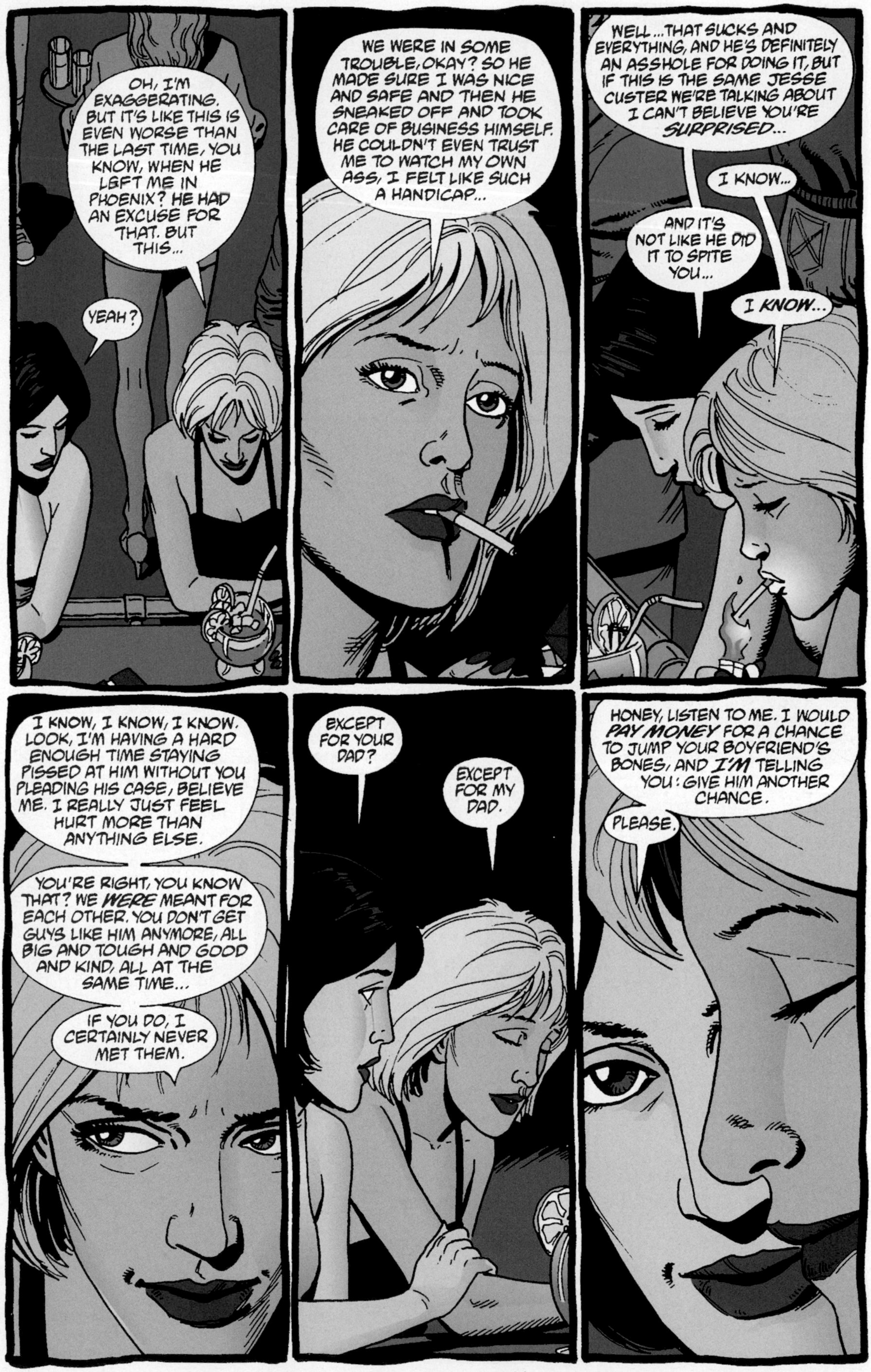
OH, I'M EXAGGERATING. BUT IT'S LIKE THIS IS EVEN WORSE THAN THE LAST TIME, YOU KNOW, WHEN HE LEFT ME IN PHOENIX? HE HAD AN EXCUSE FOR THAT. BUT THIS...
YEAH?
WE WERE IN SOME TROUBLE, OKAY? SO HE MADE SURE I WAS NICE AND SAFE AND THEN HE SNEAKED OFF AND TOOK CARE OF BUSINESS HIMSELF. HE COULDN'T EVEN TRUST ME TO WATCH MY OWN ASS, I FELT LIKE SUCH A HANDICAP...
WELL... THAT SUCKS AND EVERYTHING, AND HE'S DEFINITELY AN ASSHOLE FOR DOING IT, BUT IF THIS IS THE SAME JESSE CUSTER WE'RE TALKING ABOUT I CAN'T BELIEVE YOU'RE SURPRISED...
I KNOW...
AND IT'S NOT LIKE HE DID IT TO SPITE YOU...
I KNOW...
I KNOW, I KNOW, I KNOW. LOOK, I'M HAVING A HARD ENOUGH TIME STAYING PISSED AT HIM WITHOUT YOU PLEADING HIS CASE, BELIEVE ME. I REALLY JUST FEEL HURT MORE THAN ANYTHING ELSE.
YOU'RE RIGHT, YOU KNOW THAT? WE WERE MEANT FOR EACH OTHER. YOU DON'T GET GUYS LIKE HIM ANYMORE, ALL BIG AND TOUGH AND GOOD AND KIND, ALL AT THE SAME TIME...
IF YOU DO, I CERTAINLY NEVER MET THEM.
EXCEPT FOR YOUR DAD?
EXCEPT FOR MY DAD.
HONEY, LISTEN TO ME. I WOULD PAY MONEY FOR A CHANCE TO JUMP YOUR BOYFRIEND'S BONES, AND I'M TELLING YOU: GIVE HIM ANOTHER CHANCE.
PLEASE.

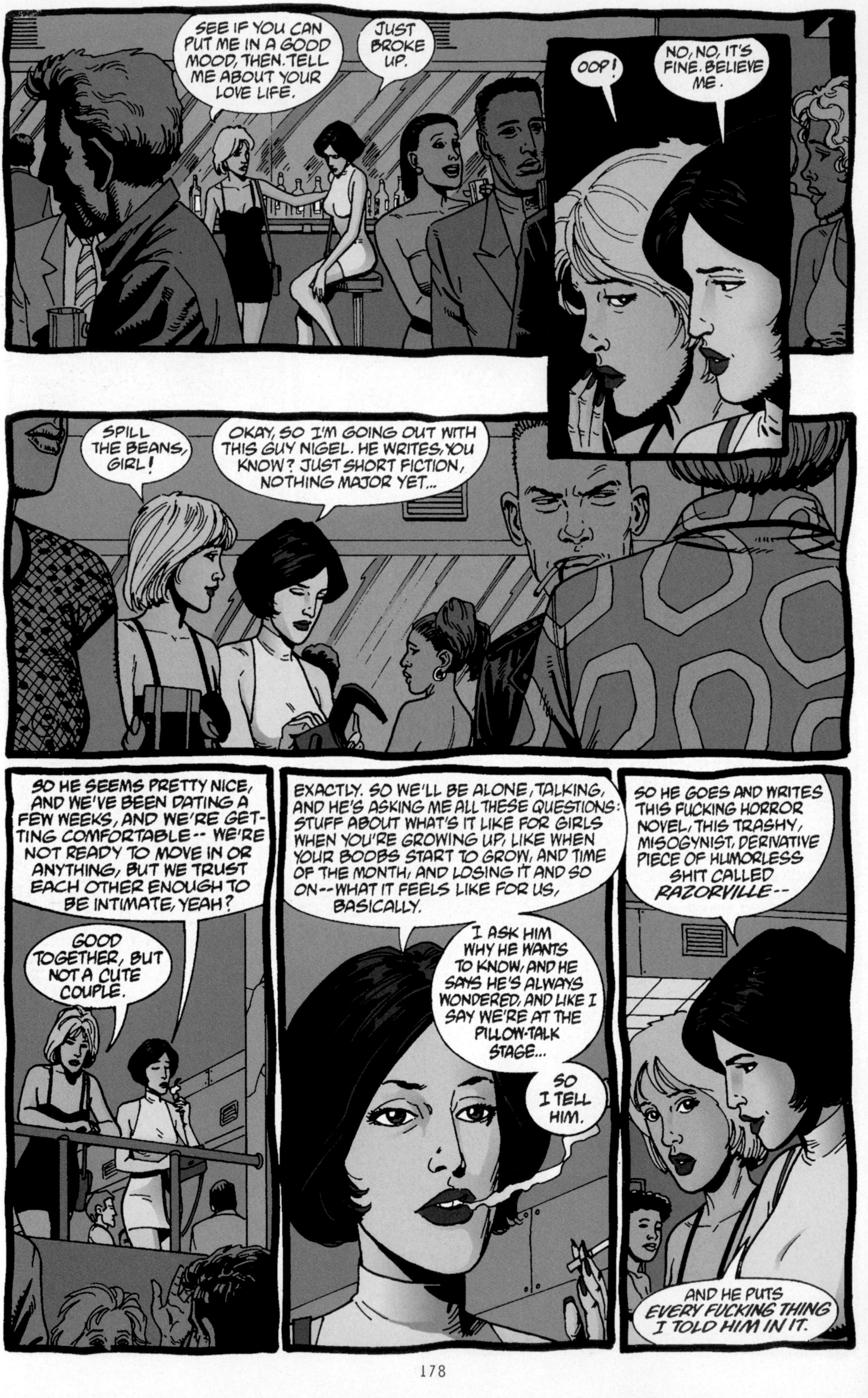
SEE IF YOU CAN PUT ME IN A GOOD MOOD, THEN. TELL ME ABOUT YOUR LOVE LIFE.
JUST BROKE UP.
OOP!
NO, NO, IT'S FINE. BELIEVE ME.
SPILL THE BEANS, GIRL!
OKAY, SO I'M GOING OUT WITH THIS GUY NIGEL. HE WRITES, YOU KNOW? JUST SHORT FICTION, NOTHING MAJOR YET...
SO HE SEEMS PRETTY NICE, AND WE'VE BEEN DATING A FEW WEEKS, AND WE'RE GETTING COMFORTABLE-- WE'RE NOT READY TO MOVE IN OR ANYTHING, BUT WE TRUST EACH OTHER ENOUGH TO BE INTIMATE, YEAH?
GOOD TOGETHER, BUT NOT A CUTE COUPLE.
EXACTLY. SO WE'LL BE ALONE, TALKING, AND HE'S ASKING ME ALL THESE QUESTIONS: STUFF ABOUT WHAT'S IT LIKE FOR GIRLS WHEN YOU'RE GROWING UP, LIKE WHEN YOUR BOOBS START TO GROW, AND TIME OF THE MONTH, AND LOSING IT AND SO ON--WHAT IT FEELS LIKE FOR US, BASICALLY.
I ASK HIM WHY HE WANTS TO KNOW, AND HE SAYS HE'S ALWAYS WONDERED, AND LIKE I SAY WE'RE AT THE PILLOW-TALK STAGE...
SO I TELL HIM.
SO HE GOES AND WRITES THIS FUCKING HORROR NOVEL, THIS TRASHY, MISOGYNIST, DERIVATIVE PIECE OF HUMORLESS SHIT CALLED *RAZORVILLE*--
AND HE PUTS *EVERY FUCKING THING* I TOLD HIM IN IT.

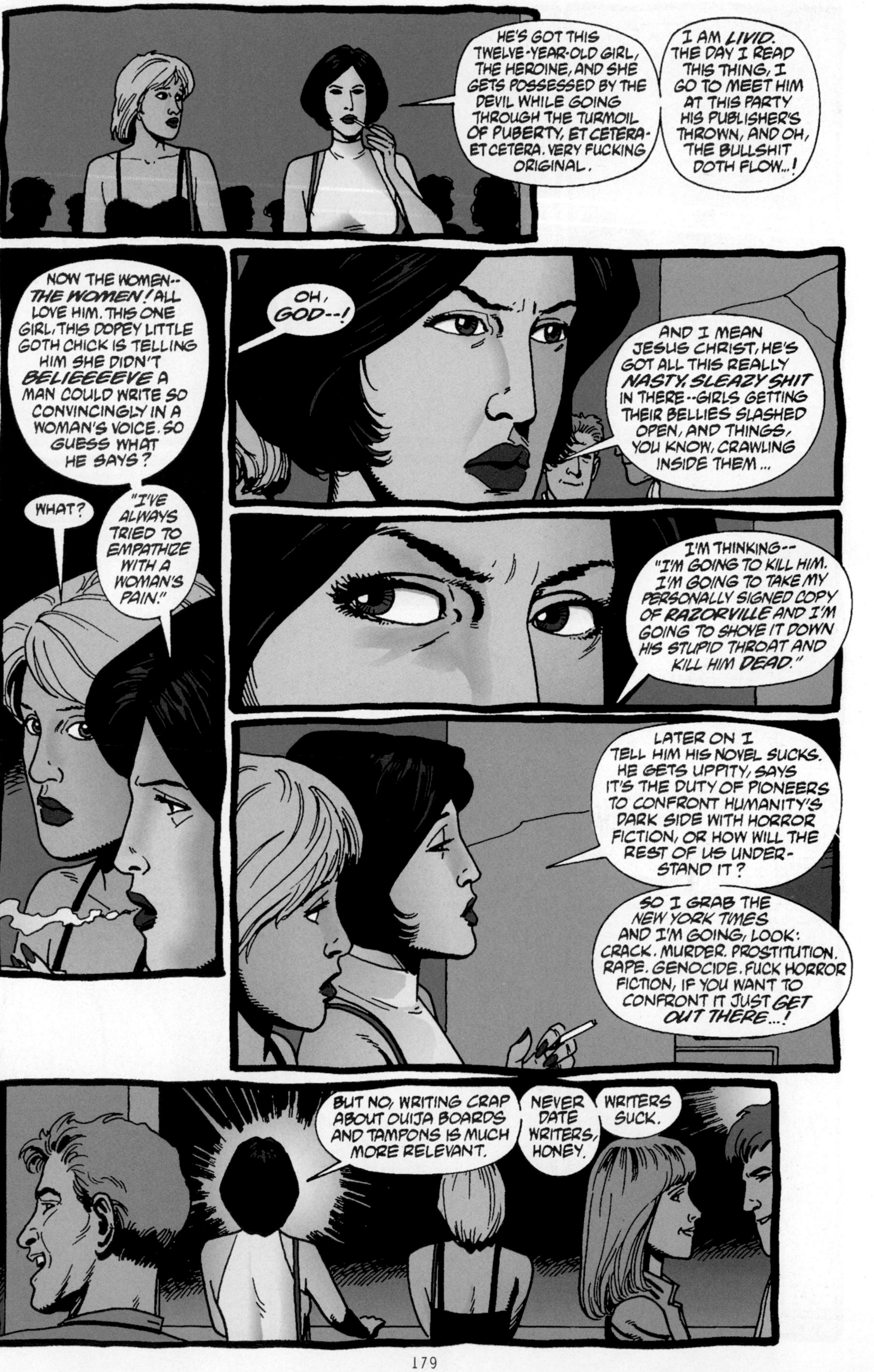
HE'S GOT THIS TWELVE-YEAR-OLD GIRL, THE HEROINE, AND SHE GETS POSSESSED BY THE DEVIL WHILE GOING THROUGH THE TURMOIL OF PUBERTY, ET CETERA ET CETERA. VERY FUCKING ORIGINAL.
I AM LIVID. THE DAY I READ THIS THING, I GO TO MEET HIM AT THIS PARTY HIS PUBLISHER'S THROWN, AND OH, THE BULLSHIT DOTH FLOW...!
NOW THE WOMEN-- THE WOMEN! ALL LOVE HIM. THIS ONE GIRL, THIS DOPEY LITTLE GOTH CHICK IS TELLING HIM SHE DIDN'T BELIEEEEVE A MAN COULD WRITE SO CONVINCINGLY IN A WOMAN'S VOICE. SO GUESS WHAT HE SAYS?
WHAT?
"I'VE ALWAYS TRIED TO EMPATHIZE WITH A WOMAN'S PAIN."
OH, GOD--!
AND I MEAN JESUS CHRIST, HE'S GOT ALL THIS REALLY NASTY, SLEAZY SHIT IN THERE --GIRLS GETTING THEIR BELLIES SLASHED OPEN, AND THINGS, YOU KNOW, CRAWLING INSIDE THEM...
I'M THINKING-- "I'M GOING TO KILL HIM. I'M GOING TO TAKE MY PERSONALLY SIGNED COPY OF RAZORVILLE AND I'M GOING TO SHOVE IT DOWN HIS STUPID THROAT AND KILL HIM DEAD."
LATER ON I TELL HIM HIS NOVEL SUCKS. HE GETS UPPITY, SAYS IT'S THE DUTY OF PIONEERS TO CONFRONT HUMANITY'S DARK SIDE WITH HORROR FICTION, OR HOW WILL THE REST OF US UNDER-STAND IT?
SO I GRAB THE NEW YORK TIMES AND I'M GOING, LOOK: CRACK. MURDER. PROSTITUTION. RAPE. GENOCIDE. FUCK HORROR FICTION, IF YOU WANT TO CONFRONT IT JUST GET OUT THERE...!
BUT NO, WRITING CRAP ABOUT OUIJA BOARDS AND TAMPONS IS MUCH MORE RELEVANT.
NEVER DATE WRITERS, HONEY.
WRITERS SUCK.

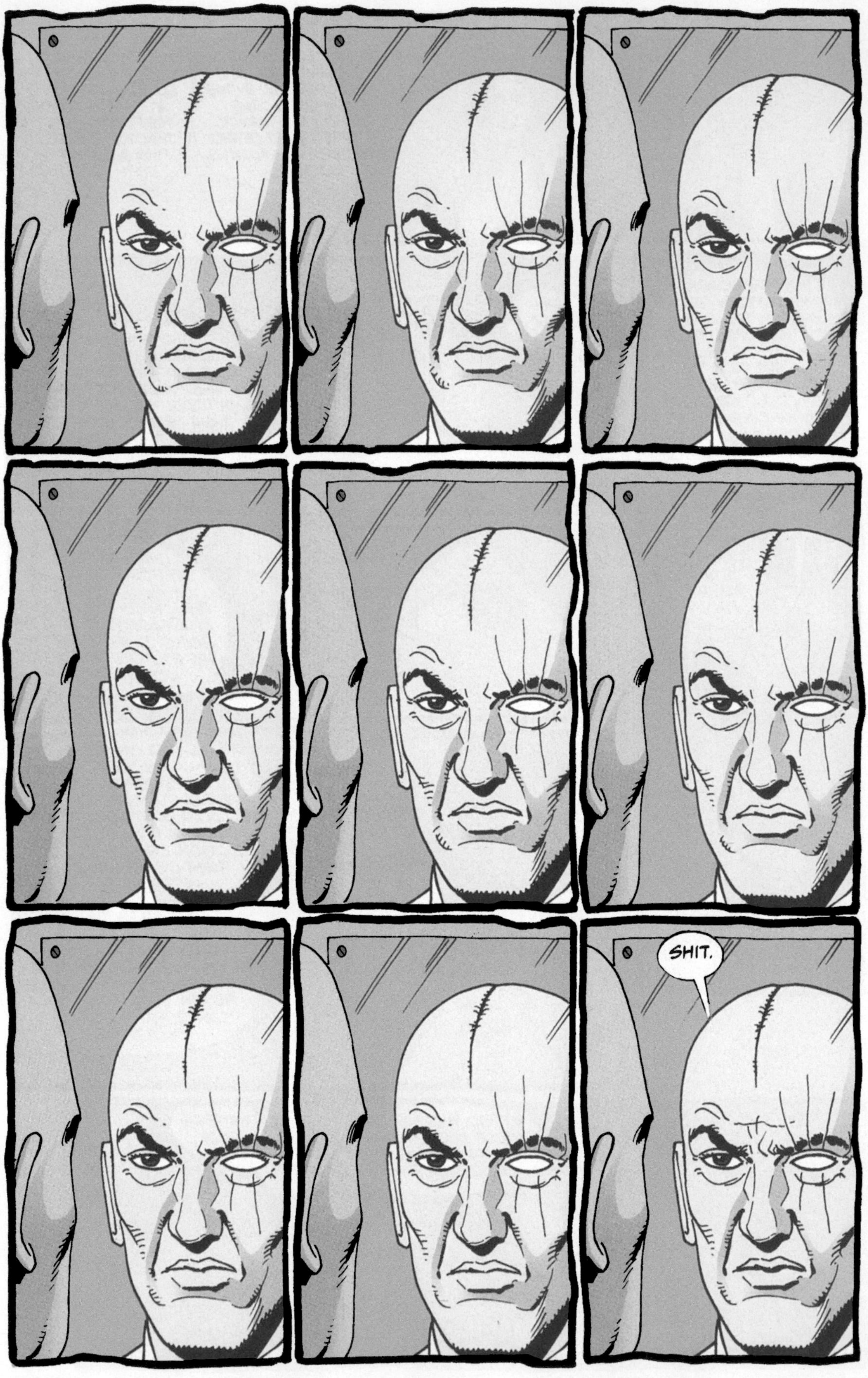
SHIT.

YEAH, AT PILCHER HIGH. IT ISN'T IDEAL, BUT IT'S NOT *DANGEROUS MINDS* JUST YET.

SEE ANYTHING YOU LIKE?

MM...WHO ARE YOU DEALING WITH, THE GUY YOU HAD IN MEMPHIS?

YOU MEAN ROY? NO, THIS IS A LOCAL GUY. PRETTY REPUTABLE, MOSTLY DEALS WITH COUPLES OR OLD FOLKS--YOU KNOW, PEOPLE WHO WANT SOMETHING FOR THE APARTMENT, JUST IN CASE?

HE TRUSTS ME WITH MONEY, SO HE WAS COOL ABOUT LEAVING THESE FOR YOU TO LOOK AT. HE'S CUTE, ACTUALLY, BUT HE'S IN A LITTLE TOO DEEP FOR ME...

AH, FROM THE COUNTRY THAT BROUGHT YOU THE UZI, YOU WANT IT IN THREE FIFTY-SEVEN OR FORTY-FOUR?

I READ YOU CAN GET 'EM IN FIFTY.

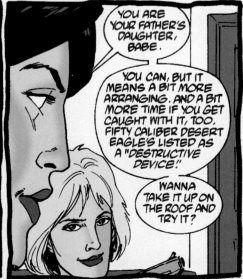

YOU ARE YOUR FATHER'S DAUGHTER, BABE.

YOU CAN, BUT IT MEANS A BIT MORE ARRANGING. AND A BIT MORE TIME IF YOU GET CAUGHT WITH IT, TOO. FIFTY CALIBER DESERT EAGLE'S LISTED AS A "DESTRUCTIVE DEVICE."

WANNA TAKE IT UP ON THE ROOF AND TRY IT?

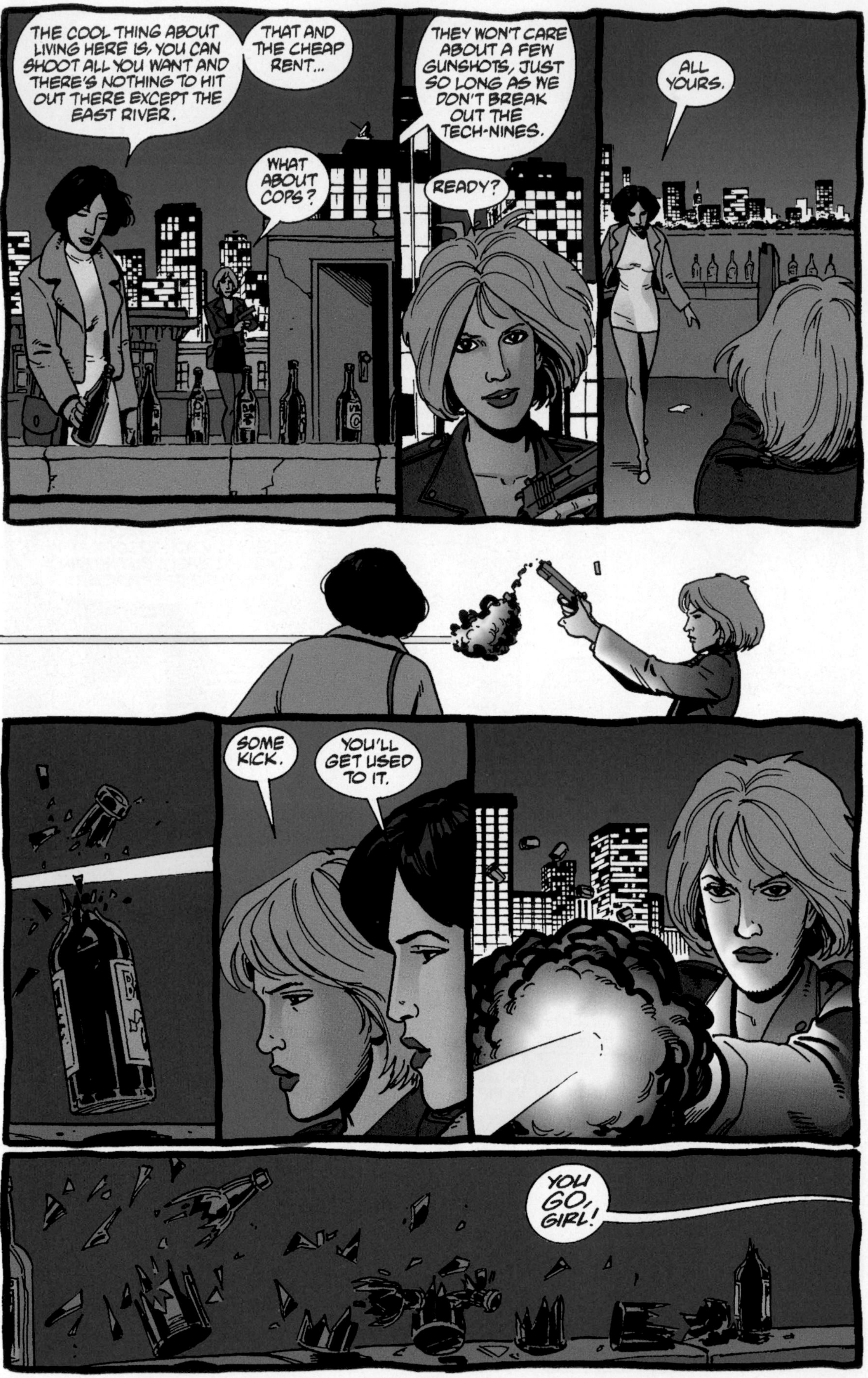
THE COOL THING ABOUT LIVING HERE IS, YOU CAN SHOOT ALL YOU WANT AND THERE'S NOTHING TO HIT OUT THERE EXCEPT THE EAST RIVER.
THAT AND THE CHEAP RENT...
WHAT ABOUT COPS?
THEY WON'T CARE ABOUT A FEW GUNSHOTS, JUST SO LONG AS WE DON'T BREAK OUT THE TECH-NINES.
READY?
ALL YOURS.
SOME KICK.
YOU'LL GET USED TO IT.
YOU GO, GIRL!

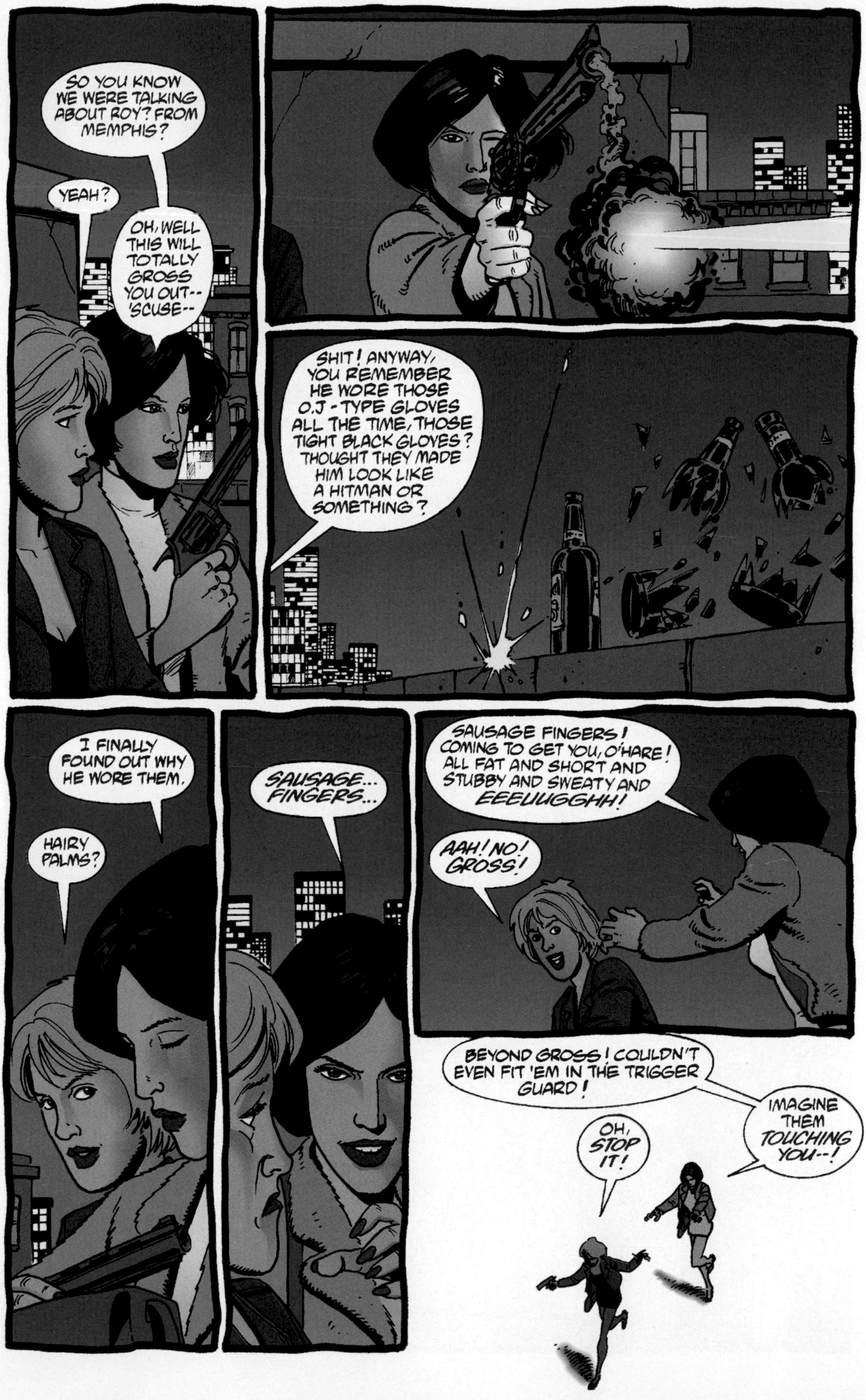
SO YOU KNOW WE WERE TALKING ABOUT ROY? FROM MEMPHIS?
YEAH?
OH, WELL THIS WILL TOTALLY GROSS YOU OUT-- 'SCUSE--
SHIT! ANYWAY, YOU REMEMBER HE WORE THOSE O.J - TYPE GLOVES ALL THE TIME, THOSE TIGHT BLACK GLOVES? THOUGHT THEY MADE HIM LOOK LIKE A HITMAN OR SOMETHING?
I FINALLY FOUND OUT WHY HE WORE THEM.
HAIRY PALMS?
SAUSAGE... FINGERS...
SAUSAGE FINGERS! COMING TO GET YOU, O'HARE! ALL FAT AND SHORT AND STUBBY AND SWEATY AND EEEUUGGHH!
AAH! NO! GROSS!
BEYOND GROSS! COULDN'T EVEN FIT 'EM IN THE TRIGGER GUARD!
IMAGINE THEM TOUCHING YOU--!
OH, STOP IT!

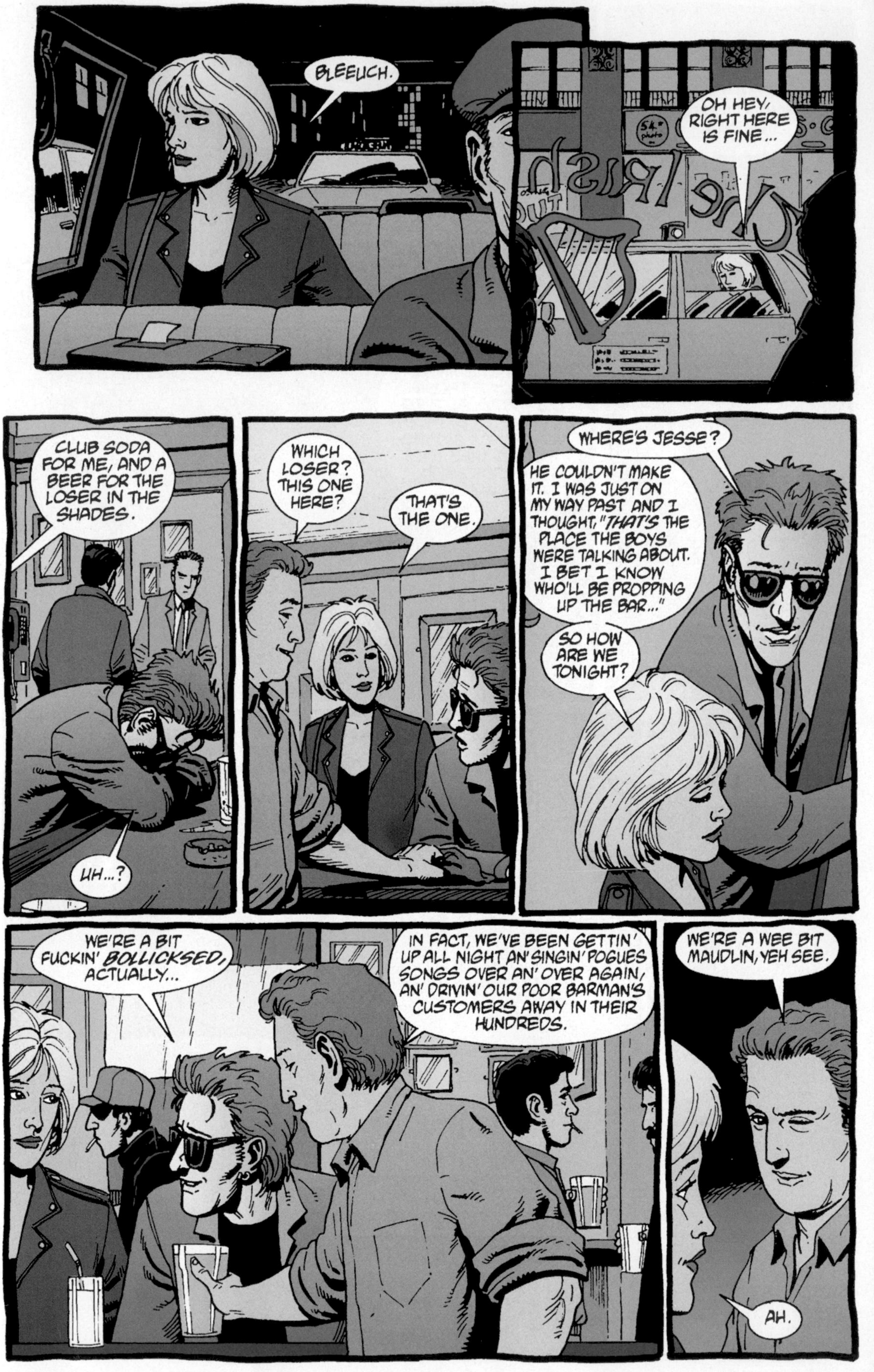
BLEEUCH.
OH HEY, RIGHT HERE IS FINE...
CLUB SODA FOR ME, AND A BEER FOR THE LOSER IN THE SHADES.
UH...?
WHICH LOSER? THIS ONE HERE?
THAT'S THE ONE.
WHERE'S JESSE?
HE COULDN'T MAKE IT. I WAS JUST ON MY WAY PAST AND I THOUGHT, "THAT'S THE PLACE THE BOYS WERE TALKING ABOUT. I BET I KNOW WHO'LL BE PROPPING UP THE BAR..."
SO HOW ARE WE TONIGHT?
WE'RE A BIT FUCKIN' BOLLICKSED, ACTUALLY...
IN FACT, WE'VE BEEN GETTIN' UP ALL NIGHT AN' SINGIN' POGUES SONGS OVER AN' OVER AGAIN, AN' DRIVIN' OUR POOR BARMAN'S CUSTOMERS AWAY IN THEIR HUNDREDS.
WE'RE A WEE BIT MAUDLIN, YEH SEE.
AH.

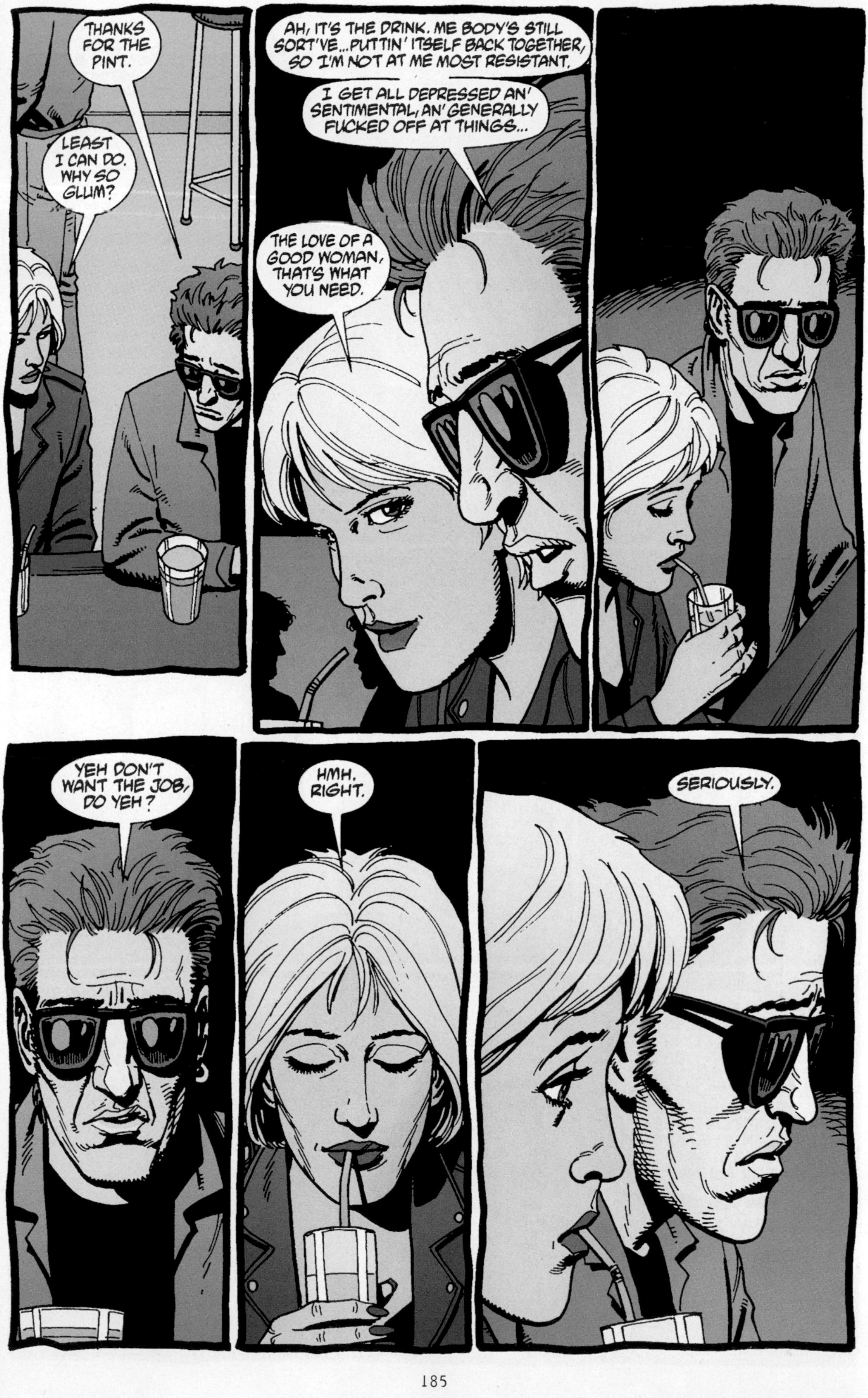
THANKS FOR THE PINT.
LEAST I CAN DO. WHY SO GLUM?
AH, IT'S THE DRINK. ME BODY'S STILL SORT'VE...PUTTIN' ITSELF BACK TOGETHER, SO I'M NOT AT ME MOST RESISTANT.
I GET ALL DEPRESSED AN' SENTIMENTAL, AN' GENERALLY FUCKED OFF AT THINGS...
THE LOVE OF A GOOD WOMAN, THAT'S WHAT YOU NEED.
YEH DON'T WANT THE JOB, DO YEH?
HMH. RIGHT.
SERIOUSLY.

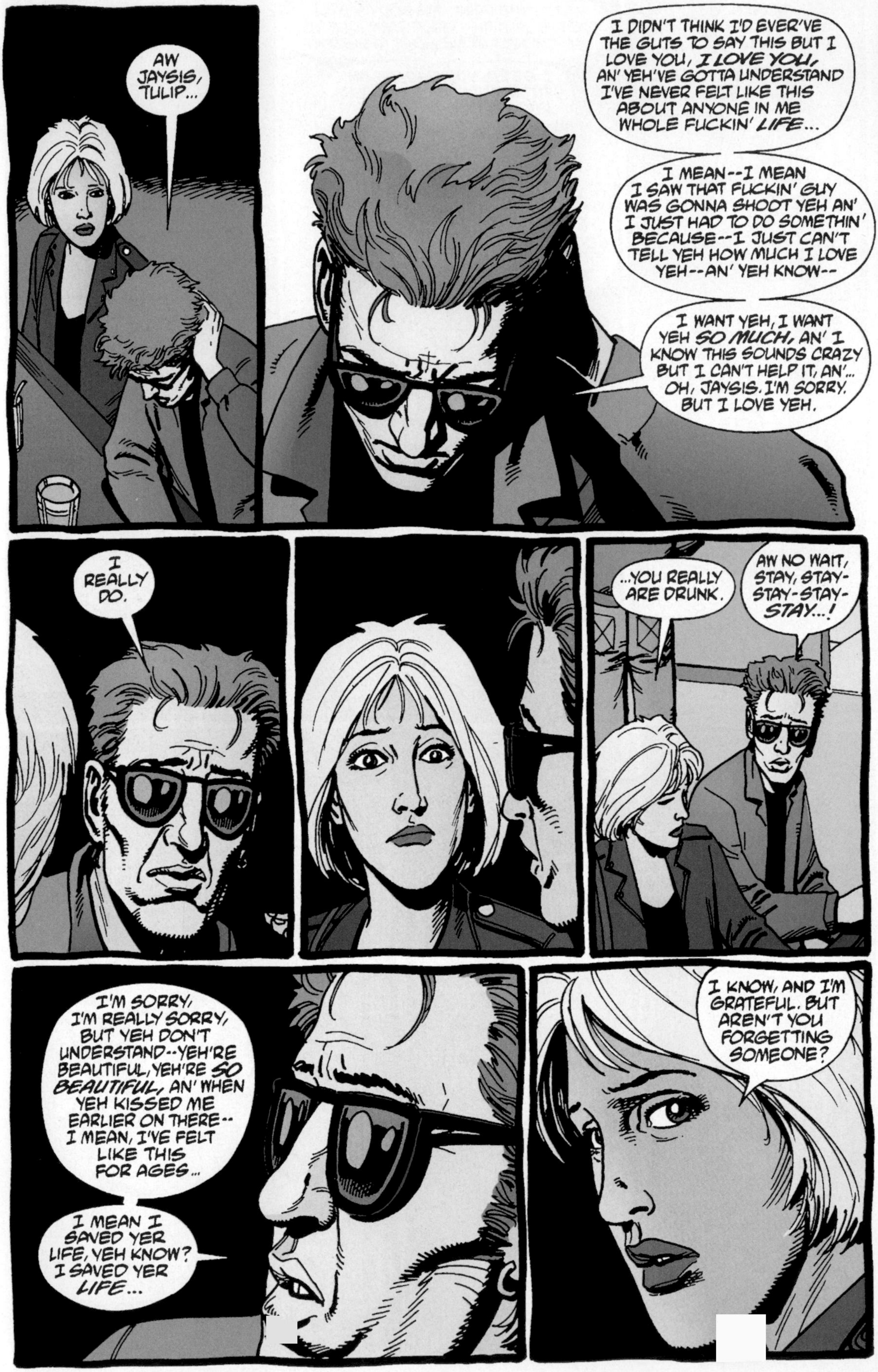
AW JAYSIS, TULIP...
I DIDN'T THINK I'D EVER'VE THE GUTS TO SAY THIS BUT I LOVE YOU, *I LOVE YOU,* AN' YEH'VE GOTTA UNDERSTAND I'VE NEVER FELT LIKE THIS ABOUT ANYONE IN ME WHOLE FUCKIN' *LIFE*...
I MEAN--I MEAN I SAW THAT FUCKIN' GUY WAS GONNA SHOOT YEH AN' I JUST HAD TO DO SOMETHIN' BECAUSE--I JUST CAN'T TELL YEH HOW MUCH I LOVE YEH--AN' YEH KNOW--
I WANT YEH, I WANT YEH *SO MUCH,* AN' I KNOW THIS SOUNDS CRAZY BUT I CAN'T HELP IT, AN'... OH, JAYSIS. I'M SORRY. BUT I LOVE YEH.
I REALLY DO.
...YOU REALLY ARE DRUNK.
AW NO WAIT, STAY, STAY-STAY-STAY-STAY-*STAY*...!
I'M SORRY, I'M REALLY SORRY, BUT YEH DON'T UNDERSTAND--YEH'RE BEAUTIFUL, YEH'RE *SO BEAUTIFUL,* AN' WHEN YEH KISSED ME EARLIER ON THERE-- I MEAN, I'VE FELT LIKE THIS FOR AGES...
I MEAN I SAVED YER LIFE, YEH KNOW? I SAVED YER *LIFE*...
I KNOW, AND I'M GRATEFUL. BUT AREN'T YOU FORGETTING SOMEONE?

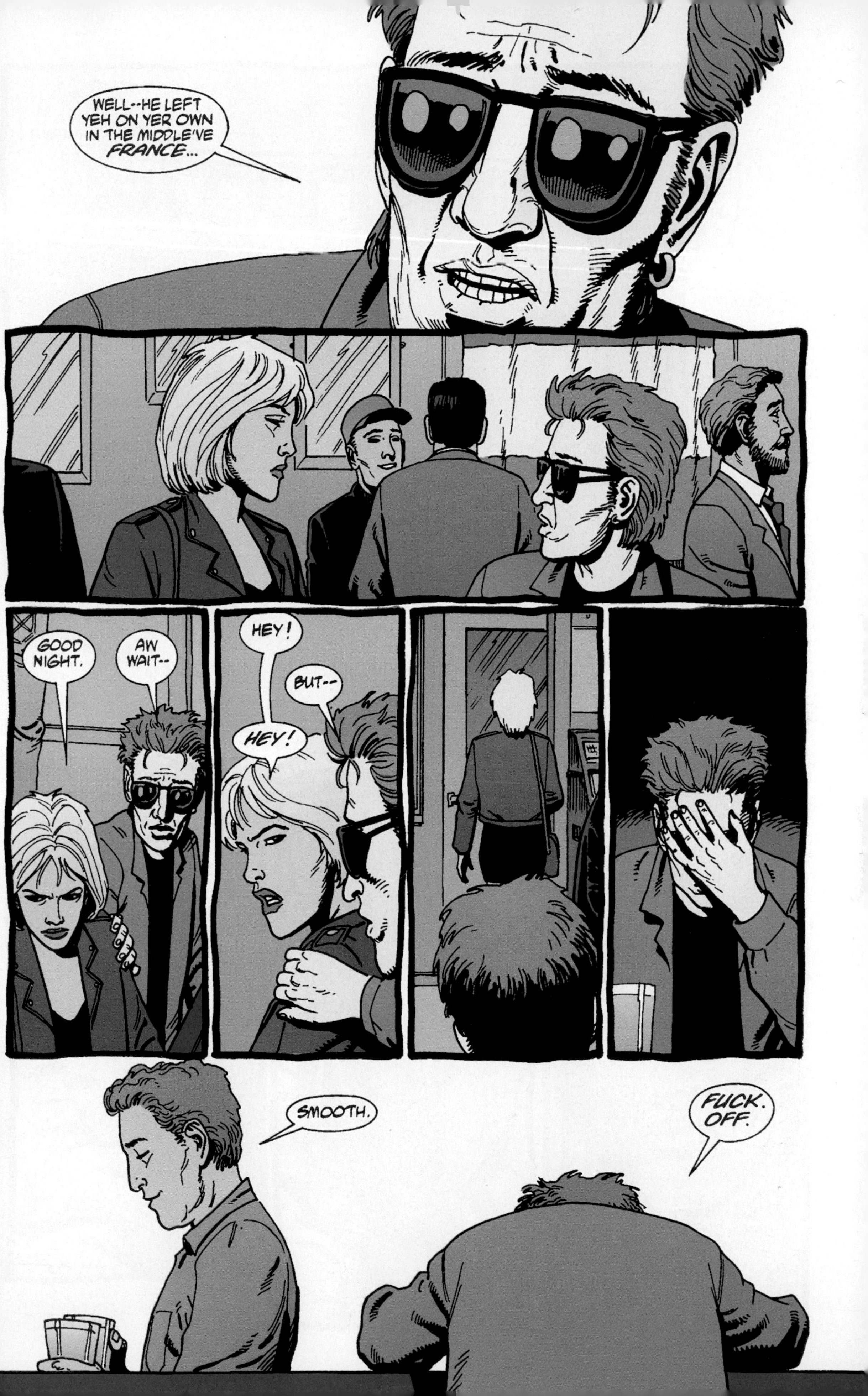
WELL--HE LEFT YEH ON YER OWN IN THE MIDDLE'VE *FRANCE*...
GOOD NIGHT.
AW WAIT--
HEY!
BUT--
*HEY!*
SMOOTH.
*FUCK. OFF.*

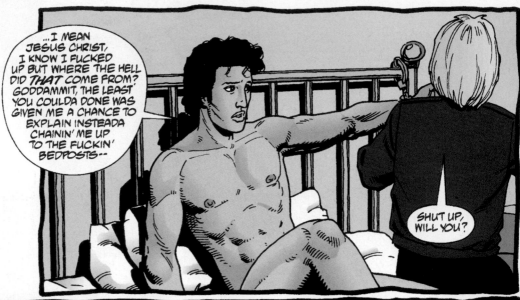

...I MEAN JESUS CHRIST, I KNOW I FUCKED UP BUT WHERE THE HELL DID *THAT* COME FROM? GODDAMMIT, THE LEAST YOU COULDA DONE WAS GIVEN ME A CHANCE TO EXPLAIN INSTEADA CHAININ' ME UP TO THE FUCKIN' BEDPOSTS--

SHUT UP, WILL YOU?

SHUT UP AND HOLD ME.

I GUESS THAT SOUNDS LIKE A PLAN.

188

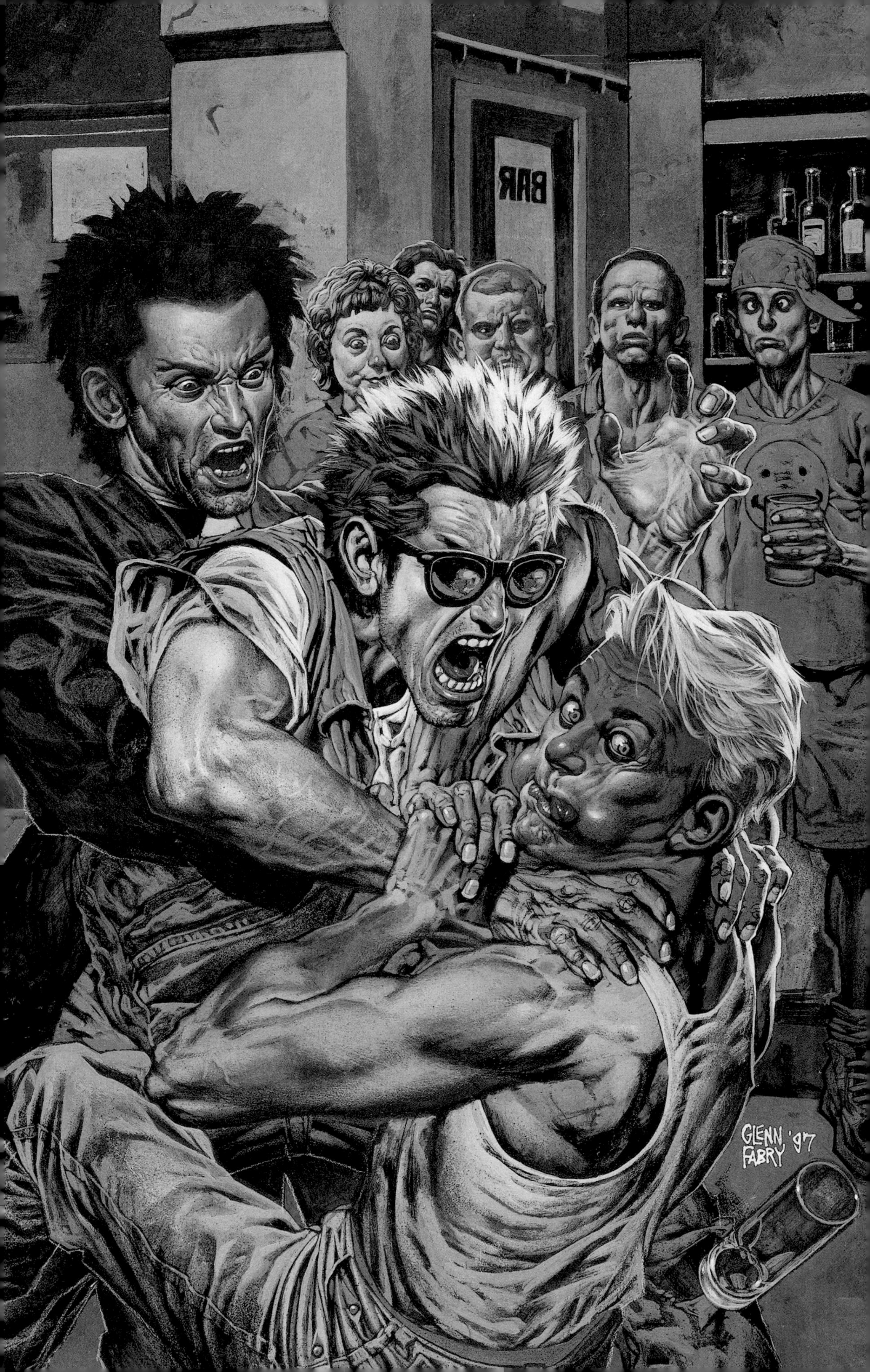
BAR
GLENN FABRY '97

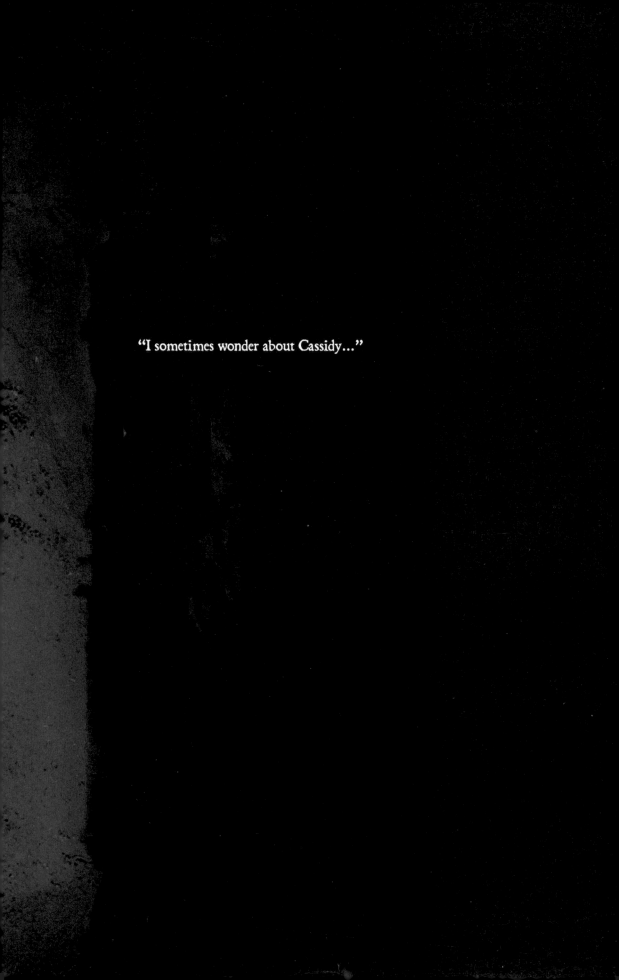

"I sometimes wonder about Cassidy..."

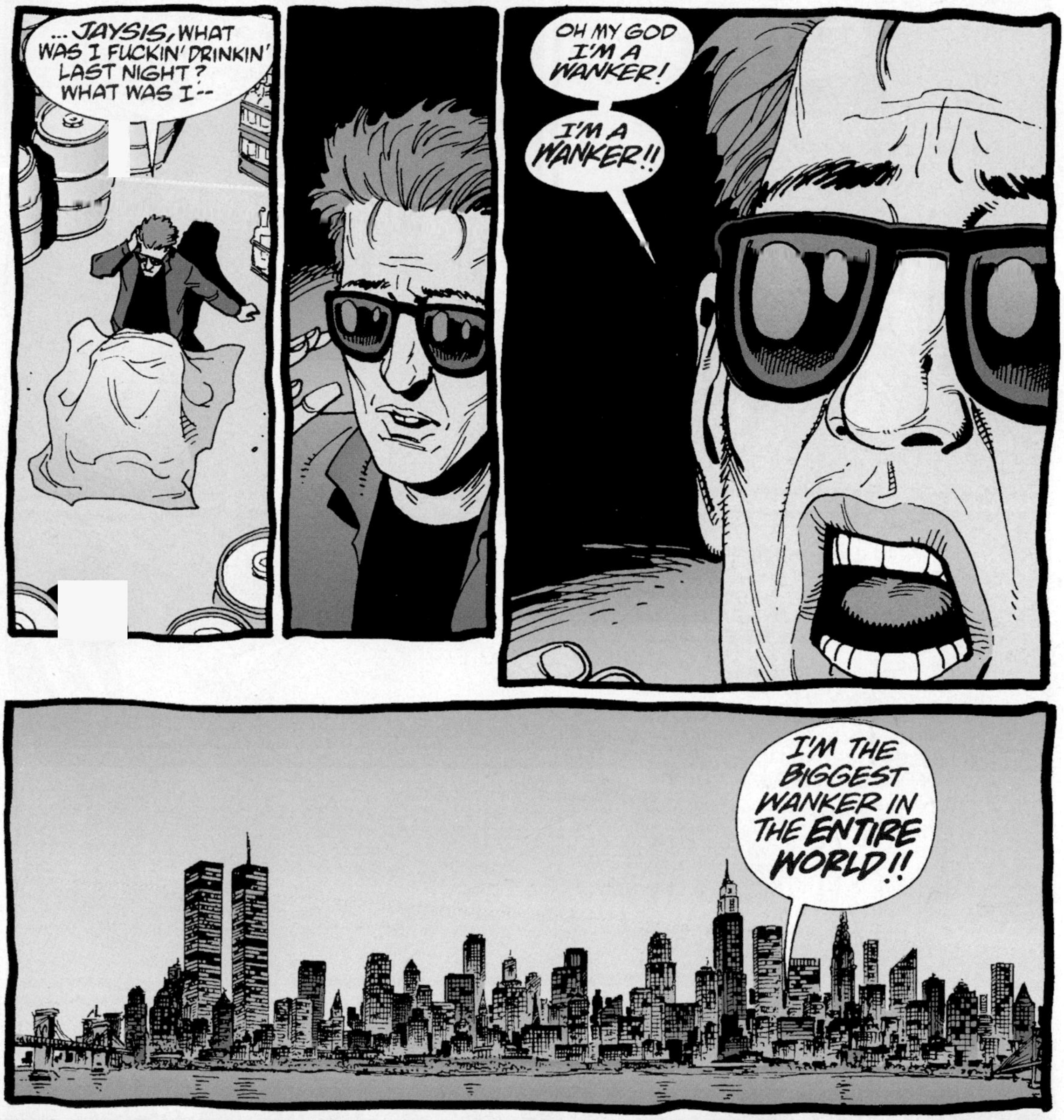
...JAYSIS, WHAT WAS I FUCKIN' DRINKIN' LAST NIGHT? WHAT WAS I--
OH MY GOD I'M A WANKER!
I'M A WANKER!!
I'M THE BIGGEST WANKER IN THE ENTIRE WORLD!!

# RUMORS OF WAR

GARTH ENNIS - Writer STEVE DILLON - Artist
MATT HOLLINGSWORTH - Colorist
CLEM ROBINS - Letterer AXEL ALONSO - Editor

PREACHER created by GARTH ENNIS and STEVE DILLON

YOU KNOW WHAT THE WORST THING ABOUT IT WAS...?

WHAT WAS THE WORST THING, BABY?

IT REMINDED ME OF WHEN I WAS EIGHT AND THE BOYS WOULDN'T LET ME PLAY SOLDIERS.

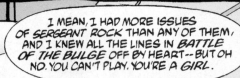

I MEAN, I HAD MORE ISSUES OF SERGEANT ROCK THAN ANY OF THEM, AND I KNEW ALL THE LINES IN *BATTLE OF THE BULGE* OFF BY HEART--BUT OH NO. YOU CAN'T PLAY. YOU'RE A *GIRL*.

AND WHEN YOU DUMPED ME IN THAT MOTEL AND RAN OFF ON YOUR BIG BOY'S ADVENTURE, I FELT JUST AS DUMB AND USELESS AND STUPID AS THEY MADE ME FEEL ALL THOSE YEARS AGO.

WELL...*uh*... I AIN'T TRYNNA GET OFF THE SUBJECT HERE OR ANYTHING, HONEY, BUT I REALLY GOTTA ASK...

HOW COME YOU WANTED TO PLAY SOLDIERS, INSTEADA LIKE WITH DOLLS AN' STUFFED TOYS AN' SHIT LIKE THAT?

REMIND ME WHY I HAVE SEX WITH YOU AGAIN?

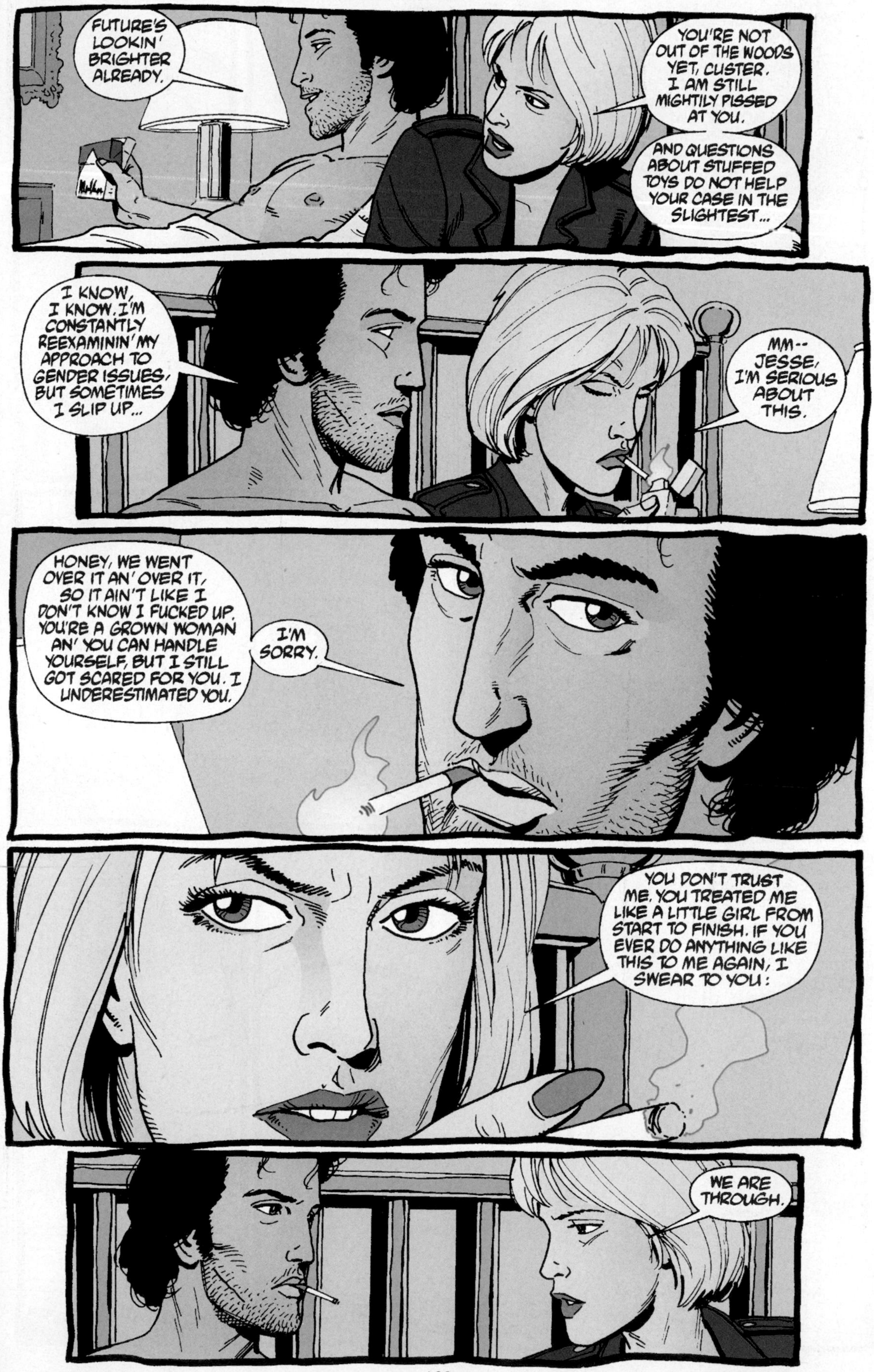
FUTURE'S LOOKIN' BRIGHTER ALREADY.
YOU'RE NOT OUT OF THE WOODS YET, CUSTER. I AM STILL MIGHTILY PISSED AT YOU.
AND QUESTIONS ABOUT STUFFED TOYS DO NOT HELP YOUR CASE IN THE SLIGHTEST...
I KNOW, I KNOW. I'M CONSTANTLY REEXAMININ' MY APPROACH TO GENDER ISSUES, BUT SOMETIMES I SLIP UP...
MM-- JESSE, I'M SERIOUS ABOUT THIS.
HONEY, WE WENT OVER IT AN' OVER IT, SO IT AIN'T LIKE I DON'T KNOW I FUCKED UP. YOU'RE A GROWN WOMAN AN' YOU CAN HANDLE YOURSELF, BUT I STILL GOT SCARED FOR YOU. I UNDERESTIMATED YOU.
I'M SORRY.
YOU DON'T TRUST ME. YOU TREATED ME LIKE A LITTLE GIRL FROM START TO FINISH. IF YOU EVER DO ANYTHING LIKE THIS TO ME AGAIN, I SWEAR TO YOU:
WE ARE THROUGH.

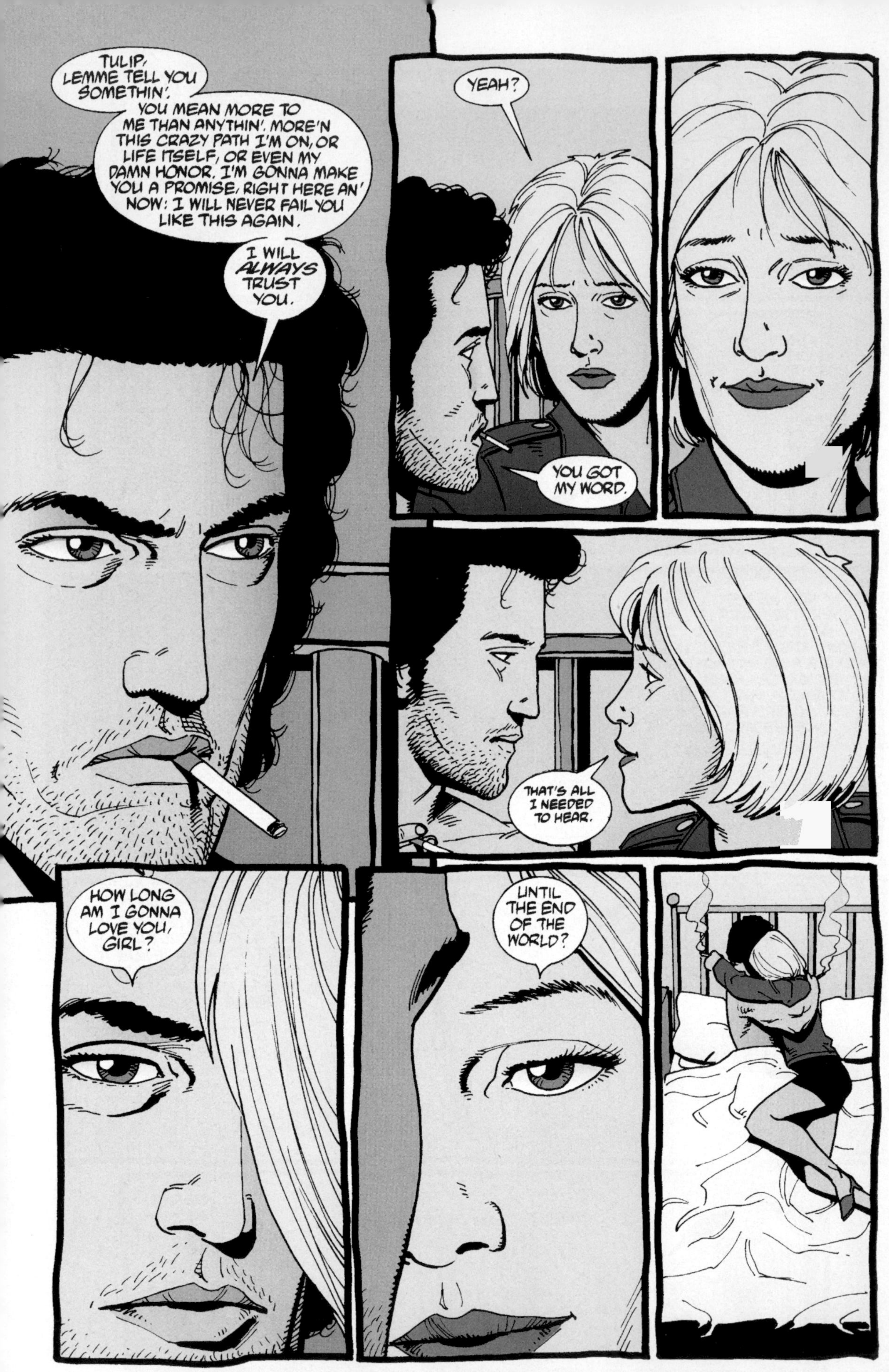
TULIP, LEMME TELL YOU SOMETHIN'.
YOU MEAN MORE TO ME THAN ANYTHIN'. MORE'N THIS CRAZY PATH I'M ON, OR LIFE ITSELF, OR EVEN MY DAMN HONOR. I'M GONNA MAKE YOU A PROMISE, RIGHT HERE AN' NOW: I WILL NEVER FAIL YOU LIKE THIS AGAIN.
I WILL *ALWAYS* TRUST YOU.
YEAH?
YOU GOT MY WORD.
THAT'S ALL I NEEDED TO HEAR.
HOW LONG AM I GONNA LOVE YOU, GIRL?
UNTIL THE END OF THE WORLD?

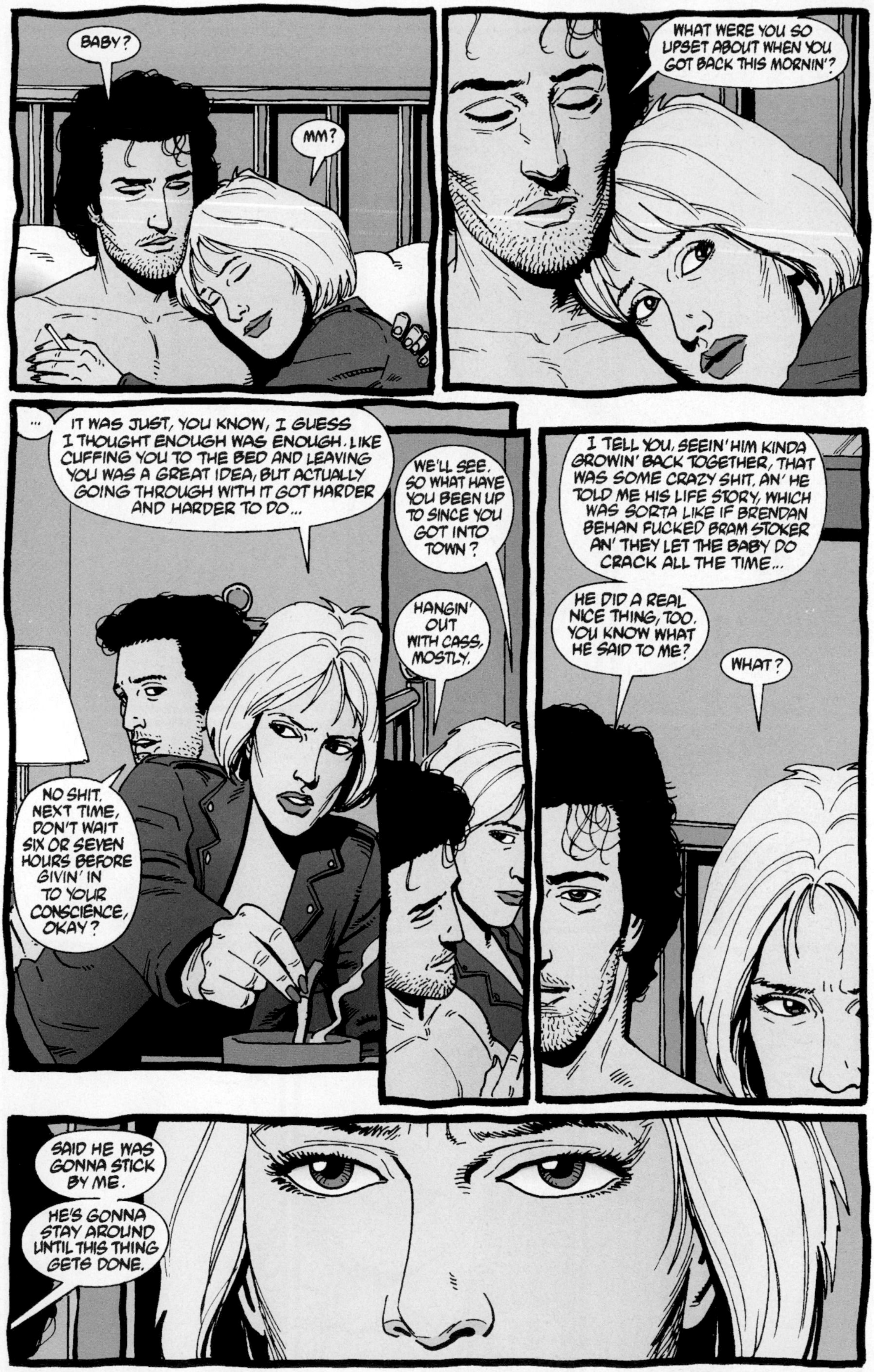
BABY?
MM?
WHAT WERE YOU SO UPSET ABOUT WHEN YOU GOT BACK THIS MORNIN'?
...
IT WAS JUST, YOU KNOW, I GUESS I THOUGHT ENOUGH WAS ENOUGH. LIKE CUFFING YOU TO THE BED AND LEAVING YOU WAS A GREAT IDEA, BUT ACTUALLY GOING THROUGH WITH IT GOT HARDER AND HARDER TO DO...
NO SHIT. NEXT TIME, DON'T WAIT SIX OR SEVEN HOURS BEFORE GIVIN' IN TO YOUR CONSCIENCE, OKAY?
WE'LL SEE. SO WHAT HAVE YOU BEEN UP TO SINCE YOU GOT INTO TOWN?
HANGIN' OUT WITH CASS, MOSTLY.
I TELL YOU, SEEIN' HIM KINDA GROWIN' BACK TOGETHER, THAT WAS SOME CRAZY SHIT, AN' HE TOLD ME HIS LIFE STORY, WHICH WAS SORTA LIKE IF BRENDAN BEHAN FUCKED BRAM STOKER AN' THEY LET THE BABY DO CRACK ALL THE TIME...
HE DID A REAL NICE THING, TOO. YOU KNOW WHAT HE SAID TO ME?
WHAT?
SAID HE WAS GONNA STICK BY ME.
HE'S GONNA STAY AROUND UNTIL THIS THING GETS DONE.

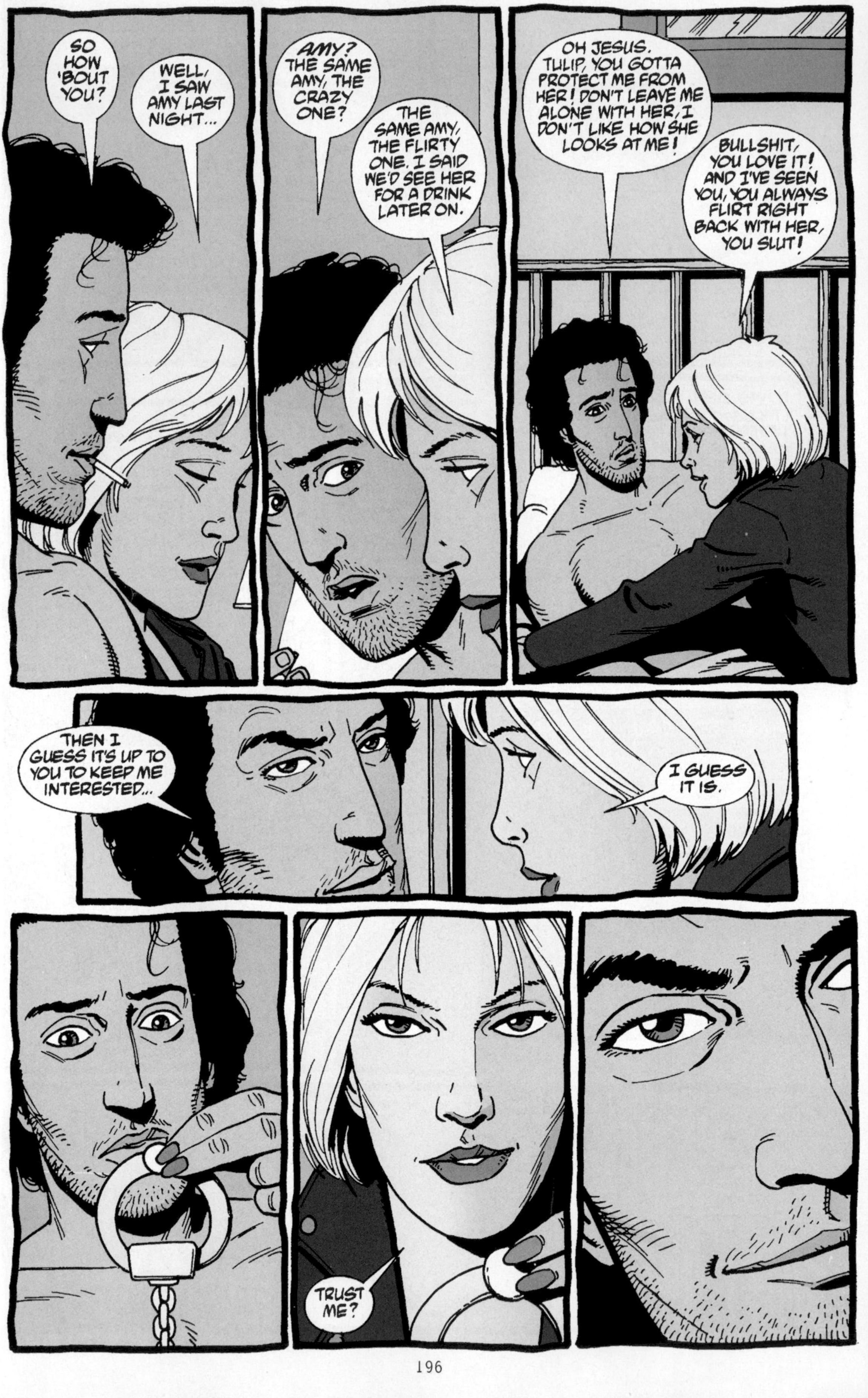
SO HOW 'BOUT YOU?
WELL, I SAW AMY LAST NIGHT...
AMY? THE SAME AMY, THE CRAZY ONE?
THE SAME AMY, THE FLIRTY ONE. I SAID WE'D SEE HER FOR A DRINK LATER ON.
OH JESUS. TULIP, YOU GOTTA PROTECT ME FROM HER! DON'T LEAVE ME ALONE WITH HER, I DON'T LIKE HOW SHE LOOKS AT ME!
BULLSHIT, YOU LOVE IT! AND I'VE SEEN YOU, YOU ALWAYS FLIRT RIGHT BACK WITH HER, YOU SLUT!
THEN I GUESS IT'S UP TO YOU TO KEEP ME INTERESTED...
I GUESS IT IS.
TRUST ME?

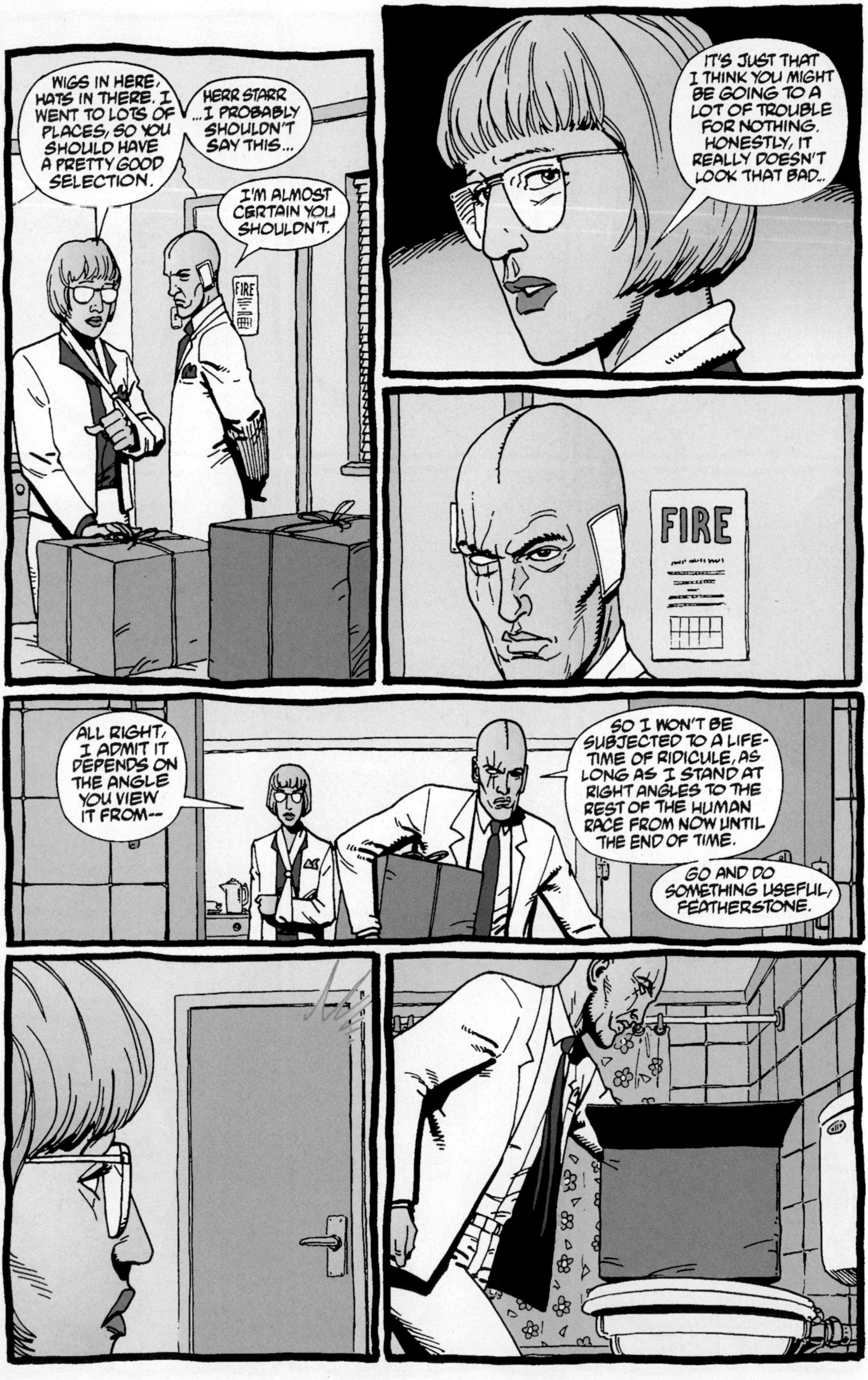
WIGS IN HERE, HATS IN THERE. I WENT TO LOTS OF PLACES, SO YOU SHOULD HAVE A PRETTY GOOD SELECTION.
HERR STARR ...I PROBABLY SHOULDN'T SAY THIS...
I'M ALMOST CERTAIN YOU SHOULDN'T.
FIRE
IT'S JUST THAT I THINK YOU MIGHT BE GOING TO A LOT OF TROUBLE FOR NOTHING. HONESTLY, IT REALLY DOESN'T LOOK THAT BAD...
FIRE
ALL RIGHT, I ADMIT IT DEPENDS ON THE ANGLE YOU VIEW IT FROM--
SO I WON'T BE SUBJECTED TO A LIFETIME OF RIDICULE, AS LONG AS I STAND AT RIGHT ANGLES TO THE REST OF THE HUMAN RACE FROM NOW UNTIL THE END OF TIME.
GO AND DO SOMETHING USEFUL, FEATHERSTONE.

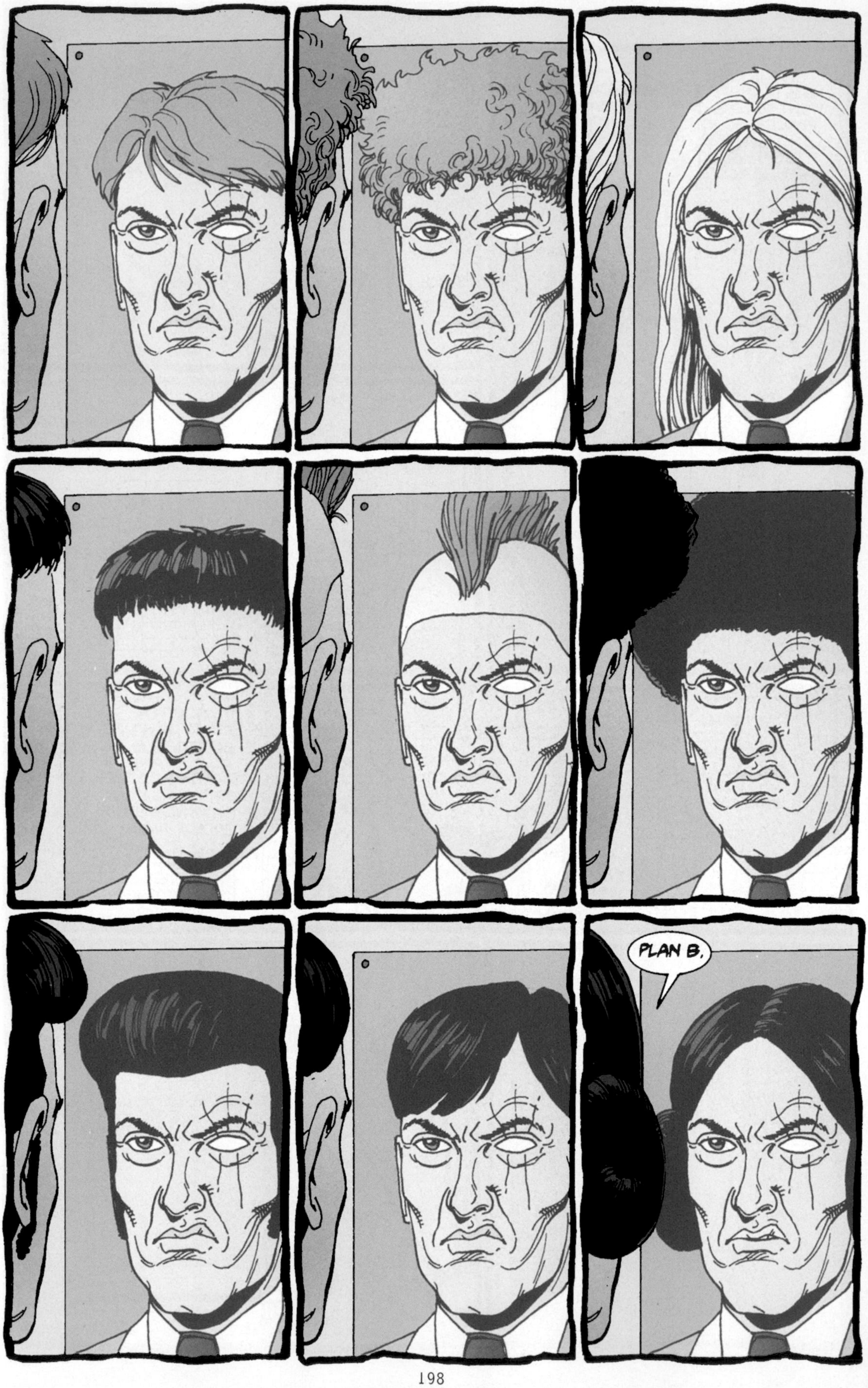
PLAN B.

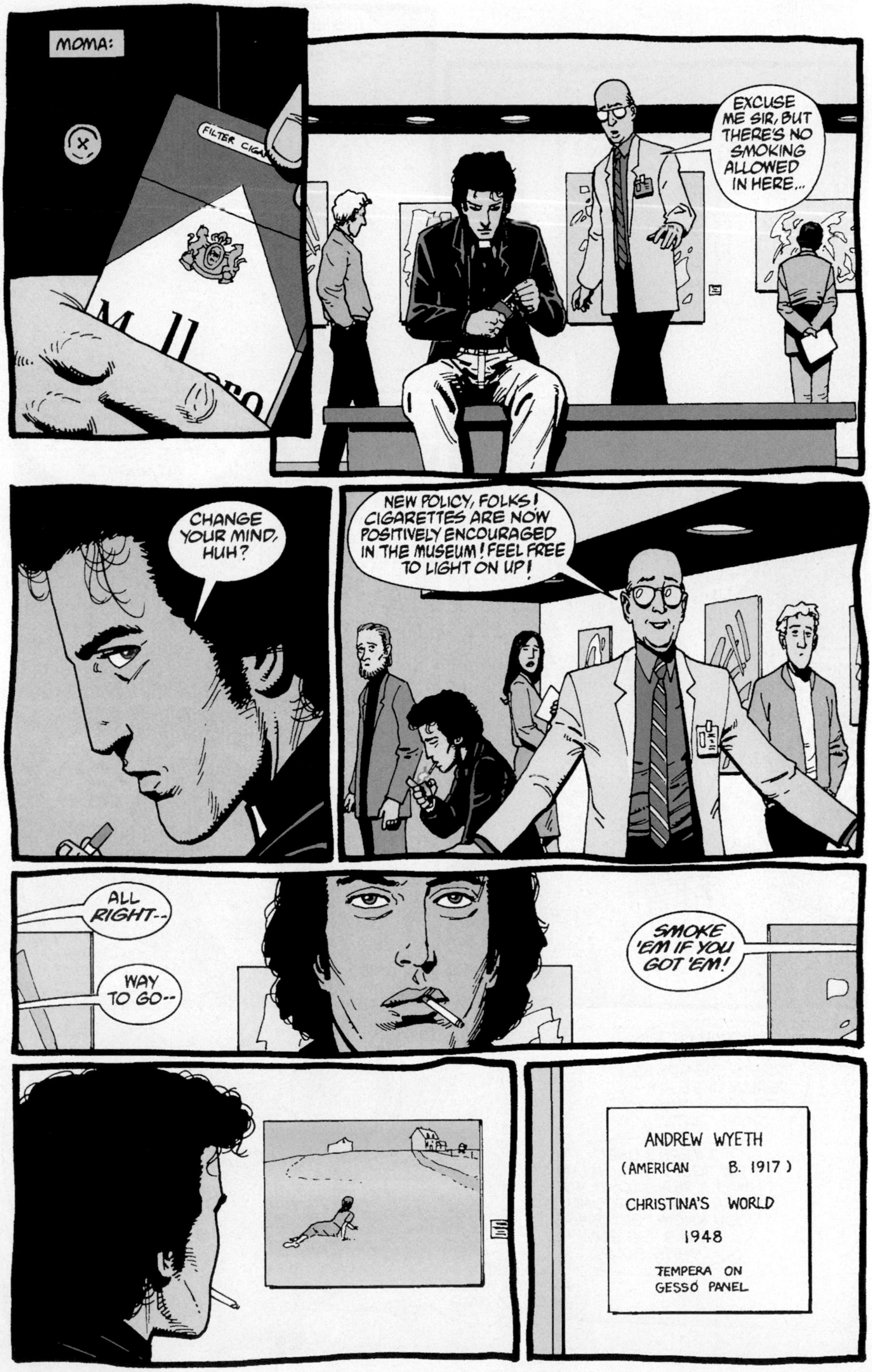
MOMA:
FILTER CIGA
EXCUSE ME SIR, BUT THERE'S NO SMOKING ALLOWED IN HERE...
CHANGE YOUR MIND, HUH?
NEW POLICY, FOLKS! CIGARETTES ARE NOW POSITIVELY ENCOURAGED IN THE MUSEUM! FEEL FREE TO LIGHT ON UP!
ALL RIGHT--
WAY TO GO--
SMOKE 'EM IF YOU GOT 'EM!
ANDREW WYETH
(AMERICAN B. 1917)
CHRISTINA'S WORLD
1948
TEMPERA ON GESSO PANEL

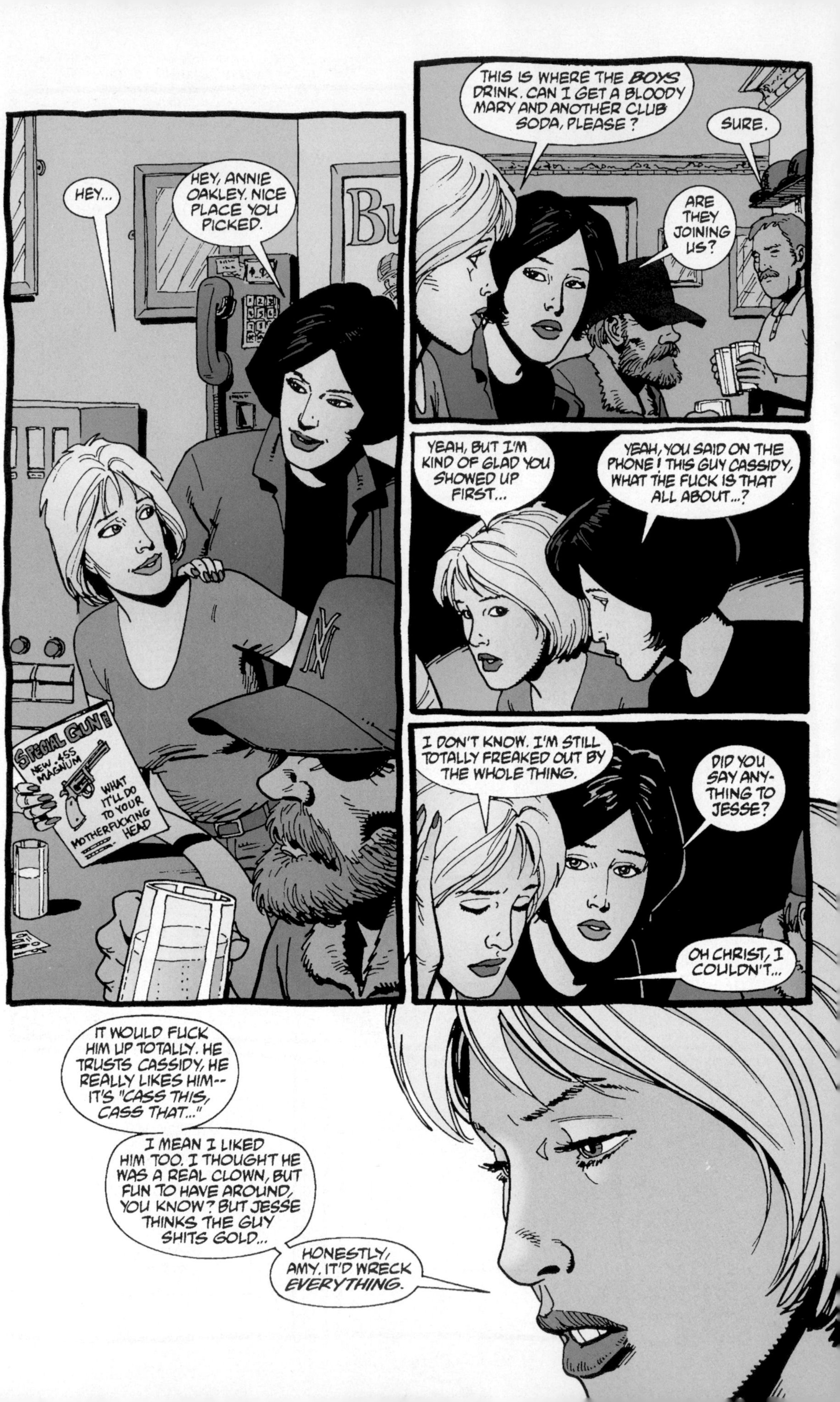
HEY...
HEY, ANNIE OAKLEY. NICE PLACE YOU PICKED.
SPECIAL GUN! NEW .455 MAGNUM WHAT IT'LL DO TO YOUR MOTHERFUCKING HEAD
THIS IS WHERE THE BOYS DRINK. CAN I GET A BLOODY MARY AND ANOTHER CLUB SODA, PLEASE?
SURE.
ARE THEY JOINING US?
YEAH, BUT I'M KIND OF GLAD YOU SHOWED UP FIRST...
YEAH, YOU SAID ON THE PHONE! THIS GUY CASSIDY, WHAT THE FUCK IS THAT ALL ABOUT...?
I DON'T KNOW. I'M STILL TOTALLY FREAKED OUT BY THE WHOLE THING.
DID YOU SAY ANYTHING TO JESSE?
OH CHRIST, I COULDN'T...
IT WOULD FUCK HIM UP TOTALLY. HE TRUSTS CASSIDY, HE REALLY LIKES HIM-- IT'S "CASS THIS, CASS THAT..."
I MEAN I LIKED HIM TOO. I THOUGHT HE WAS A REAL CLOWN, BUT FUN TO HAVE AROUND, YOU KNOW? BUT JESSE THINKS THE GUY SHITS GOLD...
HONESTLY, AMY. IT'D WRECK EVERYTHING.

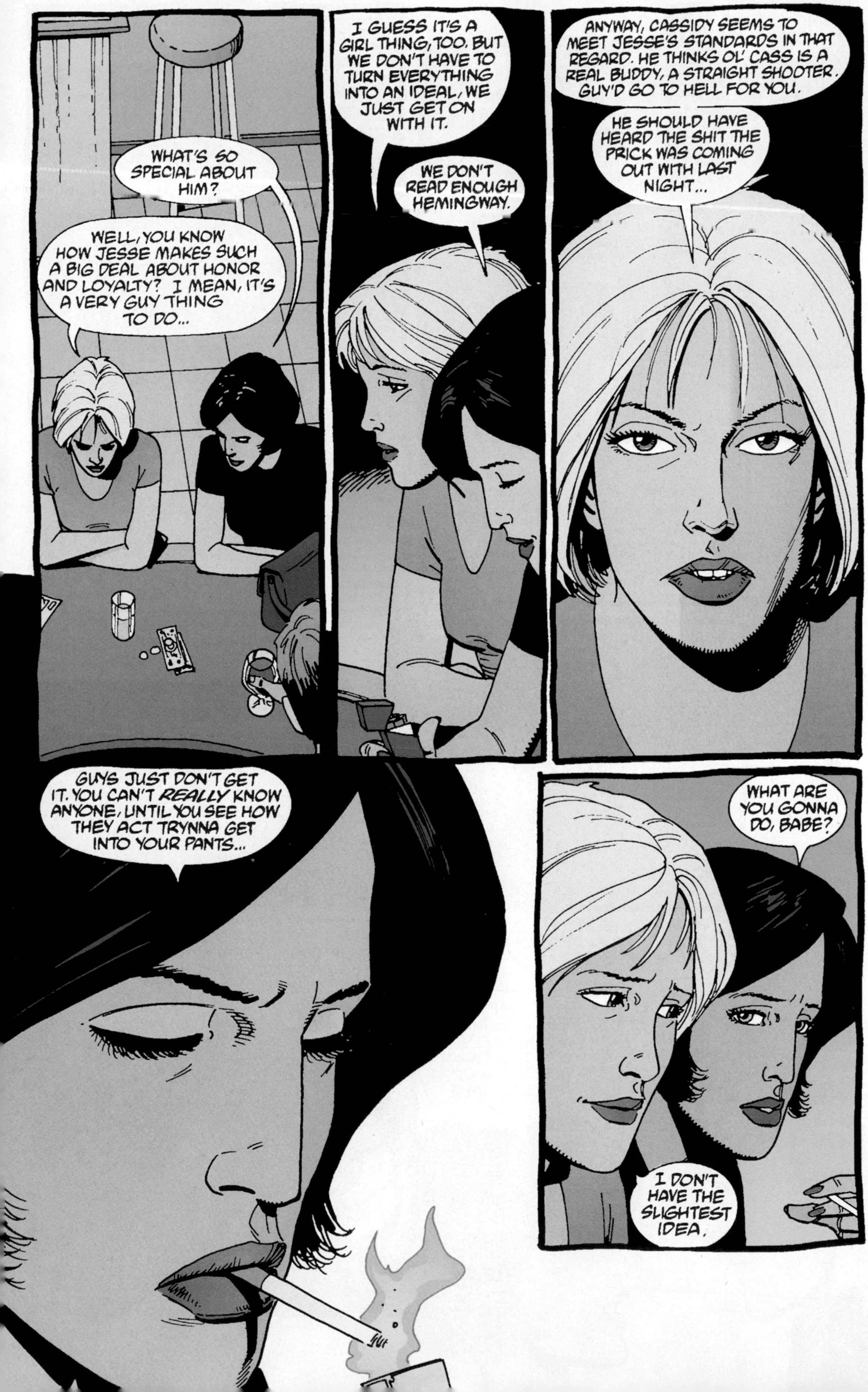
WHAT'S SO SPECIAL ABOUT HIM?
WELL, YOU KNOW HOW JESSE MAKES SUCH A BIG DEAL ABOUT HONOR AND LOYALTY? I MEAN, IT'S A VERY GUY THING TO DO...
I GUESS IT'S A GIRL THING, TOO. BUT WE DON'T HAVE TO TURN EVERYTHING INTO AN IDEAL, WE JUST GET ON WITH IT.
WE DON'T READ ENOUGH HEMINGWAY.
ANYWAY, CASSIDY SEEMS TO MEET JESSE'S STANDARDS IN THAT REGARD. HE THINKS OL' CASS IS A REAL BUDDY, A STRAIGHT SHOOTER. GUY'D GO TO HELL FOR YOU.
HE SHOULD HAVE HEARD THE SHIT THE PRICK WAS COMING OUT WITH LAST NIGHT...
GUYS JUST DON'T GET IT. YOU CAN'T *REALLY* KNOW ANYONE, UNTIL YOU SEE HOW THEY ACT TRYNNA GET INTO YOUR PANTS...
WHAT ARE YOU GONNA DO, BABE?
I DON'T HAVE THE SLIGHTEST IDEA.

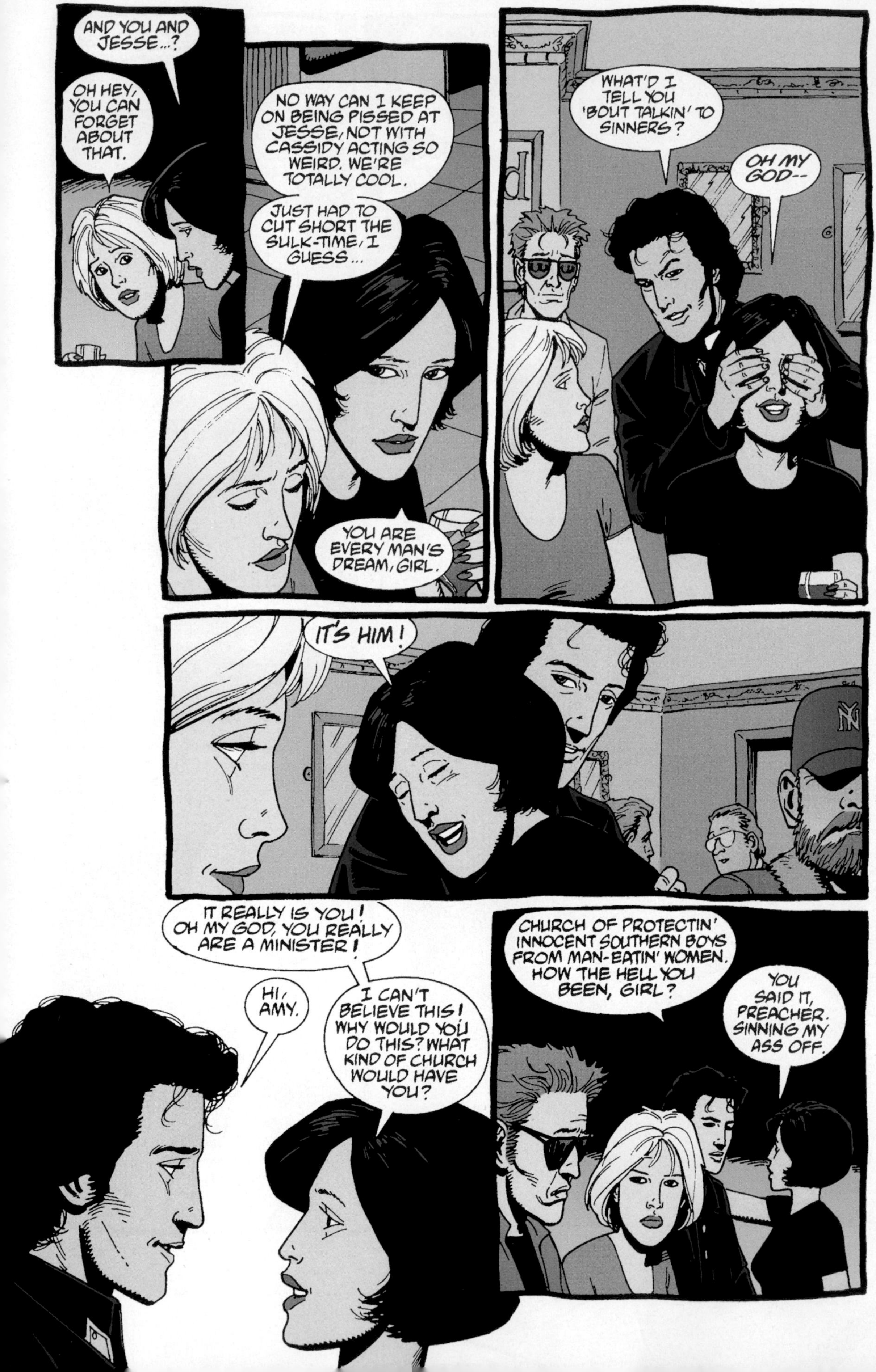
AND YOU AND JESSE...?
OH HEY, YOU CAN FORGET ABOUT THAT.
NO WAY CAN I KEEP ON BEING PISSED AT JESSE, NOT WITH CASSIDY ACTING SO WEIRD. WE'RE TOTALLY COOL.
JUST HAD TO CUT SHORT THE SULK-TIME, I GUESS...
YOU ARE EVERY MAN'S DREAM, GIRL.
WHAT'D I TELL YOU 'BOUT TALKIN' TO SINNERS?
OH MY GOD--
IT'S HIM!
IT REALLY IS YOU! OH MY GOD, YOU REALLY ARE A MINISTER!
HI, AMY.
I CAN'T BELIEVE THIS! WHY WOULD YOU DO THIS? WHAT KIND OF CHURCH WOULD HAVE YOU?
CHURCH OF PROTECTIN' INNOCENT SOUTHERN BOYS FROM MAN-EATIN' WOMEN. HOW THE HELL YOU BEEN, GIRL?
YOU SAID IT, PREACHER. SINNING MY ASS OFF.

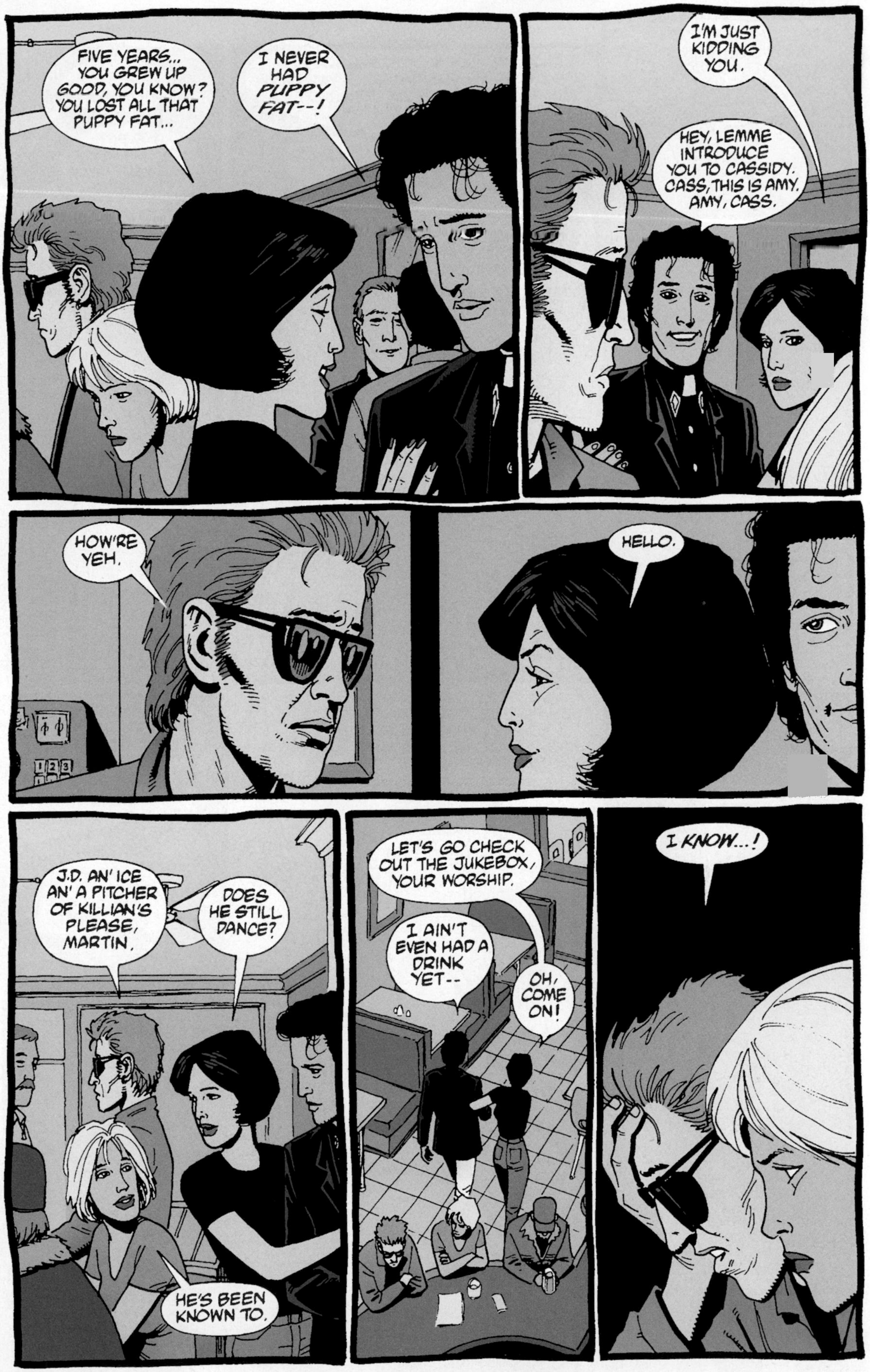
FIVE YEARS... YOU GREW UP GOOD, YOU KNOW? YOU LOST ALL THAT PUPPY FAT...
I NEVER HAD PUPPY FAT--!
I'M JUST KIDDING YOU.
HEY, LEMME INTRODUCE YOU TO CASSIDY. CASS, THIS IS AMY. AMY, CASS.
HOW'RE YEH.
HELLO.
J.D. AN' ICE AN' A PITCHER OF KILLIAN'S PLEASE, MARTIN.
DOES HE STILL DANCE?
HE'S BEEN KNOWN TO.
LET'S GO CHECK OUT THE JUKEBOX, YOUR WORSHIP.
I AIN'T EVEN HAD A DRINK YET--
OH, COME ON!
I KNOW...!

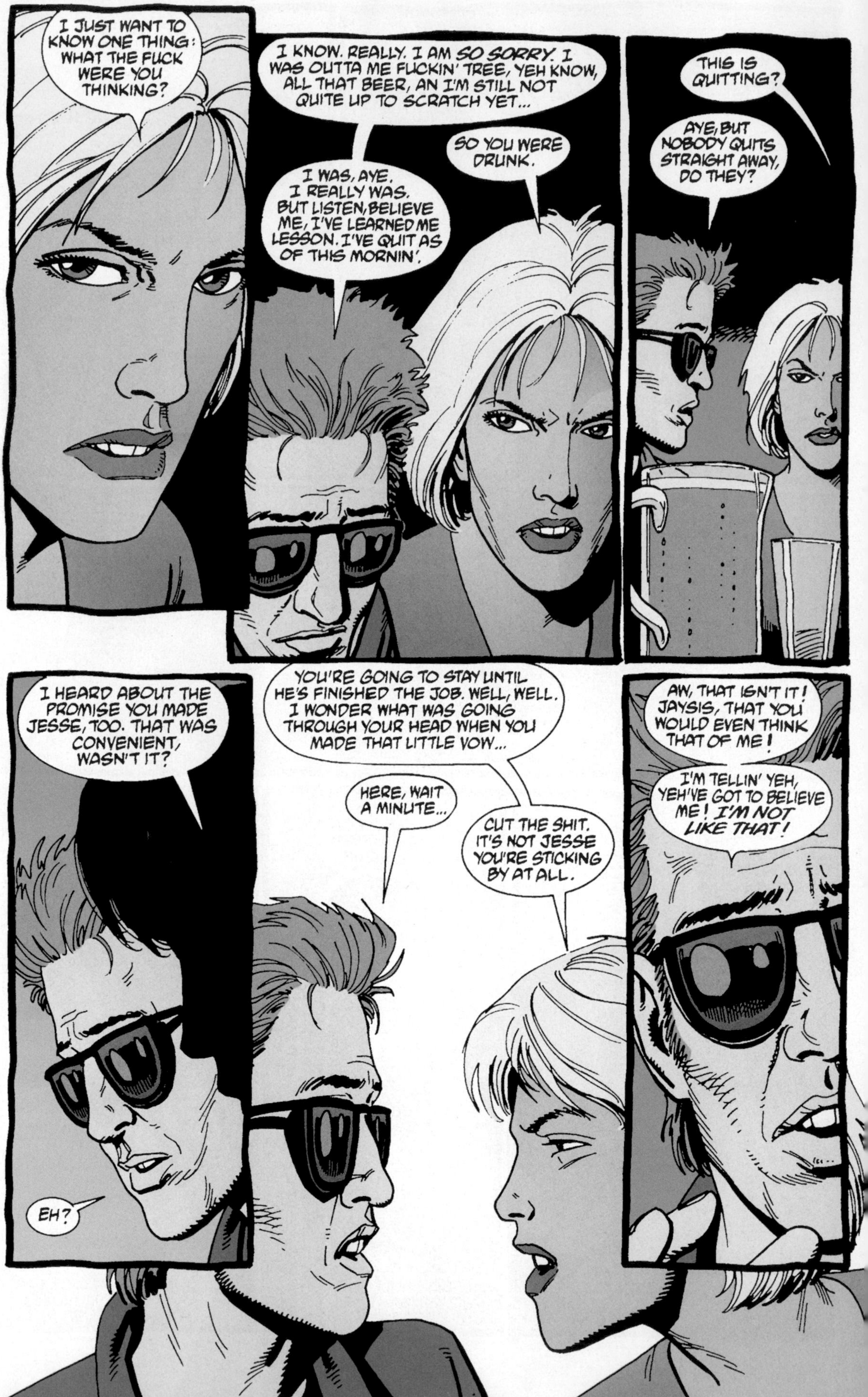
I JUST WANT TO KNOW ONE THING: WHAT THE FUCK WERE YOU THINKING?
I KNOW. REALLY. I AM *SO SORRY*. I WAS OUTTA ME FUCKIN' TREE, YEH KNOW, ALL THAT BEER, AN I'M STILL NOT QUITE UP TO SCRATCH YET...
SO YOU WERE DRUNK.
I WAS, AYE. I REALLY WAS. BUT LISTEN, BELIEVE ME, I'VE LEARNED ME LESSON. I'VE QUIT AS OF THIS MORNIN'.
THIS IS QUITTING?
AYE, BUT NOBODY QUITS STRAIGHT AWAY, DO THEY?
I HEARD ABOUT THE PROMISE YOU MADE JESSE, TOO. THAT WAS CONVENIENT, WASN'T IT?
EH?
YOU'RE GOING TO STAY UNTIL HE'S FINISHED THE JOB. WELL, WELL. I WONDER WHAT WAS GOING THROUGH YOUR HEAD WHEN YOU MADE THAT LITTLE VOW...
HERE, WAIT A MINUTE...
CUT THE SHIT. IT'S NOT JESSE YOU'RE STICKING BY AT ALL.
AW, THAT ISN'T IT! JAYSIS, THAT YOU WOULD EVEN THINK THAT OF ME!
I'M TELLIN' YEH, YEH'VE GOT TO BELIEVE ME! *I'M NOT LIKE THAT!*

♪ ARMORED CARS AND TRUCKS AND GUNS, COME TO TAKE AWAY OUR SONS-- ♪

WHAT THE FUCK IS THIS?

I THINK IT'S THIS OR THE MACARENA...

♪ EVERY MAN MUST STAND BEHIND, THE MEN BEHIND THE WY-ERRR! ♪

YOU CONVINCED ME!

D'YEH NOT THINK THE TWO'VE THEM LOOK A WEE BIT COZY...?

I KNOW THEM. I *TRUST* THEM. DON'T EVEN *TRY* TO CHANGE THE SUBJECT, OKAY?

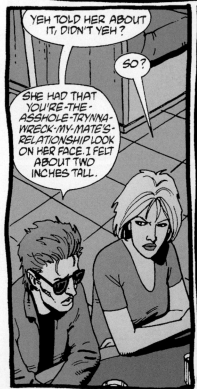

YEH TOLD HER ABOUT IT, DIDN'T YEH?

SO?

SHE HAD THAT YOU'RE-THE-ASSHOLE-TRYNNA-WRECK-MY-MATE'S-RELATIONSHIP LOOK ON HER FACE. I FELT ABOUT TWO INCHES TALL.

SHE'S MY FRIEND. I'LL TELL HER WHATEVER THE FUCK I WANT TO, THANKS.

BESIDES, NEVER MIND ABOUT AMY. WHAT *YOU* SHOULD BE WORRYING ABOUT--

IS WHAT'S GOING TO HAPPEN IF I TELL *JESSE.*

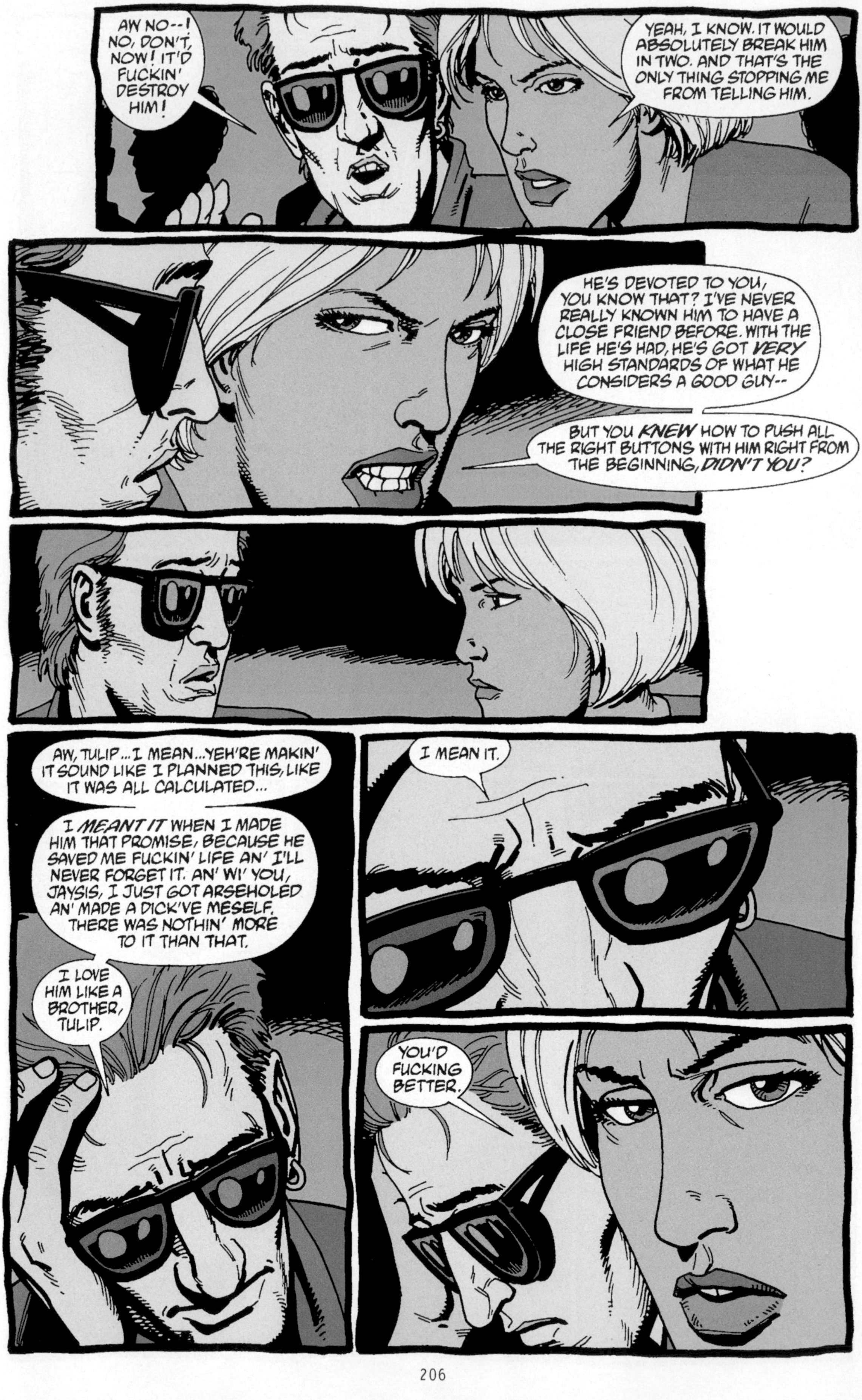

AW NO--! NO, DON'T, NOW! IT'D FUCKIN' DESTROY HIM!
YEAH, I KNOW. IT WOULD ABSOLUTELY BREAK HIM IN TWO. AND THAT'S THE ONLY THING STOPPING ME FROM TELLING HIM.
HE'S DEVOTED TO YOU, YOU KNOW THAT? I'VE NEVER REALLY KNOWN HIM TO HAVE A CLOSE FRIEND BEFORE. WITH THE LIFE HE'S HAD, HE'S GOT *VERY* HIGH STANDARDS OF WHAT HE CONSIDERS A GOOD GUY--
BUT YOU *KNEW* HOW TO PUSH ALL THE RIGHT BUTTONS WITH HIM RIGHT FROM THE BEGINNING, *DIDN'T YOU?*
AW, TULIP...I MEAN...YEH'RE MAKIN' IT SOUND LIKE I PLANNED THIS, LIKE IT WAS ALL CALCULATED...
I *MEANT IT* WHEN I MADE HIM THAT PROMISE, BECAUSE HE SAVED ME FUCKIN' LIFE AN' I'LL NEVER FORGET IT. AN' WI' YOU, JAYSIS, I JUST GOT ARSEHOLED AN' MADE A DICK'VE MESELF. THERE WAS NOTHIN' MORE TO IT THAN THAT.
I LOVE HIM LIKE A BROTHER, TULIP.
I MEAN IT.
YOU'D FUCKING BETTER.

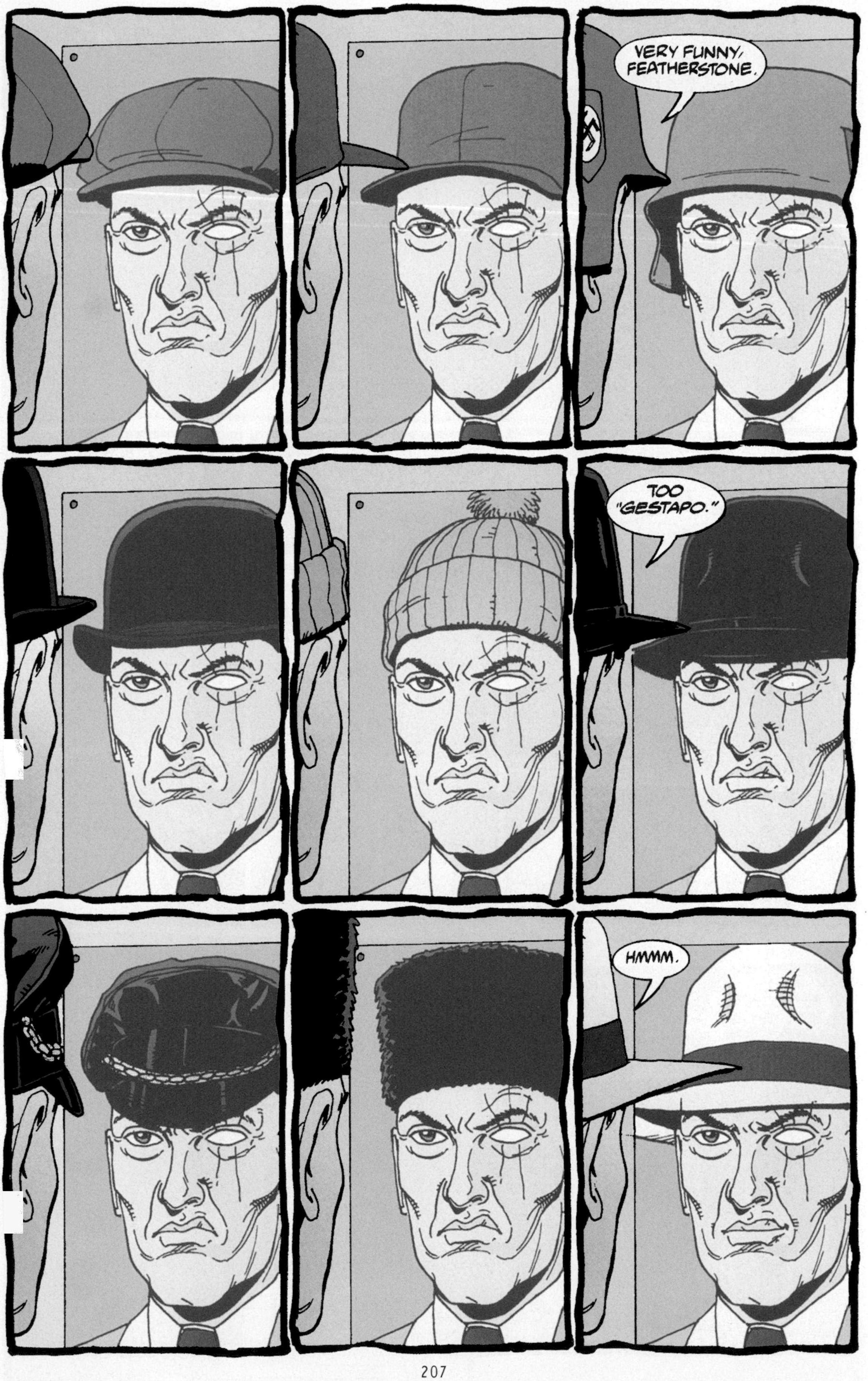
VERY FUNNY, FEATHERSTONE.
TOO "GESTAPO."
HMMM.

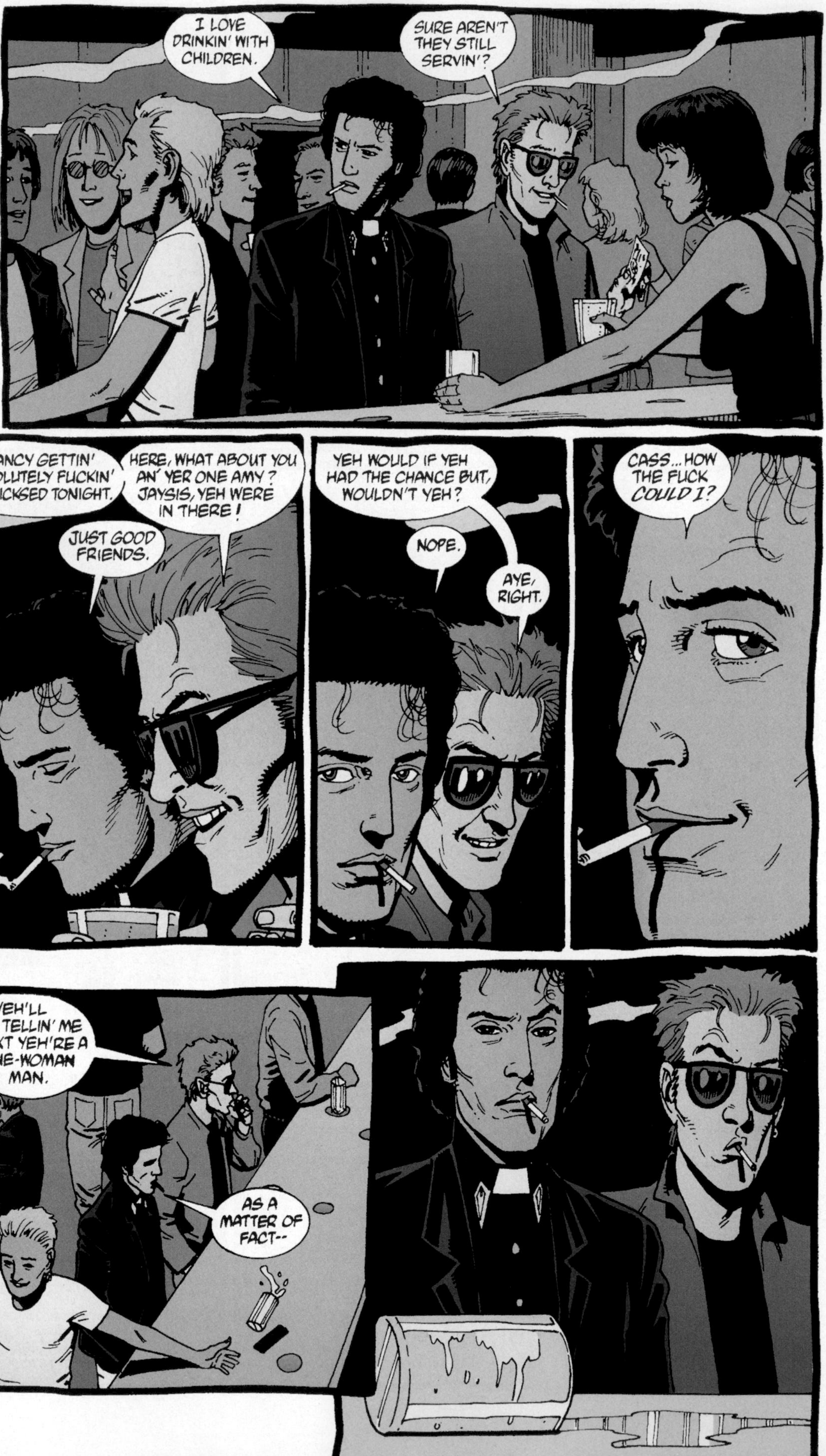
I LOVE DRINKIN' WITH CHILDREN.
SURE AREN'T THEY STILL SERVIN'?
I FANCY GETTIN' ABSOLUTELY FUCKIN' BOLLICKSED TONIGHT.
HERE, WHAT ABOUT YOU AN' YER ONE AMY? JAYSIS, YEH WERE IN THERE!
JUST GOOD FRIENDS.
YEH WOULD IF YEH HAD THE CHANCE BUT, WOULDN'T YEH?
NOPE.
AYE, RIGHT.
CASS... HOW THE FUCK *COULD I*?
YEH'LL BE TELLIN' ME NEXT YEH'RE A ONE-WOMAN MAN.
AS A MATTER OF FACT--

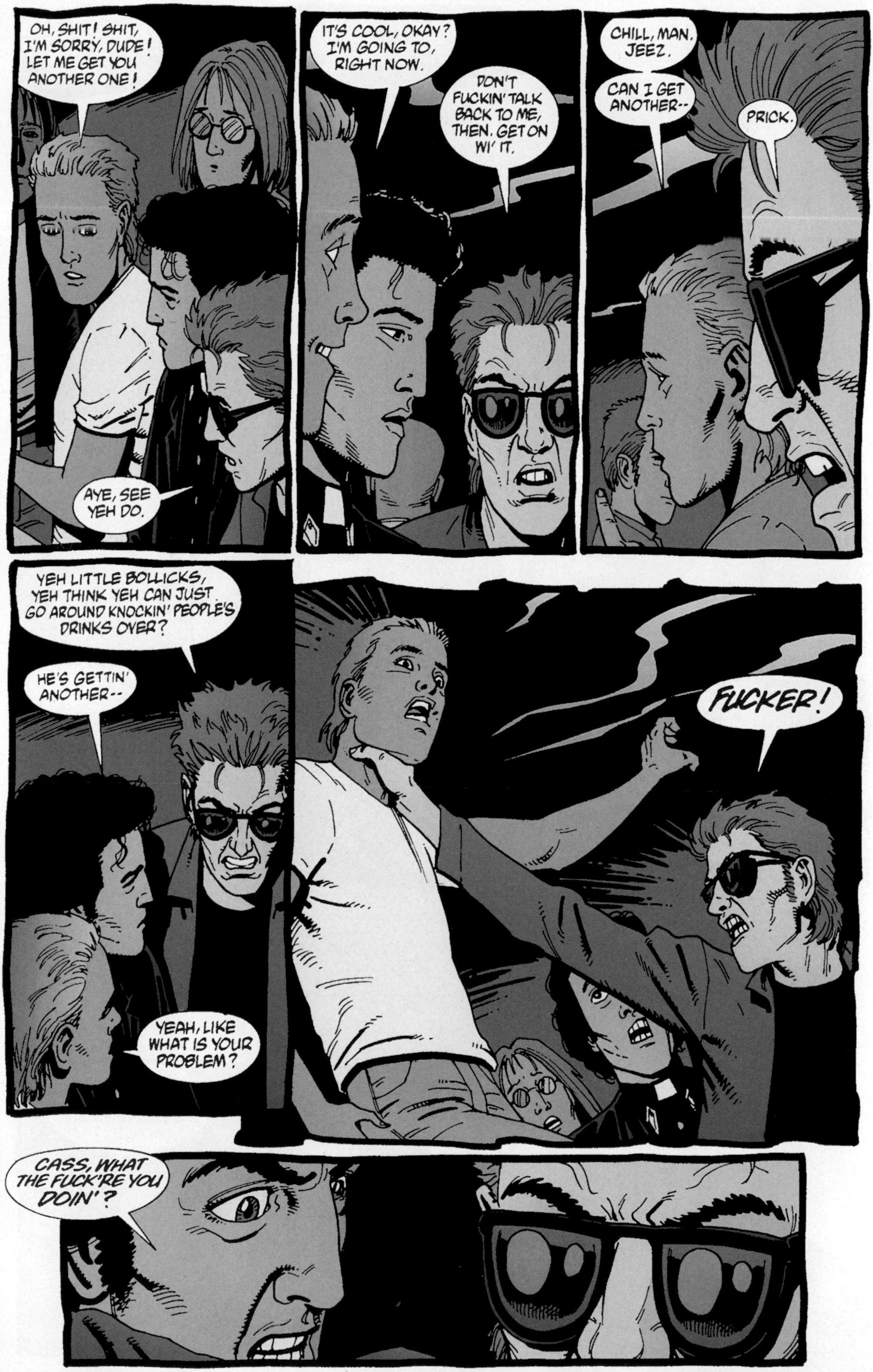
OH, SHIT! SHIT, I'M SORRY, DUDE! LET ME GET YOU ANOTHER ONE!
AYE, SEE YEH DO.
IT'S COOL, OKAY? I'M GOING TO, RIGHT NOW.
DON'T FUCKIN' TALK BACK TO ME, THEN. GET ON WI' IT.
CHILL, MAN. JEEZ.
CAN I GET ANOTHER--
PRICK.
YEH LITTLE BOLLICKS, YEH THINK YEH CAN JUST GO AROUND KNOCKIN' PEOPLE'S DRINKS OVER?
HE'S GETTIN' ANOTHER--
YEAH, LIKE WHAT IS YOUR PROBLEM?
FUCKER!
CASS, WHAT THE FUCK'RE YOU DOIN'?

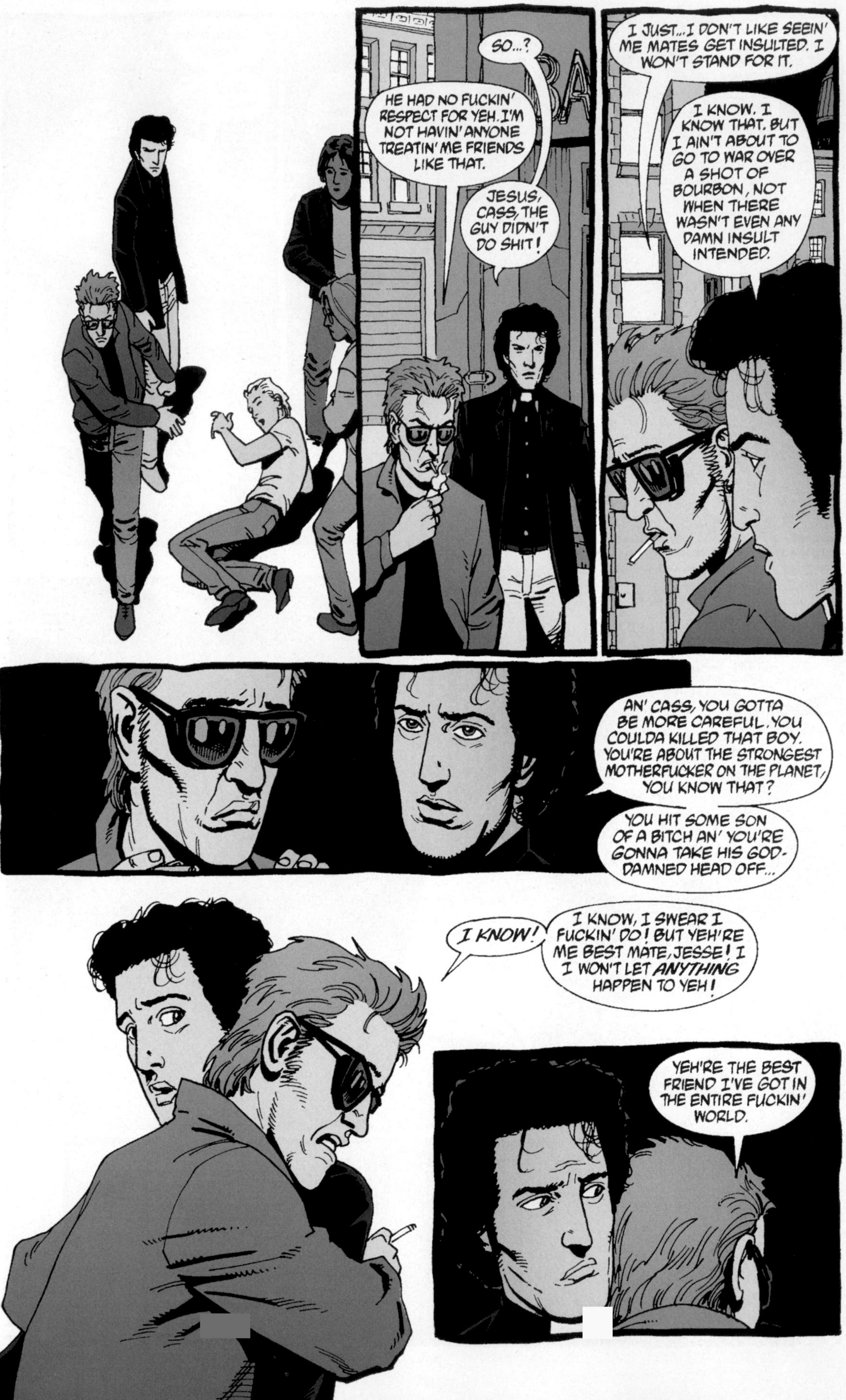
SO...?
HE HAD NO FUCKIN' RESPECT FOR YEH. I'M NOT HAVIN' ANYONE TREATIN' ME FRIENDS LIKE THAT.
JESUS, CASS, THE GUY DIDN'T DO SHIT!
I JUST... I DON'T LIKE SEEIN' ME MATES GET INSULTED. I WON'T STAND FOR IT.
I KNOW. I KNOW THAT. BUT I AIN'T ABOUT TO GO TO WAR OVER A SHOT OF BOURBON, NOT WHEN THERE WASN'T EVEN ANY DAMN INSULT INTENDED.
AN' CASS, YOU GOTTA BE MORE CAREFUL. YOU COULDA KILLED THAT BOY. YOU'RE ABOUT THE STRONGEST MOTHERFUCKER ON THE PLANET, YOU KNOW THAT?
YOU HIT SOME SON OF A BITCH AN' YOU'RE GONNA TAKE HIS GOD-DAMNED HEAD OFF...
I KNOW!
I KNOW, I SWEAR I FUCKIN' DO! BUT YEH'RE ME BEST MATE, JESSE! I WON'T LET ANYTHING HAPPEN TO YEH!
YEH'RE THE BEST FRIEND I'VE GOT IN THE ENTIRE FUCKIN' WORLD.

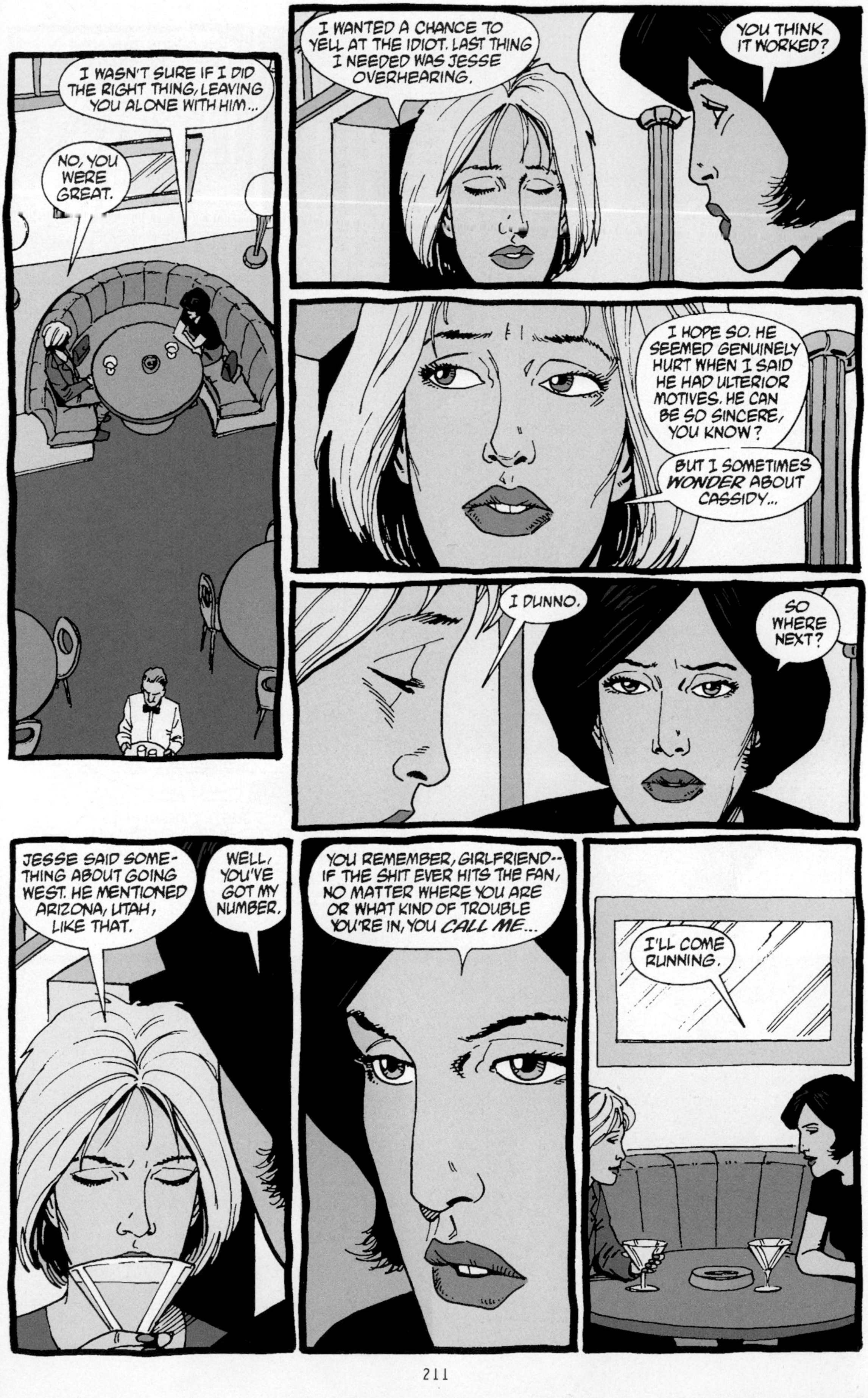
I WASN'T SURE IF I DID THE RIGHT THING, LEAVING YOU ALONE WITH HIM...
NO, YOU WERE GREAT.
I WANTED A CHANCE TO YELL AT THE IDIOT. LAST THING I NEEDED WAS JESSE OVERHEARING.
YOU THINK IT WORKED?
I HOPE SO. HE SEEMED GENUINELY HURT WHEN I SAID HE HAD ULTERIOR MOTIVES. HE CAN BE SO SINCERE, YOU KNOW?
BUT I SOMETIMES WONDER ABOUT CASSIDY...
I DUNNO.
SO WHERE NEXT?
JESSE SAID SOMETHING ABOUT GOING WEST. HE MENTIONED ARIZONA, UTAH, LIKE THAT.
WELL, YOU'VE GOT MY NUMBER.
YOU REMEMBER, GIRLFRIEND-- IF THE SHIT EVER HITS THE FAN, NO MATTER WHERE YOU ARE OR WHAT KIND OF TROUBLE YOU'RE IN, YOU CALL ME...
I'LL COME RUNNING.

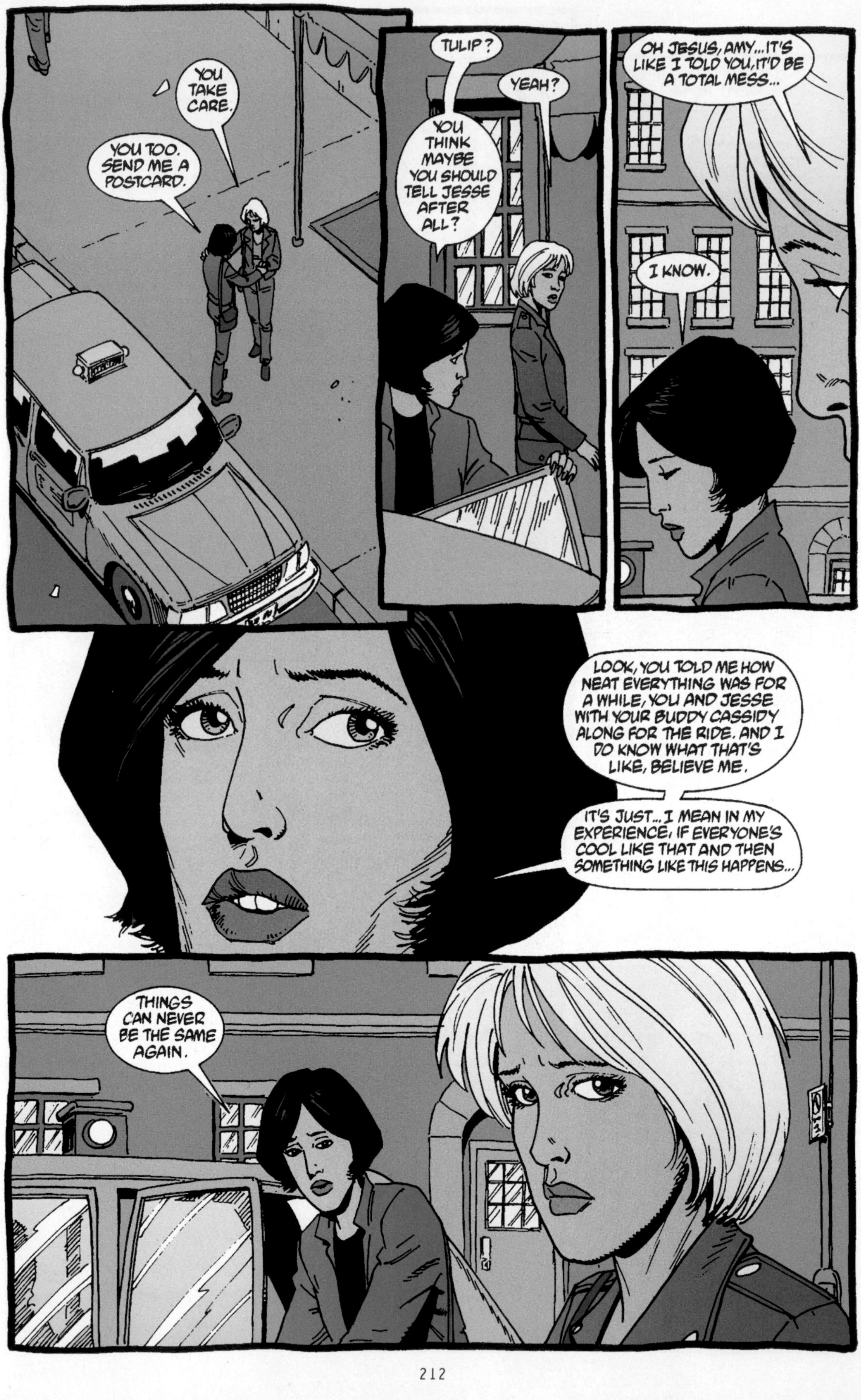
YOU TAKE CARE.
YOU TOO. SEND ME A POSTCARD.
TULIP?
YEAH?
YOU THINK MAYBE YOU SHOULD TELL JESSE AFTER ALL?
OH JESUS, AMY...IT'S LIKE I TOLD YOU, IT'D BE A TOTAL MESS...
I KNOW.
LOOK, YOU TOLD ME HOW NEAT EVERYTHING WAS FOR A WHILE, YOU AND JESSE WITH YOUR BUDDY CASSIDY ALONG FOR THE RIDE. AND I DO KNOW WHAT THAT'S LIKE, BELIEVE ME.
IT'S JUST... I MEAN IN MY EXPERIENCE, IF EVERYONE'S COOL LIKE THAT AND THEN SOMETHING LIKE THIS HAPPENS...
THINGS CAN NEVER BE THE SAME AGAIN.

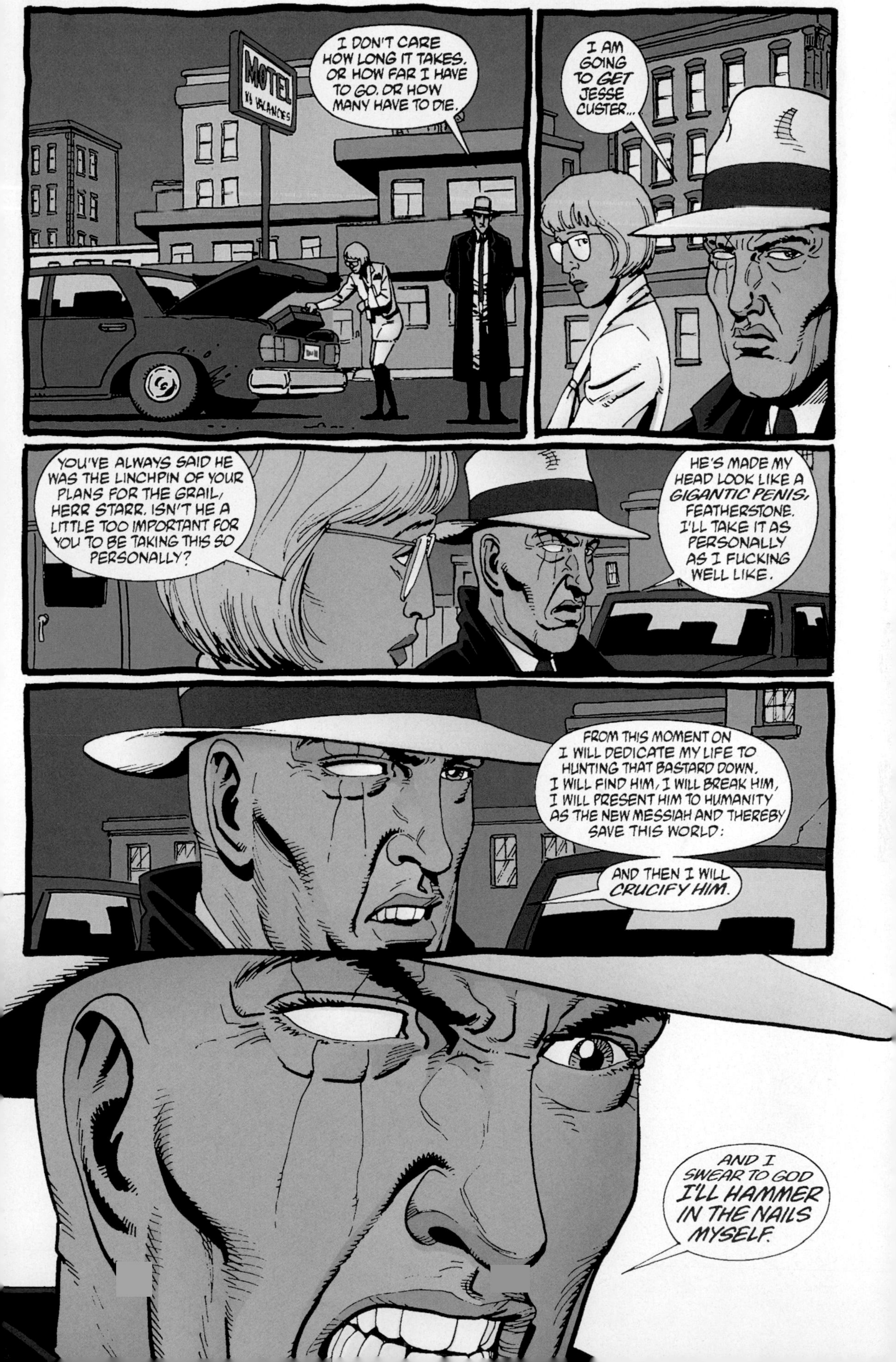
MOTEL
NO VACANCIES
I DON'T CARE HOW LONG IT TAKES. OR HOW FAR I HAVE TO GO. OR HOW MANY HAVE TO DIE.
I AM GOING TO GET JESSE CUSTER...
YOU'VE ALWAYS SAID HE WAS THE LINCHPIN OF YOUR PLANS FOR THE GRAIL, HERR STARR. ISN'T HE A LITTLE TOO IMPORTANT FOR YOU TO BE TAKING THIS SO PERSONALLY?
HE'S MADE MY HEAD LOOK LIKE A GIGANTIC PENIS, FEATHERSTONE. I'LL TAKE IT AS PERSONALLY AS I FUCKING WELL LIKE.
FROM THIS MOMENT ON I WILL DEDICATE MY LIFE TO HUNTING THAT BASTARD DOWN. I WILL FIND HIM, I WILL BREAK HIM, I WILL PRESENT HIM TO HUMANITY AS THE NEW MESSIAH AND THEREBY SAVE THIS WORLD:
AND THEN I WILL CRUCIFY HIM.
AND I SWEAR TO GOD I'LL HAMMER IN THE NAILS MYSELF.

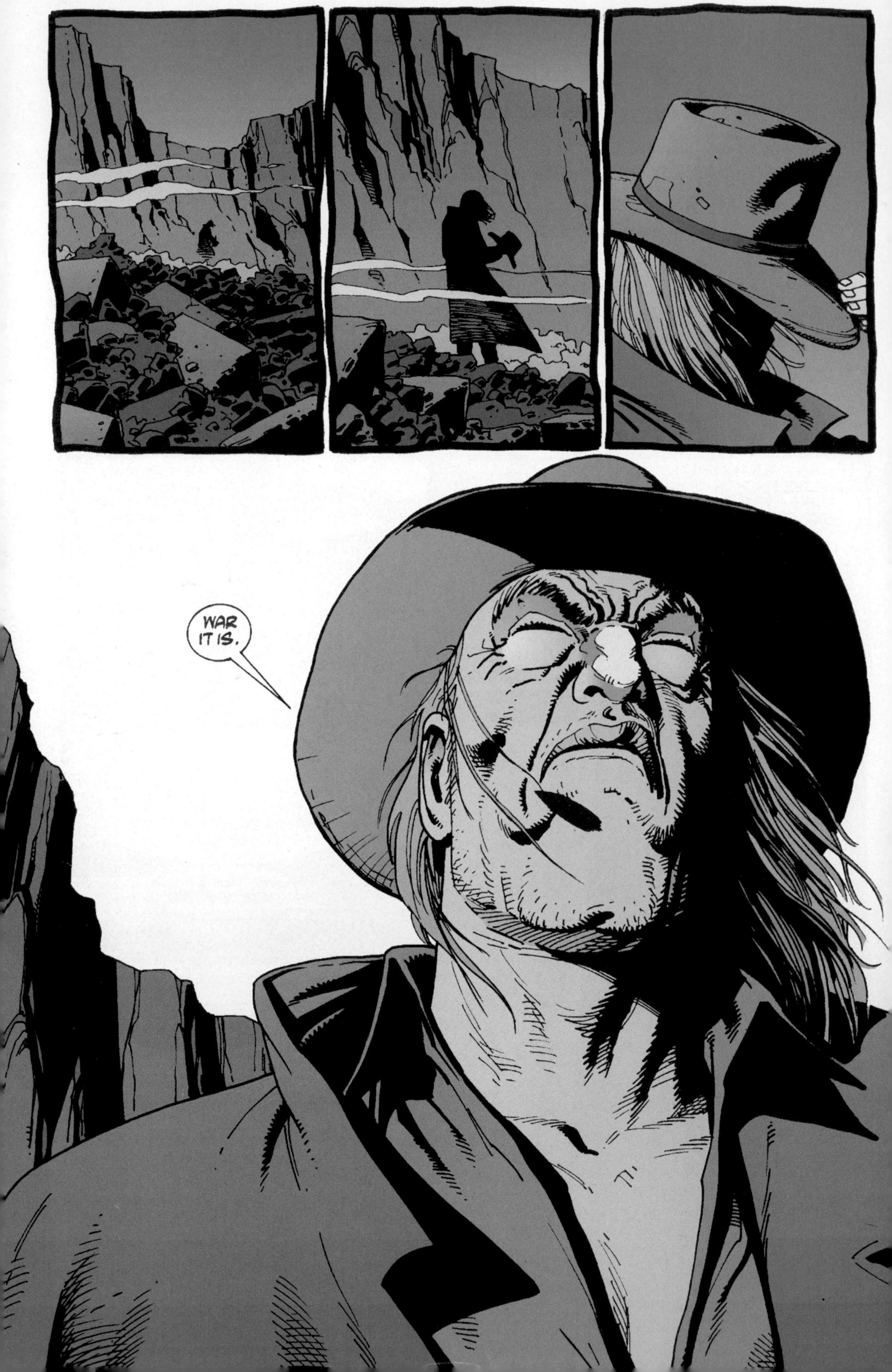
WAR IT IS.

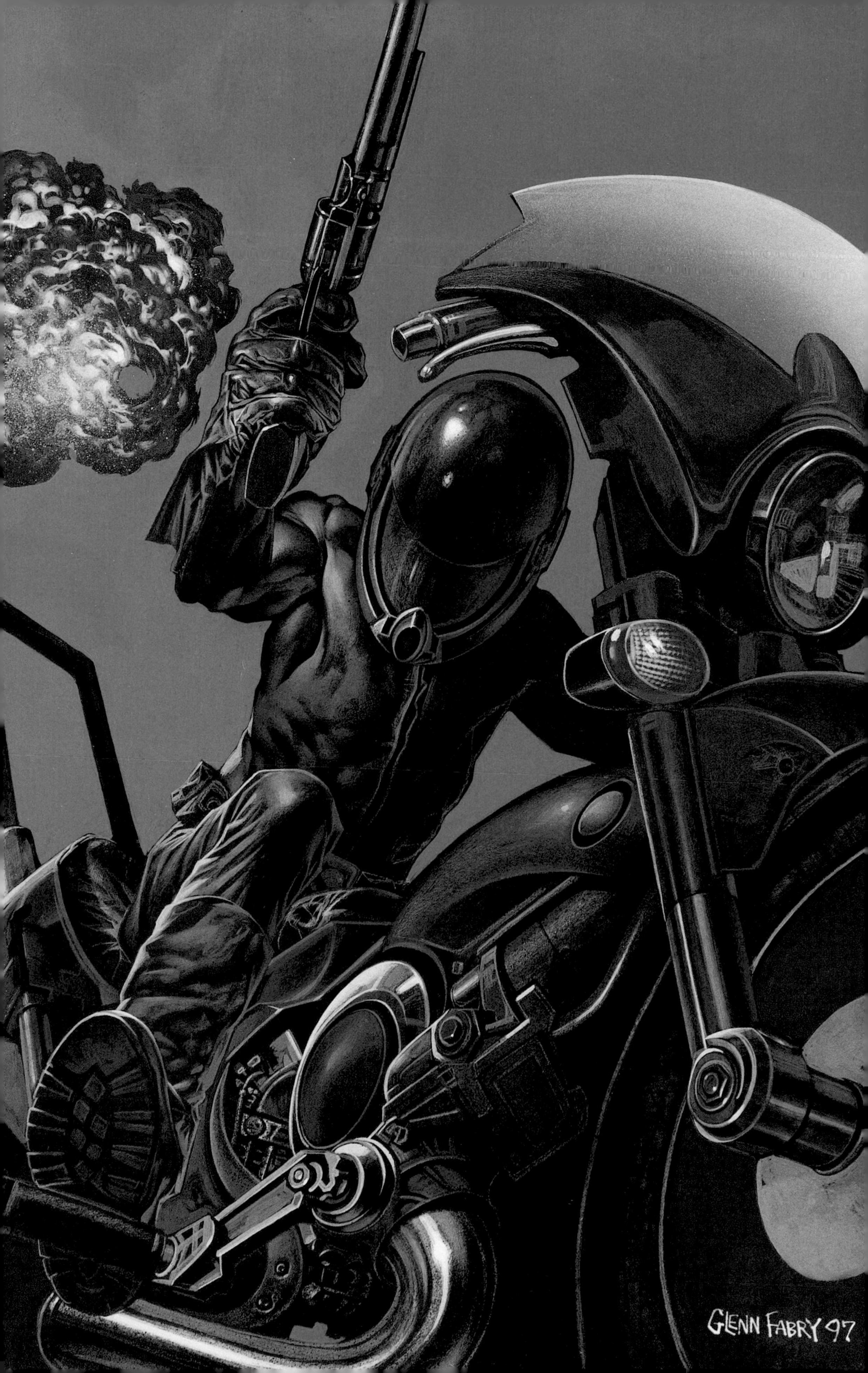
GLENN FABRY 97

"Is he anything like your other *mate*,
the one who turned out to be a serial killer and almost murdered us all?"

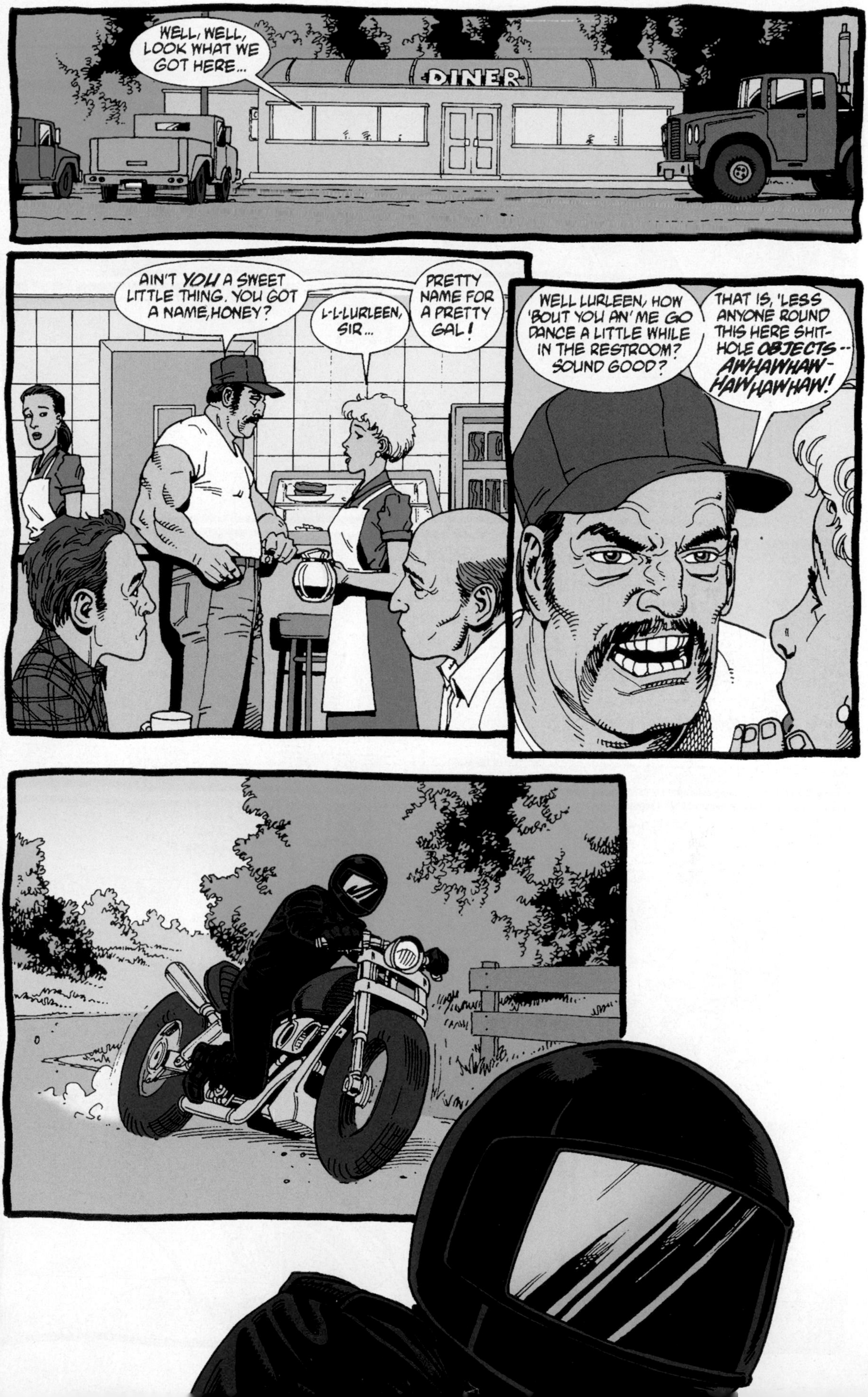
WELL, WELL, LOOK WHAT WE GOT HERE...
DINER
AIN'T YOU A SWEET LITTLE THING. YOU GOT A NAME, HONEY?
L-L-LURLEEN, SIR...
PRETTY NAME FOR A PRETTY GAL!
WELL LURLEEN, HOW 'BOUT YOU AN' ME GO DANCE A LITTLE WHILE IN THE RESTROOM? SOUND GOOD?
THAT IS, 'LESS ANYONE ROUND THIS HERE SHIT-HOLE OBJECTS-- AWHAWHAW-HAWHAWHAW!

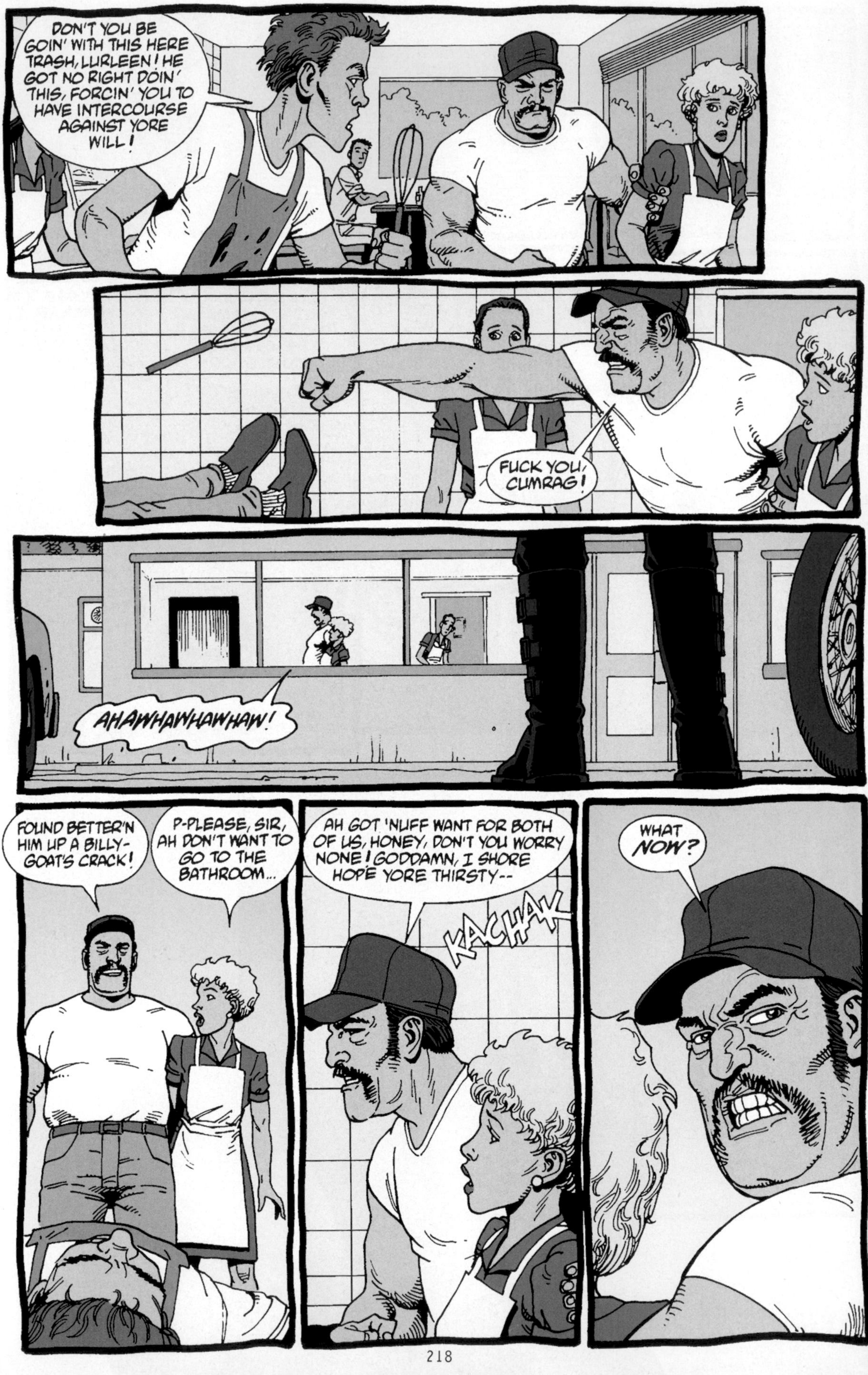

DON'T YOU BE GOIN' WITH THIS HERE TRASH, LURLEEN! HE GOT NO RIGHT DOIN' THIS, FORCIN' YOU TO HAVE INTERCOURSE AGAINST YORE WILL!
FUCK YOU, CUMRAG!
AHAWHAWHAWHAW!
FOUND BETTER'N HIM UP A BILLY-GOAT'S CRACK!
P-PLEASE, SIR, AH DON'T WANT TO GO TO THE BATHROOM...
AH GOT 'NUFF WANT FOR BOTH OF US, HONEY, DON'T YOU WORRY NONE! GODDAMN, I SHORE HOPE YORE THIRSTY--
KACHAK
WHAT *NOW*?

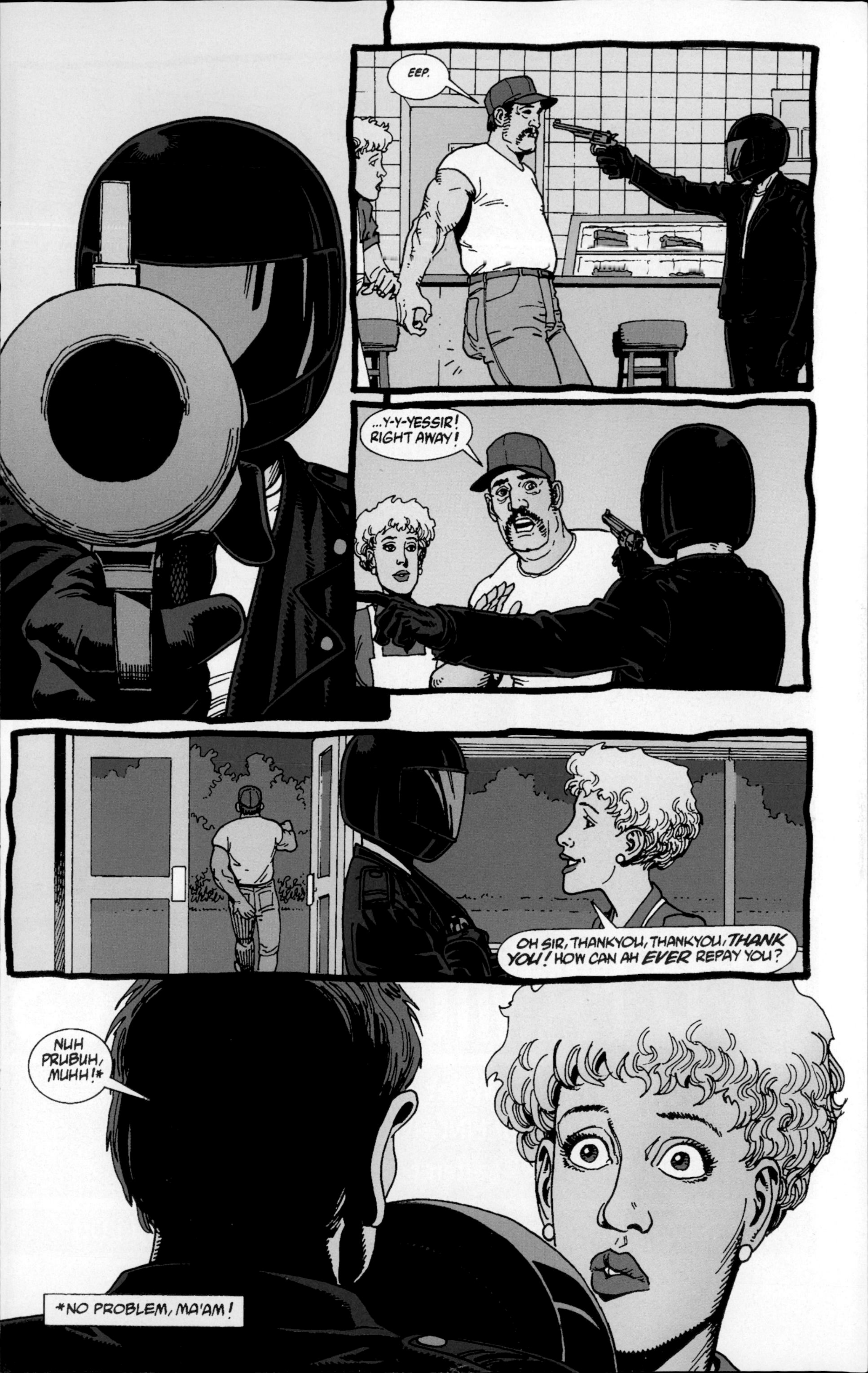
EEP.
...Y-Y-YESSIR! RIGHT AWAY!
OH SIR, THANKYOU, THANKYOU, THANK YOU! HOW CAN AH EVER REPAY YOU?
NUH PRUBUH, MUHH!*
*NO PROBLEM, MA'AM!

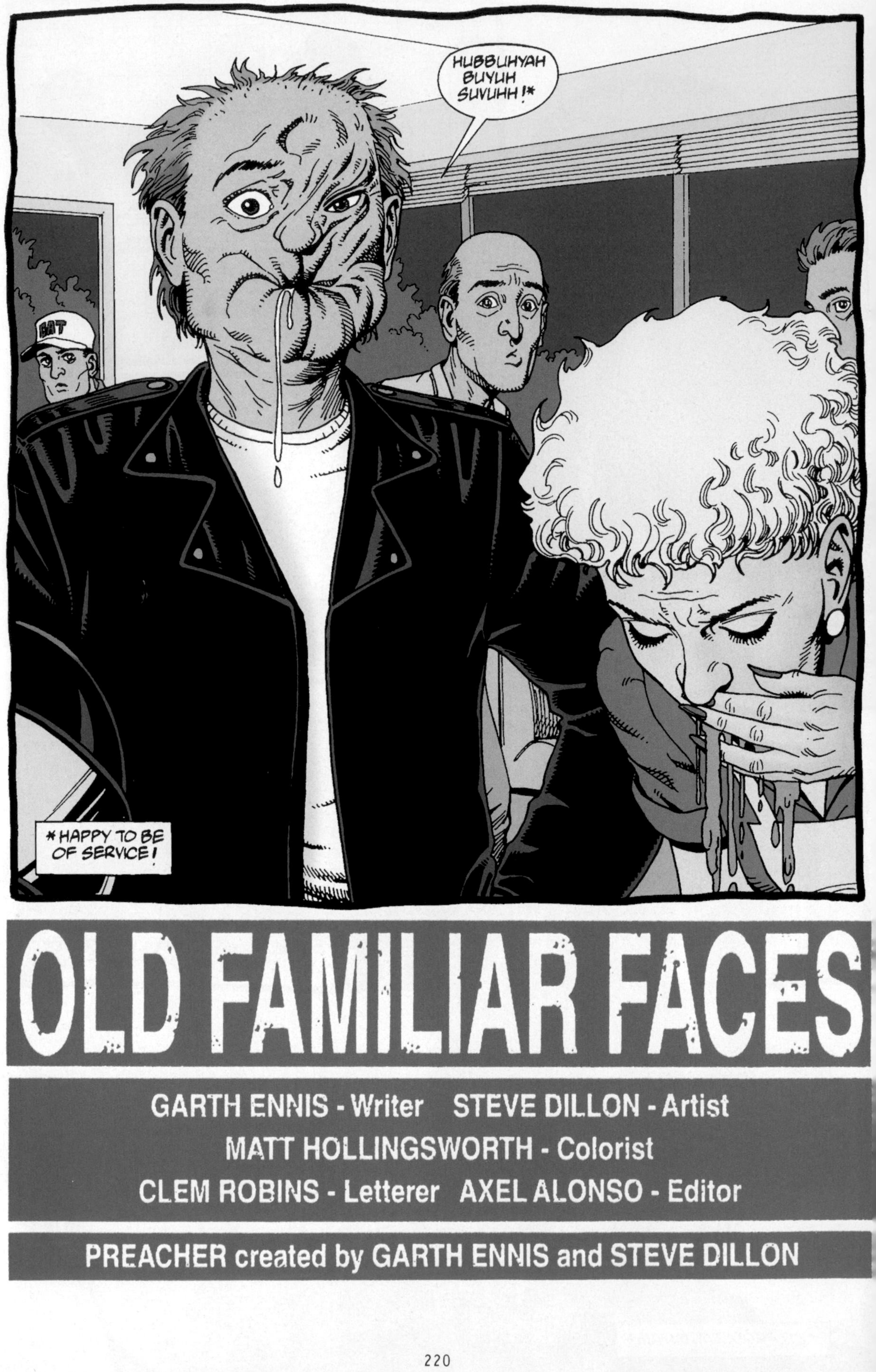
HUBBUHYAH BUYUH SUVUHH!*
BAT
*HAPPY TO BE OF SERVICE!

# OLD FAMILIAR FACES

GARTH ENNIS - Writer STEVE DILLON - Artist
MATT HOLLINGSWORTH - Colorist
CLEM ROBINS - Letterer AXEL ALONSO - Editor

PREACHER created by GARTH ENNIS and STEVE DILLON

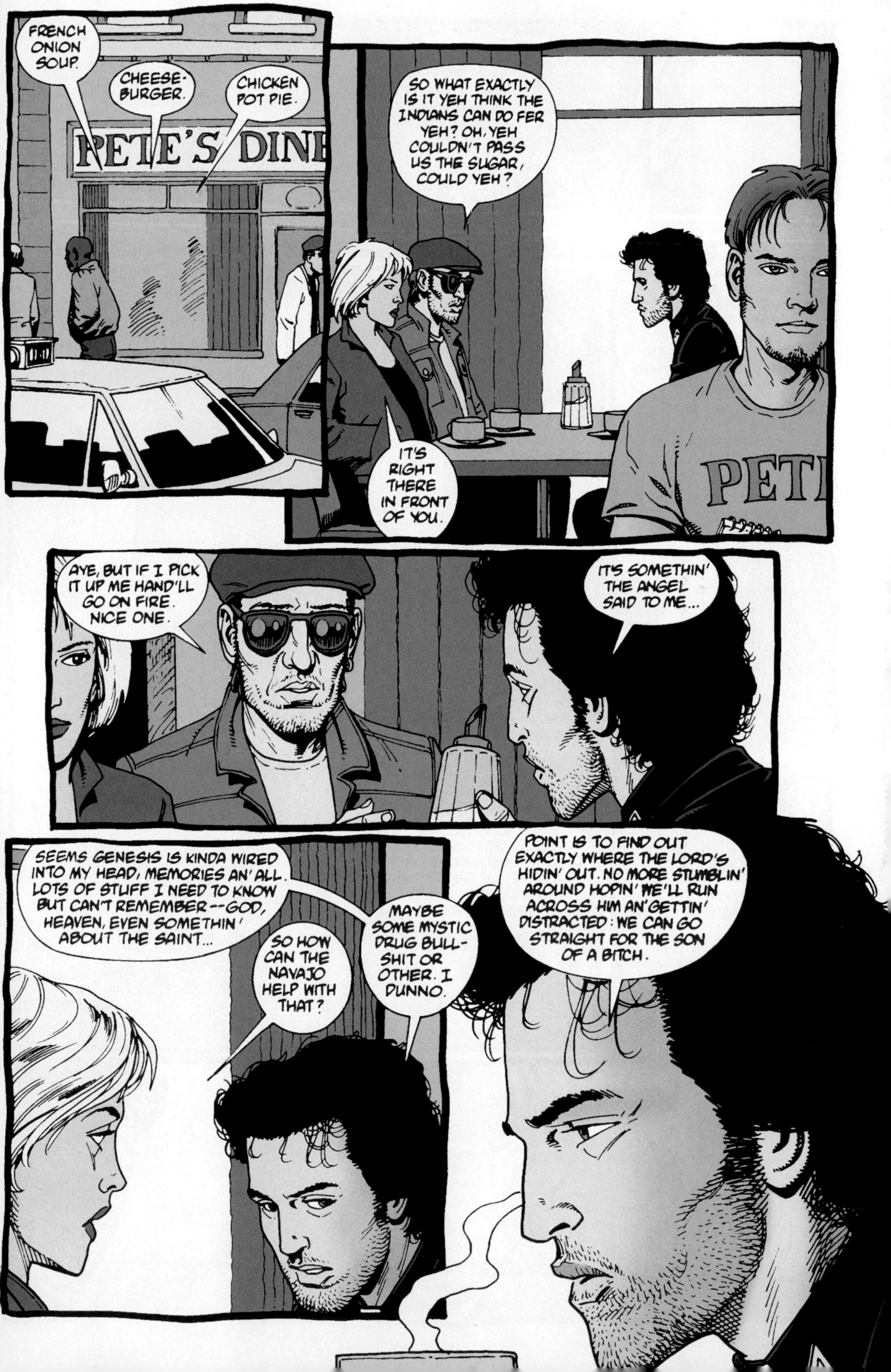
FRENCH ONION SOUP.
CHEESE-BURGER.
CHICKEN POT PIE.
PETE'S DINE
SO WHAT EXACTLY IS IT YEH THINK THE INDIANS CAN DO FER YEH? OH, YEH COULDN'T PASS US THE SUGAR, COULD YEH?
IT'S RIGHT THERE IN FRONT OF YOU.
PETE
AYE, BUT IF I PICK IT UP ME HAND'LL GO ON FIRE. NICE ONE.
IT'S SOMETHIN' THE ANGEL SAID TO ME...
SEEMS GENESIS IS KINDA WIRED INTO MY HEAD, MEMORIES AN' ALL. LOTS OF STUFF I NEED TO KNOW BUT CAN'T REMEMBER--GOD, HEAVEN, EVEN SOMETHIN' ABOUT THE SAINT...
SO HOW CAN THE NAVAJO HELP WITH THAT?
MAYBE SOME MYSTIC DRUG BULL-SHIT OR OTHER. I DUNNO.
POINT IS TO FIND OUT EXACTLY WHERE THE LORD'S HIDIN' OUT. NO MORE STUMBLIN' AROUND HOPIN' WE'LL RUN ACROSS HIM AN' GETTIN' DISTRACTED: WE CAN GO STRAIGHT FOR THE SON OF A BITCH.

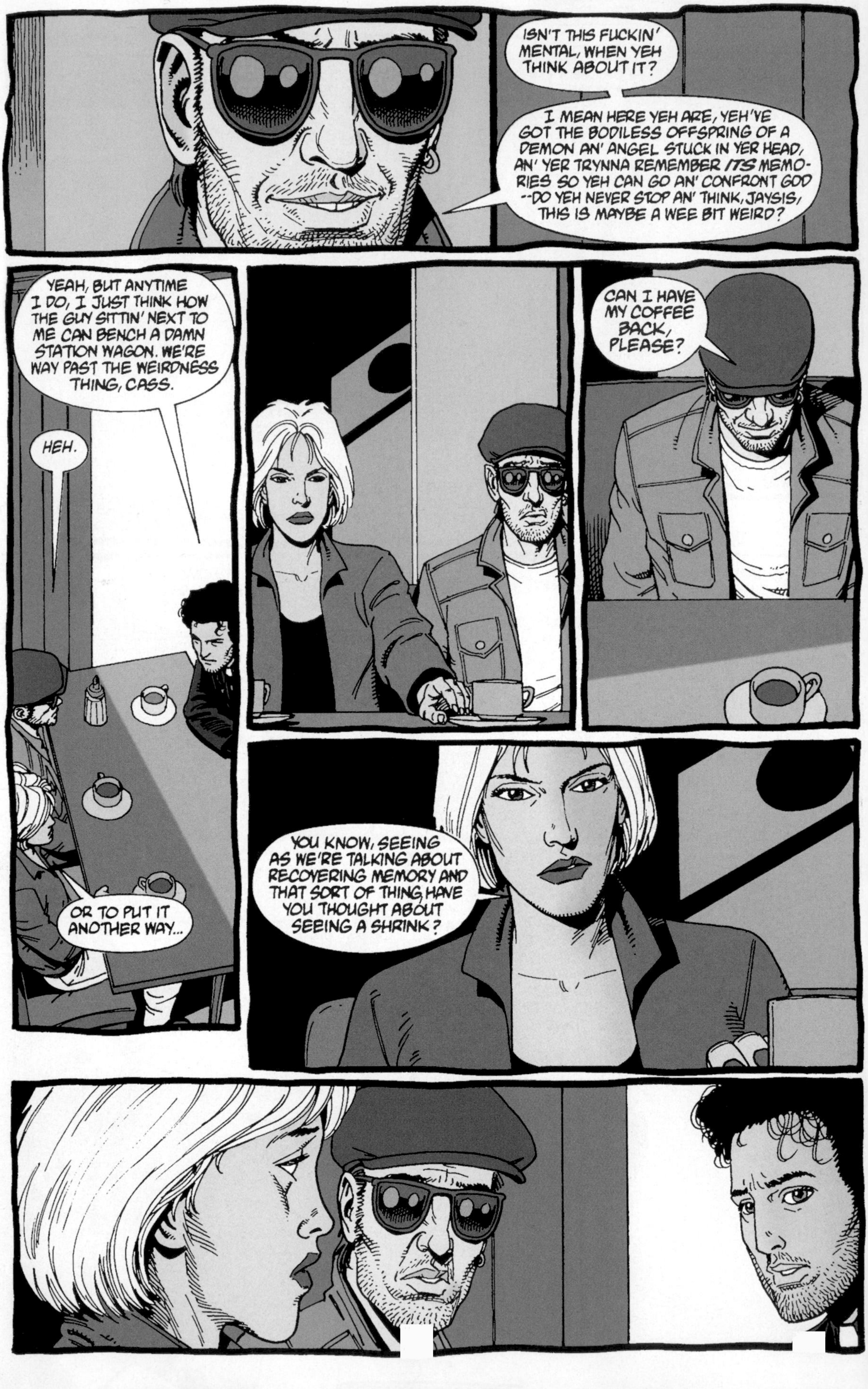
ISN'T THIS FUCKIN' MENTAL, WHEN YEH THINK ABOUT IT?
I MEAN HERE YEH ARE, YEH'VE GOT THE BODILESS OFFSPRING OF A DEMON AN' ANGEL STUCK IN YER HEAD, AN' YER TRYNNA REMEMBER *ITS* MEMORIES SO YEH CAN GO AN' CONFRONT GOD --DO YEH NEVER STOP AN' THINK, JAYSIS, THIS IS MAYBE A WEE BIT WEIRD?
YEAH, BUT ANYTIME I DO, I JUST THINK HOW THE GUY SITTIN' NEXT TO ME CAN BENCH A DAMN STATION WAGON. WE'RE WAY PAST THE WEIRDNESS THING, CASS.
HEH.
OR TO PUT IT ANOTHER WAY...
CAN I HAVE MY COFFEE BACK, PLEASE?
YOU KNOW, SEEING AS WE'RE TALKING ABOUT RECOVERING MEMORY AND THAT SORT OF THING, HAVE YOU THOUGHT ABOUT SEEING A SHRINK?

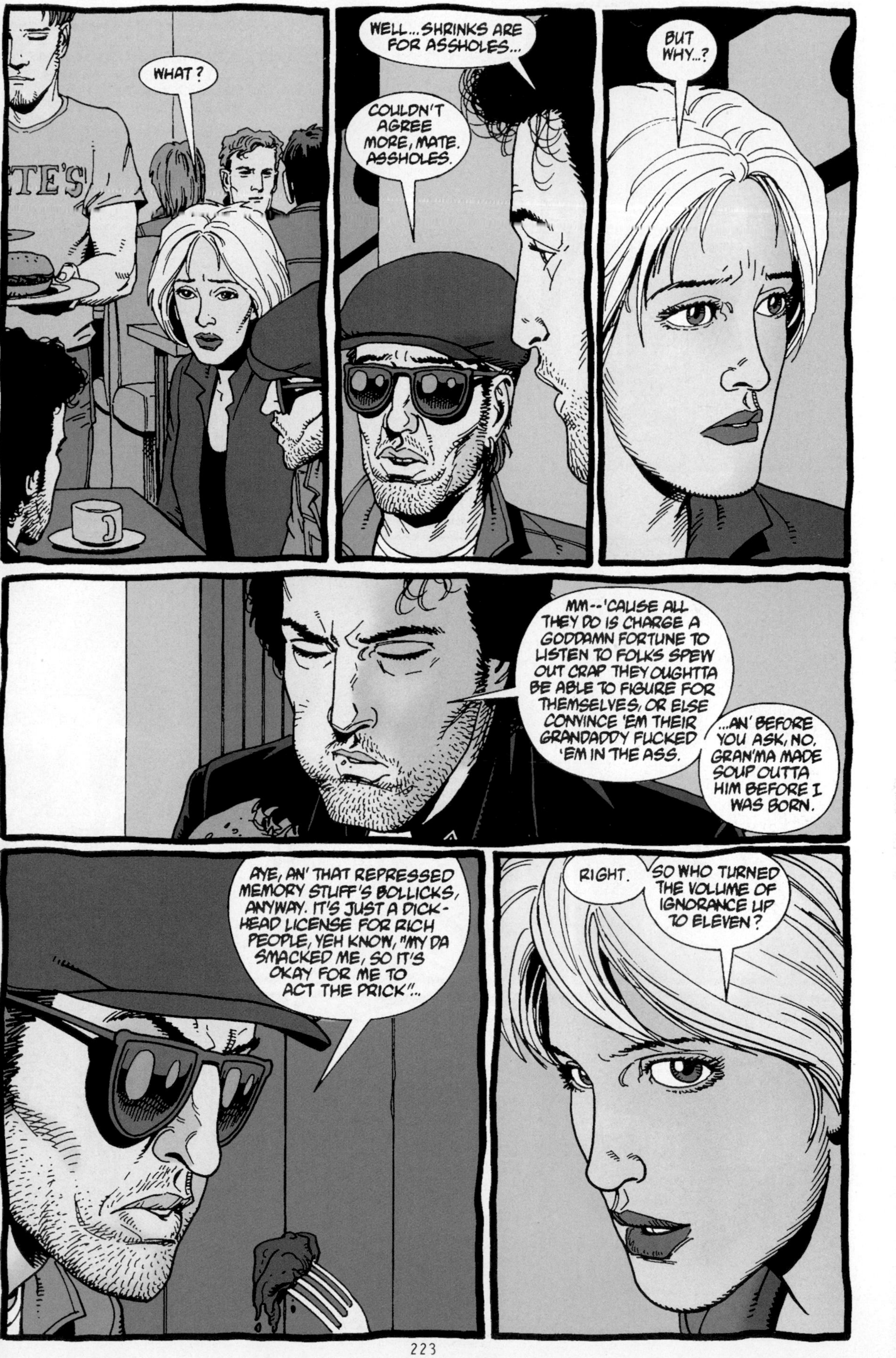

WHAT?
WELL... SHRINKS ARE FOR ASSHOLES...
COULDN'T AGREE MORE, MATE. ASSHOLES.
BUT WHY...?
MM--'CAUSE ALL THEY DO IS CHARGE A GODDAMN FORTUNE TO LISTEN TO FOLKS SPEW OUT CRAP THEY OUGHTTA BE ABLE TO FIGURE FOR THEMSELVES, OR ELSE CONVINCE 'EM THEIR GRANDADDY FUCKED 'EM IN THE ASS.
...AN' BEFORE YOU ASK, NO, GRAN'MA MADE SOUP OUTTA HIM BEFORE I WAS BORN.
AYE, AN' THAT REPRESSED MEMORY STUFF'S BOLLICKS, ANYWAY. IT'S JUST A DICK-HEAD LICENSE FOR RICH PEOPLE, YEH KNOW, "MY DA SMACKED ME, SO IT'S OKAY FOR ME TO ACT THE PRICK"...
RIGHT.
SO WHO TURNED THE VOLUME OF IGNORANCE UP TO ELEVEN?

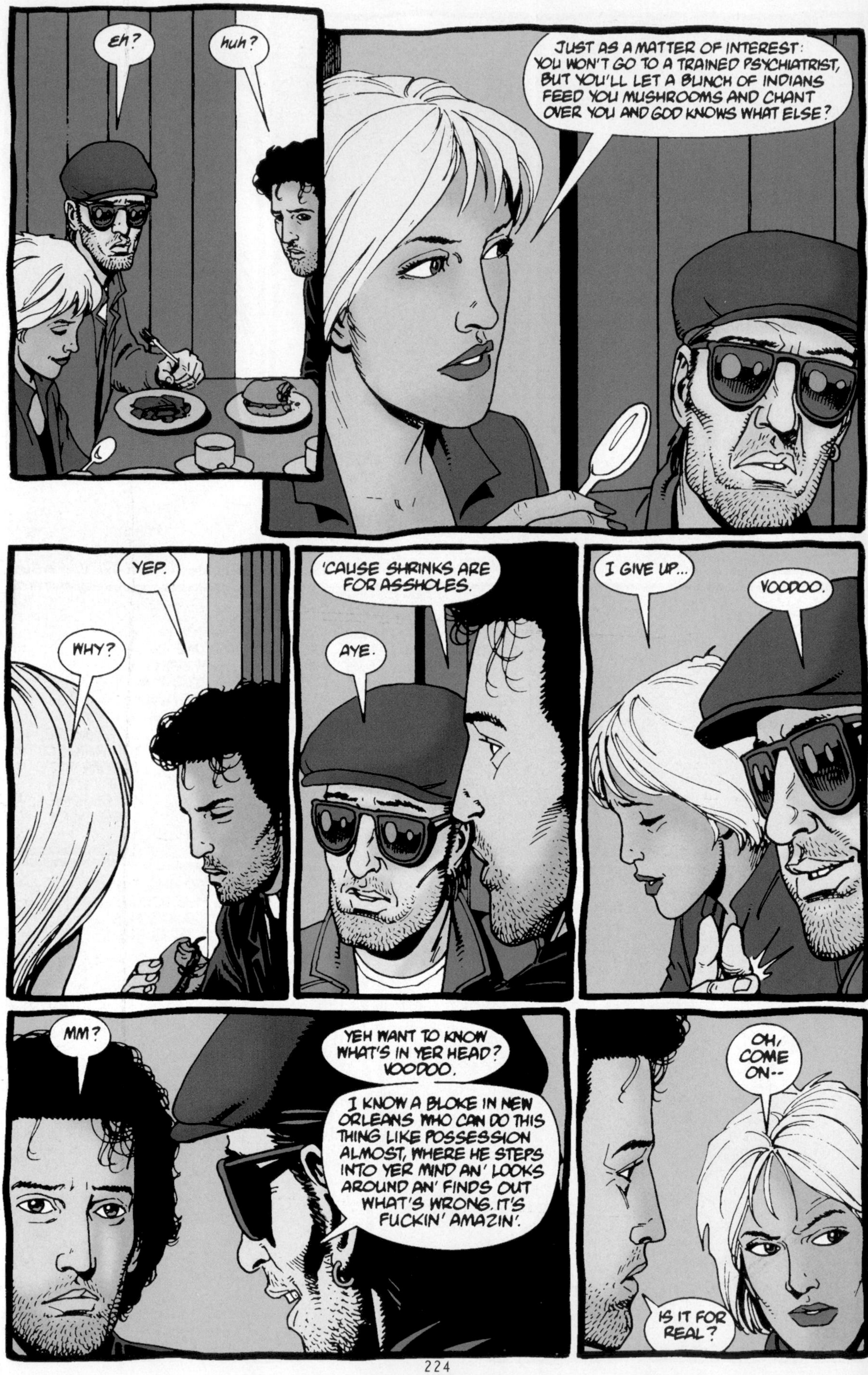

Eh?
huh?
JUST AS A MATTER OF INTEREST: YOU WON'T GO TO A TRAINED PSYCHIATRIST, BUT YOU'LL LET A BUNCH OF INDIANS FEED YOU MUSHROOMS AND CHANT OVER YOU AND GOD KNOWS WHAT ELSE?
YEP.
WHY?
'CAUSE SHRINKS ARE FOR ASSHOLES.
AYE.
I GIVE UP...
VOODOO.
MM?
YEH WANT TO KNOW WHAT'S IN YER HEAD? VOODOO.
I KNOW A BLOKE IN NEW ORLEANS WHO CAN DO THIS THING LIKE POSSESSION ALMOST, WHERE HE STEPS INTO YER MIND AN' LOOKS AROUND AN' FINDS OUT WHAT'S WRONG. IT'S FUCKIN' AMAZIN'.
OH, COME ON--
IS IT FOR REAL?

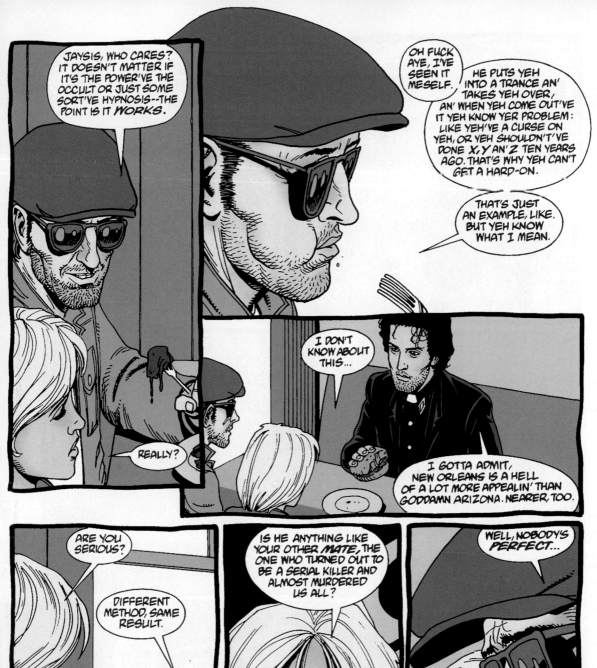

JAYSIS, WHO CARES? IT DOESN'T MATTER IF IT'S THE POWER'VE THE OCCULT OR JUST SOME SORT'VE HYPNOSIS--THE POINT IS IT *WORKS*.

OH FUCK AYE, I'VE SEEN IT MESELF.

HE PUTS YEH INTO A TRANCE AN' TAKES YEH OVER, AN' WHEN YEH COME OUT'VE IT YEH KNOW YER PROBLEM: LIKE YEH'VE A CURSE ON YEH, OR YEH SHOULDN'T'VE DONE *X, Y* AN'*Z* TEN YEARS AGO. THAT'S WHY YEH CAN'T GET A HARD-ON.

THAT'S JUST AN EXAMPLE, LIKE. BUT YEH KNOW WHAT I MEAN.

REALLY?

I DON'T KNOW ABOUT THIS...

I GOTTA ADMIT, NEW ORLEANS IS A HELL OF A LOT MORE APPEALIN' THAN GODDAMN ARIZONA. NEARER, TOO.

ARE YOU SERIOUS?

DIFFERENT METHOD, SAME RESULT.

I'M TELLIN' YEH, TULIP, IT' WORKS EVERY TIME. THIS MATE'VE MINE'S FANTASTIC...

IS HE ANYTHING LIKE YOUR OTHER *MATE*, THE ONE WHO TURNED OUT TO BE A SERIAL KILLER AND ALMOST MURDERED US ALL?

WELL, NOBODY'S *PERFECT*...

NO.

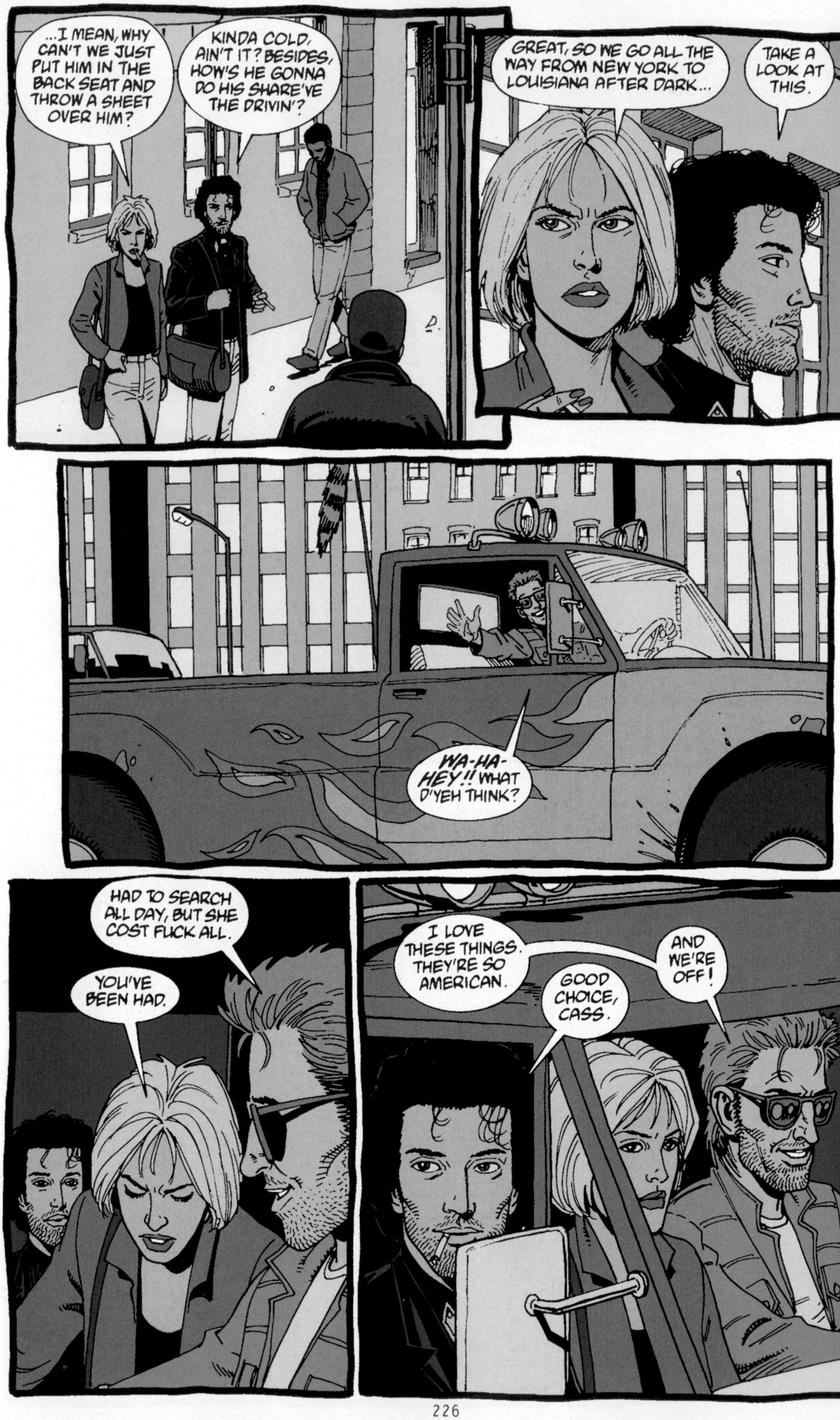
...I MEAN, WHY CAN'T WE JUST PUT HIM IN THE BACK SEAT AND THROW A SHEET OVER HIM?
KINDA COLD, AIN'T IT? BESIDES, HOW'S HE GONNA DO HIS SHARE'VE THE DRIVIN'?
GREAT, SO WE GO ALL THE WAY FROM NEW YORK TO LOUISIANA AFTER DARK...
TAKE A LOOK AT THIS.
WA-HA-HEY!! WHAT D'YEH THINK?
HAD TO SEARCH ALL DAY, BUT SHE COST FUCK ALL.
YOU'VE BEEN HAD.
I LOVE THESE THINGS. THEY'RE SO AMERICAN.
GOOD CHOICE, CASS.
AND WE'RE OFF!

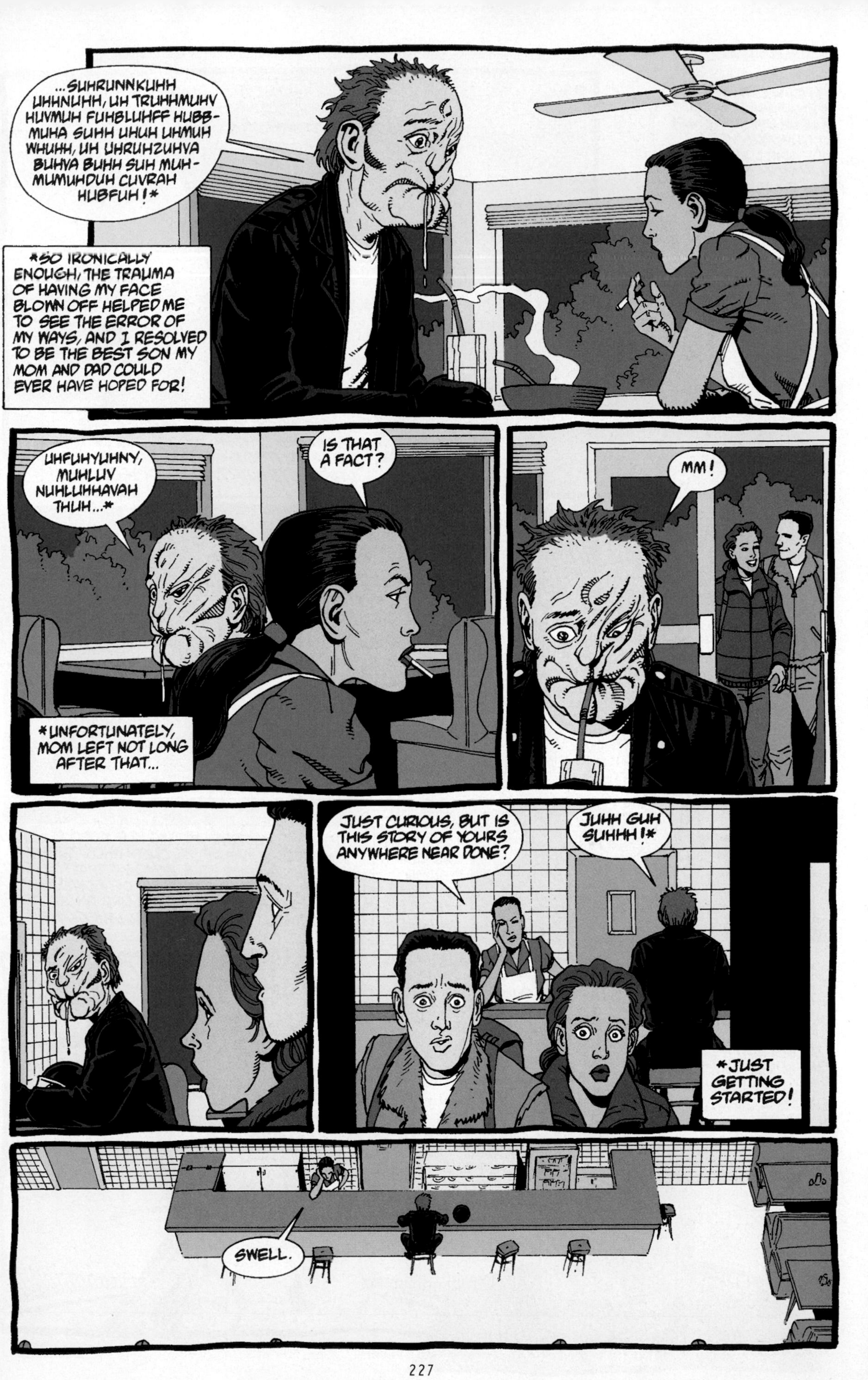
...SUHRUNNKUHH UHHNUHH, UH TRUHHMUHV HUVMUH FUHBLUHFF HUBB-MUHA SUHH UHUH UHMUH WHUHH, UH UHRUHZUHVA BUHVA BUHH SUH MUH-MUMUHDUH CUVRAH HUBFUH!*
*SO IRONICALLY ENOUGH, THE TRAUMA OF HAVING MY FACE BLOWN OFF HELPED ME TO SEE THE ERROR OF MY WAYS, AND I RESOLVED TO BE THE BEST SON MY MOM AND DAD COULD EVER HAVE HOPED FOR!
UHFUHYUHNY, MUHLUV NUHLUHHAVAH THUH...*
IS THAT A FACT?
*UNFORTUNATELY, MOM LEFT NOT LONG AFTER THAT...
MM!
JUST CURIOUS, BUT IS THIS STORY OF YOURS ANYWHERE NEAR DONE?
JUHH GUH SUHHH!*
*JUST GETTING STARTED!
SWELL.

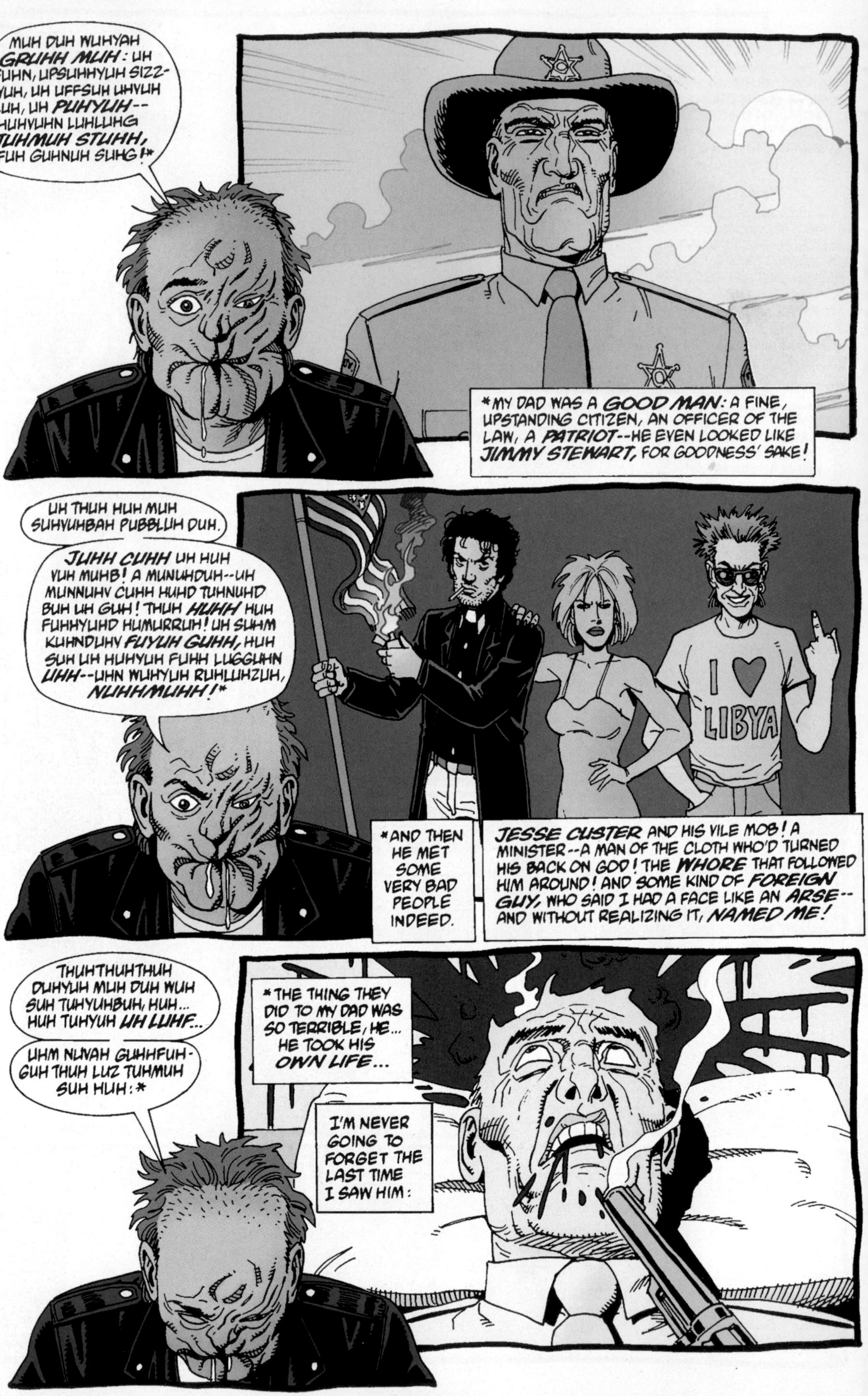
MUH DUH WUHYAH GRUHH MUH: UH FUHN, UPSUHHYUH SIZZ-YUH, UH UFFSUH UHYUH LUH, UH PUHYUH--HUHYUHN LUHLUHG JUHMUH STUHH, FUH GUHNUH SUHG!*
*MY DAD WAS A GOOD MAN: A FINE, UPSTANDING CITIZEN, AN OFFICER OF THE LAW, A PATRIOT--HE EVEN LOOKED LIKE JIMMY STEWART, FOR GOODNESS' SAKE!
UH THUH HUH MUH SUHVUHBAH PUBBLUH DUH.
JUHH CUHH UH HUH VUH MUHB! A MUNUHDUH--UH MUNNUHV CUHH HUHD TUHNUHD BUH UH GUH! THUH HUHH HUH FUHHYUHD HUMURRUH! UH SUHM KUHNDUHV FUYUH GUHH, HUH SUH UH HUHYUH FUHH LUGGUHN UHH--UHN WUHYUH RUHLUHZUH, NUHHMUHH!*
I ♥ LIBYA
*AND THEN HE MET SOME VERY BAD PEOPLE INDEED.
JESSE CUSTER AND HIS VILE MOB! A MINISTER--A MAN OF THE CLOTH WHO'D TURNED HIS BACK ON GOD! THE WHORE THAT FOLLOWED HIM AROUND! AND SOME KIND OF FOREIGN GUY, WHO SAID I HAD A FACE LIKE AN ARSE--AND WITHOUT REALIZING IT, NAMED ME!
THUHTHUHTHUH DUHYUH MUH DUH WUH SUH TUHYUHBUH, HUH... HUH TUHYUH UH LUHF...
UHM NUVAH GUHHFUH-GUH THUH LUZ TUHMUH SUH HUH:*
*THE THING THEY DID TO MY DAD WAS SO TERRIBLE, HE... HE TOOK HIS OWN LIFE...
I'M NEVER GOING TO FORGET THE LAST TIME I SAW HIM:

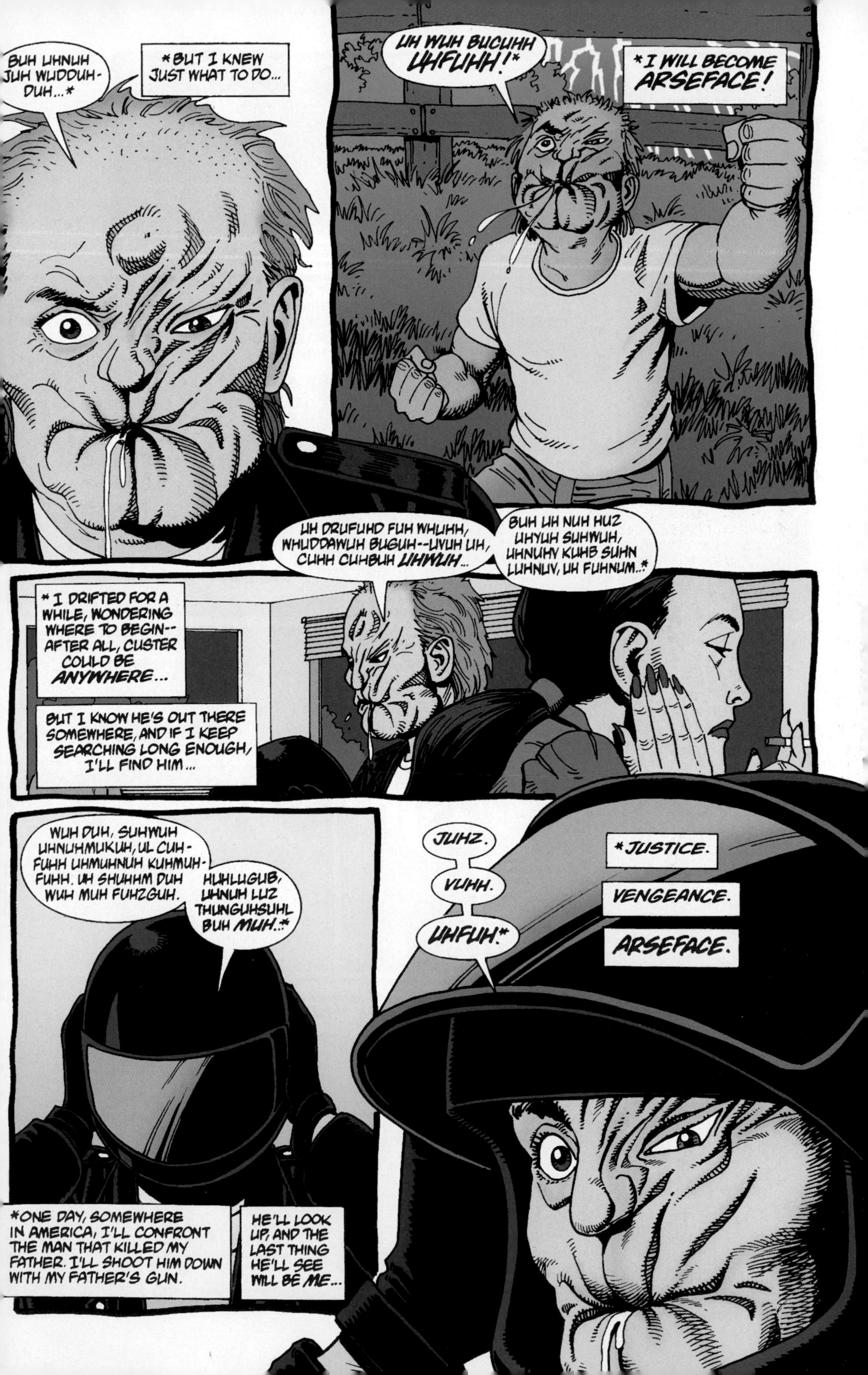
BUH UHNUH JUH WUDDUH-DUH...*
*BUT I KNEW JUST WHAT TO DO...
UH WUH BUCUHH UHFUHH!*
*I WILL BECOME ARSEFACE!
UH DRUFUHD FUH WHUHH, WHUDDAWUH BUGUH--UVUH UH, CUHH CUHBUH UHWUH...
BUH UH NUH HUZ UHYUH SUHWUH, UHNUHV KUHB SUHN LUHNUV, UH FUHNUM...*
*I DRIFTED FOR A WHILE, WONDERING WHERE TO BEGIN-- AFTER ALL, CUSTER COULD BE ANYWHERE...
BUT I KNOW HE'S OUT THERE SOMEWHERE, AND IF I KEEP SEARCHING LONG ENOUGH, I'LL FIND HIM...
WUH DUH, SUHWUH UHNUHMUKUH, UL CUH-FUHH UHMUHNUH KUHMUH-FUHH. UH SHUHHM DUH WUH MUH FUHZGUH.
HUHLUGUB, UHNUH LUZ THUNGUHSUHL BUH MUH..*
*ONE DAY, SOMEWHERE IN AMERICA, I'LL CONFRONT THE MAN THAT KILLED MY FATHER. I'LL SHOOT HIM DOWN WITH MY FATHER'S GUN.
HE'LL LOOK UP, AND THE LAST THING HE'LL SEE WILL BE ME...
JUHZ.
VUHH.
UHFUH.*
*JUSTICE.
VENGEANCE.
ARSEFACE.

THAT'LL BE EIGHT-FIFTY. DON'T LET THE DOOR HIT YOU IN THE ASS ON THE WAY OUT.

SHUH THUH!*

*SURE THING!

THIS *ALWAYS* HAPPENS...

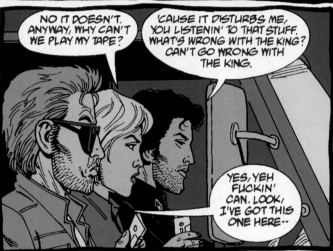

NO IT DOESN'T. ANYWAY, WHY CAN'T WE PLAY MY TAPE?

'CAUSE IT DISTURBS ME, YOU LISTENIN' TO THAT STUFF. WHAT'S WRONG WITH THE KING? CAN'T GO WRONG WITH THE KING.

YES, YEH FUCKIN' CAN. LOOK, I'VE GOT THIS ONE HERE--

KLIK

LONDON IS FLOODING, IIIIII LIVE BY THE RIVAAAHH--

KLIK

AN' YOU LIGHT MY MORNIN' SKYYYY, BURNIN' LUHUVV...

KLIK

KNEW A CRACK DEALER BY THE NAME OF PETAH, HAD TO BUCK 'IM DOWN WIT' MY NINE MILLIMETAH...

KLIK

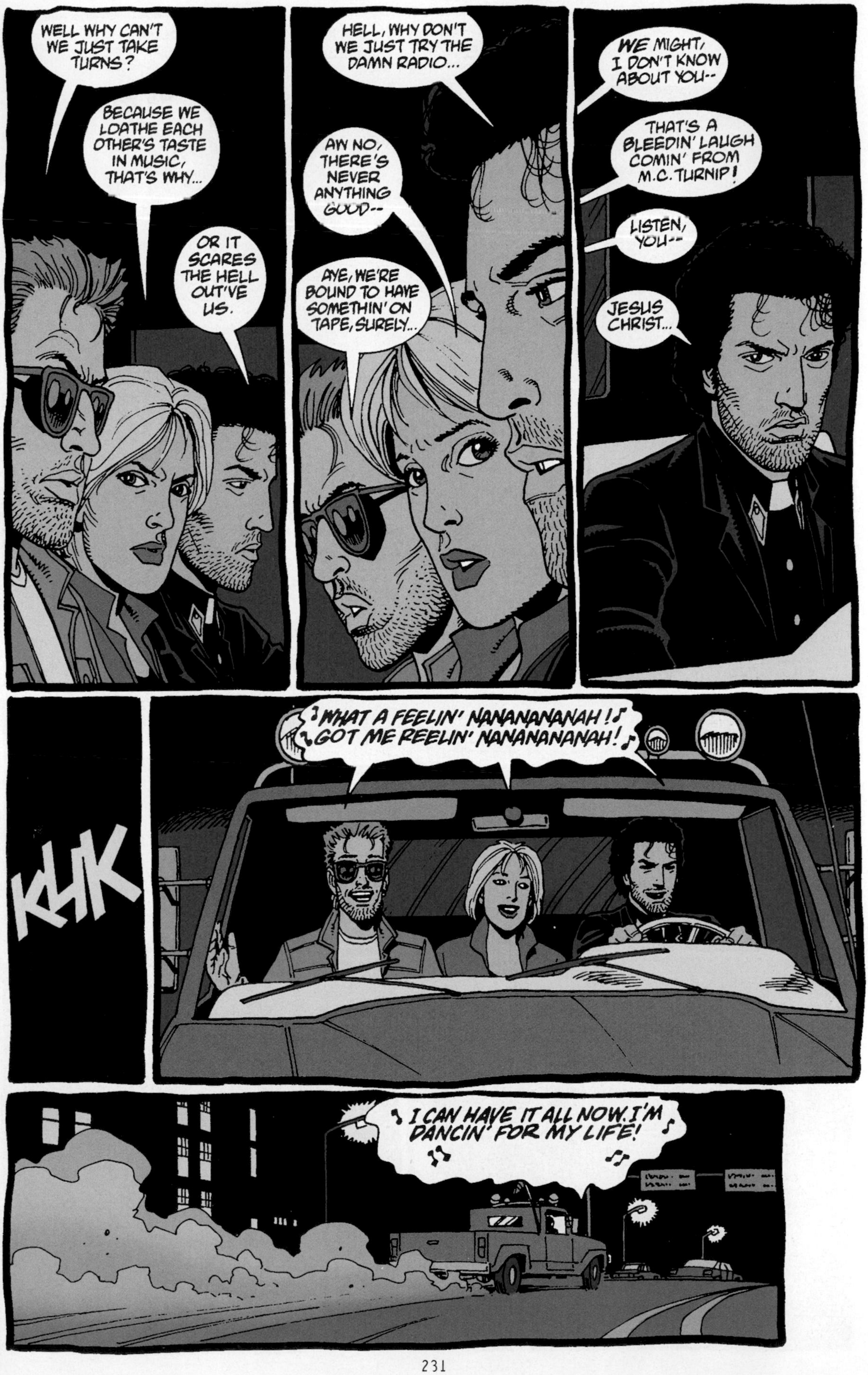

WELL WHY CAN'T WE JUST TAKE TURNS?
BECAUSE WE LOATHE EACH OTHER'S TASTE IN MUSIC, THAT'S WHY...
OR IT SCARES THE HELL OUT'VE US.
HELL, WHY DON'T WE JUST TRY THE DAMN RADIO...
AW NO, THERE'S NEVER ANYTHING GOOD--
AYE, WE'RE BOUND TO HAVE SOMETHIN' ON TAPE, SURELY...
WE MIGHT, I DON'T KNOW ABOUT YOU--
THAT'S A BLEEDIN' LAUGH COMIN' FROM M.C. TURNIP!
LISTEN, YOU--
JESUS CHRIST...
KLIK
WHAT A FEELIN' NANANANANAH! GOT ME REELIN' NANANANANAH!
I CAN HAVE IT ALL NOW. I'M DANCIN' FOR MY LIFE!

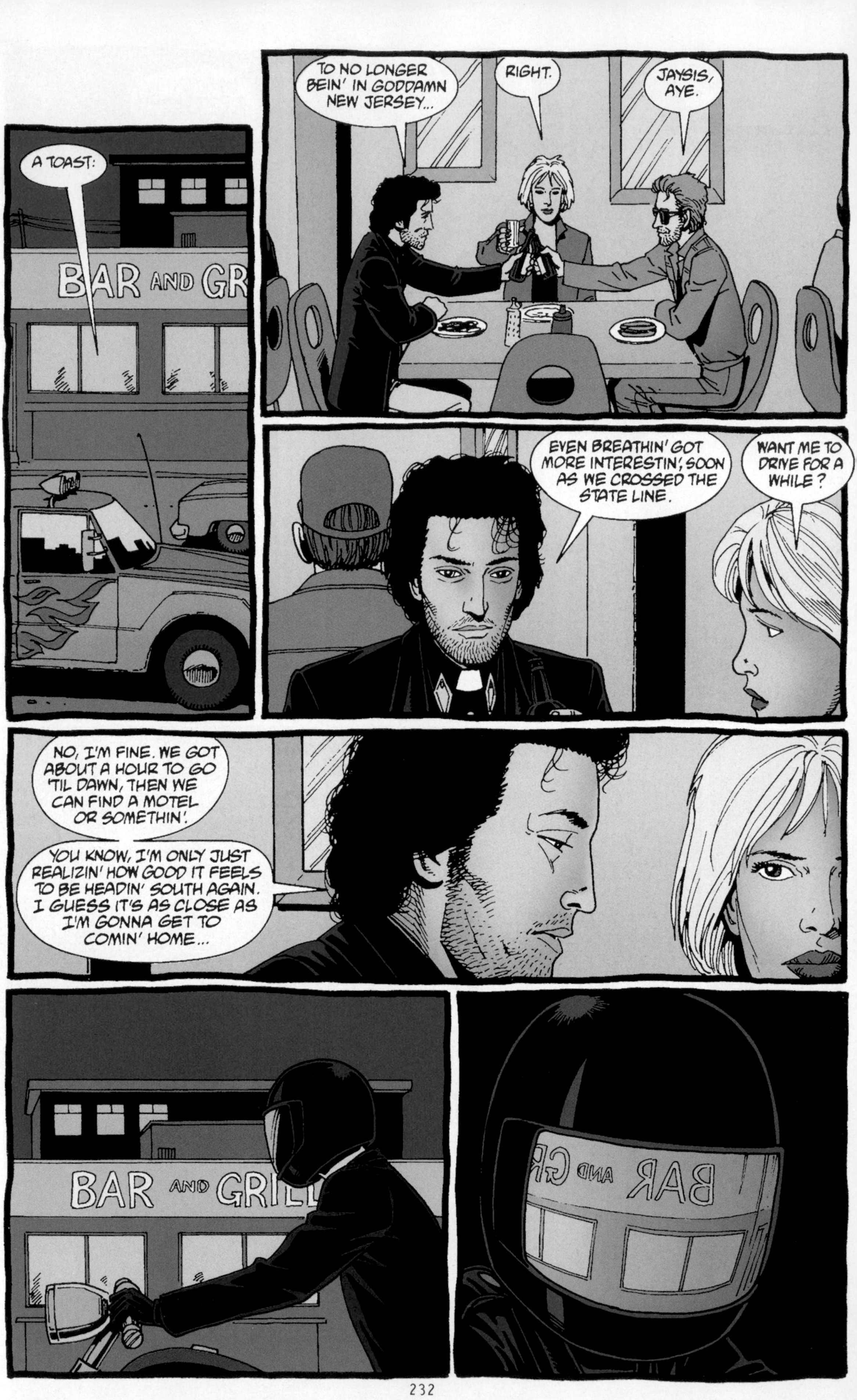
A TOAST:
BAR AND GR
TO NO LONGER BEIN' IN GODDAMN NEW JERSEY...
RIGHT.
JAYSIS, AYE.
EVEN BREATHIN' GOT MORE INTERESTIN', SOON AS WE CROSSED THE STATE LINE.
WANT ME TO DRIVE FOR A WHILE?
NO, I'M FINE. WE GOT ABOUT A HOUR TO GO 'TIL DAWN, THEN WE CAN FIND A MOTEL OR SOMETHIN'.
YOU KNOW, I'M ONLY JUST REALIZIN' HOW GOOD IT FEELS TO BE HEADIN' SOUTH AGAIN. I GUESS IT'S AS CLOSE AS I'M GONNA GET TO COMIN' HOME...
BAR AND GRILL

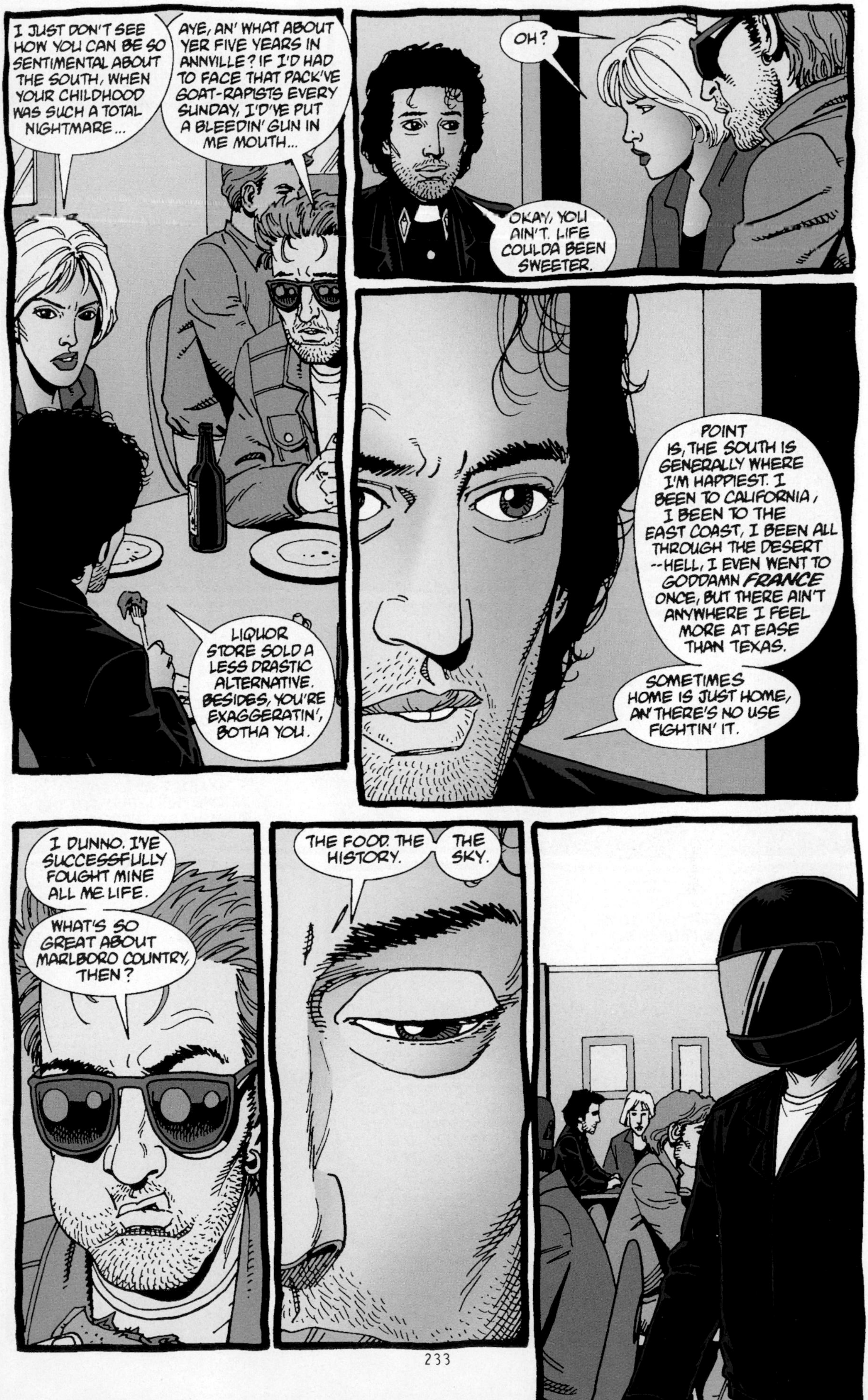
I JUST DON'T SEE HOW YOU CAN BE SO SENTIMENTAL ABOUT THE SOUTH, WHEN YOUR CHILDHOOD WAS SUCH A TOTAL NIGHTMARE...
AYE, AN' WHAT ABOUT YER FIVE YEARS IN ANNVILLE? IF I'D HAD TO FACE THAT PACK'VE GOAT-RAPISTS EVERY SUNDAY, I'D'VE PUT A BLEEDIN' GUN IN ME MOUTH...
LIQUOR STORE SOLD A LESS DRASTIC ALTERNATIVE. BESIDES, YOU'RE EXAGGERATIN', BOTHA YOU.
OH?
OKAY, YOU AIN'T. LIFE COULDA BEEN SWEETER.
POINT IS, THE SOUTH IS GENERALLY WHERE I'M HAPPIEST. I BEEN TO CALIFORNIA, I BEEN TO THE EAST COAST, I BEEN ALL THROUGH THE DESERT --HELL, I EVEN WENT TO GODDAMN FRANCE ONCE, BUT THERE AIN'T ANYWHERE I FEEL MORE AT EASE THAN TEXAS.
SOMETIMES HOME IS JUST HOME, AN' THERE'S NO USE FIGHTIN' IT.
I DUNNO. I'VE SUCCESSFULLY FOUGHT MINE ALL ME LIFE.
WHAT'S SO GREAT ABOUT MARLBORO COUNTRY, THEN?
THE FOOD. THE HISTORY.
THE SKY.

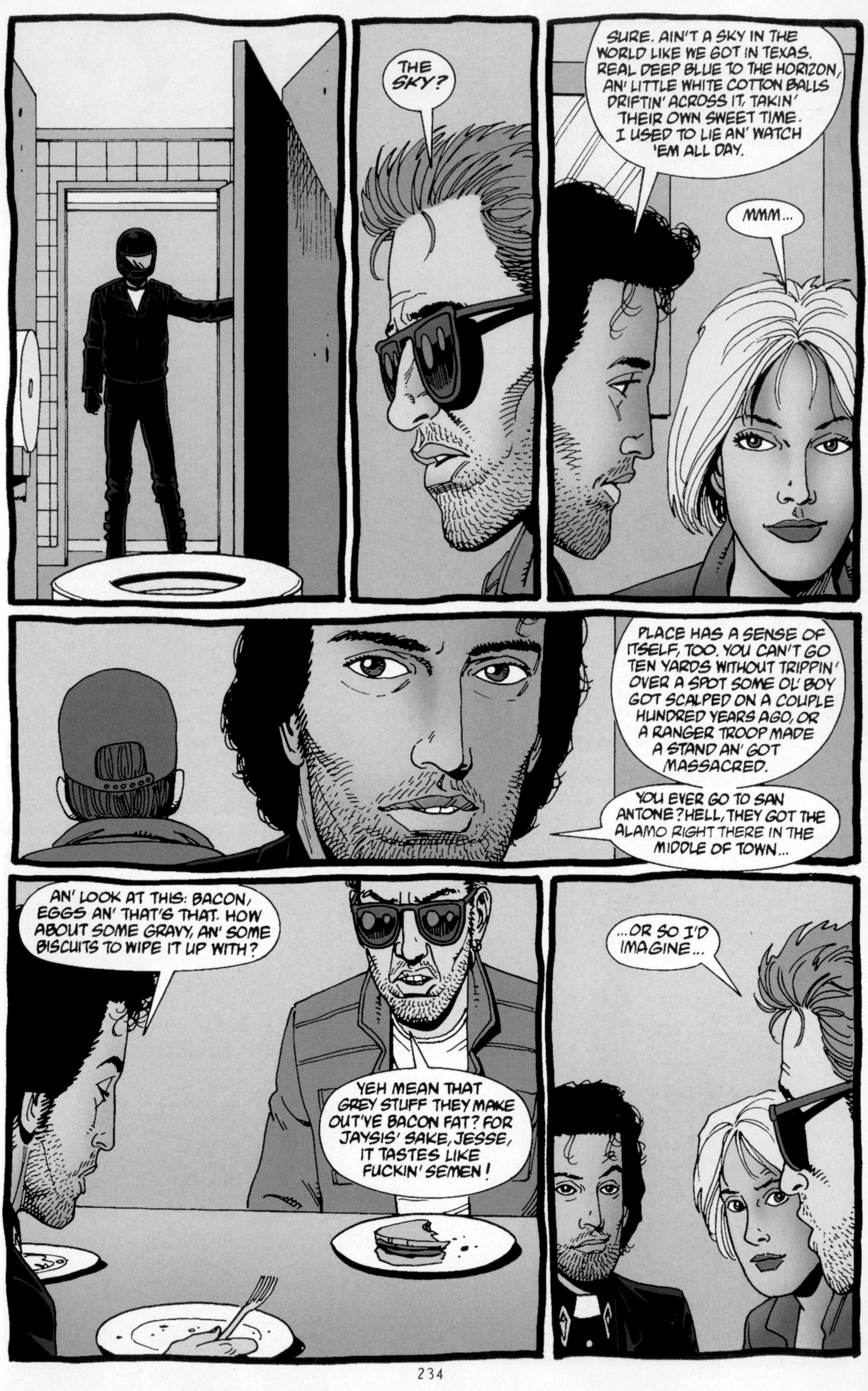
THE SKY?
SURE. AIN'T A SKY IN THE WORLD LIKE WE GOT IN TEXAS. REAL DEEP BLUE TO THE HORIZON, AN' LITTLE WHITE COTTON BALLS DRIFTIN' ACROSS IT, TAKIN' THEIR OWN SWEET TIME. I USED TO LIE AN' WATCH 'EM ALL DAY.
MMM...
PLACE HAS A SENSE OF ITSELF, TOO. YOU CAN'T GO TEN YARDS WITHOUT TRIPPIN' OVER A SPOT SOME OL' BOY GOT SCALPED ON A COUPLE HUNDRED YEARS AGO, OR A RANGER TROOP MADE A STAND AN' GOT MASSACRED.
YOU EVER GO TO SAN ANTONE? HELL, THEY GOT THE ALAMO RIGHT THERE IN THE MIDDLE OF TOWN...
AN' LOOK AT THIS: BACON, EGGS AN' THAT'S THAT. HOW ABOUT SOME GRAVY, AN' SOME BISCUITS TO WIPE IT UP WITH?
YEH MEAN THAT GREY STUFF THEY MAKE OUT'VE BACON FAT? FOR JAYSIS' SAKE, JESSE, IT TASTES LIKE FUCKIN' SEMEN!
...OR SO I'D IMAGINE...

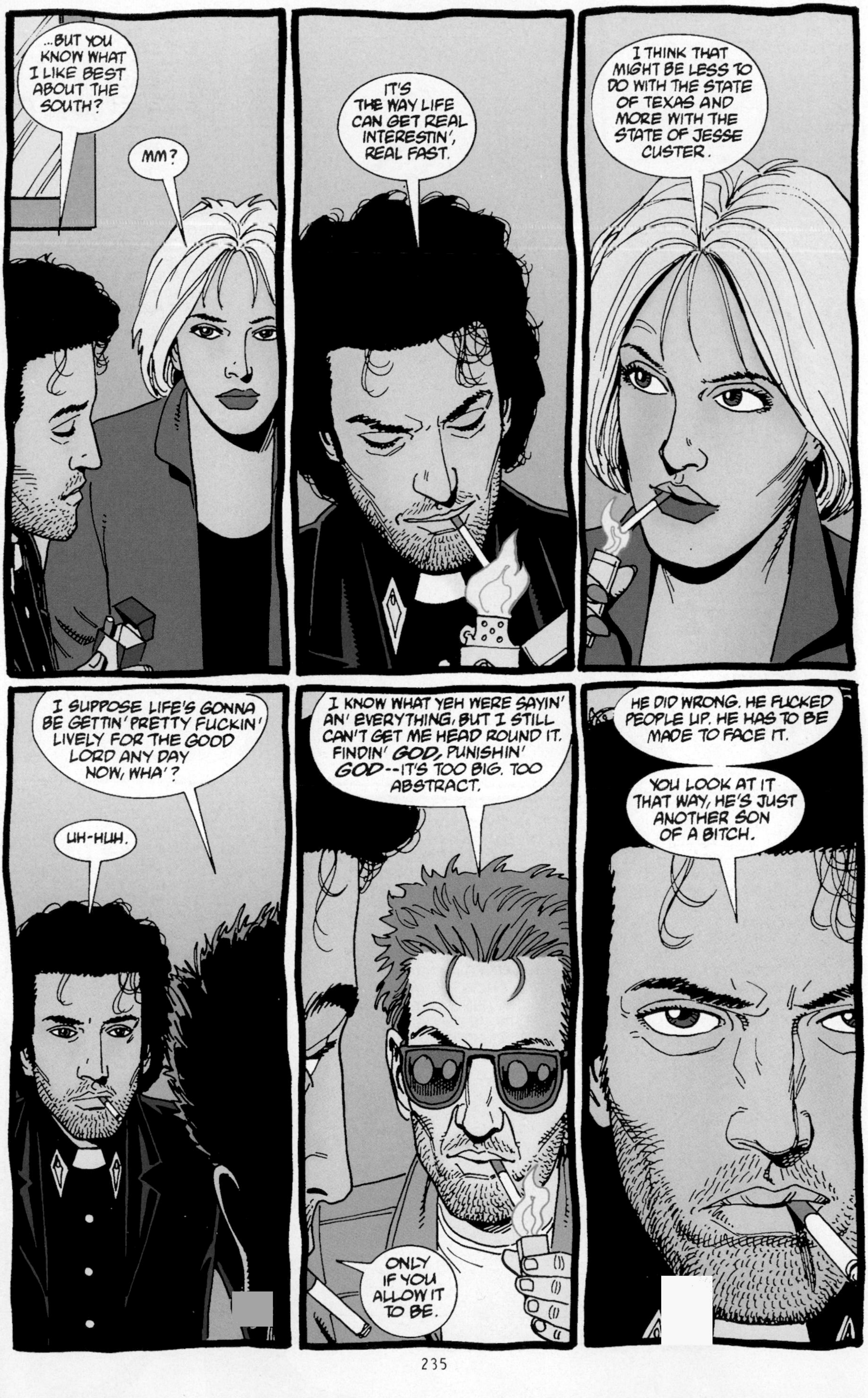
...BUT YOU KNOW WHAT I LIKE BEST ABOUT THE SOUTH?
MM?
IT'S THE WAY LIFE CAN GET REAL INTERESTIN', REAL FAST.
I THINK THAT MIGHT BE LESS TO DO WITH THE STATE OF TEXAS AND MORE WITH THE STATE OF JESSE CUSTER.
I SUPPOSE LIFE'S GONNA BE GETTIN' PRETTY FUCKIN' LIVELY FOR THE GOOD LORD ANY DAY NOW, WHA'?
UH-HUH.
I KNOW WHAT YEH WERE SAYIN' AN' EVERYTHING, BUT I STILL CAN'T GET ME HEAD ROUND IT. FINDIN' GOD, PUNISHIN' GOD--IT'S TOO BIG. TOO ABSTRACT.
ONLY IF YOU ALLOW IT TO BE.
HE DID WRONG. HE FUCKED PEOPLE UP. HE HAS TO BE MADE TO FACE IT.
YOU LOOK AT IT THAT WAY, HE'S JUST ANOTHER SON OF A BITCH.

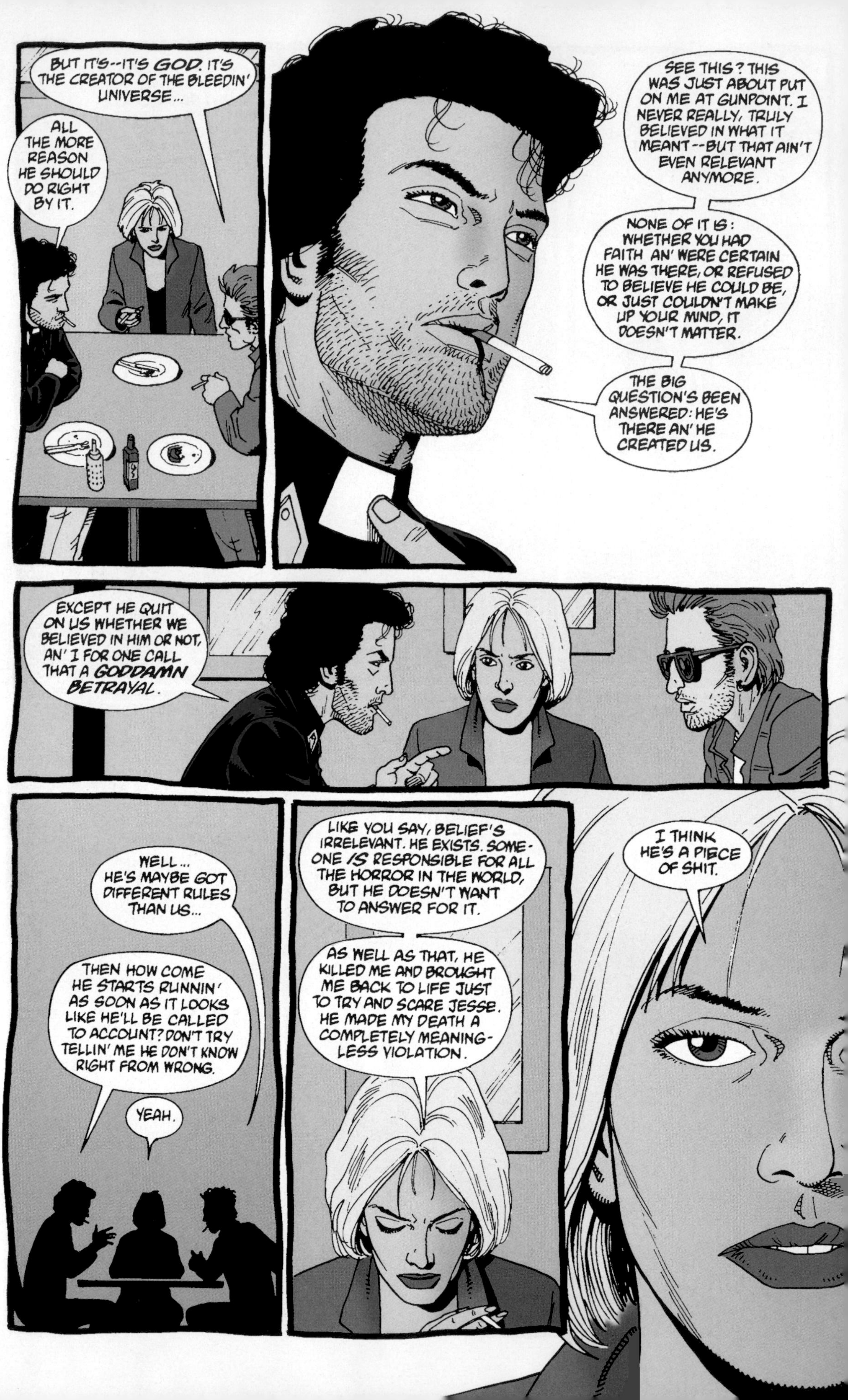
BUT IT'S--IT'S GOD. IT'S THE CREATOR OF THE BLEEDIN' UNIVERSE...
ALL THE MORE REASON HE SHOULD DO RIGHT BY IT.
SEE THIS? THIS WAS JUST ABOUT PUT ON ME AT GUNPOINT. I NEVER REALLY, TRULY BELIEVED IN WHAT IT MEANT--BUT THAT AIN'T EVEN RELEVANT ANYMORE.
NONE OF IT IS: WHETHER YOU HAD FAITH AN' WERE CERTAIN HE WAS THERE, OR REFUSED TO BELIEVE HE COULD BE, OR JUST COULDN'T MAKE UP YOUR MIND, IT DOESN'T MATTER.
THE BIG QUESTION'S BEEN ANSWERED: HE'S THERE AN' HE CREATED US.
EXCEPT HE QUIT ON US WHETHER WE BELIEVED IN HIM OR NOT, AN' I FOR ONE CALL THAT A GODDAMN BETRAYAL.
WELL... HE'S MAYBE GOT DIFFERENT RULES THAN US...
THEN HOW COME HE STARTS RUNNIN' AS SOON AS IT LOOKS LIKE HE'LL BE CALLED TO ACCOUNT? DON'T TRY TELLIN' ME HE DON'T KNOW RIGHT FROM WRONG.
YEAH.
LIKE YOU SAY, BELIEF'S IRRELEVANT. HE EXISTS. SOMEONE IS RESPONSIBLE FOR ALL THE HORROR IN THE WORLD, BUT HE DOESN'T WANT TO ANSWER FOR IT.
AS WELL AS THAT, HE KILLED ME AND BROUGHT ME BACK TO LIFE JUST TO TRY AND SCARE JESSE. HE MADE MY DEATH A COMPLETELY MEANINGLESS VIOLATION.
I THINK HE'S A PIECE OF SHIT.

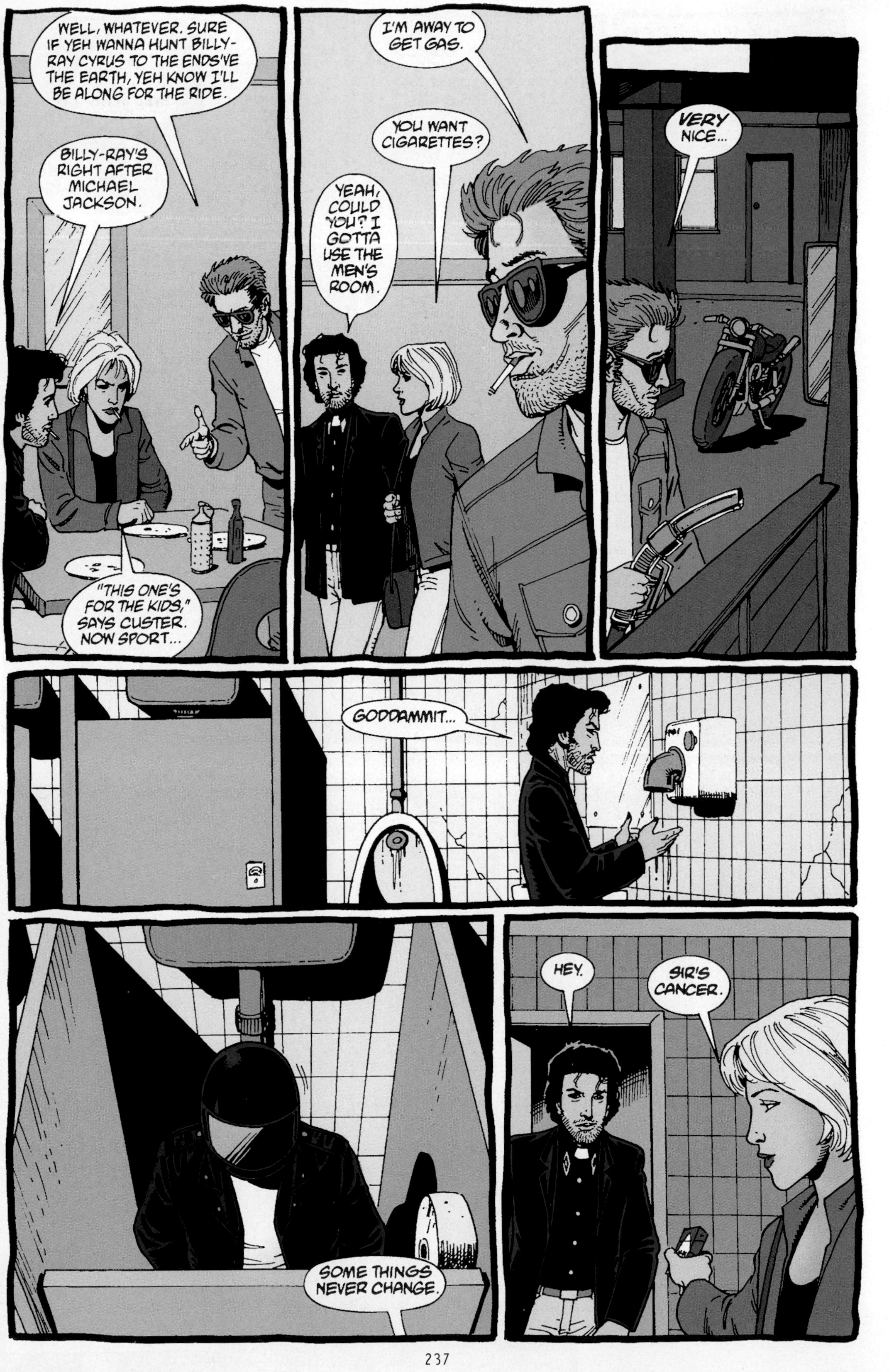
WELL, WHATEVER. SURE IF YEH WANNA HUNT BILLY-RAY CYRUS TO THE ENDS'VE THE EARTH, YEH KNOW I'LL BE ALONG FOR THE RIDE.
BILLY-RAY'S RIGHT AFTER MICHAEL JACKSON.
"THIS ONE'S FOR THE KIDS," SAYS CUSTER. NOW SPORT...
I'M AWAY TO GET GAS.
YOU WANT CIGARETTES?
YEAH, COULD YOU? I GOTTA USE THE MEN'S ROOM.
VERY NICE...
GODDAMMIT...
SOME THINGS NEVER CHANGE.
HEY.
SIR'S CANCER.

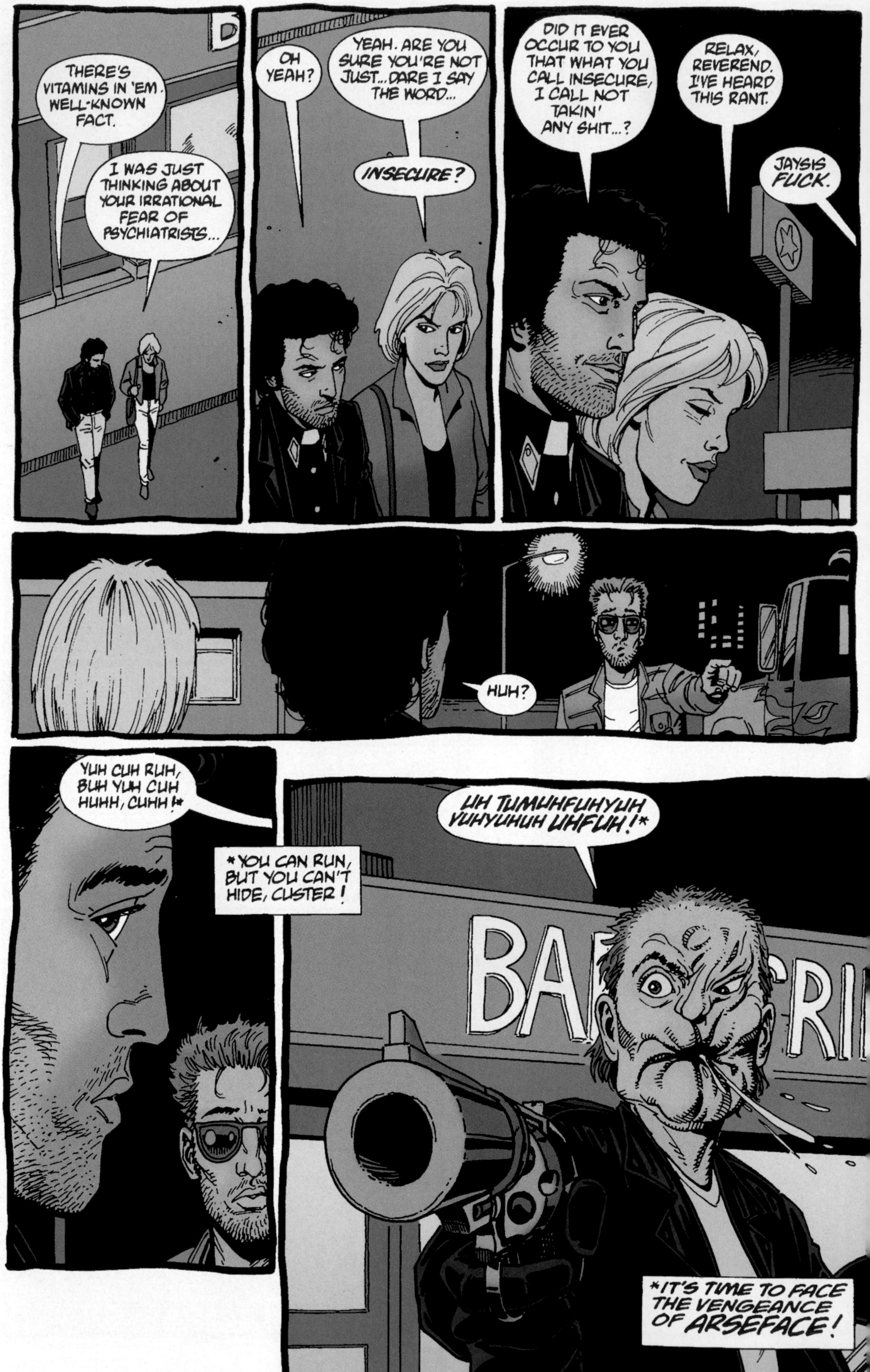
THERE'S VITAMINS IN 'EM. WELL-KNOWN FACT.
I WAS JUST THINKING ABOUT YOUR IRRATIONAL FEAR OF PSYCHIATRISTS...
OH YEAH?
YEAH. ARE YOU SURE YOU'RE NOT JUST... DARE I SAY THE WORD...
INSECURE?
DID IT EVER OCCUR TO YOU THAT WHAT YOU CALL INSECURE, I CALL NOT TAKIN' ANY SHIT...?
RELAX, REVEREND. I'VE HEARD THIS RANT.
JAYSIS FUCK.
HUH?
YUH CUH RUH, BUH YUH CUH HUHH, CUHH!*
*YOU CAN RUN, BUT YOU CAN'T HIDE, CUSTER!
UH TUMUHFUHYUH VUHYUHUH UHFUH!*
*IT'S TIME TO FACE THE VENGEANCE OF ARSEFACE!

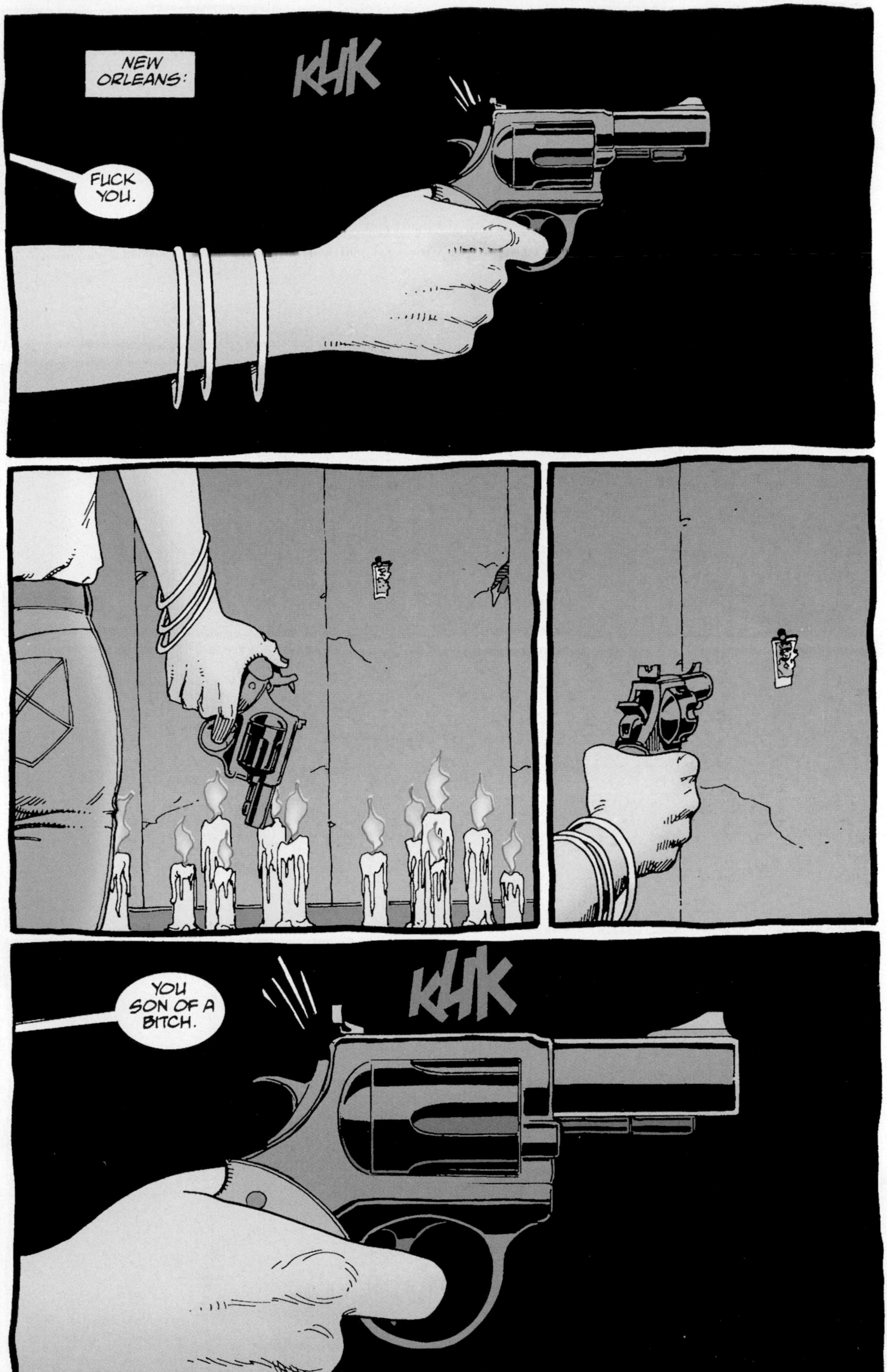
NEW ORLEANS:
KLIK
FUCK YOU.
YOU SON OF A BITCH.
KLIK

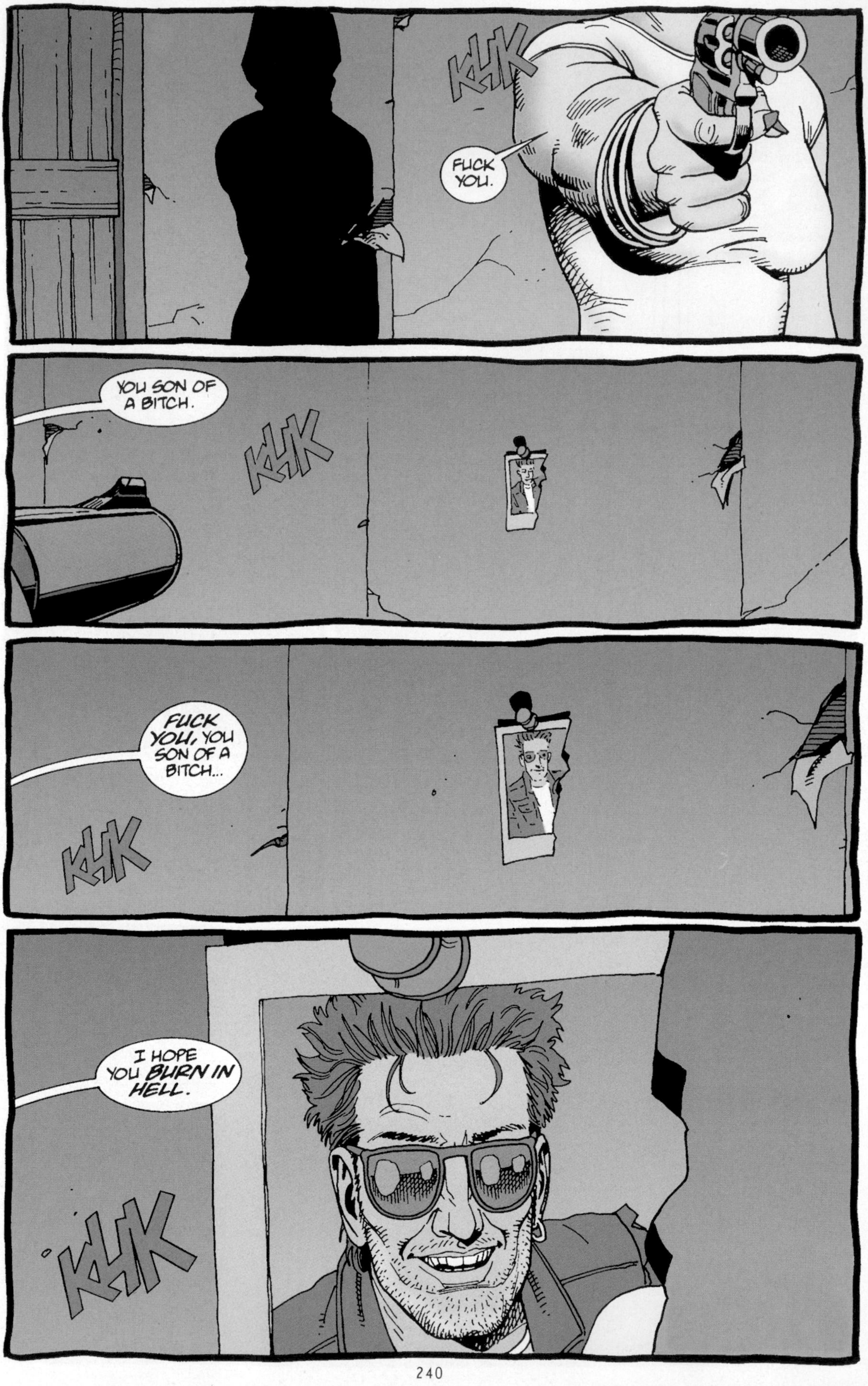
KLIK
FUCK YOU.
YOU SON OF A BITCH.
KLIK
FUCK YOU, YOU SON OF A BITCH...
KLIK
I HOPE YOU BURN IN HELL.
KLIK

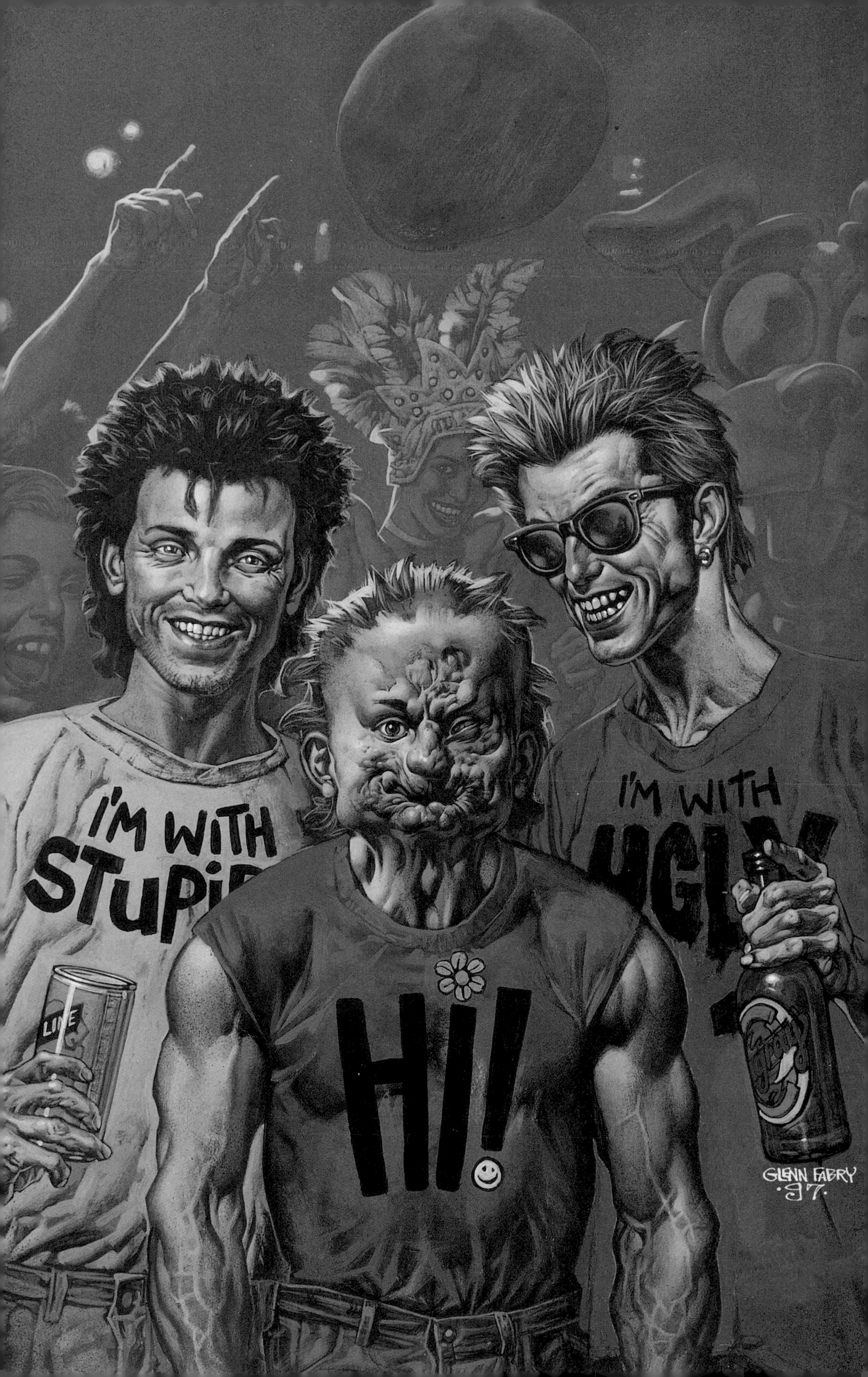
I'M WITH
STUPI
HI!
I'M WITH
UGL
GLENN FABRY
·97·

"We are gonna burn in hell for this one…"

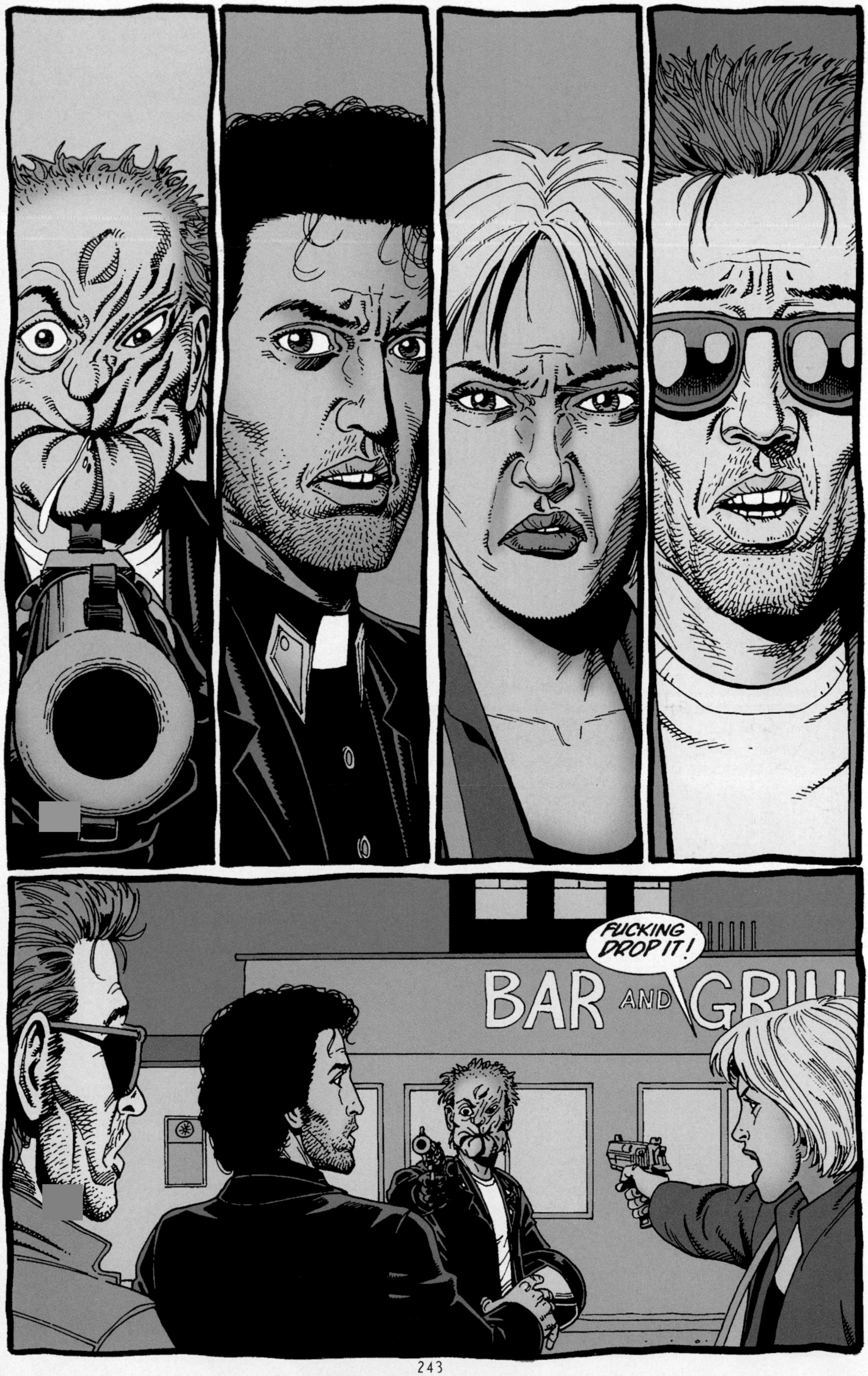
FUCKING DROP IT!
BAR AND GRILL

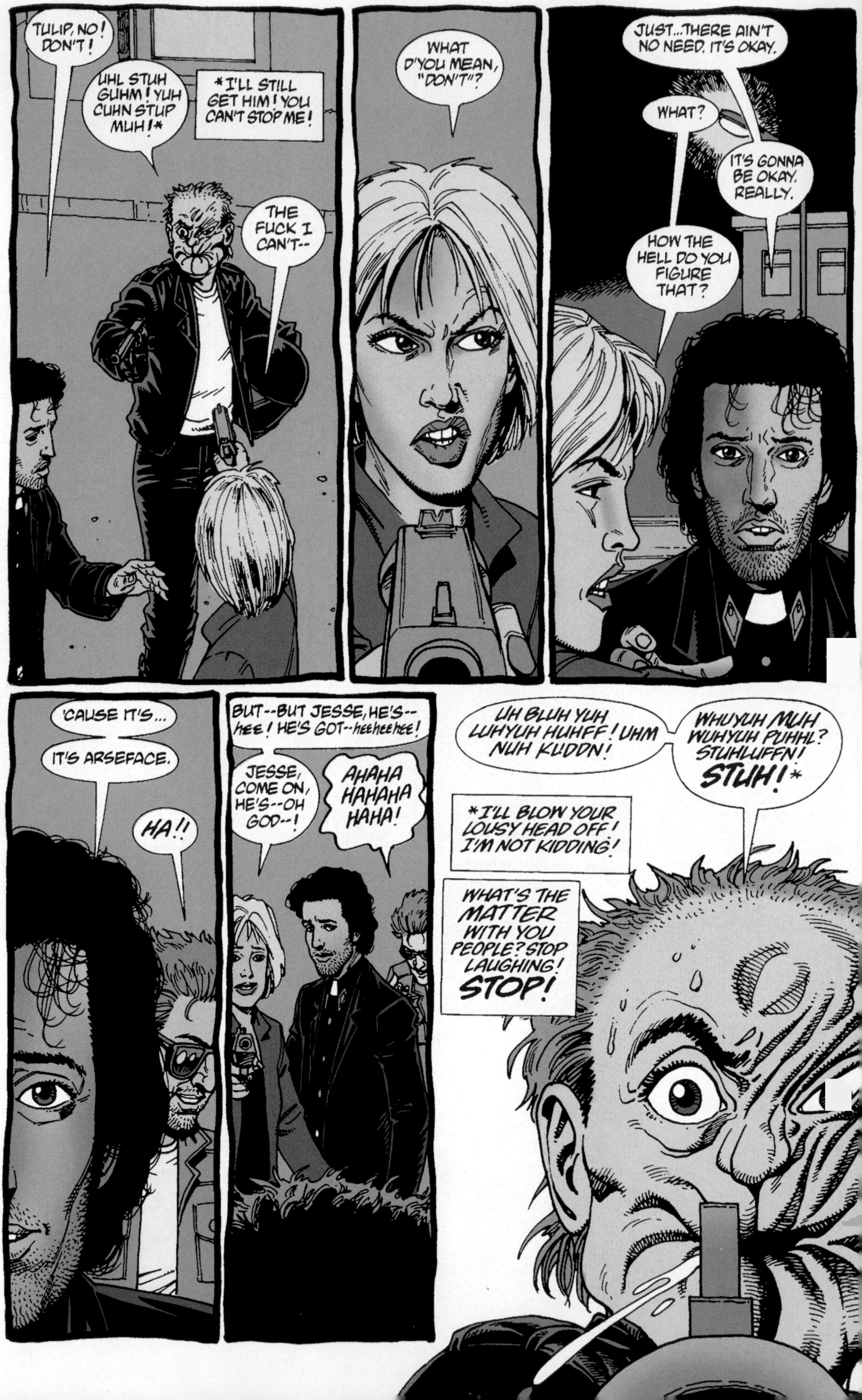
TULIP, NO! DON'T!
UHL STUH GUHM! YUH CUHN STUP MUH!*
*I'LL STILL GET HIM! YOU CAN'T STOP ME!
THE FUCK I CAN'T--
WHAT D'YOU MEAN, "DON'T"?
JUST... THERE AIN'T NO NEED. IT'S OKAY.
WHAT?
IT'S GONNA BE OKAY. REALLY.
HOW THE HELL DO YOU FIGURE THAT?
'CAUSE IT'S...
IT'S ARSEFACE.
HA!!
BUT--BUT JESSE, HE'S--hee! HE'S GOT--heeheehee!
JESSE, COME ON, HE'S--OH GOD--!
AHAHA HAHAHA HAHA!
UH BLUH YUH LUHYUH HUHFF! UHM NUH KUDDN!
WHUYUH MUH WUHYUH PUHHL? STUHLUFFN! STUH!*
*I'LL BLOW YOUR LOUSY HEAD OFF! I'M NOT KIDDING!
WHAT'S THE MATTER WITH YOU PEOPLE? STOP LAUGHING! STOP!

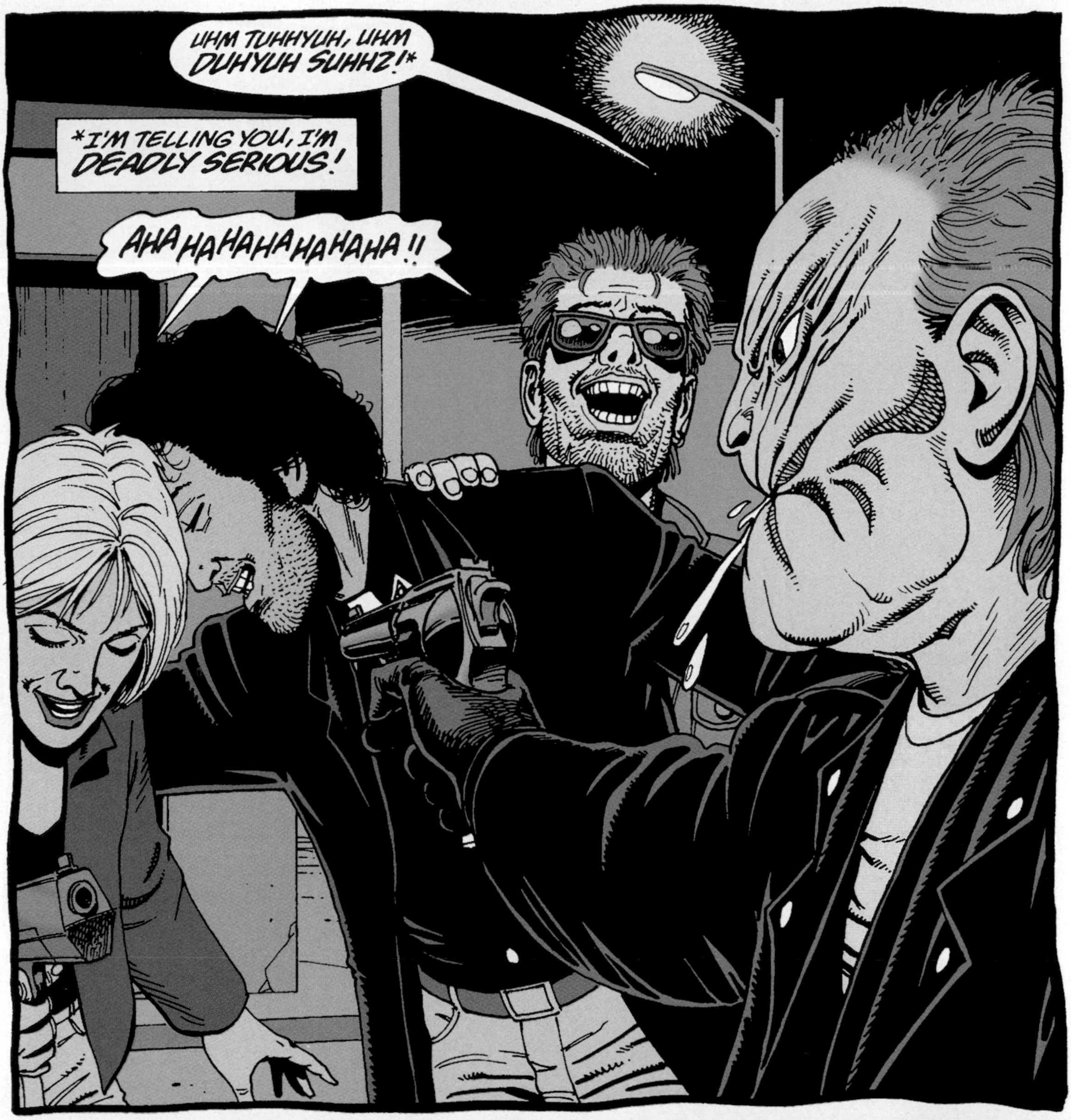
UHM TUHHYUH, UHM DUHYUH SUHHZ!*
*I'M TELLING YOU, I'M DEADLY SERIOUS!
AHAHAHAHAHAHAHAHA!!

# GOOD TIMES ROLLING

GARTH ENNIS - Writer STEVE DILLON - Artist
PAMELA RAMBO and JAMES SINCLAIR - Colorists
CLEM ROBINS - Letterer AXEL ALONSO - Editor

PREACHER created by GARTH ENNIS and STEVE DILLON

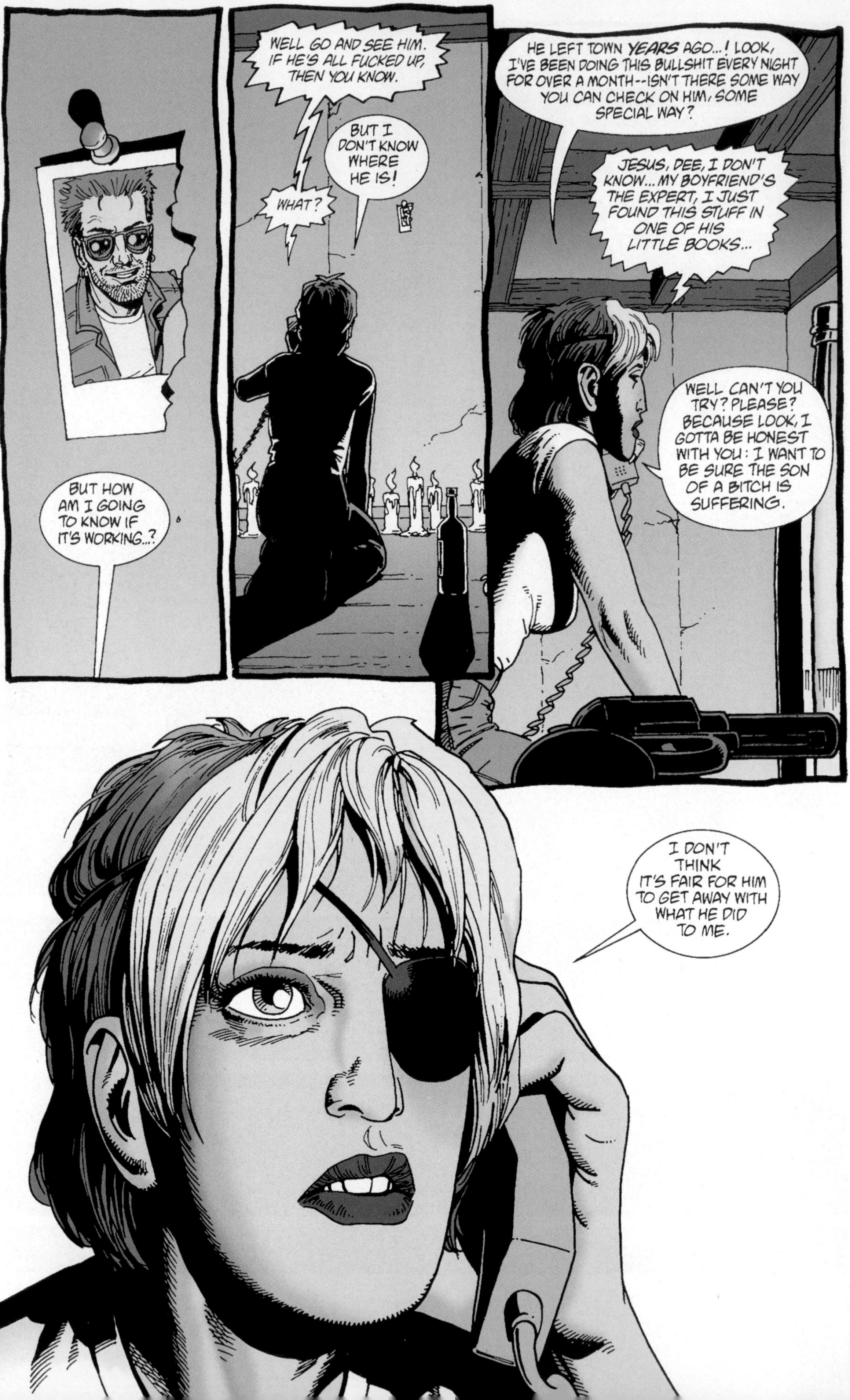

WELL GO AND SEE HIM. IF HE'S ALL FUCKED UP, THEN YOU KNOW.
WHAT?
BUT I DON'T KNOW WHERE HE IS!
HE LEFT TOWN YEARS AGO...! LOOK, I'VE BEEN DOING THIS BULLSHIT EVERY NIGHT FOR OVER A MONTH--ISN'T THERE SOME WAY YOU CAN CHECK ON HIM, SOME SPECIAL WAY?
JESUS, DEE, I DON'T KNOW... MY BOYFRIEND'S THE EXPERT, I JUST FOUND THIS STUFF IN ONE OF HIS LITTLE BOOKS...
BUT HOW AM I GOING TO KNOW IF IT'S WORKING...?
WELL CAN'T YOU TRY? PLEASE? BECAUSE LOOK, I GOTTA BE HONEST WITH YOU: I WANT TO BE SURE THE SON OF A BITCH IS SUFFERING.
I DON'T THINK IT'S FAIR FOR HIM TO GET AWAY WITH WHAT HE DID TO ME.

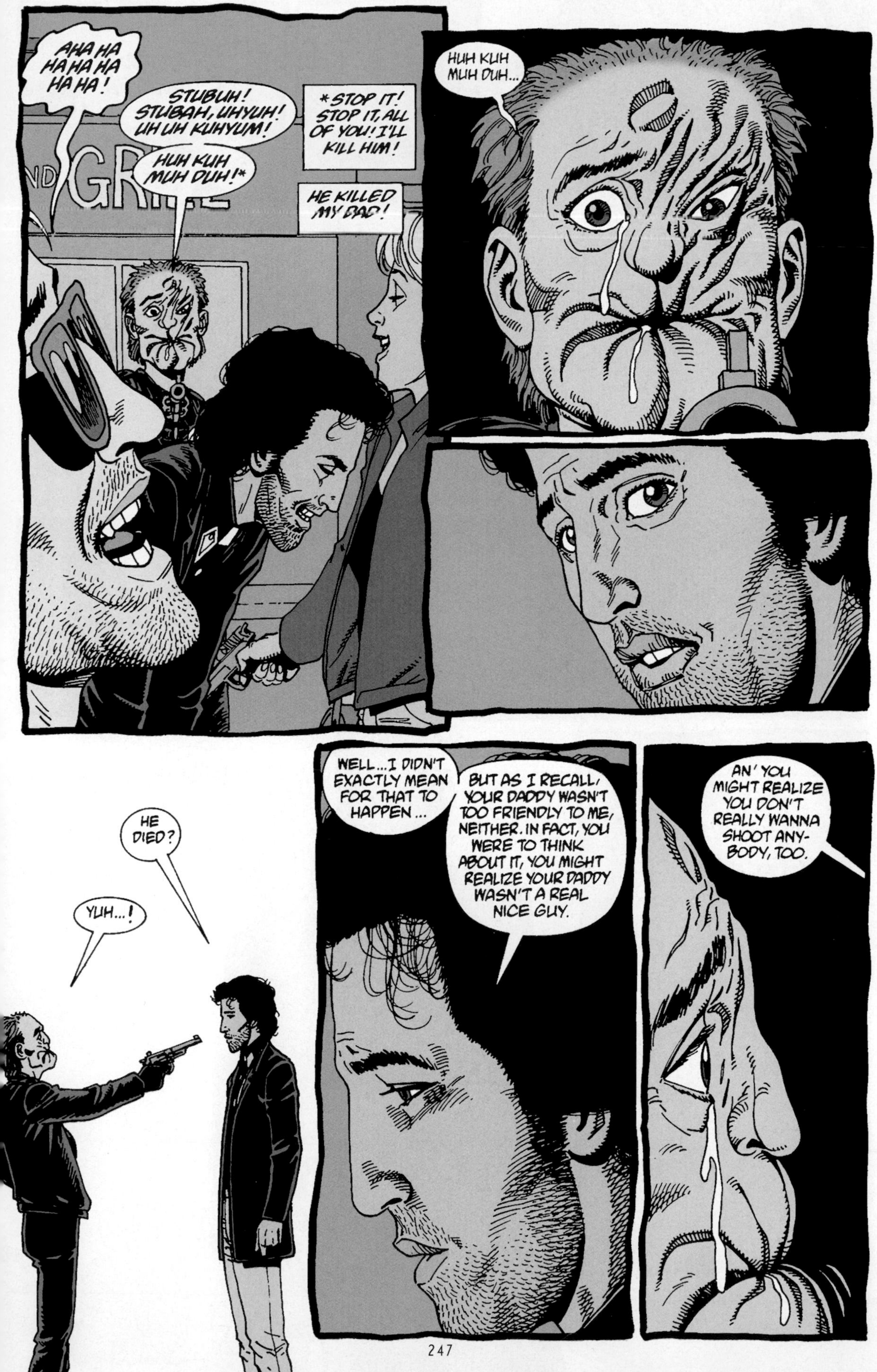

AHA HA HA HA HA HA HA!
STUBUH! STUBAH, UHYUH! UH UH KUHYUM!
HUH KUH MUH DUH!*
*STOP IT! STOP IT, ALL OF YOU! I'LL KILL HIM!
HE KILLED MY DAD!
GRI
HUH KUH MUH DUH...
HE DIED?
YUH...!
WELL...I DIDN'T EXACTLY MEAN FOR THAT TO HAPPEN...
BUT AS I RECALL, YOUR DADDY WASN'T TOO FRIENDLY TO ME, NEITHER. IN FACT, YOU WERE TO THINK ABOUT IT, YOU MIGHT REALIZE YOUR DADDY WASN'T A REAL NICE GUY.
AN' YOU MIGHT REALIZE YOU DON'T REALLY WANNA SHOOT ANY-BODY, TOO.

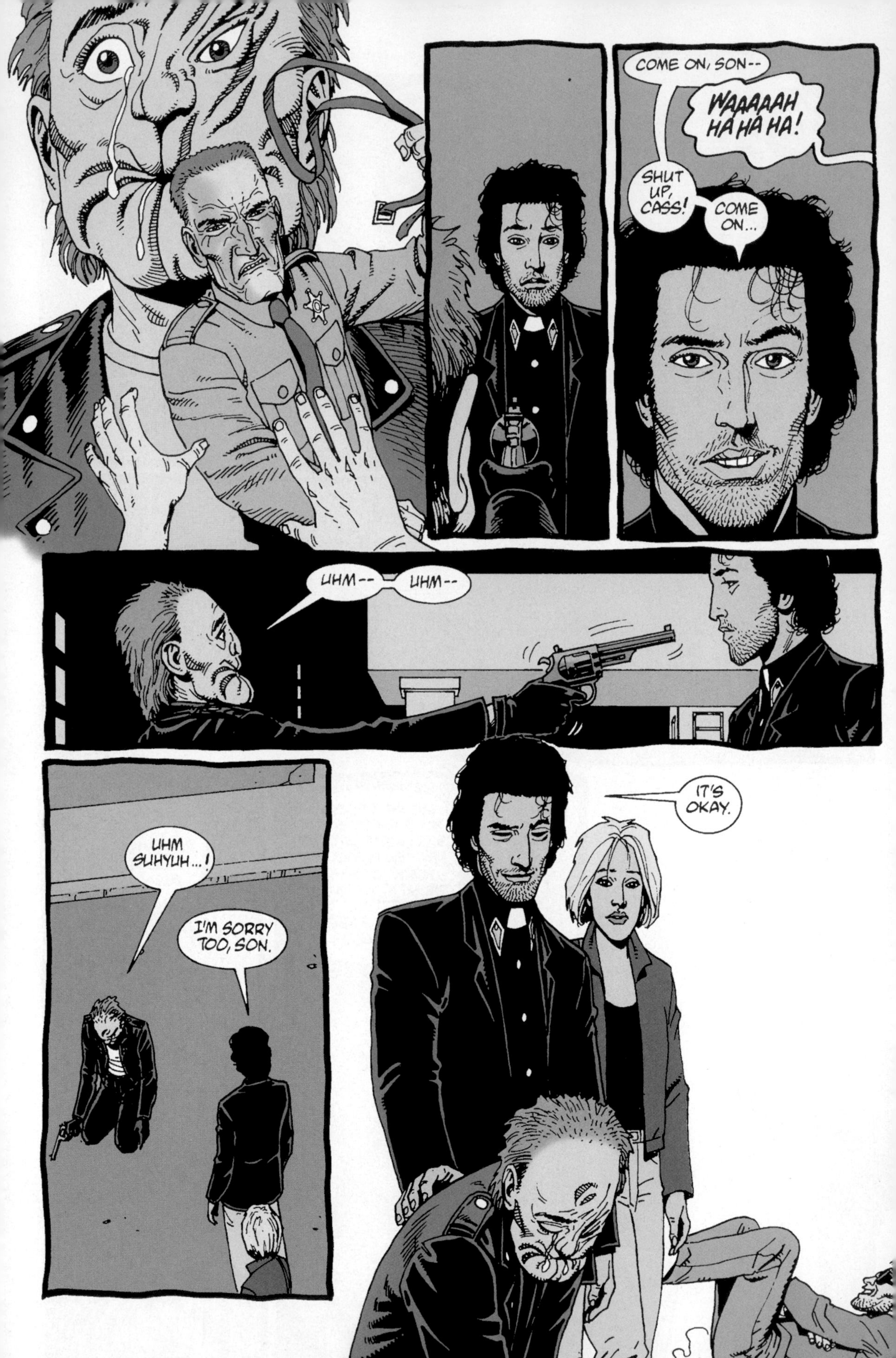
COME ON, SON--
WAAAAAH HA HA HA!
SHUT UP, CASS!
COME ON...
UHM--
UHM--
IT'S OKAY.
UHM SUHYUH...!
I'M SORRY TOO, SON.

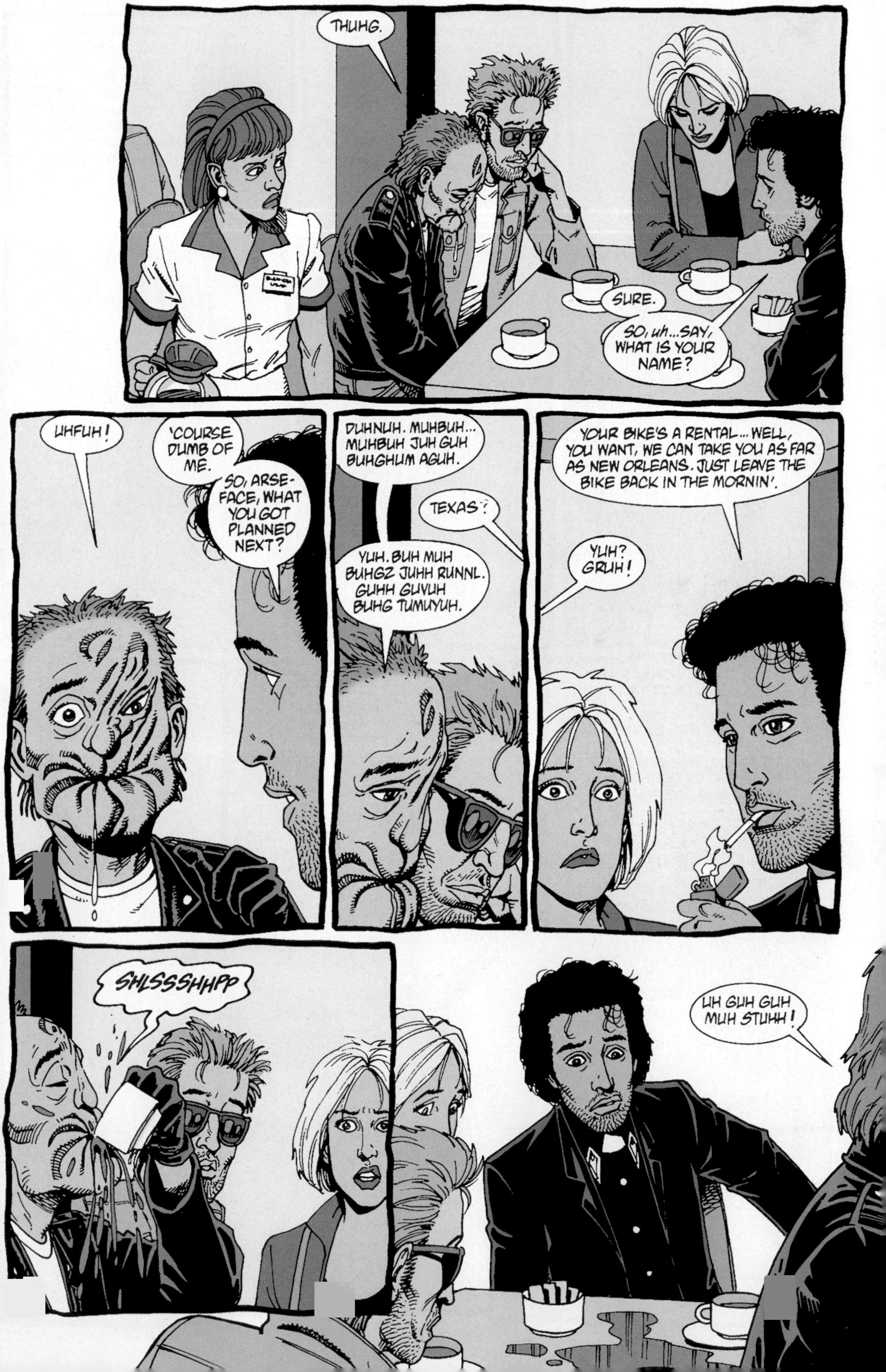
THUHG.
SURE.
SO, uh...SAY, WHAT IS YOUR NAME?
UHFUH!
'COURSE DUMB OF ME.
SO, ARSE-FACE, WHAT YOU GOT PLANNED NEXT?
DUHNUH. MUHBUH... MUHBUH JUH GUH BUHGHUM AGUH.
TEXAS?
YUH. BUH MUH BUHGZ JUHH RUNNL. GUHH GUVUH BUHG TUMUYUH.
YOUR BIKE'S A RENTAL... WELL, YOU WANT, WE CAN TAKE YOU AS FAR AS NEW ORLEANS. JUST LEAVE THE BIKE BACK IN THE MORNIN'.
YUH? GRUH!
SHLSSSHHPP
UH GUH GUH MUH STUHH!

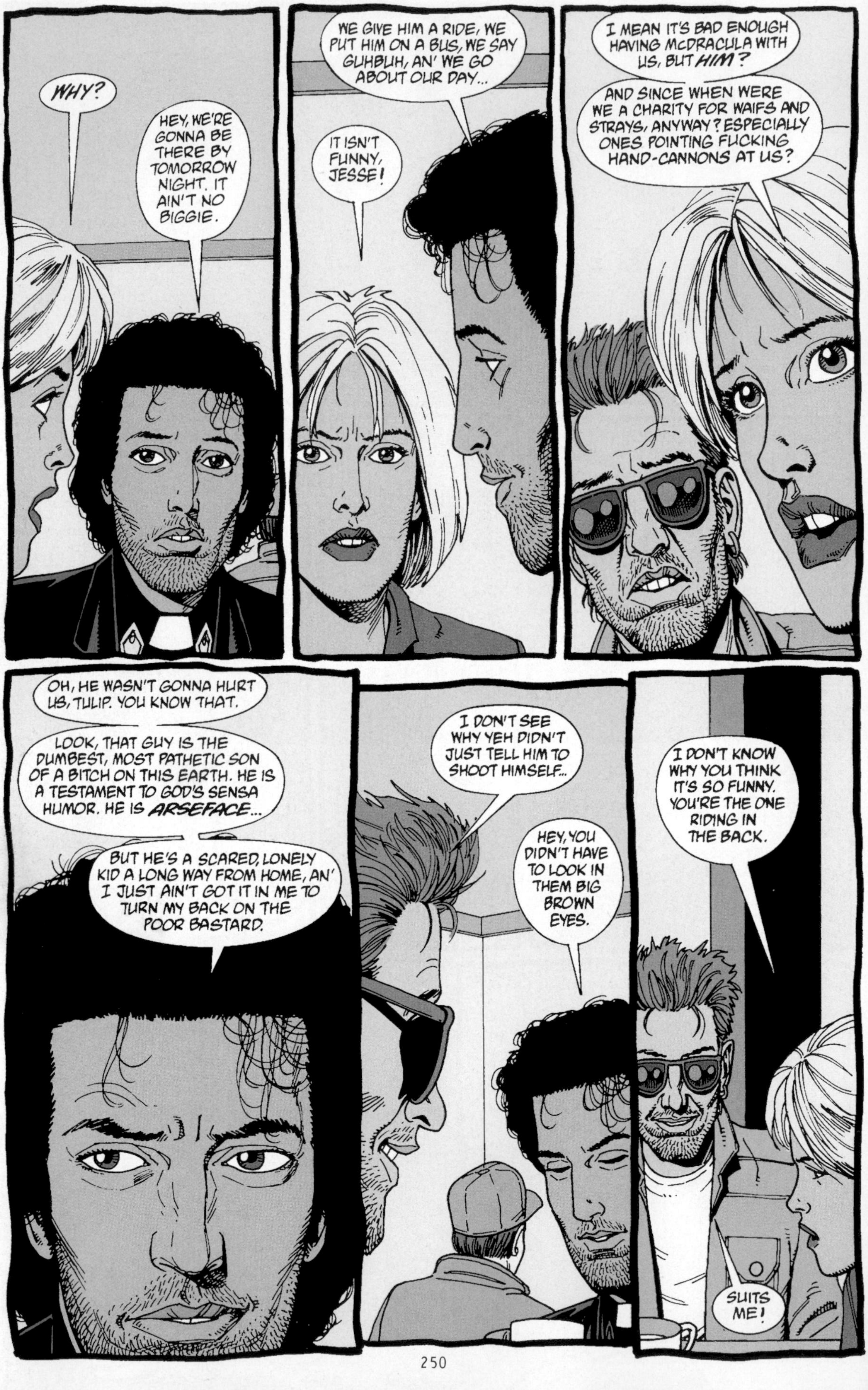
WHY?
HEY, WE'RE GONNA BE THERE BY TOMORROW NIGHT. IT AIN'T NO BIGGIE.
WE GIVE HIM A RIDE, WE PUT HIM ON A BUS, WE SAY GUHBUH, AN' WE GO ABOUT OUR DAY...
IT ISN'T FUNNY, JESSE!
I MEAN IT'S BAD ENOUGH HAVING McDRACULA WITH US, BUT HIM?
AND SINCE WHEN WERE WE A CHARITY FOR WAIFS AND STRAYS, ANYWAY? ESPECIALLY ONES POINTING FUCKING HAND-CANNONS AT US?
OH, HE WASN'T GONNA HURT US, TULIP. YOU KNOW THAT.
LOOK, THAT GUY IS THE DUMBEST, MOST PATHETIC SON OF A BITCH ON THIS EARTH. HE IS A TESTAMENT TO GOD'S SENSA HUMOR. HE IS ARSEFACE...
BUT HE'S A SCARED, LONELY KID A LONG WAY FROM HOME, AN' I JUST AIN'T GOT IT IN ME TO TURN MY BACK ON THE POOR BASTARD.
I DON'T SEE WHY YEH DIDN'T JUST TELL HIM TO SHOOT HIMSELF...
HEY, YOU DIDN'T HAVE TO LOOK IN THEM BIG BROWN EYES.
I DON'T KNOW WHY YOU THINK IT'S SO FUNNY. YOU'RE THE ONE RIDING IN THE BACK.
SUITS ME!

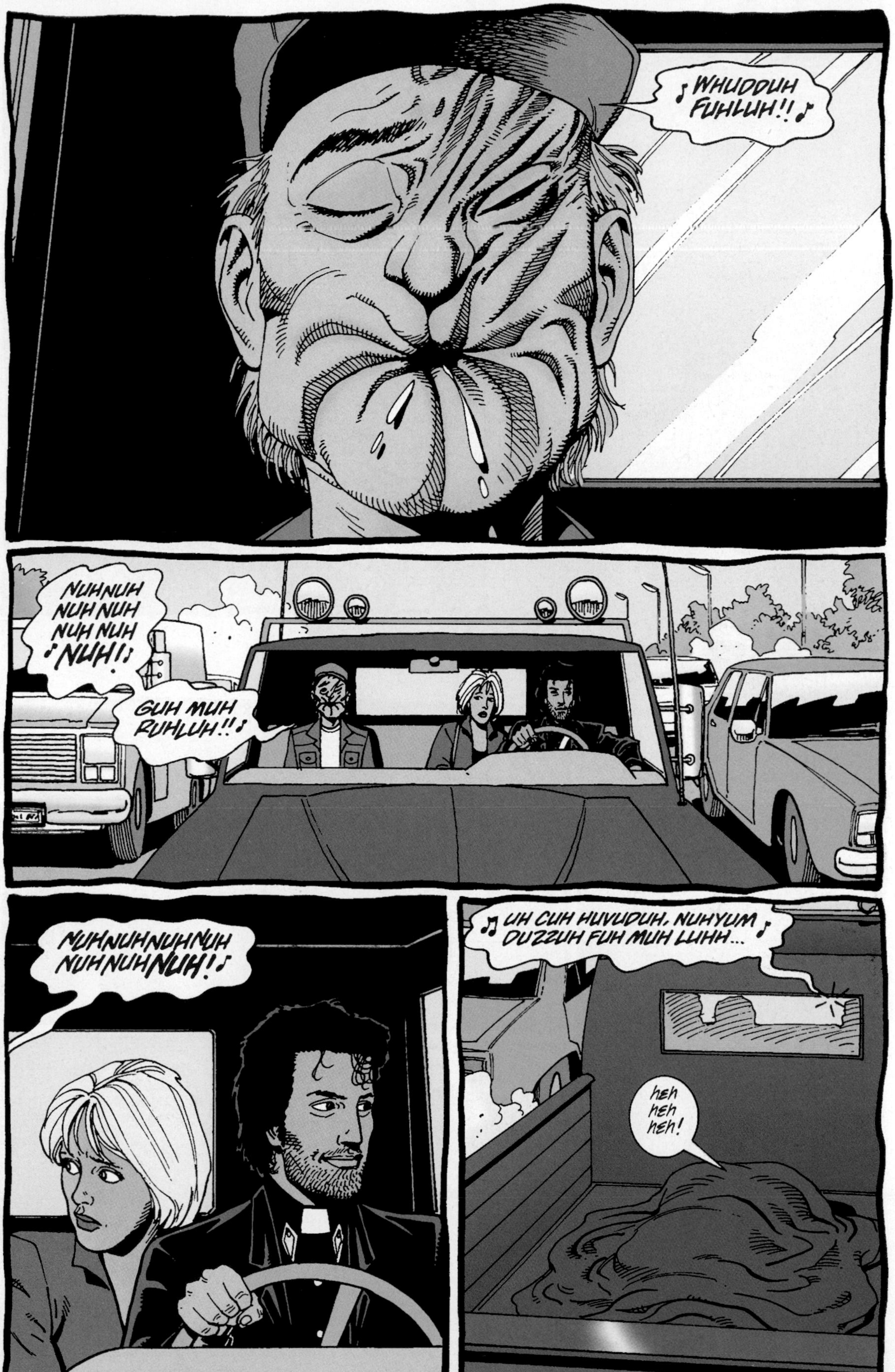
♪ WHUDDUH FUHLUH!! ♪
NUHNUH NUH NUH NUH NUH ♪ NUH! ♪
GUH MUH RUHLUH!! ♪
NUHNUHNUHNUH NUHNUHNUH! ♪
♪ UH CUH HUVUDUH, NUHYUM DUZZUH FUH MUH LUHH... ♪
heh heh heh!

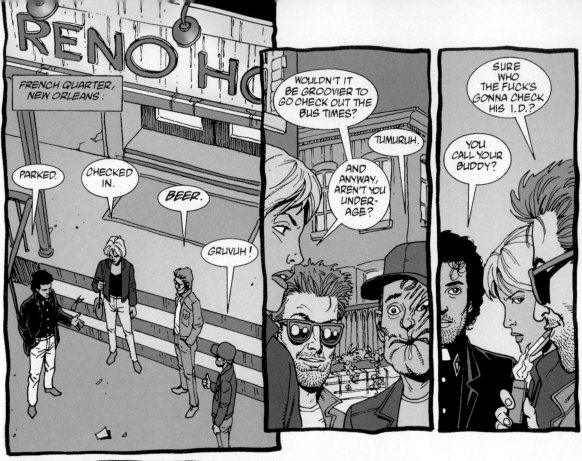

FRENCH QUARTER, NEW ORLEANS:

PARKED.

CHECKED IN.

BEER.

GRUVUH!

WOULDN'T IT BE GROOVIER TO GO CHECK OUT THE BUS TIMES?

TUMURUH.

AND ANYWAY, AREN'T YOU UNDER-AGE?

SURE WHO THE FUCK'S GONNA CHECK HIS I.D.?

YOU CALL YOUR BUDDY?

AYE, HE'S MEETIN' US AT THE PLACE. AN' IS HE IN FOR A SHOCK...

GUESS SO.

NO, I MEANT AT ME KNOCKIN' AROUND WI' THE CLERGY.

THAT THAT THAT THAT'S HIM...

WHERE'S YOUR FUCKING PHONE?!

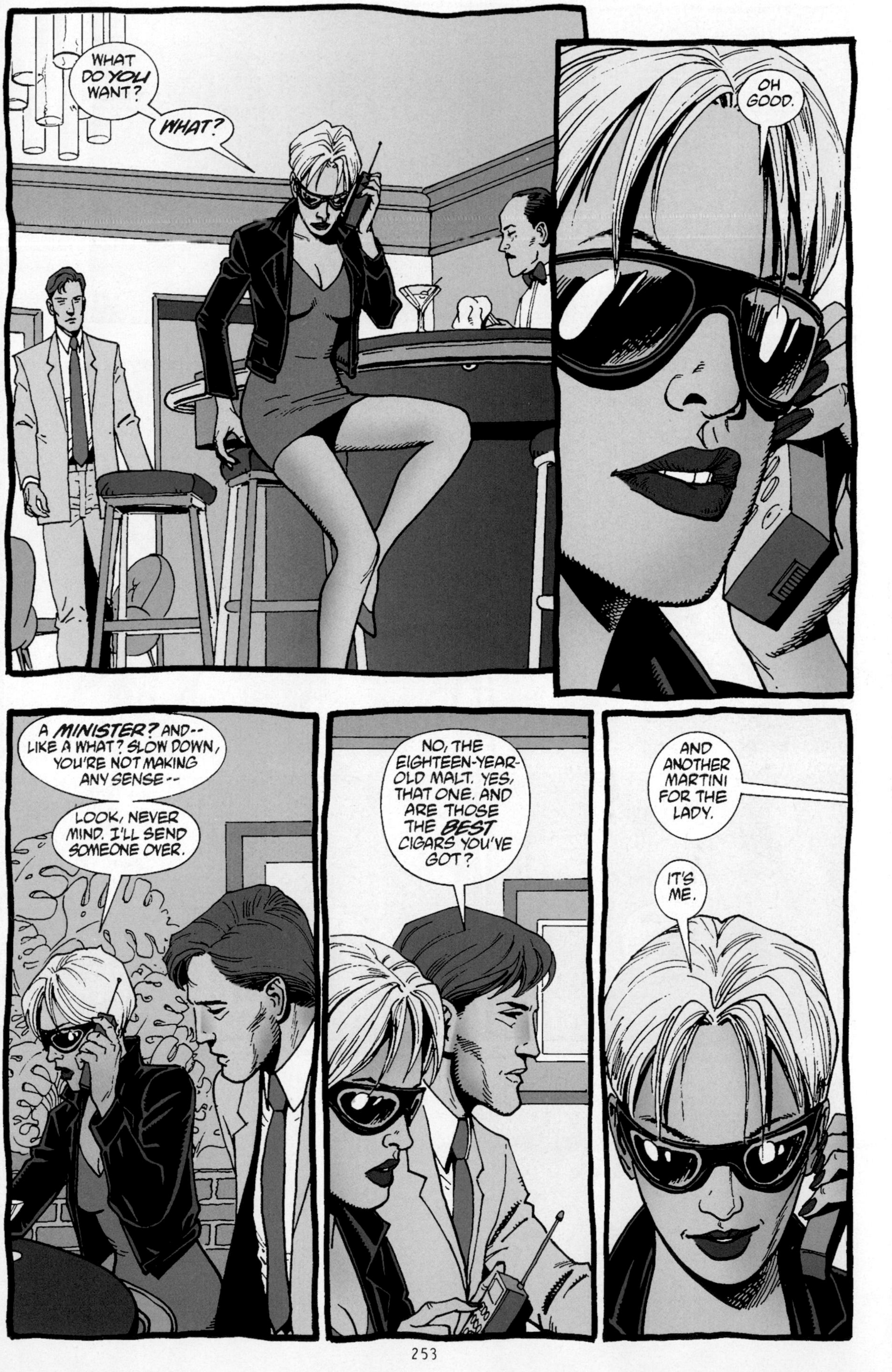
WHAT DO YOU WANT?
WHAT?
OH GOOD.
A MINISTER? AND-- LIKE A WHAT? SLOW DOWN, YOU'RE NOT MAKING ANY SENSE--
LOOK, NEVER MIND. I'LL SEND SOMEONE OVER.
NO, THE EIGHTEEN-YEAR-OLD MALT. YES, THAT ONE. AND ARE THOSE THE BEST CIGARS YOU'VE GOT?
AND ANOTHER MARTINI FOR THE LADY.
IT'S ME.

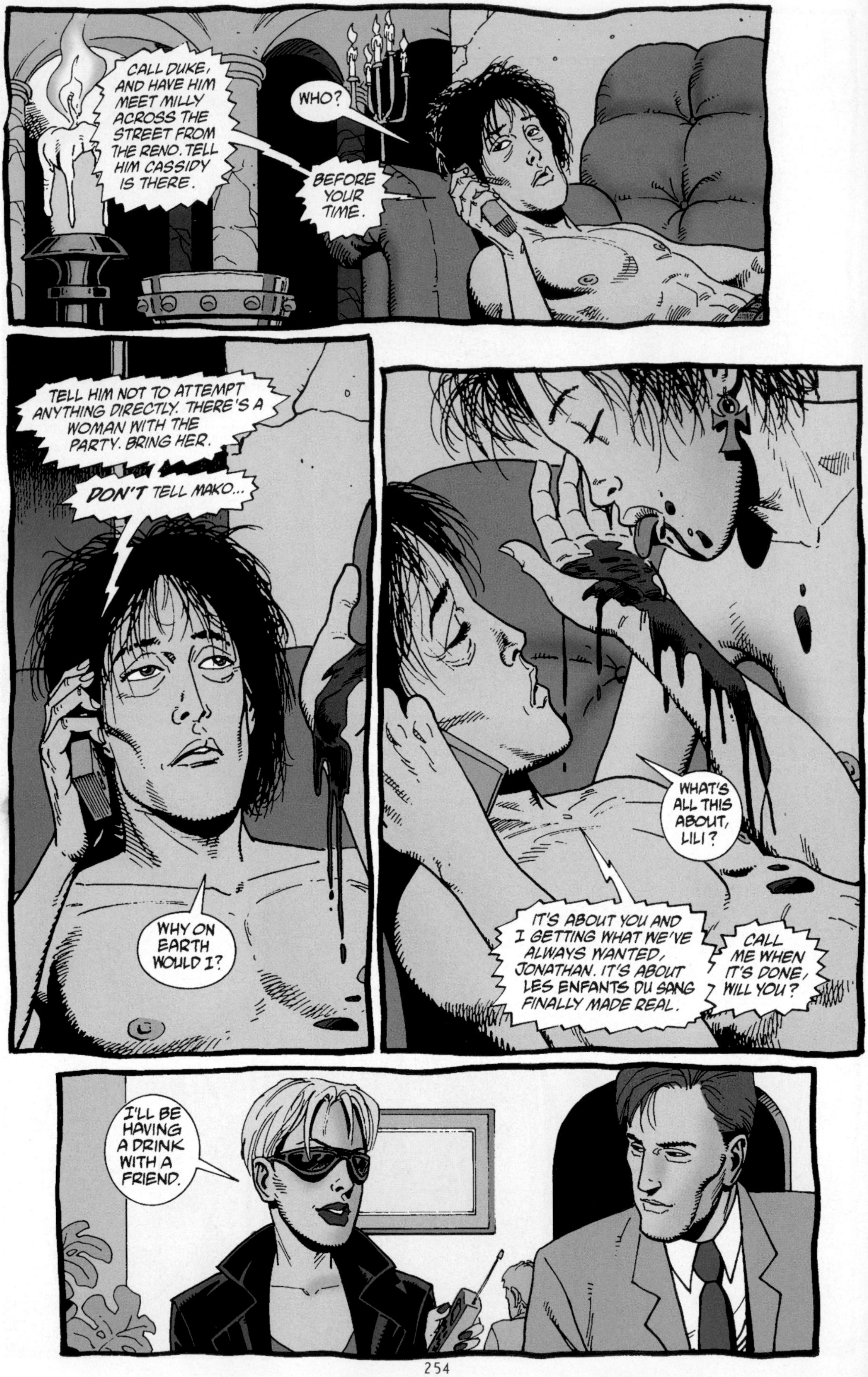
CALL DUKE, AND HAVE HIM MEET MILLY ACROSS THE STREET FROM THE RENO. TELL HIM CASSIDY IS THERE.
WHO?
BEFORE YOUR TIME.
TELL HIM NOT TO ATTEMPT ANYTHING DIRECTLY. THERE'S A WOMAN WITH THE PARTY. BRING HER.
DON'T TELL MAKO...
WHY ON EARTH WOULD I?
WHAT'S ALL THIS ABOUT, LILI?
IT'S ABOUT YOU AND I GETTING WHAT WE'VE ALWAYS WANTED, JONATHAN. IT'S ABOUT LES ENFANTS DU SANG FINALLY MADE REAL.
CALL ME WHEN IT'S DONE, WILL YOU?
I'LL BE HAVING A DRINK WITH A FRIEND.

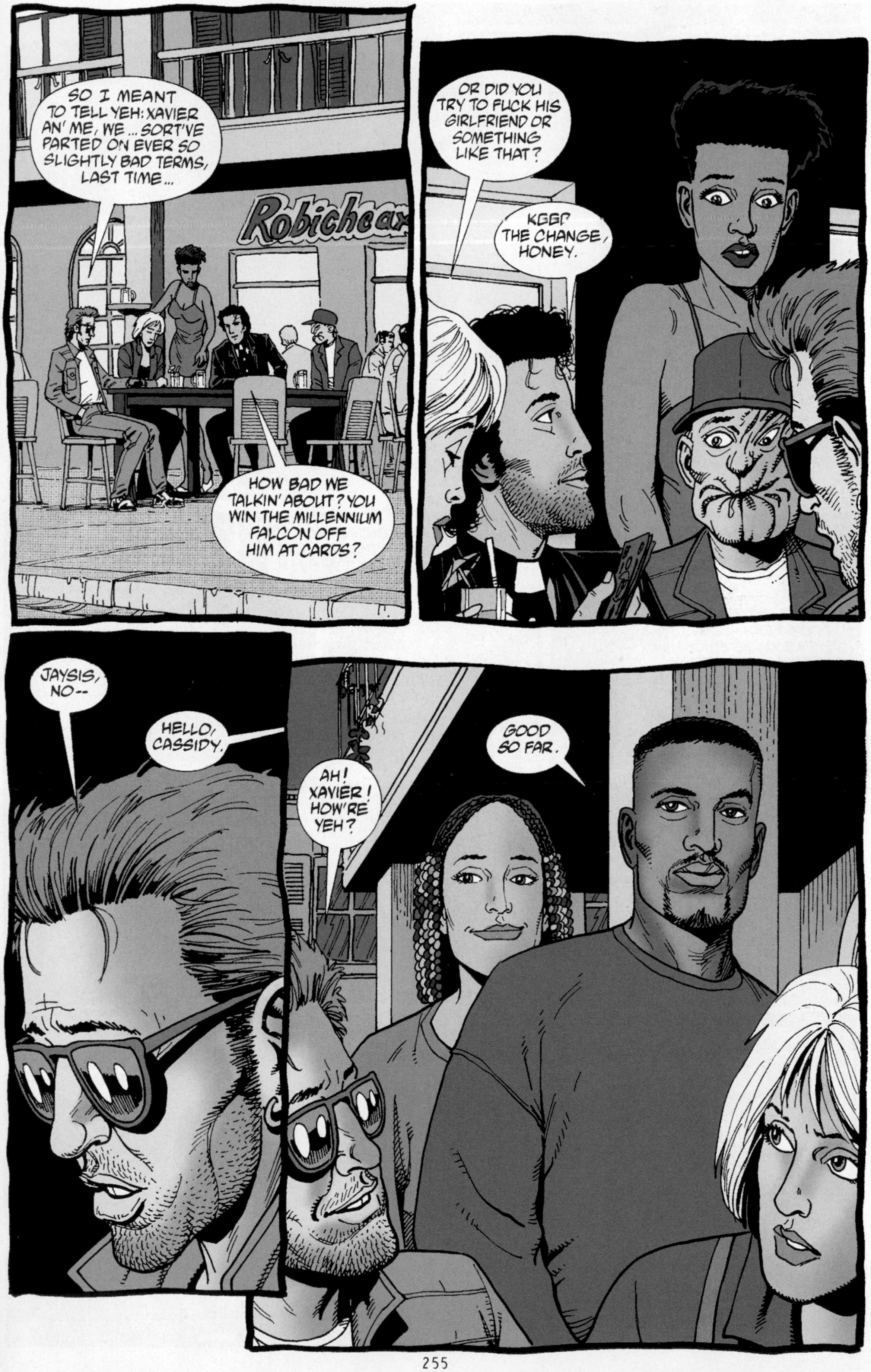
SO I MEANT TO TELL YEH: XAVIER AN' ME, WE ... SORT'VE PARTED ON EVER SO SLIGHTLY BAD TERMS, LAST TIME...
HOW BAD WE TALKIN' ABOUT? YOU WIN THE MILLENNIUM FALCON OFF HIM AT CARDS?
OR DID YOU TRY TO FUCK HIS GIRLFRIEND OR SOMETHING LIKE THAT?
KEEP THE CHANGE, HONEY.
JAYSIS, NO--
HELLO, CASSIDY.
AH! XAVIER! HOW'RE YEH?
GOOD SO FAR.

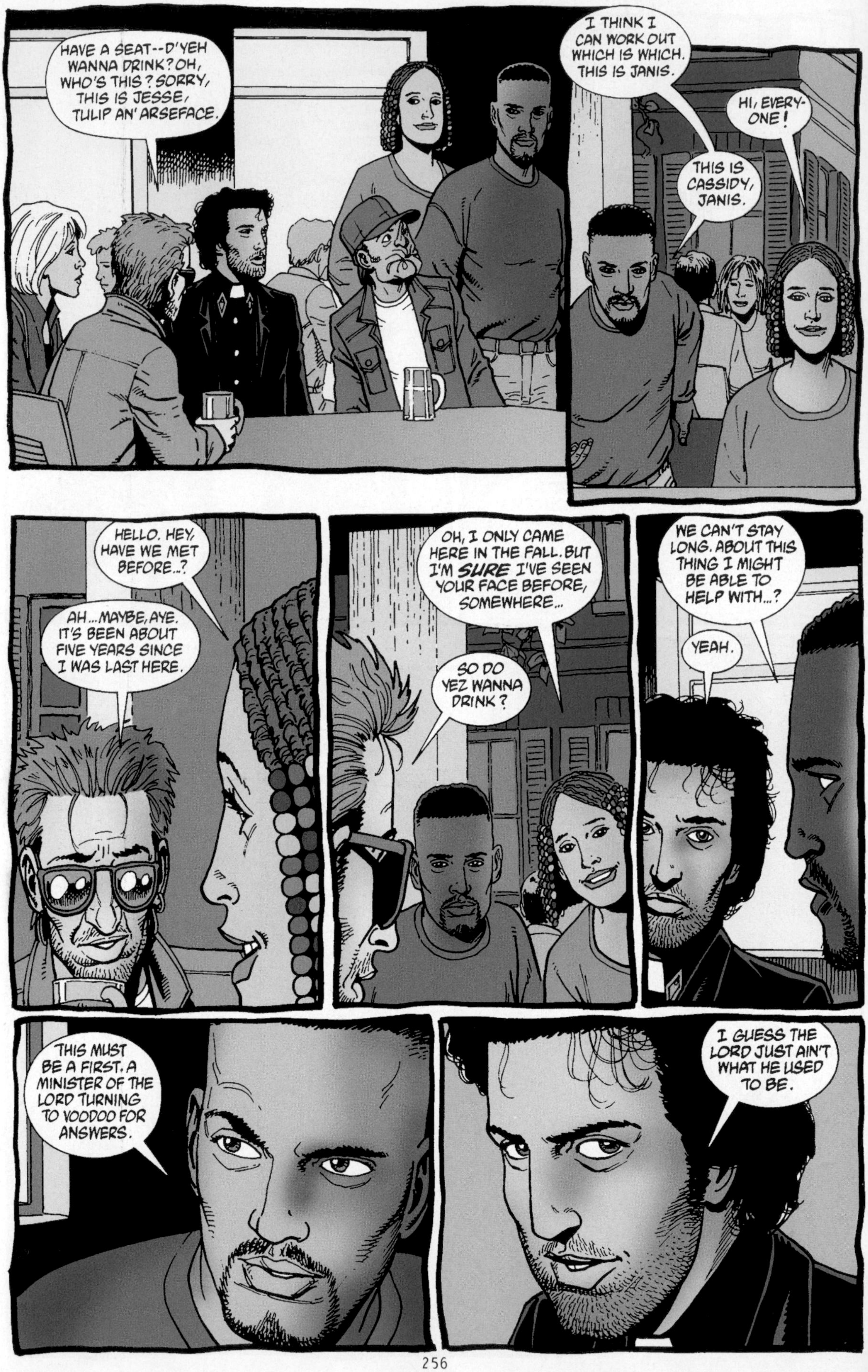
HAVE A SEAT--D'YEH WANNA DRINK? OH, WHO'S THIS? SORRY, THIS IS JESSE, TULIP AN' ARSEFACE.
I THINK I CAN WORK OUT WHICH IS WHICH. THIS IS JANIS.
THIS IS CASSIDY, JANIS.
HI, EVERY-ONE!
HELLO. HEY, HAVE WE MET BEFORE..?
AH...MAYBE, AYE. IT'S BEEN ABOUT FIVE YEARS SINCE I WAS LAST HERE.
OH, I ONLY CAME HERE IN THE FALL. BUT I'M SURE I'VE SEEN YOUR FACE BEFORE, SOMEWHERE...
SO DO YEZ WANNA DRINK?
WE CAN'T STAY LONG. ABOUT THIS THING I MIGHT BE ABLE TO HELP WITH...?
YEAH.
THIS MUST BE A FIRST. A MINISTER OF THE LORD TURNING TO VOODOO FOR ANSWERS.
I GUESS THE LORD JUST AIN'T WHAT HE USED TO BE.

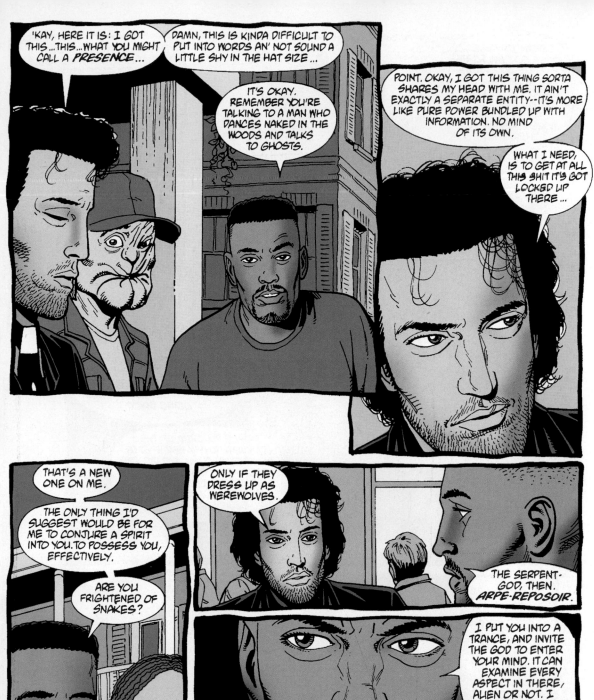

'KAY, HERE IT IS: I GOT THIS...THIS...WHAT YOU MIGHT CALL A *PRESENCE*...

DAMN, THIS IS KINDA DIFFICULT TO PUT INTO WORDS AN' NOT SOUND A LITTLE SHY IN THE HAT SIZE...

IT'S OKAY. REMEMBER YOU'RE TALKING TO A MAN WHO DANCES NAKED IN THE WOODS AND TALKS TO GHOSTS.

POINT. OKAY, I GOT THIS THING SORTA SHARES MY HEAD WITH ME. IT AIN'T EXACTLY A SEPARATE ENTITY--IT'S MORE LIKE PURE POWER BUNDLED UP WITH INFORMATION. NO MIND OF ITS OWN.

WHAT I NEED, IS TO GET AT ALL THIS SHIT IT'S GOT LOCKED UP THERE...

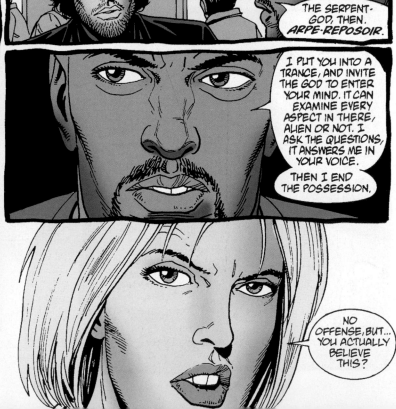

THAT'S A NEW ONE ON ME.

THE ONLY THING I'D SUGGEST WOULD BE FOR ME TO CONJURE A SPIRIT INTO YOU. TO POSSESS YOU, EFFECTIVELY.

ARE YOU FRIGHTENED OF SNAKES?

ONLY IF THEY DRESS UP AS WEREWOLVES.

THE SERPENT-GOD, THEN. *ARPE-REPOSOIR.*

I PUT YOU INTO A TRANCE, AND INVITE THE GOD TO ENTER YOUR MIND. IT CAN EXAMINE EVERY ASPECT IN THERE, ALIEN OR NOT. I ASK THE QUESTIONS, IT ANSWERS ME IN YOUR VOICE.

THEN I END THE POSSESSION.

NO OFFENSE, BUT... YOU ACTUALLY BELIEVE THIS?

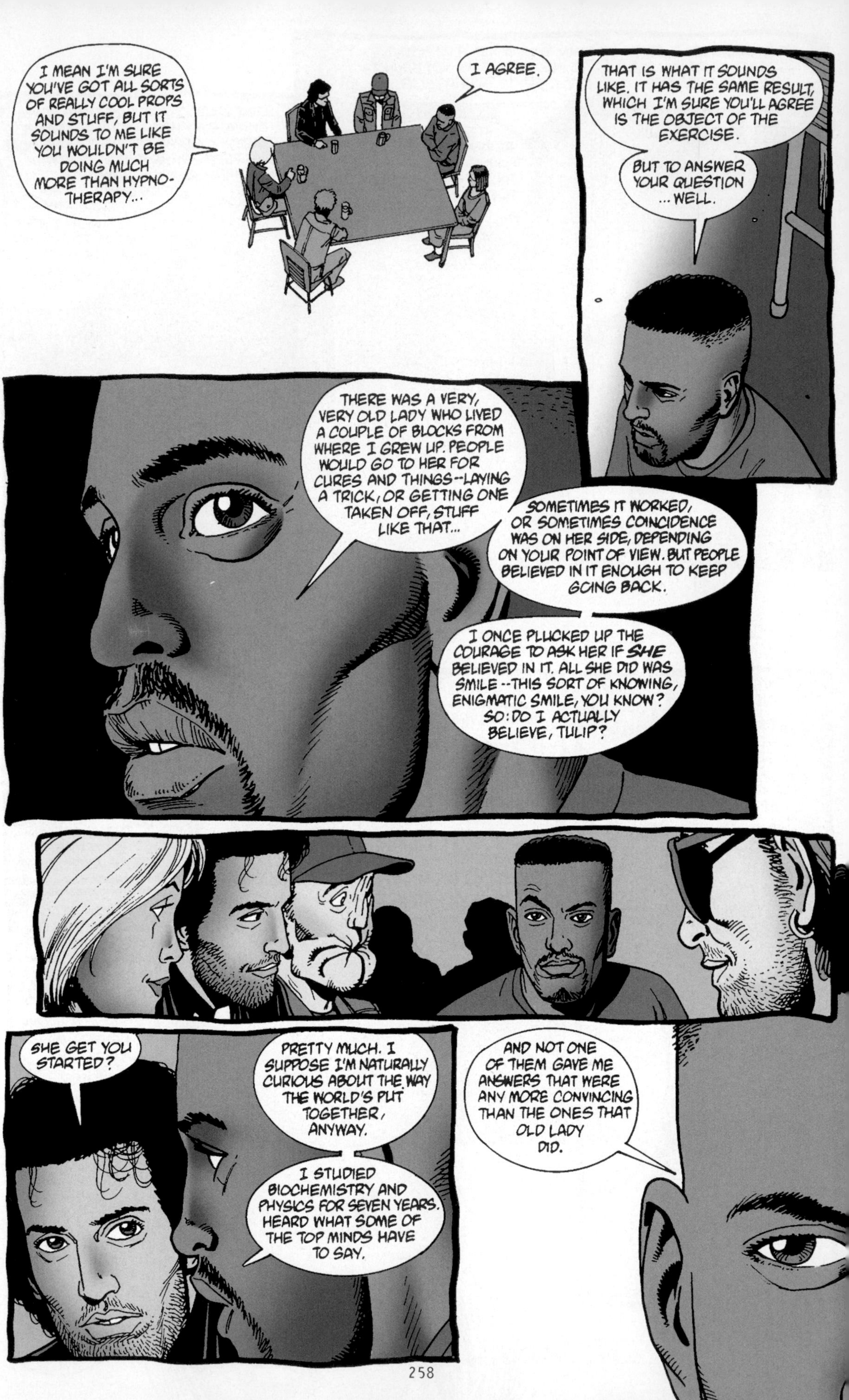
I MEAN I'M SURE YOU'VE GOT ALL SORTS OF REALLY COOL PROPS AND STUFF, BUT IT SOUNDS TO ME LIKE YOU WOULDN'T BE DOING MUCH MORE THAN HYPNO-THERAPY...
I AGREE.
THAT IS WHAT IT SOUNDS LIKE. IT HAS THE SAME RESULT, WHICH I'M SURE YOU'LL AGREE IS THE OBJECT OF THE EXERCISE.
BUT TO ANSWER YOUR QUESTION ...WELL.
THERE WAS A VERY, VERY OLD LADY WHO LIVED A COUPLE OF BLOCKS FROM WHERE I GREW UP. PEOPLE WOULD GO TO HER FOR CURES AND THINGS--LAYING A TRICK, OR GETTING ONE TAKEN OFF, STUFF LIKE THAT...
SOMETIMES IT WORKED, OR SOMETIMES COINCIDENCE WAS ON HER SIDE, DEPENDING ON YOUR POINT OF VIEW. BUT PEOPLE BELIEVED IN IT ENOUGH TO KEEP GOING BACK.
I ONCE PLUCKED UP THE COURAGE TO ASK HER IF *SHE* BELIEVED IN IT. ALL SHE DID WAS SMILE --THIS SORT OF KNOWING, ENIGMATIC SMILE, YOU KNOW? SO: DO I ACTUALLY BELIEVE, TULIP?
SHE GET YOU STARTED?
PRETTY MUCH. I SUPPOSE I'M NATURALLY CURIOUS ABOUT THE WAY THE WORLD'S PUT TOGETHER, ANYWAY.
I STUDIED BIOCHEMISTRY AND PHYSICS FOR SEVEN YEARS. HEARD WHAT SOME OF THE TOP MINDS HAVE TO SAY.
AND NOT ONE OF THEM GAVE ME ANSWERS THAT WERE ANY MORE CONVINCING THAN THE ONES THAT OLD LADY DID.

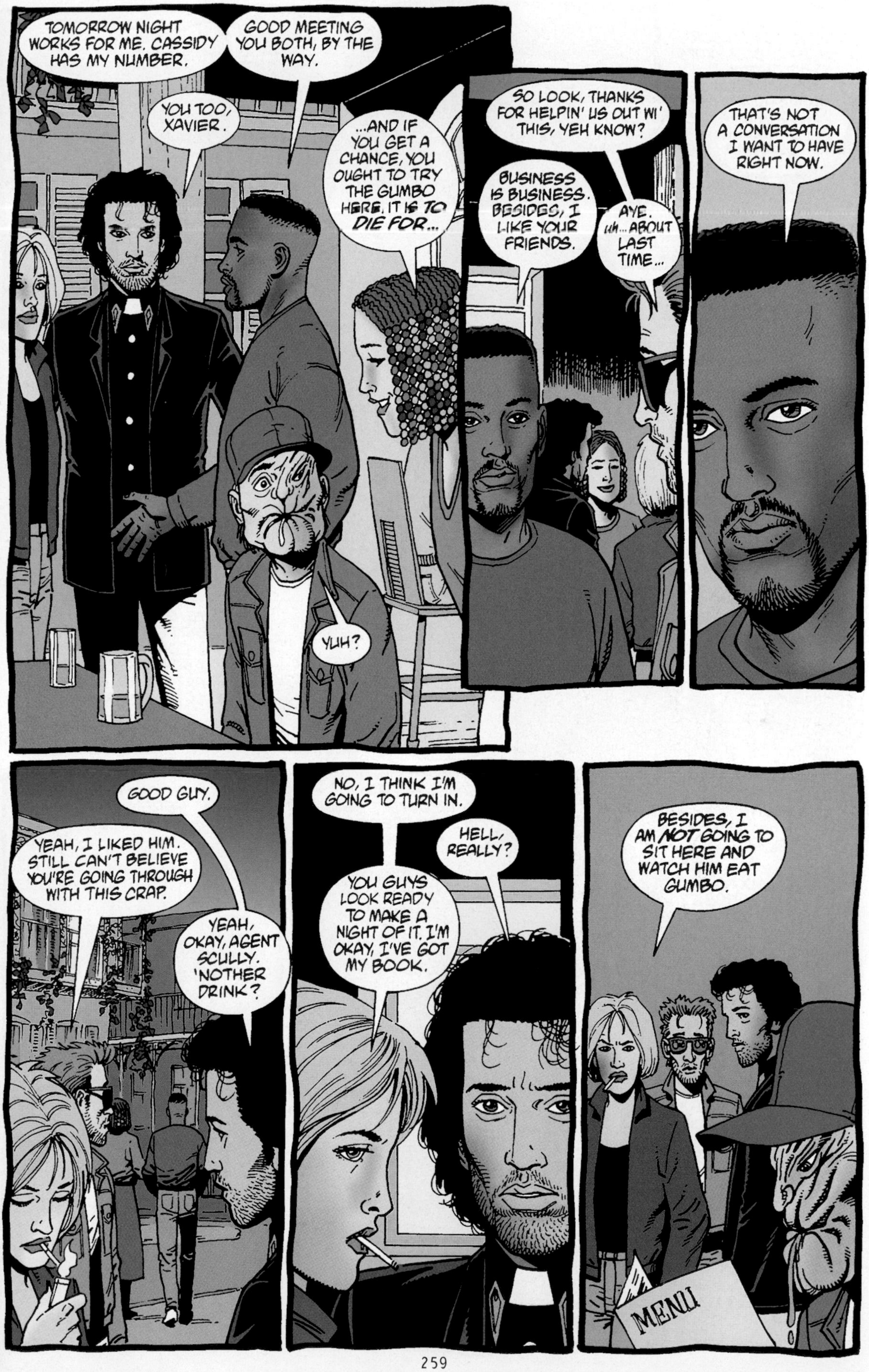
TOMORROW NIGHT WORKS FOR ME. CASSIDY HAS MY NUMBER.
GOOD MEETING YOU BOTH, BY THE WAY.
YOU TOO, XAVIER.
...AND IF YOU GET A CHANCE, YOU OUGHT TO TRY THE GUMBO HERE. IT IS *TO DIE FOR*...
YUH?
SO LOOK, THANKS FOR HELPIN' US OUT WI' THIS, YEH KNOW?
BUSINESS IS BUSINESS. BESIDES, I LIKE YOUR FRIENDS.
AYE. *uh*...ABOUT LAST TIME...
THAT'S NOT A CONVERSATION I WANT TO HAVE RIGHT NOW.
GOOD GUY.
YEAH, I LIKED HIM. STILL CAN'T BELIEVE YOU'RE GOING THROUGH WITH THIS CRAP.
YEAH, OKAY, AGENT SCULLY. 'NOTHER DRINK?
NO, I THINK I'M GOING TO TURN IN.
HELL, REALLY?
YOU GUYS LOOK READY TO MAKE A NIGHT OF IT. I'M OKAY, I'VE GOT MY BOOK.
BESIDES, I AM *NOT* GOING TO SIT HERE AND WATCH HIM EAT GUMBO.
MENU

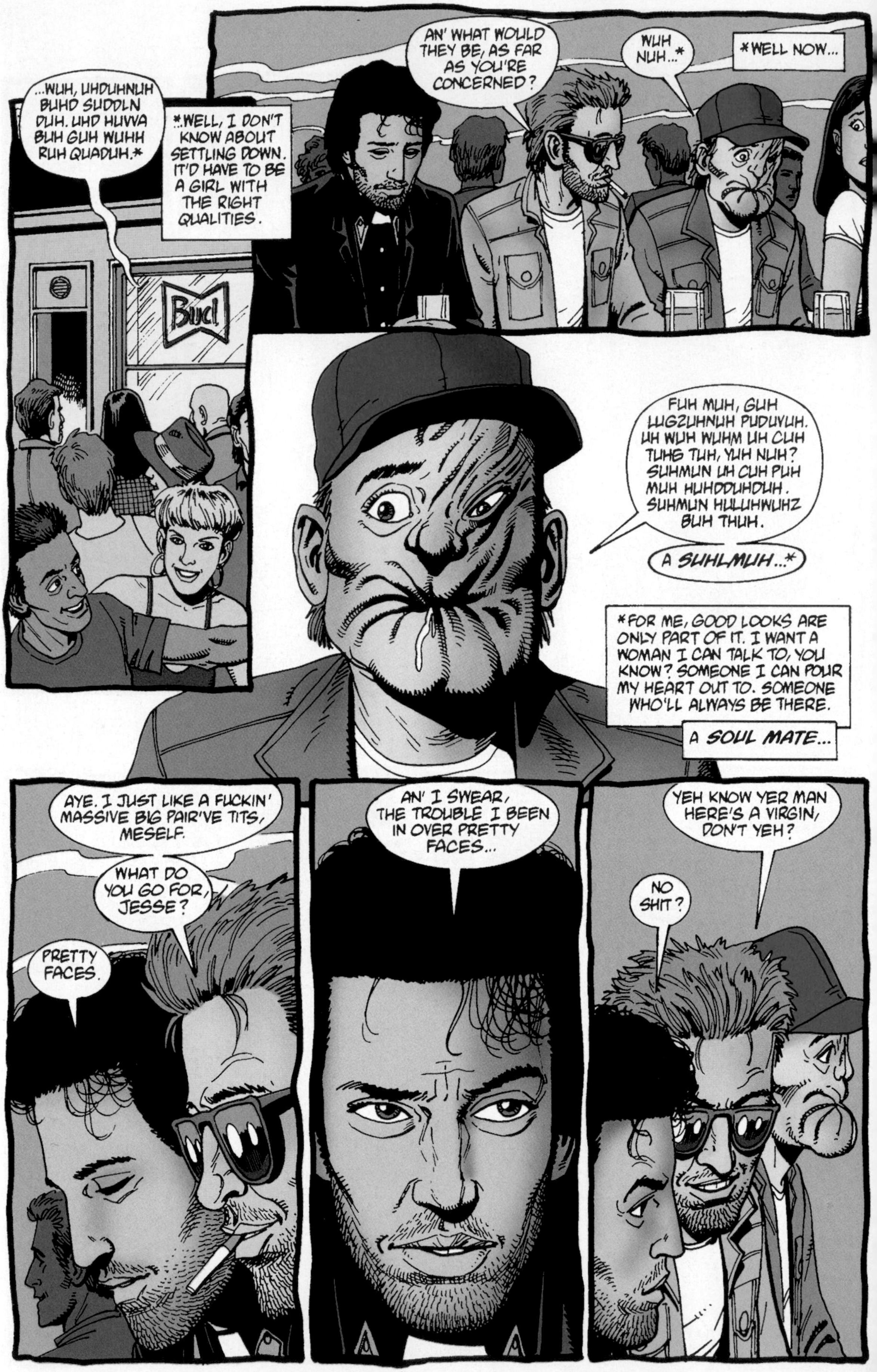
...WUH, UHDUHNUH BUHD SUDDLN DUH. UHD HUVVA BUH GUH WUHH RUH QUADUH.*
*WELL, I DON'T KNOW ABOUT SETTLING DOWN. IT'D HAVE TO BE A GIRL WITH THE RIGHT QUALITIES.
AN' WHAT WOULD THEY BE, AS FAR AS YOU'RE CONCERNED?
WUH NUH...*
*WELL NOW...
BUD
FUH MUH, GUH LUGZUHNUH PUDUVUH. UH WUH WUHM UH CUH TUHG TUH, YUH NUH? SUHMUN UH CUH PUH MUH HUHDDUHDUH. SUHMUN HULUHWUHZ BUH THUH.
A SUHLMUH...*
*FOR ME, GOOD LOOKS ARE ONLY PART OF IT. I WANT A WOMAN I CAN TALK TO, YOU KNOW? SOMEONE I CAN POUR MY HEART OUT TO. SOMEONE WHO'LL ALWAYS BE THERE.
A SOUL MATE...
AYE. I JUST LIKE A FUCKIN' MASSIVE BIG PAIR'VE TITS, MESELF.
WHAT DO YOU GO FOR, JESSE?
PRETTY FACES.
AN' I SWEAR, THE TROUBLE I BEEN IN OVER PRETTY FACES...
YEH KNOW YER MAN HERE'S A VIRGIN, DON'T YEH?
NO SHIT?

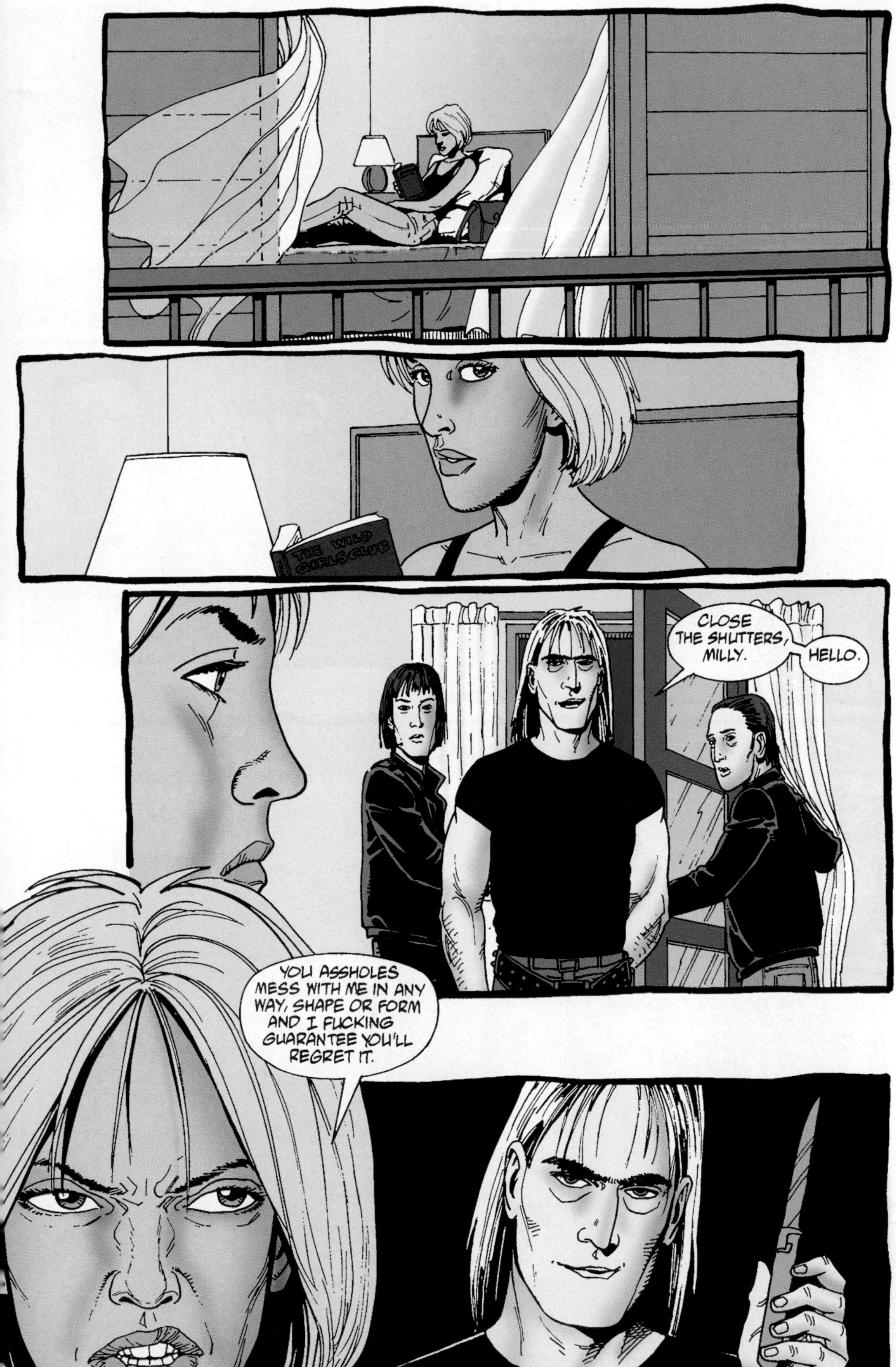
THE WILD GIRLS CLUB
CLOSE THE SHUTTERS, MILLY.
HELLO.
YOU ASSHOLES MESS WITH ME IN ANY WAY, SHAPE OR FORM AND I FUCKING GUARANTEE YOU'LL REGRET IT.

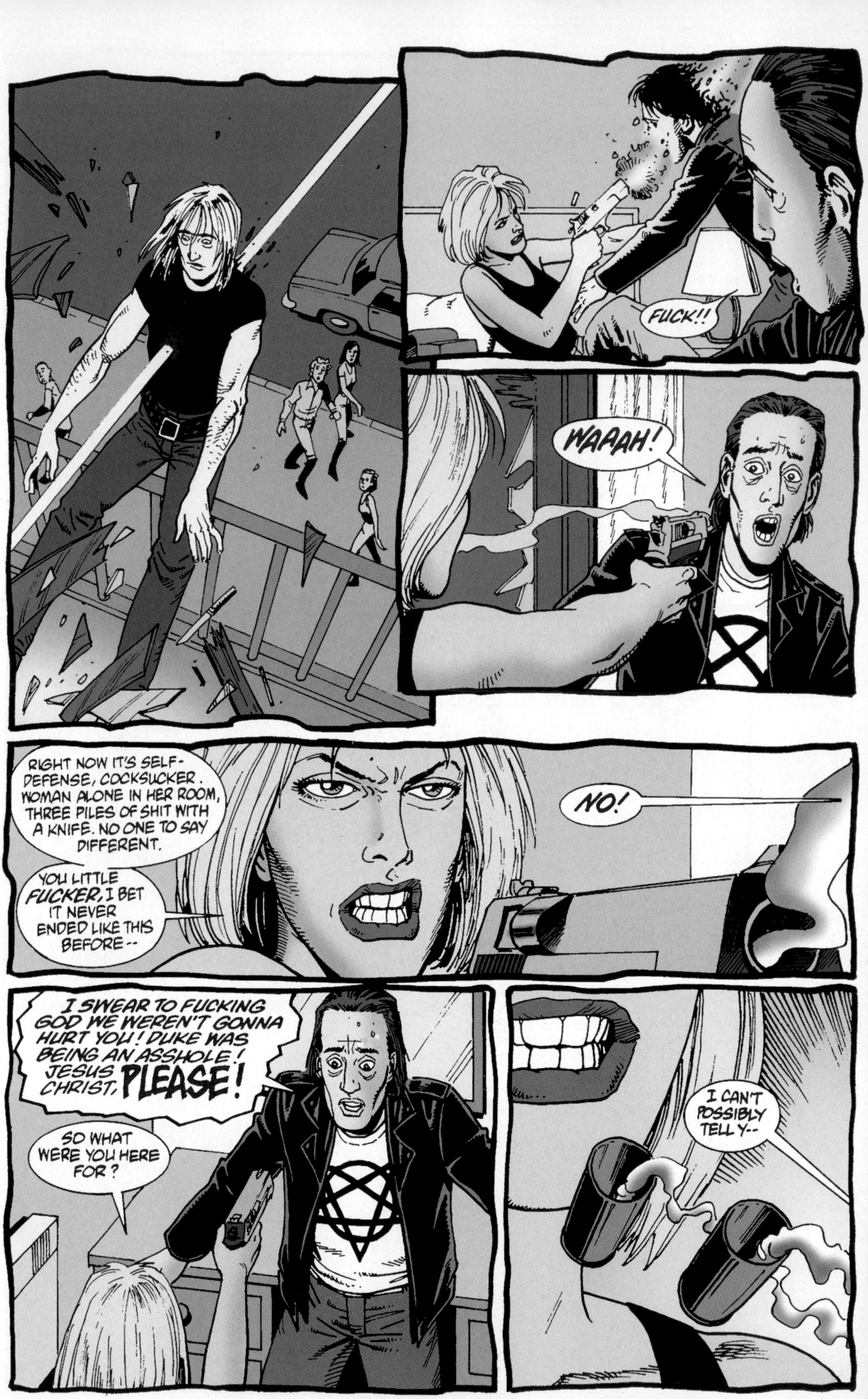
FUCK!!
WAAAH!
RIGHT NOW IT'S SELF-DEFENSE, COCKSUCKER. WOMAN ALONE IN HER ROOM, THREE PILES OF SHIT WITH A KNIFE. NO ONE TO SAY DIFFERENT.
YOU LITTLE FUCKER, I BET IT NEVER ENDED LIKE THIS BEFORE--
NO!
I SWEAR TO FUCKING GOD WE WEREN'T GONNA HURT YOU! DUKE WAS BEING AN ASSHOLE! JESUS CHRIST, PLEASE!
SO WHAT WERE YOU HERE FOR?
I CAN'T POSSIBLY TELL Y--

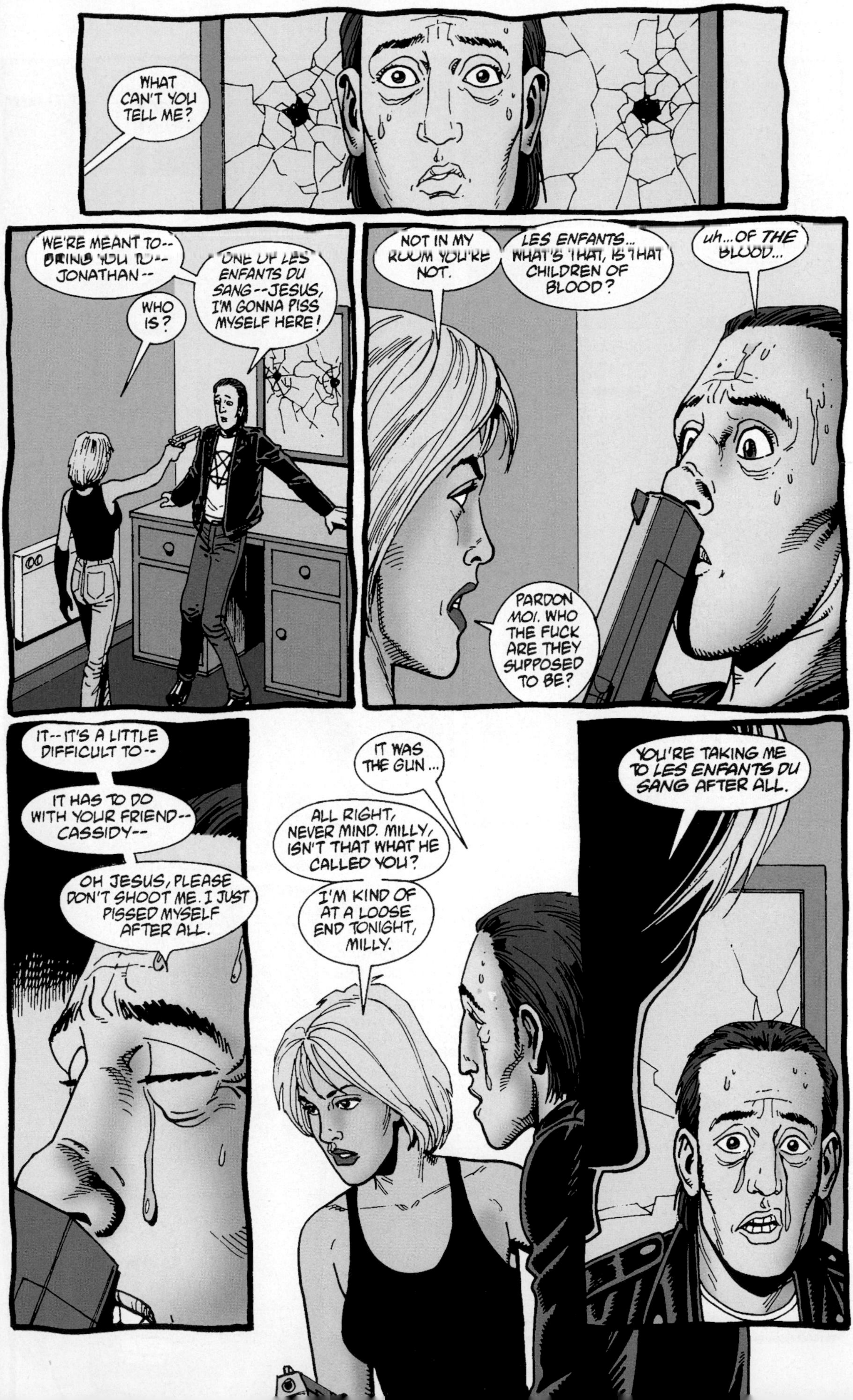
WHAT CAN'T YOU TELL ME?
WE'RE MEANT TO-- BRING YOU TO-- JONATHAN--
WHO IS?
ONE OF LES ENFANTS DU SANG--JESUS, I'M GONNA PISS MYSELF HERE!
NOT IN MY ROOM YOU'RE NOT.
LES ENFANTS... WHAT'S THAT, IS THAT CHILDREN OF BLOOD?
uh...OF THE BLOOD...
PARDON MOI. WHO THE FUCK ARE THEY SUPPOSED TO BE?
IT--IT'S A LITTLE DIFFICULT TO--
IT HAS TO DO WITH YOUR FRIEND-- CASSIDY--
OH JESUS, PLEASE DON'T SHOOT ME. I JUST PISSED MYSELF AFTER ALL.
IT WAS THE GUN...
ALL RIGHT, NEVER MIND. MILLY, ISN'T THAT WHAT HE CALLED YOU?
I'M KIND OF AT A LOOSE END TONIGHT, MILLY.
YOU'RE TAKING ME TO LES ENFANTS DU SANG AFTER ALL.

I HEARD SHOOTING--

THEY'RE BACK THERE! TWO MEN! SOMEBODY KILLED THEM! *OH GOD IT'S HORRIBLE, CALL THE POLICE!*

ROOM Nºs
31—35

OH JESUS, I CAN'T STAND BLOOD!

GUTS! BRAINS! IT'S HORRIBLE, I'VE GOT TO GET OUT!

..."I CAN'T STAND BLOOD." WHAT A *DICK.*

JESUS FUCKING CHRIST, LADY, WHAT IS IT WITH YOU?

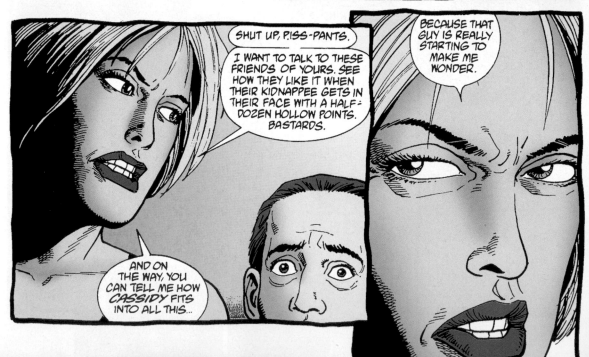

SHUT UP, P.ISS-PANTS.

I WANT TO TALK TO THESE FRIENDS OF YOURS. SEE HOW THEY LIKE IT WHEN THEIR KIDNAPPEE GETS IN THEIR FACE WITH A HALF-DOZEN HOLLOW POINTS. BASTARDS.

BECAUSE THAT GUY IS REALLY STARTING TO MAKE ME WONDER.

AND ON THE WAY, YOU CAN TELL ME HOW *CASSIDY* FITS INTO ALL THIS...

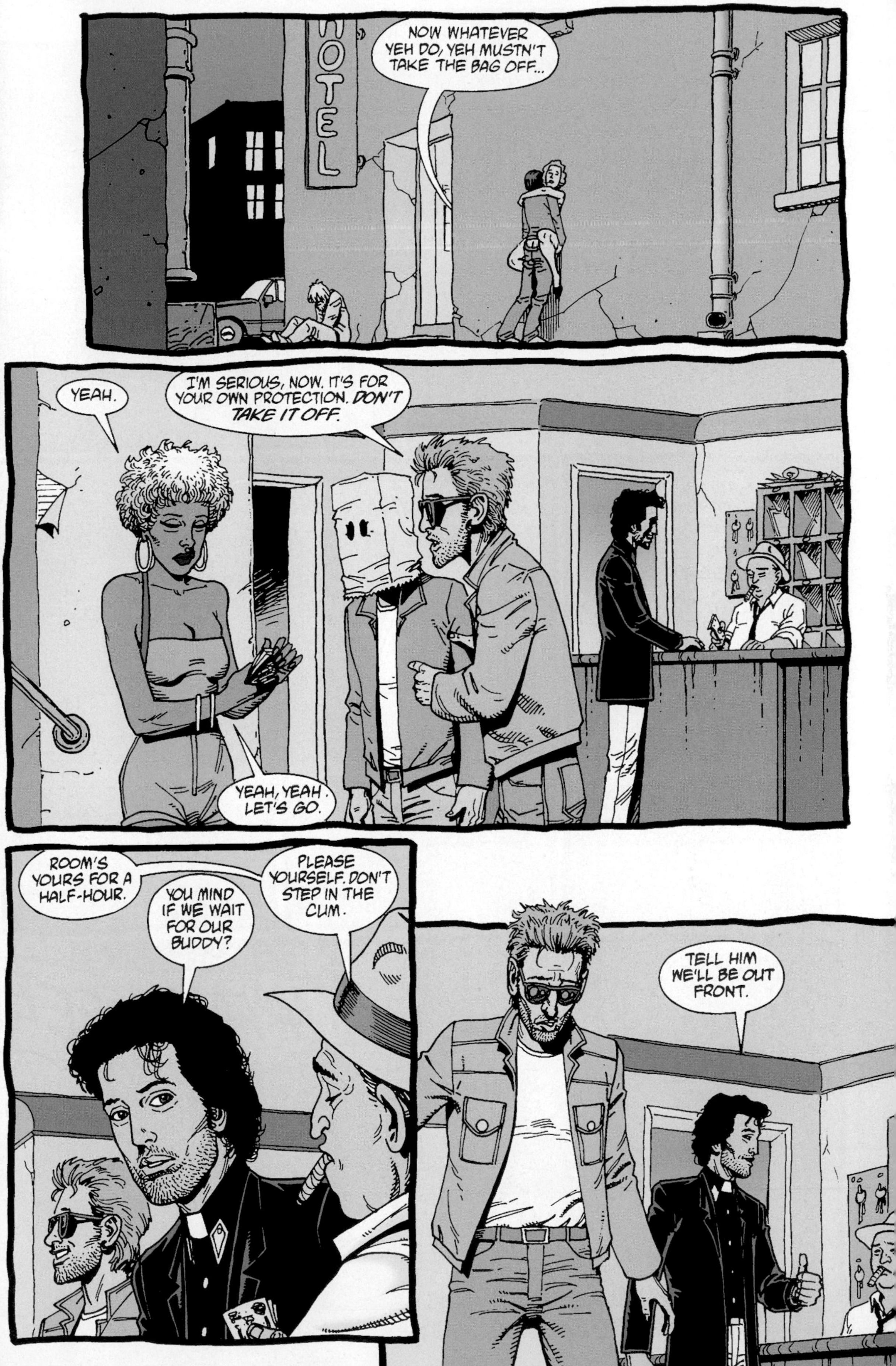

HOTEL
NOW WHATEVER YEH DO, YEH MUSTN'T TAKE THE BAG OFF...
YEAH.
I'M SERIOUS, NOW. IT'S FOR YOUR OWN PROTECTION. *DON'T TAKE IT OFF.*
YEAH, YEAH. LET'S GO.
ROOM'S YOURS FOR A HALF-HOUR.
YOU MIND IF WE WAIT FOR OUR BUDDY?
PLEASE YOURSELF. DON'T STEP IN THE CUM.
TELL HIM WE'LL BE OUT FRONT.

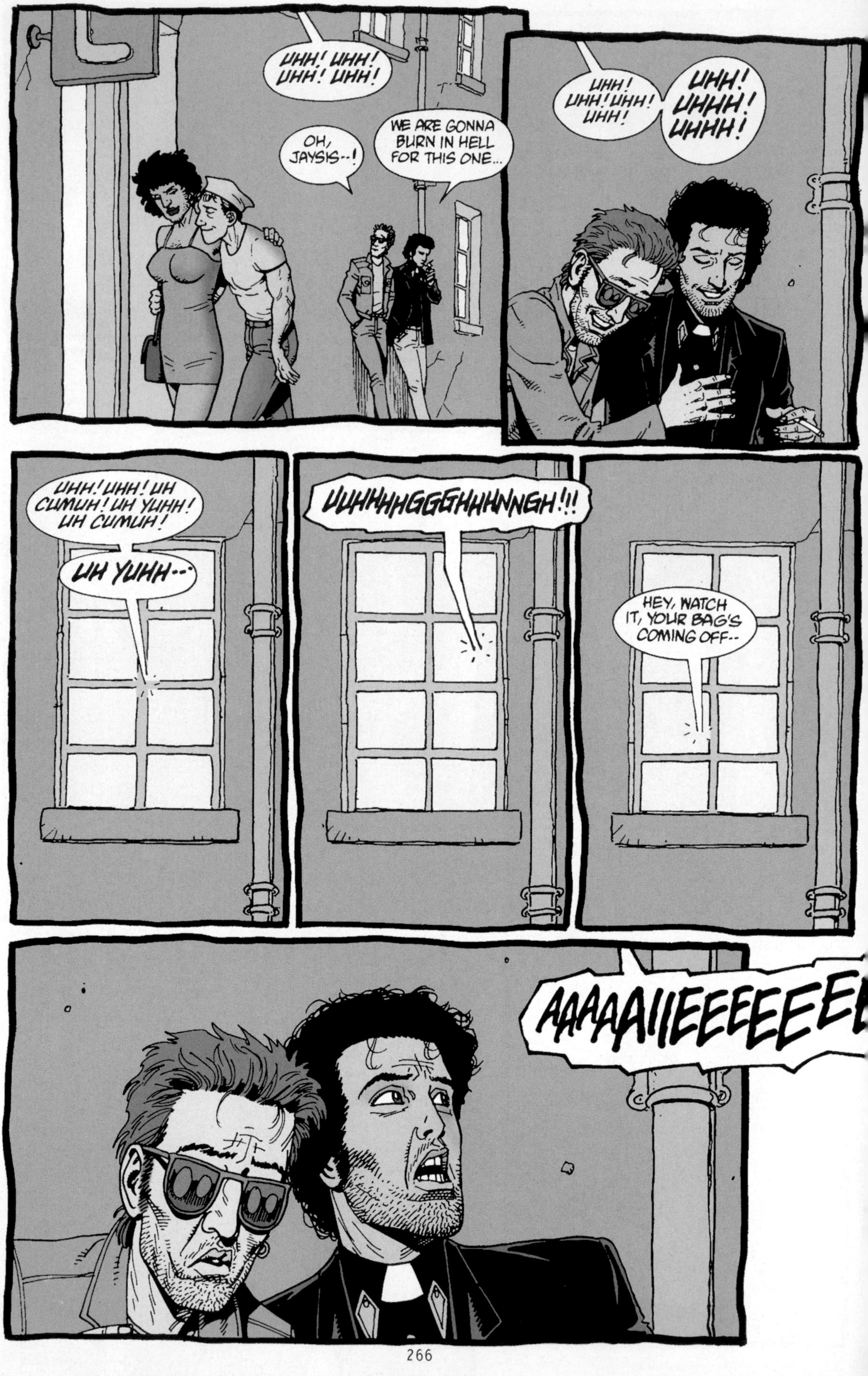
UHH! UHH! UHH! UHH!
OH, JAYSIS--!
WE ARE GONNA BURN IN HELL FOR THIS ONE...
UHH! UHH! UHH! UHH!
UHH! UHHH! UHHH!
UHH! UHH! UH CUMUH! UH YUHH! UH CUMUH!
UH YUHH--
UUHHHHGGGHHHNNGH!!!
HEY, WATCH IT, YOUR BAG'S COMING OFF--
AAAAAIIIEEEEEEE

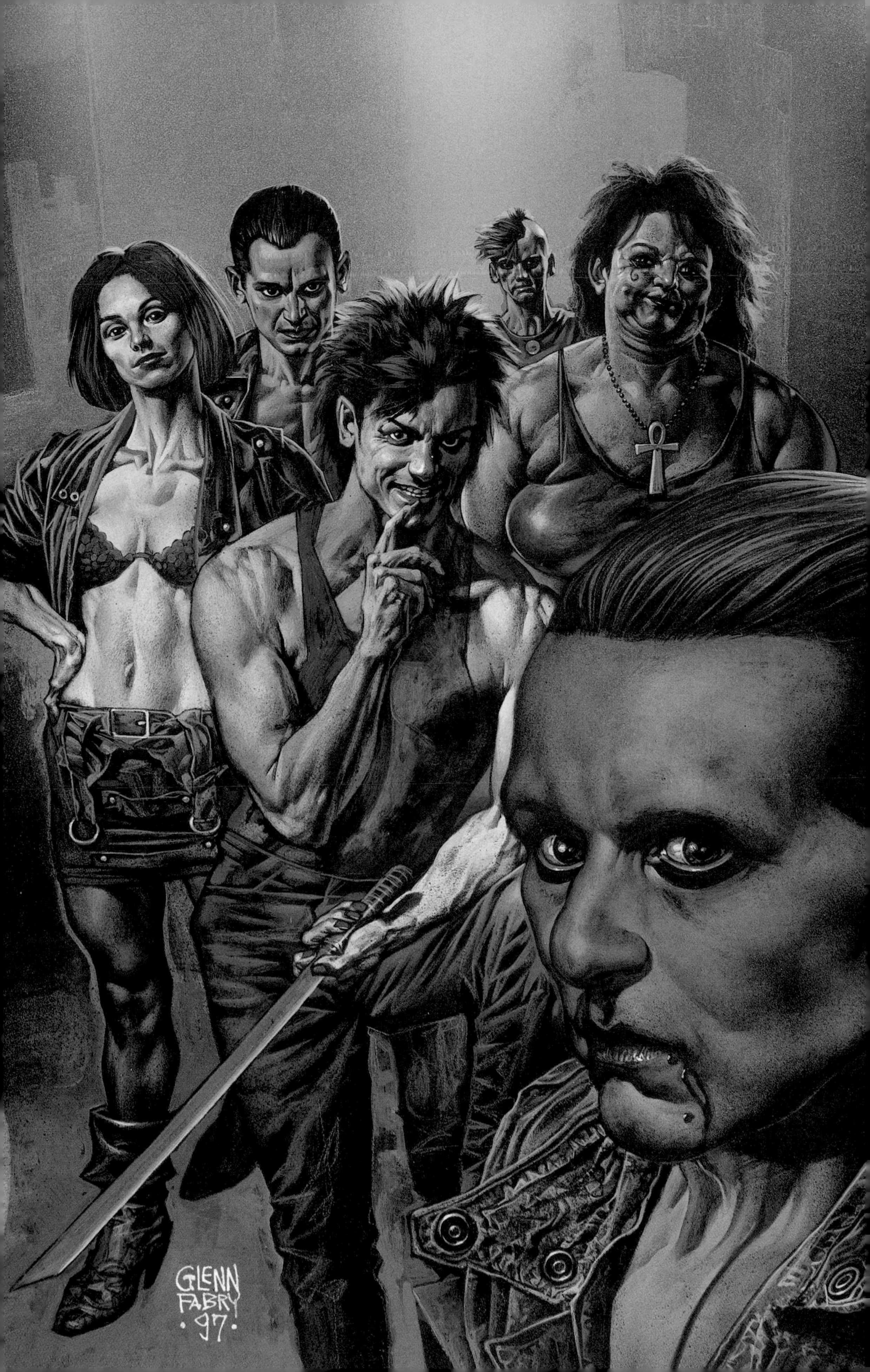
GLENN
FABRY
·97·

"Absolutely nobody fucks with me, dogshit.
That's the golden rule."

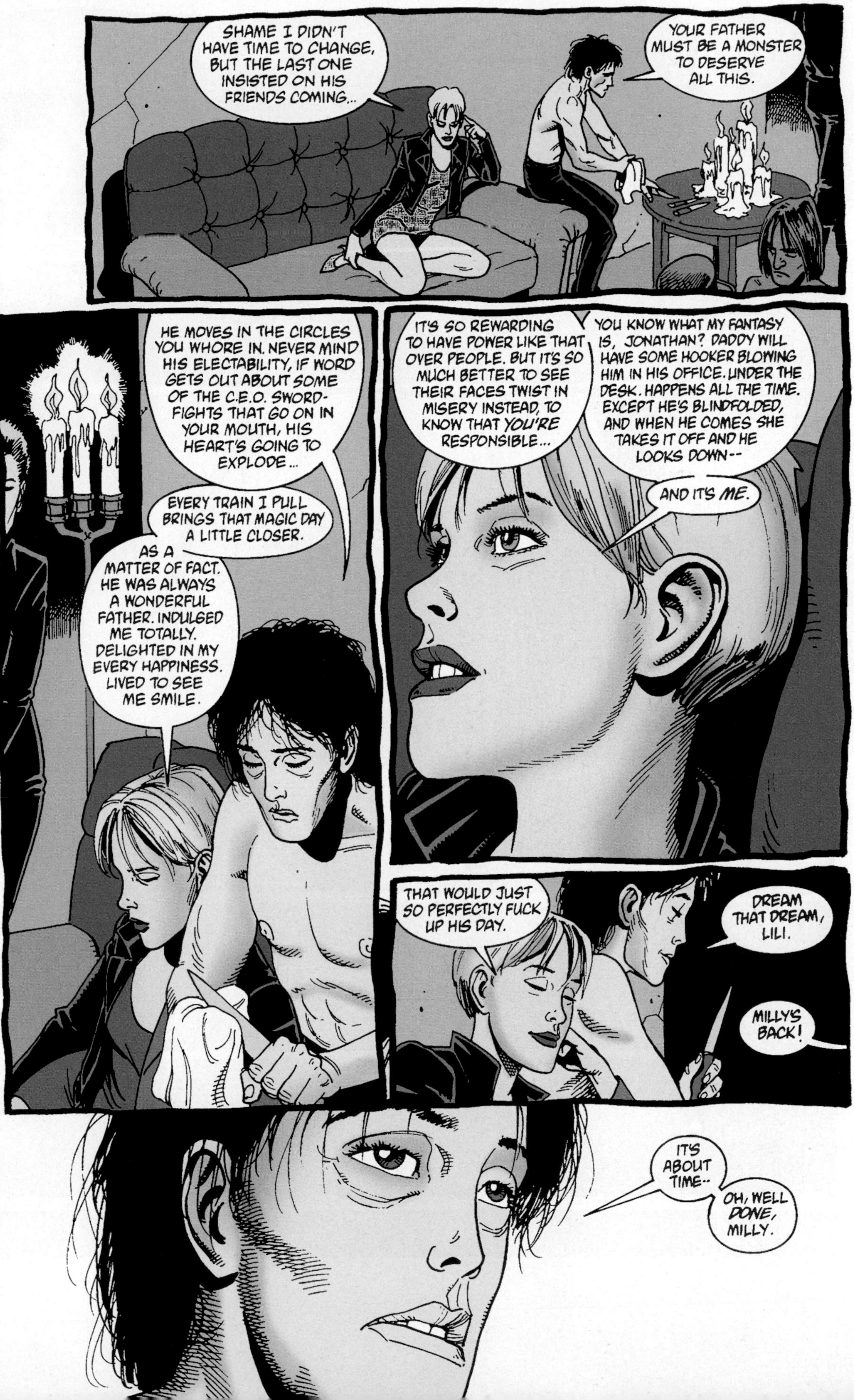
SHAME I DIDN'T HAVE TIME TO CHANGE, BUT THE LAST ONE INSISTED ON HIS FRIENDS COMING...
YOUR FATHER MUST BE A MONSTER TO DESERVE ALL THIS.
HE MOVES IN THE CIRCLES YOU WHORE IN. NEVER MIND HIS ELECTABILITY, IF WORD GETS OUT ABOUT SOME OF THE C.E.O. SWORD-FIGHTS THAT GO ON IN YOUR MOUTH, HIS HEART'S GOING TO EXPLODE...
EVERY TRAIN I PULL BRINGS THAT MAGIC DAY A LITTLE CLOSER.
AS A MATTER OF FACT. HE WAS ALWAYS A WONDERFUL FATHER. INDULGED ME TOTALLY. DELIGHTED IN MY EVERY HAPPINESS. LIVED TO SEE ME SMILE.
IT'S SO REWARDING TO HAVE POWER LIKE THAT OVER PEOPLE. BUT IT'S SO MUCH BETTER TO SEE THEIR FACES TWIST IN MISERY INSTEAD, TO KNOW THAT *YOU'RE* RESPONSIBLE...
YOU KNOW WHAT MY FANTASY IS, JONATHAN? DADDY WILL HAVE SOME HOOKER BLOWING HIM IN HIS OFFICE. UNDER THE DESK. HAPPENS ALL THE TIME. EXCEPT HE'S BLINDFOLDED, AND WHEN HE COMES SHE TAKES IT OFF AND HE LOOKS DOWN--
AND IT'S *ME*.
THAT WOULD JUST SO PERFECTLY FUCK UP HIS DAY.
DREAM THAT DREAM, LILI.
MILLY'S BACK!
IT'S ABOUT TIME--
OH, WELL *DONE*, MILLY.

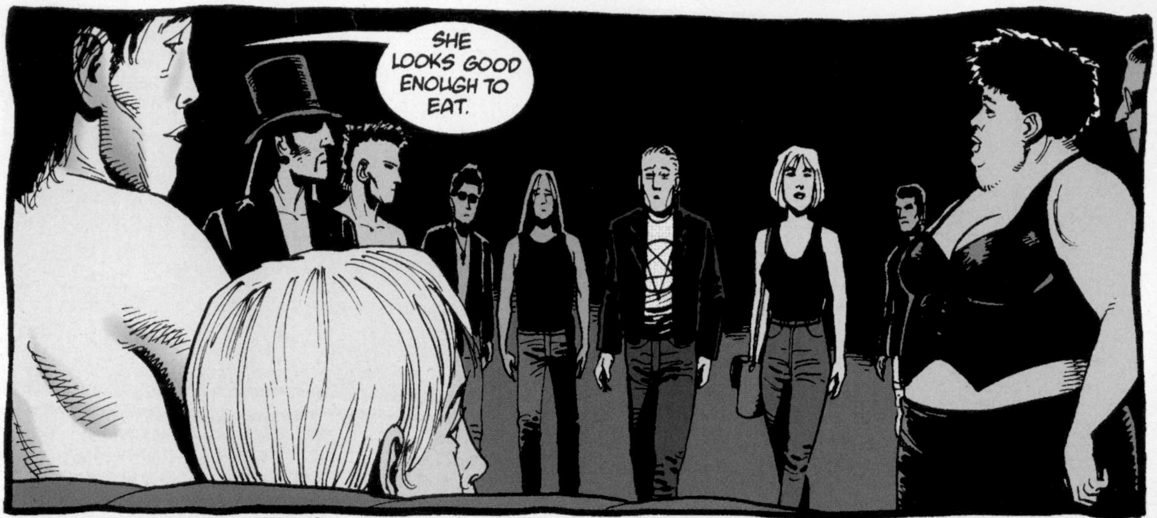
SHE LOOKS GOOD ENOUGH TO EAT.

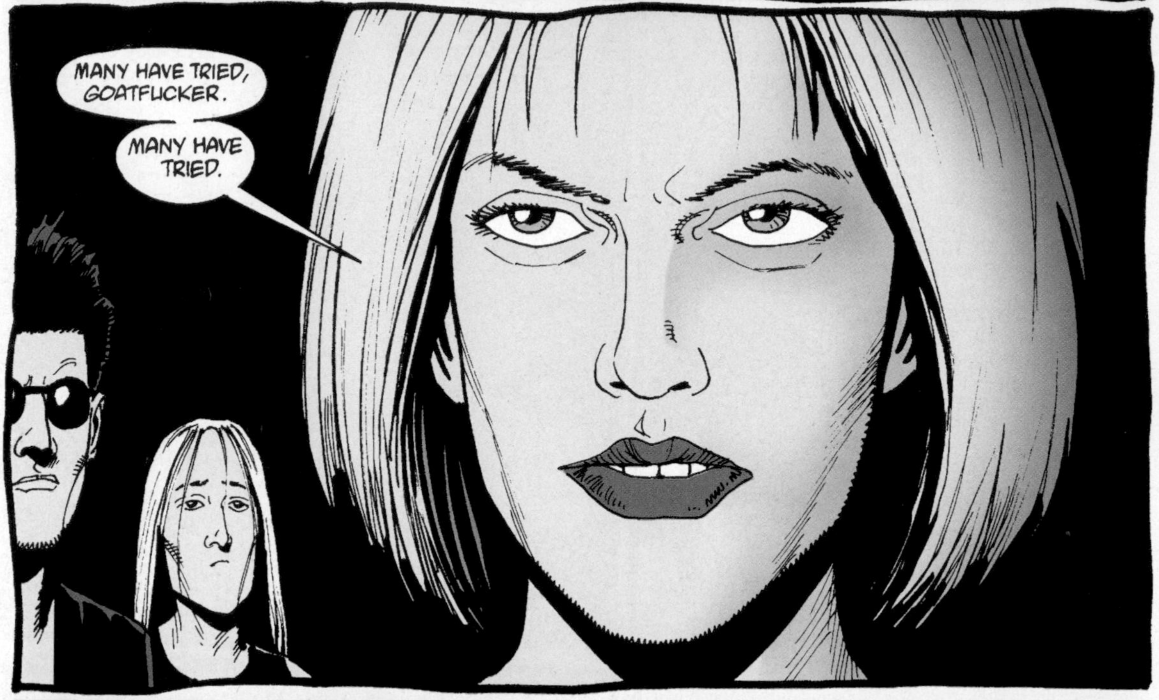
MANY HAVE TRIED, GOATFUCKER.
MANY HAVE TRIED.

# UNDERWORLD

GARTH ENNIS - Writer STEVE DILLON - Artist
PAMELA RAMBO - Colorist
CLEM ROBINS - Letterer AXEL ALONSO - Editor

PREACHER created by GARTH ENNIS and STEVE DILLON

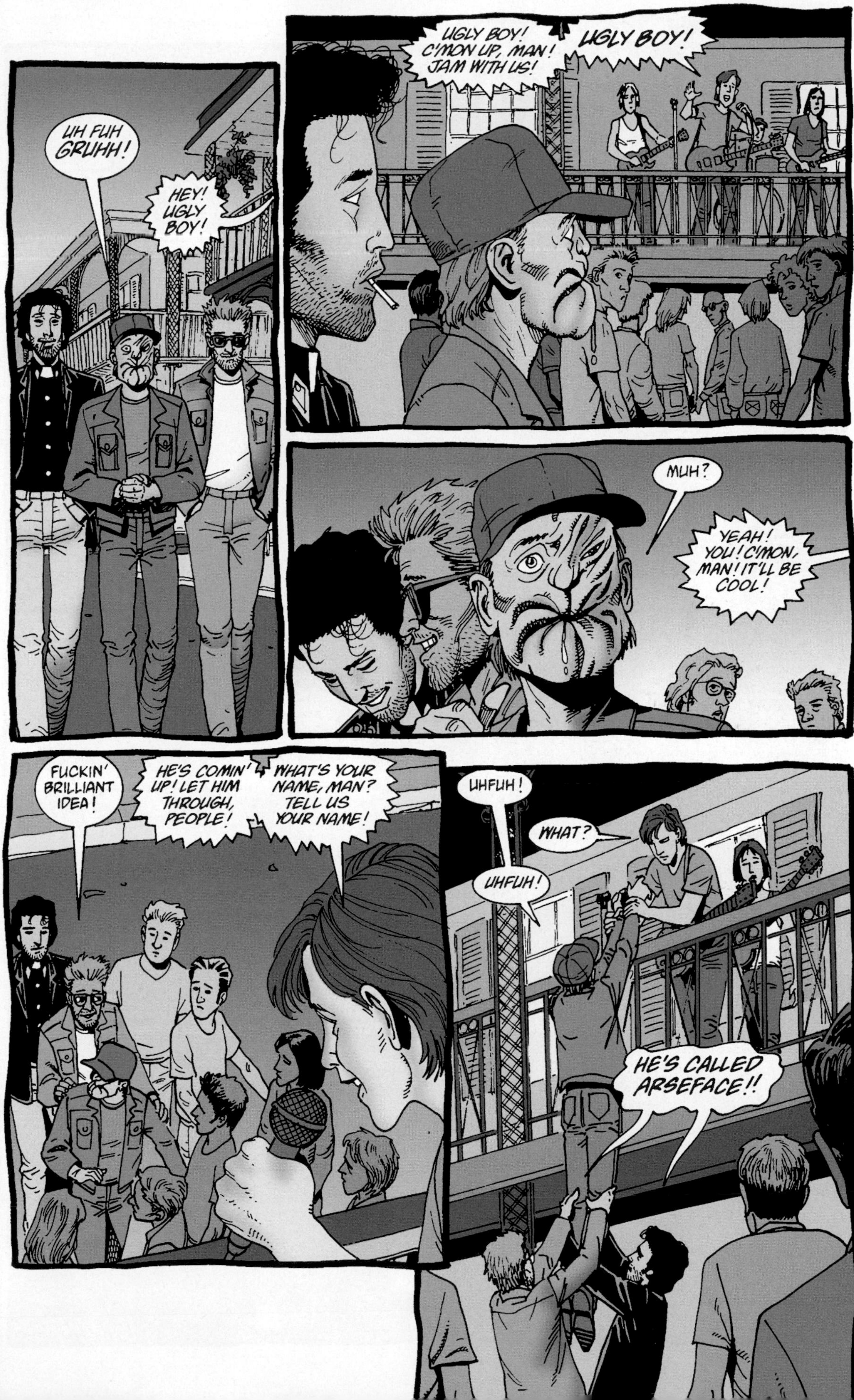
UH FUH GRUHH!
HEY! UGLY BOY!
UGLY BOY! C'MON UP, MAN! JAM WITH US!
UGLY BOY!
MUH?
YEAH! YOU! C'MON, MAN! IT'LL BE COOL!
FUCKIN' BRILLIANT IDEA!
HE'S COMIN' UP! LET HIM THROUGH, PEOPLE!
WHAT'S YOUR NAME, MAN? TELL US YOUR NAME!
UHFUH!
WHAT?
UHFUH!
HE'S CALLED ARSEFACE!!

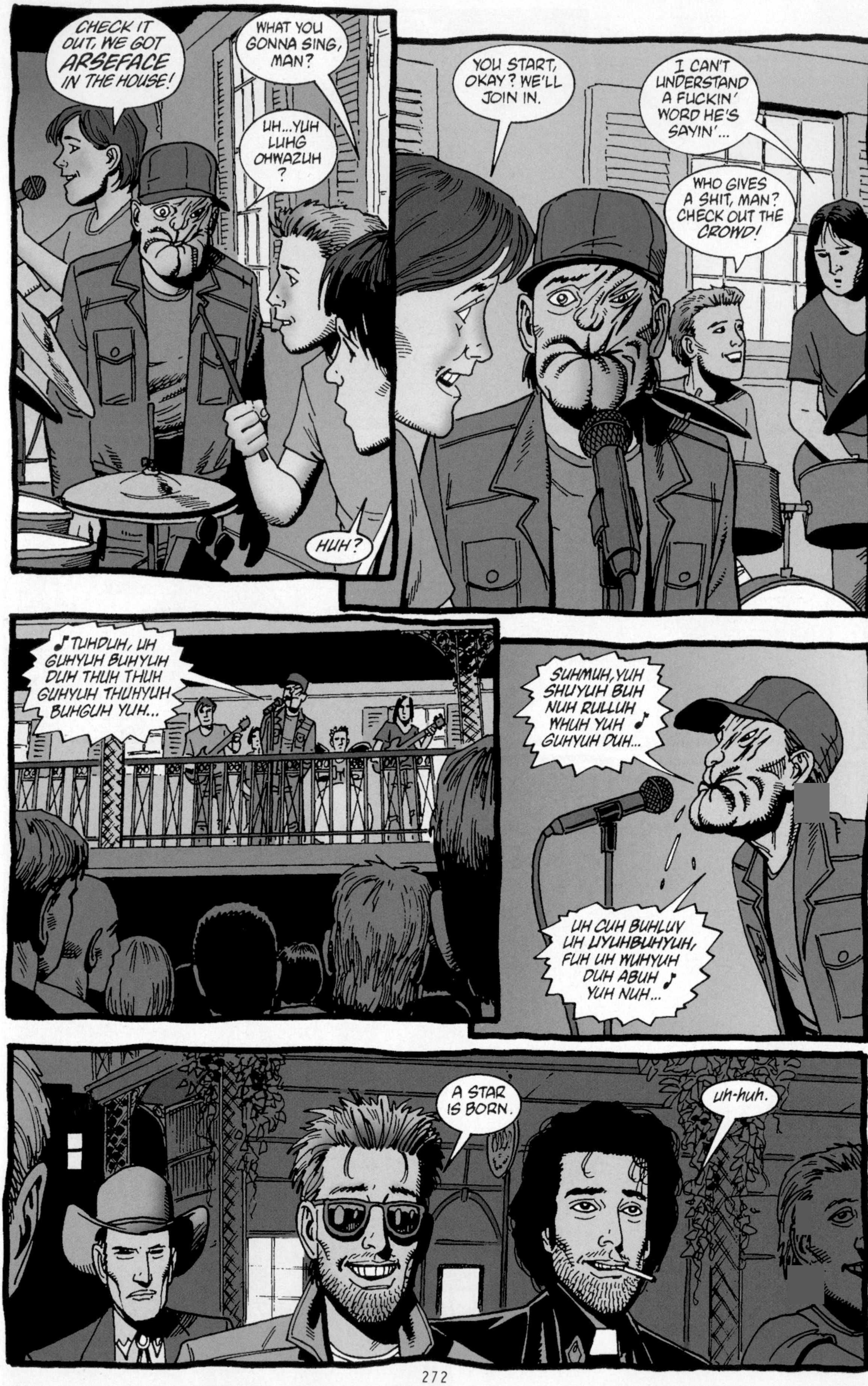
CHECK IT OUT, WE GOT ARSEFACE IN THE HOUSE!
WHAT YOU GONNA SING, MAN?
UH...YUH LUHG OHWAZUH?
HUH?
YOU START, OKAY? WE'LL JOIN IN.
I CAN'T UNDERSTAND A FUCKIN' WORD HE'S SAYIN'...
WHO GIVES A SHIT, MAN? CHECK OUT THE CROWD!
♪ TUHDUH, UH GUHYUH BUHYUH DUH THUH THUH GUHYUH THUHYUH BUHGUH YUH...
SUHMUH, YUH SHUYUH BUH NUH RULLUH WHUH YUH ♪ GUHYUH DUH...
UH CUH BUHLUV UH UYUHBUHYUH, FUH UH WUHYUH DUH ABUH ♪ YUH NUH...
A STAR IS BORN.
uh-huh.

SO WHAT DO YOU ASSHOLES WANT WITH CASSIDY?

UH, JONATHAN, SHE--

QUIET, MILLY.

WE WANT HIS POWER.

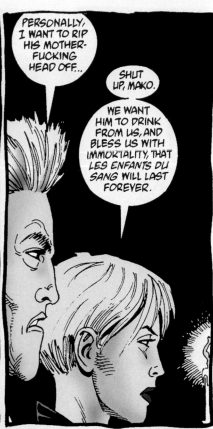

PERSONALLY, I WANT TO RIP HIS MOTHER-FUCKING HEAD OFF...

SHUT UP, MAKO.

WE WANT HIM TO DRINK FROM US, AND BLESS US WITH IMMORTALITY, THAT LES ENFANTS DU SANG WILL LAST FOREVER.

WHAT IS THIS LES ENFANTS SHIT?

LOOK, REALLY, SHE'S GOT--

MILLY.

WE ARE CHILDREN OF BLOOD, AND OF SHADOW, AND OF NIGHT. WE DRINK FROM VEINS AND ARTERY. OURS IS A PALE AND LANGUID PARADISE, AND IN OUR DREAMS WE WALK AS WOLVES AND FLY AS BATS.

AND PREY AT WILL UPON THE HUMAN HERD.

SOUNDS LIKE ONE BIG CIRCLE-JERK TO ME.

ARE YOU CASSIDY'S SOW?

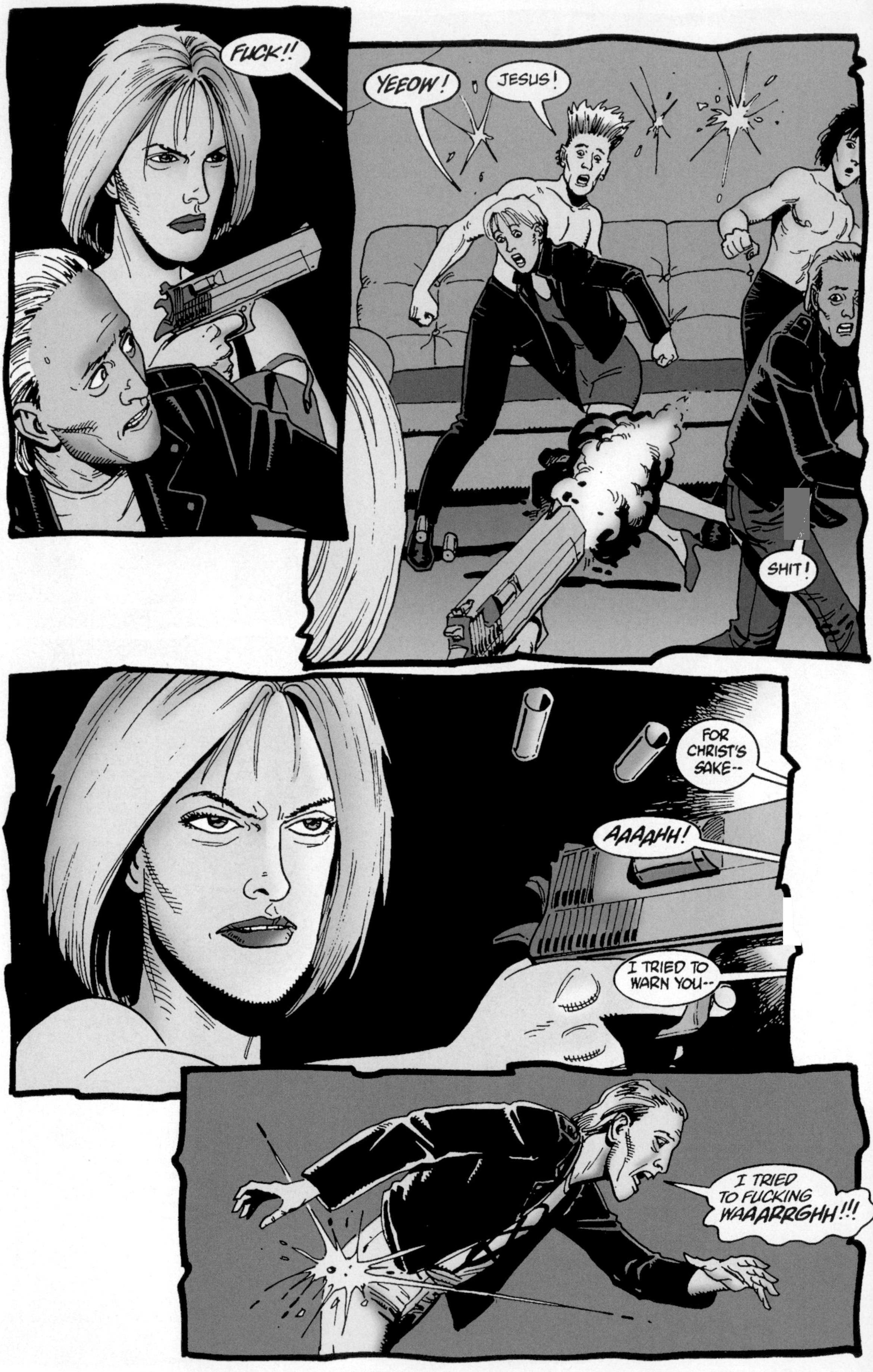
FUCK!!
YEEOW!
JESUS!
SHIT!
FOR CHRIST'S SAKE--
AAAAHH!
I TRIED TO WARN YOU--
I TRIED TO FUCKING WAAARRGHH!!!

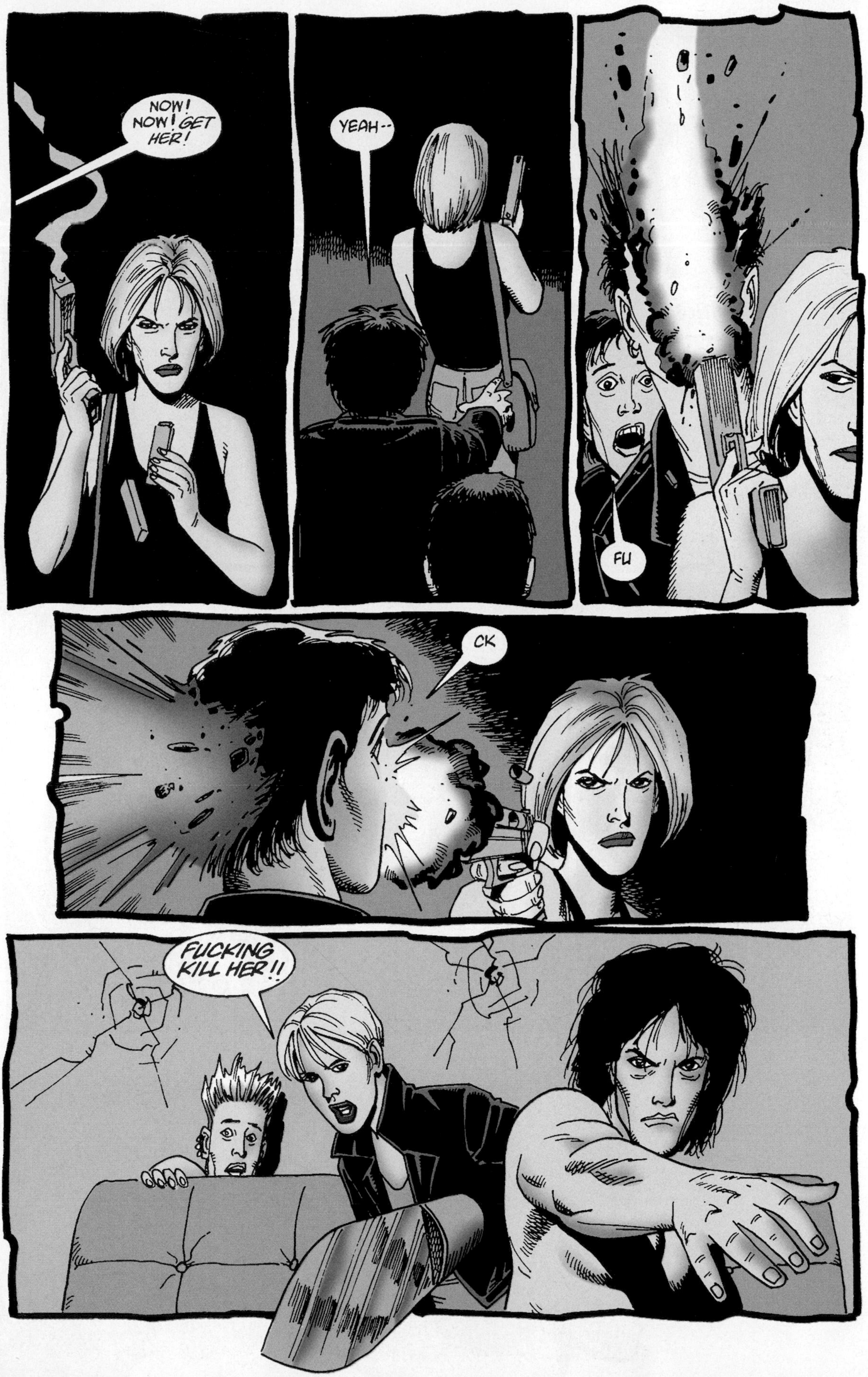
NOW! NOW! GET HER!
YEAH--
FU
CK
FUCKING KILL HER!!

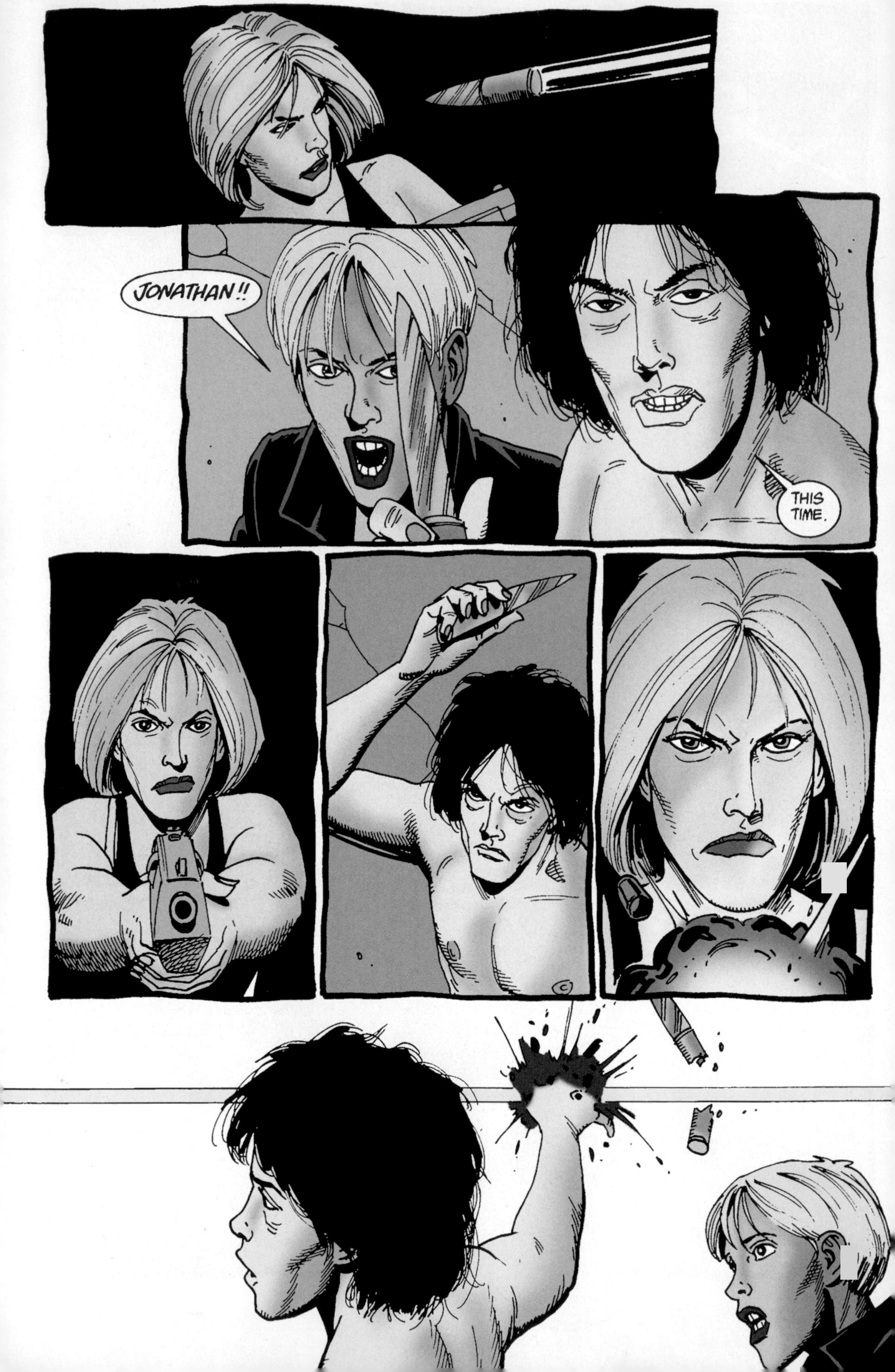
JONATHAN!!
THIS TIME.

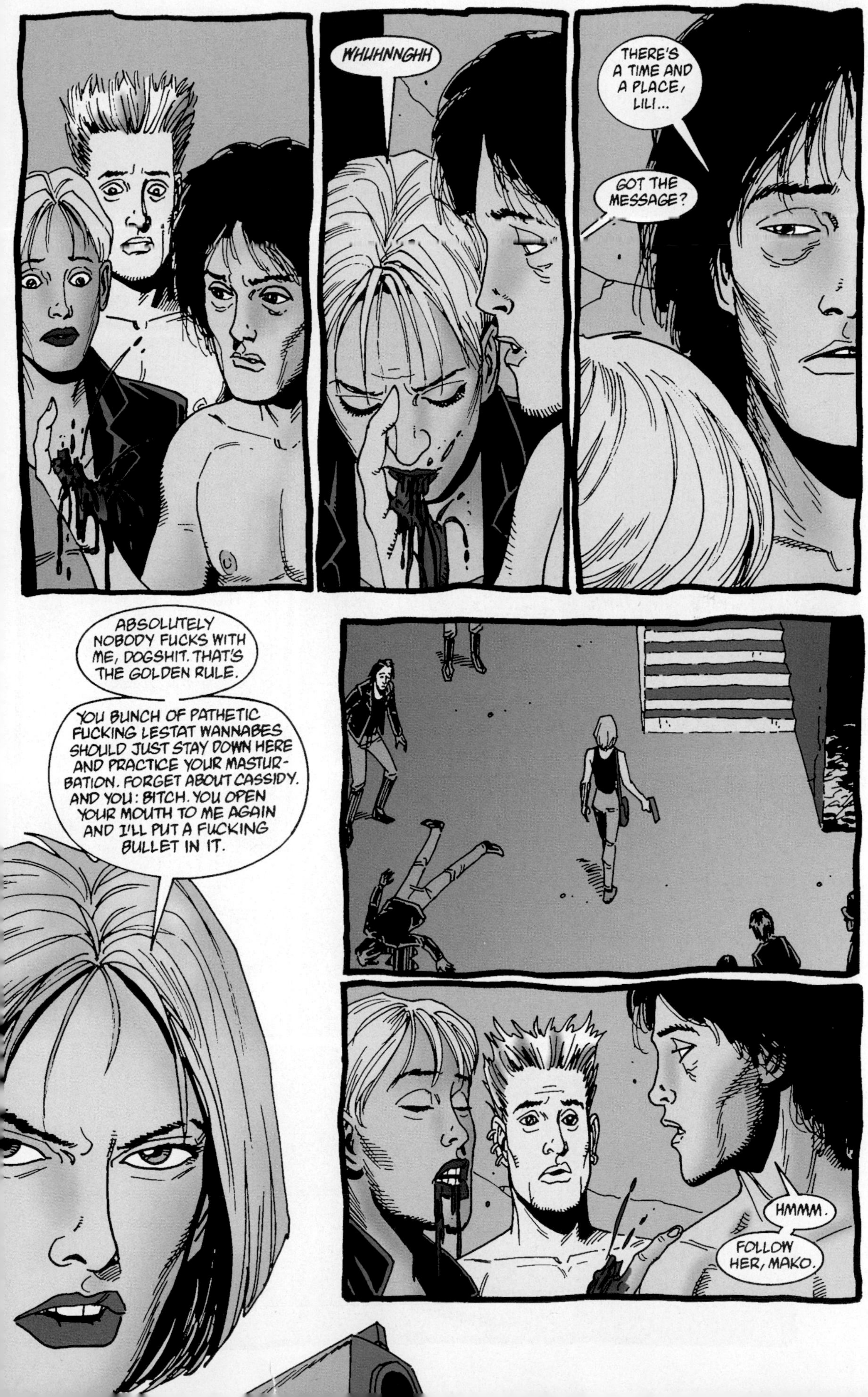
WHUHNNGHH
THERE'S A TIME AND A PLACE, LILI...
GOT THE MESSAGE?
ABSOLUTELY NOBODY FUCKS WITH ME, DOGSHIT. THAT'S THE GOLDEN RULE.
YOU BUNCH OF PATHETIC FUCKING LESTAT WANNABES SHOULD JUST STAY DOWN HERE AND PRACTICE YOUR MASTURBATION. FORGET ABOUT CASSIDY. AND YOU: BITCH. YOU OPEN YOUR MOUTH TO ME AGAIN AND I'LL PUT A FUCKING BULLET IN IT.
HMMM.
FOLLOW HER, MAKO.

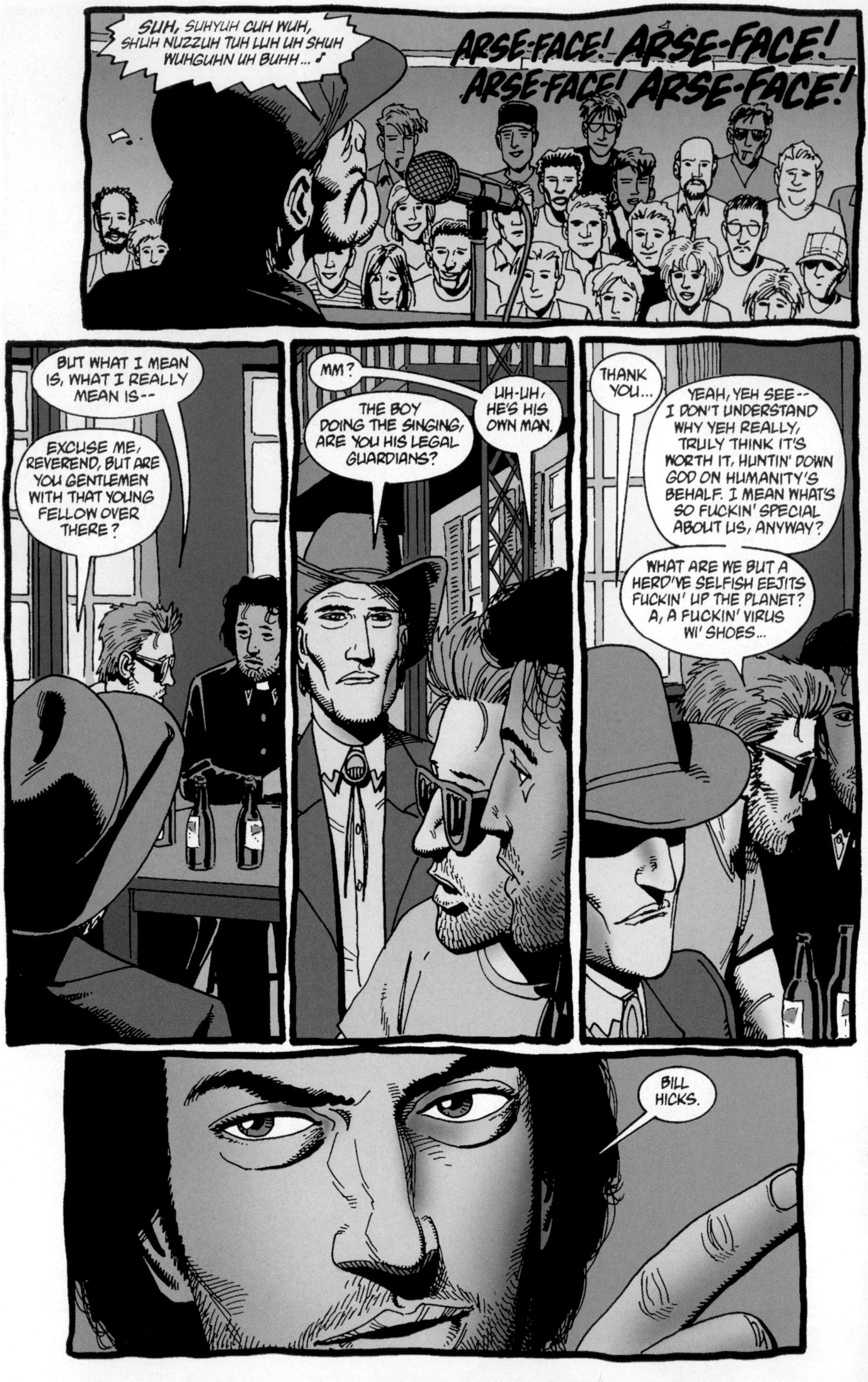
SUH, SUHYUH CUH WUH, SHUH NUZZUH TUH LUH UH SHUH WUHGUHN UH BUHH...
ARSE-FACE! ARSE-FACE! ARSE-FACE! ARSE-FACE!
BUT WHAT I MEAN IS, WHAT I REALLY MEAN IS--
EXCUSE ME, REVEREND, BUT ARE YOU GENTLEMEN WITH THAT YOUNG FELLOW OVER THERE?
MM?
THE BOY DOING THE SINGING, ARE YOU HIS LEGAL GUARDIANS?
UH-UH, HE'S HIS OWN MAN.
THANK YOU...
YEAH, YEH SEE-- I DON'T UNDERSTAND WHY YEH REALLY, TRULY THINK IT'S WORTH IT, HUNTIN' DOWN GOD ON HUMANITY'S BEHALF. I MEAN WHAT'S SO FUCKIN' SPECIAL ABOUT US, ANYWAY?
WHAT ARE WE BUT A HERD'VE SELFISH EEJITS FUCKIN' UP THE PLANET? A, A FUCKIN' VIRUS WI' SHOES...
BILL HICKS.

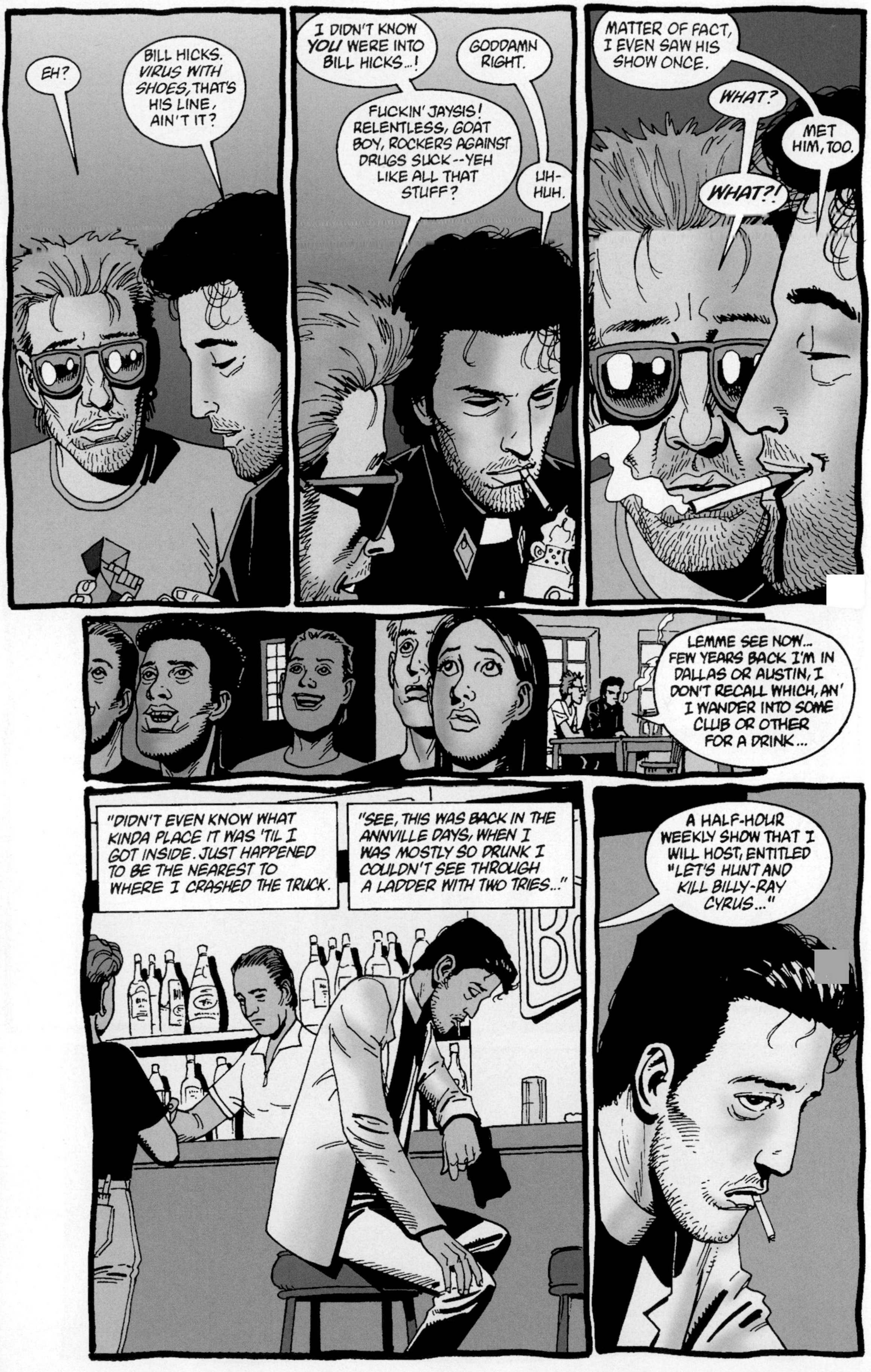
EH?
BILL HICKS. VIRUS WITH SHOES, THAT'S HIS LINE, AIN'T IT?
I DIDN'T KNOW YOU WERE INTO BILL HICKS...!
GODDAMN RIGHT.
FUCKIN' JAYSIS! RELENTLESS, GOAT BOY, ROCKERS AGAINST DRUGS SUCK--YEH LIKE ALL THAT STUFF?
UH-HUH.
MATTER OF FACT, I EVEN SAW HIS SHOW ONCE.
WHAT?
MET HIM, TOO.
WHAT?!
LEMME SEE NOW... FEW YEARS BACK I'M IN DALLAS OR AUSTIN, I DON'T RECALL WHICH, AN' I WANDER INTO SOME CLUB OR OTHER FOR A DRINK...
"DIDN'T EVEN KNOW WHAT KINDA PLACE IT WAS 'TIL I GOT INSIDE. JUST HAPPENED TO BE THE NEAREST TO WHERE I CRASHED THE TRUCK.
"SEE, THIS WAS BACK IN THE ANNVILLE DAYS, WHEN I WAS MOSTLY SO DRUNK I COULDN'T SEE THROUGH A LADDER WITH TWO TRIES..."
A HALF-HOUR WEEKLY SHOW THAT I WILL HOST, ENTITLED "LET'S HUNT AND KILL BILLY-RAY CYRUS..."

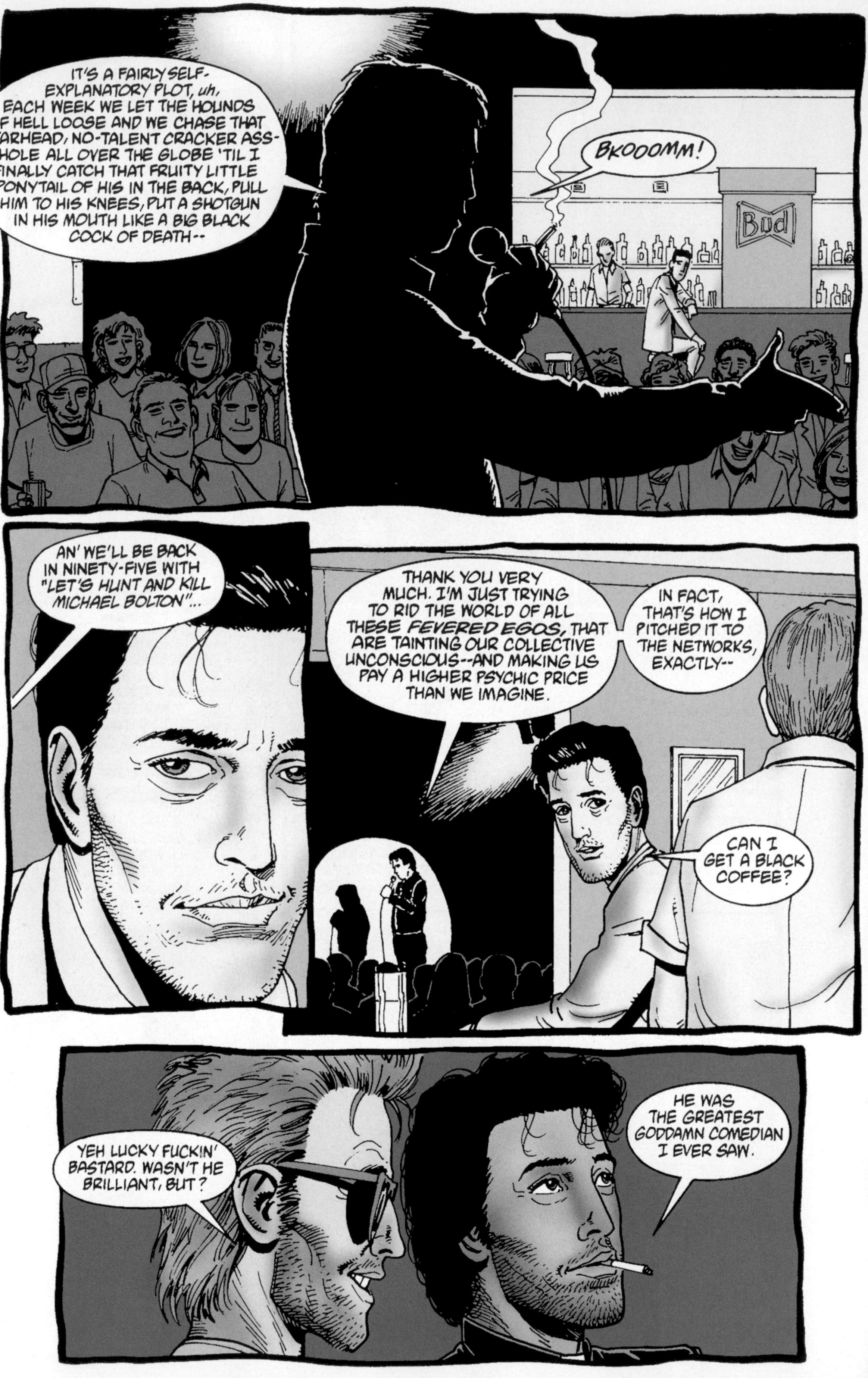
IT'S A FAIRLY SELF-EXPLANATORY PLOT, uh, EACH WEEK WE LET THE HOUNDS OF HELL LOOSE AND WE CHASE THAT JARHEAD, NO-TALENT CRACKER ASS-HOLE ALL OVER THE GLOBE 'TIL I FINALLY CATCH THAT FRUITY LITTLE PONYTAIL OF HIS IN THE BACK, PULL HIM TO HIS KNEES, PUT A SHOTGUN IN HIS MOUTH LIKE A BIG BLACK COCK OF DEATH--
BKOOOMM!
Bud
AN' WE'LL BE BACK IN NINETY-FIVE WITH "LET'S HUNT AND KILL MICHAEL BOLTON"...
THANK YOU VERY MUCH. I'M JUST TRYING TO RID THE WORLD OF ALL THESE FEVERED EGOS, THAT ARE TAINTING OUR COLLECTIVE UNCONSCIOUS--AND MAKING US PAY A HIGHER PSYCHIC PRICE THAN WE IMAGINE.
IN FACT, THAT'S HOW I PITCHED IT TO THE NETWORKS, EXACTLY--
CAN I GET A BLACK COFFEE?
YEH LUCKY FUCKIN' BASTARD. WASN'T HE BRILLIANT, BUT?
HE WAS THE GREATEST GODDAMN COMEDIAN I EVER SAW.

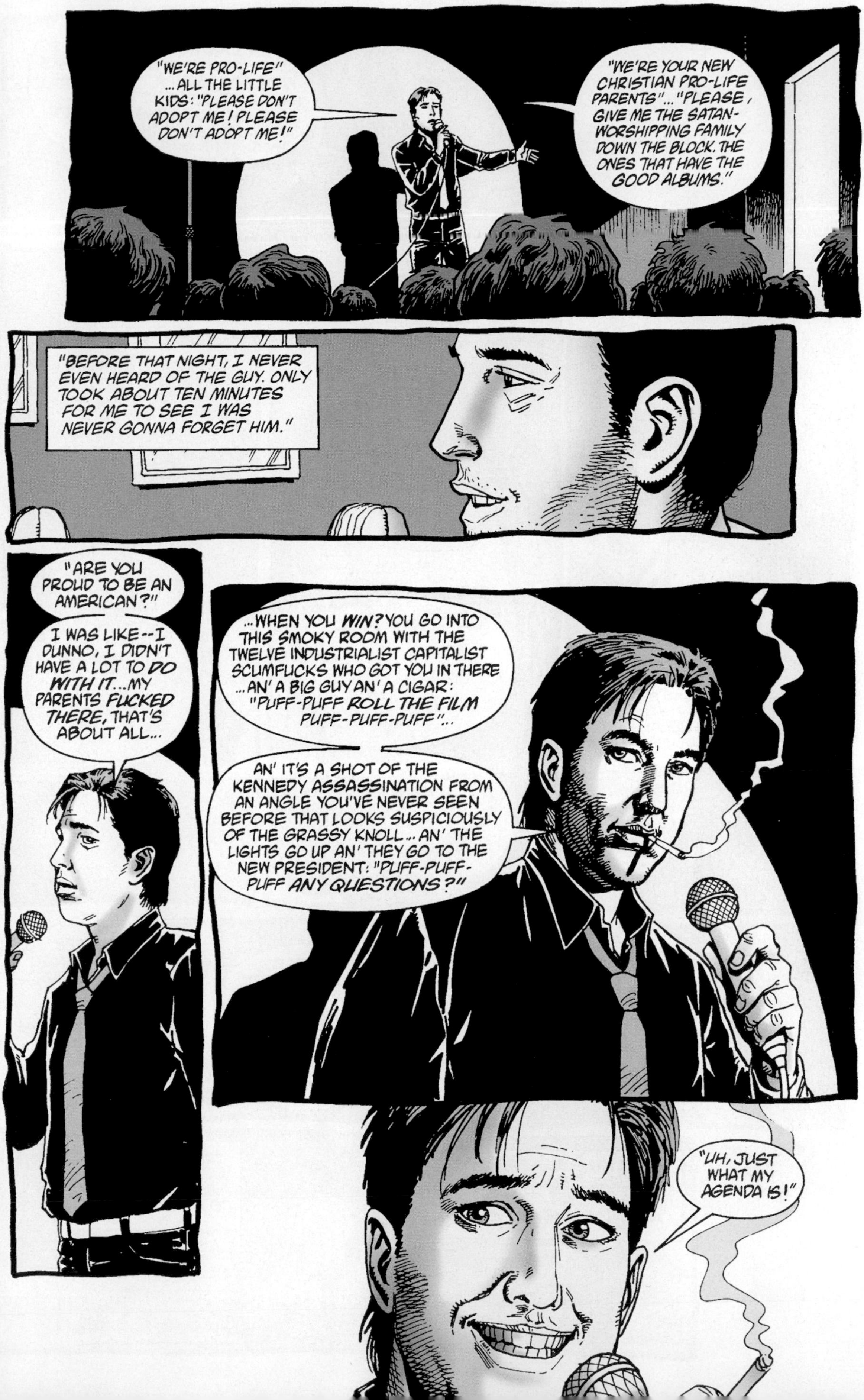
"WE'RE PRO-LIFE" ...ALL THE LITTLE KIDS: "PLEASE DON'T ADOPT ME! PLEASE DON'T ADOPT ME!"
"WE'RE YOUR NEW CHRISTIAN PRO-LIFE PARENTS"... "PLEASE, GIVE ME THE SATAN-WORSHIPPING FAMILY DOWN THE BLOCK. THE ONES THAT HAVE THE GOOD ALBUMS."
"BEFORE THAT NIGHT, I NEVER EVEN HEARD OF THE GUY. ONLY TOOK ABOUT TEN MINUTES FOR ME TO SEE I WAS NEVER GONNA FORGET HIM."
"ARE YOU PROUD TO BE AN AMERICAN?"
I WAS LIKE--I DUNNO, I DIDN'T HAVE A LOT TO DO WITH IT...MY PARENTS FUCKED THERE, THAT'S ABOUT ALL...
...WHEN YOU WIN? YOU GO INTO THIS SMOKY ROOM WITH THE TWELVE INDUSTRIALIST CAPITALIST SCUMFUCKS WHO GOT YOU IN THERE ...AN' A BIG GUY AN' A CIGAR: "PUFF-PUFF ROLL THE FILM PUFF-PUFF-PUFF"...
AN' IT'S A SHOT OF THE KENNEDY ASSASSINATION FROM AN ANGLE YOU'VE NEVER SEEN BEFORE THAT LOOKS SUSPICIOUSLY OF THE GRASSY KNOLL... AN' THE LIGHTS GO UP AN' THEY GO TO THE NEW PRESIDENT: "PUFF-PUFF-PUFF ANY QUESTIONS?"
"UH, JUST WHAT MY AGENDA IS!"

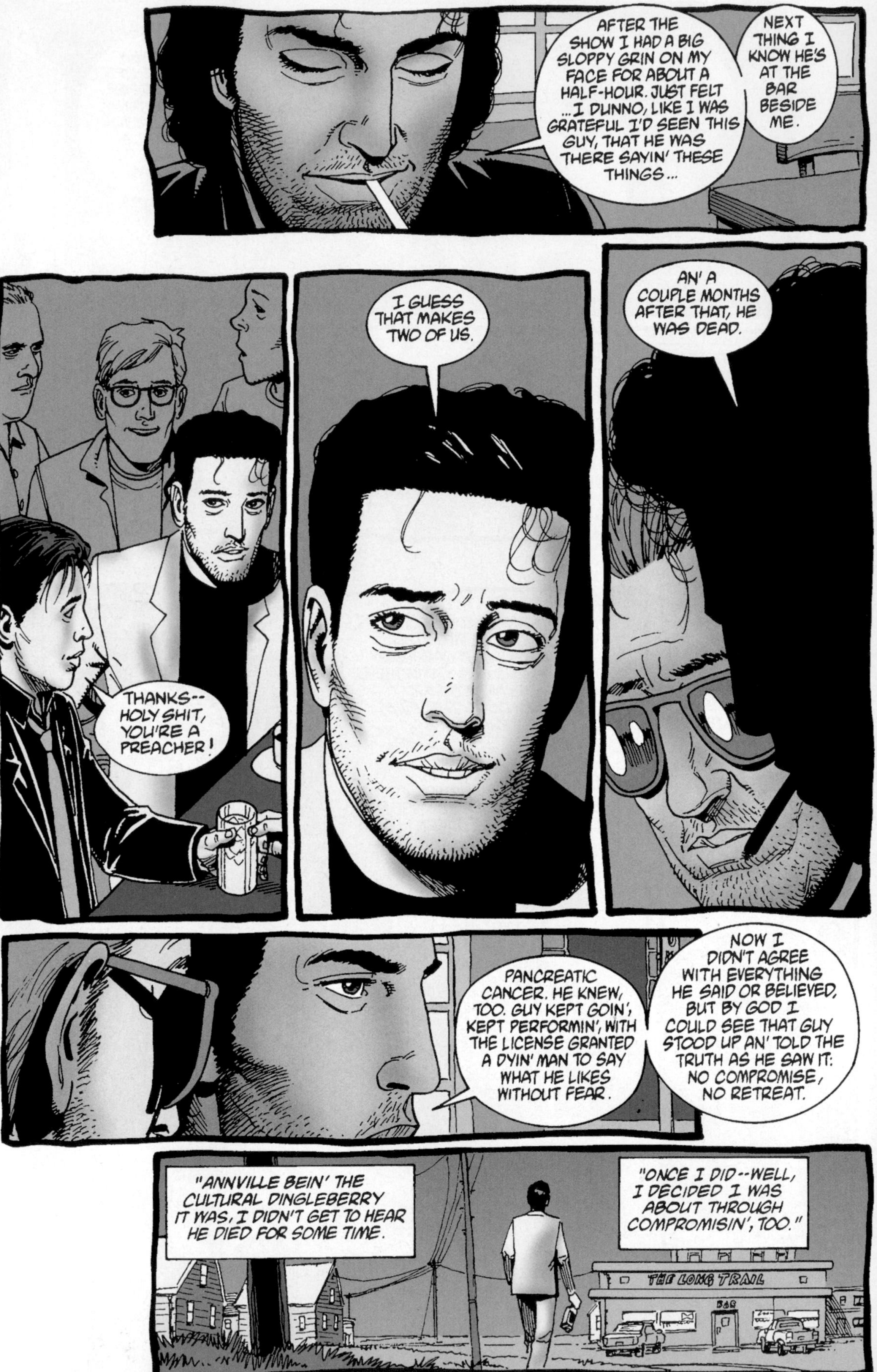
AFTER THE SHOW I HAD A BIG SLOPPY GRIN ON MY FACE FOR ABOUT A HALF-HOUR. JUST FELT ...I DUNNO, LIKE I WAS GRATEFUL I'D SEEN THIS GUY, THAT HE WAS THERE SAYIN' THESE THINGS...
NEXT THING I KNOW HE'S AT THE BAR BESIDE ME.
THANKS-- HOLY SHIT, YOU'RE A PREACHER!
I GUESS THAT MAKES TWO OF US.
AN' A COUPLE MONTHS AFTER THAT, HE WAS DEAD.
PANCREATIC CANCER. HE KNEW, TOO. GUY KEPT GOIN', KEPT PERFORMIN', WITH THE LICENSE GRANTED A DYIN' MAN TO SAY WHAT HE LIKES WITHOUT FEAR.
NOW I DIDN'T AGREE WITH EVERYTHING HE SAID OR BELIEVED, BUT BY GOD I COULD SEE THAT GUY STOOD UP AN' TOLD THE TRUTH AS HE SAW IT: NO COMPROMISE, NO RETREAT.
"ANNVILLE BEIN' THE CULTURAL DINGLEBERRY IT WAS, I DIDN'T GET TO HEAR HE DIED FOR SOME TIME.
"ONCE I DID--WELL, I DECIDED I WAS ABOUT THROUGH COMPROMISIN', TOO."
THE LONG TRAIL
BAR

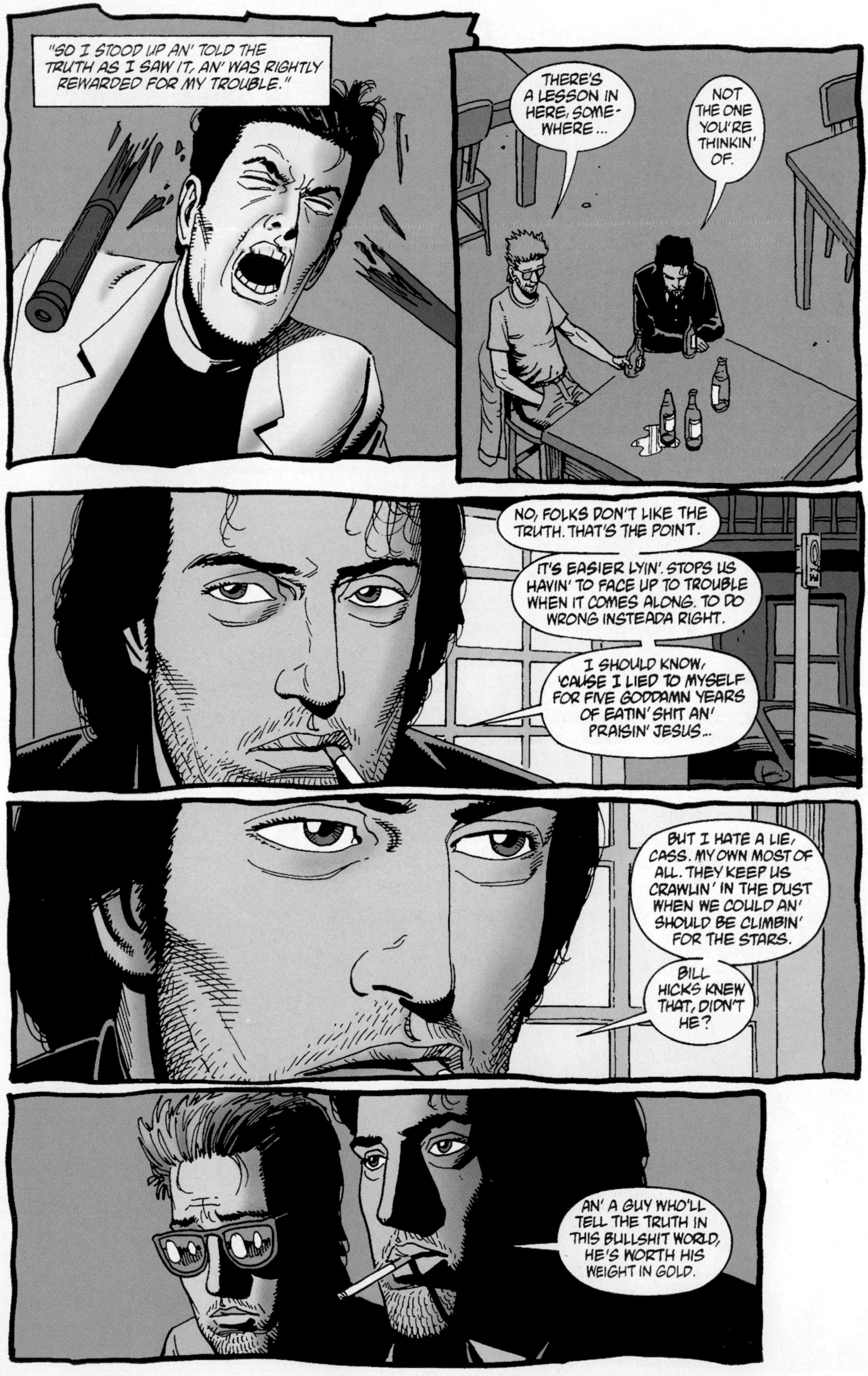
"SO I STOOD UP AN' TOLD THE TRUTH AS I SAW IT, AN' WAS RIGHTLY REWARDED FOR MY TROUBLE."
THERE'S A LESSON IN HERE, SOME-WHERE...
NOT THE ONE YOU'RE THINKIN' OF.
NO, FOLKS DON'T LIKE THE TRUTH. THAT'S THE POINT.
IT'S EASIER LYIN'. STOPS US HAVIN' TO FACE UP TO TROUBLE WHEN IT COMES ALONG. TO DO WRONG INSTEADA RIGHT.
I SHOULD KNOW, 'CAUSE I LIED TO MYSELF FOR FIVE GODDAMN YEARS OF EATIN' SHIT AN' PRAISIN' JESUS...
BUT I HATE A LIE, CASS. MY OWN MOST OF ALL. THEY KEEP US CRAWLIN' IN THE DUST WHEN WE COULD AN' SHOULD BE CLIMBIN' FOR THE STARS.
BILL HICKS KNEW THAT, DIDN'T HE?
AN' A GUY WHO'LL TELL THE TRUTH IN THIS BULLSHIT WORLD, HE'S WORTH HIS WEIGHT IN GOLD.

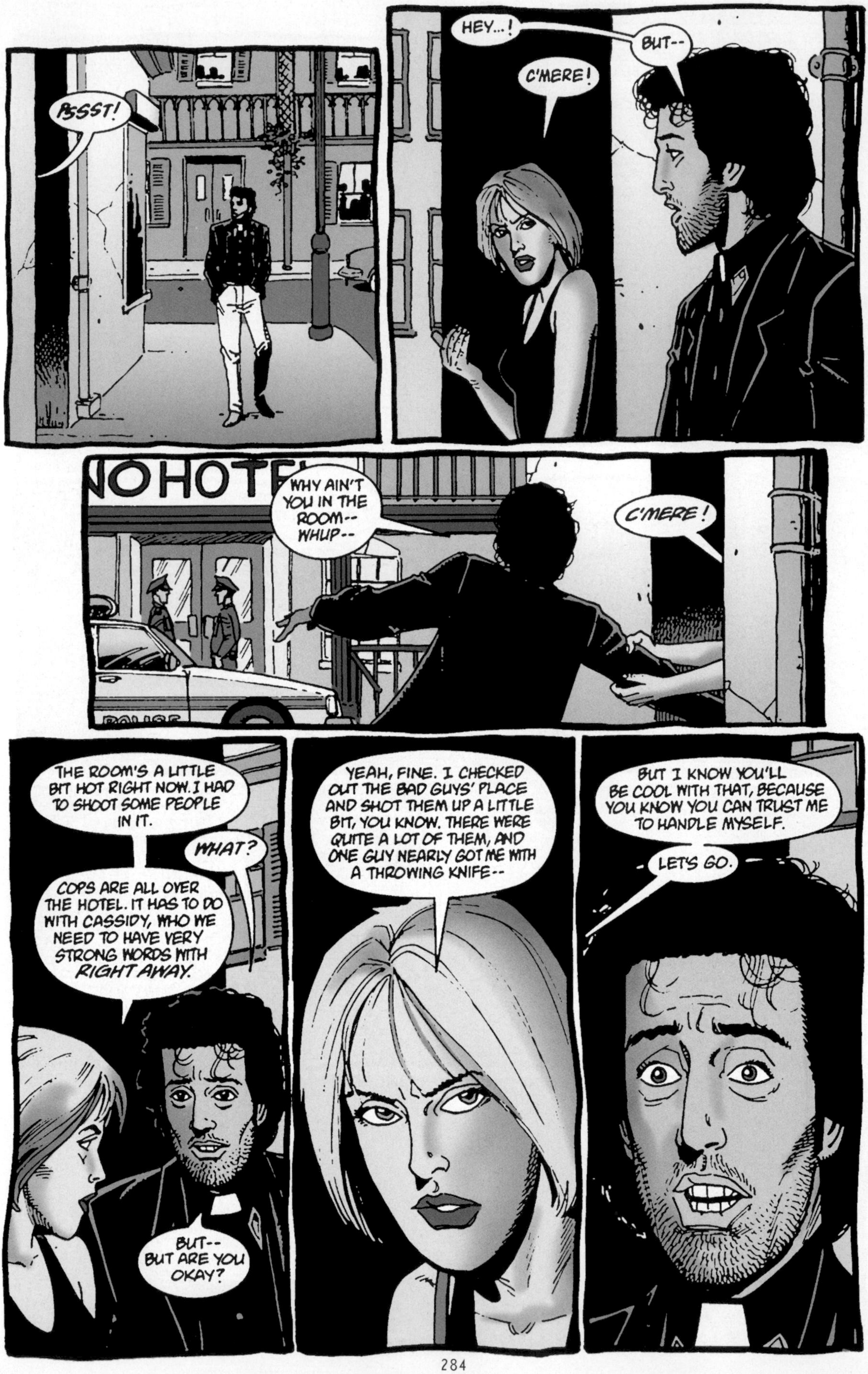
PSSST!
HEY...!
BUT--
C'MERE!
WHY AIN'T YOU IN THE ROOM-- WHUP--
C'MERE!
THE ROOM'S A LITTLE BIT HOT RIGHT NOW. I HAD TO SHOOT SOME PEOPLE IN IT.
WHAT?
COPS ARE ALL OVER THE HOTEL. IT HAS TO DO WITH CASSIDY, WHO WE NEED TO HAVE VERY STRONG WORDS WITH RIGHT AWAY.
BUT-- BUT ARE YOU OKAY?
YEAH, FINE. I CHECKED OUT THE BAD GUYS' PLACE AND SHOT THEM UP A LITTLE BIT, YOU KNOW. THERE WERE QUITE A LOT OF THEM, AND ONE GUY NEARLY GOT ME WITH A THROWING KNIFE--
BUT I KNOW YOU'LL BE COOL WITH THAT, BECAUSE YOU KNOW YOU CAN TRUST ME TO HANDLE MYSELF.
LET'S GO.

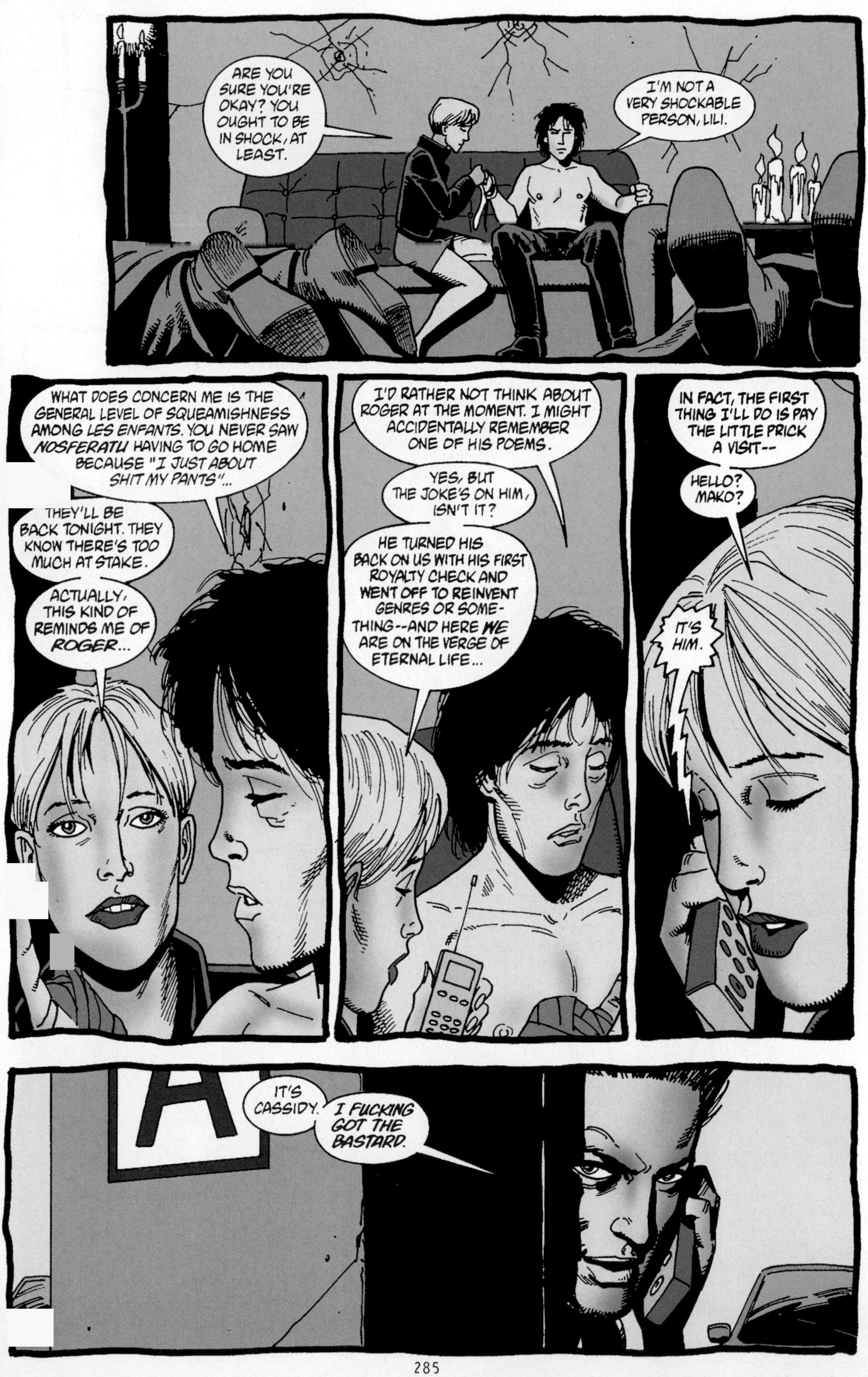
ARE YOU SURE YOU'RE OKAY? YOU OUGHT TO BE IN SHOCK, AT LEAST.
I'M NOT A VERY SHOCKABLE PERSON, LILI.
WHAT DOES CONCERN ME IS THE GENERAL LEVEL OF SQUEAMISHNESS AMONG LES ENFANTS. YOU NEVER SAW NOSFERATU HAVING TO GO HOME BECAUSE "I JUST ABOUT SHIT MY PANTS"...
THEY'LL BE BACK TONIGHT. THEY KNOW THERE'S TOO MUCH AT STAKE.
ACTUALLY, THIS KIND OF REMINDS ME OF ROGER...
I'D RATHER NOT THINK ABOUT ROGER AT THE MOMENT. I MIGHT ACCIDENTALLY REMEMBER ONE OF HIS POEMS.
YES, BUT THE JOKE'S ON HIM, ISN'T IT?
HE TURNED HIS BACK ON US WITH HIS FIRST ROYALTY CHECK AND WENT OFF TO REINVENT GENRES OR SOMETHING--AND HERE WE ARE ON THE VERGE OF ETERNAL LIFE...
IN FACT, THE FIRST THING I'LL DO IS PAY THE LITTLE PRICK A VISIT--
HELLO? MAKO?
IT'S HIM.
IT'S CASSIDY.
I FUCKING GOT THE BASTARD.

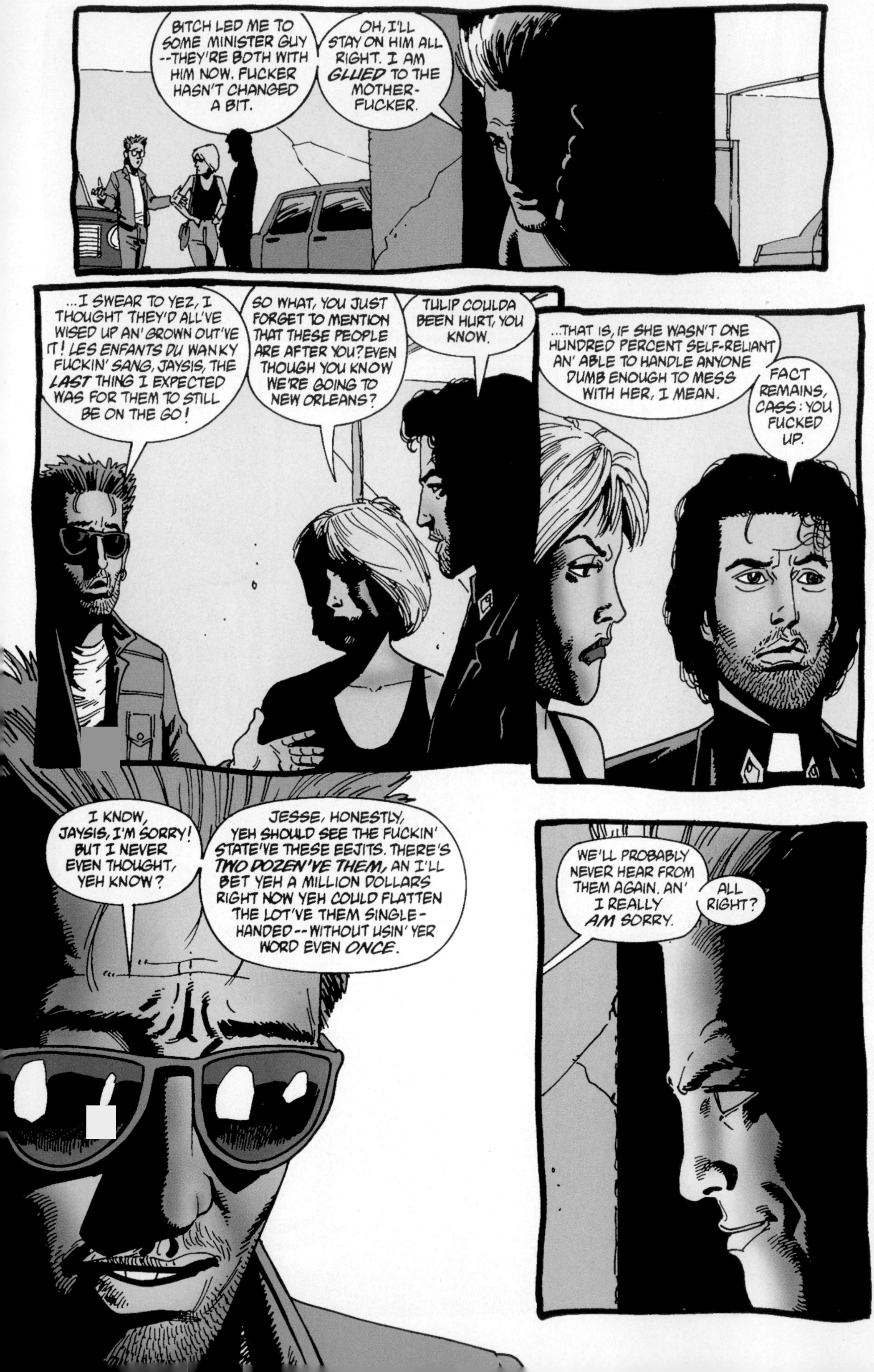
BITCH LED ME TO SOME MINISTER GUY --THEY'RE BOTH WITH HIM NOW. FUCKER HASN'T CHANGED A BIT.
OH, I'LL STAY ON HIM ALL RIGHT. I AM GLUED TO THE MOTHER-FUCKER.
...I SWEAR TO YEZ, I THOUGHT THEY'D ALL'VE WISED UP AN' GROWN OUT'VE IT! LES ENFANTS DU WANKY FUCKIN' SANG, JAYSIS, THE LAST THING I EXPECTED WAS FOR THEM TO STILL BE ON THE GO!
SO WHAT, YOU JUST FORGET TO MENTION THAT THESE PEOPLE ARE AFTER YOU? EVEN THOUGH YOU KNOW WE'RE GOING TO NEW ORLEANS?
TULIP COULDA BEEN HURT, YOU KNOW.
...THAT IS, IF SHE WASN'T ONE HUNDRED PERCENT SELF-RELIANT AN' ABLE TO HANDLE ANYONE DUMB ENOUGH TO MESS WITH HER, I MEAN.
FACT REMAINS, CASS: YOU FUCKED UP.
I KNOW, JAYSIS, I'M SORRY! BUT I NEVER EVEN THOUGHT, YEH KNOW?
JESSE, HONESTLY, YEH SHOULD SEE THE FUCKIN' STATE'VE THESE EEJITS. THERE'S TWO DOZEN'VE THEM, AN I'LL BET YEH A MILLION DOLLARS RIGHT NOW YEH COULD FLATTEN THE LOT'VE THEM SINGLE-HANDED--WITHOUT USIN' YER WORD EVEN ONCE.
WE'LL PROBABLY NEVER HEAR FROM THEM AGAIN. AN' I REALLY AM SORRY.
ALL RIGHT?

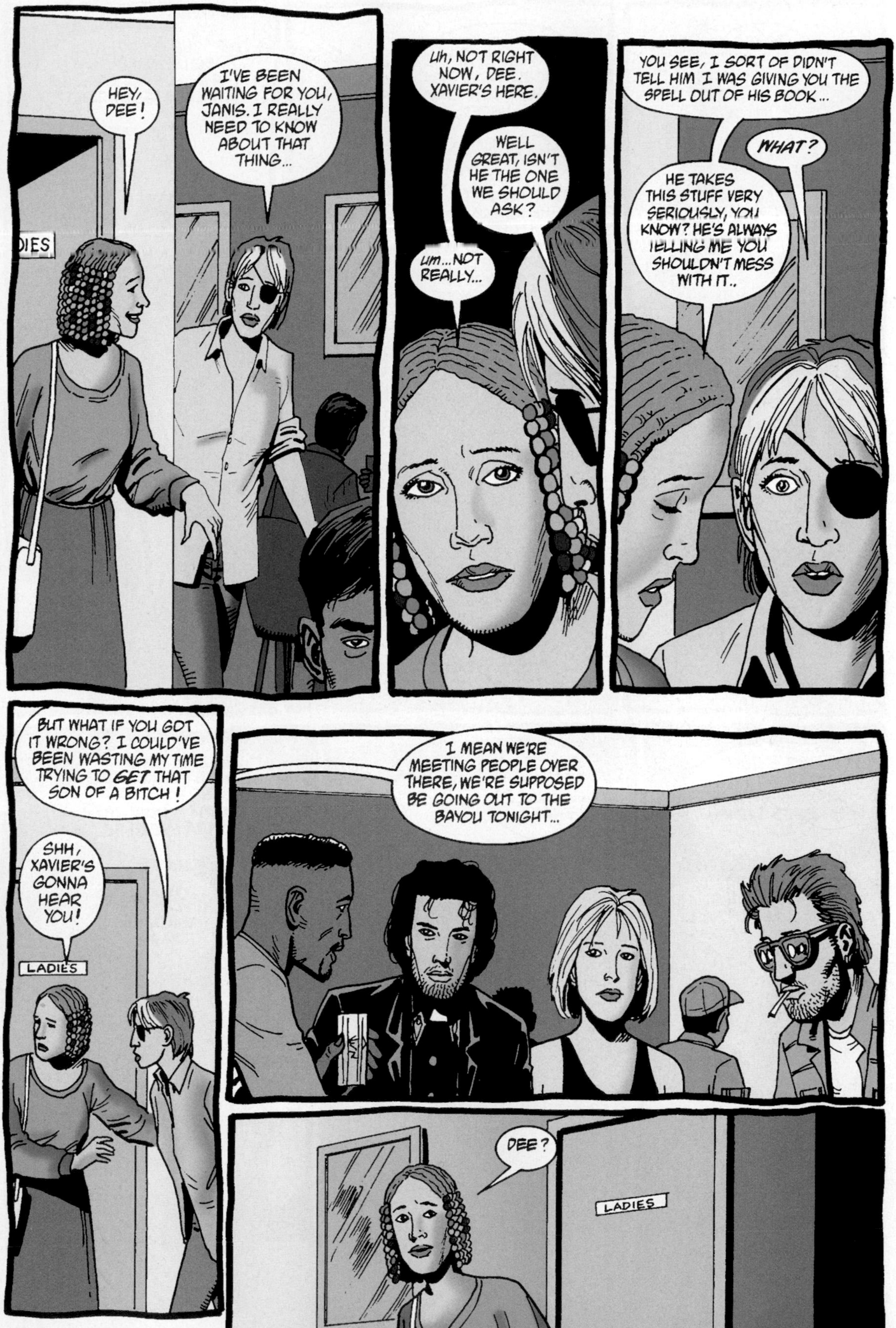
HEY, DEE!
I'VE BEEN WAITING FOR YOU, JANIS. I REALLY NEED TO KNOW ABOUT THAT THING...
DIES
UH, NOT RIGHT NOW, DEE. XAVIER'S HERE.
WELL GREAT, ISN'T HE THE ONE WE SHOULD ASK?
UM...NOT REALLY...
YOU SEE, I SORT OF DIDN'T TELL HIM I WAS GIVING YOU THE SPELL OUT OF HIS BOOK...
WHAT?
HE TAKES THIS STUFF VERY SERIOUSLY, YOU KNOW? HE'S ALWAYS TELLING ME YOU SHOULDN'T MESS WITH IT..
BUT WHAT IF YOU GOT IT WRONG? I COULD'VE BEEN WASTING MY TIME TRYING TO GET THAT SON OF A BITCH!
SHH, XAVIER'S GONNA HEAR YOU!
LADIES
I MEAN WE'RE MEETING PEOPLE OVER THERE, WE'RE SUPPOSED BE GOING OUT TO THE BAYOU TONIGHT...
DEE?
LADIES

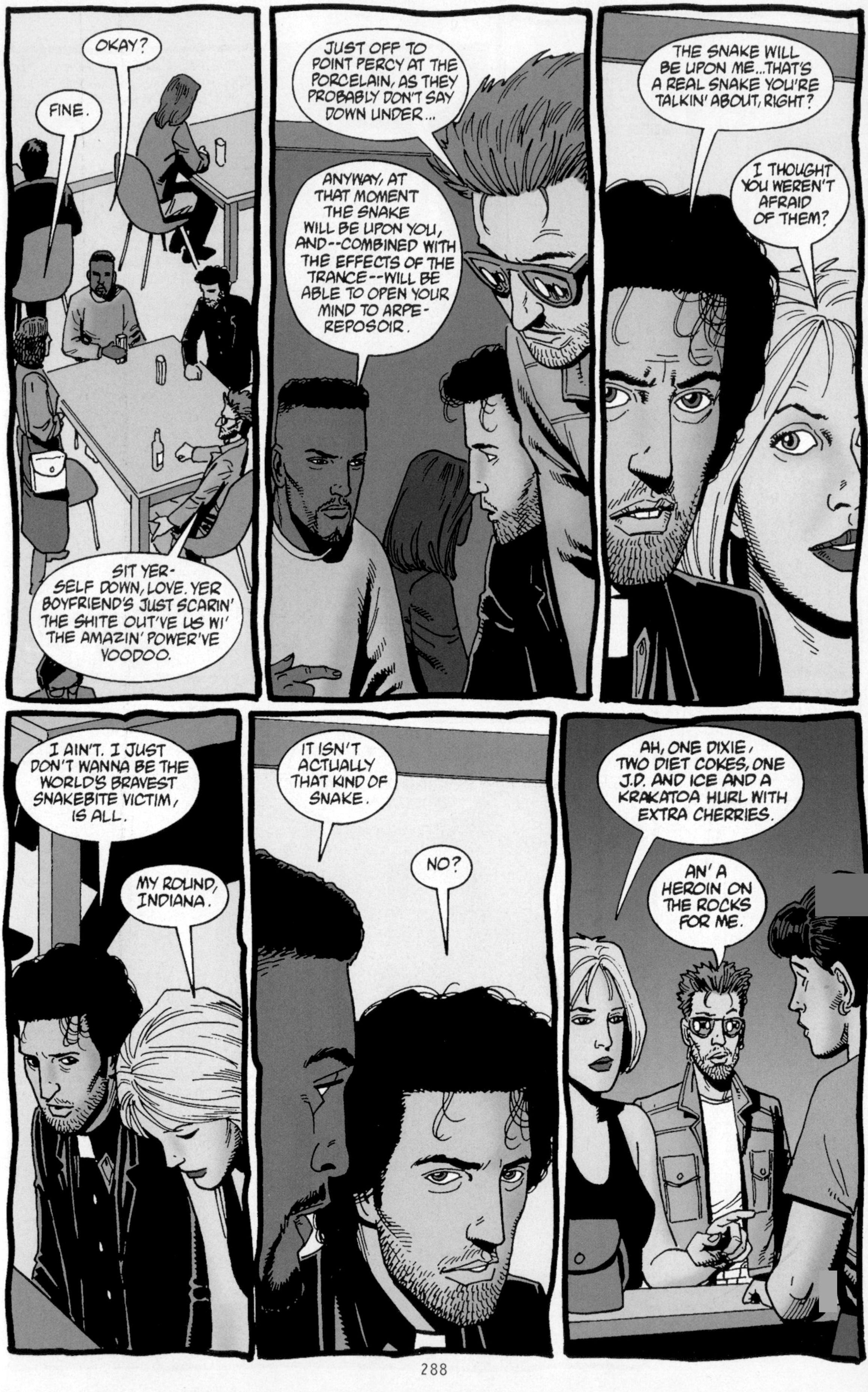
OKAY?
FINE.
SIT YER-SELF DOWN, LOVE. YER BOYFRIEND'S JUST SCARIN' THE SHITE OUT'VE US WI' THE AMAZIN' POWER'VE VOODOO.
JUST OFF TO POINT PERCY AT THE PORCELAIN, AS THEY PROBABLY DON'T SAY DOWN UNDER...
ANYWAY, AT THAT MOMENT THE SNAKE WILL BE UPON YOU, AND--COMBINED WITH THE EFFECTS OF THE TRANCE--WILL BE ABLE TO OPEN YOUR MIND TO ARPE-REPOSOIR.
THE SNAKE WILL BE UPON ME...THAT'S A REAL SNAKE YOU'RE TALKIN' ABOUT, RIGHT?
I THOUGHT YOU WEREN'T AFRAID OF THEM?
I AIN'T. I JUST DON'T WANNA BE THE WORLD'S BRAVEST SNAKEBITE VICTIM, IS ALL.
MY ROUND, INDIANA.
IT ISN'T ACTUALLY THAT KIND OF SNAKE.
NO?
AH, ONE DIXIE, TWO DIET COKES, ONE J.D. AND ICE AND A KRAKATOA HURL WITH EXTRA CHERRIES.
AN' A HEROIN ON THE ROCKS FOR ME.

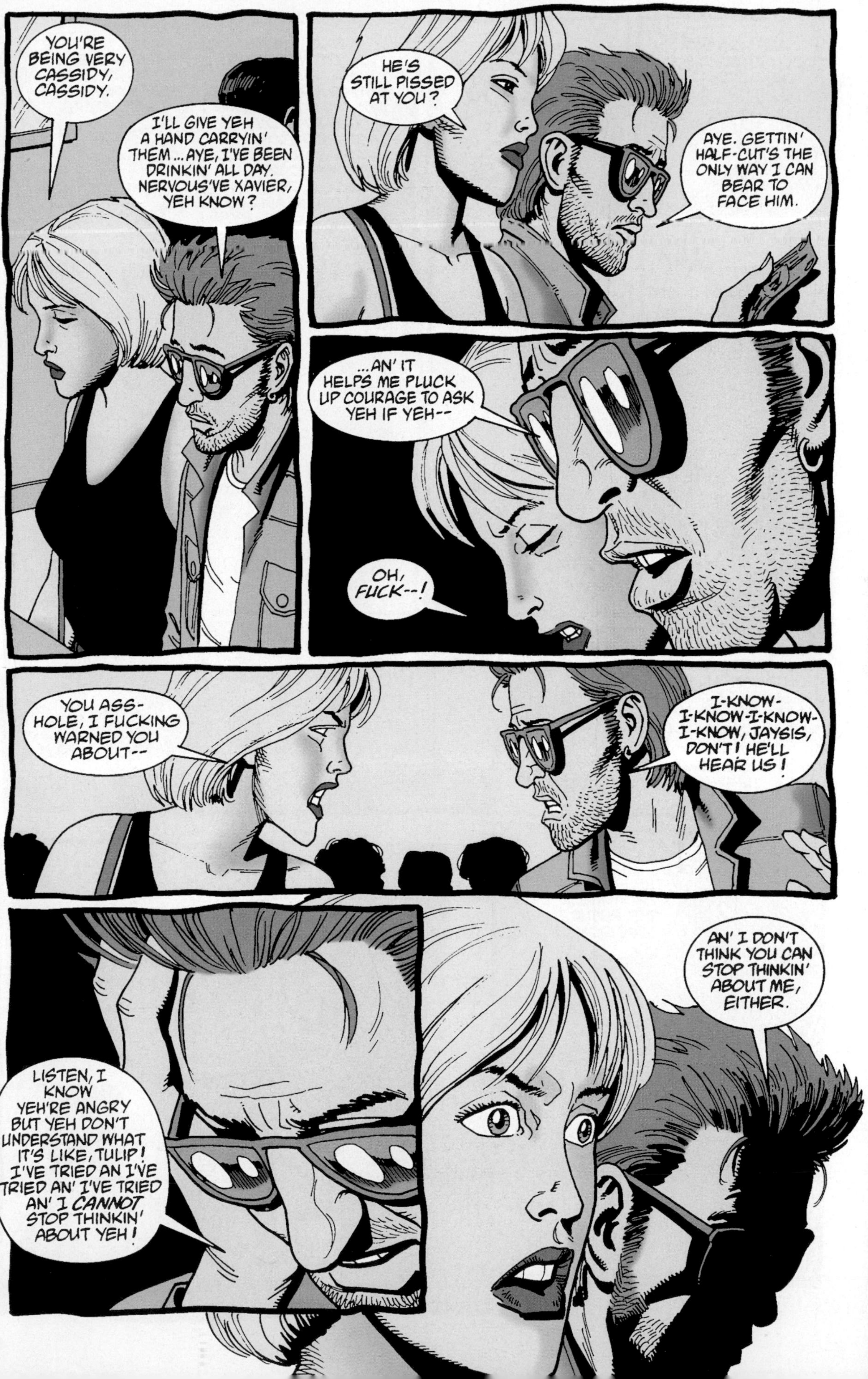
YOU'RE BEING VERY CASSIDY, CASSIDY.
I'LL GIVE YEH A HAND CARRYIN' THEM ... AYE, I'VE BEEN DRINKIN' ALL DAY. NERVOUS'VE XAVIER, YEH KNOW?
HE'S STILL PISSED AT YOU?
AYE. GETTIN' HALF-CUT'S THE ONLY WAY I CAN BEAR TO FACE HIM.
...AN' IT HELPS ME PLUCK UP COURAGE TO ASK YEH IF YEH--
OH, FUCK--!
YOU ASS-HOLE, I FUCKING WARNED YOU ABOUT--
I-KNOW-I-KNOW-I-KNOW-I-KNOW, JAYSIS, DON'T! HE'LL HEAR US!
LISTEN, I KNOW YEH'RE ANGRY BUT YEH DON'T UNDERSTAND WHAT IT'S LIKE, TULIP! I'VE TRIED AN I'VE TRIED AN' I'VE TRIED AN' I CANNOT STOP THINKIN' ABOUT YEH!
AN' I DON'T THINK YOU CAN STOP THINKIN' ABOUT ME, EITHER.

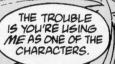

AND HOW DO YOU FIGURE THAT, EXACTLY?

BUT YEH HAVEN'T, BECAUSE YEH CAN'T DENY HOW YEH FEEL ABOUT ME.

I KNOW IT AN' YOU KNOW IT, TULIP: YOU WANT ME AS MUCH AS I WANT YOU.

OKAY, LET ME TELL YOU WHAT YOU'RE DOING HERE: YOU'RE WRITING A STORY. YOU'VE GOT THE PLOT AND THE DIALOGUE FROM *MELROSE PLACE* AND FUCKING *BAY-WATCH,* AND YOU'RE WRITING YOURSELF A LITTLE STORY IN YOUR HEAD...

THE TROUBLE IS YOU'RE USING *ME* AS ONE OF THE CHARACTERS.

YEH'D'VE TOLD HIM.

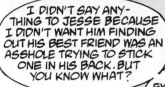

I DIDN'T SAY ANYTHING TO JESSE BECAUSE I DIDN'T WANT HIM FINDING OUT HIS BEST FRIEND WAS AN ASSHOLE TRYING TO STICK ONE IN HIS BACK. BUT YOU KNOW WHAT?

THAT'S EXACTLY WHY I SHOULD HAVE TOLD HIM.

YOU STAY THE FUCK AWAY FROM ME IN THE FUTURE, CASSIDY.

BOLLICKS.

290

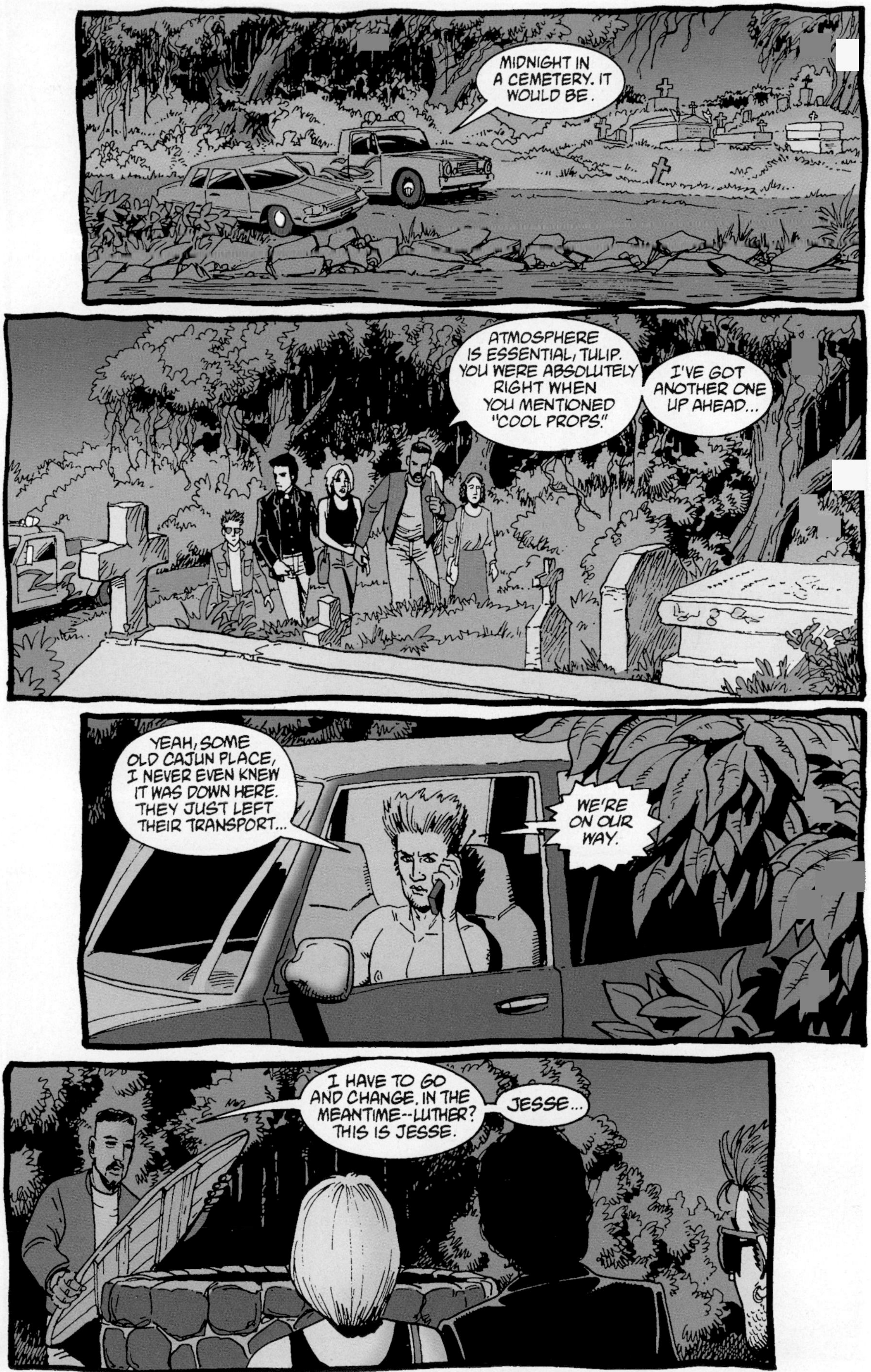
MIDNIGHT IN A CEMETERY. IT WOULD BE.
ATMOSPHERE IS ESSENTIAL, TULIP. YOU WERE ABSOLUTELY RIGHT WHEN YOU MENTIONED "COOL PROPS."
I'VE GOT ANOTHER ONE UP AHEAD...
YEAH, SOME OLD CAJUN PLACE, I NEVER EVEN KNEW IT WAS DOWN HERE. THEY JUST LEFT THEIR TRANSPORT...
WE'RE ON OUR WAY.
I HAVE TO GO AND CHANGE. IN THE MEANTIME--LUTHER? THIS IS JESSE.
JESSE...

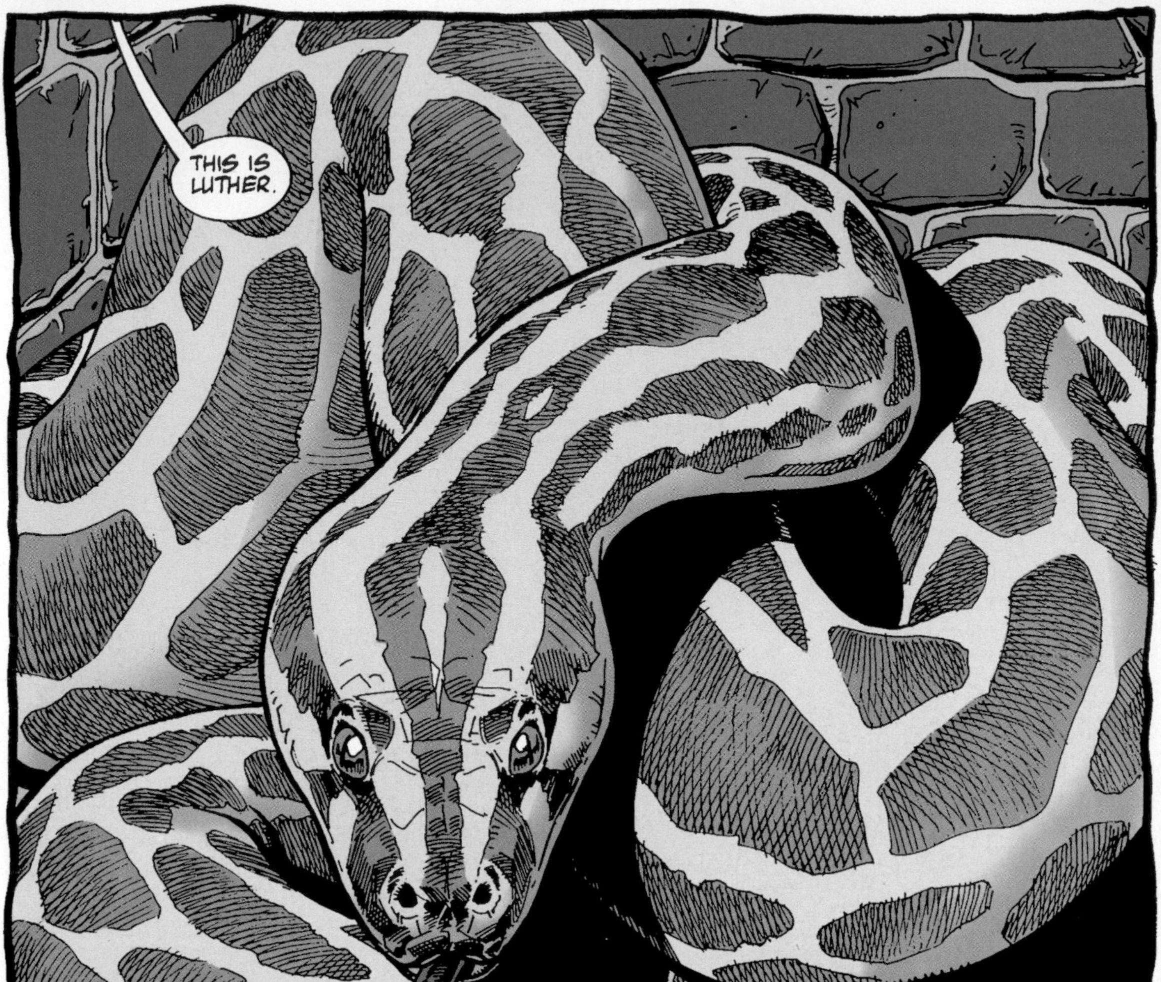
THIS IS LUTHER.

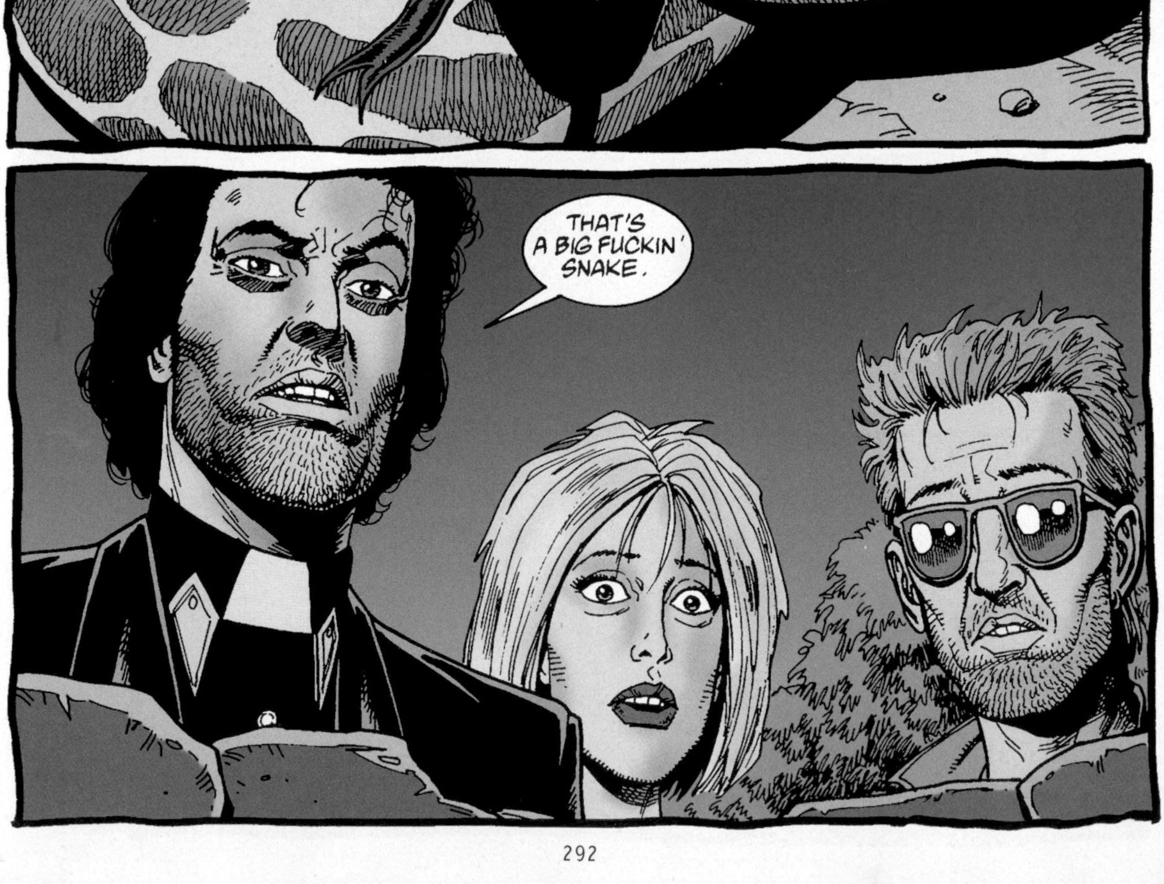
THAT'S A BIG FUCKIN' SNAKE.

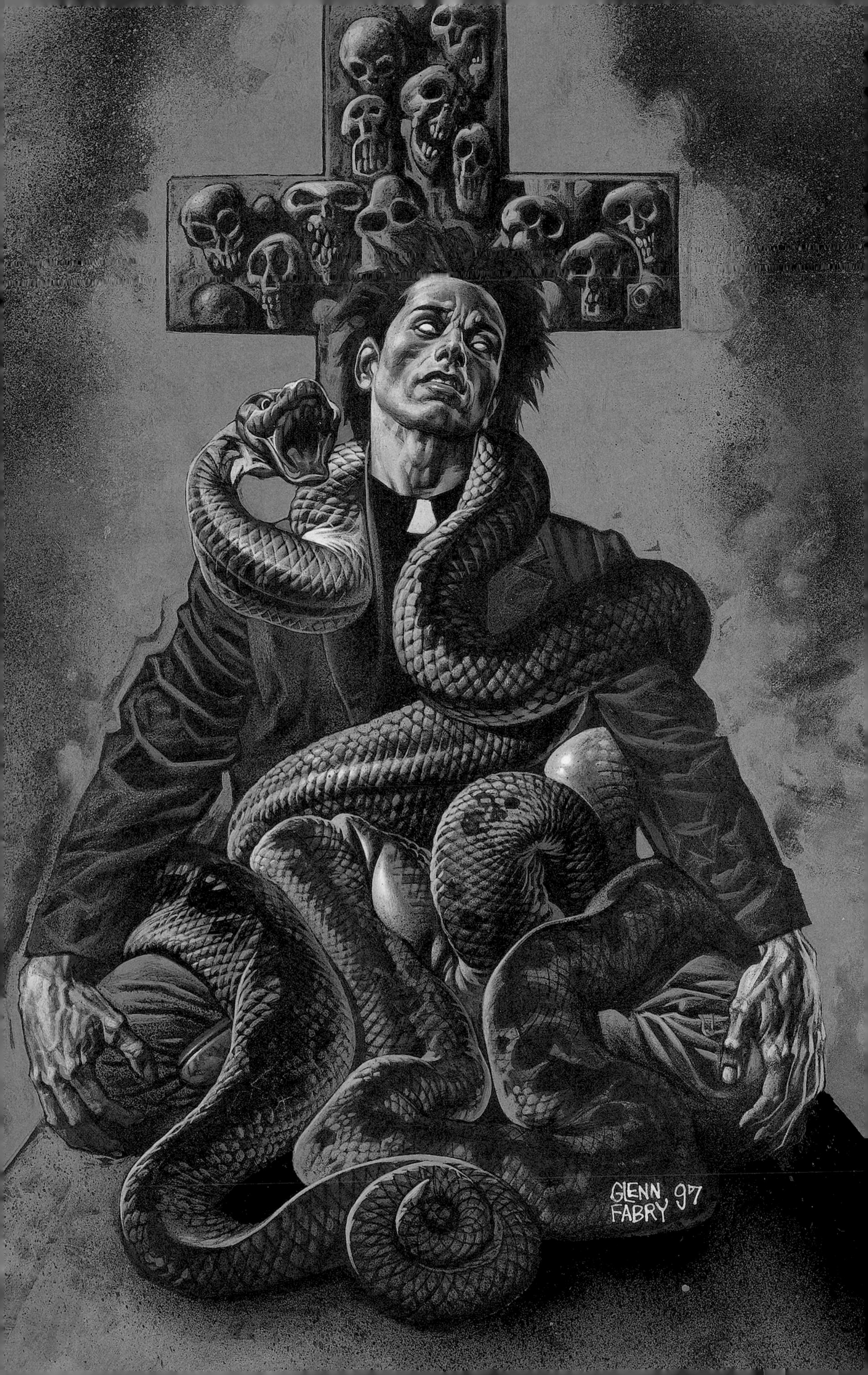
GLENN FABRY 97

"Who would have the laws of Paradise enforced
by the thunder of his guns?"

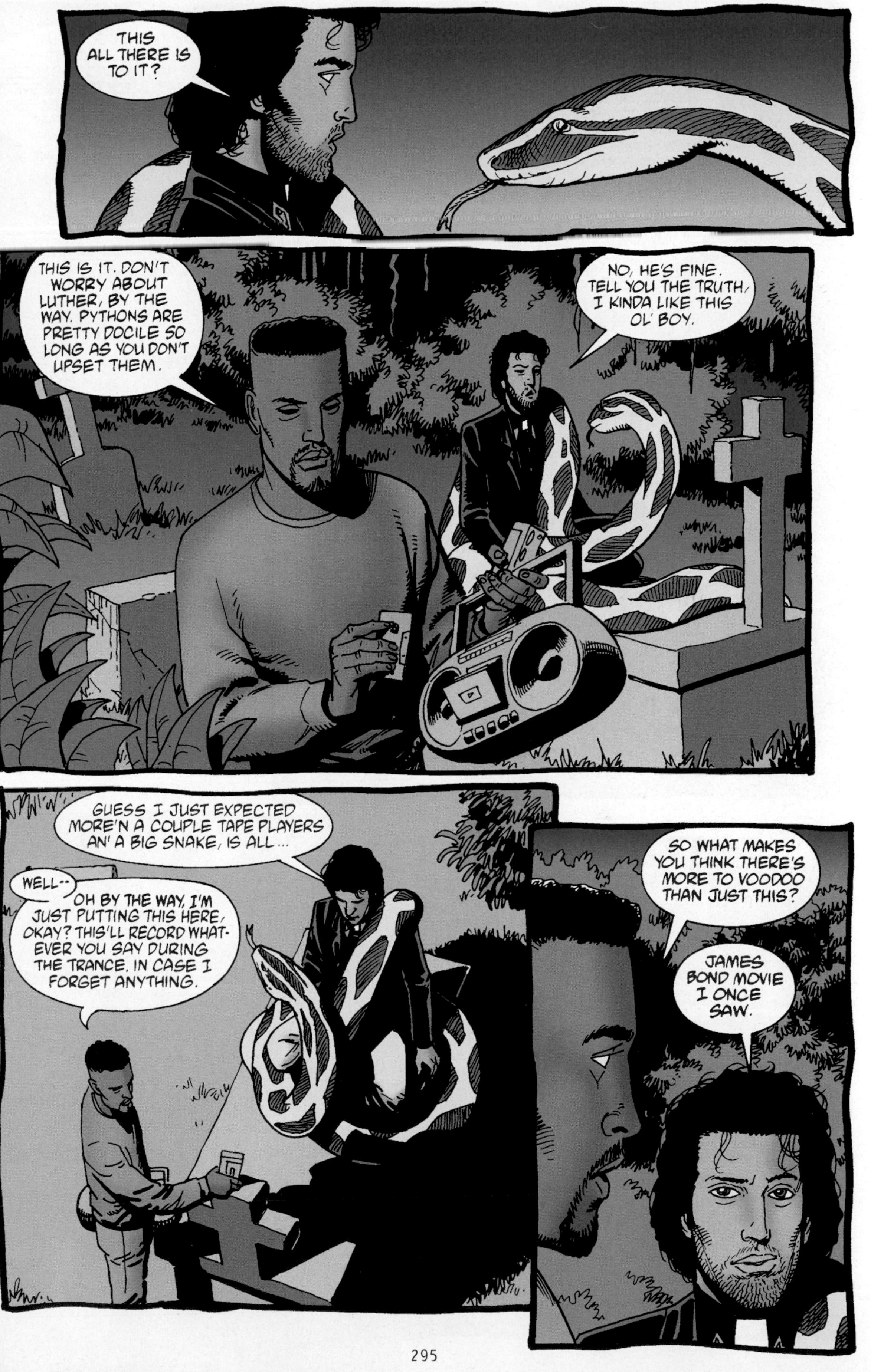

THIS ALL THERE IS TO IT?
THIS IS IT. DON'T WORRY ABOUT LUTHER, BY THE WAY. PYTHONS ARE PRETTY DOCILE SO LONG AS YOU DON'T UPSET THEM.
NO, HE'S FINE. TELL YOU THE TRUTH, I KINDA LIKE THIS OL' BOY.
GUESS I JUST EXPECTED MORE'N A COUPLE TAPE PLAYERS AN' A BIG SNAKE, IS ALL...
WELL--
OH BY THE WAY, I'M JUST PUTTING THIS HERE, OKAY? THIS'LL RECORD WHAT-EVER YOU SAY DURING THE TRANCE. IN CASE I FORGET ANYTHING.
SO WHAT MAKES YOU THINK THERE'S MORE TO VOODOO THAN JUST THIS?
JAMES BOND MOVIE I ONCE SAW.

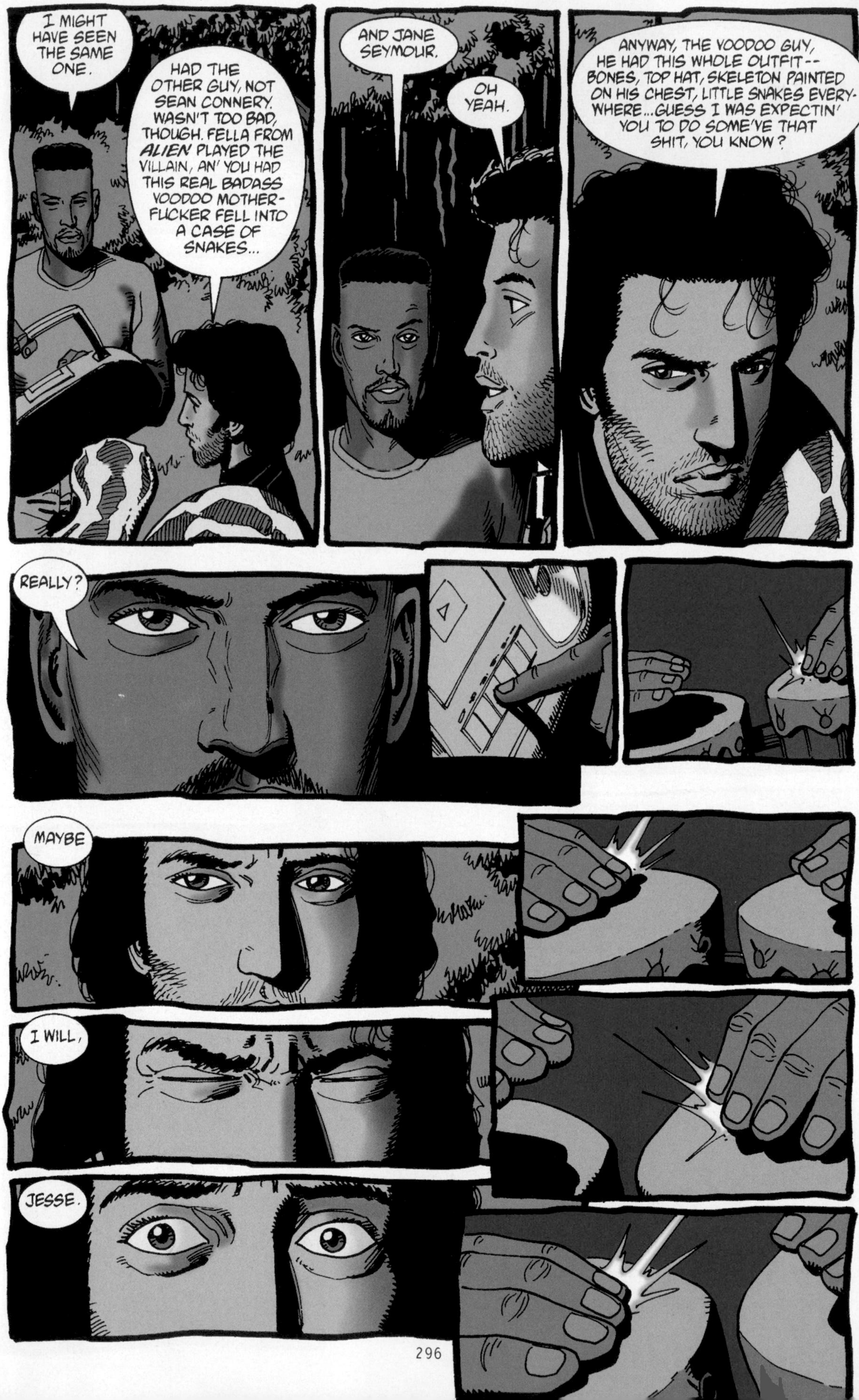
I MIGHT HAVE SEEN THE SAME ONE.
HAD THE OTHER GUY, NOT SEAN CONNERY. WASN'T TOO BAD, THOUGH. FELLA FROM *ALIEN* PLAYED THE VILLAIN, AN' YOU HAD THIS REAL BADASS VOODOO MOTHER-FUCKER FELL INTO A CASE OF SNAKES...
AND JANE SEYMOUR.
OH YEAH.
ANYWAY, THE VOODOO GUY, HE HAD THIS WHOLE OUTFIT-- BONES, TOP HAT, SKELETON PAINTED ON HIS CHEST, LITTLE SNAKES EVERY-WHERE...GUESS I WAS EXPECTIN' YOU TO DO SOME'VE THAT SHIT, YOU KNOW?
REALLY?
MAYBE
I WILL,
JESSE.

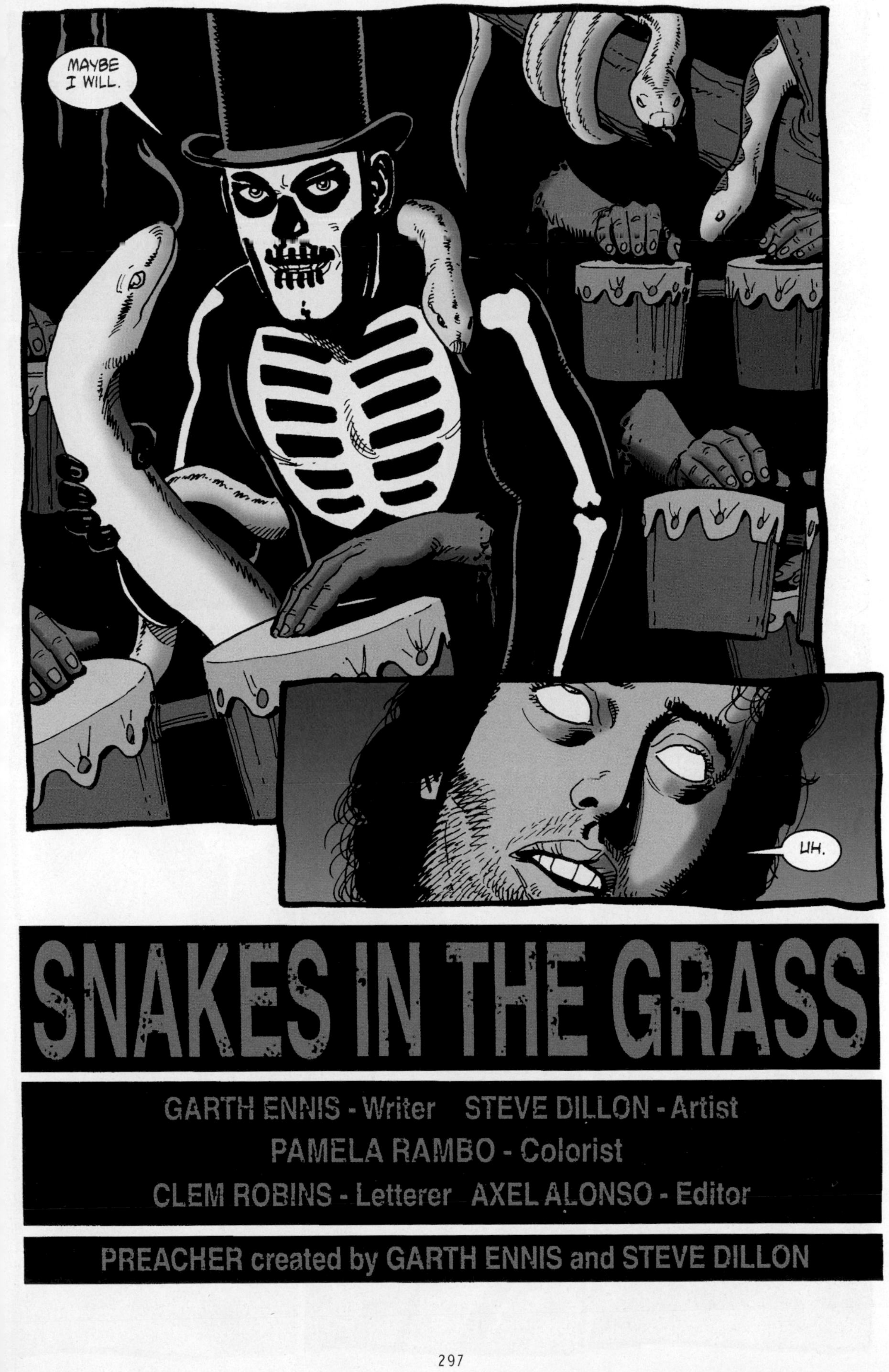

MAYBE I WILL.
UH.


# SNAKES IN THE GRASS

GARTH ENNIS - Writer STEVE DILLON - Artist
PAMELA RAMBO - Colorist
CLEM ROBINS - Letterer AXEL ALONSO - Editor

PREACHER created by GARTH ENNIS and STEVE DILLON

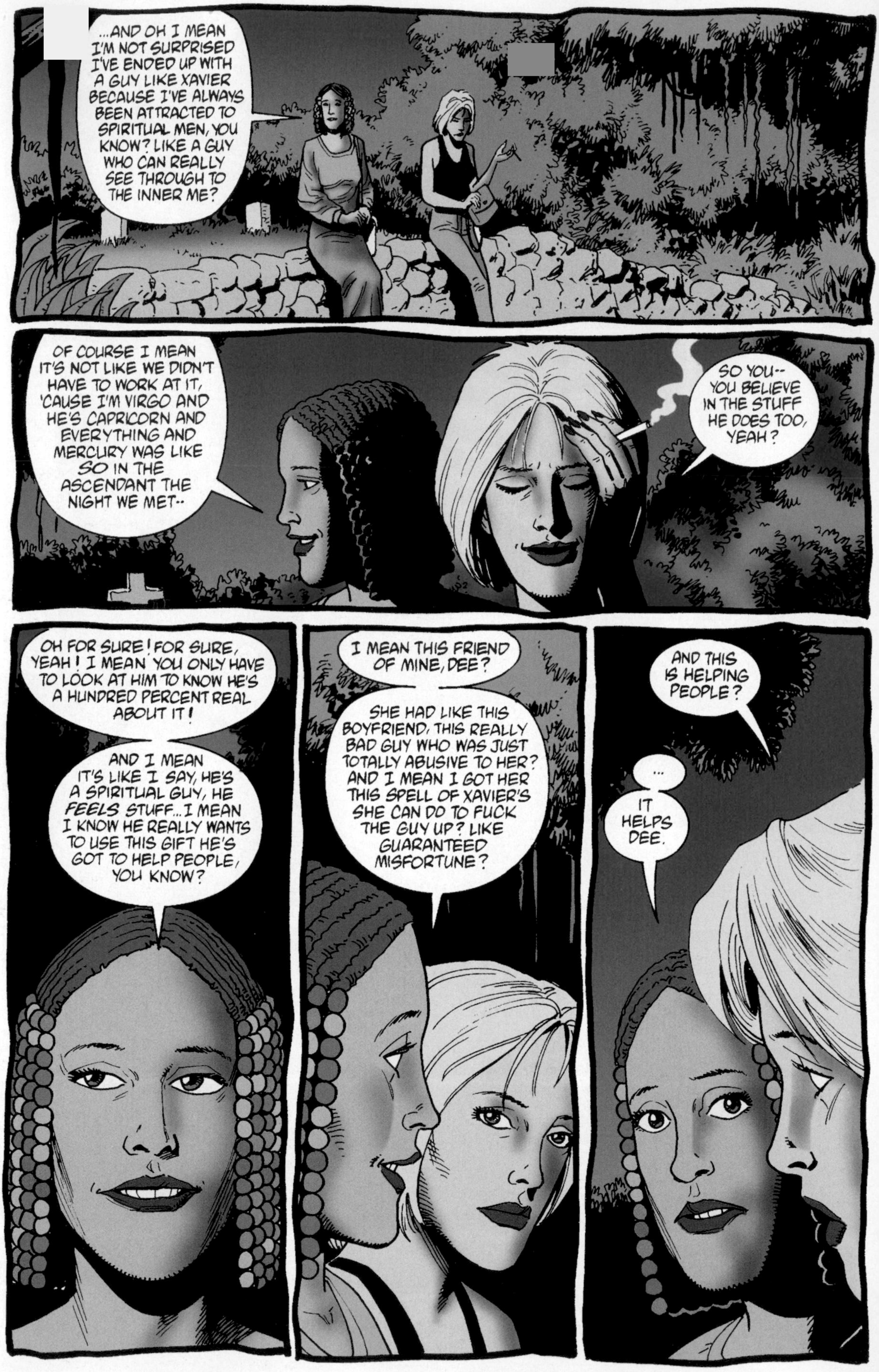
...AND OH I MEAN I'M NOT SURPRISED I'VE ENDED UP WITH A GUY LIKE XAVIER BECAUSE I'VE ALWAYS BEEN ATTRACTED TO SPIRITUAL MEN, YOU KNOW? LIKE A GUY WHO CAN REALLY SEE THROUGH TO THE INNER ME?
OF COURSE I MEAN IT'S NOT LIKE WE DIDN'T HAVE TO WORK AT IT, 'CAUSE I'M VIRGO AND HE'S CAPRICORN AND EVERYTHING AND MERCURY WAS LIKE SO IN THE ASCENDANT THE NIGHT WE MET--
SO YOU-- YOU BELIEVE IN THE STUFF HE DOES TOO, YEAH?
OH FOR SURE! FOR SURE, YEAH! I MEAN YOU ONLY HAVE TO LOOK AT HIM TO KNOW HE'S A HUNDRED PERCENT REAL ABOUT IT!
AND I MEAN IT'S LIKE I SAY, HE'S A SPIRITUAL GUY, HE FEELS STUFF... I MEAN I KNOW HE REALLY WANTS TO USE THIS GIFT HE'S GOT TO HELP PEOPLE, YOU KNOW?
I MEAN THIS FRIEND OF MINE, DEE?
SHE HAD LIKE THIS BOYFRIEND, THIS REALLY BAD GUY WHO WAS JUST TOTALLY ABUSIVE TO HER? AND I MEAN I GOT HER THIS SPELL OF XAVIER'S SHE CAN DO TO FUCK THE GUY UP? LIKE GUARANTEED MISFORTUNE?
AND THIS IS HELPING PEOPLE?
...
IT HELPS DEE.

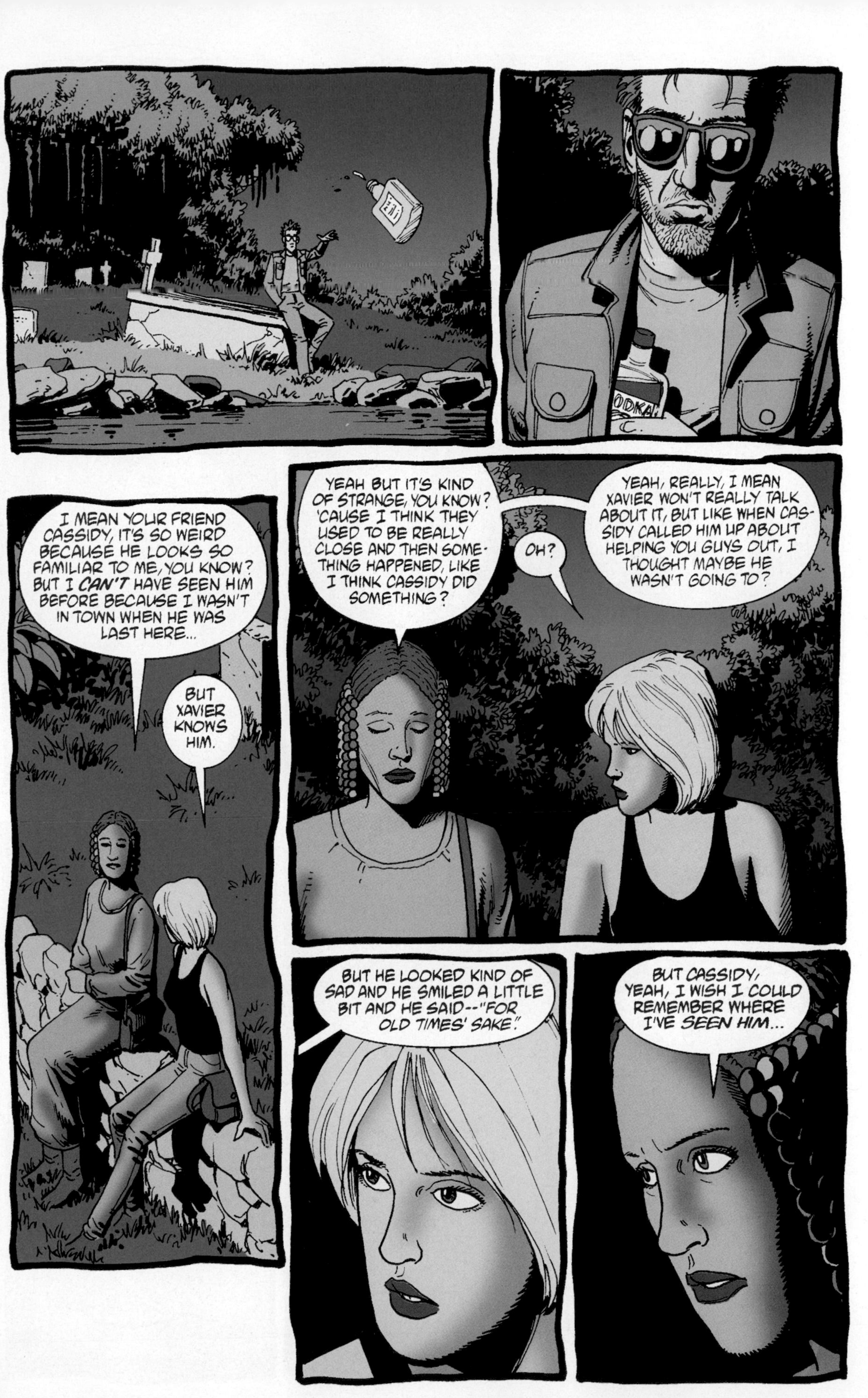

ODKA
I MEAN YOUR FRIEND CASSIDY, IT'S SO WEIRD BECAUSE HE LOOKS SO FAMILIAR TO ME, YOU KNOW? BUT I CAN'T HAVE SEEN HIM BEFORE BECAUSE I WASN'T IN TOWN WHEN HE WAS LAST HERE...
BUT XAVIER KNOWS HIM.
YEAH BUT IT'S KIND OF STRANGE, YOU KNOW? 'CAUSE I THINK THEY USED TO BE REALLY CLOSE AND THEN SOMETHING HAPPENED, LIKE I THINK CASSIDY DID SOMETHING?
OH?
YEAH, REALLY, I MEAN XAVIER WON'T REALLY TALK ABOUT IT, BUT LIKE WHEN CASSIDY CALLED HIM UP ABOUT HELPING YOU GUYS OUT, I THOUGHT MAYBE HE WASN'T GOING TO?
BUT HE LOOKED KIND OF SAD AND HE SMILED A LITTLE BIT AND HE SAID--"FOR OLD TIMES' SAKE."
BUT CASSIDY, YEAH, I WISH I COULD REMEMBER WHERE I'VE SEEN HIM...

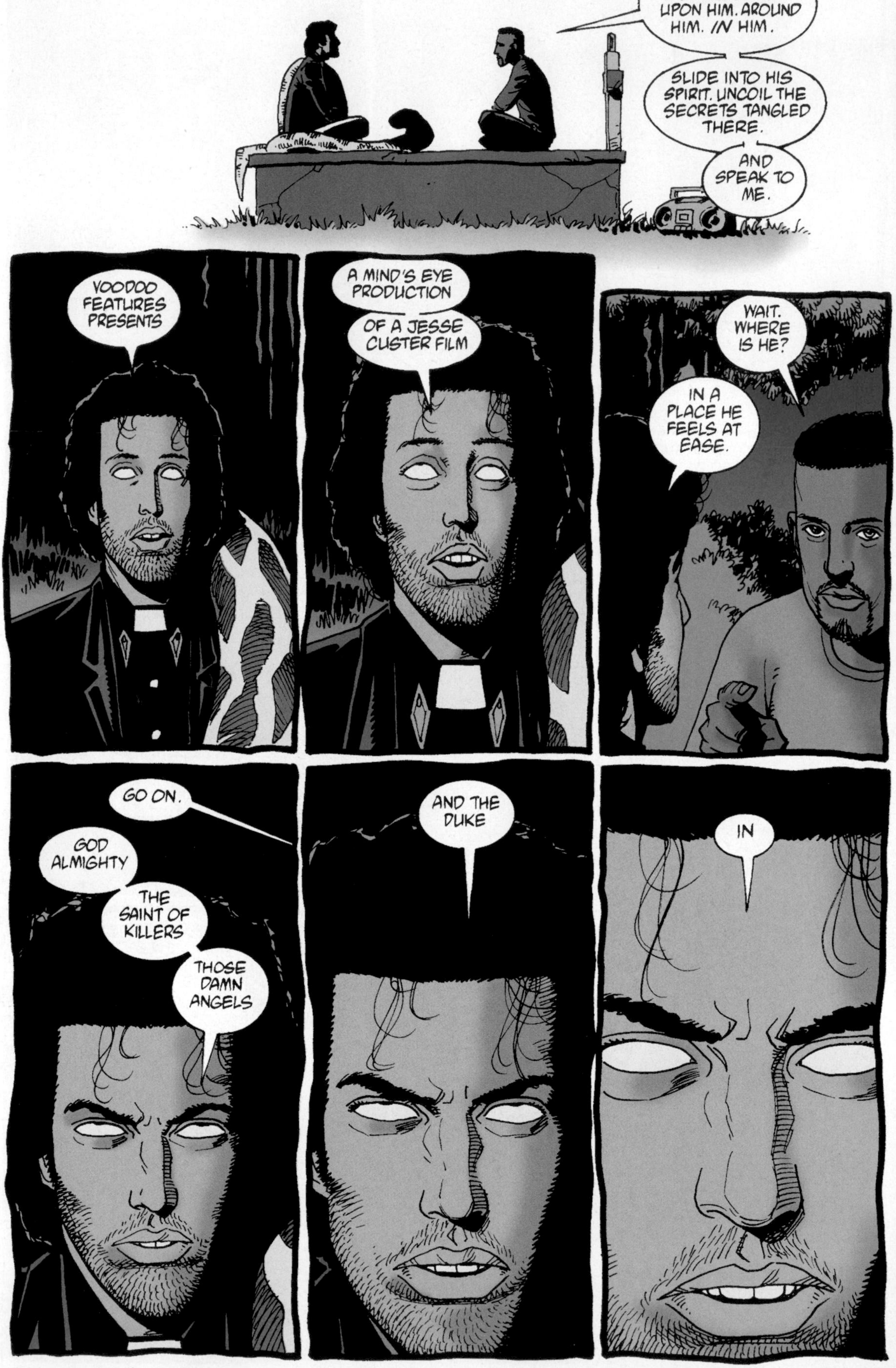
ARPE-REPOSOIR. YOU ARE ON HIM. UPON HIM. AROUND HIM. IN HIM.
SLIDE INTO HIS SPIRIT. UNCOIL THE SECRETS TANGLED THERE.
AND SPEAK TO ME.
VOODOO FEATURES PRESENTS
A MIND'S EYE PRODUCTION
OF A JESSE CUSTER FILM
WAIT. WHERE IS HE?
IN A PLACE HE FEELS AT EASE.
GO ON.
GOD ALMIGHTY
THE SAINT OF KILLERS
THOSE DAMN ANGELS
AND THE DUKE
IN

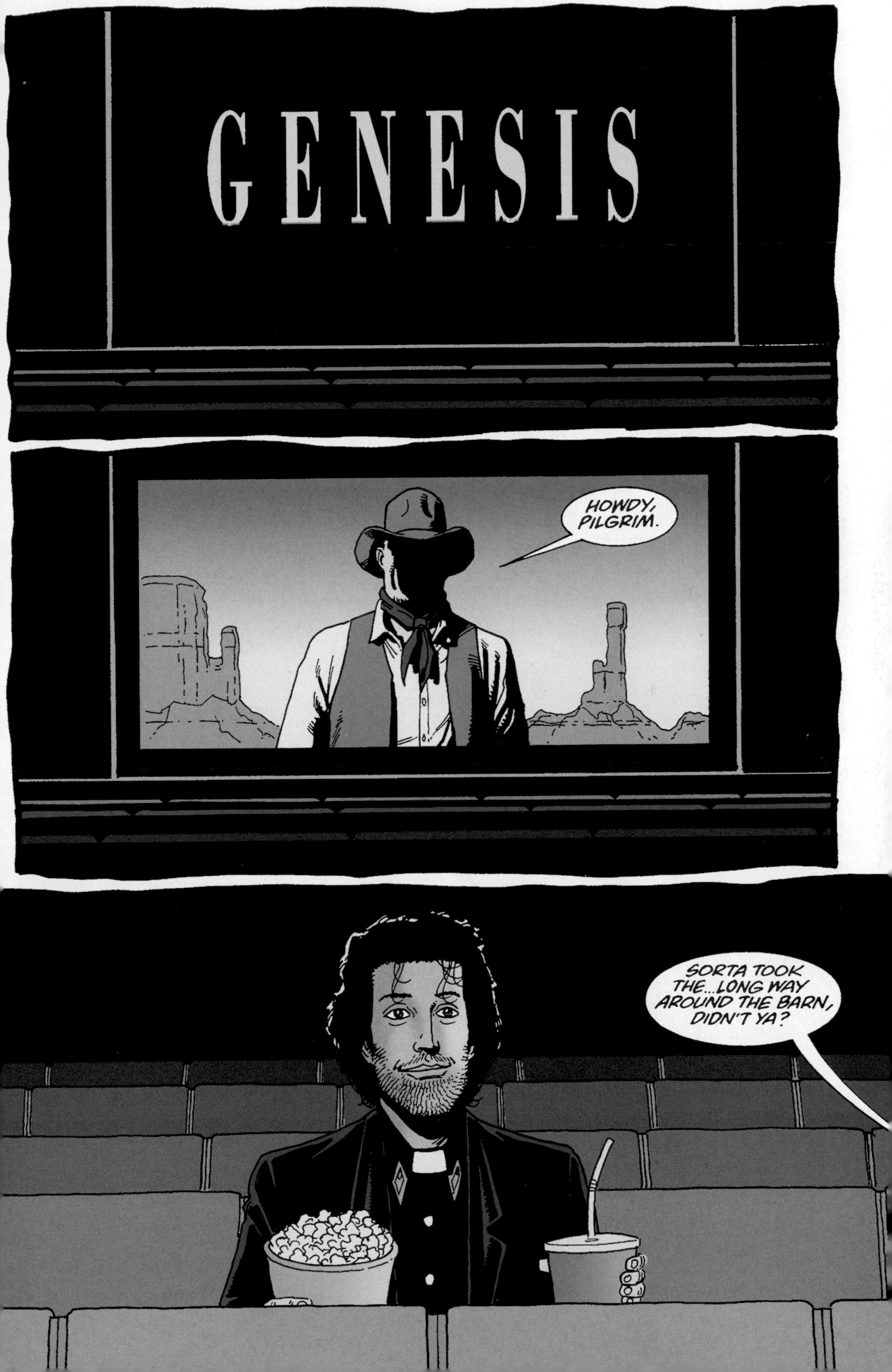
GENESIS
HOWDY, PILGRIM.
SORTA TOOK THE...LONG WAY AROUND THE BARN, DIDN'T YA?

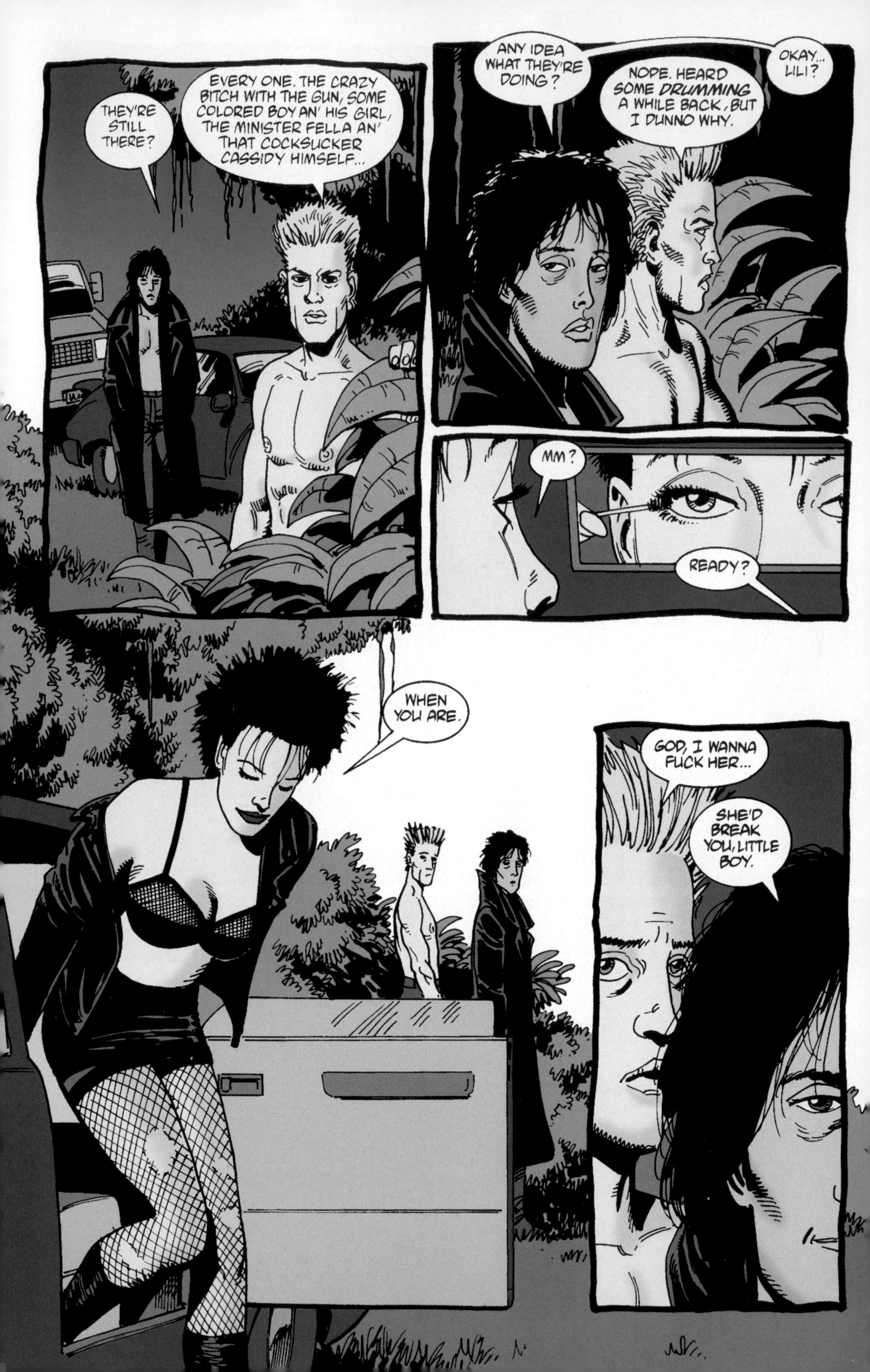
THEY'RE STILL THERE?
EVERY ONE. THE CRAZY BITCH WITH THE GUN, SOME COLORED BOY AN' HIS GIRL, THE MINISTER FELLA AN' THAT COCKSUCKER CASSIDY HIMSELF...
ANY IDEA WHAT THEY'RE DOING?
NOPE. HEARD SOME DRUMMING A WHILE BACK, BUT I DUNNO WHY.
OKAY... LILI?
MM?
READY?
WHEN YOU ARE.
GOD, I WANNA FUCK HER...
SHE'D BREAK YOU, LITTLE BOY.

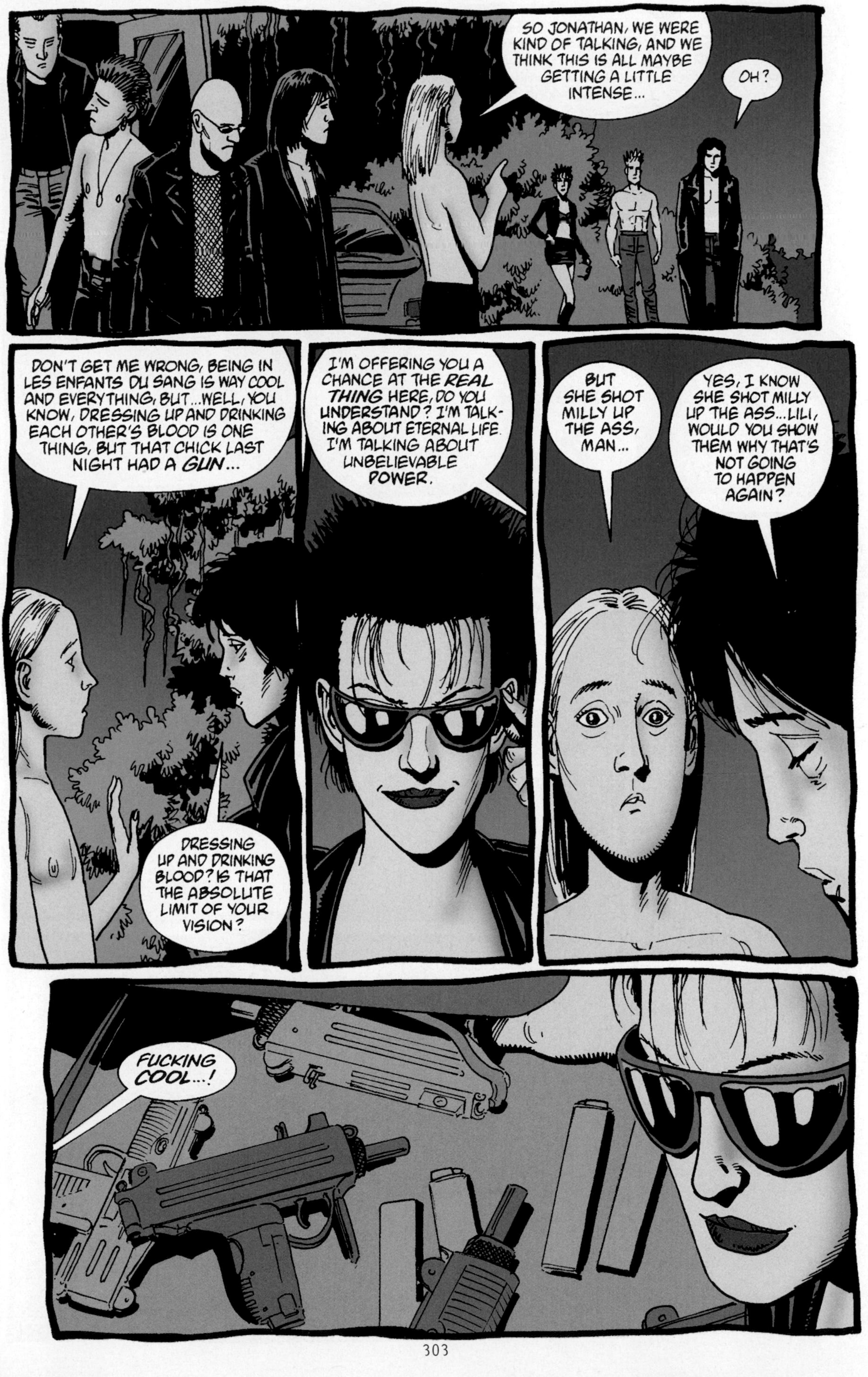
SO JONATHAN, WE WERE KIND OF TALKING, AND WE THINK THIS IS ALL MAYBE GETTING A LITTLE INTENSE...
OH?
DON'T GET ME WRONG, BEING IN LES ENFANTS DU SANG IS WAY COOL AND EVERYTHING, BUT...WELL, YOU KNOW, DRESSING UP AND DRINKING EACH OTHER'S BLOOD IS ONE THING, BUT THAT CHICK LAST NIGHT HAD A GUN...
DRESSING UP AND DRINKING BLOOD? IS THAT THE ABSOLUTE LIMIT OF YOUR VISION?
I'M OFFERING YOU A CHANCE AT THE REAL THING HERE, DO YOU UNDERSTAND? I'M TALKING ABOUT ETERNAL LIFE. I'M TALKING ABOUT UNBELIEVABLE POWER.
BUT SHE SHOT MILLY UP THE ASS, MAN...
YES, I KNOW SHE SHOT MILLY UP THE ASS...LILI, WOULD YOU SHOW THEM WHY THAT'S NOT GOING TO HAPPEN AGAIN?
FUCKING COOL...!

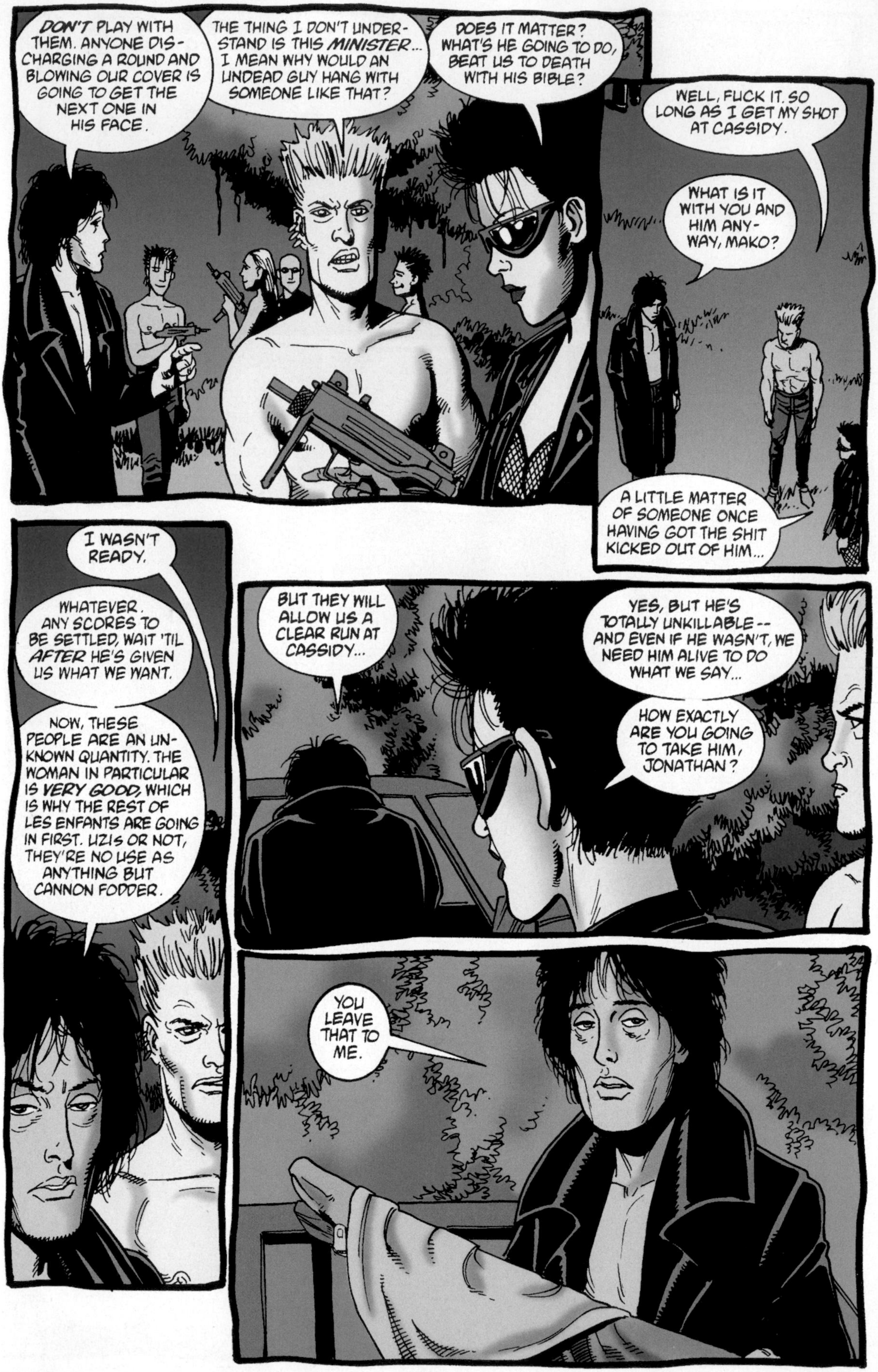
DON'T PLAY WITH THEM. ANYONE DIS-CHARGING A ROUND AND BLOWING OUR COVER IS GOING TO GET THE NEXT ONE IN HIS FACE.
THE THING I DON'T UNDER-STAND IS THIS MINISTER... I MEAN WHY WOULD AN UNDEAD GUY HANG WITH SOMEONE LIKE THAT?
DOES IT MATTER? WHAT'S HE GOING TO DO, BEAT US TO DEATH WITH HIS BIBLE?
WELL, FUCK IT. SO LONG AS I GET MY SHOT AT CASSIDY.
WHAT IS IT WITH YOU AND HIM ANY-WAY, MAKO?
A LITTLE MATTER OF SOMEONE ONCE HAVING GOT THE SHIT KICKED OUT OF HIM...
I WASN'T READY.
WHATEVER. ANY SCORES TO BE SETTLED, WAIT 'TIL AFTER HE'S GIVEN US WHAT WE WANT.
NOW, THESE PEOPLE ARE AN UN-KNOWN QUANTITY. THE WOMAN IN PARTICULAR IS VERY GOOD, WHICH IS WHY THE REST OF LES ENFANTS ARE GOING IN FIRST. UZIS OR NOT, THEY'RE NO USE AS ANYTHING BUT CANNON FODDER.
BUT THEY WILL ALLOW US A CLEAR RUN AT CASSIDY...
YES, BUT HE'S TOTALLY UNKILLABLE -- AND EVEN IF HE WASN'T, WE NEED HIM ALIVE TO DO WHAT WE SAY...
HOW EXACTLY ARE YOU GOING TO TAKE HIM, JONATHAN?
YOU LEAVE THAT TO ME.

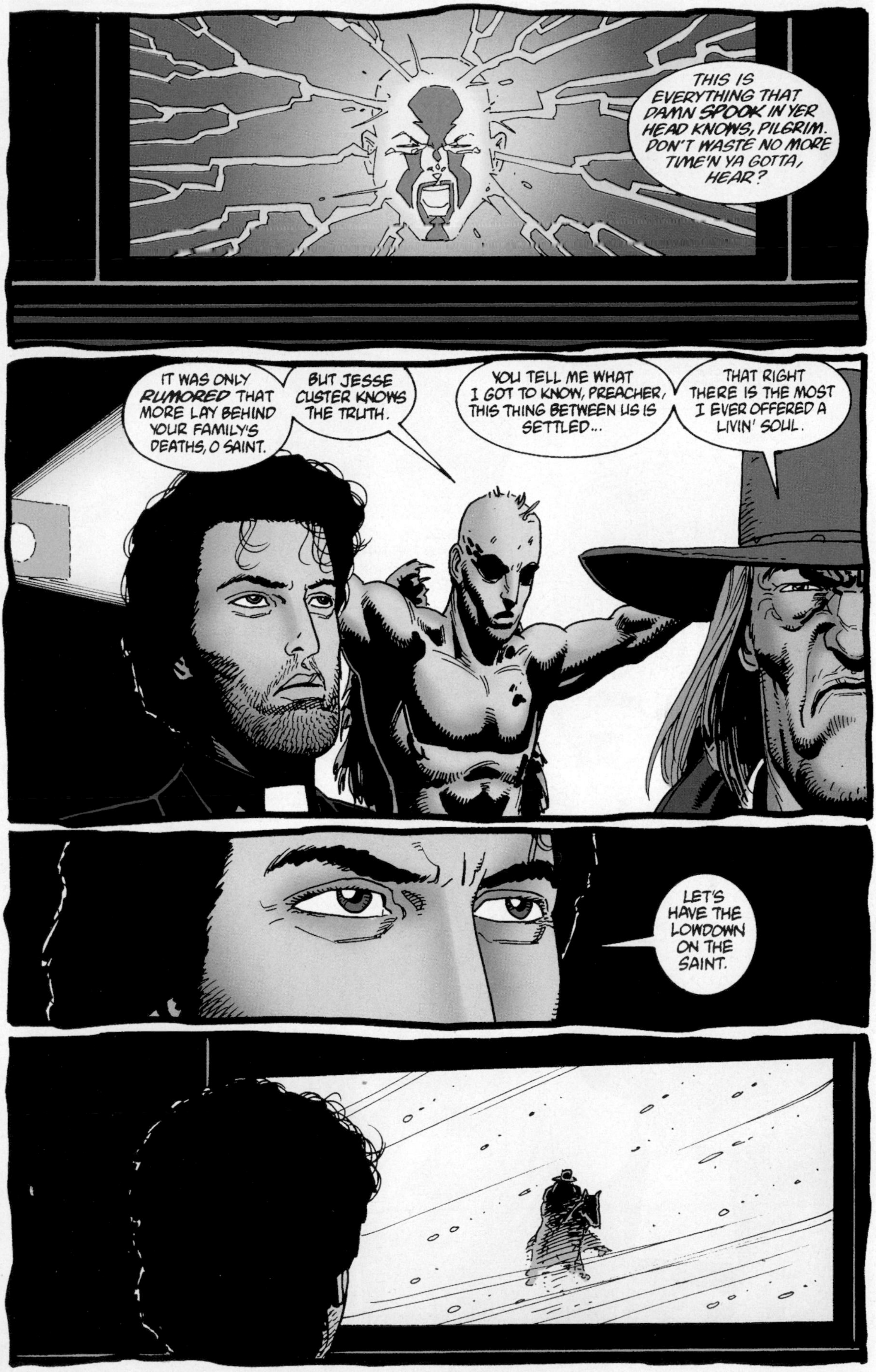
THIS IS EVERYTHING THAT DAMN SPOOK IN YER HEAD KNOWS, PILGRIM. DON'T WASTE NO MORE TIME'N YA GOTTA, HEAR?
IT WAS ONLY RUMORED THAT MORE LAY BEHIND YOUR FAMILY'S DEATHS, O SAINT.
BUT JESSE CUSTER KNOWS THE TRUTH.
YOU TELL ME WHAT I GOT TO KNOW, PREACHER, THIS THING BETWEEN US IS SETTLED...
THAT RIGHT THERE IS THE MOST I EVER OFFERED A LIVIN' SOUL.
LET'S HAVE THE LOWDOWN ON THE SAINT.

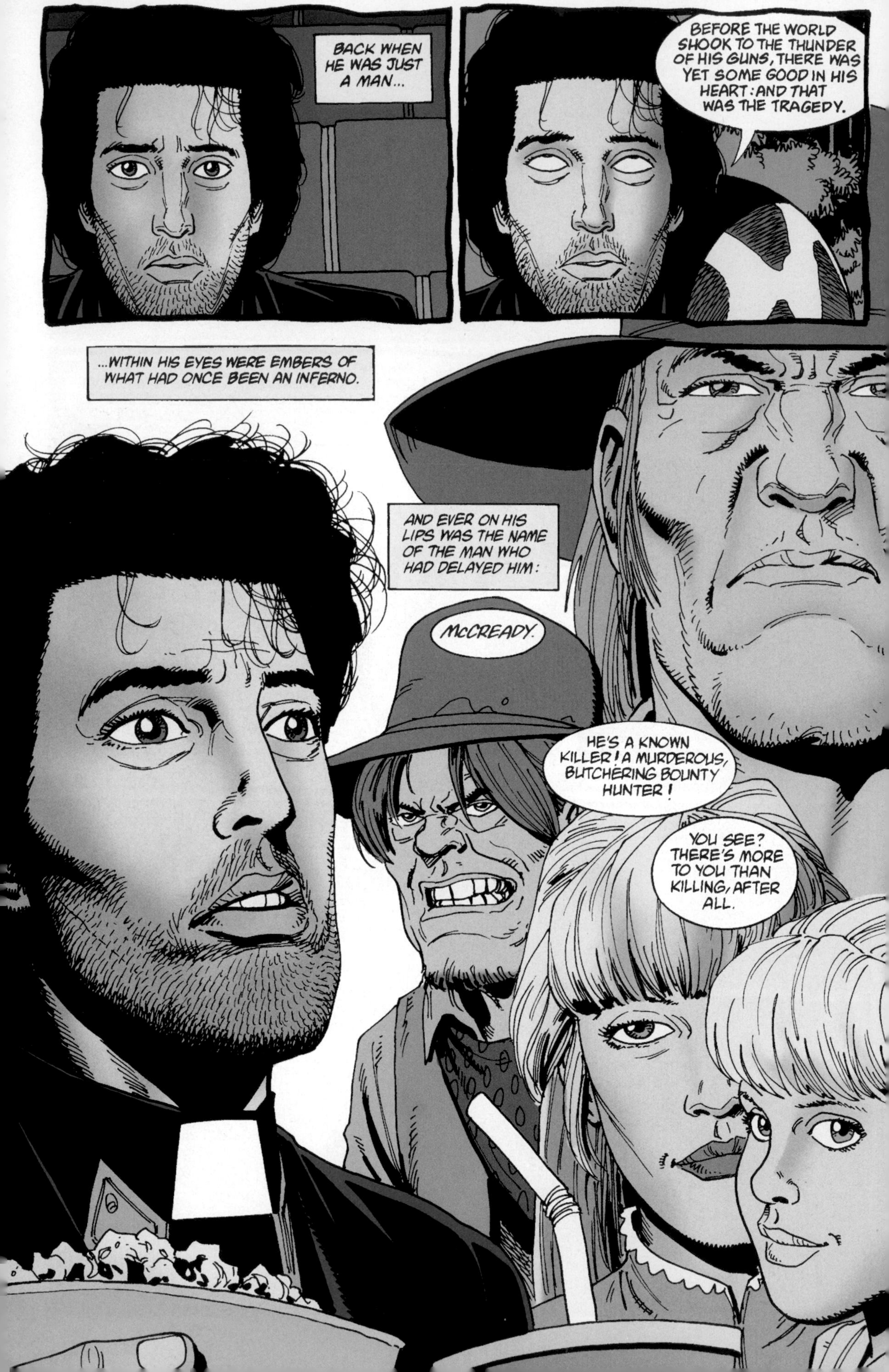
BACK WHEN HE WAS JUST A MAN...
BEFORE THE WORLD SHOOK TO THE THUNDER OF HIS GUNS, THERE WAS YET SOME GOOD IN HIS HEART: AND THAT WAS THE TRAGEDY.
...WITHIN HIS EYES WERE EMBERS OF WHAT HAD ONCE BEEN AN INFERNO.
AND EVER ON HIS LIPS WAS THE NAME OF THE MAN WHO HAD DELAYED HIM:
McCREADY.
HE'S A KNOWN KILLER! A MURDEROUS, BUTCHERING BOUNTY HUNTER!
YOU SEE? THERE'S MORE TO YOU THAN KILLING, AFTER ALL.

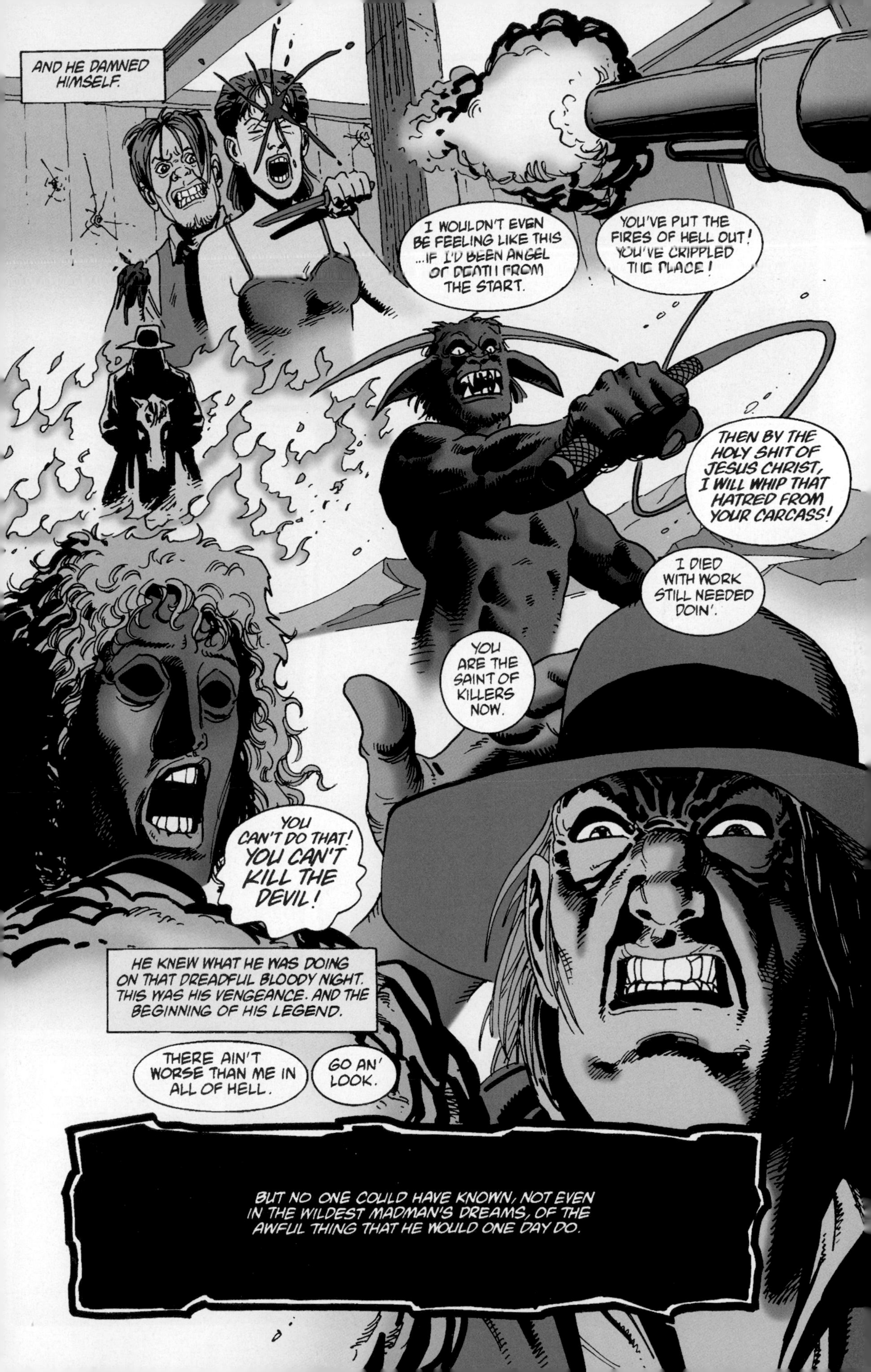

AND HE DAMNED HIMSELF.
I WOULDN'T EVEN BE FEELING LIKE THIS ...IF I'D BEEN ANGEL OF DEATH FROM THE START.
YOU'VE PUT THE FIRES OF HELL OUT! YOU'VE CRIPPLED THE PLACE!
THEN BY THE HOLY SHIT OF JESUS CHRIST, I WILL WHIP THAT HATRED FROM YOUR CARCASS!
I DIED WITH WORK STILL NEEDED DOIN'.
YOU ARE THE SAINT OF KILLERS NOW.
YOU CAN'T DO THAT! YOU CAN'T KILL THE DEVIL!
HE KNEW WHAT HE WAS DOING ON THAT DREADFUL BLOODY NIGHT. THIS WAS HIS VENGEANCE. AND THE BEGINNING OF HIS LEGEND.
THERE AIN'T WORSE THAN ME IN ALL OF HELL.
GO AN' LOOK.
BUT NO ONE COULD HAVE KNOWN, NOT EVEN IN THE WILDEST MADMAN'S DREAMS, OF THE AWFUL THING THAT HE WOULD ONE DAY DO.

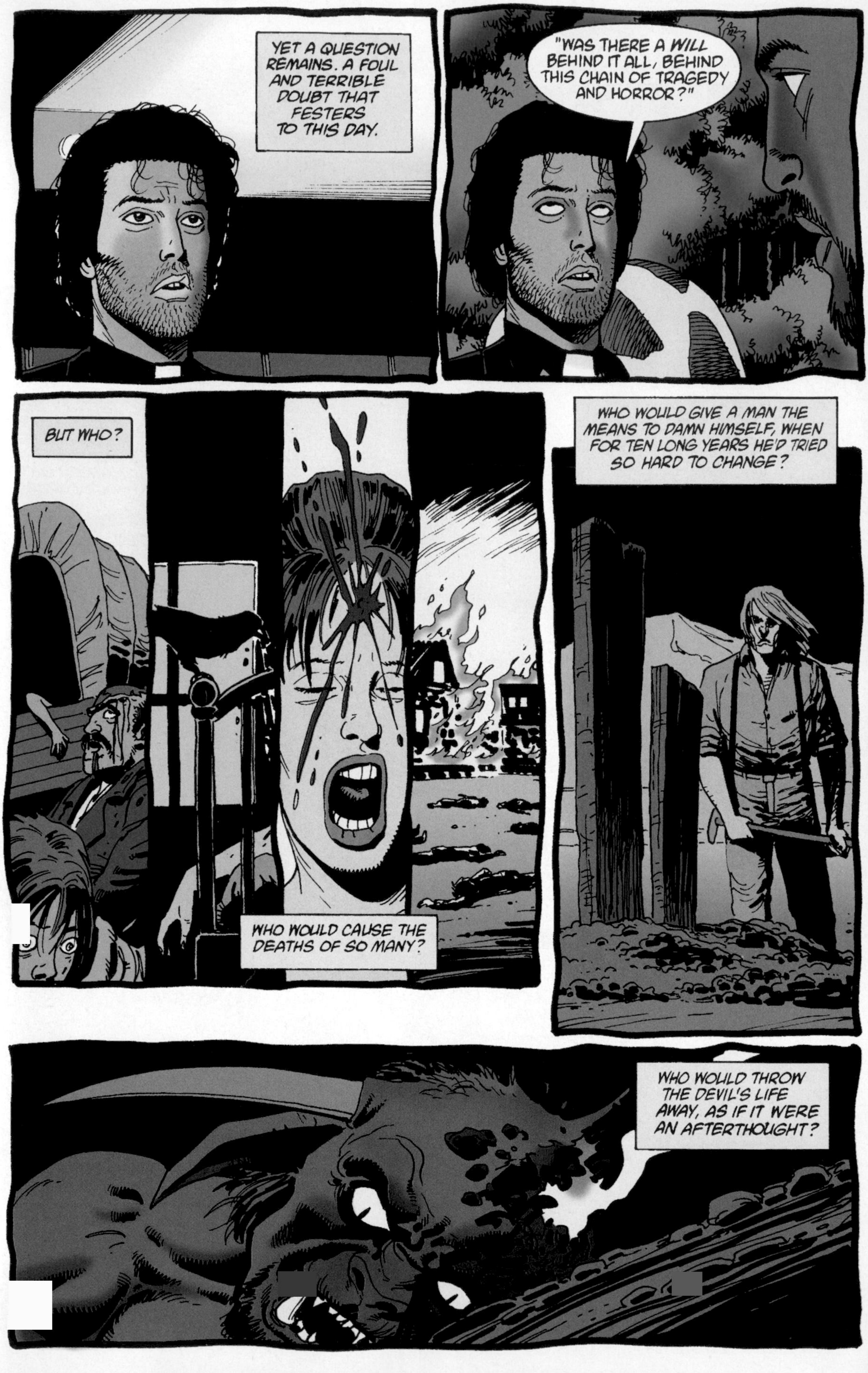
YET A QUESTION REMAINS. A FOUL AND TERRIBLE DOUBT THAT FESTERS TO THIS DAY.
"WAS THERE A WILL BEHIND IT ALL, BEHIND THIS CHAIN OF TRAGEDY AND HORROR?"
BUT WHO?
WHO WOULD CAUSE THE DEATHS OF SO MANY?
WHO WOULD GIVE A MAN THE MEANS TO DAMN HIMSELF, WHEN FOR TEN LONG YEARS HE'D TRIED SO HARD TO CHANGE?
WHO WOULD THROW THE DEVIL'S LIFE AWAY, AS IF IT WERE AN AFTERTHOUGHT?

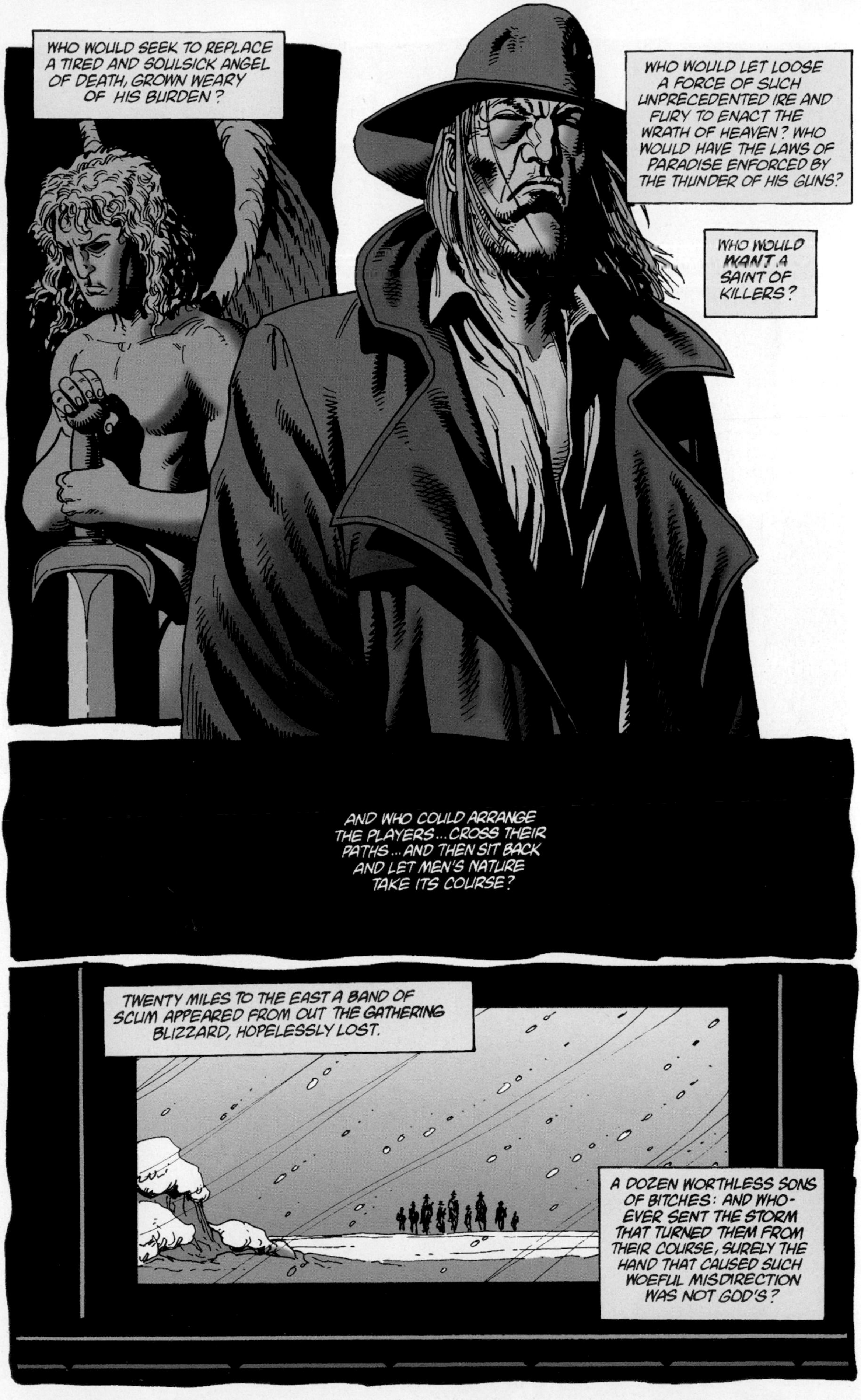
WHO WOULD SEEK TO REPLACE A TIRED AND SOULSICK ANGEL OF DEATH, GROWN WEARY OF HIS BURDEN?
WHO WOULD LET LOOSE A FORCE OF SUCH UNPRECEDENTED IRE AND FURY TO ENACT THE WRATH OF HEAVEN? WHO WOULD HAVE THE LAWS OF PARADISE ENFORCED BY THE THUNDER OF HIS GUNS?
WHO WOULD WANT A SAINT OF KILLERS?
AND WHO COULD ARRANGE THE PLAYERS... CROSS THEIR PATHS... AND THEN SIT BACK AND LET MEN'S NATURE TAKE ITS COURSE?
TWENTY MILES TO THE EAST A BAND OF SCUM APPEARED FROM OUT THE GATHERING BLIZZARD, HOPELESSLY LOST.
A DOZEN WORTHLESS SONS OF BITCHES: AND WHO-EVER SENT THE STORM THAT TURNED THEM FROM THEIR COURSE, SURELY THE HAND THAT CAUSED SUCH WOEFUL MISDIRECTION WAS NOT GOD'S?

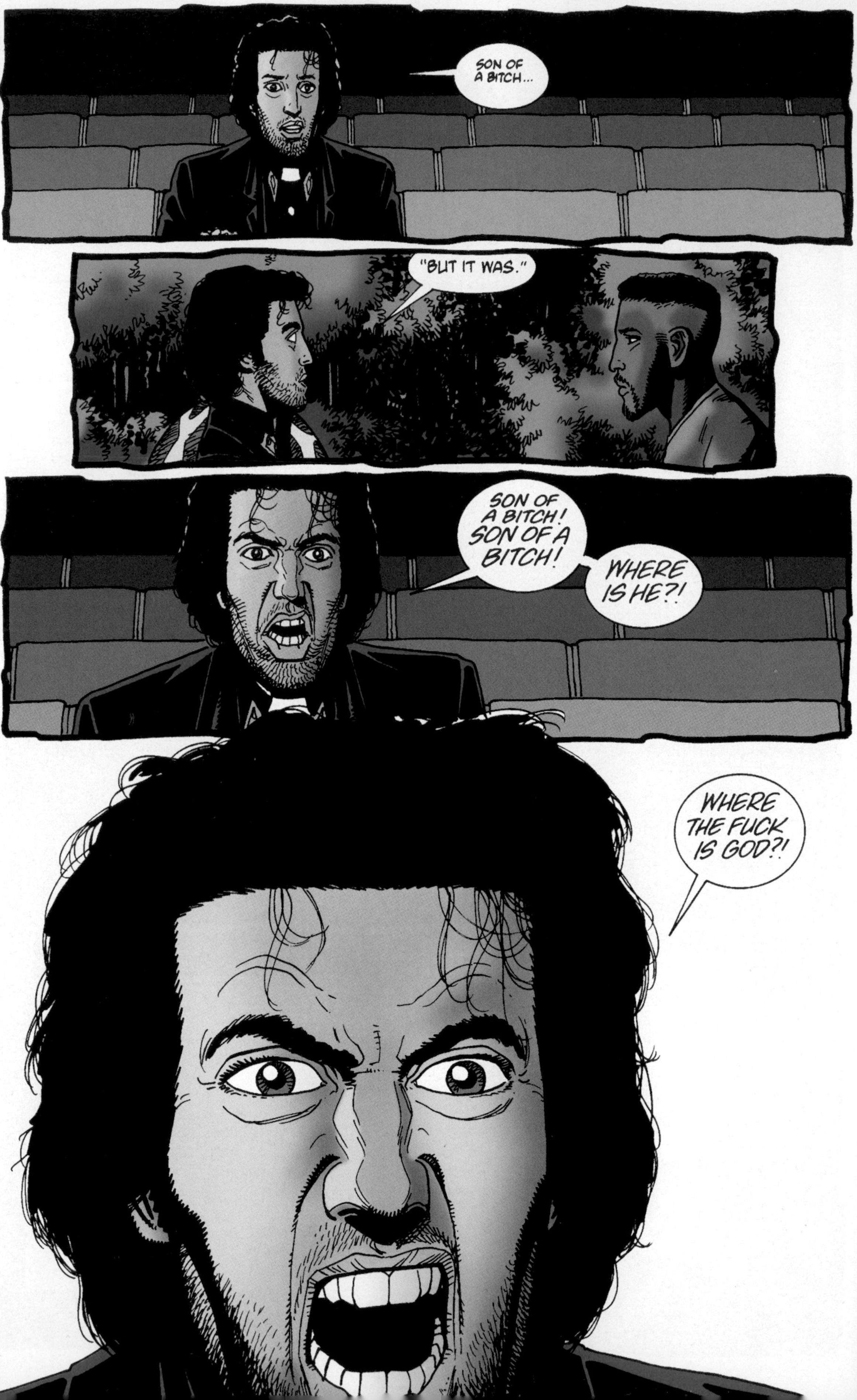
SON OF A BITCH...
"BUT IT WAS."
SON OF A BITCH! SON OF A BITCH!
WHERE IS HE?!
WHERE THE FUCK IS GOD?!

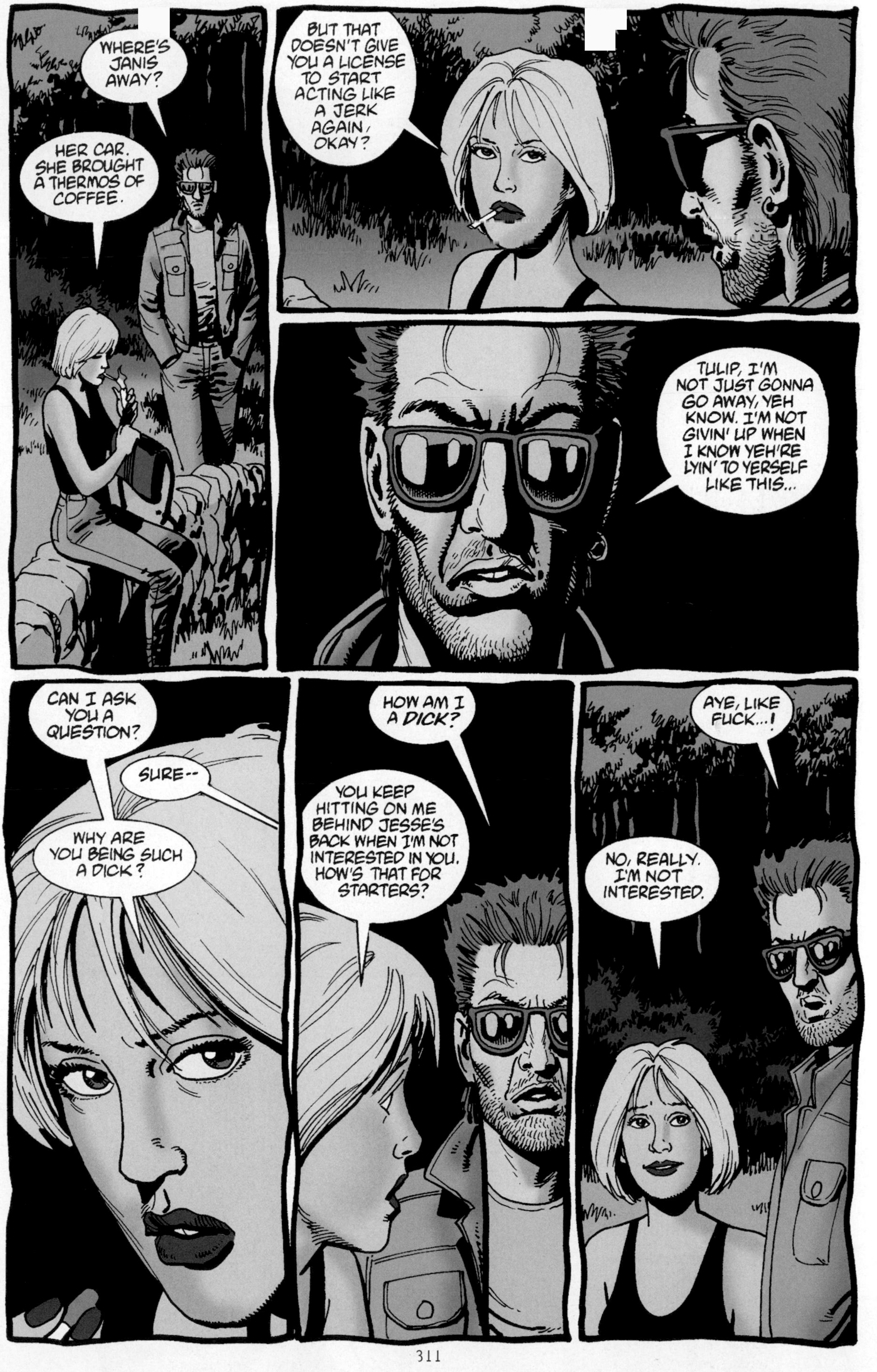
WHERE'S JANIS AWAY?
HER CAR. SHE BROUGHT A THERMOS OF COFFEE.
BUT THAT DOESN'T GIVE YOU A LICENSE TO START ACTING LIKE A JERK AGAIN, OKAY?
TULIP, I'M NOT JUST GONNA GO AWAY, YEH KNOW. I'M NOT GIVIN' UP WHEN I KNOW YEH'RE LYIN' TO YERSELF LIKE THIS...
CAN I ASK YOU A QUESTION?
SURE--
WHY ARE YOU BEING SUCH A DICK?
HOW AM I A DICK?
YOU KEEP HITTING ON ME BEHIND JESSE'S BACK WHEN I'M NOT INTERESTED IN YOU. HOW'S THAT FOR STARTERS?
AYE, LIKE FUCK...!
NO, REALLY. I'M NOT INTERESTED.

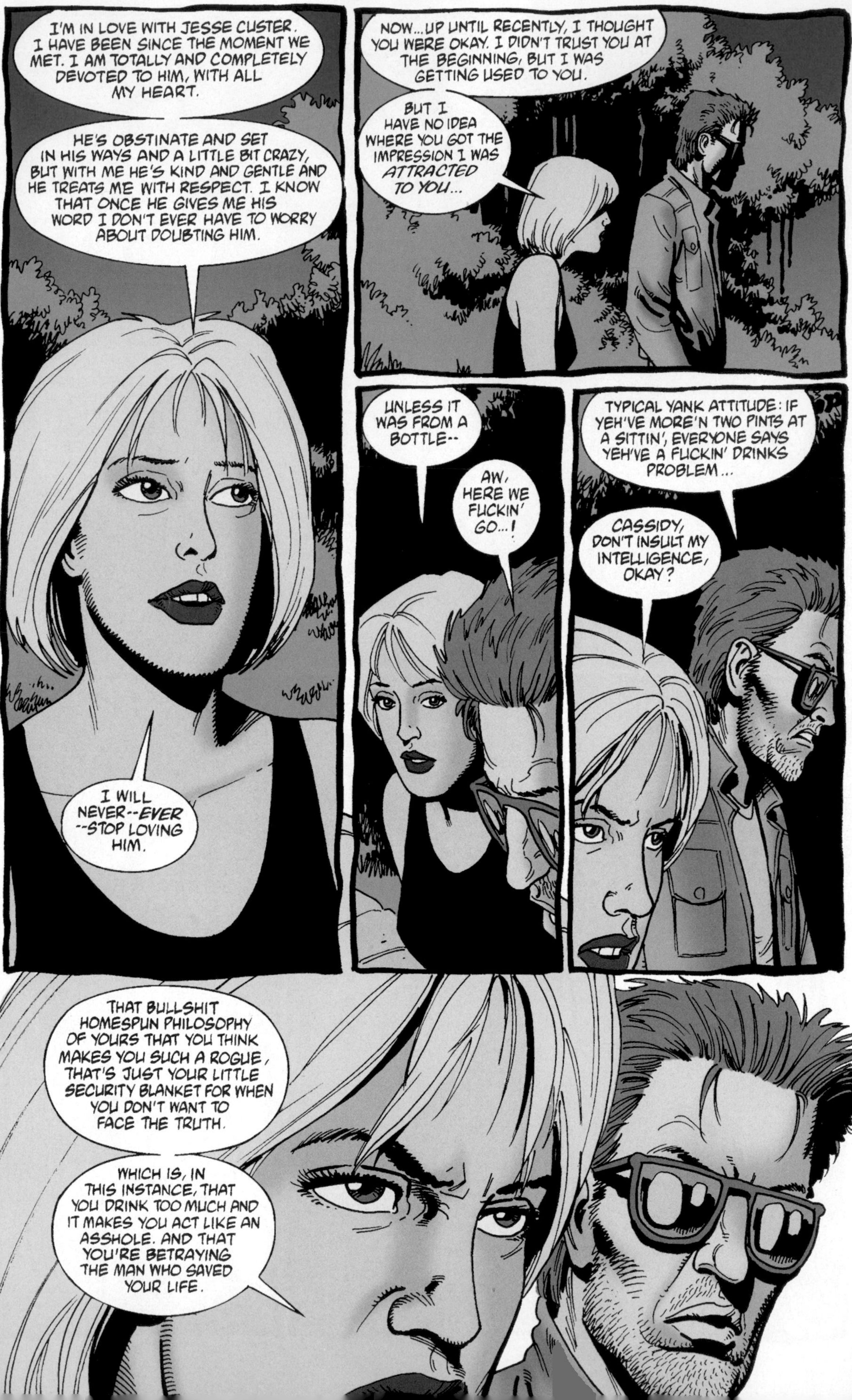

I'M IN LOVE WITH JESSE CUSTER. I HAVE BEEN SINCE THE MOMENT WE MET. I AM TOTALLY AND COMPLETELY DEVOTED TO HIM, WITH ALL MY HEART.
HE'S OBSTINATE AND SET IN HIS WAYS AND A LITTLE BIT CRAZY, BUT WITH ME HE'S KIND AND GENTLE AND HE TREATS ME WITH RESPECT. I KNOW THAT ONCE HE GIVES ME HIS WORD I DON'T EVER HAVE TO WORRY ABOUT DOUBTING HIM.
I WILL NEVER--*EVER*--STOP LOVING HIM.
NOW...UP UNTIL RECENTLY, I THOUGHT YOU WERE OKAY. I DIDN'T TRUST YOU AT THE BEGINNING, BUT I WAS GETTING USED TO YOU.
BUT I HAVE NO IDEA WHERE YOU GOT THE IMPRESSION I WAS *ATTRACTED TO YOU*...
UNLESS IT WAS FROM A BOTTLE--
AW, HERE WE FUCKIN' GO...!
TYPICAL YANK ATTITUDE: IF YEH'VE MORE'N TWO PINTS AT A SITTIN', EVERYONE SAYS YEH'VE A FUCKIN' DRINKS PROBLEM...
CASSIDY, DON'T INSULT MY INTELLIGENCE, OKAY?
THAT BULLSHIT HOMESPUN PHILOSOPHY OF YOURS THAT YOU THINK MAKES YOU SUCH A ROGUE, THAT'S JUST YOUR LITTLE SECURITY BLANKET FOR WHEN YOU DON'T WANT TO FACE THE TRUTH.
WHICH IS, IN THIS INSTANCE, THAT YOU DRINK TOO MUCH AND IT MAKES YOU ACT LIKE AN ASSHOLE. AND THAT YOU'RE BETRAYING THE MAN WHO SAVED YOUR LIFE.

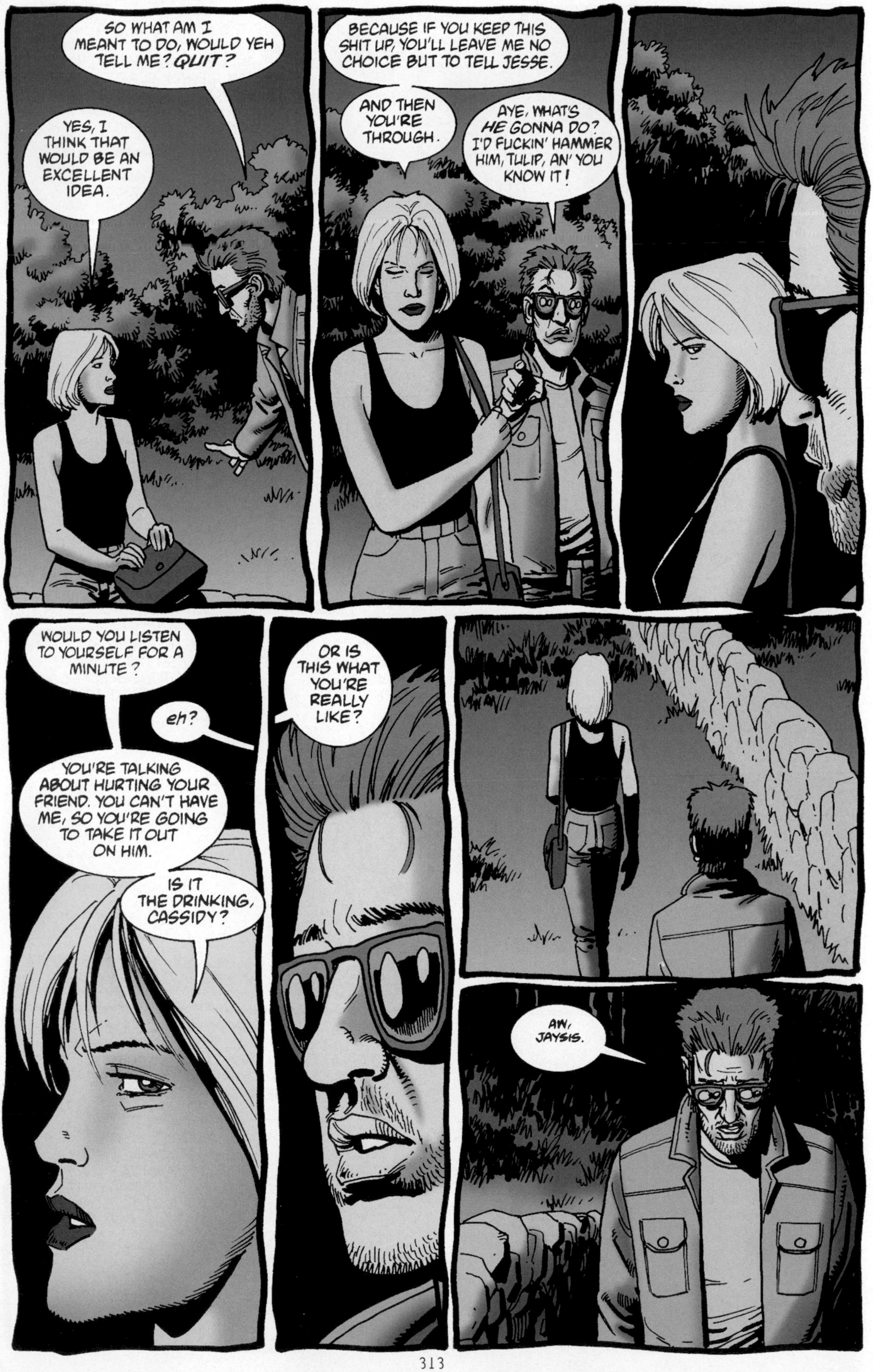

SO WHAT AM I MEANT TO DO, WOULD YEH TELL ME? QUIT?
YES, I THINK THAT WOULD BE AN EXCELLENT IDEA.
BECAUSE IF YOU KEEP THIS SHIT UP, YOU'LL LEAVE ME NO CHOICE BUT TO TELL JESSE.
AND THEN YOU'RE THROUGH.
AYE, WHAT'S HE GONNA DO? I'D FUCKIN' HAMMER HIM, TULIP, AN' YOU KNOW IT!
WOULD YOU LISTEN TO YOURSELF FOR A MINUTE?
eh?
YOU'RE TALKING ABOUT HURTING YOUR FRIEND. YOU CAN'T HAVE ME, SO YOU'RE GOING TO TAKE IT OUT ON HIM.
IS IT THE DRINKING, CASSIDY?
OR IS THIS WHAT YOU'RE REALLY LIKE?
AW, JAYSIS.

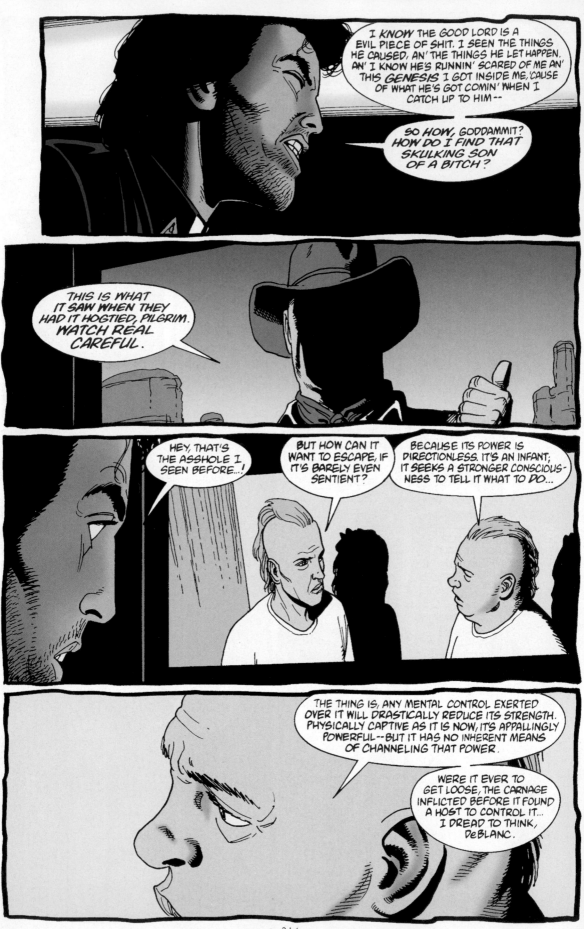

I *KNOW* THE GOOD LORD IS A EVIL PIECE OF SHIT. I SEEN THE THINGS HE CAUSED, AN' THE THINGS HE LET HAPPEN. AN' I KNOW HE'S RUNNIN' SCARED OF ME AN' THIS *GENESIS* I GOT INSIDE ME, 'CAUSE OF WHAT HE'S GOT COMIN' WHEN I CATCH UP TO HIM--

SO *HOW,* GODDAMMIT? HOW DO I FIND THAT SKULKING SON OF A BITCH?

THIS IS WHAT IT SAW WHEN THEY HAD IT HOGTIED, PILGRIM. *WATCH REAL CAREFUL.*

HEY, THAT'S THE ASSHOLE I SEEN BEFORE...!

BUT HOW CAN IT WANT TO ESCAPE, IF IT'S BARELY EVEN SENTIENT?

BECAUSE ITS POWER IS DIRECTIONLESS. IT'S AN INFANT; IT SEEKS A STRONGER CONSCIOUSNESS TO TELL IT WHAT TO *DO....*

THE THING IS, ANY MENTAL CONTROL EXERTED OVER IT WILL DRASTICALLY REDUCE ITS STRENGTH. PHYSICALLY CAPTIVE AS IT IS NOW, IT'S APPALLINGLY POWERFUL--BUT IT HAS NO INHERENT MEANS OF CHANNELING THAT POWER.

WERE IT EVER TO GET LOOSE, THE CARNAGE INFLICTED BEFORE IT FOUND A HOST TO CONTROL IT... I DREAD TO THINK, DeBLANC.

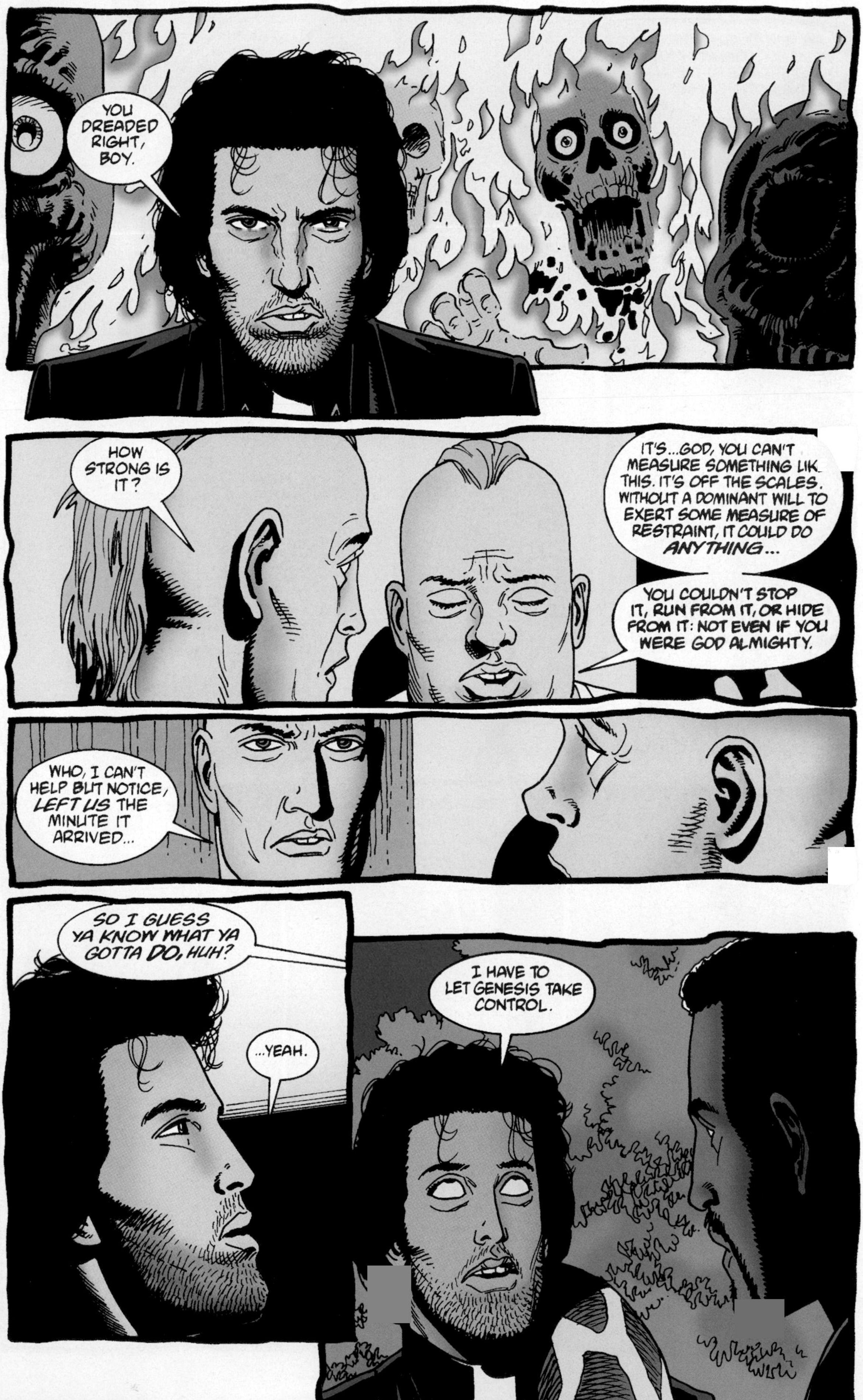
YOU DREADED RIGHT, BOY.
HOW STRONG IS IT?
IT'S...GOD, YOU CAN'T MEASURE SOMETHING LIK THIS. IT'S OFF THE SCALES. WITHOUT A DOMINANT WILL TO EXERT SOME MEASURE OF RESTRAINT, IT COULD DO ANYTHING...
YOU COULDN'T STOP IT, RUN FROM IT, OR HIDE FROM IT: NOT EVEN IF YOU WERE GOD ALMIGHTY.
WHO, I CAN'T HELP BUT NOTICE, LEFT US THE MINUTE IT ARRIVED...
SO I GUESS YA KNOW WHAT YA GOTTA DO, HUH?
...YEAH.
I HAVE TO LET GENESIS TAKE CONTROL.

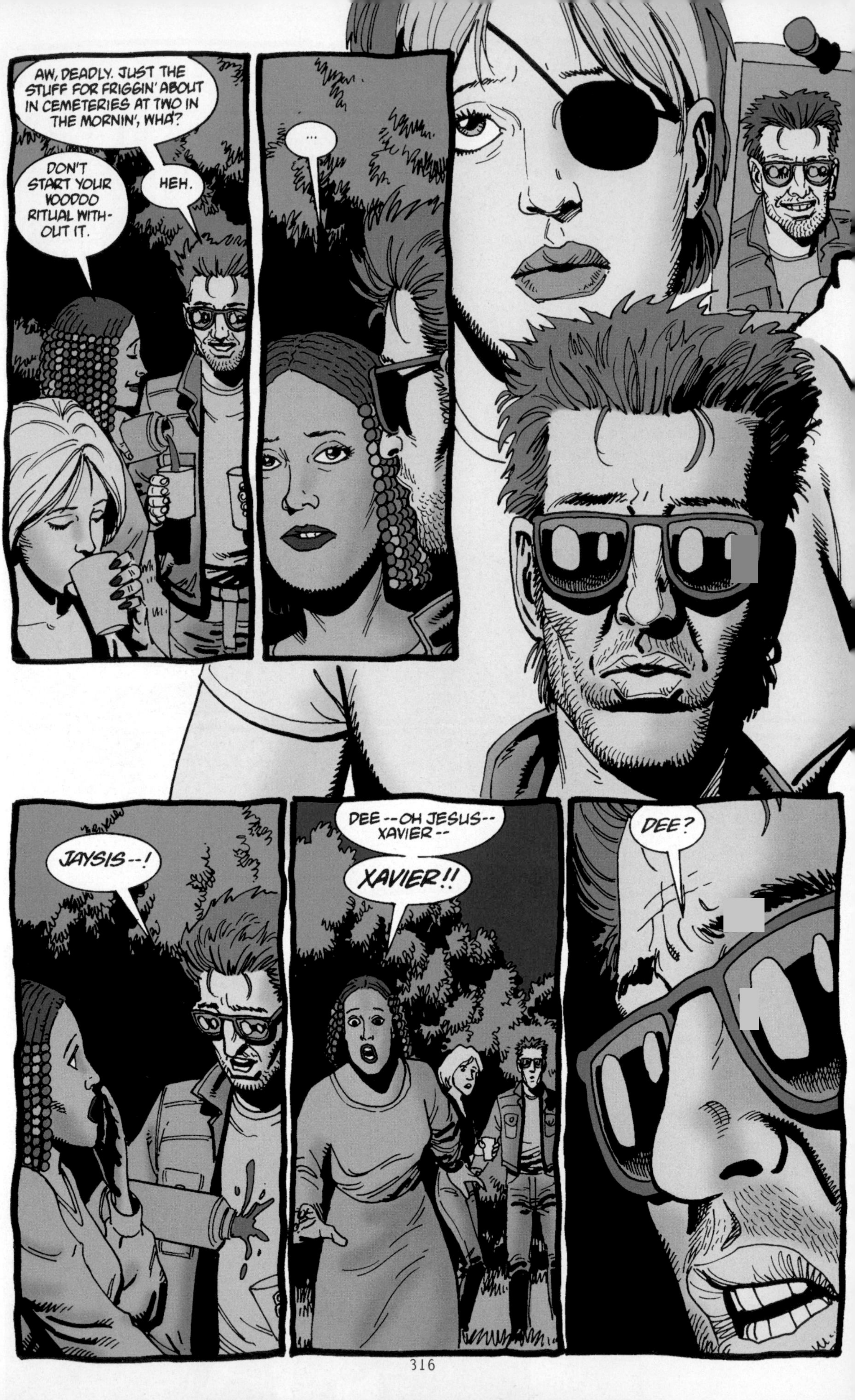
AW, DEADLY. JUST THE STUFF FOR FRIGGIN' ABOUT IN CEMETERIES AT TWO IN THE MORNIN', WHA'?
DON'T START YOUR VOODOO RITUAL WITH-OUT IT.
HEH.
...
JAYSIS--!
DEE--OH JESUS-- XAVIER--
XAVIER!!
DEE?

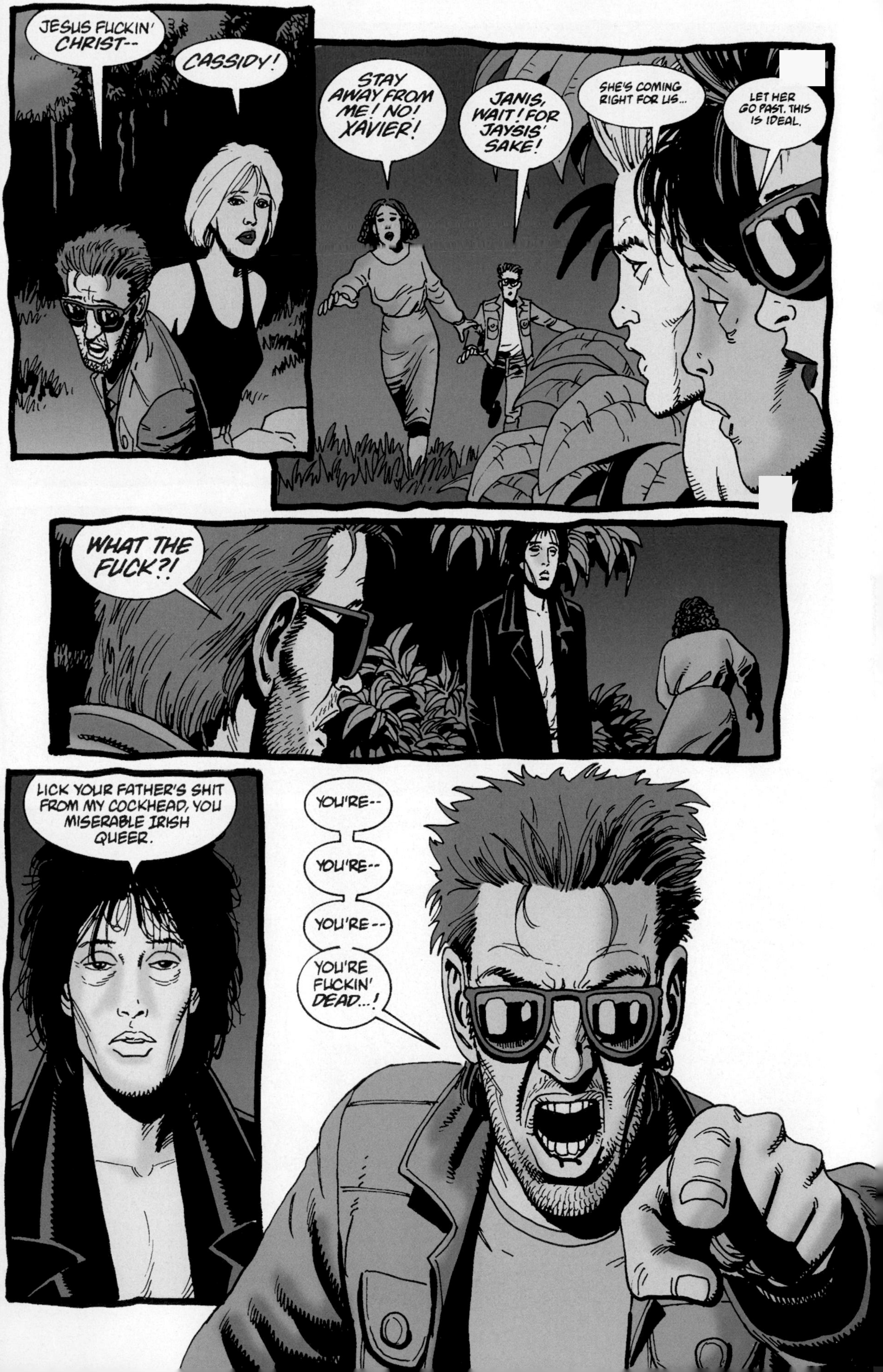
JESUS FUCKIN' CHRIST--
CASSIDY!
STAY AWAY FROM ME! NO! XAVIER!
JANIS, WAIT! FOR JAYSIS' SAKE!
SHE'S COMING RIGHT FOR US...
LET HER GO PAST. THIS IS IDEAL.
WHAT THE FUCK?!
LICK YOUR FATHER'S SHIT FROM MY COCKHEAD, YOU MISERABLE IRISH QUEER.
YOU'RE--
YOU'RE--
YOU'RE--
YOU'RE FUCKIN' DEAD...!

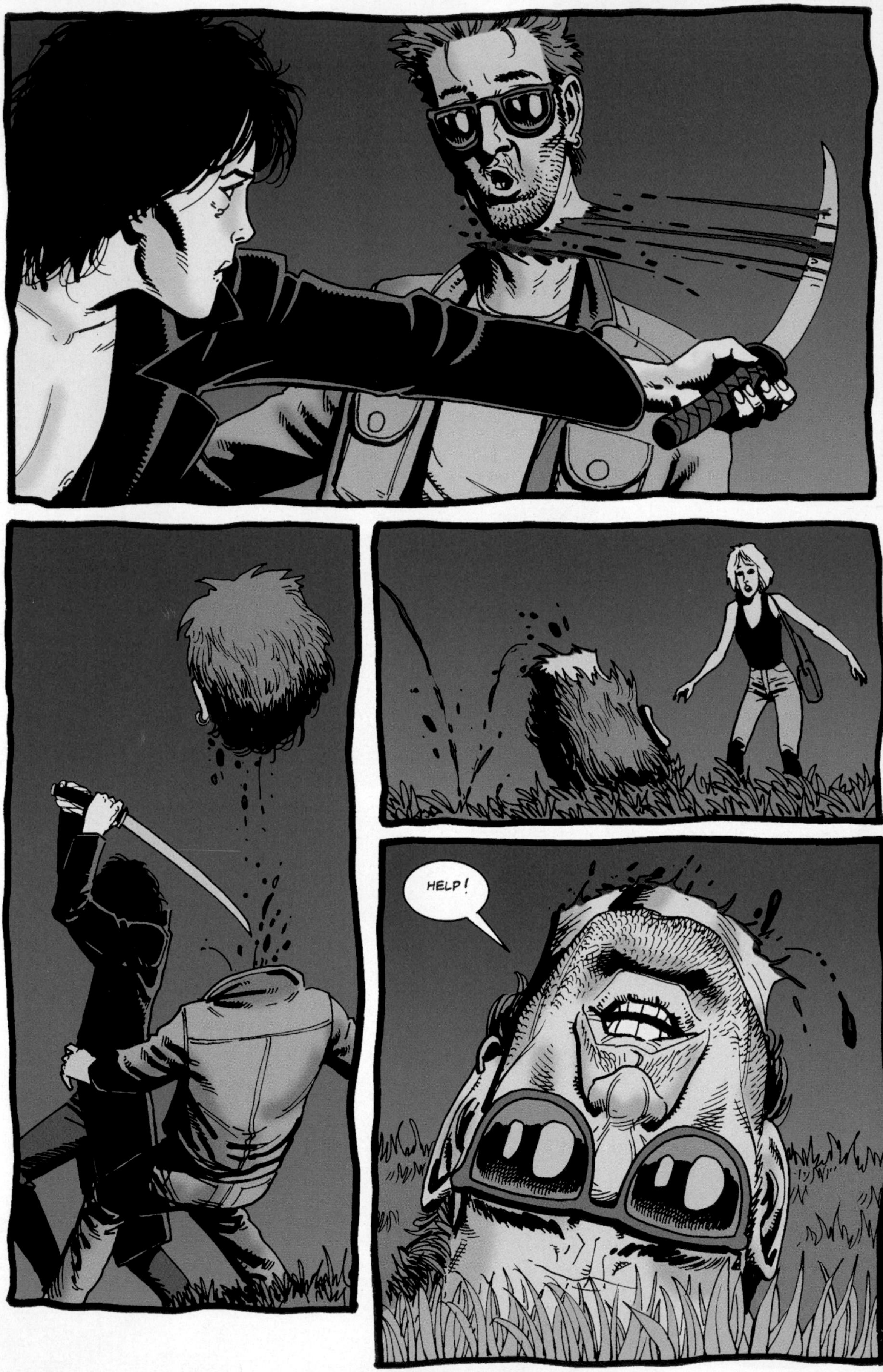
HELP!

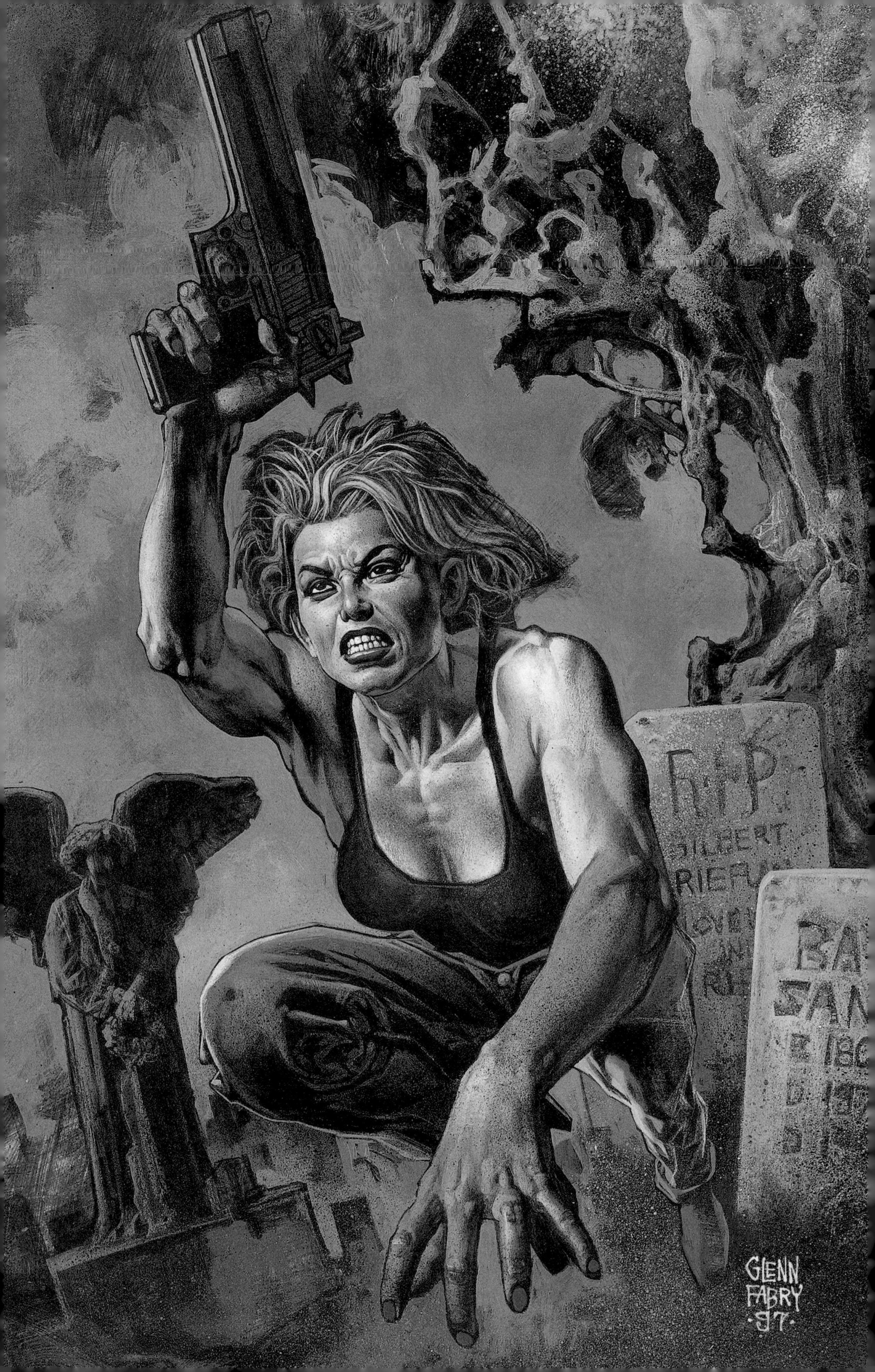
R.I.P.
GILBERT
GLENN
FABRY
97

"I'd try *anything*, to make you pay for what you did."

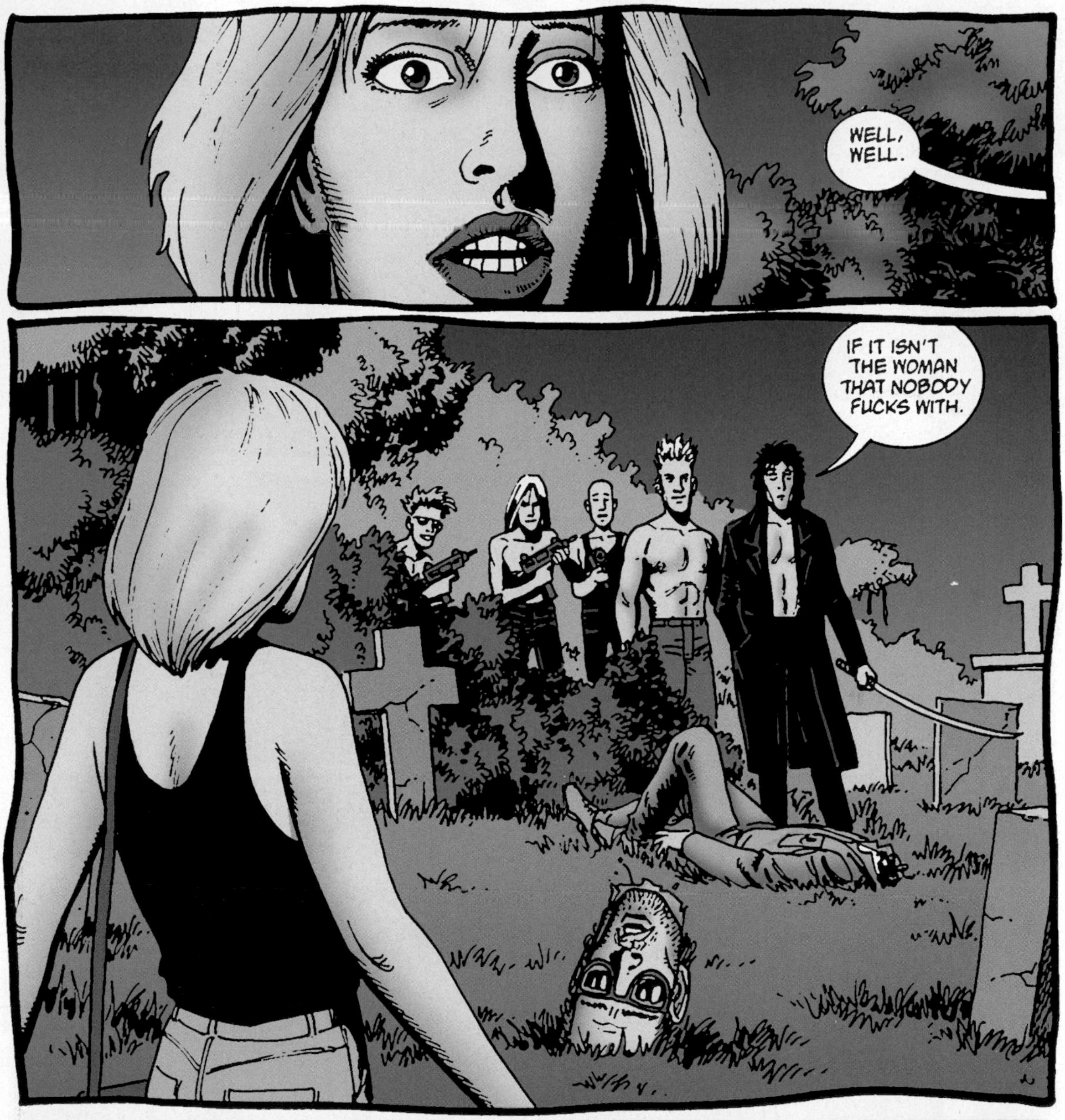
WELL, WELL.
IF IT ISN'T THE WOMAN THAT NOBODY FUCKS WITH.

# PRICE OF NIGHT

GARTH ENNIS - Writer STEVE DILLON - Artist
PAMELA RAMBO - Colorist
CLEM ROBINS - Letterer AXEL ALONSO - Editor

PREACHER created by GARTH ENNIS and STEVE DILLON

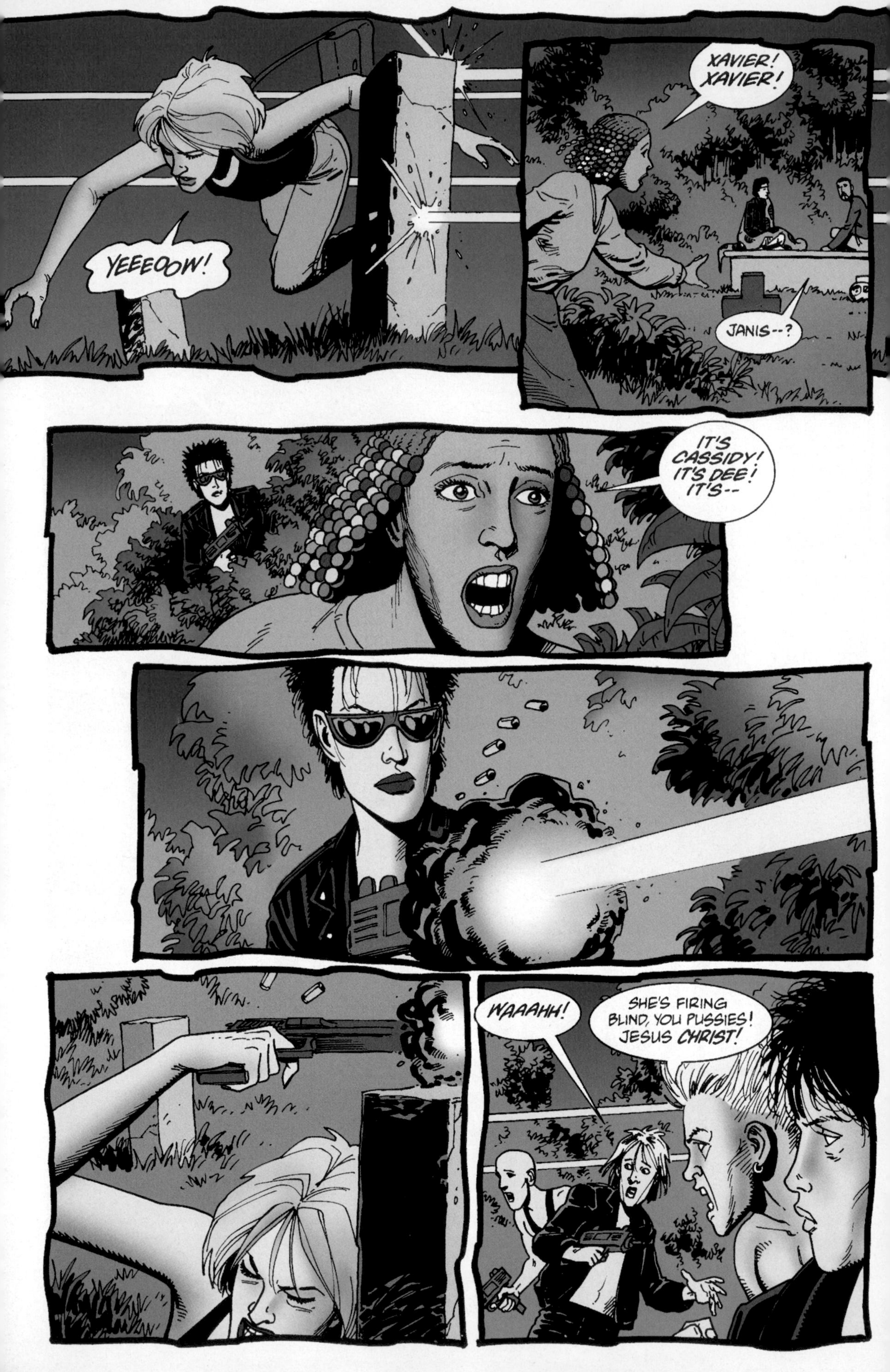
YEEEOOW!
XAVIER! XAVIER!
JANIS--?
IT'S CASSIDY! IT'S DEE! IT'S--
WAAAHH!
SHE'S FIRING BLIND, YOU PUSSIES! JESUS CHRIST!

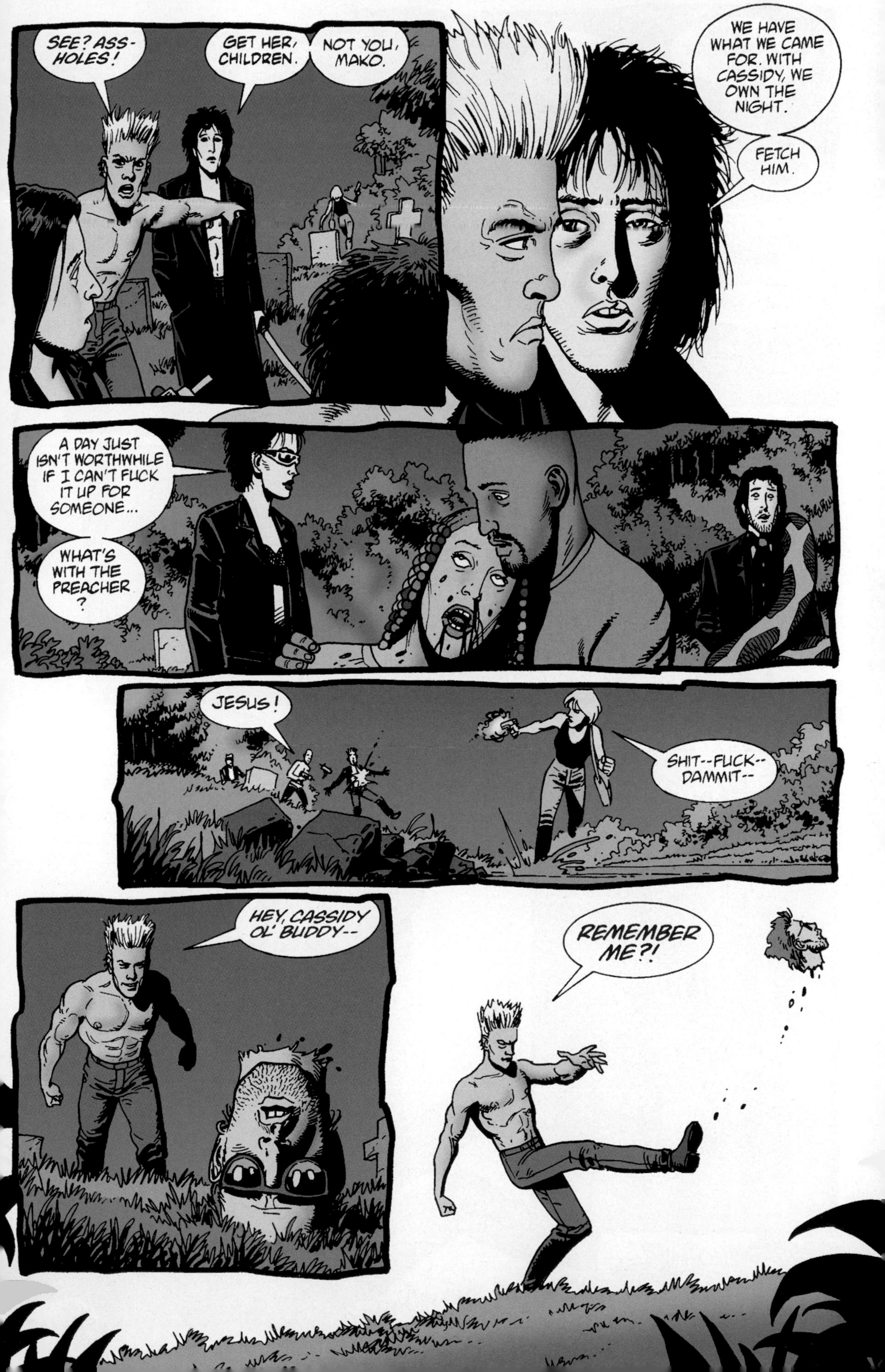
SEE? ASS-HOLES!
GET HER, CHILDREN.
NOT YOU, MAKO.
WE HAVE WHAT WE CAME FOR. WITH CASSIDY, WE OWN THE NIGHT.
FETCH HIM.
A DAY JUST ISN'T WORTHWHILE IF I CAN'T FUCK IT UP FOR SOMEONE...
WHAT'S WITH THE PREACHER?
JESUS!
SHIT--FUCK--DAMMIT--
HEY, CASSIDY OL' BUDDY--
REMEMBER ME?!

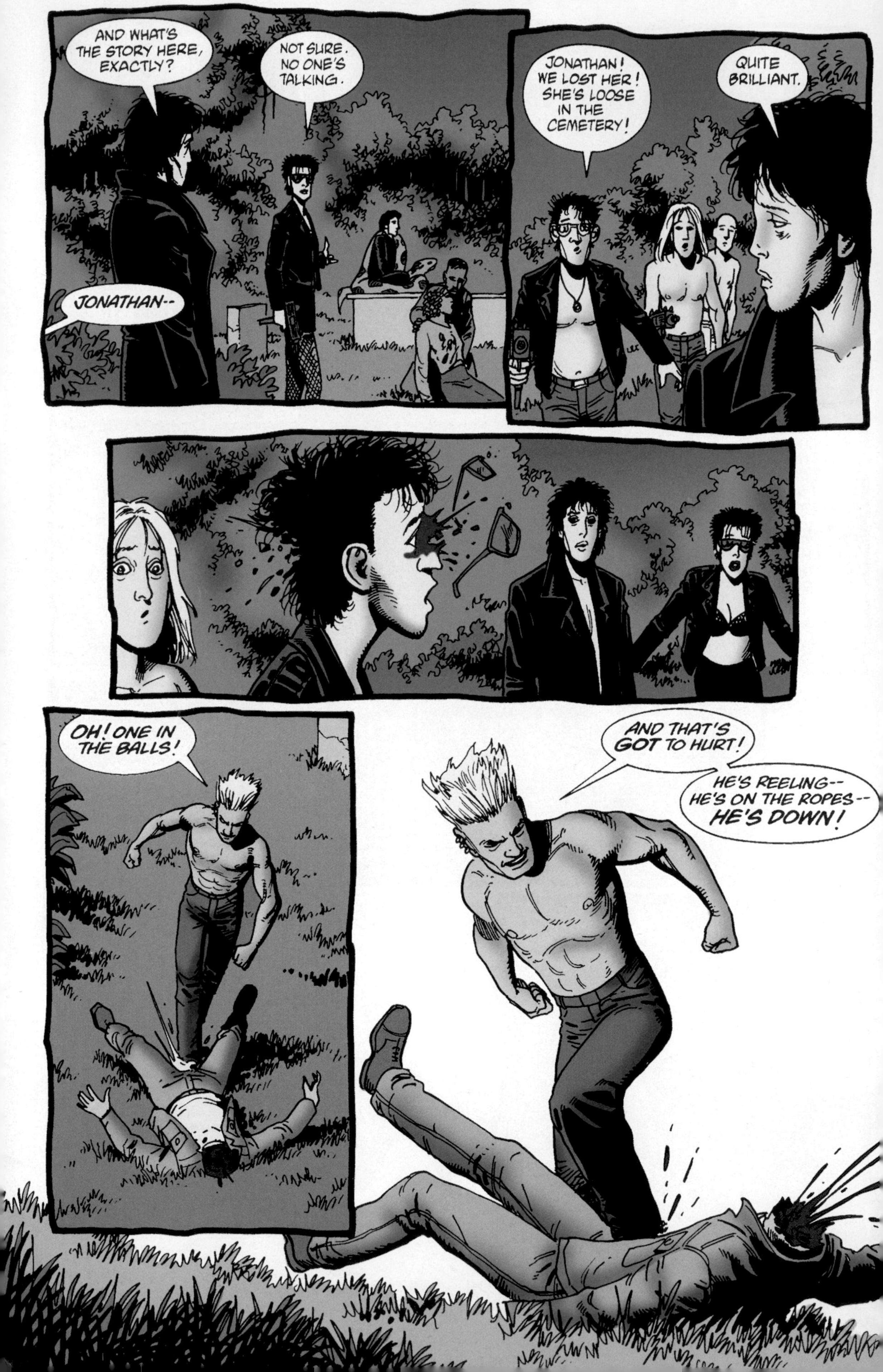
AND WHAT'S THE STORY HERE, EXACTLY?
NOT SURE. NO ONE'S TALKING.
JONATHAN--
JONATHAN! WE LOST HER! SHE'S LOOSE IN THE CEMETERY!
QUITE BRILLIANT.
OH! ONE IN THE BALLS!
AND THAT'S GOT TO HURT!
HE'S REELING-- HE'S ON THE ROPES-- HE'S DOWN!

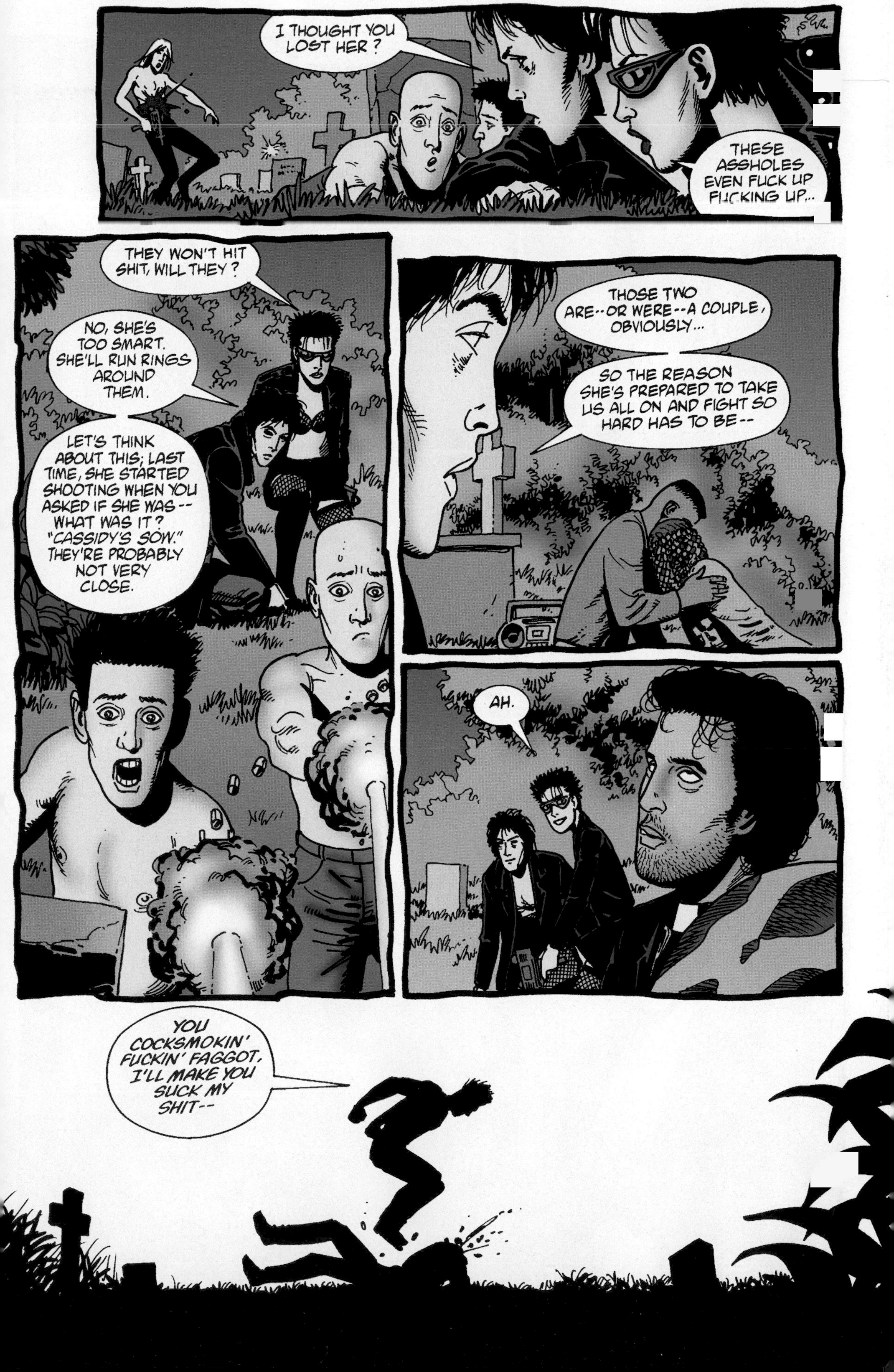

I THOUGHT YOU LOST HER ?
THESE ASSHOLES EVEN FUCK UP FUCKING UP...
THEY WON'T HIT SHIT, WILL THEY ?
NO, SHE'S TOO SMART. SHE'LL RUN RINGS AROUND THEM.
LET'S THINK ABOUT THIS; LAST TIME, SHE STARTED SHOOTING WHEN YOU ASKED IF SHE WAS-- WHAT WAS IT? "CASSIDY'S SOW." THEY'RE PROBABLY NOT VERY CLOSE.
THOSE TWO ARE--OR WERE--A COUPLE, OBVIOUSLY...
SO THE REASON SHE'S PREPARED TO TAKE US ALL ON AND FIGHT SO HARD HAS TO BE--
AH.
YOU COCKSMOKIN' FUCKIN' FAGGOT, I'LL MAKE YOU SUCK MY SHIT--

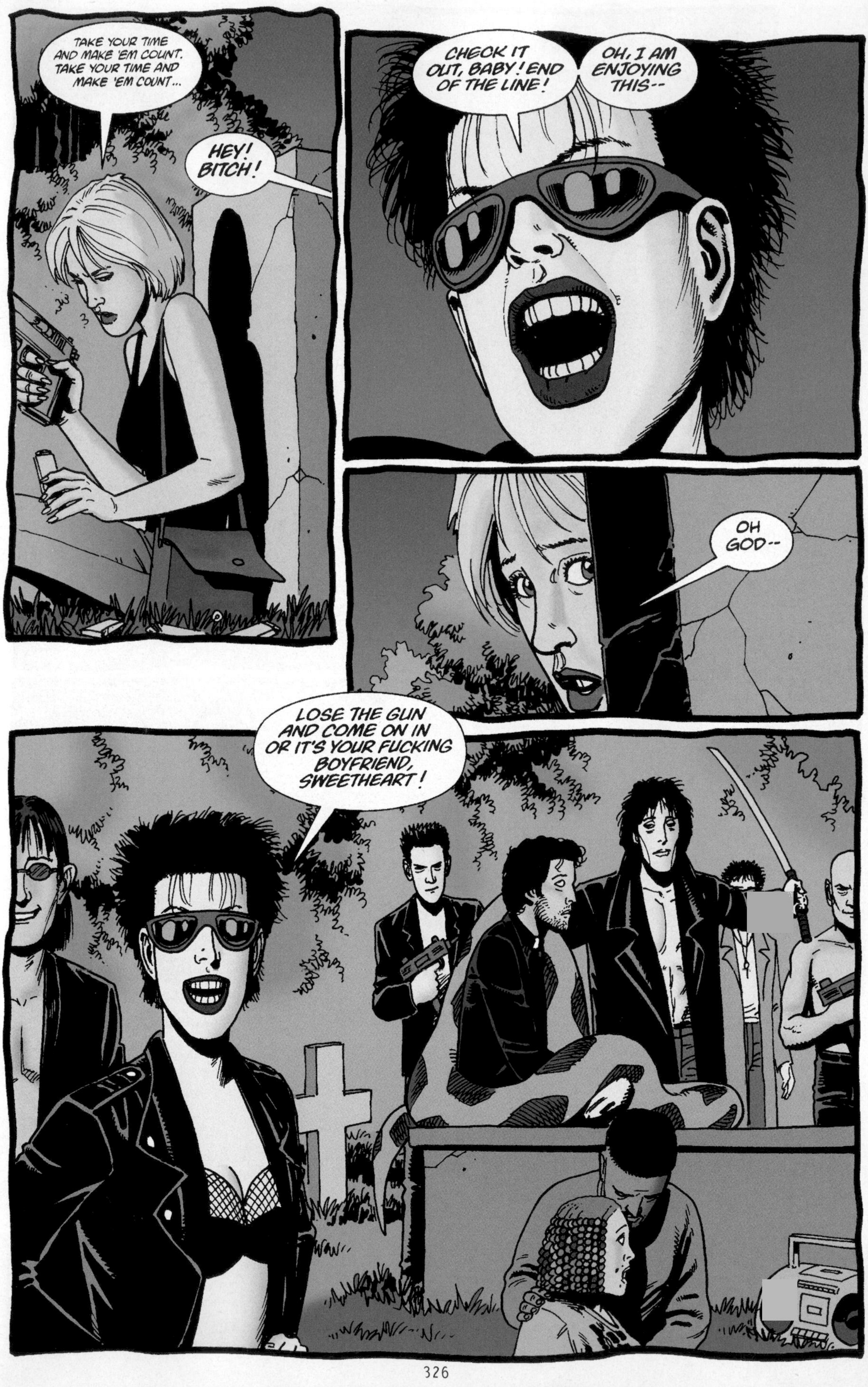
TAKE YOUR TIME AND MAKE 'EM COUNT. TAKE YOUR TIME AND MAKE 'EM COUNT...
HEY! BITCH!
CHECK IT OUT, BABY! END OF THE LINE!
OH, I AM ENJOYING THIS--
OH GOD--
LOSE THE GUN AND COME ON IN OR IT'S YOUR FUCKING BOYFRIEND, SWEETHEART!

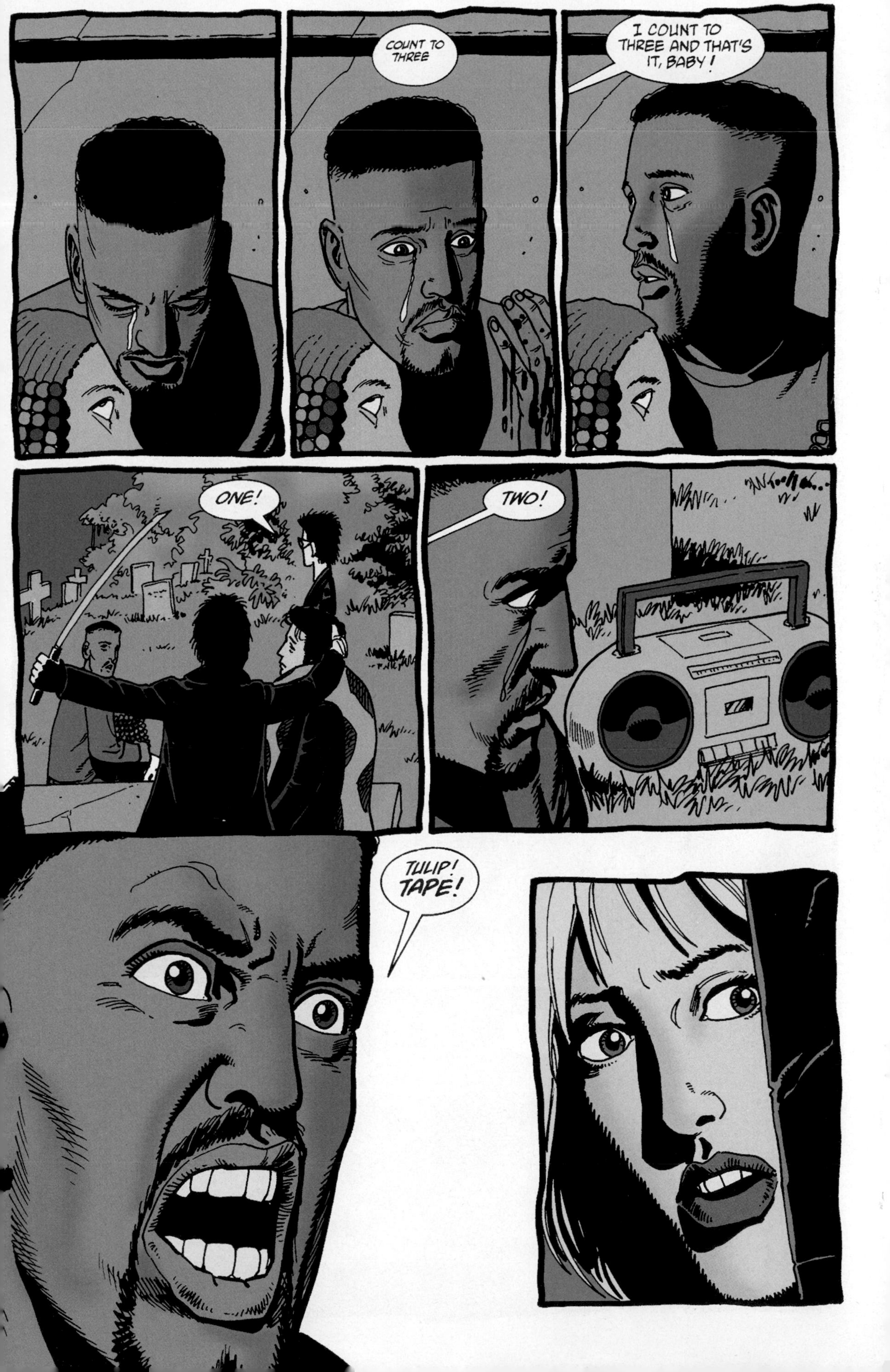
COUNT TO THREE
I COUNT TO THREE AND THAT'S IT, BABY!
ONE!
TWO!
TULIP! TAPE!

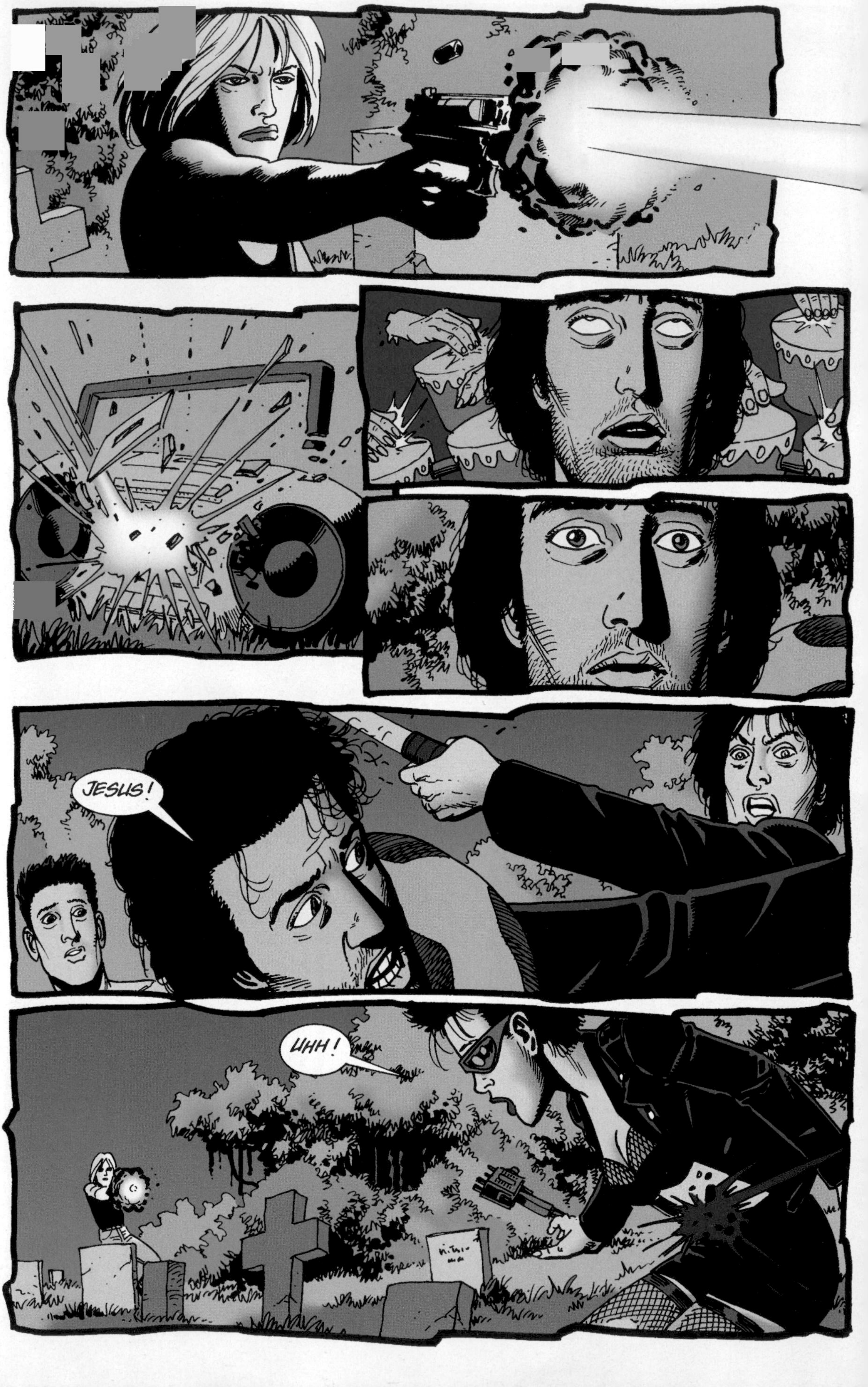
JESUS!
UHH!

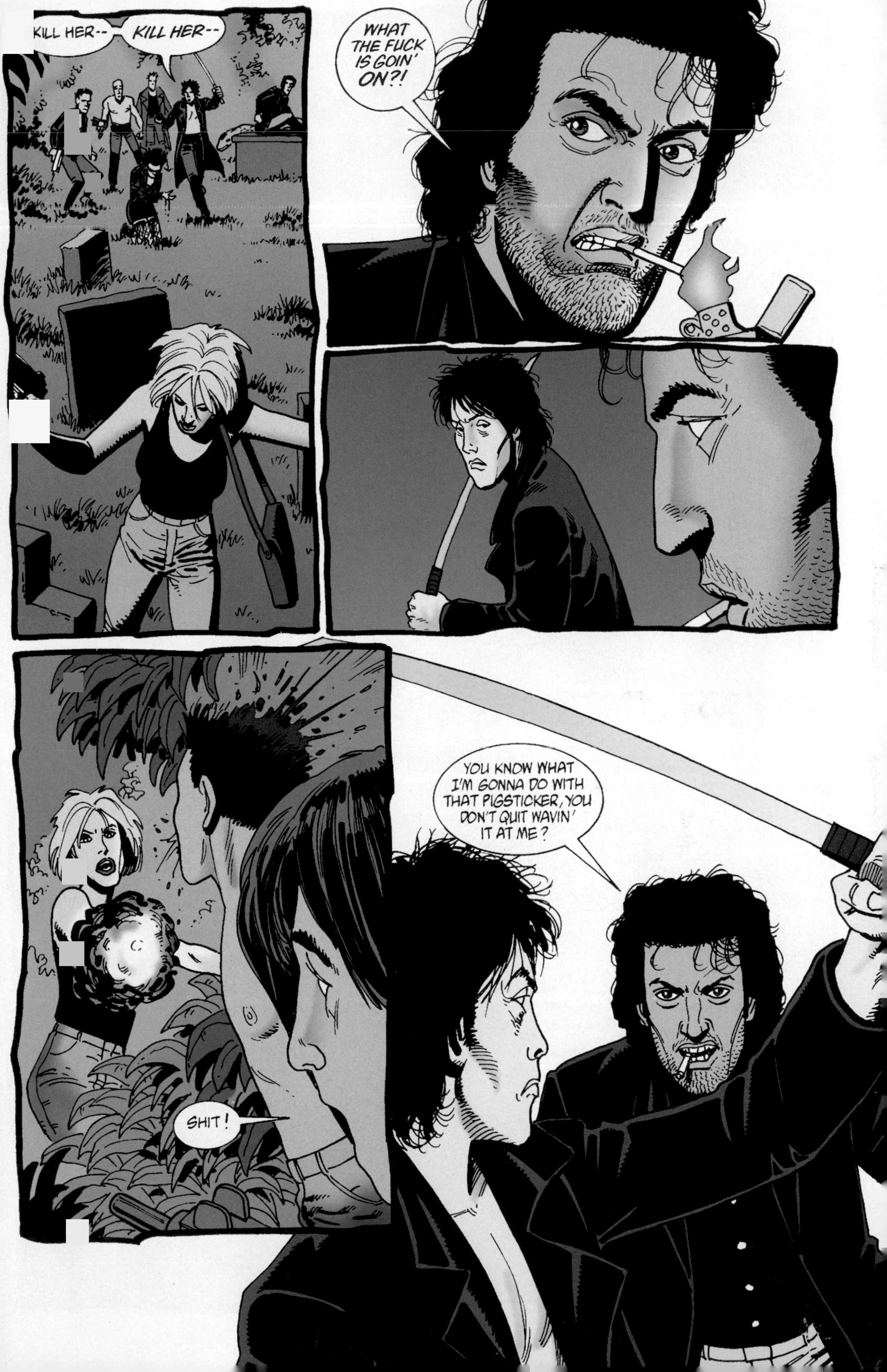
KILL HER--
KILL HER--
WHAT THE FUCK IS GOIN' ON?!
YOU KNOW WHAT I'M GONNA DO WITH THAT PIGSTICKER, YOU DON'T QUIT WAVIN' IT AT ME?
SHIT!

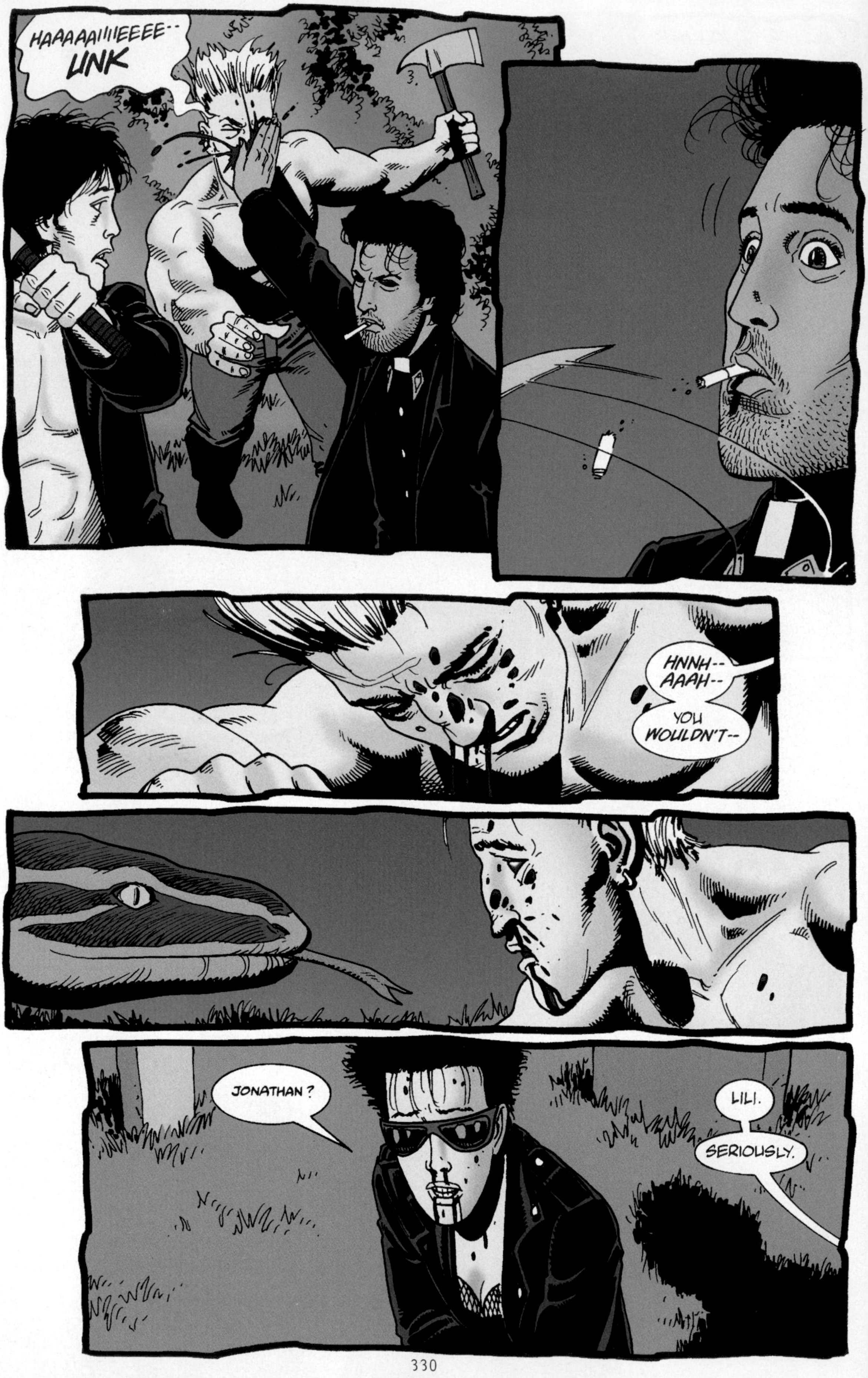
HAAAAAIIIIEEEE--
UNK
HNNH--
AAAH--
YOU WOULDN'T--
JONATHAN?
LILI.
SERIOUSLY.

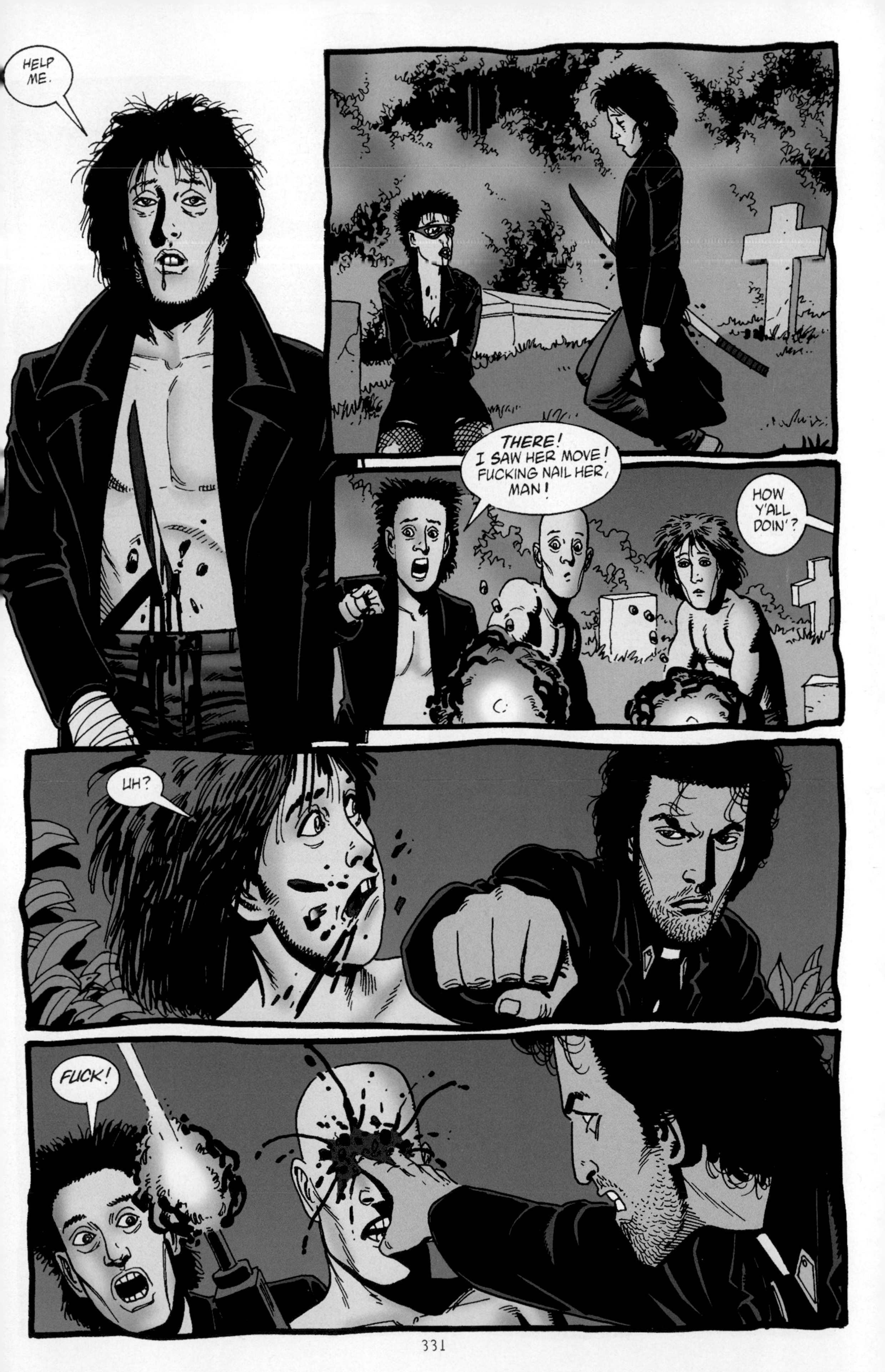
HELP ME.
THERE! I SAW HER MOVE! FUCKING NAIL HER, MAN!
HOW Y'ALL DOIN'?
UH?
FUCK!

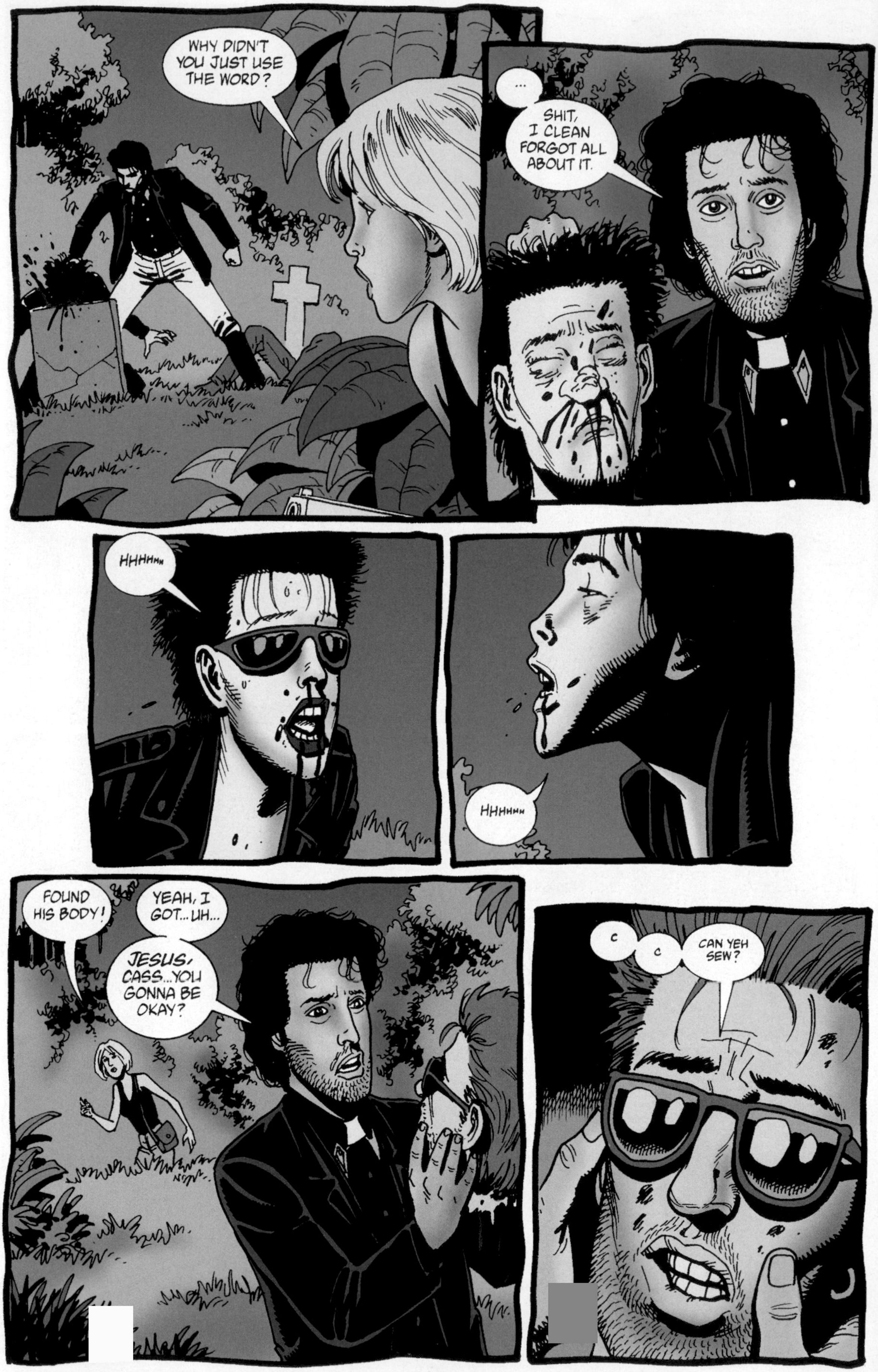
WHY DIDN'T YOU JUST USE THE WORD?
...
SHIT, I CLEAN FORGOT ALL ABOUT IT.
HHHHHH
HHHHHH
FOUND HIS BODY!
YEAH, I GOT... UH...
JESUS, CASS... YOU GONNA BE OKAY?
C
C
CAN YEH SEW?

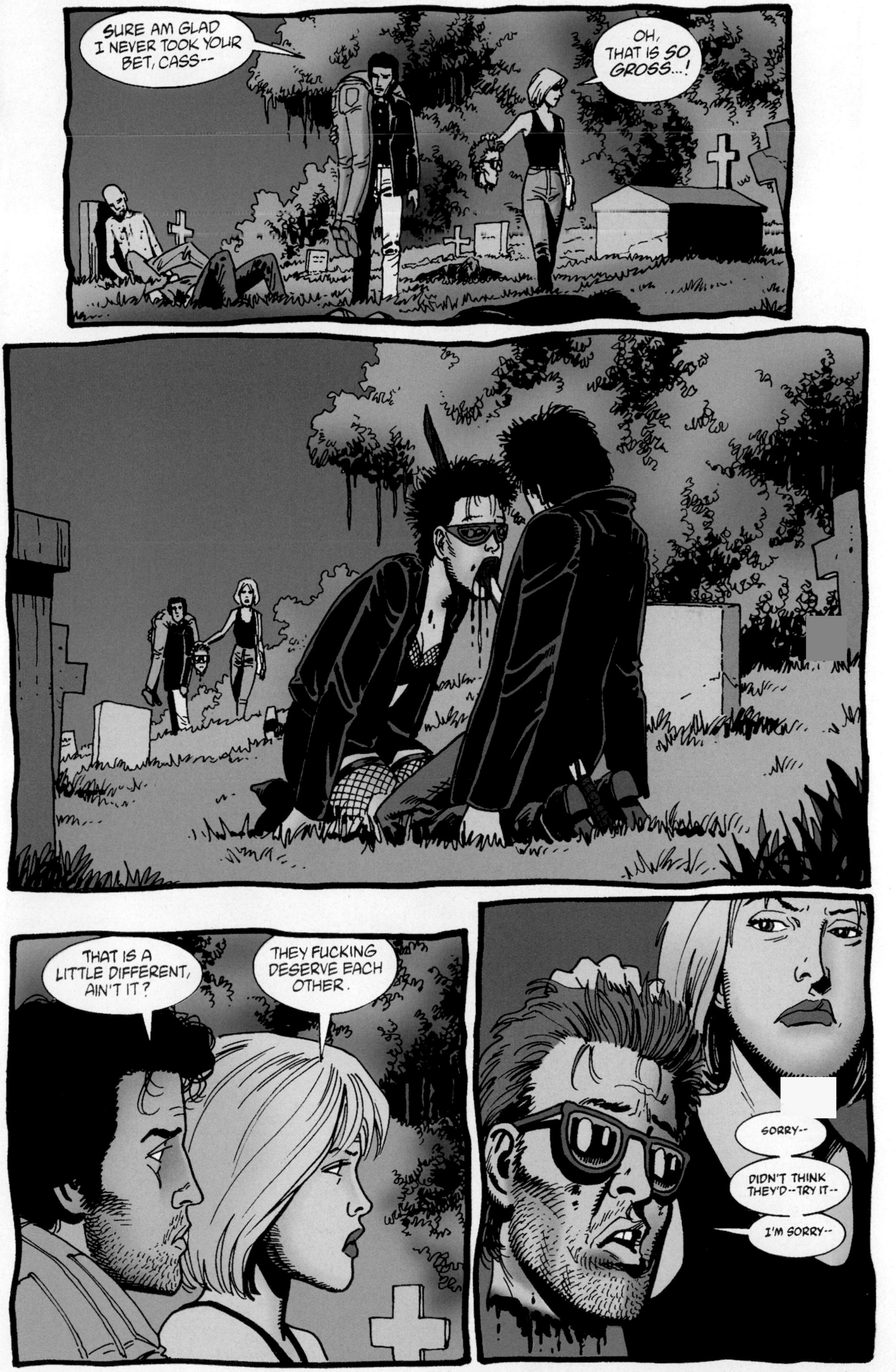

SURE AM GLAD I NEVER TOOK YOUR BET, CASS--
OH, THAT IS SO GROSS...!
THAT IS A LITTLE DIFFERENT, AIN'T IT?
THEY FUCKING DESERVE EACH OTHER.
SORRY--
DIDN'T THINK THEY'D--TRY IT--
I'M SORRY--

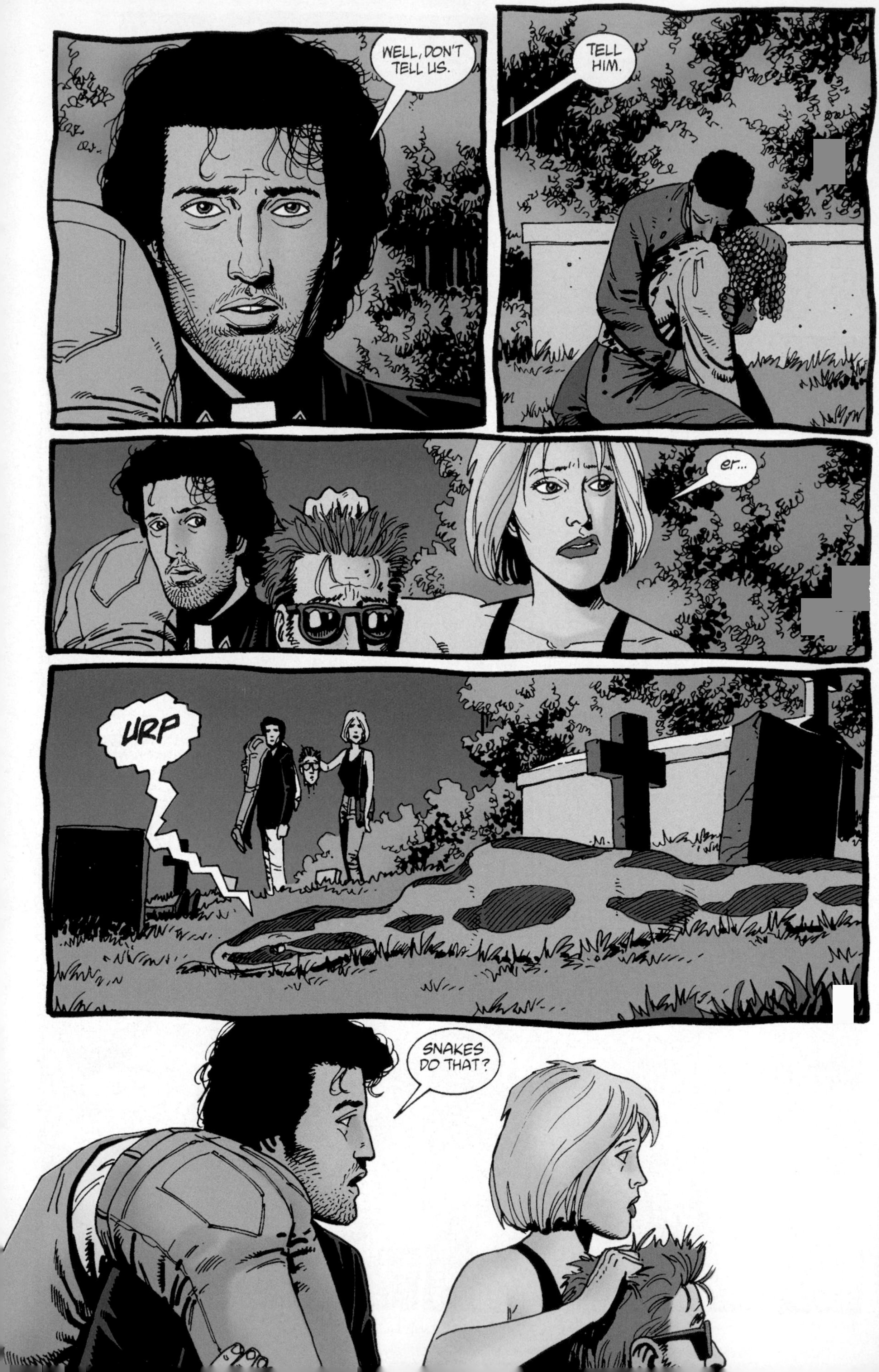
WELL, DON'T TELL US.
TELL HIM.
er...
URP
SNAKES DO THAT?

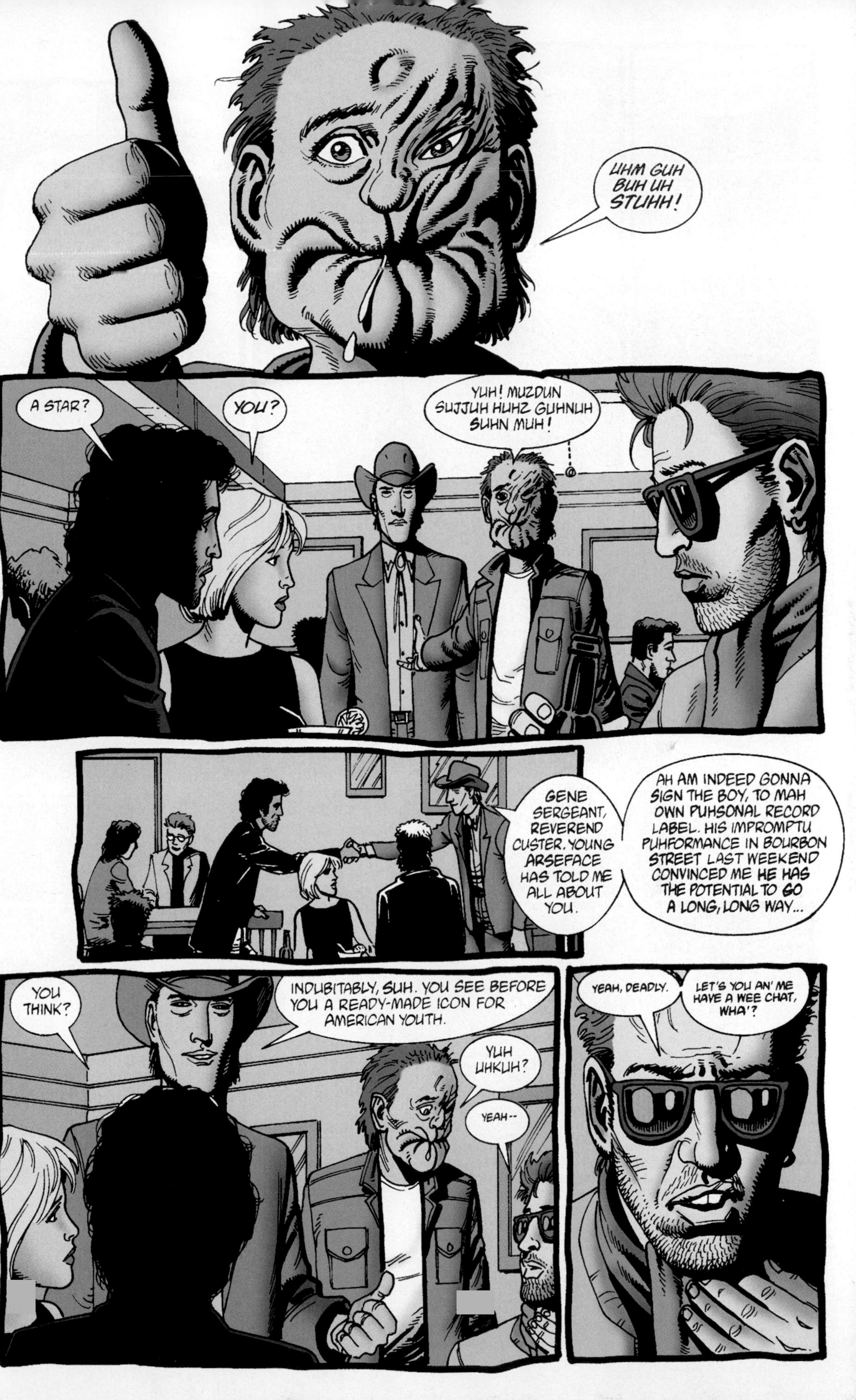
UHM GUH BUH UH STUHH!
A STAR?
YOU?
YUH! MUZDUN SUJJUH HUHZ GUHNUH SUHN MUH!
GENE SERGEANT, REVEREND CUSTER. YOUNG ARSEFACE HAS TOLD ME ALL ABOUT YOU.
AH AM INDEED GONNA SIGN THE BOY, TO MAH OWN PUHSONAL RECORD LABEL. HIS IMPROMPTU PUHFORMANCE IN BOURBON STREET LAST WEEKEND CONVINCED ME HE HAS THE POTENTIAL TO GO A LONG, LONG WAY...
YOU THINK?
INDUBITABLY, SUH. YOU SEE BEFORE YOU A READY-MADE ICON FOR AMERICAN YOUTH.
YUH UHKUH?
YEAH--
YEAH, DEADLY.
LET'S YOU AN' ME HAVE A WEE CHAT, WHA'?

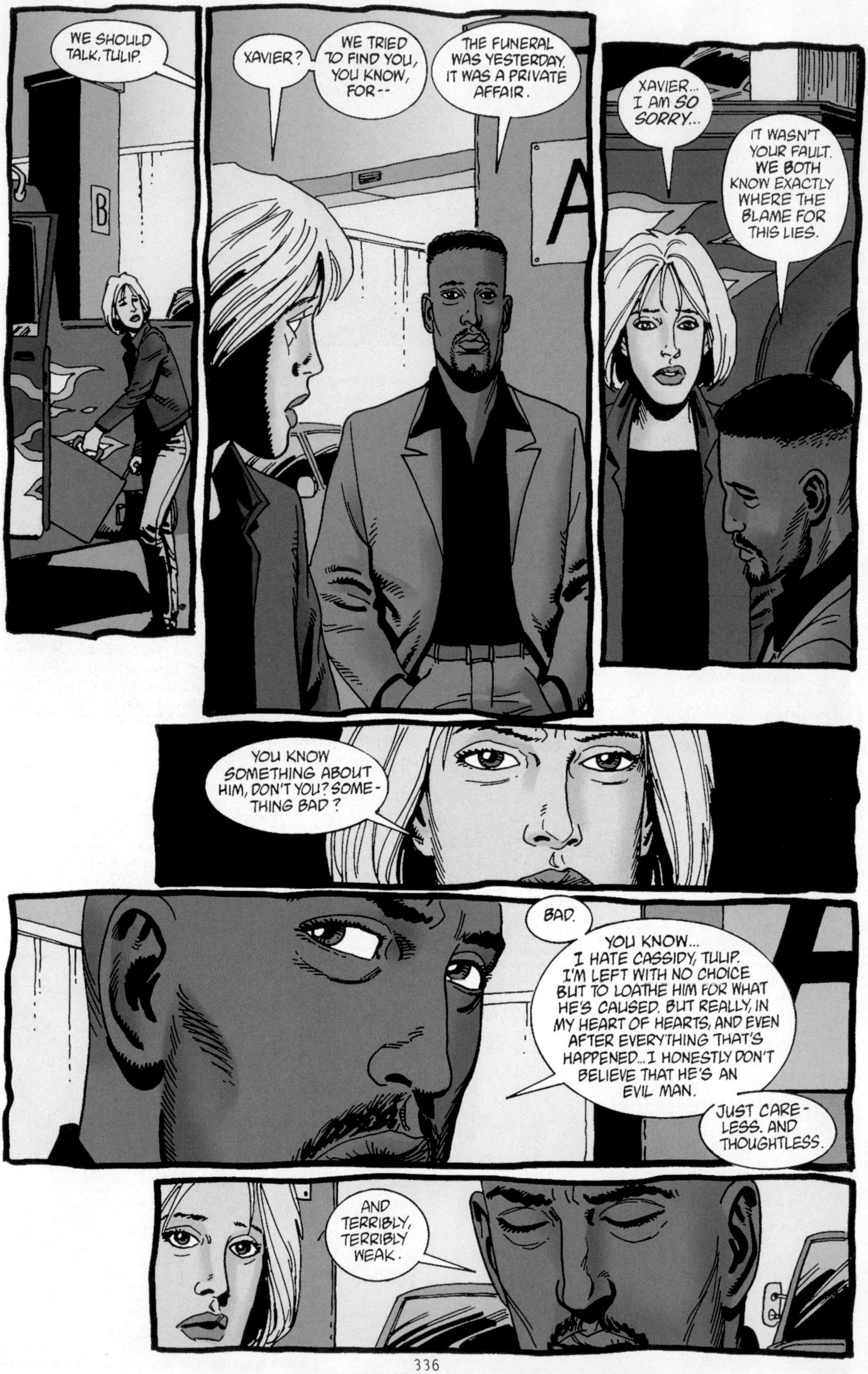
WE SHOULD TALK, TULIP.
XAVIER?
WE TRIED TO FIND YOU, YOU KNOW, FOR--
THE FUNERAL WAS YESTERDAY. IT WAS A PRIVATE AFFAIR.
B
A
XAVIER... I AM SO SORRY...
IT WASN'T YOUR FAULT. WE BOTH KNOW EXACTLY WHERE THE BLAME FOR THIS LIES.
YOU KNOW SOMETHING ABOUT HIM, DON'T YOU? SOMETHING BAD?
BAD.
YOU KNOW... I HATE CASSIDY, TULIP. I'M LEFT WITH NO CHOICE BUT TO LOATHE HIM FOR WHAT HE'S CAUSED. BUT REALLY, IN MY HEART OF HEARTS, AND EVEN AFTER EVERYTHING THAT'S HAPPENED... I HONESTLY DON'T BELIEVE THAT HE'S AN EVIL MAN.
JUST CARELESS. AND THOUGHTLESS.
AND TERRIBLY, TERRIBLY WEAK.

WHAT HAPPENED BETWEEN THE TWO OF YOU, ANYWAY?

A WOMAN.

CASSIDY SEDUCED HER WHILE I WAS OUT OF TOWN.

SEDUCED...THEY WERE DRUNK AND THEY FUCKED. IT WAS HER AS MUCH AS HIM.

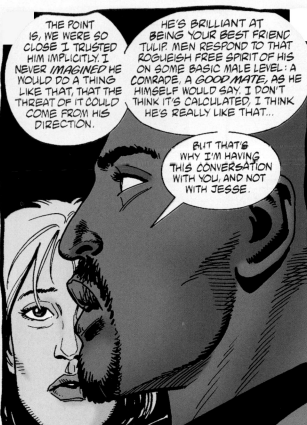

THE POINT IS, WE WERE SO CLOSE I TRUSTED HIM IMPLICITLY. I NEVER IMAGINED HE WOULD DO A THING LIKE THAT, THAT THE THREAT OF IT COULD COME FROM HIS DIRECTION.

HE'S BRILLIANT AT BEING YOUR BEST FRIEND, TULIP. MEN RESPOND TO THAT ROGUEISH FREE SPIRIT OF HIS ON SOME BASIC MALE LEVEL: A COMRADE, A GOOD MATE, AS HE HIMSELF WOULD SAY. I DON'T THINK IT'S CALCULATED, I THINK HE'S REALLY LIKE THAT...

BUT THAT'S WHY I'M HAVING THIS CONVERSATION WITH YOU, AND NOT WITH JESSE.

EVERY TIME HE CAME TO TOWN WAS AN OCCASION. I LOVED HIM SO MUCH I LET HIM CLIMB RIGHT INSIDE OF ME, UNTIL I COULDN'T IMAGINE LIFE WITHOUT HIM.

AND THEN HE LET ME DOWN.

YOU THINK THAT'S HOW IT ALWAYS IS WITH HIM?

I THINK HE GOES THROUGH LIFE WITHOUT A SENSE OF CONSEQUENCE.

HE DIDN'T CARE THAT LES ENFANTS MIGHT BE DANGEROUS, THAT THEY'D STILL BE OUT TO GET HIM AFTER WHATEVER HAPPENED BEFORE. IT DIDN'T EVEN OCCUR TO HIM.

TOO BAD FOR JANIS, MM?

IT'S JUST CASSIDY, TULIP.

SHIT HAPPENS IN HIS WAKE.

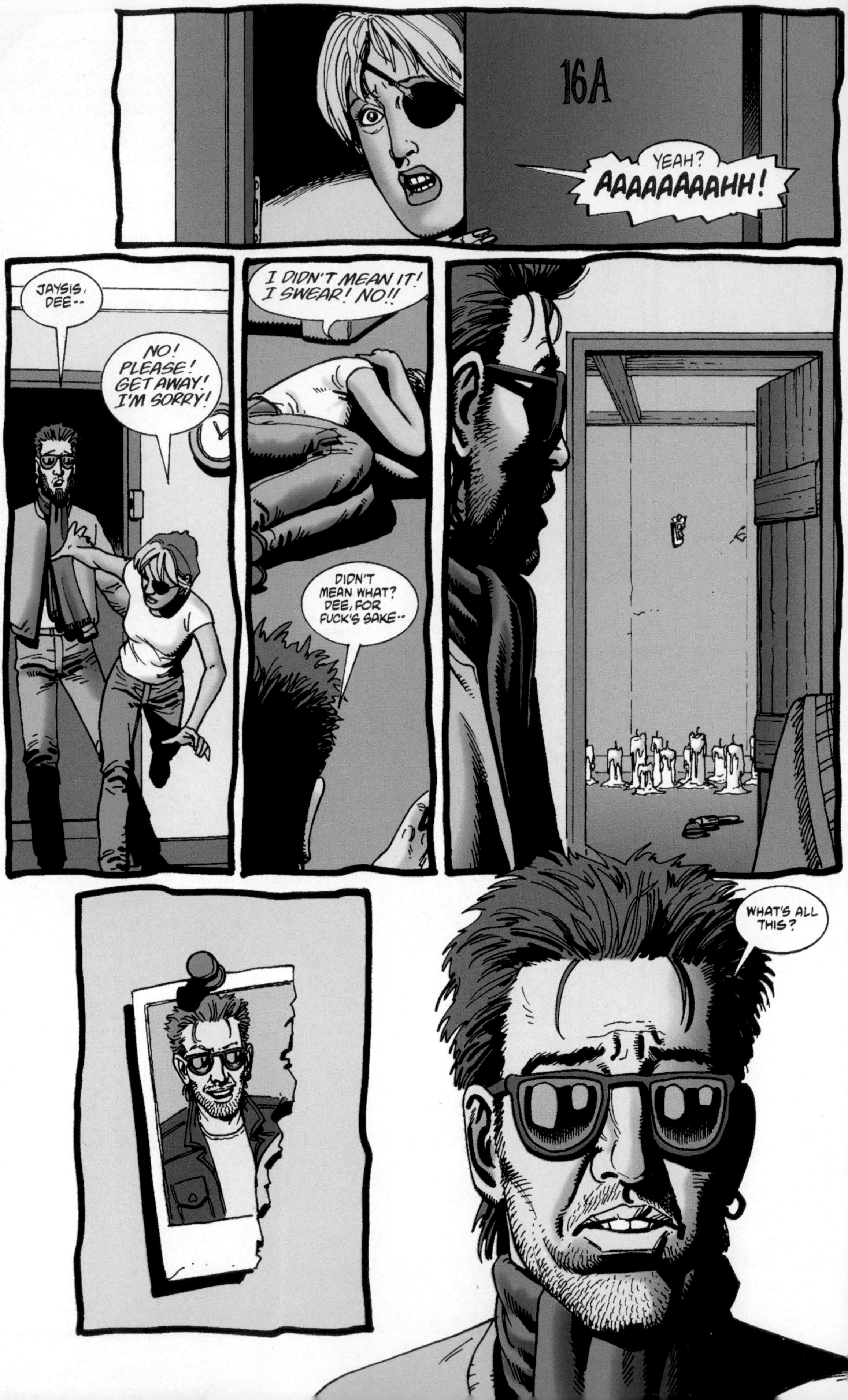
16A
YEAH?
AAAAAAAAHH!
JAYSIS, DEE--
NO! PLEASE! GET AWAY! I'M SORRY!
I DIDN'T MEAN IT! I SWEAR! NO!!
DIDN'T MEAN WHAT? DEE, FOR FUCK'S SAKE--
WHAT'S ALL THIS?

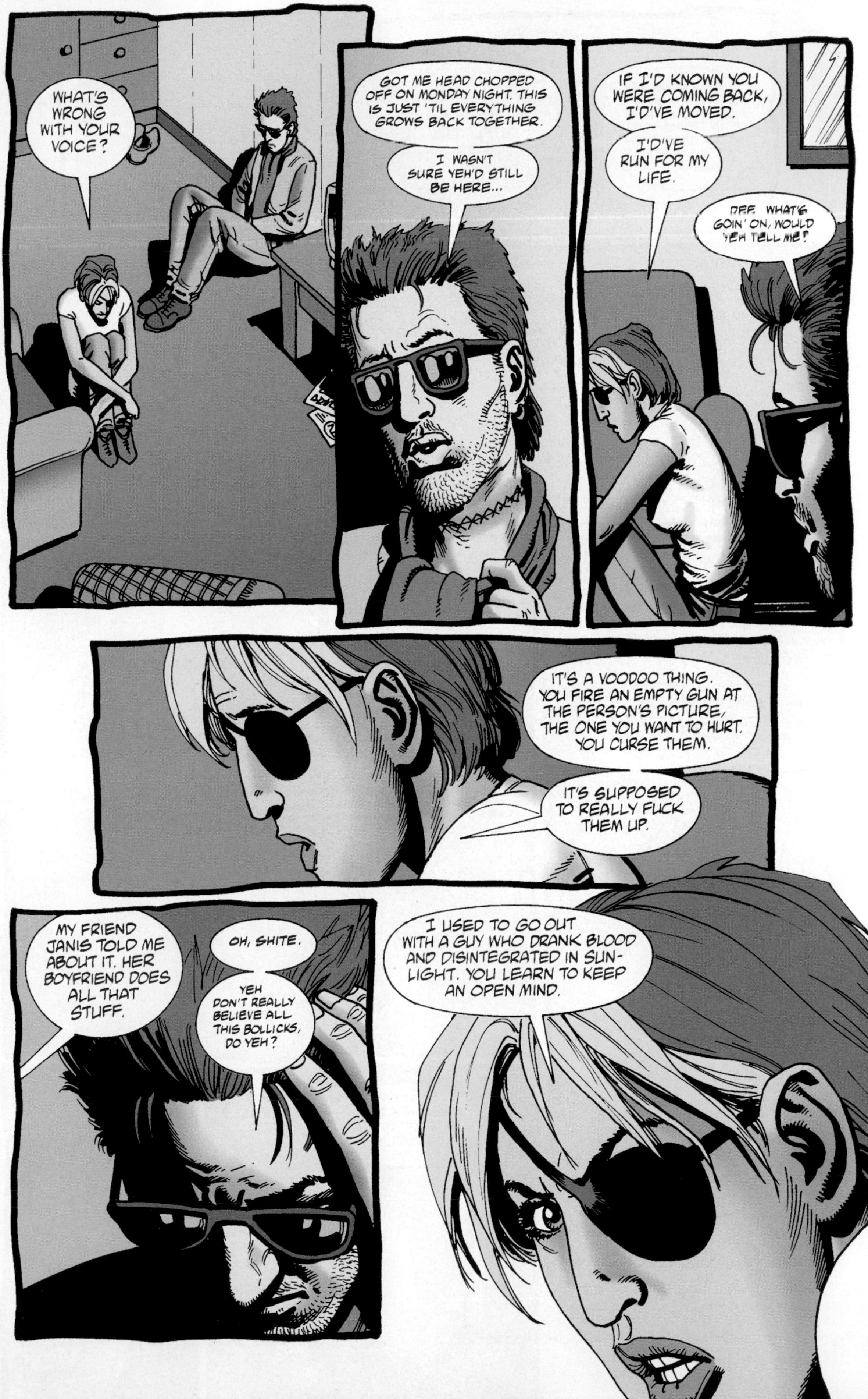
WHAT'S WRONG WITH YOUR VOICE?
GOT ME HEAD CHOPPED OFF ON MONDAY NIGHT. THIS IS JUST 'TIL EVERYTHING GROWS BACK TOGETHER.
I WASN'T SURE YEH'D STILL BE HERE...
IF I'D KNOWN YOU WERE COMING BACK, I'D'VE MOVED.
I'D'VE RUN FOR MY LIFE.
DEE. WHAT'S GOIN' ON, WOULD YEH TELL ME?
IT'S A VOODOO THING. YOU FIRE AN EMPTY GUN AT THE PERSON'S PICTURE, THE ONE YOU WANT TO HURT. YOU CURSE THEM.
IT'S SUPPOSED TO REALLY FUCK THEM UP.
MY FRIEND JANIS TOLD ME ABOUT IT. HER BOYFRIEND DOES ALL THAT STUFF.
OH, SHITE.
YEH DON'T REALLY BELIEVE ALL THIS BOLLICKS, DO YEH?
I USED TO GO OUT WITH A GUY WHO DRANK BLOOD AND DISINTEGRATED IN SUNLIGHT. YOU LEARN TO KEEP AN OPEN MIND.

ALL THE SAME, YEH WERE ALWAYS SUCH A SMART WEE GIRL... I MEAN JAYSIS, WHY WOULD YEH BOTHER WI' THIS SORT'VE CRAP?

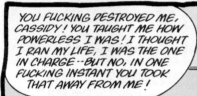

BECAUSE OF THIS, YOU ASSHOLE!

AND THAT'S WHY I'D TRY ANYTHING, TO MAKE YOU PAY FOR WHAT YOU DID.

YOU FUCKING DESTROYED ME, CASSIDY! YOU TAUGHT ME HOW POWERLESS I WAS! I THOUGHT I RAN MY LIFE, I WAS THE ONE IN CHARGE--BUT NO, IN ONE FUCKING INSTANT YOU TOOK THAT AWAY FROM ME!

BECAUSE STRONGEST ALWAYS WINS! AND THERE'S ALWAYS SOME FUCKING SAVAGE LIKE YOU TO PROVE IT!!

UH, YER PAL JANIS... SHE'S THE ONE MENTIONED YEH. I KNEW HER, YEH SEE.

I'M AFRAID SHE'S...WELL, SHE'S DEAD...

I'M NOT SURPRISED.

GET OUT.

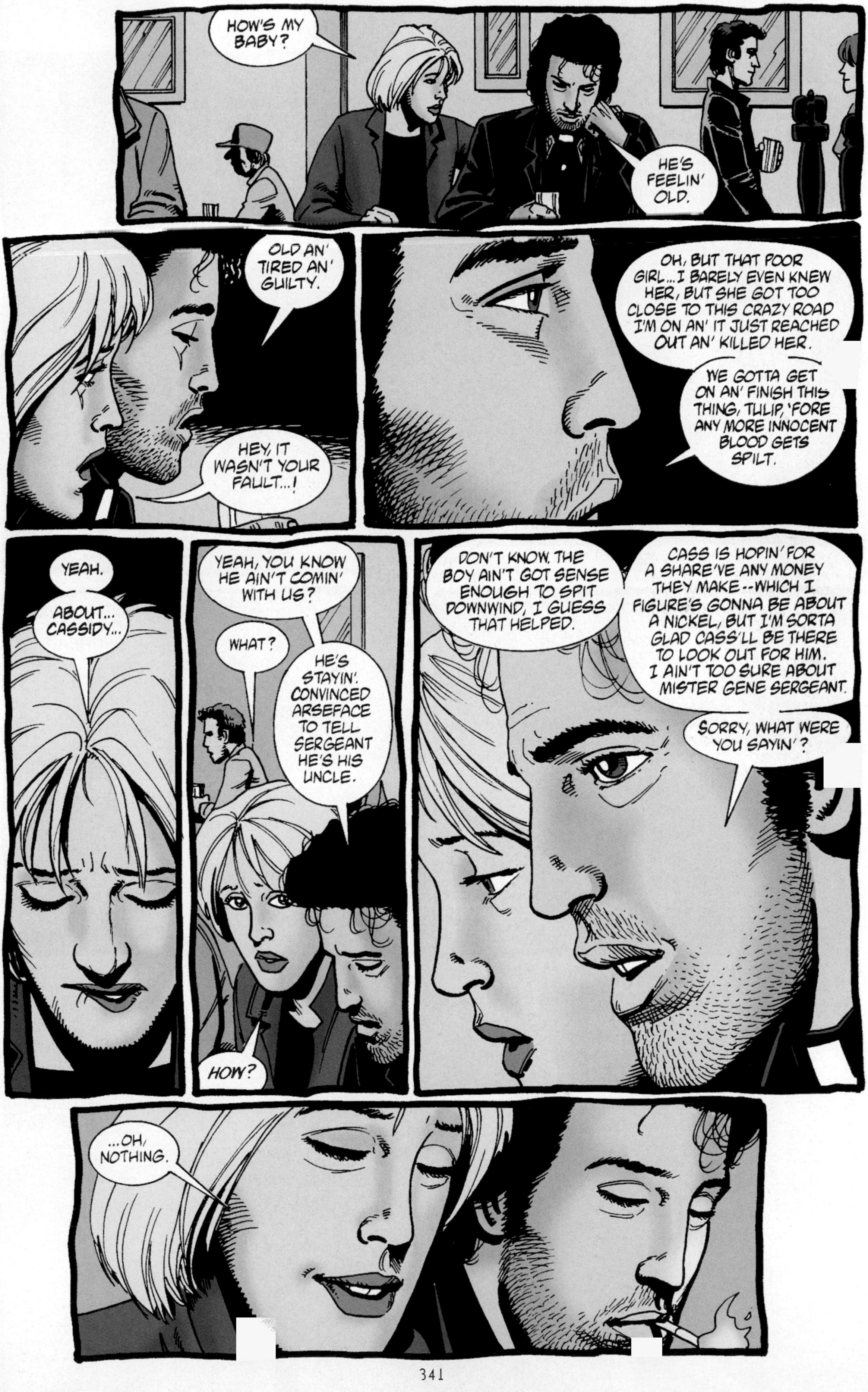
HOW'S MY BABY?
HE'S FEELIN' OLD.
OLD AN' TIRED AN' GUILTY.
HEY, IT WASN'T YOUR FAULT...!
OH, BUT THAT POOR GIRL... I BARELY EVEN KNEW HER, BUT SHE GOT TOO CLOSE TO THIS CRAZY ROAD I'M ON AN' IT JUST REACHED OUT AN' KILLED HER.
WE GOTTA GET ON AN' FINISH THIS THING, TULIP, 'FORE ANY MORE INNOCENT BLOOD GETS SPILT.
YEAH.
ABOUT... CASSIDY...
YEAH, YOU KNOW HE AIN'T COMIN' WITH US?
WHAT?
HE'S STAYIN'. CONVINCED ARSEFACE TO TELL SERGEANT HE'S HIS UNCLE.
HOW?
DON'T KNOW. THE BOY AIN'T GOT SENSE ENOUGH TO SPIT DOWNWIND, I GUESS THAT HELPED.
CASS IS HOPIN' FOR A SHARE'VE ANY MONEY THEY MAKE--WHICH I FIGURE'S GONNA BE ABOUT A NICKEL, BUT I'M SORTA GLAD CASS'LL BE THERE TO LOOK OUT FOR HIM. I AIN'T TOO SURE ABOUT MISTER GENE SERGEANT.
SORRY, WHAT WERE YOU SAYIN'?
...OH, NOTHING.

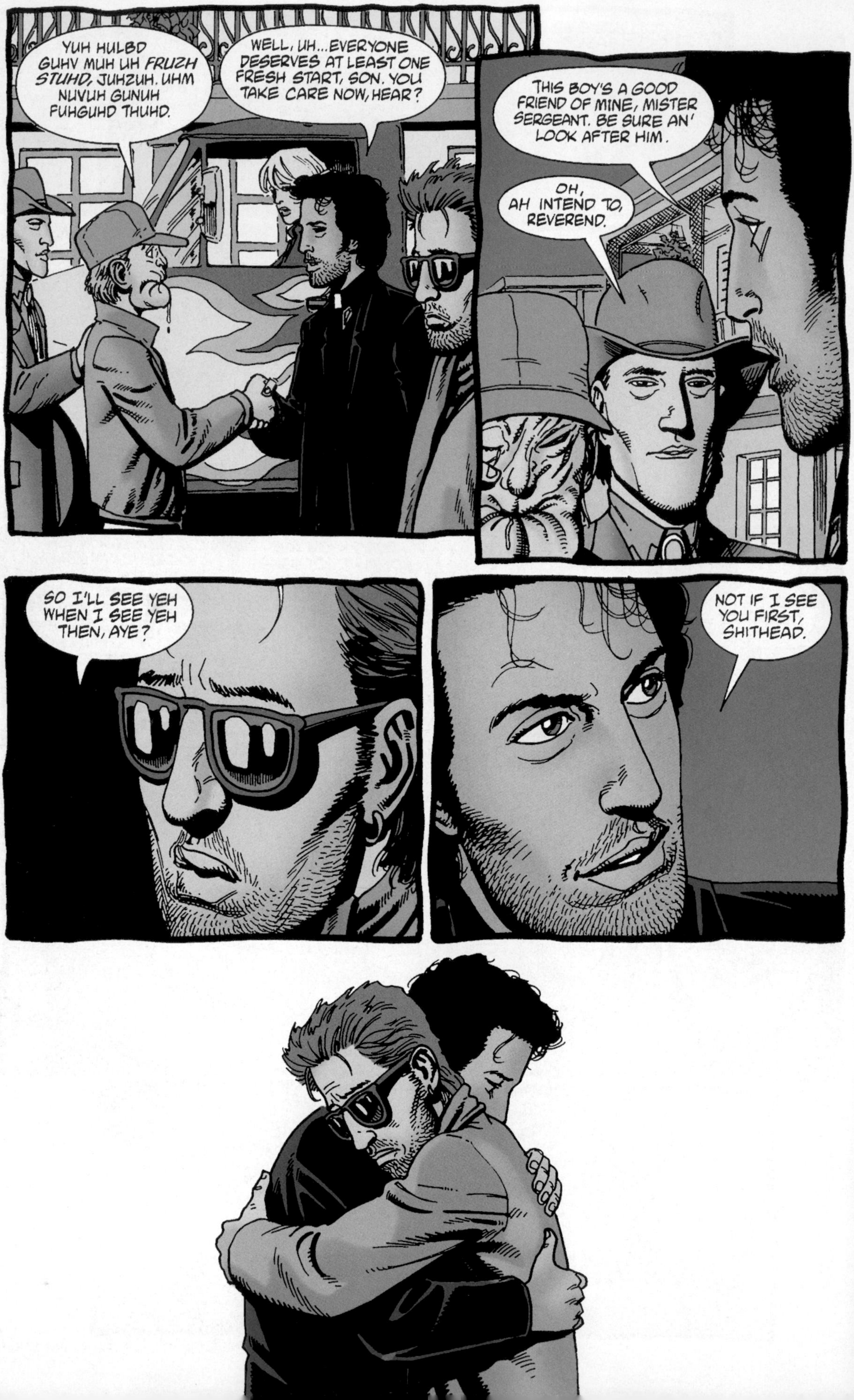
YUH HULBD GUHV MUH UH *FRUZH STUHD*, JUHZUH. UHM NUVUH GUNUH FUHGUHD THUHD.
WELL, UH...EVERYONE DESERVES AT LEAST ONE FRESH START, SON. YOU TAKE CARE NOW, HEAR?
THIS BOY'S A GOOD FRIEND OF MINE, MISTER SERGEANT. BE SURE AN' LOOK AFTER HIM.
OH, AH INTEND TO, REVEREND.
SO I'LL SEE YEH WHEN I SEE YEH THEN, AYE?
NOT IF I SEE YOU FIRST, SHITHEAD.

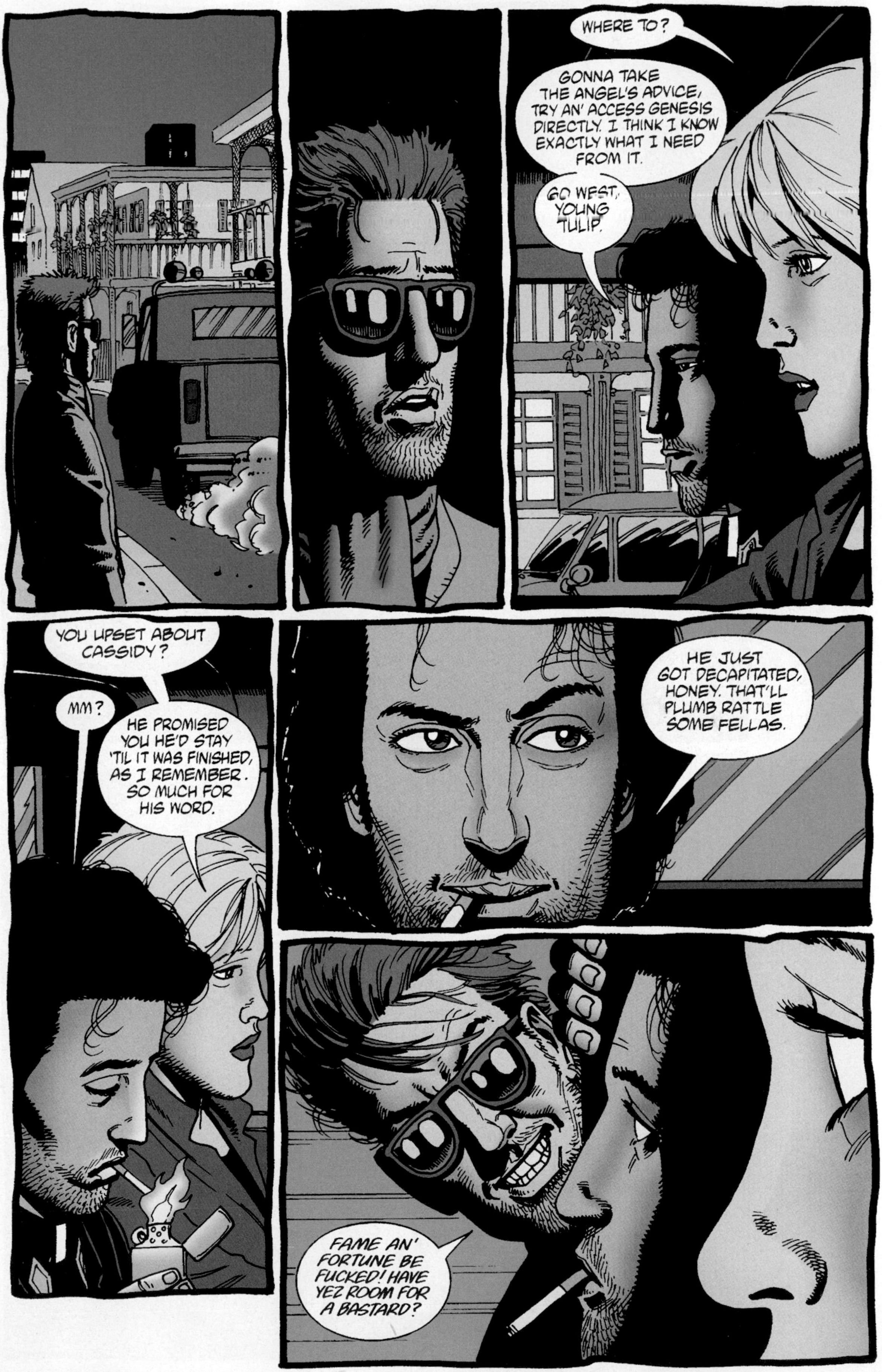
WHERE TO?
GONNA TAKE THE ANGEL'S ADVICE, TRY AN' ACCESS GENESIS DIRECTLY. I THINK I KNOW EXACTLY WHAT I NEED FROM IT.
GO WEST, YOUNG TULIP.
YOU UPSET ABOUT CASSIDY?
MM?
HE PROMISED YOU HE'D STAY 'TIL IT WAS FINISHED, AS I REMEMBER. SO MUCH FOR HIS WORD.
HE JUST GOT DECAPITATED, HONEY. THAT'LL PLUMB RATTLE SOME FELLAS.
FAME AN' FORTUNE BE FUCKED! HAVE YEZ ROOM FOR A BASTARD?

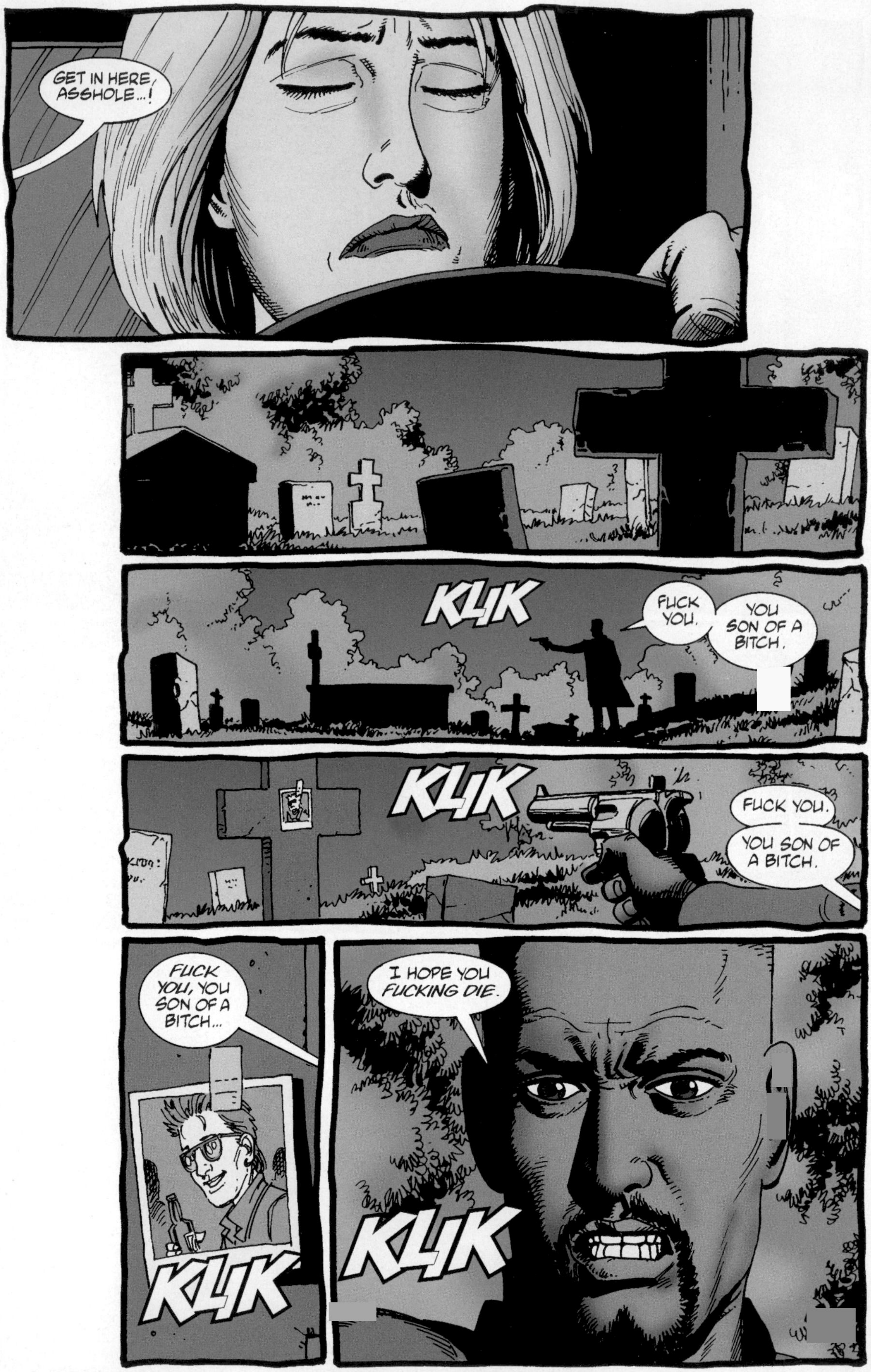
GET IN HERE, ASSHOLE...!
KLIK
FUCK YOU.
YOU SON OF A BITCH.
KLIK
FUCK YOU.
YOU SON OF A BITCH.
FUCK YOU, YOU SON OF A BITCH...
KLIK
I HOPE YOU FUCKING DIE.
KLIK

# COLLECTIBLES

## A PREACHER Gallery by Glenn Fabry

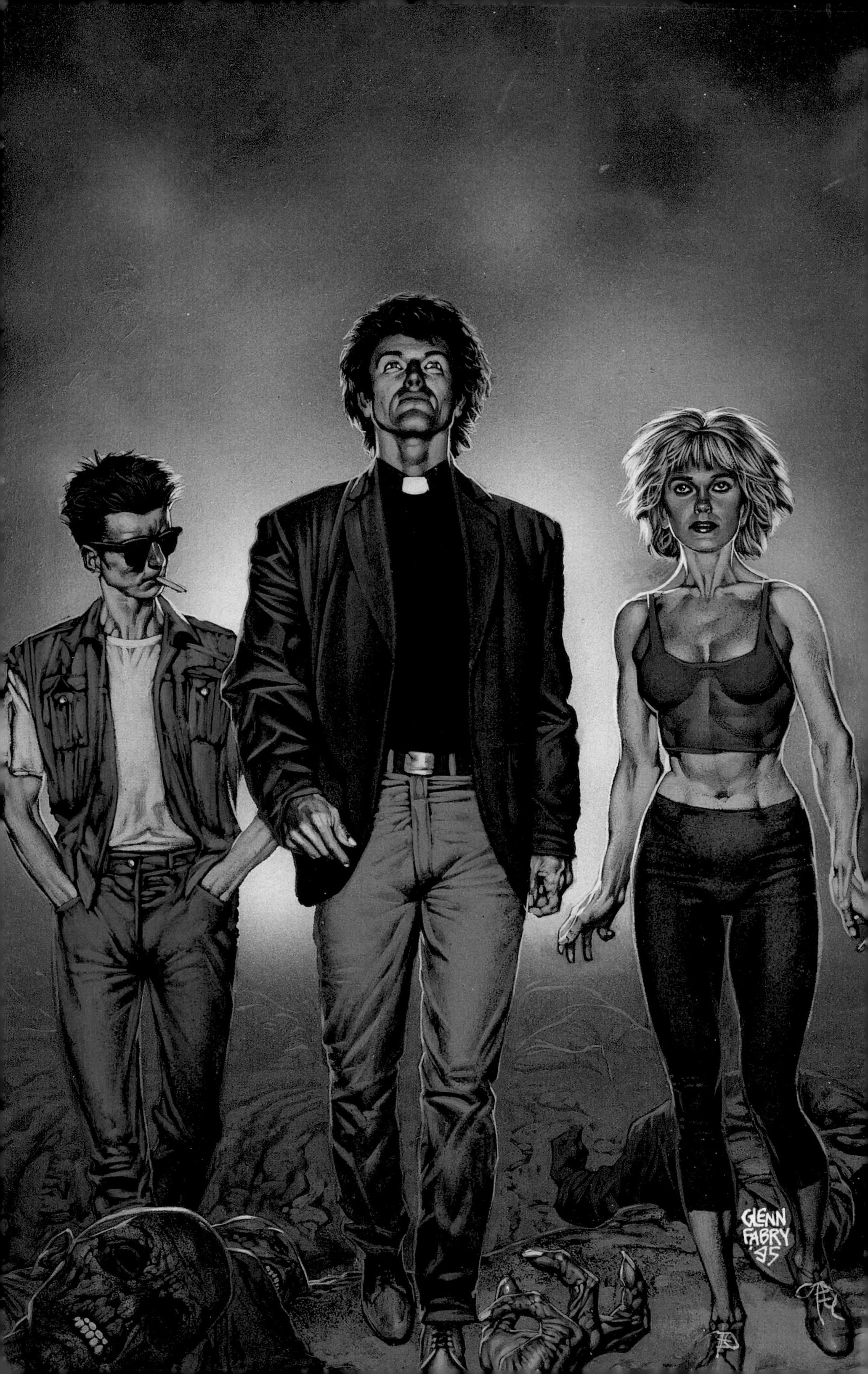
GLENN
FABRY
'95

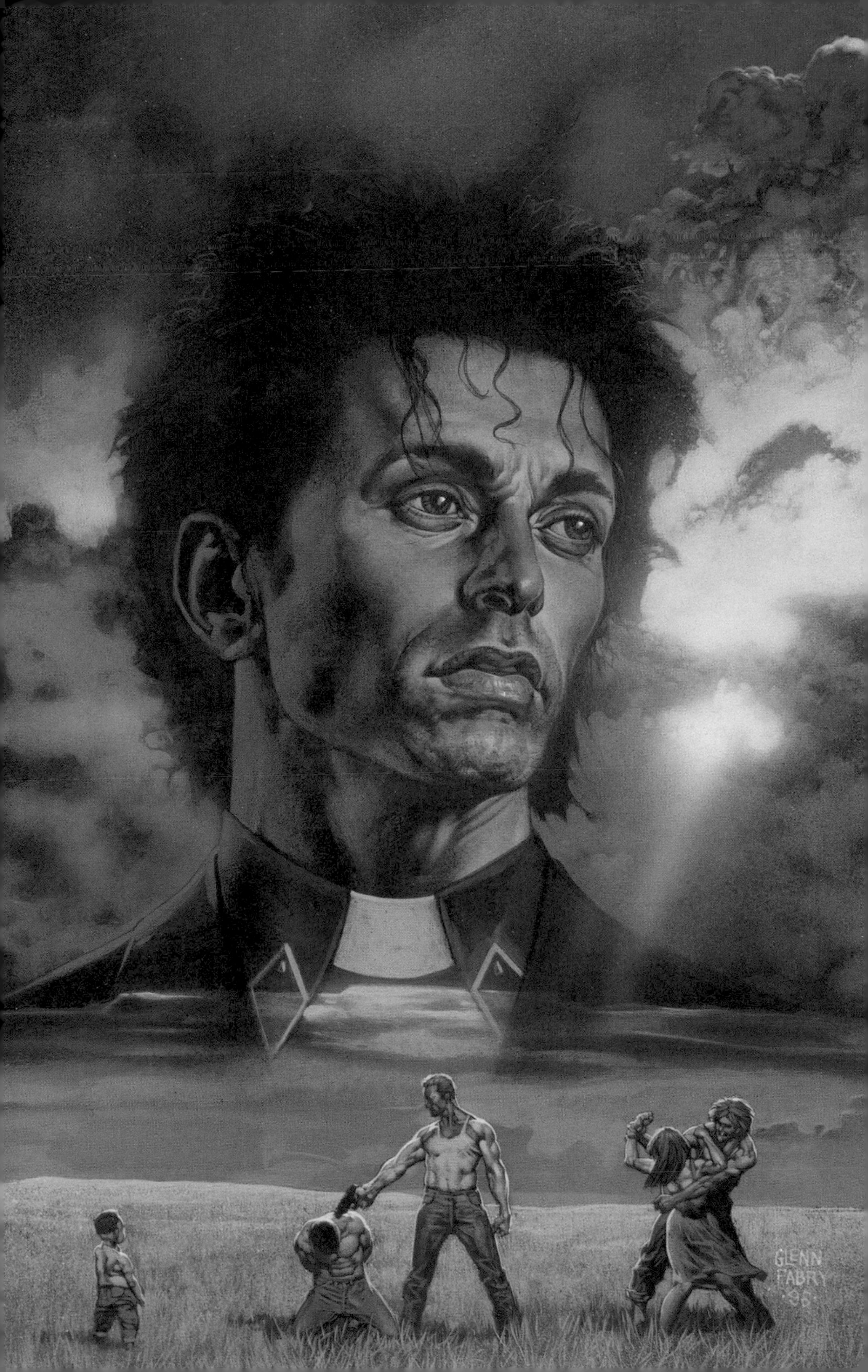
GLENN
FABRY
96

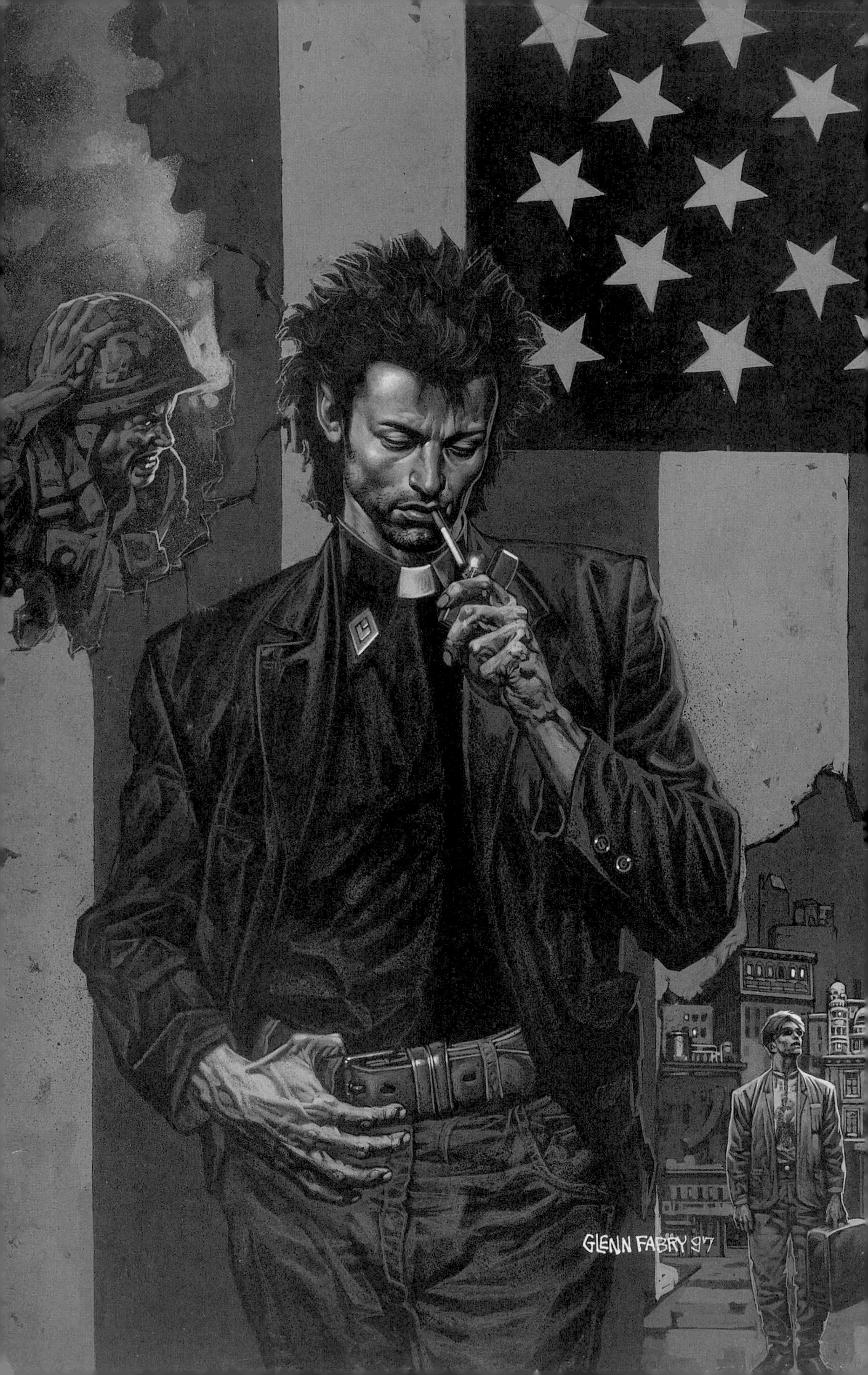
GLENN FABRY '97

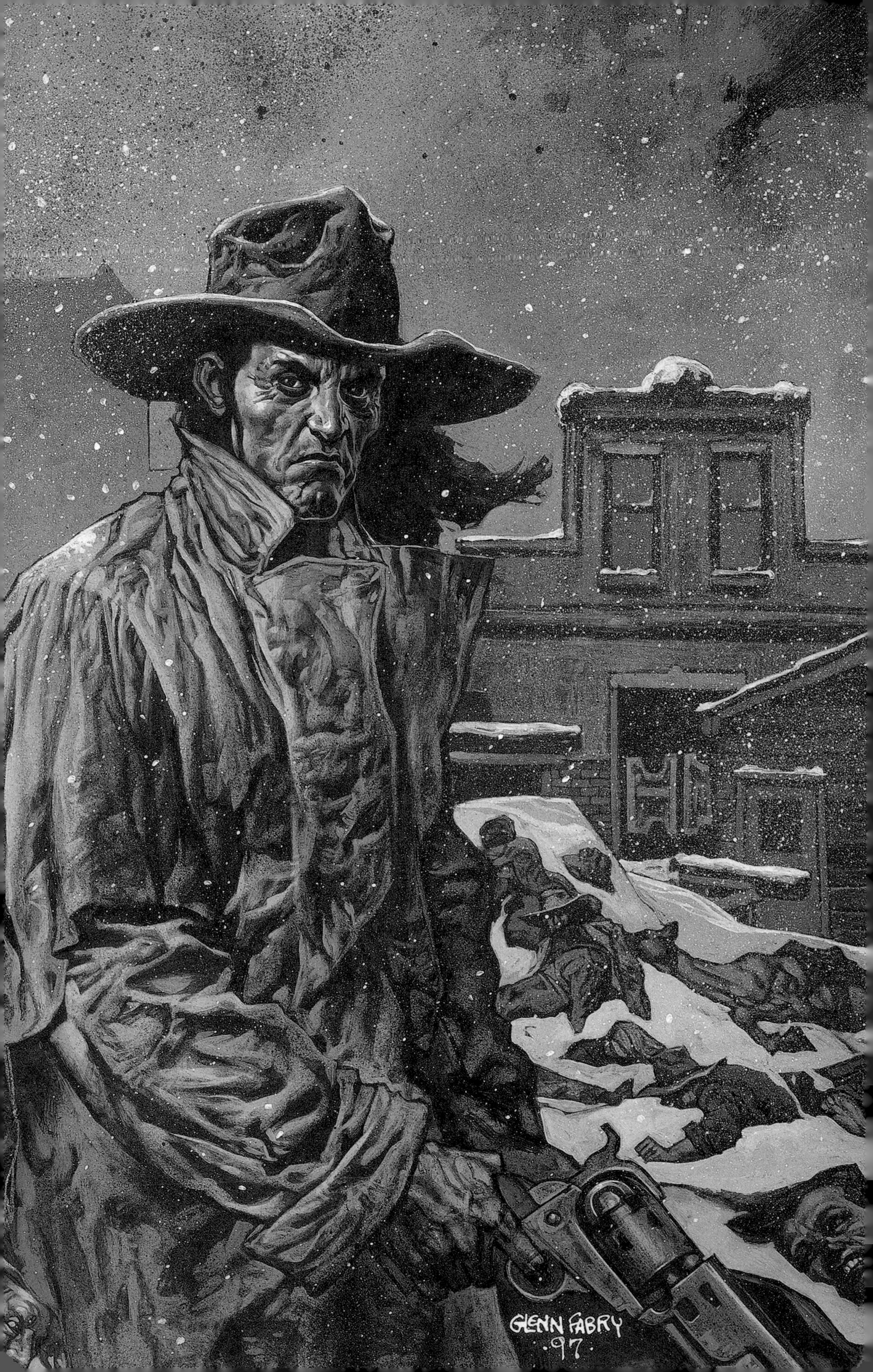
GLENN FABRY
·97

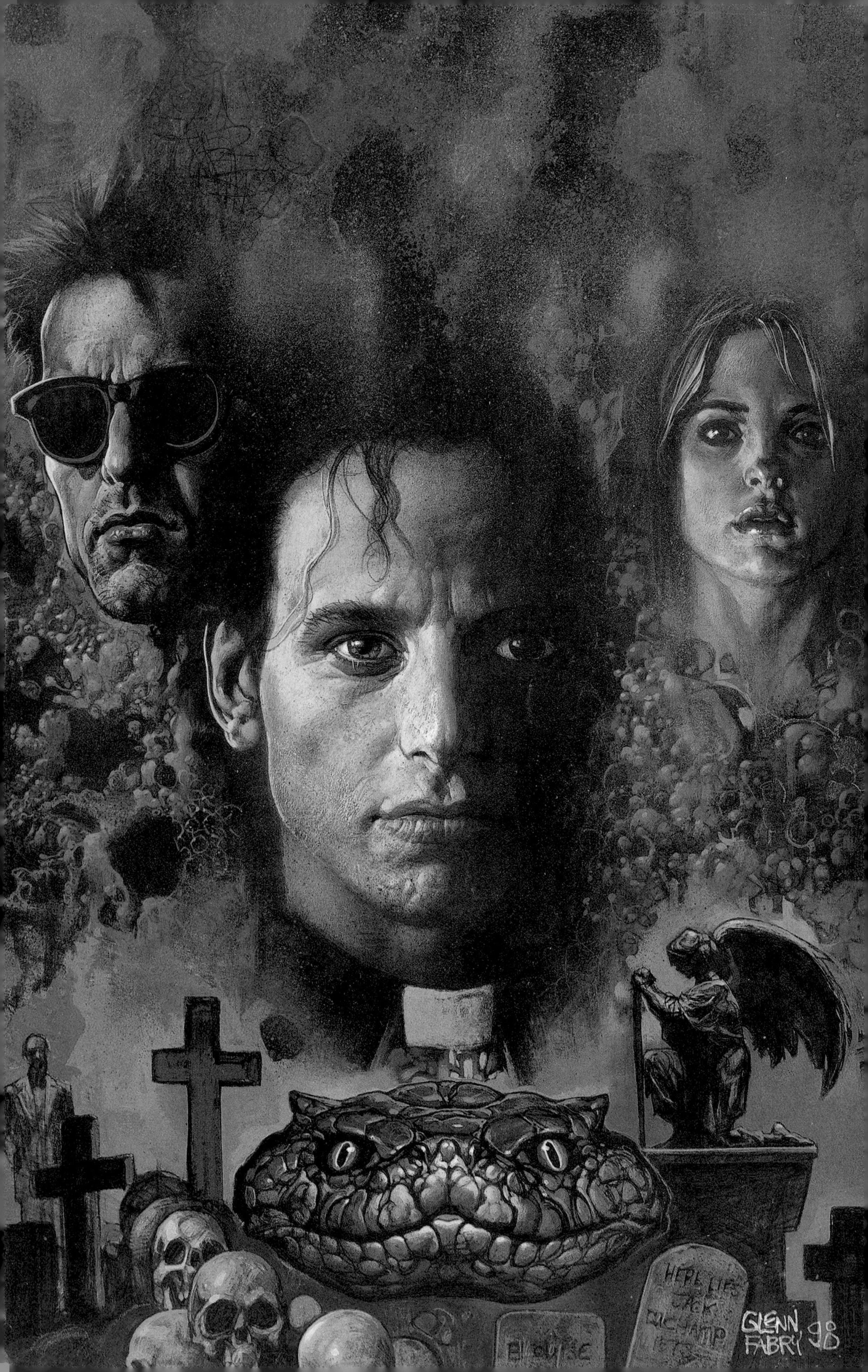
HERE LIES
GLENN FABRY 98

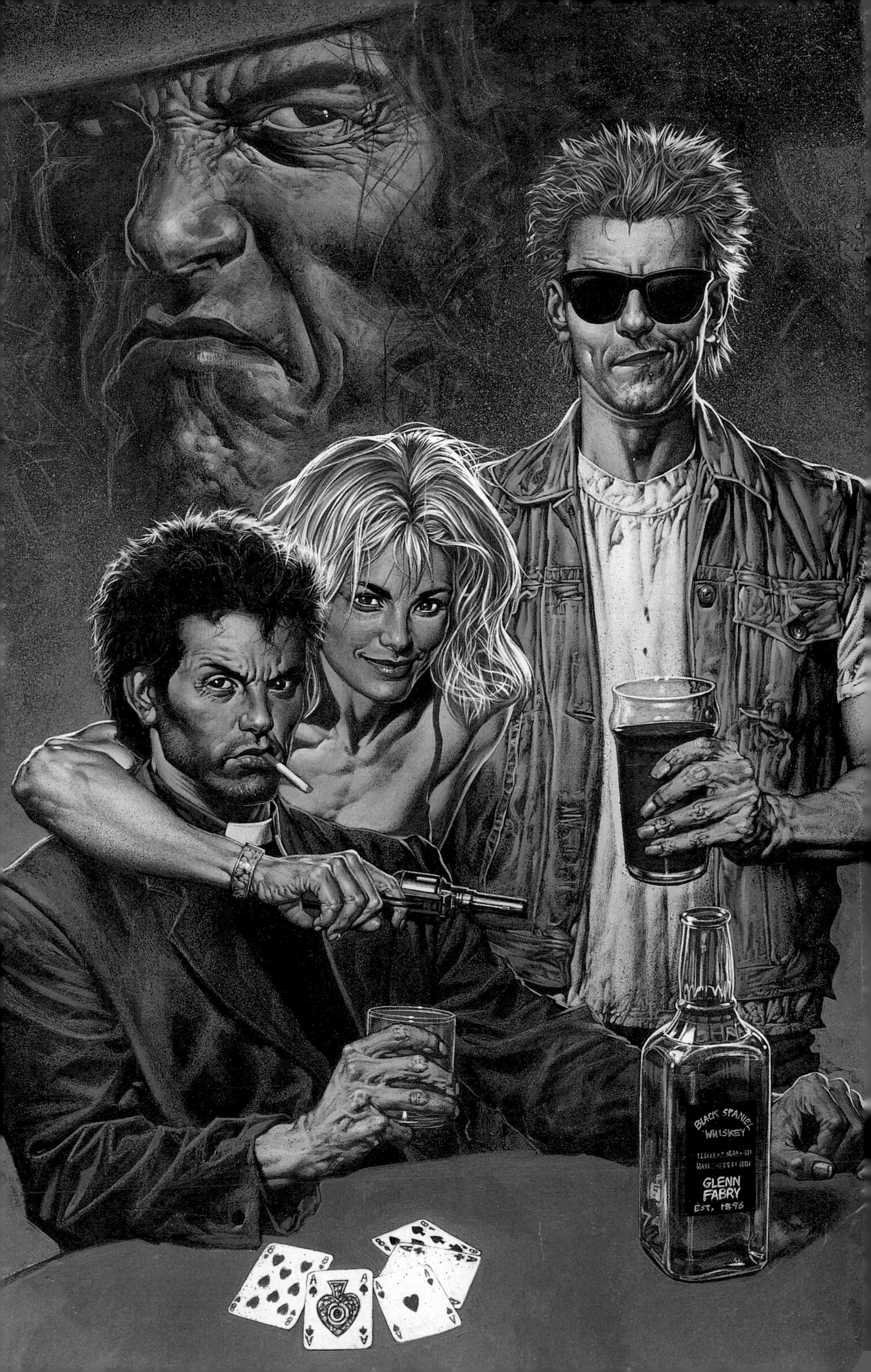
BLACK SPANIEL WHISKEY
GLENN FABRY
EST. 1896

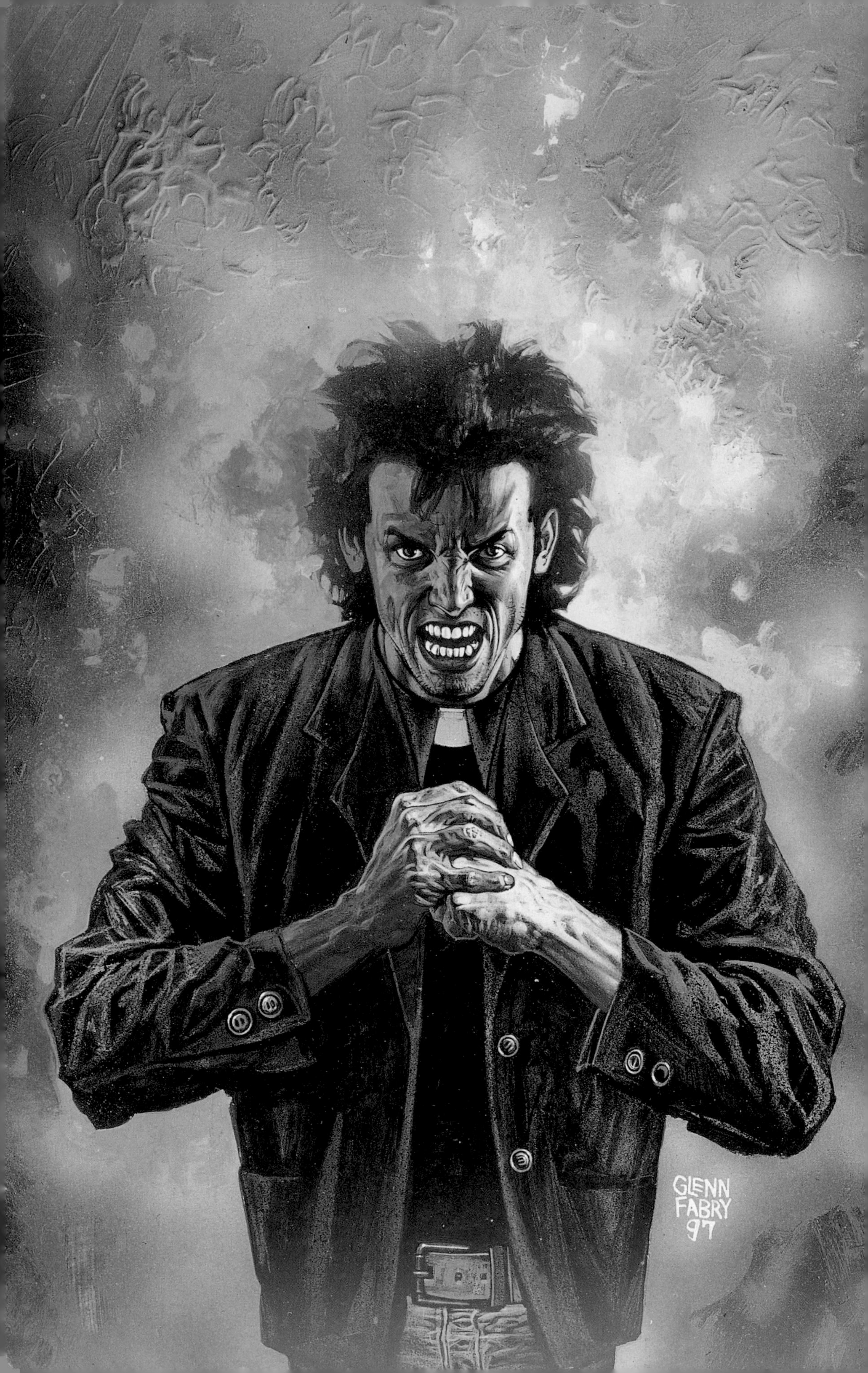
GLENN
FABRY
97